26/8/03
2 8 AUG 2003
LS/PTC
11/9/03 C
- 4 MAY 2004
27 MAY 2004
1 6 JUN 2004

COUNTY STORE

C.L. 69.

929.71   Duren

C003181889

This book is due for return on or before the last date shown above: it may, subject to the book not being reserved by another reader, be renewed by personal application, post, or telephone, quoting this date and details of the book.

H.Q. Account

HAMPSHIRE COUNTY COUNCIL
County Library

 100% recycled paper

ORDERS OF KNIGHTHOOD AND OF MERIT

ORDERS OF KNIGHTHOOD AND OF MERIT

The Pontifical, Religious and Secularised
Catholic-founded Orders
and their relationship to
the Apostolic See

Peter Bander van Duren

COLIN SMYTHE
Gerrards Cross, 1995

Copyright © 1995 by Peter Bander van Duren

First published in 1995 by Colin Smythe Limited,
Gerrards Cross, Buckinghamshire SL9 8XA

The right of Peter Bander van Duren to be identified as the Author of this work has been asserted in accordance with the Copyright, Designs and Patents Act, 1988

All rights reserved. Apart from any fair dealing for the purposes of research or private study, or criticism or review, as permitted under the Copyright, Designs and Patents Act, 1988, this publication may be reproduced, stored or transmitted, in any forms or by any means, only with the prior permission in writing of the publishers, or in the case of reprographic reproduction in accordance with the terms of licences issued by the Copyright Licensing Agency. Inquiries concerning reproduction outside these terms should be sent to the publishers at the undermentioned address.

British Library Cataloguing in Publication Data

A catalogue record for this book is available from the British Library

ISBN 0-86140-371-1
ISBN 0-86140-380-0 ltd signed edition

HAMPSHIRE COUNTY LIBRARY	
	0861403711
	C003181889

Text generated by AJT Photoset Ltd., Beaconsfield,
film and colour separations produced by Kempston Graphics Ltd., Bedford,
colour illustrations printed by Cheney & Sons Ltd. Banbury;
text printed by Lawrence-Allen Ltd., Weston-super-Mare,
and bound by Cedric Chivers Ltd., Bristol.

Courtesy: *Cecil Drake pinx*

DEDICATED TO THE MEMORY OF HYGINUS EUGENE CARDINALE
Titular Archbishop of Nepte
1916-1983

CONTENTS

Acknowledgements	xiii
INTRODUCTION	1

CHAPTER ONE
I:	The involvement of the Apostolic See and the Holy See in the field of chivalry	19
II:	The origin and evolution of Orders of Knighthood	46

CHAPTER TWO: THE PONTIFICAL ORDERS OF KNIGHTHOOD
I:	The origin and evolution of Pontifical Orders of Knighthood and the attitude of individual pontiffs to the Orders	55
II:	The Supreme Order of Christ	64
III:	The Order of the Golden Spur or The Golden Militia etc	75
IV:	The Golden Collar of the Pian Order	85
V:	The Order of Pius IX	87
VI:	The Order of St. Gregory the Great	99
VII:	The Order of Pope St. Sylvester	115
VIII:	Corollary on non-Catholic Knights of the Pontifical Equestrian Order of St. Gregory the Great	126

CHAPTER THREE: PAPAL KNIGHTS — 129
I:	The role and function of the Pontifical Equestrian Orders	136
II:	The procedure for admission to the Pontifical Orders of Knighthood	142
III:	The implications of the Supreme Pontiff being the *fons honorum* of Pontifical Knighthoods	145

CHAPTER FOUR: PONTIFICAL RELIGIOUS AWARDS OF MERIT — 149
I:	The Golden Rose	152
II:	The Cross 'Pro Ecclesia et Pontifice'	157
III:	The Medal 'Benemerenti'	160

CHAPTER FIVE: RELIGIOUS BUT NON-PONTIFICAL ORDERS OF KNIGHTHOOD — 167
I:	The Sovereign Military Hospitaller Order of St. John of Jerusalem, of Rhodes and of Malta	171
	The Order of Merit	184
	The Insignia of the Order	184

II:	The Most Venerable Order of the Hospital of St. John of Jerusalem	187
III:	The Equestrian Order of the Holy Sepulchre of Jerusalem	195

CHAPTER SIX: A TRANSFORMED RELIGIOUS ORDER OF KNIGHTHOOD:

	The Teutonic Order or Fratres Domus Hospitalis Sanctae Mariae Teutonicorum in Jerusalem	211

CHAPTER SEVEN: CATHOLIC-FOUNDED DYNASTIC ORDERS

	The nature, role and function of Catholic-founded dynastic Orders of non-regnant Royal Houses and their relationship with the Apostolic See	217
I:	THE NOBLE ORDER OF THE GOLDEN FLEECE OF BURGUNDY (from 1430 to 1724)	235
II:	THE IMPERIAL AND ROYAL HOUSE OF HABSBURG-LORRAINE	243
	The Noble Order of the Golden Fleece of Austria	243
	The Order of the Dames of the Starry Cross	246
III:	THE ROYAL HOUSE OF BRAGANÇA OF PORTUGAL	
	The historical background leading to the present role and function of the Duke of Bragança	248
	The Order of Our Lady of the Conception of Vila Viçosa	266
	The Royal Order of Saint Isabel	270
IV:	THE ROYAL HOUSE OF BOURBON OF THE TWO SICILIES	
	The historical background leading to the Dynasty's present-day status	271
	The Sacred Military Constantinian Order of St. George	294
	The Royal Order of St. Januarius	303
V:	THE ROYAL HOUSE OF SAVOY – ITALY	
	the historical background and the status of the Royal House after King Umberto II went into exile	306
	The Supreme Order of the Most Holy Annunziata	312
	The Order of SS. Maurice and Lazarus	314
VI:	THE ROYAL HOUSE OF BAVARIA – WITTELSBACH	
	A brief historical background to the Dynasty	319
	The Order of St. George, Defender of the Faith in the Immaculate Conception	322
	The Order of St. Hubert	324
	The Order of St. Michael	326
VII:	THE ROYAL HOUSE OF BOURBON OF FRANCE – THE ROYAL HOUSE OF BOURBON ORLÉANS	328
	The Order of the Holy Ghost	329
	The Royal and Military Order of St. Louis	331
	The Order of St. Michael of France	333

VIII:	THE DUCAL HOUSE OF HABSBURG-TUSCANY; THE GRAND DUCHY OF TUSCANY	337
	The Order of St. Stephen	339
	The Order of St. Joseph	340
	Nota Bene. Concerning the former categories of exalted and less exalted Orders of Knighthood	341

CHAPTER EIGHT: SECULARISED CATHOLIC-FOUNDED ORDERS OF KNIGHTHOOD STILL BESTOWED AS CROWN OR STATE ORDERS

	From the *Res Publica Christiana* through the Reformation and the Age of Absolutism to the secularisation of the Orders of Knighthood and to the new concept of Orders of Merit	343
I:	DENMARK	
	The Order of the Elephant	348
	The Order of the Dannebrog	351
II:	THE UNITED KINGDOM OF GREAT BRITAIN AND NORTHERN IRELAND	
	The Most Noble Order of the Garter	355
	The Most Ancient and Most Noble Order of the Thistle	364
	The Most Honourable Order of the Bath	368
	Knights Bachelor	373
III:	THE PRINCIPALITY OF MONACO	
	The Order of St. Charles	378
IV:	THE REPUBLIC OF POLAND	381
	The Order of the White Eagle	387
	The Order of the Rebirth of Poland or 'Polonia Restituta' (as successor to the Catholic-founded former Order of St. Stanislaus)	389
V:	THE REPUBLIC OF PORTUGAL	393
	The Riband of the Three Orders	396
	The Military Order of the Tower and the Sword, of Valour, Loyalty and Merit (not a Catholic-founded Order)	399
	The Military Order of Christ	404
	The Military Order of Avis	408
	The Military Order of St. James of the Sword	413
V:	THE REPUBLIC OF SAN MARINO	
	The Equestrian Order of St. Marino	419
	The Equestrian Order of St. Agatha	423
VI:	THE KINGDOM OF SPAIN	425
	The Noble Order of the Golden Fleece (Spanish Branch)	427
	The Four Monastic Orders of Knighthood:	432
	The Military Order of Alcantara	434
	The Military Order of Calatrava	434

	The Military Order of Montesa	435
	The Military Order of Santiago	436
	The Most Distinguished Order of Carlos III	438
	The Order of Isabella the Catholic	440
	The Military Order of St. Ferdinand	443
	The Royal and Military Order of St. Hermenegildus	443
	The Order of Cisneros	444
	The Order of the Cross of St. Raymond de Peñafort	445
VII:	THE KINGDOM OF SWEDEN	447
	The Royal Order of the Sword, *otherwise known as* The Order of the Yellow Ribbon	447
	The Royal Order of the Seraphim	448

CHAPTER NINE: EXTINCT CATHOLIC-FOUNDED ORDERS OF KNIGHTHOOD

I:	The criteria for an Order of Knighthood being regarded extinct and the *raison d'être* for an Order's continued existence	451
II:	Short-lived Orders of Knighthood with special reference to Awards placed in abeyance	456
	The Lateran Cross	458
	The Lauretan Cross	458
	The Holy Land Pilgrim's Cross	459
	The Cross of the Advocates of St. Peter	459
	The Order of the Fleet, *otherwise known as* The Order of the Two Moons, *otherwise known as* The Order of the Ship and the Crescent	463
	The Order of the Hatchet, *or* Hacha	463
	The Order of the Holy Vial	464
	The Order of the Military Cincture	465
	The Order of Montjoie (*separating to form* The Order of Montfrac *and* The Order of Truxillo)	465
	The Order of Our Lady of Bethlehem	465
	The Order of St. George of Ravenna	465
	The Sacred and Military Order of Our Lady of Mercy, *otherwise known as* The Order of Our Lady of Ransom	466
	The Order of the Sword-Bearers	466
	The Royal Order of St. Ferdinand and of Merit	466
	The Royal and Military Order of St. George of the Reunion	467
	The Order of St. Louis	469
	The Order of the Slaves of Virtue	470
	The Imperial Order of St. Elizabeth	471
	The Order of Merit for Catholic Priests in Military Service	472
	The Order of Our Lady of Guadalupe	473

CONTENTS xi

	The Order of St. Charles	475
	The Order of St. Faustin	476
III:	Short-lived Orders Founded by Private Initiative	
	The Order of St. Anne (München – Bavaria)	477
	The Order of St. Anne (Würzburg – Bavaria)	478
	The Order of St. Elizabeth (of Sultzbach)	478
	The Order of St. Rupert of Salzburg	478
	The Knightly Order of the Old Nobility, *or*	478
	The Order of the Four Emperors	478
IV:	Long-lived Orders of Knighthood. A general survey of Orders surviving for more than a century and the amalgamation of Orders	479
	The Order of the Knights Templars	483
	The Order of St. James of Altopascio	486
	The Order of the Holy Ghost of Montpellier	487
	The Order of St. George of Alfama	487
	The Order of St. George in Caranthia	487
	The Order of St. George of Burgundy	488
	The Order of the Swan	488
	The Order of St. Hubert of Lorraine, *or* The Order of the Bar	489
	The Order of Our Lady of Carmel and of St. Lazarus of Jerusalem (*amalgamated*)	489
	The Military Order of St. Henry	490
	The Royal Hungarian Order of St. Stephen the Apostolic King	491

CHAPTER TEN: THE MILITARY AND HOSPITALLER ORDER OF ST. LAZARUS OF JERUSALEM 495

CHAPTER ELEVEN: RECOGNIZED KNIGHTLY ORGANISATIONS 515
I: The Association of the Knights of Columbus 517
II: The Knights and Dames of St. Michael of the Wing 519

CHAPTER TWELVE: THE SPIRIT OF CHRISTIAN CHIVALRY TODAY
St. John Ambulance – Malteser Hilfsdienst – Lazarus Hilfswerk 525

CHAPTER THIRTEEN: UNRECOGNISED ORGANISATIONS STYLING THEMSELVES ORDERS OF KNIGHTHOOD 545

APPENDICES:

I:	Pontifical Equestrian Orders: Papal Letters of Foundation and Decrees	561
II:	Additional Guidelines for Papal Knights and Investitures	
	1. Additional Guidance on the wearing of Dress Uniform	606
	2. Preparation for an Investiture	610
	3. The Investiture of a Papal Knight	615
	4. Conferment of Insignia upon newly-created Members	619
III:	Conferment of Pontifical Religious Awards	621
IV:	The Pontifical Medal	624
V:	The Pontifical Corps of Guards	631
	1. The Corps of the Pontifical Noble Guard	634
	2. The Corps of the Pontifical Swiss Guard	635
	3. The Corps of the Palatine Guard of Honour	638
	4. The Corps of the Pontifical Gendarmerie	639
VI:	Perrot's list of Extinct Orders	641
VII:	On Chronological Lists of Orders of Knighthood	646
VIII:	The Prerogatives of the Dukes of Bragança	650
IX:	Bull of Foundation of the Portuguese Order of Christ and Royal Brief of Acceptance	662
X:	Insignia as *objets d'art*	676
XI:	Orders and Decorations of the Republic of Poland	679
XII:	Appointment of S.A.R. Don Carlos de Bórbon-Dos Sicilias y Bórbon-Parma as Infante of Spain	684

SELECT BIBLIOGRAPHY 687

Index 695

Colour plates are paginated in roman numerals, and are fully indexed.

ACKNOWLEDGEMENTS

In the Introduction I pay special tribute to four gentlemen without whom this book could never have been written in the literal sense, and two whose work has so greatly enhanced the published result: my late friend and mentor for many years, Archbishop Cardinale, the pioneer of the work in this field and from whom I took over when he died in 1983, Their Eminences Cardinal Agostino Casaroli, whose trust and support, and the late Cardinal Jacques Martin, whose practical help and counsel were invaluable in realising the project I envisaged, my friend and colleague Prof. Colin Smythe, whose eponymous company publishes this book and who has worked with me on it since 1987, and finally, the two Pontifical Photographers, Messrs. Felici and Mr. Arturo Mari (*L'Osservatore Romano*), devoted friends of Mons. Cardinale and Cardinal Martin, who both generously supplied so many photographs.

However, a book like this does not just present statistical facts, laws, rules and regulations: it deals with issues that often go far deeper and involve relationships between collective entities, individuals and attitudes that change because of political expediency. It needs the assistance and good will of many experts in many different subjects to ensure that it is both factually correct and free from prejudices and innuendoes that distort the truth. Phaleristics is not a new subject, and scholars have written for centuries about Orders of Knighthood and of Merit; however, many writers only copied what others before them had written, so that some serious errors were perpetuated, sometimes for hundreds of years.

Those to whom I am indebted fall into different categories; some experts spent days and weeks in supplying me with information needed for a single Order of Knighthood or collectively for those of a country, others furnished me with their expert opinion on legal points, and many supplied me with photographs. Wherever possible, I have credited the latter with a courtesy line which, I hope, expresses my gratitude to them.

There are, of course, the many people who helped Archbishop Cardinale, and whose contribution has therefore indirectly helped me. They are mentioned in all the editions of Mons. Cardinale's *Orders of Knighthood, Awards and the Holy See*, and I have again mentioned them here when they have assisted me on this book.

Among those who have given many days of their time to researching ancient records of Orders, provided me with source material and illustrations and whose contribution to this book was substantial, are Dr. José Vicente de Bragança, Secretary-General of the Presidency of the Portuguese Republic and of all Orders the Republic, whose contribution to the Portuguese Catholic-founded Orders (and those that were not but had always been assumed to have been) has enabled me to correct the record that has been obscured by misinformation for centuries; Mr. Krzysztof Barbarski, Curator of the Sikorski Museum, London, whose assistance in so many fields of chivalry, but especially his unsurpassed knowledge of the history of Polish Orders were invaluable to me; Mr. Charles J. Burnett, Ross Herald of Arms at the Court of the Lord Lyon, Edinburgh; Mr. Peter J. Begent, Chronicler of the Most Noble Order of the Garter and of St. George's Chapel, Windsor Castle; Mr. David L. Garrison, Texas, USA, whose generous gift of photographs of the insignia of rare and extinct Orders in his collection was most welcome; the historian and biographer Mr. Kenneth Rose, perhaps better known to most readers as 'Albany' of the *Sunday Telegraph*, who with his great knowledge of constitutional matters relating to Orders of Knighthood was able to clarify difficult problems to me, not just about the British Catholic-founded Orders of the Crown but also with regard to the Noble Order of the Spanish Golden Fleece; Herr Klaus-Peter Pokolm, Germany, who supplied me with hundreds of photographs taken in Poland, Hungary, Russia and the former Yugoslavia to select from, as well as with many verified copies of documents and agreements drawn up between the Commissioners of the European Union and the Lazarus Hilfswerk; Dr.(h.c.) don Achille di Lorenzo, Naples, Italy, a living encyclopedia, who has been active in the chivalric world for over six decades; Comm. Dott. Pierre Blanchard, Vatican City, a close collaborator of Archbishop Cardinale, my friend since the days we both worked for Mons. Cardinale, and always a most reliable source of information; Mr. Stephen J. Connelly of Spink & Son Ltd., London, who never tired of being of assistance when asked. Archbishop Dr Bruno Heim, who retired in 1985 as Apostolic Nuncio in London, helped me particularly with the section on Pontifical Medals. I end this section by mentioning Dr. Andrzej Ciechanowiecki: in 1983, when Archbishop Cardinale was already in a coma, he offered to check some sections of *Orders of Knighthood, Awards and the Holy See* for possible factual errors. He discovered that some paragraphs in two sections contained major errors which the publishers decided had to be corrected before publication, so thirty-two pages were revised and reprinted. I am most grateful to him for having helped me in a field about which I knew little, and he made me realise that it was generously scattered with mines it would be difficult to avoid.

Those who have given me much help with the chapters on the Pontifical Equestrian Orders are the late President of the Academy for Diplomats of the Holy See, Archbishop Cesare Zacchi, Canon of St. Peter's Basilica, Vatican; Apostolic Nuncio Archbishop Luigi Barbarito, Doyen of the Diplomatic Corps to the Court of St. James; the late Mons Gerald Mahon, Auxiliary Bishop of Westminster; Canon Adrian

Arrowsmith of Westminster Cathedral; Primatial Canon of Warsaw, Mons. Wladislaw Wyszowadski, who facilitated special photographs to be taken for the section on the guidelines for Papal Knights; and Mr. Nicola Vecchione, KSG; last but not least, Major-General His Grace the Duke of Norfolk, KG, GCVO, CB, MC, Earl Marshal of England, a Knight Grand Cross of the Pian Order and President of the Papal Knights in Great Britain, whose good humour and ability to pour oil on troubled waters has always been appreciated.

The Ven. Frà Oberto, Marchese Pallavicini, of the Sovereign Council of the Sovereign Military Order of Malta, its High Historical Consultant, Frà Cyril, Prince Toumanoff, as well as several members of the Grand Magisterium of the Equestrian Order of the Holy Sepulchre of Jerusalem, have all furnished me with updated information on the two Religious Orders of Knighthood. The administration of the Most Venerable Order of St. John at St. John's Gate, London, has done everything in its power to assist me and supply photographs of the Order and of St. John Ambulance in action. However I must mention two members of the Order who have always given me their unstinting help: Miss Pamela Willis, the Curator of the St. John Museum, and Dr. John Tanner, CBE, formerly a member of the Chapter General of the Order.

There were many who supplied information concerning the Catholic-founded dynastic Orders. Special thanks must go to Their Royal Highnesses O Senhor Dom Duarte, Duke of Bragança, and Prince Vittorio Emanuele, Duke of Savoy, for their personal help and to their Grand Chancelleries for their assistance.

The only difficulties I encountered concerned the Royal House of the Two Sicilies. In fact, I wrote and rewrote that chapter well over ten times in the last few years. Although the legal arguments were straightforward, and the decision for the Apostolic See had been made by Pope John XXIII in 1960, it has been extremely difficult to be utterly detached from personal conflicts and arguments and be objective in my assessment of all the evidence made available to me. I do not think that the family conflict in the House of the Two Sicilies will be solved as quickly as have the juridical aspects when on 16 December 1994, His Majesty King Juan Carlos of Spain created one member of the family a Spanish Infante, thus ending an argument that has raged since 1960. I am grateful to all who have supplied me with information on this matter. Of course, the above-mentioned Dr.(h.c.) don Achille di Lorenzo owns such vast archives on the House of the Two Sicilies that historians could spend years on them, and he has never failed to supply me with any documentary evidence I asked for. Similarly, Mr. Guy Stair Sainty, representing the Marquês de la Conquista Real, and therefore the other party in the family dispute, supplied me with other information, especially on the four Military Monastic Orders of Spain, which was difficult to come by, without prejudice. Among those who were always there when I needed their assistance with some of the dynastic Orders were Dr. Manuel de Noronha e Andrade, Marquês de Arena e Pascarolla; Prof.Catedrático Dr. Antonio de Sousa Lara, Conte di Guedes; and Prof.Arq. Marcello de Moraes.

Some of those who gave me invaluable help on the chapter on Catholic-founded secularised Orders that are conferred as State or Crown Orders, have already been mentioned earlier. Yet there were those who laid the foundation for some fundamental changes with regard to the position some Orders occupy in the international fraternity of chivalry. First and foremost I must mention His Majesty King Juan Carlos of Spain who personally and with the assistance of the then Jeffe de Protocolo del Estado, Ambassador Joaquin Martinez-Correcher, Count de la Sierragorda, explained to me the very special rôle of the Spanish Order of the Golden Fleece, the intricate and complicated evolution of that Order from a purely Catholic dynastic Order to the preeminent position of the Golden Fleece as the principal Order of the Realm His Majesty aimed at, placing it on a par with the Order of the Garter. I am most grateful to His Majesty for receiving me so graciously and to the Count de la Sierragorda for furnishing me with all the information and documents I needed.

The knightly Orders or Associations are well represented. I am grateful for the assistance I was given by the Supreme Knight of the Knights of Columbus, Mr. Virgil C. Dechant, the most highly decorated layman in the Church, and I owe a debt of gratitude to Mr. Malcolm Howe of the Knights and Dames of St. Michael of the Wing (Portugal) for the wealth of historical information he supplied.

Finally, I want to thank Dr. Hans von Leden, the Grand Prior of America of the Military Hospitaller Order of St. Lazarus for making available to me all the information and documentation I needed and requested.

Over the years, I have been helped by many people in different countries: the list numbers hundreds of people whose interest in the subjects under discussion in this work has in some way been of assistance in increasing my knowledge and understanding. It would be invidious to mention some of them at the expense of the others, yet it is impossible for me to name them all I would produce mere pages of names. I hope I am forgiven, therefore, if I restrict myself to naming only those whose help has been essential to my completion of this book.

PBvD

INTRODUCTION

This work is not a revised edition of Archbishop H.E. Cardinale's *Orders of Knighthood, Awards and the Holy See*. However, without his pioneering work, I would not have been asked to revise his book twice (1984 and 1985), nor would I have rewritten and restructured what he began in 1978, shortly after the election of Pope John Paul II. Mons. Cardinale was the pioneer of this work. In retrospect, I, more than anyone, can appreciate the difficulties he faced and the obstacles he had to overcome in obtaining correct information.

As I explain later, had Archbishop Cardinale, a loyal and important member of the Holy See, known of the dichotomy between the *Holy* See and the *Apostolic* See that has been created by Canon 361 of the 1983 *Codex Iuris Canonici*, I do not think he would have undertaken the task of writing *Orders of Knighthood, Awards and the Holy See*. Although it had always been my intention to use Mons. Cardinale's name as co-author of my completely rewritten book, I was persuaded by many friends, all of whom experts in phaleristics, that doing so might create the impression that Mons. Cardinale shared my views and criticism of certain matters that ultimately involve the Holy See. During my long friendship with him I learned that he would rather not have written anything at all than discuss matters that might – however slightly – criticise something in which the Holy See was involved. I also know that on many occasions he took up with the Pope and the Cardinal Secretary of State some of the controversial issues I now discuss openly. However, he would in the end, and without question or qualification, express only the views of the Holy See.

Both His Holiness Pope John Paul II and His Eminence Agostino Cardinal Casaroli, the former Secretary of State, were anxious that an authoritative book should be written about the relationship between the Holy See and the Pontifical, Religious and Catholic Orders of Knighthood, but that was in 1979 and before the above-mentioned Canon 361 juridically invalidated what Archbishop Cardinale had written. Had it only been a question of correcting factual errors and omissions, I would have merely written an extensively revised edition of his work. As I said above, his pioneering work has been invaluable, and I always highlight those issues he personally dealt with and which are not affected by the metamorphosis that has taken place inside the Vatican. My book is dedicated to him because he sowed the seeds that finally grew into this work, though he had no way of knowing that those seeds would produce hybrids within the span of a single decade.

I was one of three friends whom Archbishop Cardinale asked to assist him collecting data or, in my case, to take responsibility for the section on self-styled Orders, and later, that on the S.M. Constantinian Order of St. George. The latter was at the centre of a family dispute, and the involvement of several of his colleagues who were taking opposite sides, as well as his own awareness of the situation as a result of his previous position as Chief of Protocol to Pope John XXIII who had made the attitude of the Papacy quite clear, caused Mons. Cardinale embarrassment in his diplomatic mission. His position as Doyen of the Diplomatic Corps accredited to the European Economic Community made his task all the more difficult, but he made it clear that he personally would keep overall control of the project.

As I was also on the board of directors of the publishing house that was to publish his book on 25 March 1983, a date chosen to coincide with the opening of the Extraordinary Holy Year, I saw Mons. Cardinale's typescript as it arrived, chapter by chapter. There were no illustrations of insignia and decorations, and only most reluctantly did he agree to the inclusion of line drawings of the insignia of most Orders. However, he supplied several of the colour photographs for the colour plates and also photographs of solemn occasions.

Both Messrs. Felici and Arturo Mari (*L'Osservatore Romano*) generously furnished us with all the photographs we requested. The unstinting cooperation of the Pontifical Photographers has always been greatly appreciated. I owe to both Pontifical Photographers a great debt; they continued their unstinting cooperation when I was privileged to work with Cardinal Jacques Martin, the Prefetto Emerito della Casa Pontificia, on his work and the Cardinal assisted me with this book.

I spent much time at the Apostolic Nunciature in Brussels, and I was singularly fortunate that Mons. Cardinale placed at my disposal the diaries he had meticulously kept throughout his diplomatic mission in Rome and later abroad. He was especially anxious that I should familiarise myself with events in which he had been personally involved, such as the dispute between the Holy See and the Sovereign Military Order of Malta, and decisions taken concerning Orders such as the Constantinian Order of the Royal House of the Two Sicilies – during the time he was responsible for the meetings and audiences of Pope John XXIII, as well as *Assessore* of Secretariat of State of his Holiness.

However, one of Mons. Cardinale's voluntary researchers, a gentleman who had spent his life in the Vatican from the reign of Pope St. Pius X to that of Paul VI, and who was in his nineties, often supplied information that was obviously out of date. For example, he insisted that all the Pontifical Knights still wore white pantaloons. I tried in vain to convince Mons. Cardinale to ignore this clearly outdated information as I had the statutes of the Pontifical Orders, promulgated on 7 February 1905 by St. Pius X, which gave the colour of the trousers as black with gold stripes for the Order of Pius IX and as dark green with silver stripes for Knights of St. Gregory the Great. Alas, white pantaloons it had to be in the 1983 edition.

Similarly, I voiced some apprehension about certain phrases he had used in the chapter on the Sovereign Military Order of Malta. Whilst his presentation of the legal status of the Order under international law was impeccable, certain other matters were bound to evoke memories of the unhappy period of the interregnum between 1951 and 1962. His diaries showed that he had played an active part, working for both Cardinal Canali and Mons. (later Cardinal) Dell'Acqua, the senior prelates who represented the interests of the Holy See in the dispute with the Sovereign Military Order of Malta. Archbishop Cardinale was firm and refused to change anything. He always said: 'Quod scripsi, scripsi!'

In 1981 he mentioned that he suffered from painful dental troubles; he controlled the pain as much as possible with painkillers. In 1982 he told me in confidence of the excruciating pain he was suffering, of his sleepless nights and his general feeling of exhaustion, and he made me promise not to tell anyone. As the months went by, his suffering got worse. He camouflaged it as much as possible with painkillers because his work was so important to him. He was the first to rise and the last to retire. Unfortunately, our original intention to have advance copies of the book sent out before 25 March 1983 had to be abandoned. He was very worried about letting us down, but the ever-increasing pain he suffered and the strain and stress of work, (he simply would not delegate any of his diplomatic work in two countries and the European Economic Community, although he had two most senior and efficient Counsellors at the Nunciature), finally took its toll. When I visited the Nunciature in Brussels at the end of November and early December 1982, I felt very concerned about his state of health and well being. He spoke much about the sudden death of his friend Cardinal Benelli and hinted at the important and great work which had been planned and now would never be done. He insisted on accompanying me to the airport and arranged for us to be there early so that he could talk to me in private in the diplomats' lounge. He spoke of certain people wanting him to take three months leave and go into a clinic for treatment, but that he had declined firmly. His dental surgeon was satisfied that his weekly appointments would eventually lead to a complete alleviation of his troubles, and apart from suffering symptoms of being overworked there was little wrong with him. Without being specific on this occasion, he hinted at two things: first that he wished he could find the time to go to England where he had several doctor friends, but more important, that his days as Nuncio in Brussels were numbered. He would be going to Italy. It appeared a foregone conclusion that the Holy Father would raise him to the College of Cardinals, but such matters are never mentioned prior to the official announcement.

Shortly before Christmas 1982 at what was to be their last meeting, both Archbishop Cardinale and the author attended the festivities in honour of the Belgian Royal House in Brussels. This photograph, probably the last ever of Mons. Cardinale, was taken just after the official function to which the Nuncio had been appointed Pontifical Legate and the author acted as his lay attendant for the occasion.

Photo: +Monteiro de Castro

After my return to England he wrote almost daily to me, and he seemed to be deeply troubled by events that unfolded themselves inside the Vatican and were sensationally written about in the press. Although he promised to give his continued support and help to the publishers to meet the publication date, from his private letters I realised that far more important issues occupied his mind almost all the time.

His Christmas message to me contained, seen in retrospect, an almost prophetic note. He sent me a beautiful limited edition of a book on the Order of the Golden Fleece of Burgundy. He dated his presentation with the proposed date of the publication of his own book and wrote behind it "dies irae – but what fun!". These are the opening words of the *Sequentia* on the day of death and of the funeral of a faithful. When I received the book, the inscription made no sense to me. In March 1983, the words 'dies irae' had taken on an almost sinister meaning, though I never had the opportunity of asking my friend personally what he had been trying to tell me.

In the last week of January 1983 he telephoned me after midnight; I realised that he was feverish, and as soon as he had replaced the receiver, I telephoned one of the Counsellors at the Nunciature to warn him of the Nuncio's serious condition. Mons. Cardinale was taken to a clinic where he slipped into a coma in which he remained until the life-support system was switched off on 24 March 1983, on the eve of the opening of the extraordinary Holy Year.

The book went through its final stages of production, somewhat half-heartedly, because the author was in a coma in hospital. As soon as we received them from the printers, copies of the book were sent to Cardinal Casaroli and other members of the Holy See, the Sovereign Military Order of Malta and several Chiefs of Protocol of Governments who had supplied me with additional illustrations.

Shortly afterwards, I went to Rome. During the long audience granted me by Cardinal Casaroli, it gradually became obvious to me that the protests he had received – quite apart from his personal objection to certain parts of it – spelled disaster for the book. His Eminence was anxious to learn what could be done about correcting matters, and he first sent me to see members of the Sovereign Council of the Sovereign Military Order of Malta. He also gave me a list of errors that were essential to correct, and he conveyed two requests of the Holy Father concerning changes if the book were to be revised. His Eminence was apprehensive that certain other persons might make a request to undertake this task and he indicated that he would in that case prefer if the project were to be abandoned. When I agreed to undertake the revision of Archbishop Cardinale's book, I had no idea of the magnitude of my promise to Cardinal Casaroli.

I am glad to say that following the removal of the most offensive errors and the book being edited as much as pagination allowed, the publishers were immediately given an order for several thousand copies; but it was no secret that the financial losses would still be substantial.

Following the second edition in 1984, I started immediately on the third, but I kept to the old pagination so as to lessen the publishers's production costs. Because Colin Smythe Limited had used the Van Duren imprint for the book, it had cast me in the role of author and publisher, a dual position which Cardinal Casaroli felt might create the wrong impression. I withdrew from the role as publisher, and the Van Duren imprint, whilst still being used by Colin Smythe Limited for some books, was considered confusing to the readership of any future project dealing with Catholic-founded Orders of Knighthood. However, we retained the imprint for the revised editions of Archbishop Cardinale's book and my supplementary volume which appeared in 1987. We added another four colour plates to the twenty already in the book, and I also removed the line drawings and obtained as many photographs of insignia as possible.

At that meeting in 1983 Cardinal Casaroli made a prediction to me: it would take ten years, after the book had been written and rewritten before I would get to know the chivalric fraternity, and they me, well enough to become accepted by it as the authority on this vast subject.

The publication of the second revised edition in 1985 was quite successful, though I soon received further complaints, not just from the self-styled Orders, but also genuine grievances from legitimate Orders and many requests from papal knights for further information. For example, the papal decrees concerning their privileges and uniforms had been reproduced in the Latin original which was of little help to those knights who were looking for guidance. I had been able to carry out the Holy Father's wishes with regard to the Polish Order of the White Eagle and correcting its status from extinct to extant, but the Royal House of Bragança of Portugal felt equally aggrieved because the Catholic-founded dynastic Orders of the Immaculate Conception of Our Lady of Vila Viçosa and of Saint Isabel had also been placed into the category of extinct Orders because the ambassador of Portugal in Brussels at the time Mons. Cardinale enquired about them, told him they had been abolished. This was not correct, and to prove it I received certified statements from the Portuguese Embassy in London that neither Order had ever been claimed by the Republic; they belonged the Royal House of Bragança, the Head of which was resident in Portugal.

Subsequently I wrote a supplementary book to *Orders of Knighthood, Awards and the Holy See*, and called it *The Cross on the Sword*. Even at time of publication of that work, it had become obvious that an entirely new book was needed as any more revisions or addenda would only create a worse patch work.

Before placing on record the subsequent events, I must once again reiterate that without Archbishop Cardinale's pioneering work, no such book as this could or would have been possible. I was fortunate in finding in Cardinal Jacques Martin a scholar of protocol, phaleristics, history, heraldry and several related disciplines second to none. Once we had finished his Heraldry in the Vatican, he gave me every assistance on my new project. I owe him a great debt.

Similarly, Cardinal Agostino Casaroli and his Private Secretary, Mons. Luigi Ventura, always answered my questions, and the Secretariat of State also tried to be helpful, though I soon realised that I was faced with a dichotomy: on the one hand the original title of the book had been *Orders of Knighthood and the Holy See*, while on the other, the only Catholic-founded Orders the Holy See was prepared to recognise were the Pontifical Orders of Knighthood, the two Religious Orders of Knighthood, the Sovereign Military Order of Malta and the Equestrian Order of the Holy Sepulchre and, being a sovereign entity under international law, the Orders of Knighthood and Merit of those States with which the Holy See entertained diplomatic relations.

I realised suddenly that between the time when Archbishop Cardinale was preparing his book, drawing also on his earlier work *The Holy See and the International Order* published in 1976, and 1987, when I contemplated rewriting a book on Catholic-founded Orders, a major metamorphosis inside the Vatican had brought about changes to many rules, formed new concepts and generally caused different values that had to be adopted. They took place far more rapidly than those in the past, and because of the rapidity of change in attitudes and values, much of what was accepted as a matter of fact in the days of Archbishop Cardinale, seemed to me to become more and more irrelevant and even contradictory. The most obvious contradiction that concerned the book was its very title. *Orders of Knighthood, Awards and the Holy See* only applied to a relatively small section: the Pontifical Orders of Knighthood, the Sovereign Military Order of Malta and the Equestrian Order of the Holy Sepulchre.

The vast majority of Catholic-founded Orders were of no concern to the *Holy* See in its capacity as the government of the Church, the Curia and the Vatican City State. On the other hand the *Apostolic* See had retained a relationship with many of the extant Catholic-founded Orders.

The Apostolic See and successive Pontiffs had always recognised the dynastic character of Orders belonging to those 'Catholic' dynasties with which the Apostolic See had entertained relations for hundreds of years, although most of the dynasties were now non-regnant. Many of these dynastic Orders are still active in the ceremonial of the Church and in an active lay apostolate.

It is therefore necessary to examine the role and function of the *Holy* See and that of the *Apostolic* See, but the 1983 edition of the *Codex Iuris Canonici* only confuses matters by trying – in a somewhat ambiguous manner – to equate the *Holy* See with the *Apostolic* See, what are two, quite separate juridical entities. Throughout this book I make a strict distinction between them.

The often liberal use of the term 'Holy See' begs the question of the authority that is attached to it. Canon and international lawyers have written many volumes on the definition of '*Holy* See' (*Sancta Sedes*) and '*Apostolic* See' (*Sedes Apostolica*). In the context of Catholic-founded Orders of Knighthood, both terms are used in Papal Bulls and Papal Briefs.

The *Holy* See came to be the usual term for the central ecclesiastical government of the Holy Roman Church. During the journey of Pope Martin V (1417-1431) from Constance to Rome it frequently occurred that the Pope and the ecclesiastical authorities and government were separated from each other. Even in the fifteenth century the official location of the *Holy* See, insofar as this was legally important, was not yet authoritatively fixed. In the Middle Ages it was assumed that the Holy Roman Court of the Pontiff was the seat of ecclesiastical authority and the phrase 'Ubi Papa, ibi Curia' expresses the assumption that the machinery of administration or Curia always surrounded the pope.

This uncertainty caused Pope Clement VIII (1592-1605) to draw up the Constitution *Cum ob nonnullas*, in which it is laid down that, if the pope and the pontifical administration should not reside in the same place, the utterances of both are authoritative, provided they are in agreement with each other.[1]

The term '*Apostolic* See' expresses, according to contemporary theologians and canon lawyers, an abstract notion of authority; it is the core of authority of the Holy Roman Church, continuing the Apostolic succession and the functions of St. Peter, Prince of the Apostles. The *Apostolic* See is thus personified as the Representative of the Prince of the Apostles. This is quite clearly laid down in Pope Leo II's confirmation of the Sixth General Council (Constantinople, 680-681) : 'Id circo et Nos et per nostrum officium haec veneranda Sedes Apostolica his quae difinita sunt, consenti beati Petri Apostoli auctoritate confirmat.' (Therefore We, and also through Our office this venerable Apostolic See, give assent to the things that have been defined, and confirm them by the authority of the Blessed Apostle Peter.)

In more recent times it has been noticeable that those who wished to minimise papal authority used the term 'Curia' in preference to Apostolic See or Holy See. In the Lateran Treaty of 1929, sovereignty was placed with the Holy See, not with the papacy and not with the Vatican. However, even some serious writers, who ought to know better, frequently refer to the Vatican when they mean the Holy See. Diplomats are accredited to the Holy See, not to the Vatican, in the same way that diplomats are accredited to the Court of St. James, not to the United Kingdom of Great Britain.

There is a very subtle distinction between the terms 'Apostolic See' and 'Holy See'; but in each case, the Sovereign Pontiff is its head. From ancient times a distinction has been made between the Apostolic See and its actual occupant: between *sedes* and *sedens*. The intention was neither to discriminate between the two nor to subordinate one to the other, but rather to set forth their intimate connection. The Apostolic See, and indeed the Holy See, are by their nature permanent, whereas their occupant holds that authority but for a time and inasmuch as he occupies the See of St. Peter.

In my definition of phrases I must inevitably restrict myself to those that have had, and continue to have, an impact on Catholic-founded

---

[1]'provided that they are in agreement which each other' is as ambiguous as Canon 361 in the 1983 *Codex Iurus Canonici*, Section I, Chapter IV, which states: '...the terms Apostolic See or Holy See mean not only the Roman Pontiff, but also, unless the contrary is clear from the nature of things or from the context, the Secretariat of State, the Council for the Public Affairs of the Church, and other Institutes of the Roman Curia'. The Council for the Public Affairs of Church has since been abolished and many new changes have been made to the Curia.

Orders of Knighthood. First, I have to define the basis upon which the relationship of the Catholic-founded Orders of Knighthood with its true *fons honorum* began in the Res Publica Christiana and developed into the most powerful force that created what we today call 'Western Civilisation', until the Age of Feudalism and the Reformation moved the *fons honorum* and those many Orders of Catholic knights that had grown up under its umbrella, more towards a state of coexistence than, as previously, interdependence. Only then can one discern why each side used words and phrases that had in the course of time assumed a different linguistic meaning to the other.

A typical example is the word 'suppressed' which time and again has been used by Pope Paul VI in his constitution *Regimini Ecclesiae Universae* and also by Archbishop Cardinale in *Orders of Knighthood, Awards and the Holy See*. Pope Paul's meaning of the word was that something or some function had been transferred to another department; Archbishop Cardinale used it to mean 'abolished' or sometimes 'illegally suppressed and therefore still extant', but no indication is given what he meant when using the word. Whilst it is not my task to comment on a papal constitution, in the context of this work the word 'suppressed' has a very specific meaning.

Another ambiguity involves the use of the word 'Catholic' (meaning that it belongs to the Roman Catholic Church and may even speak and act on behalf of the Church). As the *Holy* See always reiterates, there are only two expressly Catholic Orders of Knighthood that it recognises, the two Religious Orders. However, two expressly Catholic Orders of Knighthood, the Austrian Order of the Golden Fleece of the Imperial and Royal House of Habsburg and the Sacred Military Constantinian Order of St. George of the Royal House of the Two Sicilies, are acknowledged as such and held in high esteem by the *Apostolic* See; membership of these two Orders is only open to those who confess the Roman Catholic religion. However, there exist and have existed many Catholic-founded Orders of Knighthood. Those founded prior to the Reformation were undoubtedly Catholic; but except for the above-mentioned four Orders that are extant today and qualify to be called 'Catholic', all the other Orders were, as time passed by, opened to members of other Christian denominations or even other faiths.

Certainly since 1922, but probably as early as 1885, after the infamous Bismarck incident[1], only Roman Catholics received the Supreme Order of Christ, and since the Apostolic Letter *Equestres Ordines*, issued by Paul VI in 1966, reserving the Order to Christian Heads of State, only President Saragat of Italy received the Order (in February 1966); it was not until on 4 July 1987, twenty-one years later, that Pope John Paul II conferred it on

---

[1] Although he had declared himself publicly to be an atheist, Bismarck blackmailed Pope Leo XIII into giving him the Order of Christ. See also Chapter Two, under The Supreme Order of Christ.

H.M.E.H. Frà Angelo de Mojana di Cologna, Prince and Grand Master of the Sovereign Military Order of Malta, who died six months later, leaving one solitary Knight of the Order of Christ alive, King Baudouin of the Belgians, who died in 1993.

Without wishing to involve myself in papal politics, it has remained a mystery to me why His Majesty, Juan Carlos I, King of Spain, successor of generations of Spanish Kings, all of whom bore the exalted title 'Most Catholic Majesty' and were Knights of the Order of Christ, has not received the Order twenty years after ascending the throne of Spain. I was three times informed by an impeccable source that conferment was imminent, but it never materialised. What really puzzled me was that while Paul VI conferred the Pian Collar in 1977 on King Juan Carlos, in 1983, when John Paul II was on his way to Haiti, he made a stopover in Spain and met King Juan Carlos. The very next day, however, he conferred the same Order on the infamous dictator of Haiti, Jean Claude Duvalier.

Although this appeared in print in *The Cross on the Sword* in 1987, I received many letters about it, especially from Papal Knights, though I remember at the time of the conferment, the international press commented on the Pope's 'generosity of spirit', or words to that effect. Similar hostile comments appeared in August 1994 in connection with Dr. Kurt Waldheim.[1]

I started on this book as soon as *The Cross on the Sword* had been published, but had I foreseen the magnitude of the task I had undertaken, I might not have done so. As both publications gradually became widely known internationally, I received many letters about them. Some pointed out errors on my part, but others, mainly from self-styled Orders, complained, claiming that they were *ipso facto* recognised by the Vatican and demanding that I publish corrections, but the majority concerned personal queries about papal decorations and especially papal titles conferred on an ancestor, and I was usually asked, whether I could confirm that they had inherited the right to bear that title. On occasion such letters contained many pages of family trees and photocopies of ancient and not so ancient documents, but I never saw an original document of conferment.

In 1987 I noticed in the Roman Curia a sudden change of attitude towards Orders of Knighthood in general and Pontifical Orders in particular. It is difficult to say in retrospect where and when this subject began to occupy some of the prelates, but I became very conscious of it when, after the publication of *The Cross on the Sword*, one senior prelate voiced serious criticism that I had given a whole chapter to the conferment of the title Knight Commander of the Order of St. Gregory the

---

[1] A powerful Jewish lobby protested strongly against the Pope conferring the Pian Order on the former Secretary General of UNO and then President of Austria, Kurt Waldheim.

Great on a Jew. He felt that I had opened the flood gates to future conferments. After a while I became aware of a small minority of prelates who openly canvassed for the Holy See to have nothing to do with Orders, and the pontifical and dynastic honours came under their scrutiny.

Slowly but continuously, I worked on this book, first building a scaffolding for a new structure and gathering first-hand information, and later, correcting names, dates and other details. Previously I had restricted my revisions to those points that had been specifically submitted to me to for revision. Now, I had to check the names and dates of every pope, emperor, king as well as the dates of foundation, restoration or abolition of all the Catholic-founded Orders. I never cease to be amazed how many reference books seem to copy from one another and how many errors are thus perpetuated.

I have lost track of the number of Pandora's Boxes that found their way onto my desk, the contents of which never failed to cause more trouble.

However, probably my rudest awakening came in 1990. I had already decided not to use the phrase 'Holy See' in the title, as it only worked in the limitations imposed upon it by its sovereign status. The Holy See wanted nothing to do with dynastic Catholic-founded Orders nor with those Catholic-founded Orders that subsequently had become Orders of Merit of their States, other than recognise those Orders belonging to states with which it had diplomatic relations. But such recognition amounts really to nothing more than abiding by an international convention that it was obliged to observe as a sovereign power. Secondly, I had already decided to delete the episcopal 'We' in the text, because it was both inappropriate and archaic. When Archbishop Cardinale wrote his books, especially *The Holy See and the International Order* and later *Orders of Knighthood, Awards and the Holy See*,[1] a different world order prevailed. Although Pope John Paul II refers to himself in the first person singular when he speaks and writes, one had to be in the somewhat privileged position of working and living, even if only for short periods, inside the walls of the Vatican City to notice the metamorphosis taking place. After three years I realised that the hitherto authoritative 'We' no longer

---

[1] Mons. Cardinale researched and wrote theses on this subject as early as 1960. He spoke not for himself but for the Pontiff, the Holy See and the Roman Curia. The episcopal 'We' indicated that he wrote with authority and expressed the view of the highest administration in the Church Although new Draconian rules and regulations had been introduced after the Second Vatican Council (of which Mons. Cardinale was a member), and many changes were made, they were probably more noticeable on the level of the Local Church than inside the Vatican. Both Paul VI and John XXIII continued to use the Apostolic 'We' in their official pronouncements, and Archbishop Cardinale did so in his books because when he began his work on them, there was one unified voice, that of the Pontiff and of the Holy See. The Apostolic See was a reality, but an abstract of the continued occupancy of the See of St. Peter. He truly acted and wrote with authority. However, being so close to that See of St. Peter himself, he probably did not see the authority slowly eroding, although being domiciled in Brussels, this is surprising since Belgium is well known for its dissidents and innovators.

existed. Those who dissented from an 'official view' (as long as it did not concern matters of dogma) voiced their own ideas and views. It may perhaps be a democratic attribute but it seemed singularly out of place in the Roman Curia.

It became more and more difficult to get a consensus of opinion on any question I asked. I am sure that there have always been differences of opinion in the Vatican, but they were probably sorted out behind closed doors. At no time would anybody try, for example, to countermand an express wish of the Holy Father. Although the case which comes to mind did not concern a matter of faith but was merely a personal wish of the Pope, I realised for the first time how drastic the metamorphosis inside the Roman Curia had been, when I was indirectly drawn into a situation where one dignitary tried to persuade another of the same rank to ignore a personal wish of the Holy Father and follow his advice instead. It became quite obvious that I would act under false pretences if I claimed to express the Holy See's view of, and attitude to, Catholic-founded Orders of Knighthood in this book. In fact, all I can claim is to have been given privileges, valuable information, the assistance of some of the Roman Hierarchy's greatest experts, and on several occasions, an opportunity of being 'inside looking out', but also looking at the inside.

I have endeavoured to remain scrupulously detached from controversies and to be fair to those I write about and the last thing I want to do is pontificate. However, having worked in this field for fifteen years, and since 1983 occupied the role that my late friend Archbishop Cardinale filled as chronicler of the Catholic-founded Orders and of their past or present relations with the Apostolic See, I speak with experience rather than authority. I am not speaking for the Apostolic See, but about it and its relations with Catholic-founded Orders of Knighthood and of Merit. Only the Supreme Pontiff, the successor of St. Peter and Christ's Vicar on Earth can speak *for* the Apostolic See because it is he who occupies it; that is one role even the Pope cannot delegate.

Having made my position absolutely clear, I now venture to comment on some of the contents of this book.

With regard to the Pontifical Orders of Knighthood (Chapter One), there is no doubt that recent events only herald further changes in the not too distant future. If I appear impatient and aggravated in some paragraphs of that chapter, it is only because I found myself frustrated at not receiving straightforward answers to my questions. I felt annoyed that even the Apostolic Nuncio in London was given information about the admission of women to the Pontifical Orders which those who gave it must have known to be incorrect. The Nuncio subsequently issued a statement on the situation which was read out to the Papal Knights in Great Britain at their annual dinner, and if it is any comfort to His Excellency, he initially received the same reply I got, with one difference: I continued to receive that reply for two weeks after the Nuncio had been told the opposite to be true. It is of no concern of mine nor my role to criticise or venture a written opinion on the admission of women to the Pontifical Orders of Knighthood – even if the statutes were never changed. In fact, as I explain in Chapter One, I would have welcomed it as a day of joy and happiness for all members of the Orders that have now been opened to women. What I object to and found distasteful was the secretive manner in which it was done. How could the Archbishop of Los Angeles publicise the investiture of women into the Order of St. Gregory the Great many months before it was officially announced that it had pleased the Holy Father to open three Orders to women? There are words which aptly describe such practices; alas, I am neither judge nor jury, but I reserve my right to point out practices which I consider unchivalrous, to say the least.

I have no doubt that Archbishop Cardinale would never have voiced his annoyance or frustration publicly. His duty to the Holy See, of which he was an important member, would have silenced him, and he would have merely said that three of the Orders are now open to women, with no further comment. There was nothing wrong in the Pope opening the three Orders to women. All pontifical honours are in the Pontiff's absolute gift and he can do with them as he pleases, so there was no need for denials that it was about to happen – unless if those whom one would expect to know about such matters only discovered it had happened by reading about it in the world's press.

I have always held the Holy See in high esteem and I believe I have served it well and to the best of my ability, but I will not be accused of sweeping uncomfortable truths under the proverbial carpet. I could not ignore the letters and information, backed up by documentary proof, that I received from Catholics living in the Archdiocese of Los Angeles, that showed just how many people are only too aware of what has been going on. In a work of this nature one does not criticize an accidental mistake but when something happens that fundamentally changes a centuries-old tradition, the matter is too important to ignore, and if I mention it, I must also give an explanation. My personal credibility and academic integrity would be called in doubt if I passed over this momentous event without putting it in perspective. Personally I believe that the Secretariat of State was faced with a *fait accompli*, about which it could do nothing. The carpet had been pulled from under its feet.

On a different note, following the press coverage of the investiture as a Papal Knight Commander of a devout Jew who has been working for many years on establishing good relations between the Catholic Church and the Jewish community, I had many letters from (Catholic) Papal Knights, asking why they had not been invested at a similar ceremony. I could only explain to them that at the request of the Cardinal Archbishop of Westminster the ceremony had been specially devised by me with the help of the late Mons. Gerald Mahon, Auxiliary Bishop of Westminster. Because of the many letters from Papal Knights which continued to arrive, Bishop Mahon and Canon Adrian Arrowsmith, also of Westminster Cathedral, and Archbishop Cesare Zacchi, President of the Pontifical Ecclesiastical Academy for Diplomats in Rome, who was staying with me at the time, helped me to devise variations for different investiture ceremonies. Cardinal Jacques Martin checked them and made occasional suggestions, and I was able to publish various guidelines for an investiture of a Catholic Papal Knight in *The Cross on the Sword*.

With regard to Chapter Three, 'Pontifical Awards of Merit', it has been the consensus of opinion among the Hierarchy, that the Cross 'Pro Ecclesia et Pontifice' and the Medal 'Benemerenti' are strictly Religious Awards, unlike Papal Knighthoods, which are chivalric Orders of Merit and thus should receive recognition as such by all governments that entertain diplomatic relations with the Holy See.

Archbishop Cardinale featured a chapter on the Pontifical Medals which he described not as an award, but as a token of the Holy Father's appreciation. Since the role of the Pontifical Medal underwent a change in the fourth year of the pontificate of John Paul II, I thought it more appropriate now to place the section about it in the Appendices.

In Chapter Five, 'Religious but not Pontifical Orders of Knighthood' I have strictly adhered to Archbishop Cardinale's text of matters concerning the juridical status of the Sovereign Military Order of Malta, which the Sovereign Council of the Order of Malta corrected and purged of any errors of fact or judgement.

The Catholic-founded dynastic Orders in Chapter Seven are preceded by an introduction to the dynasties that bestow the Order. Instead of classifying dynasties into 'exalted' and 'less exalted', as was done before, I have explained which of the dynasties and orders participate in the ceremonial of the Local Church or are otherwise are engaged in a lay apostolate. It is sometimes important to examine the infrastructure of a dynasty to understand historical facts which could have an influence on future developments. In the case of the Royal House of Bourbon of the Two Sicilies, I used some facsimile letters and also a genealogical table which reflects the legal position of various parties with regard to the headship of the Royal House and the grand-mastership of the Constantinian Order.

Catholic-founded and secularised Crown and State Orders in Chapter Eight are preceded by a brief introduction. As far as the Republic of Poland is concerned, only the Orders of the White Eagle and of Polonia Restituta are relevant to this book. However, as no published record exists of the precedence among the Polish Orders and Decorations other than in the *Polish Law Gazette*, I have added a comprehensive list as an appendix.

December 22, 1990 was a proud day, not only for the Poles, whose democratically elected President was sworn in, but also for me. Having restored the Order of the White Eagle to its rightful place among the Orders of Knighthood in the 1985 revised edition of *Orders of Knighthood, Awards and the Holy See*, I was delighted when the new President accepted from the outgoing President-in-Exile the Grand-Mastership of that Order as the principal Order of Knighthood of the new Republic.

Other appendices deal further and more extensively with extinct Orders that are dealt with in detail in Chapter Nine.

To those who have read *Orders of Knighthood, Awards and the Holy See* and *The Cross on the Sword*, Chapter Ten will come as a surprise, and some readers might conclude that I finally gave in to some strong lobbying. I wish to make it absolutely clear that I was under no pressure from any group: it is there because the Holy Father made it known that it was his wish to see recognised the chivalric and hospitaller work of those knights who have given and continue to give enormous support to the Polish and other peoples when and where they most need it. I had a straightforward choice: to abide by the Holy Father's express wish or to take the easy way out and join those who do not wish the subject matter given any public mention. I have no desire whatever to be confrontational or controversial: my complete loyalty to His Holiness decided the matter for me, and I very much hope that it will be read in the spirit of the Holy Father's wishes.

Chapter Eleven deals with knightly organisations whose work in their lay apostolate is held in high esteem. It was Cardinal Casaroli who originally voiced the idea that the true spirit of Christian chivalry is no exclusive reserve of Orders of Knighthood; he singled out the Knights of Columbus in America as a typical example and he felt most unhappy that Archbishop Cardinale had only given them a brief 'corollary' appended to the chapter on self-styled Orders.

I have headed Chapter Twelve 'The Spirit of Christian Chivalry Today': if one photograph can speak a thousand words with a few extra by me, how much can ten or more? The organisations that put such a chivalric spirit into action and at the same time revive the hospitaller spirit of the ancient Orders of Knighthood that fought in the Crusades, are not themselves Orders of Knighthood, but foundations of those extant Orders which also support them financially and in other ways. It raises an interesting point for discussion which does not belong in the chapters on the Orders of Knighthood: at the time of the Crusades, members of the ancient Orders were originally divided into Hospitallers and Military Knights. The latter protected the pilgrims to the Holy Places and defended them against the invading forces of Islam who were attempting to reconquer Christian holy shrines and Christian land. The Hospitallers looked after the needs of sick pilgrims and, of course, their own wounded

Military Knights. Is there perhaps a case to be made now for the reinstatement of the distinct roles and functions of Military and Hospitaller Knights? Although today's Knights are often actively engaged in some of the hospitaller work, Chapter Twelve could have been headed 'The Hospitallers of Today'.

Chapter Thirteen deals with the perennial matter of self-styled orders that claim chivalric status without any justification, often adopting names or imitating styles of extant legitimate Orders of Knighthood, and in other cases using names of long extinct Catholic-founded Orders.

I have thanked in the Acknowledgements all those who in their different ways have contributed to this book by providing me with information and illustrations, but I must at the outset single out three gentlemen in particular: without each and every one of them I would have been unable to write this book. First, His Eminence Agostino Cardinal Casaroli, who put so much trust in me in 1983 and who has encouraged me ever since. It was a proud day when I saw His Eminence receive the prestigious dignity of Doctor in Sacra Theologia from Oxford University. His definition of what a Christian Knight should be, is what this book is about.

While giving wholehearted place of honour to the dedication Archbishop Cardinale wrote for His Holiness Pope John Paul II in the first edition of his book *Orders of Knighthood, Awards and the Holy See*, I dedicate this book to three great Priests, His late Excellency Archbishop Hyginus Eugene Cardinale, His Eminence Agostino Cardinal Casaroli, and His late Eminence Jacques Cardinal Martin, whose practical help, assistance and support have made much of this book possible. Cardinal Martin became a mentor and friend, who never tired of spending many hours hunting out documents for me that even his fictional fellow-countryman Detective Inspector Maigret would not have found.

When I had taken my leave of Cardinal Martin in September 1992, and as I approached the door to his apartment in the Palazzo di S.Carlo, he asked me to stop a moment. He told me that he wished to give me a special Blessing, which he did. Afterwards he said: 'Don't forget, Peter, that was a very special Blessing.' A few days later, on 27 September, I received a telephone call from the Vatican, informing me that His Eminence had unexpectedly died of a heart attack during the night. Cardinal Jacques Martin lives on in this book which owes so much to him.

Last but not least, I want to thank my friend and colleague Colin Smythe. It is quite incidental that he is the publisher of this book; whilst being grateful for his professional work in publishing it – any good publisher could have done that – I must thank him for the countless hours he spent reading and rereading every chapter, some of them more than ten times, such as the section on the House of the Two Sicilies, which

IOANNI PAULO II

Pontifici Maximo

Qui in universa Ecclesia Catholica

sub Deo

omnium Fons est Honorum

benigne annuenti

hoc quantulumcumque est opus

Hyginus Cardinale

observantissimo filii animo

inscribit

dedicat

Archbishop Cardinale dedicated his book to Pope John Paul II. In his 1983 edition he used a reproduction of a painting of the Pope which the author was subsequently asked to replace by the above photograph in the revised editions.

I wrote and rewrote at least that often. During the last year of my work, hardly a day passed when he was not engaged in reading what I had written, making suggestions for alterations, additions and deletions, and sometimes arguing with me so fiercely that an outsider might have thought we were quarrelling. Yet all he aimed at has been the pursuit of excellence, and he has put his mark on this book far beyond the imprint of his publishing house.

Gerrards Cross,
Buckinghamshire,
November 1994   Peter Bander van Duren

CHAPTER ONE

I

THE INVOLVEMENT OF THE APOSTOLIC SEE AND THE HOLY SEE IN THE FIELD OF CHIVALRY

The involvement of the Holy See[1] in the field of chivalry goes back to the first Papal Bull granting indulgences to those who took part in the Crusades against the Muslims. The first of these Crusade Bulls, which concerned Spain, was that of the French Pope Urban II (1088-1099) to the Counts Berenguer Ramón de Barcelona and Armengal de Besalú in 1089

Pope Urban II (1088-1099) who instigated the Crusades with his former teacher, St. Bruno, whom he called to Rome in 1094 as his counsellor. Urban II can therefore also be regarded as the founder of the chivalric and hospitaller spirit that permeated the first Orders of Knighthood.

[1]Until the Lateran Treaty came into force in 1929, there is no reason to distinguish between the 'Apostolic See' and the 'Holy See'.

at the time of the reconquest of Tarragona. The wars waged by the Spaniards against the Moors constituted a continual Crusade from the eleventh to the sixteenth century.

By definition, Crusades were expeditions undertaken in fulfilment of a solemn vow to deliver the Holy Places from Mohammedan tyranny. Since the Middle Ages the meaning of the word 'Crusade' has been extended to include all wars undertaken in pursuance of a vow, and directed against infidels, particularly against Mohammedans, but modern writers have abused the word by applying it to all wars of a religious character. The idea of the Crusade corresponds to a political conception that was realised in Christendom only from the eleventh to the fifteenth century, and it presupposes a union of all peoples and sovereigns under the direction of the popes.

The popes alone had maintained a just estimate of Christian unity; they realised to what extent the interests of Europe were threatened by Islam, and they alone had a coherent foreign policy whose traditions were formed under Pope Leo IX (1049-1054) and Pope Gregory VII (1073-1085). At that time Europe was divided into numerous states whose sovereigns were absorbed in tedious and petty territorial disputes, while the Emperor, in theory the temporal head of Christendom, was wasting his strength in a quarrel over Investitures. Hence, none but the popes could inaugurate the international movement that culminated in the Crusades.

It has been customary to describe the Crusades as eight in number. This division is arbitrary and excludes many important expeditions, among them those of the fourteenth and fifteenth centuries. In reality, the Crusades continued until the end of the seventeenth century.

From the sixteenth century European policy was swayed exclusively by state interest and the idea of a crusade seemed antiquated. The leaders of the Reformation disapproved of crusades, and Martin Luther even declared that it was a sin to make war against the Turks because God had made Islam His instrument in punishing the sins of His people.

Although the idea of a crusade was not wholly lost, therefore, it took on a new form and adapted itself to the new conditions. The Conquistadores who, since the fifteenth century, had been going forth to discover new lands, considered themselves the auxiliaries of the Crusade. The Infante Dom Henrique, Vasco da Gama, Albuquerque and others each wore the Cross on his breast and, when seeking the means of reaching Asia by routes from its East, they thought of attacking Islam from the rear, and the popes strongly encouraged these expeditions. On the other hand, among the Great Powers of Europe, the House of Habsburg, which was directly threatened by the Turks and Islam, and which had supreme control of the Mediterranean, realised that it would be to its advantage to maintain a certain interest in the concept of the Crusade.

Until the end of the seventeenth century, when a diet of German princes was held in Ratisbon, the question of war against the Turks and Islam was frequently raised. In 1528 and 1529 Martin Luther himself, modifying his first opinion, exhorted the German nobility and knights to defend Christendom. The war in Austro-Hungary always had the character of a Crusade with, on various occasions, French knights enlisting under the imperial banner. In 1664 Louis XIV, hoping to extend his influence in Europe, sent the Emperor a contingent which repulsed the Turks in the battle of St. Gothard. Soon, alas, petty jealousy made the French change sides: in order to maintain a balance of power in Europe against the House of Austria, they had no hesitation in making treaties with the Turks and Islam. When in 1683 30,000 Turks advanced on Vienna, the French made no move, and it was to John Sobieski, King of Poland, that the Emperor of Austria owed his safety. Islam, overwhelmed by the victories of Prince Eugene at the close of the seventeenth century, thenceforth became a passive power. The emergence and rapid growth of Islamic Fundamentalism since the 1970s once more poses a threat to the very existence of Christian values and what we have come to accept as 'Western Civilisation'. However, the world order has changed, mainly through scientific advance in communication and general indifference which hides behind the more respectable façade of liberalism. Historically, it appears that we are on the threshold of a worldwide Islamic expansion; the difference between now and the events at the end of the seventeenth century is there for all to see. There is no need for 30,000 Turks to advance on Vienna. The struggle – if one were to develop – would be from within the frontiers of certain Western countries, not from without, and not a single country that embraces Western Civilisation will be immune. It is neither fashionable nor politically correct to speak or write of this reality, but it has already taught us that history will repeat itself. The logical question is therefore: what can the Christian Knights of the 21st century do about it? Very little.

John Owen (1560-1622) gives the reason in his famous epigram, which is usually only quoted in part; in fact, his epigram is a dialogue:

'Tempora mutantur nos et mutamur in illis.'
'Quomodo?'
'Fit semper tempore pejor homo!'

['Times change, and we change with them too.' 'And why is this?' 'With time mankind only grows worse!']

The Crusades are an integral part of the history of the popes and the Holy Roman Church, and they were essentially an enterprise of the Apostolic See. The idea of quelling all dissensions among Christians, of uniting them under the same standard and sending them forth against the aggressions of Islam, was conceived in the eleventh century, at a time when there were no organised states in Europe, when Islam threatened to invade Europe, and the Byzantine Empire was unable to withstand the enemies that surrounded it.

Among the many Orders of Knighthood, none worked harder to defend Christendom against the onslaught of Islam than the Knights of St. John of Jerusalem, known today as the Sovereign Military Order of Malta. If, indeed, the Christian civilisation of Europe has become a universal culture in the highest sense, the glory rebounds, in no small measure, to the Crusades and to the many Catholic-founded Orders of Knighthood that were active from the eleventh to the beginning of the eighteenth century. The Apostolic See has throughout these centuries maintained its supreme rôle of *Mater et Magistra* of those Orders of Knighthood.

Although there undoubtedly existed some chivalric communities before the Crusades, none of them survived. Many of those Orders whose names are synonymous with the Crusades and which continued after they ended still exist today: the Order of St. John of Jerusalem – the Sovereign Military Order of Malta, founded in 1048; the Order of St. Lazarus of Jerusalem (founded in 1060 – partly amalgamated with the Order of St. Maurice of the House of Savoy in 1434 and recognised as an amalgamated Order in 1572 by Pope Gregory XIII, most of the French knights amalgamated with the newly-founded Order of Our Lady of Mount Carmel in 1608 by Pope Paul V, abolished in 1830 by Pius VIII, and continued by independent groups who refused to recognise the amalgamations and abolition); the Order of the Holy Sepulchre of Jerusalem, founded in 1099; the Knights Templars, founded in 1119, but suppressed by Pope Clement V at the instigation of King Philip the Fair of France in 1312; the Portuguese Order of Avis, founded in 1143; the Spanish Order of Calatrava, founded in 1158; the Spanish Order of St. James of the Sword, founded in 1170; the Spanish Order of Alcantara, founded in 1177 (but only took the title in 1212); the Teutonic Order, founded in 1190, and which became a Religious Order by decree of Pius XI in 1929; the S.M. Constantinian Order, founded in 1190; the Danish Order of the Dannebrog, founded in 1219; the Spanish Order of Montesa, founded in 1317; the Portuguese Order of Christ, founded in 1317; the Portuguese Order of St. James of the Sword, founded in 1320; the Polish Order of the White Eagle, founded in 1325); the English Order of the Garter, founded in 1346; the Swedish Order of the Seraphim, founded in 1334; the Savoyan Order SS. Annunziata, founded in 1362; the English Order of the Bath, founded in 1399; the Order of the Golden Fleece, founded in 1430; the Savoyan Order of St. Maurice, founded in 1434; the Bavarian Order of St. Hubert, founded in 1444; the Danish Order of the Elephant, founded in 1464; the French Order of St. Michael, founded in 1469; the Swedish Order of the Sword, founded in 1523; the Pontifical

Order of the Golden Spur or the Golden Militia, founded in 1559; and the French Order of the Holy Ghost, founded in 1578.

After the victory over the Turks at Vienna, several more Catholic Orders of Knighthood were founded; among the more prominent ones are the Order of St. Januarius of the Two Sicilies (1738); the Spanish Order of Carlos III (1771); and the Portuguese Order of Our Lady of the Conception of Vila Viçosa (1819).

All these Orders of Knighthood, and many more, had the full support of the Apostolic See and successive popes. Most of the Orders founded from the time of the first Crusade to the defeat of the Turks at Vienna were expressly established to defend Christian civilisation against the onslaught of Islam. The *raison d'être* of the Orders founded later was without exception that of rewarding merit. Most of these Orders adopted in their statutes the ideals of the ancient Orders, but it is fair to say that few of them ever practised those ideals. In many cases, it became a matter of national pride and prestige to have an Order that was on par with such illustrious Orders as The Burgundian Golden Fleece, The English Garter, The Danish Elephant or the Savoyan Annunziata. It is interesting that many of these Orders had in their statutes the defence of the belief in the Immaculate Conception of the Blessed Virgin as one of the criteria.

The Papacy has not only encouraged the foundation of secular Orders of Knighthood under its auspices or patronage, but there is a history of popes founding Pontifical Orders of Knighthood and Orders of Merit, besides countless Crosses and Medals.

The conferment of papal honours on members of the laity for distinguished services and as a means of recognising and rewarding loyalty is a very ancient custom, but at first they were granted mainly within the framework of the Pontifical Order of Christ and the Order of the Golden Militia. Although recipients were usually required to prove noble ancestry and lineage, those who could not prove nobility were automatically ennobled by the Orders to which they were admitted.

Papal honours for laymen were not restricted to knighthoods; titles of nobility and ranks of office at the papal court were also much sought after, and occasionally, depending on the attitude – or sometimes financial need – of individual popes, such honours were conferred rather lavishly on not very meritorious men.

In the sixteenth century popes began founding a number of *Collegia Militum*, Colleges of Militia, though few of them survived their founders. Among many others, the best known was the Collegium Sancti Petri, the College of St. Peter, which was established by Leo X (1513-1521) in 1520. This College had all the appearances of an Order of Knighthood, but was in reality an association of gentlemen who gave substantial financial help to the Pope and the papal court, receiving as their reward all kinds of honours, titles and tributes. In 1540 Paul III (1534-1549) founded the

Collegium Militum Sancti Pauli, the College of the Militia of St. Paul, and in 1546, he established the Order of the Knights of the Lily. An Order of Pian Knights was founded in 1559 by Pius IV (1559-1565).

Sixtus V (1585-1590) founded the Order of the Lauretan Knights in 1586 because assaults on the Holy House of Loreto by pirates in the Adriatic Sea were on the increase. The Holy House of Loreto was one of the most famous, popular and therefore wealthy shrines; it is reputed to have been the house of the Holy Family at Nazareth which, according to tradition, had first been miraculously translated in 1291 to Fiume Illyria, from there in 1294 to Recanti, and finally to the estate of a Lady Lauretta, after whom the town Loreto takes its name. It is situated three miles from the Adriatic Sea in central Italy, and its reputation as a holy shrine where miracles took place grew rapidly. The Order of the Lauretan Knights was short-lived, and 300 years later, Leo XIII (1878-1903) instituted the Lauretan Cross in gold, silver and bronze for benefactors of the Holy House of Loreto. This award has no connection with the long-extinct Order of the Lauretan Knights and it was placed in abeyance by Pius XII (1938-1958).

During the seventeenth and eighteenth centuries and in the early 1800s, many more Orders of Knighthood and honours of various kinds were instituted in the Papal States. They were all short-lived. Among them were the Equestrian Order of the Moretto, founded by Pius VII (1800-1823) to honour the chairmen of the Accademia di San Luca, an academy of painters, sculptors and architects, and the Equestrian Order of St. Cecilia, founded in 1847 by Pius IX (1846-1878), to be conferred on the guardians, the chairmen, the secretaries and the *camerlengo* of the Musical Academy of St. Cecilia.

The nineteenth century saw an increase of abuses perpetrated in the conferment of honours, knighthoods, and privileges, but especially of nobiliary titles and other favours. At the same time Europe witnessed a widespread resentment and even revolution against nobility and the privileges associated with it.

The criteria upon which honours were bestowed had changed completely. With many European States changing their system of awarding honours and knighthoods to one based on merit, proof of noble lineage was no longer required. With the exception of a very few Hospitaller Orders, such as St. John of Jerusalem and the Order of the Holy Sepulchre of Jerusalem (which at that time still used the appellation 'Sacred and Military', the appellation 'Equestrian' only being adopted in 1930), and the Teutonic Order, by the nineteenth century none of the Orders of Knighthood had retained the original characteristics of those Orders founded at the time of the Crusades. Because the threat of Islam had disappeared at the end of the seventeenth century with the victory over the Turks at Vienna, the military functions of Orders of Knighthood were no longer valid criteria for their continued existence.

The Papacy therefore decided to reform its own sys[tem of] honours, basing it mainly on the new criterion of per[sonal merit.] [It is at] the beginning of the nineteenth century that we see th[e change in] the meaning of term 'Order', which previously ap[plied] more often applied to its insignia and decorations [than to a] knightly entity. It is important to note that this new sys[tem, as] it changes of attitude towards rules and statutes. To become a knight, most Orders no longer implied submission to a religious rule or even statutes, which hitherto had allowed a knight to bear some cross or symbol on his surcoat and thus bear public witness to his faith and allegiance.

Pius VII began the reform when he ordered the suppression of the title of Count Palatine which was given to, among others, the Knights of the Golden Militia. However, great confusion with regard to existing papal titles of nobility and papal knighthoods persisted until St. Pius X (1903-1914) established some uniformity when he wrote his Apostolic Letter of 7 February 1905 *Multum ad excitandos*, which reconstituted and remodelled the statutes and constitution of the Pontifical Orders of Knighthood.

St. Pius X defined the Pontifical Orders of Knighthood as 'corporations, instituted by the Roman Pontiffs to reward persons who deserved special recognition on account of the services rendered by them to the Church and society'. These Orders are called 'Pontifical' because they were founded and are awarded by the Sovereign Pontiff either directly (*motu proprio*) or indirectly, following a request submitted to the Secretariat of State.

St. Pius X reconfirmed the Supreme Order of Christ and the Pontifical Equestrian Order of St. Gregory the Great without making any changes, but he reconstituted the Order of the Golden Spur or Golden Militia, and the Order no longer conferred the title of Count Palatine. He instituted the Pontifical Equestrian Order of Pope St. Sylvester as a separate Order, and he reconfirmed the Order of Pius IX with the prerogative to confer the appellation *nobile* for the first and second class. This title did not confer actual nobility, but qualified the person to be listed among the 'untitled nobility'. The privilege of receiving or using the appellation *nobile* in connection with the Order of Pius IX was abolished by Pius XII on 11 November 1939.

During the second half of the pontificate of Pius XII, the Apostolic See discouraged the use of all titles of papal nobility and also discouraged those who claimed hereditary papal titles from using them. The reasons for these measures were twofold: the Holy See was endeavouring to adapt its practice of bestowing Orders of Merit as much as possible to present day society, and the Pontiffs had for almost 100 years attempted to further reduce the temporal aspects in the exercise of their sovereignty.

ORDERS OF KNIGHTHOOD AND OF MERIT

Pope Pius VII (1800-1823) began the reform of the Pontifical Orders of Knighthood.

His Eminence Agostino Cardinal Casaroli was the first Grand Chancellor of all the Pontifical Orders of Knighthood since 1905 to have made an official statement defining the role and functions of a Christian Knight.

Courtesy: *L'Osservatore Romano*

Pope Pius XII (1939-1958) endeavoured throughout his pontificate to further reduce the temporal aspects of the Holy See's sovereignty by abolishing all titles of nobility associated with Pontifical Orders of Knighthood.

It had long been felt and also publicly expressed that the conferment of titles of nobility was a secular practice, not in conformity with the spiritual aims of the Church. As a result, the Pontifical Equestrian Orders attracted more attention and became even more sought after.

There is no doubt that this desire to obtain a papal knighthood or promotion to a higher rank in an Order can, on occasion, lead to an abuse of the system; it happens only rarely, but those who obtain such an honour under false pretences, and even more so, those who facilitate a conferment of a decoration or promotion for reasons which do not qualify under the criterion of merit as intended by the founders of the Orders, namely to render exceptional service to the Pontiff or the Holy See, only devalue the honour; in the section 'Admission to a Pontifical Equestrian Order', I shall elaborate on some of these abuses which, in all fairness to the Holy See, are rare. Nevertheless, once they become known, they cause much consternation among the Papal Knights and usually lead to extensive correspondence. Particular resentment is shown by meritorious Papal Knights who were rewarded for valuable service rendered to the Pontiff, the Holy See or the Church, about those who it is discovered have acquired a decoration as a result of paying large sums of money to somebody who subsequently facilitated the conferment of a papal knighthood. These cases are fortunately rare; several bishops are known to have vetoed any application or proposal for a knighthood, where there has been a hint of a monetary transaction.

I shall return to the question of papal titles, because over the years I have received many enquiries concerning them, as they are usually assumed to have been inherited from an ancestor who, sometimes centuries ago, had received a papal honour which also conferred a title.

There is a fundamental difference between the Pontifical Orders and the Religious-Military, but non-Pontifical Orders of Knighthood, such as the Sovereign Military Order of Malta and the Equestrian Order of the Holy Sepulchre of Jerusalem. Their foundation was a result of private initiative, later approved by the Papacy, but from their beginning, as with the other early Monastic-Military Orders of Knighthood, they were orientated towards the Church by reason of their very constitution and motivation. These Orders are fully recognised by the Holy See in their respective different status.

When the then Papal Secretary of State, Cardinal Casaroli, wrote to me about the expressed satisfaction of His Holiness with 'this compendium of facts which hitherto could only be found in scattered and often hard-to-find sources', he referred to a one particular subject which is widely misunderstood and often misrepresented by parties with vested interests: the Vatican Archives. Whilst there are millions of documents carefully filed in thousands of sections, there are hundreds of thousands of documents that have been 'mislaid', wrongly filed, lost or were destroyed during the pillages of the Apostolic Palace. Many papal rulings and memoranda were never entered in the archives and often left in bundles, usually just marked 'Miscellanea', in drawers of cupboards or writing desks, which, in turn, had been stored away in one of the large storehouses in the Vatican.

As I have already acknowledged, Cardinal Jacques Martin gave me much help in the preparation of this book. He had already made a substantial contribution and also written the introduction to the section on Pontifical Equestrian Orders in my book *The Cross on the Sword* (1987). Having lived in the Vatican for almost sixty years and worked for six Popes, he was a legend in his own lifetime. In the course of his work, especially as Prefect of the Apostolic Palaces and later Prefect of the Pontifical Court, he was given many papal memoranda by the Pontiffs whom he served, and he found over the years many memoranda written by their predecessors, among which were also detailed notes on protocol and the functions of Papal Knights, especially those of the Order of St. Gregory the Great, that were drawn up by St. Pius X. Cardinal Martin gave me all the relevant information from them before placing the memoranda of past popes, which he had discovered in those anonymous bundles of 'Miscellanea' in the archives of the Holy See.

His Eminence Jacques Cardinal Martin (1908-1992) was the only Prefect of the Papal Court in the history of the papacy who served in that capacity under three Pontiffs, a position he filled for fourteen years. He lived in the Vatican for well over half a century, and his knowledge of the Vatican and those who had lived there since Pope Eugene IV (1431) was phenomenal, his advice being sought by many scholars.

Courtesy: *L'Osservatore Romano*

He also drew my attention to facts which with his experience appeared obvious to him, but had often been overlooked, or their significance had not been realised by others. As well as the Apostolic Brief by St. Pius X of 7 February 1905 *Multum ad excitandos*, the same date also saw the promulgation of the Apostolic Brief of Foundation for the Order of Pope St. Sylvester, Briefs of Reconstitution of the Orders of the Golden Spur and of Pius IX, and Briefs confirming the Supreme Order of Christ and the Order of St. Gregory the Great, all of which gave details about the decorations, ranks and uniforms of these Pontifical Orders in separate, but attached Papal Briefs. These were signed *Ex Cancelleria* by Luigi Cardinal Macchi, Grand Chancellor of the Pontifical Equestrian Orders, and they were the first and only documents ever to emanate from the Chancellery of the Pontifical Orders of Knighthood and to have been signed by a Grand Chancellor of all Pontifical Orders.

It must be remembered, however, that the only constitutional appointment of a Grand Chancellor to a Pontifical Equestrian Order that had taken place was in 1831, when Pope Gregory XVI included such an appointment in the Constitution of the Pontifical Equestrian Order of St. Gregory the Great: 'the Cardinal Secretary of Briefs *pro tempore* [later Cardinal Secretary of State] is to be the Grand Chancellor of this great Order.'

I enquired what had happened to the Chancellery of the Pontifical Equestrian Orders and the Grand Chancellor mentioned in that Apostolic Brief of 7 February 1905, as they had never been heard of since. Cardinal Martin had the answer: he produced a copy of the Constitution *Regimini Ecclesiae Universae*, promulgated and published by Pope Paul VI on 15 August 1967, in which a substantial part of the Roman Curia was reorganised. Many Commissions, Secretariats and Chancelleries were henceforth 'suppressed'. The word 'suppressed' definitely has a different meaning in the Constitution from its common usage: in the juridical context of this Constitution 'suppressed' did not mean that the Chancelleries, Secretariats and Commissions had been abolished, placed in abeyance or suspended, but that their functions had been reassigned to larger departments in the administration of the Holy See, such as the Secretariat of State or the Prefecture of the Apostolic Palaces (later renamed the Prefettura della Casa Pontificia). It is in the Constitution of Paul VI that the Chancellery of the Pontifical Equestrian Orders is mentioned for the first time since 1905. I therefore directed my further enquiries to the Secretary of State, Cardinal Casaroli, and his Private Secretary, Mons. Luigi Ventura, and was informed that the Chancellery had indeed been 'suppressed' by Paul VI and its functions assigned to the Secretariat of State, and *ex officio* the rôle of Grand Chancellor of all the

Pope Paul VI (1963-1978) promulgated in 1967 the Pontifical Constitution *Regimini Ecclesiae Universae* which reorganised the Roman Curia. He placed the Chancery of the Pontifical Orders of Knighthood with the Secretariat of State and gave to the Cardinal Secretary of State the position of Grand Chancellor with the authority to sign Papal Briefs concerning Orders of Knighthood *non de mandato*.

Courtesy: *L'Osservatore Romano*

Pontifical Equestrian Orders had been assigned to the Cardinal Secretary of State.

There is one more complication which needs clarifying: according to the *Annuario Pontificio*, the Secretariat of State has a Commission for Pontifical Honours (Commissione per le Onorificenze). Those familiar with the annual publication *L'Attività della Santa Sede* may recall that until 1966 this voluminous book carried a large section entitled 'Onorificenze Pontificie'. The first part listed the ecclesiastical honours of *Protonotario Apostolico*, *Prelato d'Onore* and *Cappellano di Sua Santità* the Pope had bestowed during the past year; the second part listed the appointments to, and promotions in, the Pontifical Equestrian Orders. From 1966 onwards, *L'Attività della Santa Sede* has listed only the ecclesiastical appointments. However appointments to, and promotions in, the Pontifical Equestrian Orders continue to be published regularly in the official bulletin of the Holy See, *Acta Apostolicae Sedis*.

In 1987 Cardinal Martin informed me that the Monsignori assigned by the Cardinal Secretary of State to the Commissione per le Onorificenze were now only dealing with ecclesiastical honours, and that matters relating to papal knighthoods, such as the processing of applications, the preparation of the Papal Briefs, and gazetting in the *Acta Apostolicae Sedis*, had become a collective responsibility of the Secretariat of State, the necessary tasks being carried out by officials who had been assigned to that particular function.

In his Constitution *Regimini Ecclesiae Universae*, Paul VI has also given specific instructions concerning the signature of the Cardinal Secretary of State on Papal Briefs of appointment to and promotion in Pontifical Equestrian Orders. Previously, Cardinals who had been given the mandate to sign such Briefs did so *De speziali mandato SSmi*, holding the special mandate of His Holiness for this act. Paul VI decreed that the Cardinal Secretary of State no longer needed a special mandate to sign Papal Briefs concerning Pontifical Equestrian Orders but could sign *non de mandato*, in his own right as the Papal Secretary of State in whom the powers of the former Grand Chancellor had been vested by the new Constitution. Papal Briefs of Pontifical Knights are therefore signed by the Cardinal Secretary of State and bear the Seal of his Office, not that of a Grand Chancellor. I do not think that this decision of Paul VI was widely known; but it has had far-reaching juridical implications.

Whilst not wishing to criticise in any way the Constitution *Regimini Ecclesiae Universae*, I confess that it has become a rather complicated exercise when trying to obtain information on Pontifical Equestrian Orders because, having assigned the many tasks involved in administering the Orders to the Secretariat of State, the largest department of the Holy See, it has created a collective responsibility which can cause confusion and often makes it impossible to trace the person responsible, especially when, for example, an appointment or promotion has not been gazetted in the *Acta Apostolicae Sedis*. Finally, the Constitution *Regimini Ecclesiae Universae* decrees that all controversial matters and disputes concerning papal honours are to be 'referred back' for the personal attention of the Supreme Pontiff. Since the Constitution *Regimini Ecclesiae Universae* came into force in 1967, it is very unlikely that the Supreme Pontiff would have personally dealt with a particular matter concerning papal honours in the first place, so it could hardly be 'referred back' to His Holiness since he would have never seen the documentation before. Also, one has to be realistic and accept that the Supreme Pontiff has quite enough to do without having referred to him the never-ending stream of controversies and complaints, especially from those suffering from what can be best described as 'the Order-sickness' and their unending craving for more and higher pontifical honours.

It is therefore of paramount importance that Pope St. Pius X, who laid the foundation of the present structure of the Pontifical Equestrian Orders, defined their juridical status as *ente*, a 'corporation' which comprises a group of *individual* knights; the Orders themselves are not authorised to act as a legal entities. Every knight appointed to a Pontifical Equestrian Order is personally and directly responsible to the Supreme Pontiff, the *fons honorum*, whence he received the gift of knighthood. St. Pius X also decreed that the Pontifical Equestrian Orders do not have the capacity of perpetual succession. This means that any reigning pope can change the constitutions of the Pontifical Equestrian Orders and even abolish the Orders if he so desires.

Pope St. Pius X, the foremost reformer of the Pontifical Equestrian Orders, followed the practice of endowing some of the Orders of Knighthood with special privileges; however, unlike his predecessors, he did not enshrine such privileges in Papal Briefs. (I shall return to the privileges that were granted to the Order of St. Gregory the Great in the next chapter). St. Pius X, when committing to paper those privileges and directives about ceremonial and precedence, did so in the form of memoranda to his Masters of Ceremonies. It is entirely due to the unsurpassed knowledge, diligence and scholarship of Cardinal Jacques Martin that many of these memoranda were discovered, preserved and finally placed in the archives, and they form the basis of my guidelines. The directives were addressed to the Papal Masters of Ceremonies, but at the time they were not considered sufficiently important to be entered in the archives as official papal decrees. Similarly, in 1911 St. Pius X drew up an order of precedence of heads of royal houses, both regnant and non-regnant. This also was an informal guideline for his Master of Ceremonies prior to a major reception at the Apostolic Palace. St. Pius X also distinguished between *pió eminente* – most exalted – and *eminente* – exalted – dynasties and dynastic Orders of Knighthood. It is probably the last record of this kind to have been drawn up by a reigning Pope, and I have made use of it in the sequence in which I have listed the dynasties that confer Catholic-founded Orders. However, I made one change: because the Spanish Order of the Golden Fleece has been assigned the principal position among the Orders of the Kingdom of Spain, I moved it from its previous position among the dynastic Orders, stressing, however, that this does not constitute an infringement on the dynastic rights and privileges that His Majesty King Juan Carlos enjoys as Grand Master of the Noble Order.

St. Pius X had placed His Most Catholic Majesty the King of Spain immediately after the Emperor of the House of Habsburg, followed by His Most Faithful Majesty the King of Portugal, who, at the time St. Pius X compiled the list, had already gone into exile. Until 1911, the order of precedence of Catholic monarchs and Catholic sovereign dukes was that prepared in 1504 during the pontificate of Pope Julius II (1503-1513) on the occasion of King Henry VII of England's visit to the Vatican[1]. Having been observed for over four hundred years, it shows a generally stable relationship between the Pontiff and the Catholic Monarchs; it was one of the Supreme Pontiff's prerogatives to fix the order of precedence among the Sovereigns, and the list reflects the esteem in which the Pope held the Sovereigns of the different countries. Apart from the Monarchs and Dukes who soon were to succumb to the upheavals of the Reformation and ceased to be part of this illustrious and important political alliance, the only official change in that list of precedence was made in 1517, when Leo X issued a Bull (which is kept in the Vatican Secret Archives) in which the place of honour was given to the King of France, who had been third in the original *Ordo*.

Moving on 400 years from the pontificate of Julius II and turning our attention to the Pontifical Equestrian Orders, they have not only evolved as Orders of Merit, but because of the careful reconstitution of these Orders by St. Pius X, who also gave them a legal status, national and regional associations of Papal Knights are voluntary associations which cannot legally represent any of the Pontifical Orders or the individual knights. National or regional priories, associations, regencies or lieutenancies of the Religious Orders of Knighthood, the Sovereign Military Order of Malta and the Equestrian Order of the Holy Sepulchre of Jerusalem, are legal entities and part of the infrastructure of the two Orders; membership of those Orders depends on belonging to one of the national or regional organisations. Both Religious Orders of Knighthood have their own, separate Order of Merit which does not confer membership and is in the gift of the Prince and Grand Master of the Sovereign Order or the Cardinal Grand Master of the Equestrian Order.

---

[1] H.E. Cardinale, *The Holy See and the International Order* (Gerrards Cross, 1976).

By far the most controversial subject is that of hereditary papal titles, almost all of which are attributed to the conferment of a Pontifical Equestrian Order on an ancestor prior to 1841, though a number who claim the more popular papal title of 'Count', rather than the rarer title of Papal 'Baron', trace it back as recently as the pontificate of Pius XI (1922-1930), but it is doubtful that any are dated after the Lateran Treaty of 1929. In fairness to the *fontes honorum* alleged to have conferred the titles, and to the claimants who usually have certified copies, armorials or entries from one of the armorials which also list titles and honours, the original documentation has usually been lost. It is therefore very difficult, if not impossible, to check on the conferment of such titles. Unless an original Papal Brief has been preserved, the only alternative source of confirmation of papal honours is the *Acta Apostolicae Sedis* which in its present form dates from the decree by St. Pius X of 29 June 1908. Between 1865 and 1908 the Apostolic See published the periodical *Acta Sanctae Sedis*, which contained the main papal decrees but lacked centralised control and therefore many omissions occurred. None of the claimants who submitted their documentation to the Apostolic Nunciature in London or, for that matter, were directed to me, produced an entry in the *Acta Apostolicae Sedis* as evidence.

I have already mentioned the rarer title of 'Papal Baron'. In the fifteen years I have been dealing with claims that found their way onto my desk via the Apostolic Nunciature, I have only come across one person claiming to be a Papal Baron. Legal actions were taken against him for four times defrauding a credit card company, each time for tens of thousands of US dollars. His defence was that he acted as the Pope's racing manager and had needed the money to buy horses for the Pope in Ireland.

In spite of the Apostolic Brief of St. Pius X in 1905, when His Holiness reconstituted the Order of the Golden Spur and firmly reiterated the abolition of the title Count Palatine given by his predecessor, Gregory XVI, and repeated reminders of this in *L'Osservatore Romano*, a number of gentlemen still use the title Papal Count Palatine, and for good measure some of them add the appellation 'Hereditary Knight of the Golden Spur'. In the entire history of Pontifical Orders of Knighthood, there has never been a hereditary knighthood. On one occasion, an unmarried lady styled herself Papal Countess Palatine, wishing to bequeath the title to her favourite nephew, thus carrying the illegal process one step further.

Until 1841 the Order of the Golden Spur or the Golden Militia was conferred in two classes; the first class conferred the title *Comes Palatinus Maior*, and entitled the recipient's sons to inherit the title under the clause: 'Equites potientur privilegio nobilitatis in filios transmittendae' (The Knights shall enjoy the title which can be inherited by their sons). Gregory XVI, who promulgated this clause, expressly used the word 'filii' (sons) and not the word 'heres' (heirs) or 'filiae' (daughters).

It is on this clause that legal objections to the title Papal Count Palatine being inherited *ad infinitum* are based. Although the instructions by Pius XII to entirely stop using the title Papal Count Palatine should be sufficient to abolish these papal titles of nobility, eminent canon lawyers have found it necessary to elaborate on the legal interpretation of the clause promulgated by Gregory XVI. According to Cardinal Martin, the use of the phrase 'in filios transmittendae' and the omission of the word 'heres' placed the title in a category not unlike that of a British Life Peerage. Whilst the children of a Life Peer receive and inherit a courtesy title ('The Honourable'), sons of a Major Count Palatine inherited the title of their father. Grandchildren of a Life Peer are not entitled to a courtesy title. Had it been the intention of Gregory XVI that the title Count Palatine should be inherited by the original recipient's grandsons and his heirs in the male line or by primogeniture, he would have used the word 'heres', as can be found in other documents.

The title 'Papal Count Palatine' (which must not be confused with the title of a 'Count of the Holy Roman Empire') was also attached to certain offices held at the Papal Court. However, these belong in the second category of that honour: *Comes Palatinus Minor*, which was conferred *ad personam* and was not inherited by the bearer's sons. From much correspondence I received, many claim the title because one of their ancestors held certain honorary offices at the papal court. Similarly, the second class of the Order of the Golden Spur or the Golden Militia conferred the title *Comes Palatinus Minor*.

The involvement of the Apostolic See in the field of chivalry went through several stages over the centuries. Traditionally it maintains a friendly relationship with those Catholic-founded dynastic Orders of Knighthood that have continued to participate in the ceremonial and liturgical activities of their national Churches. A detailed account of these is given in the appropriate chapters.

As mentioned above, the Holy See is also considered an international juristic person. It possesses the characteristics of that status which is required by international law inasmuch as it exists and operates within the international community as the juridical personification of the Church, and it enjoys the right to negotiate agreements and treaties with other international subjects (*jus foederum ac tractatuum*), as well as exercises the active and passive right of legation (*jus legationis*). Therefore, the Holy See is bound by international law only to recognise on an internationally mutual basis the Orders of Knighthood and of Merit of other sovereign states with which it entertains diplomatic relations.

Questions therefore arise as to where to draw the line when speaking of recognition by the Apostolic See of an Order of Knighthood, and what 'recognition by the Holy See' means. The answer to the last question is very simple: the Holy See only recognises the above-mentioned Orders. Those listed as very exalted (or less exalted) dynastic Orders of Knighthood obviously enjoy varying degrees of good will of the Apostolic See, which continues to recognise their chivalric status, and continues a tradition which goes back to the days when the Grand Masters of these Orders were reigning Sovereigns who had close relations with the Apostolic See.

The Holy See was recognised as a person in international law long before the Lateran Treaty was signed on 11 February 1929; this is attested by the position the Pope held in the international community by virtue of his spiritual authority and temporal sovereignty from the Middle Ages to the present day, and the fact that the Holy See was one of the two parties to the negotiations and the signing of the Lateran Treaty (and not the Supreme Pontiff himself) was based on its capacity to act relevantly in the international domain.[1] By Holy See we therefore understand the supreme organ of government of the Church, as was without any ambiguity laid down in Canon 7 of the *Codex Iuris Canonici* which was in force from 1917 until it was revised in 1983.

In recent years questions have been asked far more frequently about the criteria upon which the Apostolic See recognises Orders of Knighthood other than its own, the two Religious Orders and those of sovereign states. The recognition of the chivalric status of some of the dynastic Orders goes obviously beyond their participation in ceremonial and liturgical activities. Although Pope Paul VI abolished the office of a Cardinal Patron other than for the Sovereign Military Order of Malta, the Apostolic See's recognition of these Orders of Knighthood is based on their history and legitimacy. All but two of the dynastic Orders – the Catholic Order of the Golden Fleece of the House of Habsburg-Lorraine and the Sacred Military Constantinian Order of St. George of the House of the Two Sicilies (disregarding the internal family dispute) – have become totally secularised, though several Orders have retained remnants of their former strictly Catholic character; some require that those admitted to the Order must profess the Christian religion though not necessarily the Catholic faith.

Whilst ten years ago Archbishop Cardinale could speak authoritatively about 'the Holy See's view of, and attitude to, Orders of Knighthood', because the Holy See and Apostolic See, under its Supreme Pontiff, spoke with one voice on such matters, this is simply no longer the case. The continued role of the Holy See as *Mater et Magistra* of Christian chivalry has been seriously questioned for several decades. As I explain in Chapter Ten, 'Lazare Veni Foras!', the view of what constitutes chivalry is far from unanimous. In the opinion of His Holiness and a large number of

---

[1] H.E. Cardinale, *The Holy See and the International Order* (Gerrards Cross, 1976).

members of the Roman Curia, outstanding chivalric and hospitaller deeds are deserving of recognition. However, the Holy See cannot and does not rule on matters such as the status of an Order of Knighthood under, for example, dynastic laws. The basic criteria laid down by Cardinal Casaroli concerning the prerequisites of a truly Christian knight are fully endorsed by Pope John Paul II and all members of the Holy See:

> A Knight is a man who intends to place himself at the service of a noble and difficult cause, a pure and arduous ideal; fighting evil, promoting good, defending the weak and the oppressed against injustice.
> Becoming a Knight does not merely mean receiving a title of honour, even though it is well-deserved, it presupposes a solemn commitment.

Città del Vaticano
June 1984

Agostino Card. Casaroli

Of course, I was very conscious that any form of recognition based on these criteria alone would be very ambiguous. Cardinal Casaroli spoke of an ideal.

There was no lack of attempts to persuade me to ignore the expressed wishes of the Holy Father: if I were to record the Pope's expressed wish to see the outstanding chivalric and hospitaller deeds of, for example, the American, German and Austrian Grand Priories of the Military and Hospitaller Order of St. Lazarus of Jerusalem recognised, so it was argued, I would arbitrarily grant chivalric status to those whom the Holy Father had singled out for special praise because they had done something for Poland.

I do not agree with those views and I absolute refute the suggestion that I can grant chivalric status through including an Order in this book. I am in no position to grant such a status. My brief has been in the first place to revise the work of the late Archbishop H.E. Cardinale, and now, because revision could only have been further patchwork, I have had to rewrite and restructure this book so as to continue to reflect the *Apostolic* See's view of, and attitude to, Orders of Knighthood, though I cannot reiterate strongly enough that I distinguish between the *Apostolic* See the *Holy* See to a far greater extent than Archbishop Cardinale did. When he wrote his seminal work *The Holy See and the International Order* the concept that the words *Holy* See and *Apostolic* See are interchangeable in the manner the 1983 *Codex Iuris Canonici* suggests were unthinkable. The use of these words was then based on totally different criteria. The Holy See, the Apostolic See and the Roman Curia are no longer speaking with one voice on matters concerning Orders of Knighthood and Merit.

In fact, I have found myself several times in a serious dilemma; because there are Catholic-founded Equestrian Orders, and matters appertaining to them that have in the last few years caused concern, not only to me but also to others, bishops, priests and laymen alike, I had to ask myself more than once how one could possibly justify any attempt to reflect the Apostolic See's view of, and attitude to, this subject. Not only are there serious differences of opinion inside the Roman Curia concerning the

Pontifical Equestrian Orders of Knighthood, but Cardinals, Patriarchs, Archbishops, Bishops and Prelates are in open disagreement concerning the other Equestrian Orders, even those which participate actively in the ceremonial of the Church or fulfil a lay apostolate in the Church.

As I have said before, in 1982, Archbishop Cardinale could still use the episcopal 'We' when making statements and pronouncements on Orders of Knighthood. He knew that he spoke for the Supreme Pontiff, the Apostolic See and the Holy See, who were unanimous in their opinion.

Also, the rather vague definition of 'Holy See' and 'Apostolic See' in the post-1983 *Codex Iuris Canonici* did not exist when Archbishop Cardinale wrote his books.[1] At the time Pope St. Pius X reconstituted the Pontifical Orders of Knighthood, one would mainly refer to the 'Apostolic See'; 'Apostolic' was a general term which applied to everything that derived its authority directly from the Apostles and that constituted apostolicity. The Roman Catholic Church had always declared itself the Apostolic Church, and the papal chair the Apostolic See, on the ground of an unbroken series of Roman bishops from the Prince of the Apostles, St. Peter, to the present day. According to the *Codex Iuris Canonici* between 1917 and 1983, the Apostolic See was part of the Apostolic Tradition that had been handed down from the Apostles themselves[2].

The 'Holy See', as distinct from the 'Apostolic See', gained its immense importance in the administration, not only of the Church but especially of the Papal States, as well as in the secular spheres in which the Church has operated and continues to do. The Lateran Treaty of 1929 expressly assigned the sovereignty to the Holy See. During the period of *Sede Vacante*, after the death of a pope and before the new pope has been elected, the sovereignty of the Holy See remains undiminished. A *Camerlengo* heads the government of the Church, of the Holy See and of the Vatican City State as a caretaker for the next Sovereign Pontiff.

Cardinal Jacques Martin wrote in 1987: 'There is in the idea and in the word 'decoration' and in the titles 'Knight', 'Knight Commander' and 'Grand Officer', in all insignia – civil and military – conferred in recognition of merits, real or supposed, something temporal and secular that seems to go against the idea that a spiritual power like the Holy See should make use of them. Nevertheless this book[3] attests to the fact that there is nothing more ancient, more venerable, more diversified than the

---

[1] In his seminal work *The Holy See and the International Order*, which is still the authoritative text for canon lawyers, he states, referring to the Holy See and the Apostolic See: 'Since these two terms are often interchanged, some confusion may arise between the canonically distinct entities which they designate.'

[2] Hence the term 'Apostolic See'; 'Apostolic Blessing', the blessing of the pope as the successor of St. Peter; 'Apostolic Vicar', a cardinal who represents the pope in extraordinary missions; and even the title 'Apostolic Majesty', which was conferred by the Pope on Stephen, the first King of Hungary, still belongs to the Head of the Royal House of Habsburg of Austria as his successor.

[3] *The Cross on the Sword* (Gerrards Cross, 1987).

Orders of Chivalry that have existed or still exist, and none are more desired, more sought after by certain people, than a papal decoration.'

His Eminence went on to justify the alignment of the Holy See with secular states, but he also underlines the essential differences between temporal decorations and those conferred by the Sovereign Pontiff and the Pope's attitude to Orders of Knighthood which the Holy See cannot recognise. In other words, Cardinal Martin distinguished between the functions of the Holy See and those of the Apostolic See, though both are personified by the successor of St. Peter.

On several occasions Cardinal Martin expressed his apprehension about the dichotomy between the spiritual power and the temporal power exercised by the Sovereign Pontiff if what had been regarded for centuries as a symbol of the supreme power of the Pontiff, the placement of the temporal in a spiritual framework, were to be abandoned in the mistaken belief that it would enhance the spiritual power of a pope. He referred to an event on 3 September 1978, when Cardinal Albino Luciani, who not only came from a decidedly poor home[1] but from a strong, outspoken socialist background, announced that he would dispense with the traditional and century-old papal coronation, and chose to be only invested with the *Pallium* in token of his pastoral office. His reign lasted thirty-three days, but

Pope John Paul I (1978) dispensed with the century-old tradition of being crowned with the Tiara and chose instead to be invested with the Pallium in token of his pastoral office.

Courtesy: *L'Osservatore Romano*

---

[1] His father frequently went to Switzerland as a migrant worker.

his refusal to accept the tiara, the triple crown of the popes, had already created a precedent for his successor, John Paul II, who ascended to the See of St. Peter six weeks later on 16 October. By then, those who had welcomed the liberal interpretation and concept of the papacy chosen by John Paul I, announced almost at once that there would be no coronation for the new Pope, John Paul II, but introduced a characteristic new title for the ceremony on St. Peter's Square on 21 October 1978: 'the inauguration of his ministry as universal pastor of the church'.[1]

This book deals mainly with two aspects of phaleristics:
1) Catholic-founded Orders of Knighthood and of Merit, their history, insignia and decorations, and
2) the Apostolic See's relationship with, view of, and attitude to, these Orders.

With the exception of the two Religious Orders of Knighthood, all other Orders of Knighthood belong in the category of temporal institutions, disregarding whether they are Pontifical Orders of Knighthood or dynastic, state or crown Orders that have retained a close relationship with the Apostolic See. They all are secularised, and those who claim that Pontifical Orders of Knighthood are Religious Awards have completely misunderstood the legal situation.

Inevitably, where Catholic-founded dynastic Orders are concerned, I had to deal with the dynasties as well, because they are not only the *fontes honorum* of the Orders but in several cases have retained close links with the Apostolic See, although the heads of the dynasties that fall into this category are non-regnant.

With regard to the Apostolic See's rôle as *Mater et Magistra* of all Catholic-founded Orders of Knighthood or of Merit, since the Reformation there have been those Orders which defended that rôle of the Apostolic See, whilst others considered it anachronistic and not of relevance to them. Nevertheless popes were crowned with the tiara, the triple crown, symbolic of their temporal power, since the twelfth century, whereas the *Claves Sancti Petri*, the crossed keys of St. Peter, symbolised his supreme spiritual authority which has always taken precedence over the temporal power.

In addition to the Apostolic See's ancient rôle as *Mater et Magistra* of the Catholic-founded Orders of Knighthood and of Merit, the temporal symbolism of the tiara involved the Apostolic See in a second and equally important rôle: as mediator and arbiter in disputes between Catholic States, Catholic Dynasties and Catholic-founded Orders of Knighthood, who sought the reigning Pope's counsel, intervention or judgement. In most cases the Supreme Pontiff but also the Holy See would be approached in confidence, which was always respected.

[1] *The Oxford Dictionary of Popes* (Oxford, 1986).

The last dynastic dispute to be brought before the Apostolic See is described in Chapter Seven, Part IV, when two members of the Royal House of the Two Sicilies claimed the headship of the House and the grand-mastership of the Sacred Military Constantinian Order of St. George. This took place in 1960 in the pontificate of John XXIII.

The last dispute between two Orders of Knighthood, the Sovereign Military Order of Malta and the Equestrian Order of the Holy Sepulchre of Jerusalem, lasted eleven years. It began in the pontificate of Pius XII in 1951 and was settled under John XXIII in 1962.

In retrospect, one can say that it always depended on the personality of individual popes as to whether or not they felt inclined to mediate and arbitrate in such matters.

Pope Pius XI (1922-1939), for example, was not interested in arbitration or mediation between dynasties; he had no interest in Orders of Knighthood at all and showed little patience with them if they stood in the way of some of his greater aims. For example, he readily agreed to let his Cardinal Secretary of State take measures concerning one Order because that Order was used by Mussolini's representative as a pawn in the negotiations about the future Lateran Treaty which was paramount on the agenda of Pius XI.

The charismatic personality of Pope Pius XII has given many historians

Pope John XXIII (1958-1963) was the last Pope to give an opinion in a dynastic dispute. With his Chief of Protocol, Mons. H.E.Cardinale, he discussed in detail the claims to the Dynasty of the Bourbons-Two Sicilies and found in favour of Prince don Ranieri Duke of Castro.

Courtesy: Felici

Pope Pius XI (1922-1939) showed no interest in Orders of Knighthood. He relinquished the grand-mastership of the Order of the Holy Sepulchre and in 1924 refused the appointment of a new Cardinal Patron to the S. M. Constantinian Order of St. George, because that was the wish of those with whom his representatives negotiated the Lateran Treaty.

Courtesy: Felici

the impression that the Pope liked triumphalism and encouraged all manner of pomp at the papal court. On the contrary, one of his first encyclicals removed several secular aspects of the papacy, such as the conferment of titles of nobility, from the list of pontifical honours. His spiritual life, aptly given by St. Malachy as 'Pastor Angelicus'[1], has often been overlooked, because his outstanding skills in diplomacy and his actions during the Second World War were of greater interest to historians. Pope John XXIII, though often portrayed as a jovial and rustic personality, was a shrewd and skilled diplomat, very interested and accomplished in heraldry, and his knowledge of the intricacies of dynastic law and their pragmatic application were remarkable. Although he refrained from involving himself publicly in the dispute between the above-mentioned two claimants of the Royal House of the Two Sicilies, he clearly preferred the case put to him by the Neapolitan claimant to that of the Spanish, and he explained his view and judgement in detail to his Chief of Protocol, Mons. Cardinale, whom he asked to keep an unofficial record of various meetings with the claimants. I was very privileged to have been given access to Mons. Cardinale's diaries, as he was most anxious that I should gain a comprehensive view of the problems that were caused by these claims.

[1] *The Prophecies of St. Malachy and St. Columbkille* (5th edition, Gerrards Cross, 1995).

Pope Paul VI was indifferent to genealogical or heraldic matters, though he kept the *status quo* of the relationship with various non-regnant royal houses. However, Mons. Cardinale always told me that His Holiness, if he was convinced that some injustice had been done in the past, might reverse the decision of a predecessor.

Pope John Paul II differs fundamentally from his predecessors during this and the last four centuries. His attitude and views were never conditioned by Roman politics and Roman ways of doing things. The famous proverb 'when in Rome, do as the Romans do', has most certainly never applied to John Paul II. He is politically very astute and a fighter; he is a learned theologian, probably the most accomplished linguist on the See of St. Peter, a superb communicator with the masses, and a deeply pious and good priest. All trappings of the Pontifical Court and the ways and means matters are dealt with in the Vatican are really alien to him. He is a pragmatist who will place any problem on a scale of priorities, and nothing and nobody will change his mind once he has made a decision. In the context of the Archbishop of Los Angeles making ten women knights of a Pontifical Equestrian Order, he must have been well aware of the hidden provocation but also of the hidden dangers of that act, however well camouflaged the matter may have been put to him. The

Pope John Paul II (1978-) has shown himself a pragmatist. Although His Holiness did not change the original statutes of the Pontifical Orders of Knighthood, he allowed fundamental changes to be made to the Orders of Pius IX, St. Gregory the Great, and Pope St. Sylvester, because it appeared expedient to do so and averted possible complications.

Courtesy: *L'Osservatore Romano*

place of John Paul II in history is assured. Nobody can doubt that he, almost single-handedly, defeated the Russian bear and literally brought down the walls of the Soviet Empire.

Orders and decorations mean little to John Paul II personally, though I know that he was upset when he saw in Mons. Cardinale's book that the Secretary General of the Central Committee of the Polish Communist Party had abolished the ancient Polish Order of the White Eagle. Throughout his pontificate, until the first democratically elected President of Poland was sworn in on 22 December 1990, John Paul II openly supported the Polish Government-in-exile. He received the Polish Presidents-in-exile, offering them the courtesies due to a Head of State, as well as members of the Government-in-exile, which was based in London. If one sees events in that light, they bear out what I said above: it depends on the personality of the individual pope whether or not he takes an interest in temporal matters, and if he does, in which.

Disregarding whether a pope was inclined to act as mediator or arbiter, his ancient right to do so existed and had never been revoked until, probably unintentionally, the Apostolic See relinquished that prerogative when John Paul I refused to accept the tiara, the symbol of the temporal power of the papacy, and signalled to the world the supremacy of his spiritual power.

The Tiara is the symbol of the spiritual and temporal power exercised by the Supreme Pontiff.

II

THE ORIGIN AND EVOLUTION OF ORDERS OF KNIGHTHOOD

Much justified criticism is directed against the attempted re-establishment of extinct ancient Catholic-founded Orders by individuals or organisations creating self-styled Orders of Knighthood called after the long-extinct Orders. While they are neither recognised nor approved of by the Apostolic See, it is important to make it clear that in the beginning all Orders of Knighthood of a religious, hospitaller and military character were the result of private initiative.

Once their value and credibility had been established, many of these Orders were taken under the patronage of the Papacy or of a State. It was only after the thirteenth century that Orders of Knighthood became institutionalised, requiring a formal act of establishment emanating from a sovereign power, the Apostolic See or the Head of a State. Mons. Cardinale believed that this was the natural outcome of the evolution of political and social organisations, especially required to contain excesses and suppress abuses.

Excesses and abuses of Orders of Knighthood, both internal and external, have always existed, and no formal act of establishment has ever been able to prevent them. It would be fairer not to judge an entire Order by the character or conduct of some of the individuals who were, and in some cases still are, members of legitimate Orders of Knighthood. After all, those members also became Knights as a result of a formal act of establishment emanating from a legitimate *fons honorum*. But if we want to assess the evolution of Orders of Knighthood fairly, we must not gloss over the shortcomings that have been inherent in them since their foundation.

In conformity with the social pattern of the times and also because of the hardships involved in the enterprise, men alone were admitted as full members to the ancient Orders, but women were often present in their life, rendering valuable service through the various works of mercy and charity allocated to them.

Without wishing to enter one of the most controversial arguments of the second half of the twentieth century, the rôle and function of women, the reason given that they were excluded from full membership of ancient Orders because of 'the hardships involved in the enterprise' appears to be disproved by the Order of the Hatchet which had only women members who were given the title 'Dames of the Hatchet' as a reward for their outstanding courage and bravery during the siege of Tortosa in Catalonia in 1148. They were not armed with hatchets just to cut bread or meat rations for the men.

Women were admitted to the Military Order of Santiago as early as 1175, and in 1261 Loderigo d'Andalò of Bologna founded the Order of the Glorious Saint Mary, which Pope Alexander IV approved and sanctioned. This was the first religious Order of Knighthood to grant the rank of *militissa* to women. The Order was suppressed by Sixtus V in 1585, the year of his election to the papacy. It may or may not be relevant to the suppression that in 1557 the future Pope Sixtus, Felice Peretti di Grottammare, was appointed a Counsellor to the Inquisition in Northern Italy, but was recalled from that office in 1560 because of his excess of zeal and severity as an inquisitor.

Archbishop Cardinale mentioned that in 1441, at the initiative of Catharine Baw, and ten years later of the Ladies Elizabeth, Mary and Isabella of the House of Hornes, Orders were founded which were exclusive to women of noble birth, who received the French title of *chevalière* (lady knight) or the Latin title *equitessa*. I have been unable to find any reference to these Orders, though I am sure Mons. Cardinale would not have referred to them had he not found some mention of them.

A modern example of an Order exclusive to ladies is the Order of St. Isabel (Portugal) which was founded in 1801 by the Prince Regent Dom Joâo, the future King of Portugal Dom Joâo VI, at the instigation of his wife, Princess Carlota Joaquina of Spain. It was restricted to twenty-six ladies of noble birth. The Grand Master is always the spouse of the Duke of Bragança, who is the Sovereign of the Order. On the occasion of the 350th anniversary of the Independence of Portugal in 1990, the present Duke of Bragança, H.R.H. Dom Duarte Pio, in his capacity as the Sovereign of the Order, added a Medal of Merit to the Order of St. Isabel to ensure that women from all walks of life can be rewarded for their charitable works.

Nobility was a common requirement for admission to an Order of Knighthood. Those deemed worthy of membership who were not nobles, were ennobled upon entrance into the Order. Nobody had yet devised the concept of a classless society, and only nobles and their liegemen were considered fully reliable by their sovereign princes, although, of course, titles of nobility alone have never been a guarantee of reliability or loyalty. Once again we have an example in Portugal where the Dukes of Bragança, when they became Monarchs of Portugal in 1640, retained the ducal prerogative of conferring *Foros*, six titles of nobility which had always been conferred by the Dukes of Bragança, and were conferred by them as Monarchs of Portugal either as complementary titles with other royal honours they bestowed, such as Duke, Marquis, Count etc., or separately as titles of nobility upon those whom they considered especially close to the Royal House of Bragança[1].

---

[1]See Appendix VIII, 'The Prerogatives of the Dukes of Bragança'.

When the Crusades began and the first Orders of Knighthood were founded, the feudal nobility, who had attained the summit of their power, were the main instrument of the Papacy in the struggle for the deliverance of the Holy Land.

Loyal supporters of their sovereigns, who were not of noble birth, were named 'Companions' of an Order. They wore badges resembling its insignia but were not enrolled among the members of the Order as such, and did not have the same obligations.

The original Christian concept of knighthood was delivered a severe blow first with the advance of absolutism, especially from the sixteenth century onwards, when according to the formula *cuius regio illius et religio* (religion goes with the land), the custom was that the ruler's religion was imposed upon his subjects as a State religion. From then on Orders of Knighthood became more and more an instrument of political propaganda.

Absolutism among the sovereign princes set one nation against the other and stultified any international effort to bring peoples together in the way that the early Orders of Knighthood had done. The situation for the chivalric Orders worsened when Monarchs identified the State with themselves ('l'état c'est moi') in the seventeenth century.

It was the emergence of the expressly secular state in the 1800s which finally took it upon itself to rid society and its civil institutions of all religious influence and character. In several countries many of the ancient Orders of Knighthood were consequently replaced by the State's creations, or simply changed into Orders of Merit. Some followed the pattern of the Légion d'Honneur founded by the French Republic in 1802.

The feudal loyalty demanded by the original chivalric system was no longer consistent with the tenets of the emerging modern society. The principle of equality was more and more introduced in human relations and was also applied to Orders of Knighthood, often at the expense of the nobility. It was finally realised that high-minded standards and noble actions were not the monopoly of any particular class, but the heritage and duty of all free men and women alike. Some Orders, especially those newly founded by States, were open to women as well.

Despite all efforts at secularisation, the basic principles of altruistic and gentlemanly behaviour that had always inspired the Orders of Knighthood remained unchanged and were adopted by the Orders of Merit. In fact they were instituted to reward men and women who had performed meritorious deeds and to set them up as examples to stimulate their fellow men to follow in their path. Even in our day, at a time of almost universal secularising tendencies, Orders of Merit continue to follow the structural model of the ancient Orders of Knighthood as far as emblems, titles and ranks are concerned. Nobody has any qualms about their use, though their origin is distinctly Catholic, by their use of terms such as Grand Cross, Knight Commander and Knight for the traditional three classes. The division into five classes was introduced by the French Republic when it suppressed the French Military Orders of the previous regime and replaced them with the Légion d'Honneur. Any relationship between individual members of such Orders of Merit is, however, very superficial or nonexistent, as are also, generally speaking, the obligations of the same towards the Orders themselves.

One can carry these reflections further by observing that even the Communist States imitated the general concept and pattern of ancient knighthoods, often, but not always, replacing the cross by a star or other emblems acceptable to their philosophy and excluding every reference that had an ethico-religious or chivalric connotation. The definitive book *Russian and Soviet Military Awards* (Order of Lenin State History Museum, 1989) lists eight Russian Orders of Knighthood, including – until 1917 – three Orders taken from Poland when that country was occupied in the early nineteenth century. From 1917 onwards the Soviet Union had twenty-six Orders, one of the highest being listed ten times as a different Order for different Soviet Republics. The number of Military Awards, Crosses and Medals is in excess of one hundred. *Orders, Medals and Decorations of Britain and Europe* (London 1975), lists nine Orders in Communist Hungary, six in Communist Bulgaria and so on. The Soviet Union only divided its many Orders into different classes after the Second World War.

It is rather ironic that notwithstanding the essential historical links of Orders of Knighthood with the Crusades and also their typical Christian character, Islamic and Eastern States[1] have imitated the Christian West in establishing Orders of Knighthood. Obviously, they exclude all Christian emblems from their badges and insignia and replace them with a crescent, the sun, a star, a flower or the like. However, they retain the titles and ranks of Commander and Knight which are so markedly reminiscent of an era when Christianity and Islam were fighting one another in the Crusades.

In recent times the question has been raised as to whether the Apostolic See, in continuing to recognise and patronise secularised Catholic-founded Orders of Knighthood of non-reigning dynasties perpetuates an anachronism.

Whether or not an Order of Knighthood is out of harmony with the present depends entirely on the statutes which govern its activities. In the newly evolved climate of tolerance and hoped-for coexistence, none of the Orders of Knighthood is likely to be called upon by the Papacy to

---

[1]The world of Orders is not without its lighter side. S.E.R. Archbishop Cesare Zacchi, when President of the Pontifical Ecclesiastical Academy for Diplomats, told me that one Islamic State had conferred 'The Order of Chastity' – Second Class – upon a departing Nuncio. However, as this Order does not feature in that country's official list of decorations, one cannot help feeling that the diplomat concerned had been the victim of a hoax – or the subject of a lesson, sufi-style. He also received the Grand Cordon with Collar of the official Order of Merit.

rally to the defence of Christendom against the threat of Islamic fundamentalism. In 1992 Pope John Paul II visited Islamic countries in order to strengthen interfaith ties.

While tolerance and peaceful coexistence are undoubted virtues, I believe that two fundamentally different – indeed in some matters diametrically opposed – religious beliefs and basic philosophies cannot in all conscience be aligned into some multi-faith force against some theoretical evil. Such an alignment could only be realised if both Christian and Islamic principles and articles of faith were to be abandoned, and it is inconceivable that either religion would make that sacrifice.

Christianity owes a great debt to the Arab world for keeping science alive while in Europe scientific enquiry was crushed by a blinkered Church – we owe them our numbering system and words such as alcohol, alkali, algebra, alchemy, magazine, callipers, zero (a concept invented by the Arabs), zenith, cipher, cotton, mattress, even the word for that important Christian ecclesiastical item, the baldachin. But these debts cannot mask the essential differences between the two civilisations: just as the Crusades were originally directed at the Moslem kingdoms, so were Islamic Jihads directed against Christianity.

I will give some examples – already quoted in other contexts – of irreconcilable differences that can be found in the foundation statutes of most Catholic-founded Orders: the defence of the belief in the Immaculate Conception of the Blessed Virgin Mary and her motherhood of God, and especially the divinity of Christ. This criterion was the original *raison d'être* for many Orders of Knighthood.

Although many of the Catholic-founded and secularised Orders have modified their initially uncompromising and dogmatic statutes, they have nevertheless retained fundamental vestiges of the Christian faith which permeates Western civilization as we know it.

I am not reactionary, and I have no intention to be politically provocative in any way, when I point out that tolerance and coexistence between Islam and Western civilization – based as it is on 2,000 year old Greco-Roman and especially Hebraic-Christian foundations – cannot be part of a compromise. Islamic Fundamentalism simply cannot compromise, and Christian civilisation would do so at its peril. The conquest and absorption of Christian religion and culture into Islam has been its aim since the time of Mohammed, and it can no more change on matters of principle than the Catholic Church can change its dogmas. Pragmatists of both religions understand the need for tolerance and coexistence, but these words are not in the vocabulary of any fundamentalist, of whatever faith. We must always remember that.

The late 20th century successors of those knights of Christian Orders that fought in the Crusades would certainly not be able to emulate their illustrious predecessors in military prowess. But before dismissing the existence and present-day activities of these Orders of Knighthood as anachronistic and irrelevant, we should look back at their memorable achievements over the last millennium, and remind ourselves of their role as saviours of Western civilisation as we know and enjoy it today.

While I cannot really see the Apostolic See taking up the leadership, and reassuming her role as *Mater et Magistra* of the Orders of Knighthood to undertake the defence of our Christian civilisation once again, the very presence and activities of these Orders that were its past defenders may yet prove the strongest force against a final attempt to bring that civilisation – once so strong and powerful in the service of mankind – to a very sad end.

As Archbishop Cardinale said:

> 'although the concept of chivalry was not founded by the Church, but by the laity, it was the Church who immediately set out to change and refine it according to the spirit of the Gospel. As is clearly seen above, it was the papacy who more than any other body understood , appreciated and initiated the spirit which moved the first Crusading Orders of Knighthood, spiritualised their military zeal and valour, granted them papal approval and support, inspired their chivalric system of virtues based on ethico-aesthetic categories of a secular nature with high Christian ideals. These ideals transformed a secular fighting force into disciplined, self-controlled, refined, gentle and strong defenders of the rights of God, of Christendom, of the Holy Roman Church and of society, consciously endeavouring to bring religion into daily life with service to the less fortunate, honour and courtesy to all.'

The operative criterion in the last paragraph is 'a lawful Order of Knighthood'. The chapter on self-styled orders deals at some length with the phenomenon of organisations which lay claim – without justification – to being Orders of Knighthood. Perhaps there are some aspects which mitigate against an uncompromising policy of either right or wrong, lawful or unlawful. Not everything is black or white.

It is neither my brief nor prerogative to validate the lawful status of an Order of Knighthood; I can but draw the attention of the reader to a sometimes paradoxical situation. In May 1994 I addressed in Chicago a large gathering of Knights, members of Pontifical Equestrian Orders, the Sovereign Military Order of Malta, the Equestrian Order of the Holy Sepulchre, the Venerable Order of St. John of Jerusalem (UK) and the S.M.Constantinian Order of St. George, all of whom were also members of the Military and Hospitaller Order of St. Lazarus of Jerusalem (Grand Priories of America, Canada, Germany, and Austria). When I was asked why there had been, and in some cases still was, such hostility towards the Order of St. Lazarus, and why I had never recognised them as an Order of Knighthood, I explained:

'There is a thin line between being conciliatory ·
mentioning the meritorious charitable work of an org
making unwarranted concessions, such as giving them
Order of Knighthood. In any case, I have neither the pov
to change a charitable organisation into an Order of Knig
change water into wine either. On the other hand, I could easily, so as to
avoid any confrontational issues, write something very flattering, and at
the time kill with kindness; or, to follow up on my earlier metaphor, I
could water down the wine and make it undrinkable.

'Anybody who would have told me five years ago that I would address
a meeting such as this would have been told that a month of Sundays
would come to pass before I could see myself doing so.

'After all, was not the Military and Hospitaller Order of St. Lazarus a
painful thorn in the flesh of several other Orders, and had not a senior
member of the Secretariat of State, who was also a member of one of these
Orders made it clear to me he would not even look into questions I had
asked, and that St. Lazarus would never be recognised by anybody?

'There are two presumptions in that last statement nobody had
reckoned with: first, Pope John Paul II expressly wanted recognised the
chivalric work of those, who had truly lived up to Cardinal Casaroli's
definition of a true Christian knight, who helped the poor and needy and
supported the oppressed and weak in his own native Poland, when they
most needed help and support. Secondly, my personal loyalty to the
Supreme Pontiff would always override any other advice I am given. I
subsequently examined for myself whether such chivalrous deeds
qualified those who had carried them out to be listed, as I was requested,
as an Order of Knighthood or as a charitable organisation.

'As a result of my examination of the criteria commonly used by Orders
of Knighthood to justify their continued existence, I was forced to
examine the Order's original *raison d'être* after the time of its foundation
and its continued existence. Let me explain: we no longer have military
knights endeavouring to reconquer the Holy Places or defend or
reconquer Christian soil from the Infidel invader. To be a member of some
glorified cocktail circuit that masquerades as an Order of Knighthood,
does most certainly not provide a *raison d'être* for its continued existence.

'Although there are other qualifications which are valid, I noticed in
several Orders the absence of perhaps the most important *raison d'âtre*:
namely that the members of the Order have continued to carry out the
same tasks, fill the same needs and preach the same Gospel as their
predecessors did during the Crusades or when the Order was founded.
There are very few Orders that have kept the true hospitaller spirit alive.
There are many that are justifiably conferred as Orders of Merit, but there
are also those decorations, though they are legitimate, that merely serve
the vanity of man.'

Chapter Two

THE PONTIFICAL ORDERS OF KNIGHTHOOD

I

THE ORIGIN AND EVOLUTION OF PONTIFICAL ORDERS OF KNIGHTHOOD AND THE ATTITUDE OF INDIVIDUAL PONTIFFS TO THEM

The Apostolic See has never founded a Religious or Monastic-Military Order of Knighthood. All Pontifical Equestrian Orders belong in the category of Orders of Merit. Apart from the Order of St. Gregory the Great (founded in 1831) and the Order of Pius IX (founded in 1847), which were retained in their original form though recipients of the first and second class of the Pian Order lost the entitlement to the appellation *Nobile* – Pope St. Pius X promulgated the statutes and rules for five Pontifical Orders of Knighthood in his Apostolic Brief of 7 February 1905 *Multum ad excitandos*.

Even prior to its promulgation, the Supreme Order of Christ had always been reserved to Catholics (as had, indeed, the Order of St. Gregory the Great), until Paul VI and John Paul II conferred it on rare occasions on non-Catholics and even non-Christians. None of the statutes were ever changed. Within the Pontifical Orders of Knighthood there exists an order of precedence, though it would be misleading to interpret this as representing degrees of merit:

The Supreme Order of Christ;
The Order of the Golden Spur (The Golden Militia);
The Golden Collar of the Pian Order (founded in 1939);
The Order of Pius IX;
The Order of St. Gregory the Great;
The Order of Pope St. Sylvester.

Paul VI promulgated his Apostolic Brief *Equestres Ordines*[1] on 15 April 1966; it he decreed that The Supreme Order of Christ was reserved for Christian Heads of State, The Order of the Golden Spur (or of the Golden Militia) was to be conferred on Heads of State who had to confess the Christian, though not necessarily the Catholic religion, and The Golden Collar of the Pian Order was open to all Heads of State, regardless of their religious affiliation.

---

[1] Because of the strongly religious character of the Order of Christ and the Order of the Golden Spur, the former bearing the name 'The Supreme Equestrian Order of the Militia of Our Lord Jesus Christ', the latter 'The Equestrian Order of the Golden Militia' (expressly dedicated to the Blessed Virgin Mary), Paul VI reserved them for Christians only, though the Order of Christ has only been conferred on Catholics.

Each Order has its own criteria and prerequisites for conferment, though they have not only been changed from time to time by an Apostolic Brief, but on rare occasions the statutes have been ignored.

It is very sad when a breach of the rules is compounded by camouflaging it. This, I discovered was definitely the case when the Prussian Chancellor, Prince Otto von Bismarck, had the Supreme Order of Christ bestowed upon him on 31 December 1885 by Pope Leo XIII. Otto von Bismarck was not only an atheist, but the first person on record to have publicly affirmed his dissociation with any religious belief, so I questioned the reasons given by Archbishop H.E. Cardinale. He maintained – following the customary explanations by most chroniclers of the Order – that Leo XIII had conferred the Order of Christ on Bismarck as a token of gratitude for the important part the Prussian Chancellor had played in solving the dispute between Germany and Spain about the possession of the Caroline Islands, the arbitration of which had been entrusted to the Holy See. Bearing in mind that the Prussian Chancellor got possession of the Caroline Islands he was hardly a disinterested party; it therefore seemed a far-fetched reason for giving the Order of Christ to an atheist. The other excuse, namely that the Order only received the appellation 'Supreme' in 1905 is irrelevant to the already existing statutes.

The evidence of my research indicates strongly that Pope Leo XIII had to bestow the Order of Christ on Chancellor von Bismarck as the result of

In 1885, the German Chancellor, Prince von Bismarck, demanded the Order of Christ from Pope Leo XIII (1878-1903) in exchange for the release from prison of Cardinal Ledochowski, who had been incarcerated for allowing Polish priests to preach and teach in the Polish language instead of German. Bismarck was a publicly self-proclaimed atheist, and to demand and accept the Order of Christ was the ultimate insult against the Catholic Church which was his main target in the *Kulturkampf.*

the enormous political pressure he had brought to bear upon the Pope. He literally blackmailed Leo XIII by demanding the Order of Christ so as to inflict the ultimate humiliation on the Vicar of Christ on Earth. During his *Kulturkampf* between the newly formed State of Germany, especially in Prussia, and the Catholic Church, which began in 1871 and which led to a total breakdown of relations between State and Church and the suppression of everything Catholic, Bismarck forced the resignation of the Archbishop of Gniezno-Poznan, Mons. Mieczyslaw Halka Ledochowski. After Bismarck had imprisoned him in the dungeon of Ostrowo in 1874 for refusing to yield to Bismarck's demands that all sermons and religious instruction had to be given in the German language instead of in Polish, Leo XIII created Archbishop Ledochowski a Cardinal while still a prisoner of Bismarck. Although international political opinion forced the Cardinal's release in 1876, he was banished from Prussia. During his exile in Rome, Cardinal Ledochowski continued to administer his Archdiocese. In 1885, Bismarck by threatening all possible reprisals forced the Cardinal 'voluntarily to resign from the administration of Archdiocese of Gniezno-Poznan in the interest of peace'. He also demanded from Leo XIII the Order of Christ, which he received in the same year. In 1890, Bismarck was forced to resign by Kaiser Wilhelm II. In 1892, Leo XIII appointed Cardinal Ledochowski Prefect of the Sacred Congregation *De Propaganda Fide*.

The Order of the Golden Spur (Golden Militia), reconstituted in 1905 and given new statutes and rules concerning its insignia, was not spared a breach of the rules, though the episode was rather pathetic than sinister. In 1932 it was the turn of the Italian Premier Benito Mussolini to receive a token of gratitude for the good will shown in concluding the Lateran Treaty, thus putting an end to the long dispute between the Holy See and

Benito Mussolini (right), who signed the Lateran Treaty in 1929, threatened to hand the Order of the Golden Spur back to the Pope because the cross was suspended from a ribbon. An aide to Cardinal Gasparri (left) made an impromptu switch and used the collar of a chain that had been abolished in 1905. The Italian Premier accepted the Order gratefully.

Courtesy: Felici

Italy, following the annexation of the Papal States (1870-1929). King Victor Emmanuel III of Italy had already been honoured with the Supreme Order of Christ earlier in 1932. It was fortunate that a young aide to Cardinal Secretary of State Gasparri, who greeted Benito Mussolini on his arrival in the Cortile di S. Damaso which leads, after a longish walk, to the Papal Apartments, overheard the Italian Premier say to a member of his entourage that he would refuse to accept a decoration on a ribbon and simply hand it back to the Pope; he was as much entitled to get a Collar as the King. Without losing a moment or asking anyone's advice, the young Monsignor used his own initiative and rushed to the room where he knew several trunks had been stored which contained silver-gilt Collars in their old presentation boxes, which had been used prior to 1905 for the former Order of the Golden Militia and St. Sylvester. He also managed to get to the papal apartments before Benito Mussolini arrived there, explained to the astonished Pope and Cardinal Gasparri that this had to be done to avoid an embarrassing scandal, and quickly exchanged the Collar for the ribbon. Mussolini received the Order of the Golden Spur pending from a Collar.

After 1932, the Order continued to be conferred with the Collars from the old Order and which had been retrieved from storage. Although the statutes and rules appertaining to the insignia have never been changed, the Order of the Golden Spur continues to be conferred with a Collar, although the old ones have run out, Signor Giorgio Guccione makes these prestigious Orders which are conferred at present.

Pontifical Orders of Knighthood are in the personal gift of the Pope. Nevertheless, they are conferred in conformity with the appropriate statutes. On 1 November 1993, the Pontifical Equestrian Orders were still only open to gentlemen, and although it appears that deliberate misinformation about this rule was placed in Catholic journals, presumably to confuse and sow further dissent, according to the rules laid down by Pope St. Pius X, meritorious ladies should only receive the Cross 'Pro Ecclesia et Pontifice' for equivalent activities. Suggestions that the Holy Father should create a special Order for Ladies have been received in the Vatican and considered for as long as I have been associated with this work, but no decision has yet been reached. A member of the Roman Curia who believed that matters concerning the Orders of Knighthood might be deliberately undermined, expressed his apprehension concerning this matter; he felt that as Pope John Paul II held strong views on the non-admission of women to the priesthood, Catholic feminist groups might use all the power at their disposal, especially in the United States of America where their dissent is strongest, to get female knights if they could not get female priests. Some of these groups are undoubtedly supported in their radical policies by local bishops. It is therefore not surprising that *The Texas Catholic Herald*

(Vol.30,No.9/September 24 1993) reported that in Los Angeles ten women would be made knights and that they would be 'installed' there on November 21, 1993.

John Paul II has in the past created six female Knights. On the first occasion, not long after he had ascended the throne of St. Peter, when an African Ambassador who had been accredited to the Holy See for seven years paid the customary farewell visit to His Holiness and received the obligatory Grand Cross of the Order of Pius IX. From the Ambassador's name, it was impossible to see (without actually checking first) that the potential recipient of the knighthood was a lady. In the first edition of his work, Archbishop Cardinale mentioned that Ambassador Chibesakunda of Zambia was the first lady to become a Knight Grand Cross of a Pontifical Equestrian Order, but I was asked to delete this reference in my first revision of that book as it might cause a misunderstanding.

A similar 'administrative error which could not be foreseen' happened in 1992 when, prior to the State Visit of a sovereign Monarch, the Protocol Department of the royal visitor discussed the arrangements of the visit with officials of the Papal Secretariat of State. Among the topics under discussion was the usual exchange of honours; these were allocated according to rank of the visiting dignitaries and the hosts. When the insignia allocated to certain officials accompanying the King, such as Ministers, Chief of Protocol, Private Secretary of the Monarch etc. were sent to their residences in Rome in accordance with protocol on the evening prior to the State Visit, it was realised that five of them were ladies. They had become Knights Commander and Knights of the Orders of Pius IX or Gregory the Great or Pope St. Sylvester.

A brief announcement in the Catholic journal *The Tablet* in September 1993 that Pontifical Equestrian Orders were now open to women was strongly denied on behalf of the Secretariat of State by the Apostolic Nuncio to the Court of St. James, Archbishop Luigi Barbarito, who added that nothing of the kind was in the offing. Enquiries in Rome by myself from 8 September 1993 onwards yielded no reply. On 12 October 1993, I telephoned a friend who works in the Apostolic Palace; he had assisted Archbishop Cardinale for several years, and takes a special interest in the Pontifical Equestrian Orders. I told him about the American press reports. He was baffled and assured me that he had neither been told officially nor unofficially nor had he read about any changes in the Orders in the *Acta Apostolicae Sedis* or in *L'Osservatore Romano*.

There is a procedure to which all pontiffs have adhered in the past: before making any changes to Equestrian Orders, they always consulted their advisers and the Nuncios abroad, then promulgated the changes and informed the Nuncios prior to gazetting these changes or addenda first in the *Acta Apostolicae Sedis*, then in *L'Osservatore Romano*, before finally issuing a formal statement to the world press.

It would be idle to speculate what happened prior to the story about the ten Los Angeles women making news in America. Whether His Holiness and his advisers have allowed themselves to be forced to give in to demands, as one member of the Roman Curia suggested, I don't know. Yet contrary to the official statements and denials, the Holy See obviously yielded to the vociferous pressure from some extremists in the United States, as some members of the Curia had feared.

There has never been a problem or fundamental objection to the opening one or more Pontifical Orders to women; however, under the circumstances it would be dishonest if the opening of the Pontifical Equestrian Orders of Pius IX, St. Gregory the Great and Pope St. Sylvester to women and the official reasons given for it were to be chronicled and hailed as something they were not.

One eminent member of the Roman Curia summed up the true state of affairs two years ago: 'if Pope Paul VI after the Second Vatican Council had instituted an Order of Merit for women, as many of us favoured and asked him to do, the Church might be spared much aggravation and avert what is likely to happen.' He was absolutely right and gauged developments correctly. For years, many Apostolic Nuncios have pleaded for the opening of one or two existing Pontifical Equestrian Orders to women or the establishment of such an Order, as the honours available for meritorious women were woefully inadequate and in no way equal to those honours available to gentlemen.

My task is that of a chronicler, not that of a critic or judge, but I would fail in my duty if I ignored these happenings or deliberately kept silent about them. There is no doubt, judging by the letters I have received, that the abovementioned events have caused consternation among members of the episcopate and Knights of the Pontifical Equestrian Orders. As far back as 1979, Archbishop Cardinale, during the preparation of the chapter on Pontifical Equestrian Orders, wrote several letters to fellow bishops, complaining that certain practices that had been reported to him devalued the prestige of papal knighthoods, and also corresponded with the Secretary of State on the matter. He also impressed on me the need for the Holy See to assist the Pope in the foundation of an Order of Merit for women, because he feared that otherwise the traditional structure of Pontifical Orders would be destabilized.

However, it is important to reiterate that no Pontiff is bound by the Constitutions, Papal Briefs or Decrees of their predecessors, provided that the Pope makes appropriate changes to the statutes of the Orders. The conferment of an Order of Merit is in the absolute gift of the reigning Pontiff. Although Paul VI gave to his Cardinal Secretary of State the right to sign Papal Briefs of appointment *non de mandato*, without a special mandate, I doubt that this prerogative was intended to include changing rules laid down in the Papal Briefs and Decrees of earlier popes. Only the reigning Pope can make such changes.

The rôle and function of the different Orders, the admission to a Pontifical Order of Knighthood, the conferment of the insignia, guidelines for investitures, the importance of having an admission gazetted in the *Acta Apostolicae Sedis*, and other topics are dealt with in separate sections. The Chapters on the Orders of Pius IX, of St. Gregory the Great and of Pope St. Sylvester have the statutes and rules attached to them in the English translation. The original documents in Latin have been reproduced in Appendix I.

On 9 November 1993, Archbishop Barbarito informed me verbally that he just had received a letter from the Holy See and that he would communicate its contents to the Bishops of England and Wales first, before he could give me any details. Knowing that I was waiting for a clear and definite statement from the Holy See with regard to the admission of women to Pontifical Equestrian Orders, His Excellency indicated that the admission of women to some Pontifical Orders of Knighthood would become official, but stressed that he had to speak to the Bishops first. I telephoned the Nuncio at the end of November 1993 for a written confirmation. Because the letter from the Holy See was confidential, it could not be forwarded or shown to anybody. However, in view of the circumstances, the Apostolic Nuncio sent me a letter in which he explained the basic facts:

Apostolic Nunciature
London
Ref.No. 10530 29/11/1993

Dear Mr. Bander van Duren.
Following our telephone conversation yesterday I wish to inform you that the Holy See has informed the Papal Nuncios that, in order to meet the requests of several Bishops, the Holy Father has decided to extend the following Papal Awards to women:
1) Dame Grand Cross of the order of St. Gregory the Great, of St. Sylvester and of the Pian Order.
2) Dame Commander *Con Placca* of the same Orders.
3) Dame of the same Orders. The appropriate insignia for each order remains unchanged.
    With my kind regards and very best wishes,

    Yours sincerely,
    + Luigi Barbarito
    Apostolic Pro-Nuncio

Considering the history of this matter, which goes back more than twenty years, I believe that the operative words in the Holy See's letter to the Papal Nuncios are 'in order to meet the requests of several Bishops'.

I am much obliged to His Excellency Archbishop Barbarito for writing to me and officially informing me of the changes. It was a long time afterwards that an official announcement issued by the Secretariat of State appeared in *L'Osservatore Romano*.

Another controversial issue concerning Pontifical Orders of Knighthood, which arose out of a misunderstanding, needs clarification: as mentioned above, Pontifical Equestrian Orders belong in the category of Orders of Merit and are not Religious Awards. The only difference concerning the conferment of a papal knighthood compared with one conferred by a Head of a secular foreign State is that traditionally the Supreme Pontiff, unlike secular Heads of State, has never been required to obtain prior permission of the Foreign Office of the country of the recipient upon whom he wished to confer such an honour. In Great Britain, for example, recipients of papal knighthoods received the Monarch's permission to wear the insignia in public since the reign of King Edward VII. Since May 1990 however, civil servants at the Foreign and Commonwealth Office have refused to forward to the Monarch's Private Secretary any applications from newly created Papal Knights to obtain the Sovereign's permission to wear the insignia of a Pontifical Order of Knighthood at public functions if that honour was granted after May 1990. Their argument for refusing to do so is based on the premise that since Great Britain established full diplomatic relations with the Holy See in 1982, the Pope has to ask permission of the civil service first before conferring a papal knighthood on a British subject. Yet in their argument lies a paradox: Great Britain has established diplomatic relations with the Holy See, not with the Pope, who is throughout the world recognised as supranational. Pontifical Orders of Knighthood are neither conferred by the Holy See (in which sovereignty rests under international law) nor by the Vatican City State, which is a geographical location where the Holy See resides. They are in the personal gift of the Pope and awarded by him personally as Orders of Merit in accordance with the statutes of the Founders.

Theoretically, what has been created in Great Britain is a two-tier system of Papal Knights: those who obtained the Sovereign's permission to wear the insignia of a Papal Knight at public functions prior to May 1990, and those whose applications have not been forwarded. This is probably a temporary measure which, especially in the wider European context, will be revoked sooner rather than later. Nevertheless, it shows that a small bureaucratic pebble can create large waves. The fact that three Lord Lieutenants of Counties, Her Majesty's personal representatives in these counties, have asked me for advice, as the reply they had received from a civil servant at the Foreign and Commonwealth Office led them to believe that Her Majesty probably did not know what was being done in

BUCKINGHAM PALACE

20th June, 1983.

Sir,

    I have the honour to inform you that The Queen has been graciously pleased to grant to you unrestricted permission to wear the insignia of

Knight Commander of the Order of St. Gregory the Great

which has been conferred upon you by

    His Holiness Pope John Paul II

in recognition of your services.

    I have the honour to be, Sir,

    Your obedient Servant,

Philip Moore

---

her name, seems to point to some temporary measure taken by one or more civil servants without giving much thought to the position and possible consequences.

Ceremonial uniform of a Knight of the Supreme Order of Christ.

II

THE SUPREME ORDER OF CHRIST
(Militia Domini Nostri Iesu Christi)

This is the highest of the Pontifical Orders of Knighthood in existence. It shares its early history with the Portuguese Military Order of Christ. It was founded on 14 August 1318 by King Dinis I of Portugal (1279-1325), with the aim not only of defending the country against the Islamic Moors and liberating Portugal from the invaders, but also of replacing the

Order of the Knights Templars, which had been so cruelly suppressed in 1312 by Clement V (1305-1314). The Order was originally called 'The Militia of Jesus Christ', and was approved and confirmed by Pope John XXII (1316-1334) in his Bull *Ad ea ex quibus*, issued on 14 March 1319 in Avignon. The Order was endowed with the possessions of the extinct Order of the Knights Templars and with additional means of subsistence. The Papacy was the High Protecting Power of the Order, and Knights were obliged to take the vows of poverty, chastity and obedience. The Order had the special support of successive Pontiffs.

In 1492, Pope Alexander VI (1492-1503) freed the Knights of the Military Order of Christ from taking solemn vows; this was confirmed by an Apostolic Brief of Pope Julius II (1503- 1513), but both Popes continued to regard the Papacy as the Sovereign Power, though they ceded the administration of the Order to the Kings of Portugal. In 1516, Pope Leo X (1513-1521) promulgated the Bull *Constante fide* in which the Papacy recognised King Manuel I of Portugal (1495-1521) as Grand Master of the Military Order of Christ. King Manuel I was succeeded by his son King Joâo III (1521-1557), and his position as Sovereign and Grand Master of the Military Order of Christ received unqualified confirmation in the Papal Brief *Eximiae devotionis* promulgated by Pope Adrian VI in 1522. The Papal Brief promulgated in 1551 by Pope Julius III 1550-1555) granted the sovereignty and grand-masterships of all the Military Orders, of Christ, of Avis and of St. James of the Sword to the Crown of Portugal in perpetuity.

In 1522, The Military Order of Christ of Portugal and the Order of Christ (which only received the appellation 'Supreme' in 1905) which continued to be conferred by the Papacy, became definitely divided into two different Orders, one, essentially a Pontifical Order of Merit, under the sovereignty of the Supreme Pontiff, the other, a Military Order of Merit under the sovereignty and grand-mastership of the Portuguese Crown.

In retrospect it appears that this division was not made clear enough to recipients of the Pontifical Order of Christ. Whilst it went virtually into disuse and was only conferred very rarely by Popes until undergoing a certain reform in 1878, many historians and chroniclers continued to maintain that the Supreme Pontiff had retained the right to appoint persons of all social classes knights of the Order of Christ of Portugal. This was, of course, misinformation because the Order of Christ conferred by the Pope no longer had any links with the Order of Christ of Portugal.

From contemporary drawings of the sixteenth and seventeenth centuries it appears that prior to Queen Maria I of Portugal adding the image of the Sacred Heart to the Portuguese Order in 1789, the insignia of the two distinct Orders of Christ were identical.

The Pontifical Order of Christ was completely reconstituted on 7

The Star and the Cross suspended from a military trophy, the centrepiece of the golden Collar of the Supreme Order of Christ.

February 1905 by Pope St. Pius X in his Pontifical Constitution *De Ordinibus Equestribus* under the heading by which this Papal Brief became known: *Multum ad excitandos.* The Order was given the appellation 'Supreme' and it is the only Pontifical Equestrian Order the statutes of which have appended to them a prescribed protocol of investiture for 'newly appointed *Milites* (Soldiers) to be admitted to the Supreme Order of the Militia of Our Lord Jesus Christ'. It would have been inconceivable that the Prussian Chancellor Prince Otto von Bismarck, who is mentioned above, would have sworn an oath of obedience and absolute loyalty to the Supreme Pontiff, nor would it be realistic to expect a Sovereign or Head of State, even is he is a devout Catholic, to make the unequivocal commitment demanded in the protocol. Unlike the Papal Brief and the Decree *Ex Cancellaria Ordinum Equestrium*, the protocol of investiture is not dated, and Cardinal Martin, who guided me throughout in the preparation of this chapter, suggested that the protocol of investiture and the oath of obedience and loyalty had simply been adopted from some earlier document and appended to the statutes.

On 15 April 1966, Pope Paul VI (1963-1978) decreed in his Papal Brief *Equestres Ordines* that the Supreme Order of Christ was to be conferred only for extraordinary reasons on Catholic reigning Monarchs or Catholic Heads of State on the occasion of very important events or celebrations at which the Supreme Sovereign would be personally present, or on occasions of exceptionally momentous events. Paul VI further decreed that because of the religious character of the Supreme Order of Christ, it would bear the additional appellation 'The Militia of Our Lord Jesus Christ'. However, the Order is always referred to as 'The Supreme Order of Christ'.

According to the statutes and regulations, the Supreme Order of Christ has its own ceremonial court uniform, (though this is no longer worn because it would be unsuitable for Heads of States to do so). It is made of a bright scarlet fabric with facing of white cloth and rich gold embroidery on the collar, breast and cuffs, knee breeches of white silk with gold side stripes, shoes of white silk with gold buckles, a hat with white plumes and ornamented with a knot of twisted gold cord terminating in tassels of gold. A sword with a gold and mother-of-pearl hilt and pendant tassels of twisted gold cord complete the court dress.

The Order has only one class: the Badge is worn pending from a Military Trophy on the Collar and a Star is worn on the left breast.

The Badge of the Order is a gold-rimmed, long red-enamelled Latin Cross *pattée* on which is superimposed a smaller white-enamelled Latin cross, surmounted by a crown.

The Collar, symbolic of the subjection and loyalty of the Knights to the Supreme Pontiff, is of gold and consists of enamelled plaquettes, alternately the papal insignia of the Tiara and Crossed Keys, and the

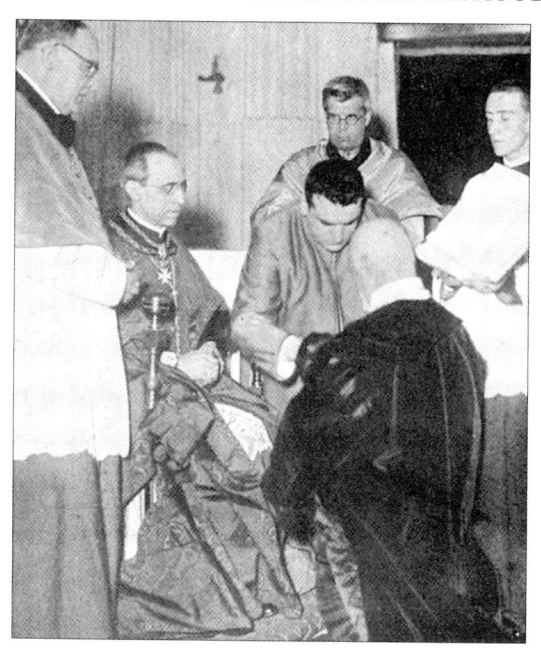

In 1933, Eugene Cardinal Pacelli (later Pope Pius XII) invested the seventy-sixth Prince and Grand Master of the Sovereign Military Order of Malta, Frà Ludovico Chigi Albani della Rovere, (also opposite) with the Supreme Order of Christ that had been conferred upon the Grand Master by Pope Pius XI.

Courtesy: SMOM

Cross of the Order surrounded by a gold laurel wreath, linked together by golden knots between two golden chains, culminating in the gold Military Trophy from which the crown of the Badge is suspended.

The Star of the Order is an eight-pointed, faceted silver star, ornamented with precious jewels and bearing in the centre the Cross of the Order surrounded by a gold laurel wreath.

The conferment of the insignia, which applies to all Collars reserved to Heads of State and Orders of other classes conferred *motu proprio* (by his own initiative) by the Supreme Pontiff follows the traditional protocol. His Holiness does not confer the insignia personally. Either on the evening prior to a State Visit by a Head of State to the Vatican, the Cardinal Secretary of State or a high dignitary of the Pope's immediate entourage will deliver the insignia to the residence of the recipient, or confer the insignia in the Apostolic Palace before the Head of State or Sovereign meets the Pope. If an Order is conferred *motu proprio* when the Pope pays a visit to a country, the Apostolic Nuncio accredited to that country will deliver the insignia to the residence of the recipient prior to His Holiness meeting him; the recipient will wear the insignia for the meeting.

I give two examples of the insignia being conferred by the Pope's representatives prior to the newly created Knights of the Supreme Order of Christ paying their official visits to the Pontiff. On 8 June 1933, His Eminence Eugene Cardinal Pacelli, Secretary of State to His Holiness,

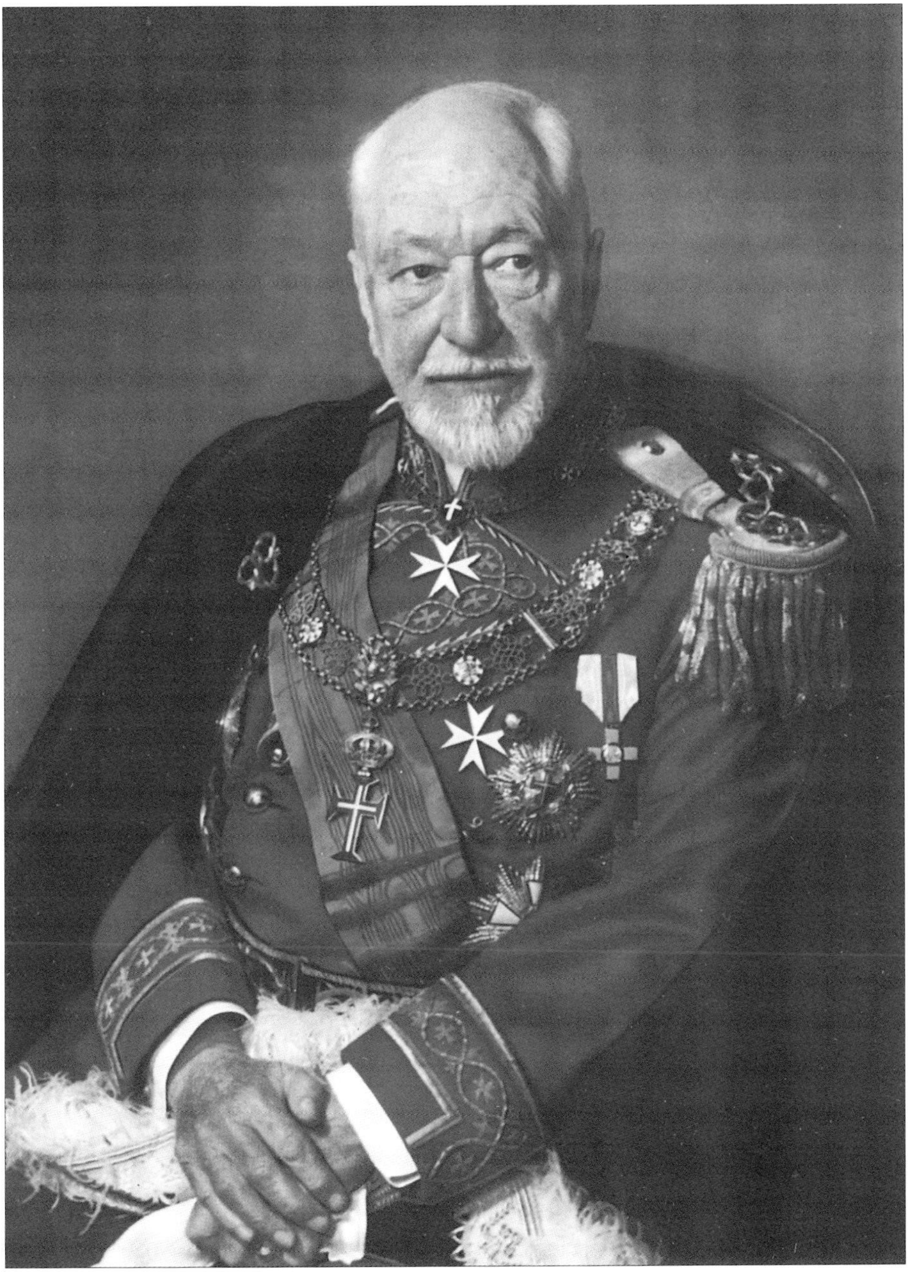

In 1987, Archbishop Giovanni Coppa bestowed the insignia of the Supreme Order of Christ on the seventy-seventh Prince and Grand Master of the Sovereign Military Order of Malta, Frà Angelo di Mojana di Cologna (also opposite)

Courtesy: SMOM

conferred the insignia of the Order of Christ on His Most Eminent Highness the Prince and Grand Master of the Sovereign Military Order of Malta, Frà Ludovico Chigi Albani della Rovere (1931-1951), before His Eminent Highness paid is customary visit to the Apostolic Palace. On 3 July 1987, His Excellency Archbishop Giovanni Coppa, special Legate of His Holiness, met His Most Eminent Highness Frà Angelo di Mojana di Cologna, 77th Prince and Grand Master of the Sovereign Military Order of Malta (1962-1988), in the Apostolic Palace and conferred the insignia of the Order of Christ on him before the Prince and Grand Master saw John Paul II in private audience. Sadly, Frà Angelo only enjoyed this highest chivalric honour six months before he died.

His Majesty King Baudouin of the Belgians had ascended the throne in 1951, and ten years later in 1961, Pope John XXIII bestowed on him (when he was only thirty-one years old) the dignity of a Knight of the Supreme Order of Christ. For several years King Baudouin was the only member of this premier Pontifical Order of Knighthood, until Frà Angelo was appointed. After his death, he was again the sole Knight of the Pontifical Supreme Order of Christ. King Baudouin died suddenly in 1993, so The Supreme Order of Christ has no members at present. Apart from Otto von Bismarck, whom I mentioned in the foregoing section, there was one other German Chancellor who was appointed a Knight of the Order of Christ, prior to Paul VI reserving it solely for Catholic Heads of State: Dr. Konrad Adenauer, on whom the Order of the Golden Spur had already been conferred.

THE PONTIFICAL ORDERS OF KNIGHTHOOD   71

Their Majesties the late King Baudouin and Queen Fabiola of the Belgians with Pope John XXIII who created the King a Knight of the Supreme Order of Christ in 1961.

Courtesy: Felici

Three Sovereign Monarchs wearing Pontifical Orders of Knighthood reserved for Heads of State: King Baudouin (Belgium), The Supreme Order of Christ; King Juan Carlos (Spain), The Golden Collar of the Pian Order; and Grand Duke Jean (Luxembourg), The Order of the Golden Spur.

Courtesy: Felici

THE PONTIFICAL ORDERS OF KNIGHTHOOD

President Charles de Gaulle of France was made a Knight of the Supreme Order of Christ in 1959 by Pope John XXIII.

Courtesy: Felici

President Antonio Segni of Italy received the Supreme Order of Christ in 1963 from Pope John XXIII one year after he had been made a Knight of the Order of Golden Spur.

Courtesy: Felici

President Éamon de Valera of the Irish Republic received the Supreme Order of Christ from Pope Paul VI.

Courtesy: Felici

Chancellor Dr. Konrad Adenauer of the Federal Republic of Germany who had already received the Order of the Golden Spur, was created a Knight of the Supreme Order of Christ by Paul VI, prior to the Pope reserving the Order solely for Heads of State.

Courtesy: Felici

III

THE ORDER OF THE GOLDEN SPUR
THE GOLDEN MILITIA
(Ordo Militia Aurata)

This is one of the most ancient Orders of Knighthood and has been the origin of several other chivalric Orders.

Although the first record of the Order of the Golden Spur, or of the Golden Militia, being conferred only appears in the Vatican archives in 1539, during the pontificate of Pope Paul III (1534-1549), it is most certainly a far more ancient institution because contemporary records refer to the Order. I want to stress here that several chroniclers of the Church whose works I consulted appear to have gone out of their way to confine the Order's early history to myth and legend and some of them are guilty of serious errors whenever they refer to Orders which are known to have had their origin in the Golden Militia, such as the S.M. Constantinian Order of St. George.

There is no evidence that the Order of the Golden Militia was an extension of the Knights of the Emperor Constantine, or that Pope St. Sylvester I (314-345) gave them the rule of St. Basil, but some contemporary writers and historians refer to the Knights of the Golden Militia prior to the Crusades, and Orders like the Sacred Military Constantinian Order of St. George were definitely given the rule of St. Basil.

Members of the Golden Militia were called Knights of the Golden Spur because of the gilt spurs with which they were presented during their investiture, and because of their military character they were called a Militia. Fifteenth century documents from all over Europe refer to golden spurs, and those who were thus knighted, were called *equites aureati* (golden knights).

From the pontificate of Pius IV (1559-1565) until that of Benedict XIV (1740-1758), recipients of the Order of the Golden Spur were awarded the title 'Palatini et Aulae Nostrae Lateranensis Comes et Miles Nobiles', Count of the Palatine and of Our Lateran Palace and Noble Soldier. From the pontificate of Clement XIII (1758-1769), until Pope Pius VII (1800-1823) for the first time tried to abolish the titles associated with the Order of the Golden Spur, two classes of the title Count Palatine were conferred: *Comes Palatinus Minor* (Minor Count Palatine), which was bestowed upon the recipient *ad personam* and could not be inherited, and *Comes Palatinus Major* (Major Count Palatine), a hereditary title.

The title Count Palatine took its name from the ancient *Comes Palatii*, who was a nobleman attached to the imperial palace in the later Roman

Empire. 'Palatine' is one of the Seven Hills – the Palatine Hill – upon which the original city of Romulus was built.

Pope Gregory XVI abolished the title previously conferred by the Order of the Golden Spur in his Apostolic Brief of 31 October 1841, and Pope St. Pius X, abolished also the two titles Pope Gregory XVI had substituted in his Apostolic Brief *Multum ad excitandos* of 7 February 1905. Pope Pius XII issued further restrictions on the use of papal titles of nobility, and frequent reminders appeared in *L'Osservatore Romano*.

Those who are styled (Papal) Count Palatine, claim inheritance from a *Comes Palatinus Major* prior to 1841. Some claimants to this title compound it by stating that they are Hereditary Knights of the Golden Spur. This is a paradox as no knighthoods can be hereditary.

Problems arise where the title Count Palatine was conferred by a secular *fons honorum*. The name of the title was the same, but its characteristics and criteria for conferring it were quite different. For

(Right): An example of the Cross of the Golden Militia prior to 1841, probably conferred by one of the ducal houses to whom the right of conferment had been delegated; (left): the Cross of the combined Order of the Golden Spur and Pope St. Sylvester. Pope Gregory XVI had added the name of Pope St. Sylvester to the Order, the bestowal of which he reserved from 1841 onwards solely to the Papacy, withdrawing all former delegated powers.

Courtesy: The Garrison Collection

example, under the Frankish Kings of the Merovingian dynasty, who preserved many of the Roman appellations, Counts Palatine enjoyed supreme judicial authority in causes that came to the Sovereign's immediate attention, and they were also sent to various parts of the Empire as judges and governors. By extension the term came to mean the districts over which palatine powers were exercised.

Under the Holy Roman Emperors, who had constituted themselves as the successors of the Roman Emperors after the collapse of the latter, and who were popularly known as the German Emperors (who ceased to exist in 1806), a Count Palatine enjoyed the prerogative of exercising jurisdiction in his own territory or province in Germany.

The title Count Palatine must not be confused with that of Count of the Holy Roman Empire. The appellation 'Holy' does not imply 'Papal', merely that it was a title granted by the emperor whose title 'Holy Roman Emperor' was obtained from the Apostolic See by Otto I who had been crowned in Rome in 962 by Pope John XII.

During the reign of Emperor Charles V (1519-1556), and under the pontificates of Leo X (1513-1521), Adrian VI (1522-1523), Clement VII (1523-1534), Paul III (1534-1549), Julius III (1550-1555), Marcellus II (1555) and Paul IV (1555-1559) the title of Count Palatine was conferred more lavishly both by the Emperor and the Popes. It often became attached to some offices at both the imperial and papal courts to increase the importance of their incumbents, without jurisdictional or territorial significance, but the title was strictly conferred *ad personam* and was not hereditary, though the Emperor could make exceptions. However, at the papal court, whatever privileges a Count Palatine enjoyed came to him as a result of being created a Knight of the Order of the Golden Spur.

I mentioned above that from the pontificate of Pius IV (1559-1565) onwards the Popes awarded the new title 'Palatini et Aulae Nostrae Lateranensis Comes et Miles Nobilis'. The prestige of the title Count Palatine had declined because of lavish and indiscriminate bestowal as a result of concessions made by those of the Popes' and Emperors' delegates who had been given the privilege of conferring the title. As far as the Papacy was concerned, the power to create Knights of the Order of the Golden Spur and grant the title (Papal) Count Palatine was delegated first to the to the Marquis de Ferrara in 1367; subsequently, that privilege was delegated to Papal Legates, Nuncios, Patriarchs, Archbishops, Bishops, Assistants at the Papal Throne, to the College of Abbreviators and, as a token for the support they had shown to the Papacy, to the Ducal House of S. Fiora, Sforza-Cesarini. In addition to the power of creating Knights of the Golden Spur and Counts Palatine, they were also given the prerogative of creating Protonotaries Apostolic. The real abuses began with the Sforza-Cesarini family after 1539 and gradually increased, depending on the individual powers of papal delegates, as more noble houses obtained that privilege.

In 1905, Pope St. Pius X separated the Order of the Golden Spur which he placed under the protection of the Blessed Virgin Mary, from the Order of Pope St. Sylvester which he made the fifth Pontifical Order of Knighthood.

Although Pope Pius IV and his successors tried hard to curb the abuses, they found themselves totally unable to control the situation as far as the Order of the Golden Spur was concerned. It was not until Pius VII who in 1815 seriously attempted to reform the Order and abolish the title Count Palatine, that the Papacy really tried to reassert its power, sadly with little success. On 31 October 1841 Gregory XVI (1831-1846) promulgated the Apostolic Brief *Cum hominum mentes* and thus finally succeeded in transforming the Order of the Golden Spur. He also withdrew on pain of excommunication all the delegated powers and reserved the bestowal of the Order exclusively to the Apostolic See. Gregory XVI also gave the Order a new name: 'The Order of St. Sylvester and of the Golden Militia'.

St. Pius X, by his Brief *Multum ad excitandos*, radically transformed the Order in 1905. He established the Order of St. Sylvester as a separate entity, and the Order of the Golden Militia was placed under the patronage of the Blessed Virgin Mary to mark the fiftieth anniversary of the proclamation of the Dogma of the Immaculate Conception, so the Apostolic See at last had an Order of Chivalry dedicated to Our Lady[1].

All titles of nobility the Order had previously conferred were suppressed and the Order could only be bestowed by papal *motu proprio* without any title. In the list of precedence it followed the Supreme Order of Christ.

On 15 April 1966, Paul VI (1963-1978) issued the Apostolic Letter *Equestres Ordines* in which he decreed that henceforth the Order would only be awarded to Christian, but not necessarily Catholic, Heads of State.[2]

The Badge of the Order is a gold yellow-enamelled Maltese cross with a golden spur hanging on the lower arms of the cross. The obverse medallion in the centre bears a crowned letter 'M' for Mary, the Immaculate Mother of Christ, the patroness of the Order, on a white-enamelled background. The medallion on the reverse bears the date 1905 in Roman numerals and the legend PIUS X. RESTITUTOR.

Until 1932, and according to the statutes of the Order, the Badge should still be suspended from a red silver-bordered ribbon. This practice was changed as a matter of expediency in 1932, however recipients of the Order of the Golden Spur continue to receive the Badge pending from a Military Trophy which is the mounting link of the Collar.[3]

The gold Collar consists of links with the Greek monogram 'XP' for Christ and a small eight-pointed star alternating.

The Star of the Order is an eight-pointed faceted star with the Badge of the Order in the centre.

---

[1]See: Introduction by Jacques Cardinal Martin to *The Cross on the Sword* (Gerrards Cross, 1987).
[2]It is interesting to note that the Pontiff mentions the Order only by the name of "The Golden Militia", whereas the Annuario Pontificio, the official yearbook, continues to call it "The Order of the Golden Spur".
[3]See: Appendix I.

The insignia of the Order of the Golden Spur as they were conferred until 1932, when a gold chain was unofficially substituted for the red ribbon with silver borders.

THE PONTIFICAL ORDERS OF KNIGHTHOOD 81

The Cross, Collar and Star as they have been conferred since 1932.

Courtesy: Guccione

The President of the Federal Republic of Germany, Dr. Theodor Heuss, received the Order of the Golden Spur from Pope Pius XII in 1957.

Courtesy: Felici

H.I.M. Mohamed Reza Pahlavi Shahinshah of Iran was created a Knight of the Golden Spur in 1958 by Pope John XXIII.

Courtesy: Felici

King Frederick IX of Denmark received the Order of the Golden Spur in 1964 from Pope Paul VI.

Courtesy: Felici

Among the Knights of the Golden Spur in the seventeenth and eighteenth centuries we find the composers Wolfgang Amadeus Mozart, Christoph Willibald Gluck, and Gaetano Donizetti, and the sculptor Antonio Canova.

Pope Pius XII instituted the Golden Collar of the Pian Order on Christmas Day 1957.

The Golden Collar and Star of the Pian Order.

Courtesy: Segretaria di Stato

THE GOLDEN COLLAR OF THE PIAN ORDER
(Torquis Aurei in Ordine Piano)

Although Pius XII instituted the Golden Collar of the Pian Order on 25 December 1957 by Papal Brief[1] as an extension to the existing Order of Pius IX, to be conferred on Sovereigns and Heads of State ('and in very exceptional circumstances on other very high authorities'), the Apostolic Letter of Paul VI, *Equestres Ordines*, of 15 April 1966, placed the Golden Collar of the Pian Order in the category of honours exclusively reserved to Sovereigns and Heads of State.

The Badge of the Golden Collar is an eight-pointed, gold-rimmed, blue-enamelled star with flamelike gold pencils of rays between the points. In the centre is a white-enamelled medallion with the inscription in gold 'A Pio XII Avctvs', which is surrounded by a gold band with the inscription 'Ordo Pianus'. The white-enamelled medallion on the reverse bears the date 'Anno MCMLVII'.

The Collar consists of gold medallions with the papal insignia, the tiara and crossed keys, alternating with white-enamelled medallions depicting the personal coat of arms of Pius XII. The mounting link of the Collar is a papal tiara between two billing doves.

[1]See: Appendix I for the Papal Brief of Foundation.

In 1967, both H.M. King Gustav Adolf VI of Sweden and H.M. King Olav V of Norway received the Collar of the Pian Order from Paul VI.

King Juan Carlos I and Queen Sophia of Spain with John Paul II in 1981. Paul VI created the King a Knight of the Pian Collar in 1977.

The Star of the Golden Collar, which is worn on the left breast, is identical to the Badge of the Order, but larger and with silver faceted pencils of rays between the points. The medallion in the centre of the Star bears the same inscription as that of the corresponding Badge.

THE ORDER OF PIUS IX
(Ordo Pianus)

The Order was instituted by Pope Pius IX (1846-1878) on 17 June 1847 by his Apostolic Letter *Romanis Pontificibus*. It was the Pope's intention that the Order should be reminiscent of that founded in 1560 by Pius IV, which, however, did not survive his pontificate.

When elected Pope in 1846, Cardinal Giovanni Maria Mastai-Ferretti was a most popular choice with the people of Rome; when he had died in 1878, and his mortal remains were for reasons of safety transferred during the night of 13 July 1881 from his temporary resting place in St. Peter's to the Basilica of St. Lawrence, a Roman mob, howling and shouting, attempted to halt the procession and throw the Pope's body into the Tiber.

Shortly after his election, and a year after founding the Order of Pius IX, he had to flee Rome in November 1848 after his Prime Minister had been murdered. He took refuge in Gaeta, in the Kingdom of the Two Sicilies, and placed himself under the protection of its King Ferdinand II. When he returned to Rome in 1850, he was confronted by many problems which culminated in the loss of the Papal States in 1870.

It is curious that after his illustrious predecessor Gregory XVI had abolished the titles of nobility associated with the Order of the Golden Spur, Pius IX introduced the nobiliary appellation *Nobile* with the conferment of the first and second class of the Order of Pius IX; he even distinguished between the appellation *Nobile* which could be inherited by the sons of recipients by right of primogeniture for recipients of the first class of the Order, and the appellation which was granted *ad personam* to those who received the second class. Knights of the third class received only the insignia. The appellation *Nobile* was abolished by Pope Pius XII on 11 November 1939 in his Apostolic Brief *Litteris suis*, and decreed that personal merit and worth should henceforth be the only titles of honour.

Initially the criteria for conferment were conspicuous deeds in Church and Society. In the twentieth century the Order of Pius IX was conferred for personal services to the Pontiff and after 1929 when the Vatican City State came into existence, especially on diplomats accredited to the Holy See, on visiting dignitaries, such as Prime Ministers and Ministers of countries, and on members of foreign delegations who attended very

Pope Pius IX, who founded the Pian Order in 1847.

The Grand Cross and Star of the Order of Pius IX, usually known as the Pian Order, is the most frequently conferred Grand Cross of all Pontifical Equestrian Orders. It is mainly given to Ambassadors, Ministers, heads of special diplomatic Missions, and in exceptional cases for oustanding services to the Supreme Pontiff.

John XXIII during the reception of the Special Mission which had come to Rome to attend the celebrations of the Pope's eightieth birthday. The late Mons. Cardinale (on the Pope's left) was then Chief of Protocol of His Holiness and *Assessore* of the Secretariat of State. Many heads of the special Mission received the Grand Cross of the Pian Order.

special functions, such as coronations of popes, anniversaries, and celebrations of Holy Years. Ambassadors Plenipotentiary who have served a minimum of two years at the papal court receive the Grand Cross either before or when they take their leave of the Pontiff. (Hence the incident of the Zambian Ambassador in 1981 which I refer to in the introduction to this chapter). Counsellors and First Secretaries of Embassies usually receive the *Commenda*[1] of the Order when leaving, and diplomats of lower rank receive the third class. Members of the apostolic administration and officers of the Swiss Guards are on occasion also honoured with the Order of Pius IX. Diplomats of Legations who represent countries that have not established full diplomatic relations with the Holy See are usually offered appropriate grades in the Order of Pope St. Sylvester.[2]

The Order has three classes: Grand Cross, Commander, (the class is divided in Commanders and Commanders with Star), and Knights.

The ribbon of the Order is dark blue with two red border stripes on either side.

---

[1]This is, depending on the rank and number of years served at an embassy accredited to the Holy See, either the rank of Knight Commander or Knight Commander with star.

[2]Some countries, such as Great Britain, do not allow their diplomats to accept a papal decoration. However, the Earl Marshal of England, the Duke of Norfolk, Britain's Premier Catholic Peer, who represented the Queen at the funerals and installations of two Popes in 1978, received and was given leave to accept the Grand Cross of the Pian Order. His Grace attended strictly as a member of the Royal Household; the political representative of the British Government at these functions did not receive a decoration.

Prime Ministers and Ministers of State who had attended the coronation of Paul VI in 1963 were invested with the Grand Cross of the Pian Order.

The Badge of the Order is a gold-rimmed, blue-enamelled eight-pointed star with gold-rimmed, flamelike pencils of rays between the points. The obverse white-enamelled medallion bears the inscription 'Pivs IX', and the gold band that surrounds the medallion has the legend 'Virtuti et Merito', for distinction and merit. The white-enamelled medallion on the reverse bears the date MDCCCXLVII.

The Badge varies in size according to rank. The Badge of the Grand Cross is worn on a sash, the Commander's Badge class is worn on a neck ribbon, and the Badge of the Knight is pending from a ribbon that is worn on the left breast.

The Star of the Order is identical to the Badge, though the Star of the Grand Cross is larger than that of the Commander.

The members of the Order wear court uniform; that for a Knight Commander is also reproduced in colour in this volume. Details about insignia and uniform for all classes are given in the statutes, which are appended here in the original and in translation.

The criteria for conferment of the Order of Pius IX were published in 1987 by the Secretariat of State as follows:

'The Order of Pius IX, founded in 1847 by Pope Pius IX to reward conspicuous deeds of merit in Church and society, and otherwise known as the Pian Order, is today conferred mainly on diplomats accredited to the Holy See, visiting statesmen or personal representatives of Sovereigns or Heads of States, or for personal services rendered to the Pope'.

THE PONTIFICAL EQUESTRIAN ORDER OF PIUS IX — THE PIAN KNIGHTS

FROM THE CHANCERY OF THE PONTIFICAL EQUESTRIAN ORDERS

February 1905

HIS HOLINESS POPE PIUS X, having given consideration to all the mandates of the Holy See promulgated to encourage virtue and to reward good conduct, wishing such rewards to be fitting and proper and, indeed, honour the Holy See itself, has on this occasion turned His attention to the Orders of Knighthood.

Hence, having discussed the matter with the undersigned Cardinal Secretary of Briefs, the Grand Chancellor of the Pontifical Orders of Knighthood, He has promulgated, besides all the regulations given this day to the other Pontifical Orders of Knighthood, all those rules concerning the uniform and decorations of the Knights of the Order of Pius IX (The Pian Knights), which have until now appeared ambiguous and lacking clear definition, and He has ordered that these matters be precisely defined according to the following regulations: —

PIAN KNIGHTS OF THE FIRST CLASS or KNIGHTS GRAND CROSS OF THE ORDER OF PIUS IX shall enjoy the privilege of hereditary nobility, which may be inherited by their sons.

Their uniform should be of dark blue cloth with coat-tails.

The collar, the cuffs and the pockets should be of red cloth.

The embroidery, all in gold thread, should be a row of laurel leaves on the collar, on the cuffs and on the pockets. There should be a double row of laurel leaves on the chest and also a narrow gilt border decorated with laurel leaves, which runs along the top and front of the collar, down the centre, along the edge of the pocket flaps, the top and side of the cuffs and along the edge of the entire tailcoat.

There should be nine buttons on the chest and three smaller buttons on each sleeve. The tail of the coat which borders on the pocket flaps should be adorned with two larger buttons, and in the centre, above the buttons should be two embroidered sprays of laurel leaves arranged in an oval circlet. At the three protruding points of the pocket flaps there should be three small buttons.

On both shoulders should be a golden braid, fastened near the collar with a button.

The trousers should be long and of dark blue cloth. A gold stripe decorated with laurel leaves, four centimetres in width, should run down the outer sides of the trousers.

The cocked hat should be of black plush velvet, adorned with a broad gold band along the top rim, with a small golden tassel at either end, and above there should be a white plume, to which the Pontifical Cockade is attached on the right side, held by four intertwined strands of gold cord and fastened at the lower end with a gilded button.

The buttons, all gilded, should be embossed with the Badge of the Order. The court sword should be worn in a sword frog, made of golden braid decorated with laurel leaves. The sword should bear on the hilt the badge of the Order. The handle should be of mother of pearl with gilded mounts and with a gilt sword-knot hanging from it. The scabbard should be of black leather with gilt boss and ferrule.

The Badge of the Order is an eight-pointed blue star superimposed on an eight-pointed star-like cluster of seven rays, each in gold, and a white enamel medallion with a broad gold border which is silver-rimmed. In the inner white circle is the name of the Founder, PIUS IX, and in the gold border is the inscription VIRTUTI ET MERITO.

The Star should be the eight-pointed blue star superimposed on an eight-pointed silver star-like cluster of rays, eight centimetres in diameter, and it is worn on the left side of the breast.

A Knight Grand Cross wears the Badge, six and a half centimetres in diameter, suspended from a sash, ten centimetres wide, which is of a dark blue moiré with two red stripes along both borders.

The Badge, Star and buttons, according to their shape and sizes, and sash, bands and stripes, according to colour and width should not vary from the patterns and designs given.

PIAN KNIGHTS OF THE SECOND CLASS OR KNIGHTS COMMANDER OF THE ORDER OF PIUS IX shall enjoy the honour of personal nobility which is not hereditary.

Their uniform should be of dark blue cloth with coat-tails.

The collar, the cuffs and the pockets should be of red cloth.

The embroidery, all in gold thread, should be a row of laurel leaves on the collar, on the cuffs and on the pockets, and a narrow gilt border,

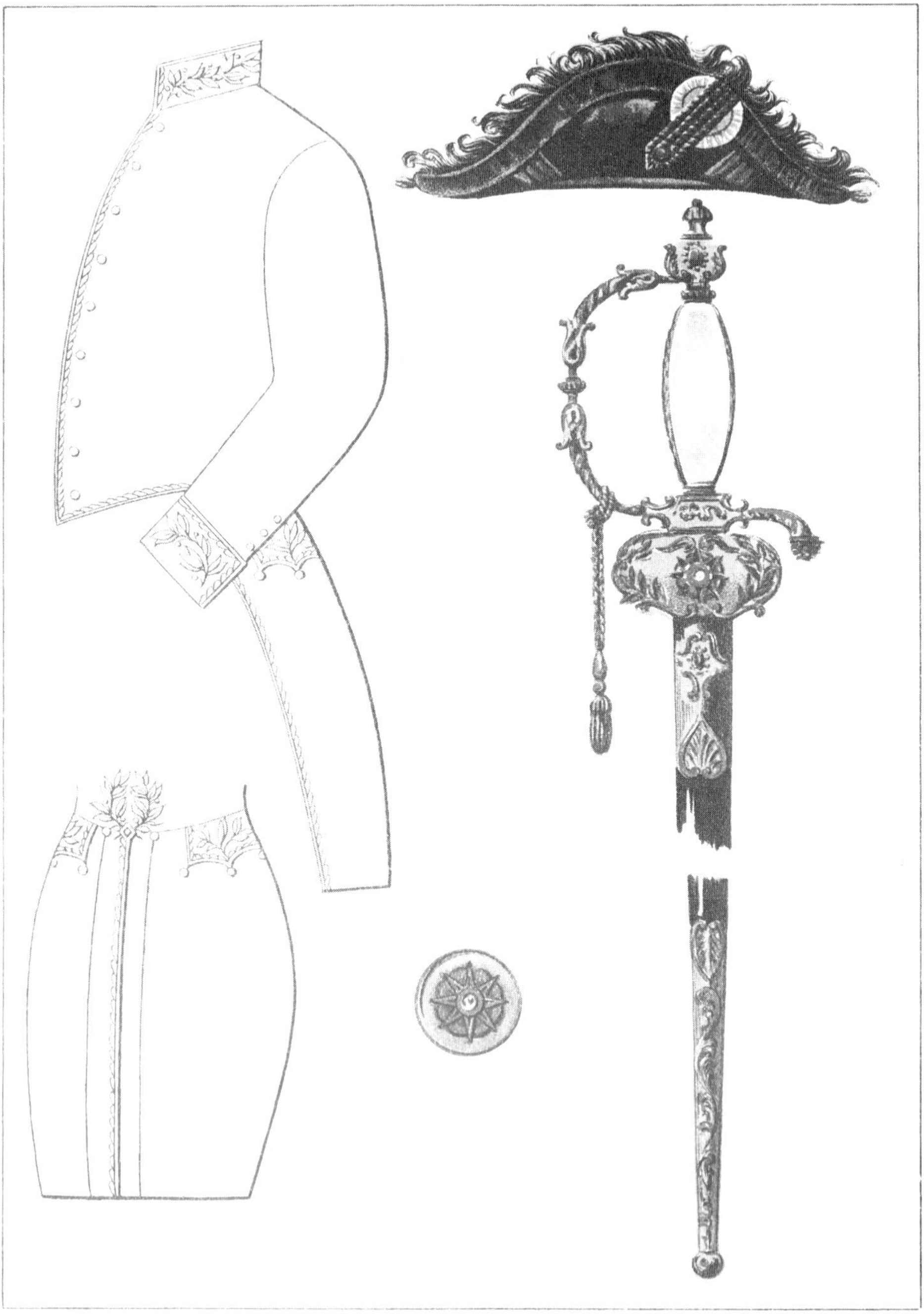

decorated with laurel leaves, which runs along the top and front of the collar, down the front, along the edge of the pocket flaps, on the top and side of the cuffs and along the edge of the entire tailcoat.

There should be nine buttons on the chest and three smaller buttons on each sleeve. The tail of the coat which borders on the pocket flaps should be adorned with two larger buttons, and in the centre, above the buttons should be two embroidered sprays of laurel leaves arranged in an oval circlet. At the three protruding points of the pocket flaps should be three small buttons.

The trousers should be long and of dark blue cloth. A gold stripe decorated with laurel leaves, four centimetres in width, should run down the outer sides of the trousers.

The cocked hat should be of black plush velvet, adorned with two black silk bands running diagonally at either end and on both sides from the upper rim of the hat to the lower part, and a third black silk band running along the top rim, with gilt tassels on both corners. The hat is surmounted with a black plume, to which the Pontifical Cockade is attached on the right side, held by four strands of intertwined gold cord and fastened at the lower end with a gilded button.

The buttons, all gilded, should be embossed with the Badge of the Order. The court sword should be worn in a sword frog, made of gold braid with laurel leaves. The sword should bear on the hilt the Badge of the Order. The handle should be of mother of pearl with gilded mounts and with a gilt sword-knot hanging from it; the scabbard should be of black leather with gilt boss and ferrule.

The Badge of the Order is an eight-pointed blue star superimposed on an eight-pointed star-like cluster of seven gold rays each, and a white enamel medallion with a broad gold border which is silver-rimmed. In the inner white circle is the name of the Founder, PIUS IX, and in the gold border is the inscription VIRTUTI ET MERITO.

A Knight Commander wears his Badge, six centimetres in diameter, on a neck riband, five centimetres wide, of dark blue moiré with two red stripes on each border.

A Knight Commander *con placca* wears in addition an eight-pointed blue Star, superimposed on a star-like cluster of seven rays in silver, seven centimetres in diameter, on the left side of his breast.

The Badge of the Order and buttons, according to their shape and sizes, and the riband, bands and stripes, according to colour and width, should not vary from the patterns and designs given.

For PIAN KNIGHTS OF THE THIRD CLASS or KNIGHTS OF THE

ORDER OF PIUS IX the uniform should be of dark blue cloth with coat-tails.

The collar, the cuffs and the pockets should be of red cloth.

The decoration should be a narrow gilt border, decorated with laurel leaves, at the top and front of the collar, at the top and side of the cuffs, running along the edge of the pockets and along the edge of the entire tailcoat.

There should be nine buttons on the chest and three smaller ones on each sleeve. The tail of the coat which borders on the pocket flaps should be adorned with two larger buttons, and in the centre, above the buttons should be two embroidered sprays of laurel leaves in gold thread arranged in a narrow oval circlet. At the three protruding points of the pockets should be three small buttons.

The trousers should be long and of dark blue cloth. A gold stripe, three centimetres wide, decorated with laurel leaves, should run down the outer sides of the trousers.

The cocked hat should be of black plush velvet, adorned with two black silk bands running diagonally on either end and on both sides from the upper rim of the hat to the lower part, and a third black silk band running along the upper rim. The hat should be surmounted by a black plume to which the Pontifical Cockade is attached on the right side, held by four strands of intertwined gold cord and fastened at the lower end with a gilded button.

The buttons, all gilded, should be embossed with the Badge of the Order. The court sword should be worn in a sword frog of golden braid, decorated with laurel leaves. The sword should bear on the hilt the Badge of the Order. The handle should be of mother of pearl with gilded mounts and with a gilt sword-knot hanging from it. The scabbard should be of black leather with gilt boss and ferrule.

The Badge of the Order is an eight-pointed blue star superimposed on an eight-pointed cluster of seven gold rays each, and a white enamel medallion with a broad gold border which is silver-rimmed. In the white circle is the name of the Founder, PIUS IX, and in the golden border is the inscription VIRTUTI ET MERITO.

A Knight of the Order of Pius IX wears the Badge five centimetres in diameter, on a dark blue ribbon with two red stripes on both sides of the border, three and a half centimetres wide, on his left breast.

The Badge and buttons, according to their shape and sizes, and the ribbon, bands and stripes, according to colour and width, should not vary from the patterns and designs given.

LUIGI CARD. MACCHI
Grand Chancellor of the Pontifical Equestrian Orders

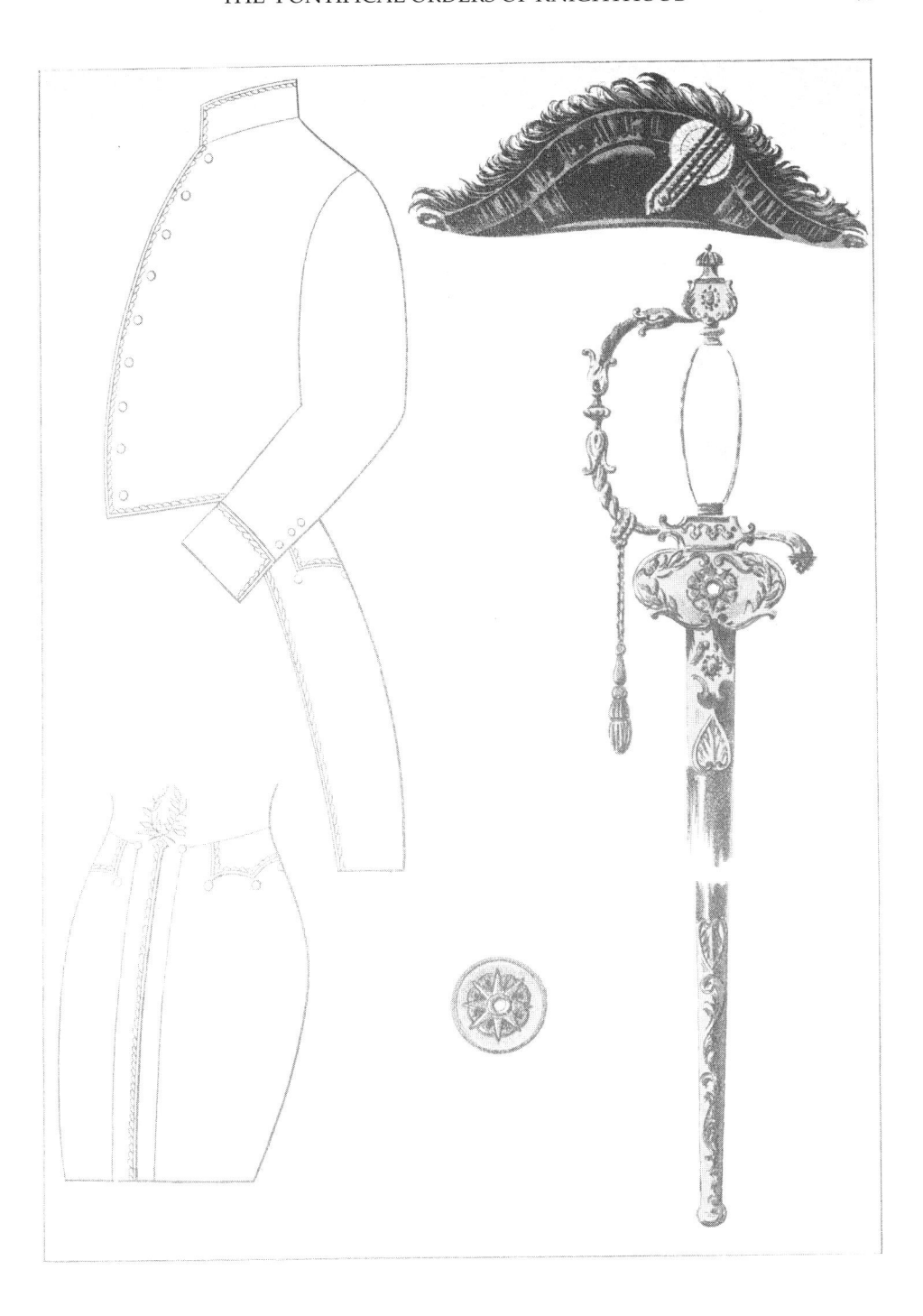

THE PONTIFICAL ORDERS OF KNIGHTHOOD

97

PAPAL BRIEF OF PIUS XII P.P. CONCERNING THE ABOLITION OF NOBILITY CONFERRED WITH THE ORDER OF PIUS IX.

FOR PERPETUAL REMEMBRANCE. Our Predecessor, Pope Pius IX by His Apostolic Letters in the form of Papal Briefs, dates 17 June 1847 and 17 June 1849, and by His Decree given at the Quirinal on 11 November 1856, created and instituted the Equestrian Order known as Pian Knights, which was to have three Classes of Knights. By these same Apostolic Letters it was decreed that those admitted to the First Class of the Pian Order should also receive the privilege of hereditary nobility which could be inherited by their sons, whereas those admitted to the Second Class should receive the privilege of nobility *ad personam* only.

In order that the Pian Order, to use the words of Our memorable Predecessor, should have as its aim "not to foment vanity and ambition, but rather solely to reward virtue and outstanding merit", We have decided that the same criteria should apply as in all the other Pontifical Orders of Knighthood, none of which enjoy the privilege of nobility. Papal Knights who have excelled either in their gifts of mind and heart, who have shown conspicuous loyalty to the Holy See, or given meritorious service to the Church, are acknowledged and rewarded by their title of rank and their insignia proper to the Order of Knighthood.

After giving careful consideration to these matters, We have decided to decree in the Lord that the status of nobility which was decreed in the aforementioned Apostolic Letters be abolished, and that as from today each and everyone admitted to any of the three Classes of the Pian Knights may legitimately use only the title of their rank and the insignia of their Class, and the status of nobility is hereby excluded.

We therefore decide, notwithstanding anything to the contrary, that this Papal Brief shall for always be inviolable and efficacious and henceforth take its full and total effect. Thus one must judge and define from now on null and void any attempt that may be made by any authority whatever, whether knowingly or in ignorance, all that is contrary to what is stated above.

Given at St. Peter's in Rome, under the Seal of the Fisherman this eleventh Day of November 1939, in the first year of Our Pontificate.

L. CARD. MAGLIONE
Secretary of State

THE ORDER OF ST. GREGORY THE GREAT
(Ordo Sancti Gregorii Magni)

This Order was founded by Pope Gregory XVI (1831-1846) by Papal Brief *Quod summis quibusque* on 1 September 1831 for the purpose of honouring loyal and meritorious gentlemen of the Papal States, and he placed it under the patronage of the great pope whose name it bears. Initially, he established four classes but reduced them to three in 1834; he also established two divisions for its members, civil and military.

Pope St. Pius X adapted the Order by his Papal Brief *Multum ad excitandos* of 7 February 1905 to the new circumstances in which Church and Society found themselves. The Papal States had been lost, and members for this Order were drawn from within the Church worldwide.

The new criteria for bestowal of this prestigious knighthood were to reward gentlemen who had distinguished themselves through conspicuous service and notable accomplishment on behalf of the Supreme Pontiff, the Apostolic and Holy See, the Holy Roman Church and society.[1]

The Order retained its three classes, Knight Grand Cross, Knight

---

[1] As briefly explained before, the perennial question that has been debated concerns the 'Catholicity' of this Order. The civil division was for over 100 years regarded as an Order strictly reserved to Catholic gentlemen. The number of non-Catholic members is still very small.

Pope Gregory XVI founded the Pontifical Equestrian Order of St. Gregory the Great in 1831 to honour loyal and meritorious gentlemen of the Papal States.

Above: Sir Harold Hood, Bt, Knight Grand Cross of the Order of St. Gregory the Great. Top right: Brigadier Gordon Viner, CBE, MC, TD, Knight Commander of the Order of St. Gregory the Great and Secretary of the Papal Knights in Great Britain. Right: Nicola Vecchione, Knight of the Order of St. Gregory the Great; he also wears the neck badge and Star of a Knight Commander of Merit of the S.M.Constantinian Order of St. George, and the Knight's Cross of the Order of 'Polonia Restituta'.

Commander and Knight, and its civil and military divisions, the latter being reserved for the various Corps of Guards and Militias attached to the Papal Court and to members of secular foreign armed forces who had rendered outstanding service to the Pope.

As stated earlier, it is entirely due to the diligent research of Cardinal Jacques Martin, with whom I worked on several projects between 1983 until two weeks before his sudden death on 27 September 1992, that much additional information about the Order of St. Gregory the Great came to light. Some of it I have placed in the Corollary at the end of this chapter.

Both the civil and military division have three classes: Knight Grand Cross, Knight Commander and Knight. The Commander's class is awarded with or without Star. The Cross of the civil division is pending from a laurel wreath, that of the military division, slightly smaller in size, is suspended from a military trophy.

The insignia of the Order of St. Gregory the Great and regulations concerning the uniform are described for all classes in the original Latin (see Appendix 1) and in the English translation in the statutes which follow.

A number of photographs of Papal Knights have been included to show Knights of Pontifical Orders, especially those belonging to the Order of St. Gregory the Great, attending upon high dignitaries during religious functions. As I explain in the Corollary, these duties of attending upon dignitaries at religious functions are open to Catholic members of all Pontifical Orders. There is no reason why non-Catholic Knights should not attend upon dignitaries at public functions.

The criteria for the conferment of the Order of St. Gregory the Great were published in 1987 by the Secretariat of State as follows:

'The Order of St. Gregory the Great, founded in 1831 by Pope Gregory XVI, is conferred as a reward for services to the Holy See on gentlemen of proved loyalty who must maintain unswerving fidelity to God and the Sovereign Pontiff'.[1]

In the Introduction I mentioned certain aspects concerning the Order of St. Gregory the Great that in the interest of fostering a confraternal spirit between Papal Knights of different Orders were previously deliberately understated. Pope Gregory XVI stated in his Decree *Cum amplissima honorum* which he promulgated in 1834: 'Magnus Cancellarius sit S.E.R. Cardinalis a Brevibus Apostolicis Litteris', thus appointing his most senior cardinal Grand Chancellor of the Order of St. Gregory the Great. It was the only Pontifical Equestrian Order that had a Grand Chancellor appointed to it, until Pope St. Pius X in his Papal Constitution *De*

---

[1] These criteria appear to exclude non-Catholics from becoming Knights of the Order of St. Gregory the Great, because no non-Catholic, especially a non-Christian could be expected to maintain unswerving loyalty to the Supreme Pontiff and Supreme Pastor of the Catholic Church.

The late Sir Geoffrey Hulton, Bt, KCSG, in attendance at the International Eucharistic Congress in Lourdes; left with Cardinal Gantin, right, with Cardinal Knox.

Two Knights of St. Gregory the Great in attendance on Cardinal Glemp of Warsaw during an official visit to London.

The Apostolic Nuncio (left) is received by the Diocesan Bishop and a Knight of St. Gregory the Great.

THE PONTIFICAL ORDERS OF KNIGHTHOOD

The Chargé d'Affaires of the Apostolic Nunciature in London, S.E.R. Mons. Rino Passigato (second from left) is attended by two Knights of the Order of St. Gregory the Great at a reception in honour of H.R.H. The Infante Dom Miguel de Bragança, Duke of Viseu, Portugal, (second from right), who is attended by Prof. Marcello de Moraes, and Prof. the Conte di Guedes.

His Grace the Metropolitan of Birmingham, Archbishop Couve de Murville was attended by three Knights of St. Gregory the Great at the Evesham Pilgrimage in 1984.

In 1990, Anthony DeSantis of Chicago, Knight Commander of the Order of St. Gregory the Great, who ten years earlier was invested by Cardinal Silvio Oddi in the Vatican, received his promotion to *Commendatore con placca* in the Order from Cardinal Joseph Bernardin of Chicago in the Grotto of St. Peter's Basilica in Rome in front of the tomb of St. Peter, an exceptional privilege which can only take place with the permission of the Canons of St. Peter's Basilica.

Courtesy: Archdiocese of Chicago

Ordinibus Equestribus in 1907 appointed the Cardinal Secretary of State *ex officio* Grand Chancellor of all Pontifical Orders of Knighthood.

Another important discovery Cardinal Jacques Martin made were the memoranda Pope St. Pius X wrote for his Masters of Ceremonies; they only concerned the Knights of the Order of St. Gregory the Great, to whom he had already allocated a place in the papal cortege. In order to foster a stronger confraternal spirit between the Knights of different Pontifical Equestrian Orders, but most of all to remove the Papal Knights once and for ever from the troublesome and perennial problem that caused continuous irritations to the Holy See, namely which uniformed or robed knights of which Order should be given precedence in processions, the privileges granted to the Knights of the Order of St. Gregory the Great were in 1987 extended to the uniformed Knights of the Orders of Pope Pius IX and Pope St. Sylvester.

Cardinal Jacques Martin discussed this matter with several leading experts on protocol and myself before asking Cardinal Secretary of State Casaroli for his opinion. He wholeheartedly agreed that all uniformed papal Knights should be given ceremonial tasks during religious functions, especially processions, which would remove them from the sometimes very undignified arguments about precedence.

THE PONTIFICAL EQUESTRIAN ORDER OF ST. GREGORY THE GREAT

FROM THE CHANCERY OF THE PONTIFICAL EQUESTRIAN ORDERS

7 February 1905

HIS HOLINESS POPE PIUS X, having given consideration to all the mandates of the Holy See promulgated to encourage virtue and to reward good conduct, wishing such rewards to be fitting and proper and, indeed, honour the Holy See itself, has on this occasion turned His attention to the Orders of Knighthood.

Hence, having discussed the matter with the undersigned Cardinal Secretary of Briefs, the Grand Chancellor of the Pontifical Orders of Knighthood, He has promulgated, besides all the regulations given this day to the other Pontifical Orders of Knighthood, all those rules concerning the uniform and decorations and their use for THE ORDER OF ST. GREGORY THE GREAT, which have until now appeared ambiguous and lacking clear definition, and He has ordered that these matters be precisely defined according to the following regulations, retaining however, unchanged the provision of having two Classes: one for Civilians, the other for the Military.

KNIGHTS GRAND CROSS OF THE CIVILIAN CLASS OF THE ORDER OF ST. GREGORY THE GREAT

Their uniform should be of a dark green cloth with coat-tails.

The embroidery, all in silver thread, should be a row of oak-leaves on the collar, on the cuffs and on the pockets. There should be a double row of oakleaves on the chest and also a silver border with oakleaves which runs along the top edge and front of the collar, along the front in the centre of the uniform and the edge of the pockets flaps, the top and sides of the cuffs and along the edge of the entire tailcoat.

There should be nine buttons on the chest and three smaller buttons on each sleeve. The tail of the coat which borders on the pocket flaps should be adorned with two larger buttons, and in the centre, above the buttons should be two embroidered branches with oakleaves arranged in a circlet. At the three protruding points of the pocket-flaps there should be three small buttons.

On both shoulders should be a silver braid, fastened near the collar with a button.

The trousers should be long and of dark green cloth. A silver stripe decorated with oakleaves, four centimetres in width, should run down the outer sides of the trousers.

The cocked hat should be of black plush velvet, adorned with a silver band along the top rim, and with a small silver tassel at either end, and above there should be a white plume, to which the Pontifical Cockade is attached on the right side, held by four intertwined strands of silver cord and fastened at the lower end with a silver button.

The buttons, all in silver, should be embossed with the Cross of the Order. The court sword should be worn in a sword frog, made of silver braid decorated with oakleaves. The sword should bear on the hilt the Cross of the Order (without the laurel wreath). The handle should be of mother of pearl with gilded mounts and with a gilt sword-knot hanging from it. The scabbard should be of black leather with gilt boss and ferrule.

The Cross of the Order (Civil Class) is an eight-pointed, gold-rimmed and ball-pointed Maltese cross of deep red enamel, with a blue medallion bearing the image of St. Gregory the Great in gold relief, and in a gold circle the inscription S. GREGORIUS MAGNUS. On the reverse side are the words PRO DEO ET PRINCIPE. The Cross is surmounted by a wreath of gold-rimmed, green enamelled oakleaves, tied at the bottom with a golden bow.

A Knight Grand Cross wears the Cross, six and a half centimetres in diameter, surmounted by the laurel wreath, three and a half centimetres wide and three centimetres deep, suspended from a sash, ten centimetres wide, which is of scarlet moiré with a yellow border either side.

The Star of a Knight Grand Cross is the Cross of the above size (but without the laurel wreath) superimposed on an eight pointed silver star, eight and a half centimetres in diameter, which is worn on the left side.

The Cross, Star and buttons, according to their shape and sizes, and the sash, bands and stripes, according to colour and width, should not vary from the patterns and designs given.

KNIGHTS COMMANDER OF THE CIVILIAN CLASS OF THE ORDER OF ST. GREGORY THE GREAT

Their uniform should be of a dark green cloth with coat-tails.

The embroidery, all in silver thread, should be a row of oakleaves on the collar, on the cuffs and on the pockets, and a silver border with oakleaves which runs along the top edge and front of the collar, down the centre of the uniform and along the edge of the entire tailcoat, along the edge of the pocket flaps and the top and side of the cuffs.

THE PONTIFICAL ORDERS OF KNIGHTHOOD 109

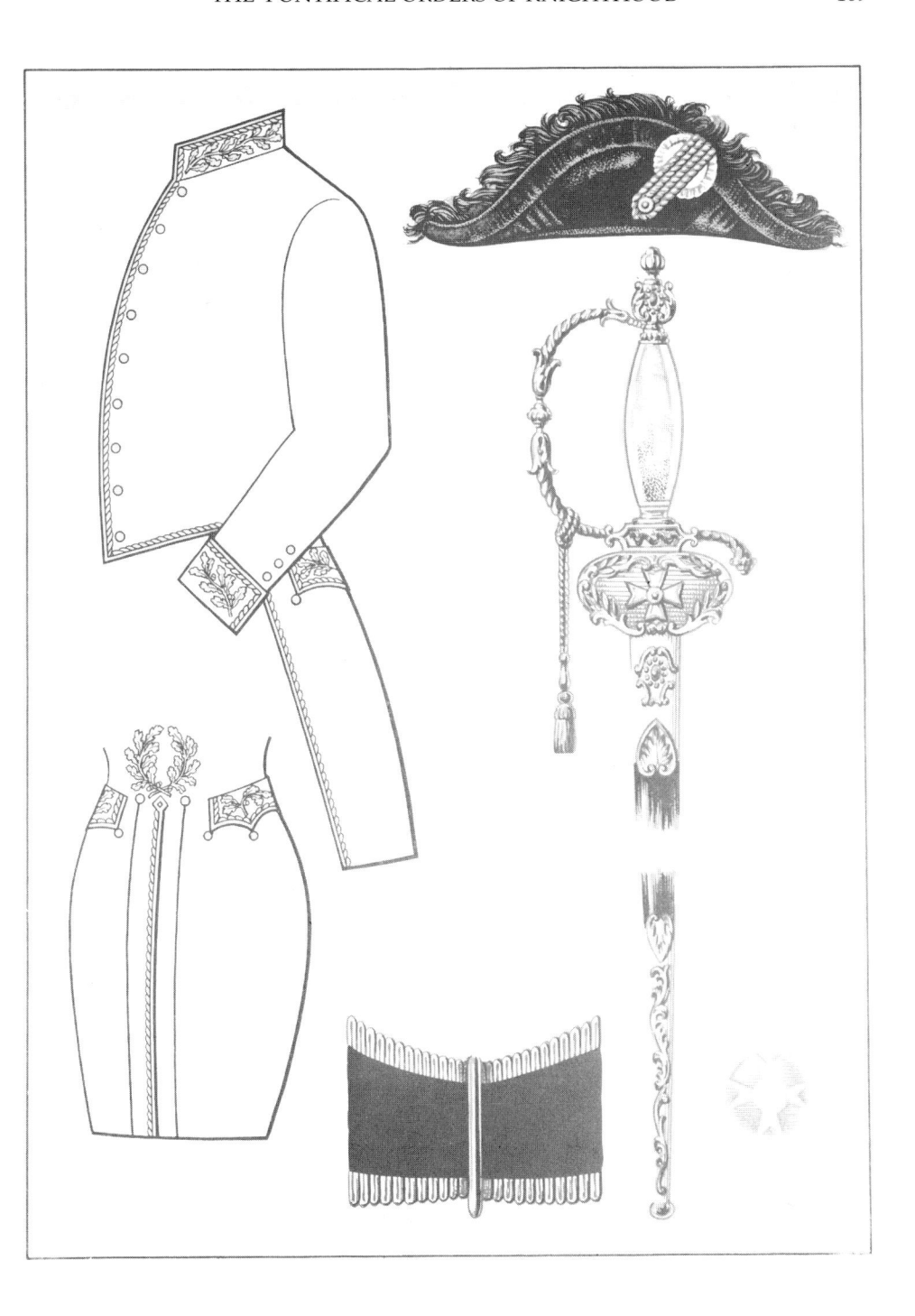

There should be nine buttons on the chest and three smaller buttons on each sleeve. The tail of the coat which borders on the pocket flaps should be adorned with two larger buttons, and in the centre, above the buttons should be two embroidered branches with oakleaves arranged in a circlet. At the three protruding points of the pocket-flaps there should be three small buttons.

The trousers should be long and of dark green cloth. A silver stripe decorated with oakleaves, four centimetres in width, should run down the outer sides of the trousers.

The cocked hat should be of black plush velvet, adorned with two black silk bands running diagonally at either end and on both sides from the upper rim of the hat to the lower part, and a third black silk band running along the top rim, with a small silver tassel at either end. The hat should be surmounted with a black plume, to which the Pontifical Cockade is attached on the right side, held by four intertwined strands of silver cord and fastened at the lower end with a silver button.

The buttons, all in silver, should be embossed with the Cross of the Order. The court sword should be worn in a sword frog, made of silver braid decorated with oakleaves. The sword should bear on the hilt the Cross of the Order (without the laurel wreath). The handle should be of mother of pearl with gilded mounts and with a gilt sword-knot hanging from it. The scabbard should be of black leather with gilt boss and ferrule.

The Cross of the Order (Civil Class) is an eight-pointed, gold-rimmed and ball-pointed Maltese cross of deep red enamel, with a blue medallion bearing the image of St. Gregory the Great in gold relief, and in a gold circle the inscription S. GREGORIUS MAGNUS. On the reverse side are the words PRO DEO ET PRINCIPE. The Cross is surmounted by a wreath of gold-rimmed, green enamelled oakleaves, tied at the bottom with a golden bow.

A Knight Commander wears his Cross, six and a half centimetres in diameter, on a neck riband, five centimetres wide, of scarlet moiré with yellow borders.

A Knight Commander *con placca* wears in addition a smaller eight-pointed silver star, seven centimetres in diameter, on which is superimposed the Cross of the Order, five centimetres in diameter, on the left side of his breast.

The Cross of the Order and buttons, according to their shape and sizes, and the riband, bands and stripes, according to colour and width, should not vary from the patterns and designs given.

KNIGHTS OF THE CIVILIAN CLASS OF THE ORDER OF ST. GREGORY THE GREAT

Their uniform should be of a dark green cloth with coat-tails.

The silver decoration should be a border with oakleaves along the top edge and front of the collar, on the cuffs and on the edge of the pocket flaps, and which runs along the front of the uniform and along the edge of the entire tail coat.

There should be nine buttons on the chest and three smaller buttons on each sleeve. The tail of the coat which borders on the pocket flaps should be adorned with two larger buttons, and in the centre, above the buttons should be two branches with oakleaves, embroidered in silver thread and arranged in a circlet. At the three protruding points of the pocket flaps there should be three small buttons.

The trousers should be long and of dark green cloth. A silver stripe decorated with oakleaves, three centimetres in width, should run down the outer sides of the trousers.

The cocked hat should be of black plush velvet, adorned with two black silk bands running diagonally at either end and on both sides from the upper rim of the hat to the lower part, and a third black silk band running along the upper rim with a small silver tassel at either end. The hat should be surmounted by a black plume to which the Pontifical Cockade is attached on the right side, held by four strands of intertwined silver cord and fastened at the lower end with a silver button.

The buttons, all in silver, should be embossed with the Cross of the Order. The court sword should be worn in a sword frog, made of silver braid decorated with oakleaves. The sword should bear on the hilt the Cross of the Order (without the laurel wreath). The handle should be of mother of pearl with gilded mounts and with a gilt sword-knot hanging from it. The scabbard should be of black leather with gilt boss and ferrule.

The Cross of the Order (Civil Class) is an eight-pointed, gold-rimmed and ball-pointed Maltese cross of deep red enamel, with a blue medallion bearing the image of St. Gregory the Great in gold relief, and in a gold circle the inscription S. GREGORIUS MAGNUS. On the reverse side are the words PRO DEO ET PRINCIPE. The Cross is surmounted by a wreath of gold-rimmed, green enamelled oakleaves, tied at the bottom with a golden bow.

A Knight of the Order wears the Cross, five centimetres in diameter, on a scarlet ribbon, three and a half centimetres wide, with yellow borders, on the left side of the chest.

The Cross and buttons, according to their shape and sizes, and the ribbon, bands and stripes, according to colour and width, should not vary from the

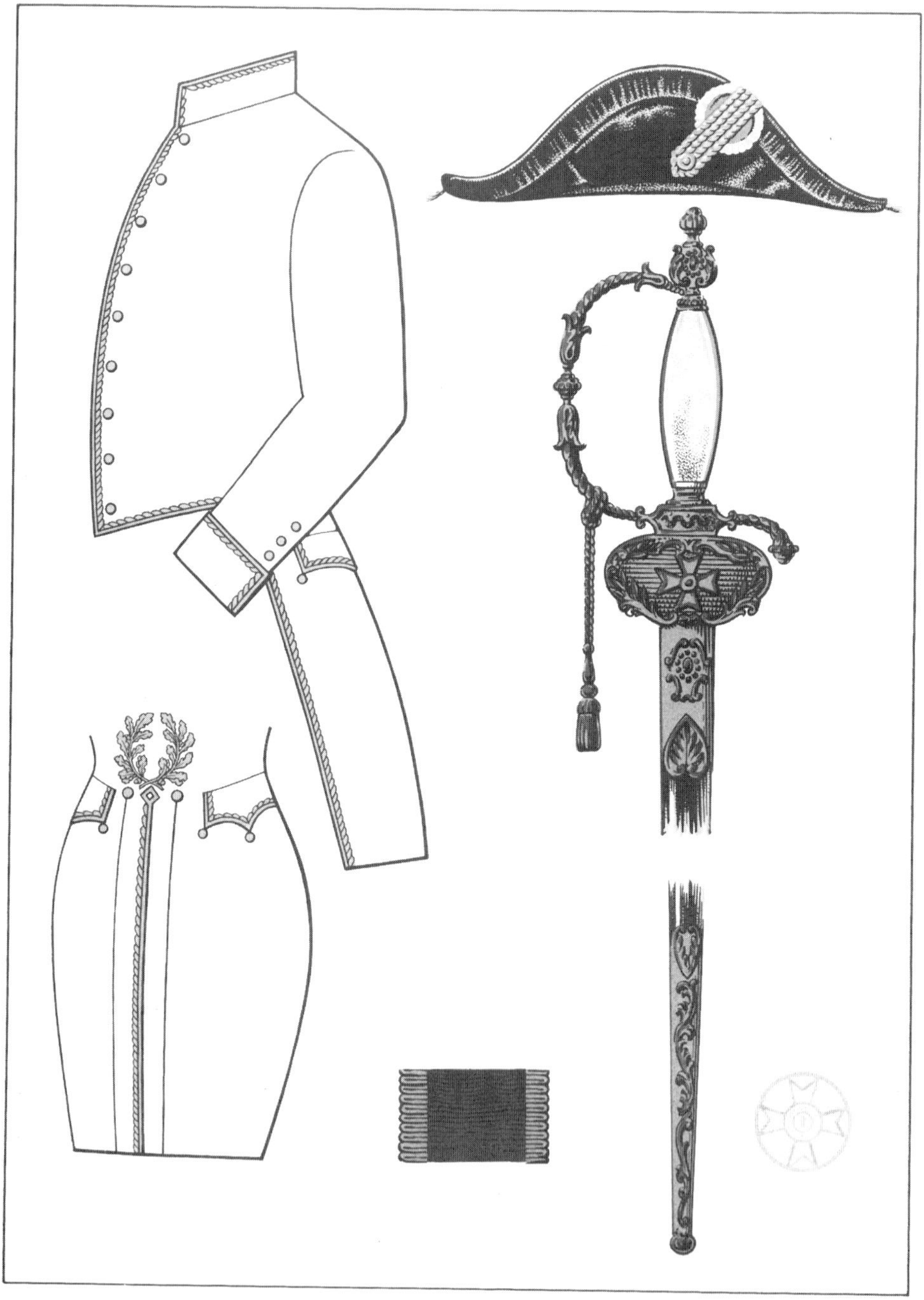

I

INVESTITURE OF A PAPAL KNIGHT COMMANDER IN THE VATICAN

Courtesy: Anthony DeSantis, KCSG

Rewards that are given to honour valour and bravery are very useful to encourage men to accomplish praiseworthy deeds because, as they do credit to persons worthy of the grateful recognition of Church and society, they also stimulate others to follow their path leading to praise and honour. So it was that Our Predecessors, the Roman Pontiffs, turned their special attention to Orders of Knighthood, as a spur towards glory.
Vatican, 7 February 1905

THE SUPREME ORDER OF CHRIST
The Collar with Cross suspended from a military trophy and the Star of the Order.

Courtesy: Guccione, Roma

THE ORDER OF THE GOLDEN SPUR OR THE GOLDEN MILITIA
The Collar with the Cross suspended from a military trophy and Star of the Order.

Courtesy: Cuccione, Roma

IV

THE GOLDEN COLLAR OF THE PIAN ORDER
The Badge suspended from a papal tiara and Star of the Order.
Courtesy: Guccione, Roma

THE ORDER OF PIUS IX – Right: insignia of a Knight and a Knight Commander; below right: a Knight Commander with Star; left: Knight Grand Cross. The uniform consists of a dark blue tail coat with gold embroidered red collar and cuffs, and trousers with gold braid, a bi-cornered hat and court sword.

Courtesy: Secretariat of State

THE ORDER OF ST. GREGORY THE GREAT. Clockwise from top left: Knight Grand Cross with Star; Knight Commander with Star; Knight Commander; Knight. The uniform is an olive-green tail coat with silver-embroidered collar and cuffs, trousers with silver braid, bi-cornered hat and court sword.

Courtesy: Secretariat of State; Photo: Giovanni Johnson, Rome

THE ORDER OF POPE ST. SYLVESTER. Clockwise from top left: Knight Grand Cross with Star; Knight Commander with Star; Knight Commander; Knight. The uniform is a black tail coat with gold embroidered collar and cuffs, trousers with gold braid, bi-cornered hat and court sword.

Courtesy: Secretariat of State, Photo Giovanni Johnson, Roma

Top row: THE CROSS PRO ECCLESIA ET PONTIFICE – left: as instituted by Leo XIII and used until Paul VI changed the insignia to that in the centre; right: as adopted by John Paul II with his name and coat of arms and reverse-coloured ribbon. Lower row left: the MEDAL CONCILIUM OECUMENICUM VATICANUM II in bronze; right: the Medal *ANNO IUBILAEI ROMAE MCMLXXV* in silver.

IX

Top row: The Medal Benemerenti – as instituted by Leo XIII in 1881; left: issued during the pontificate of Pius XII; centre: during the pontificate of John XXIII; right: conferred during the first few years of the pontificate of Paul VI. Lower row left: the new insignia introduced by Paul VI; right: as adapted by John Paul II with his own coat of arms.

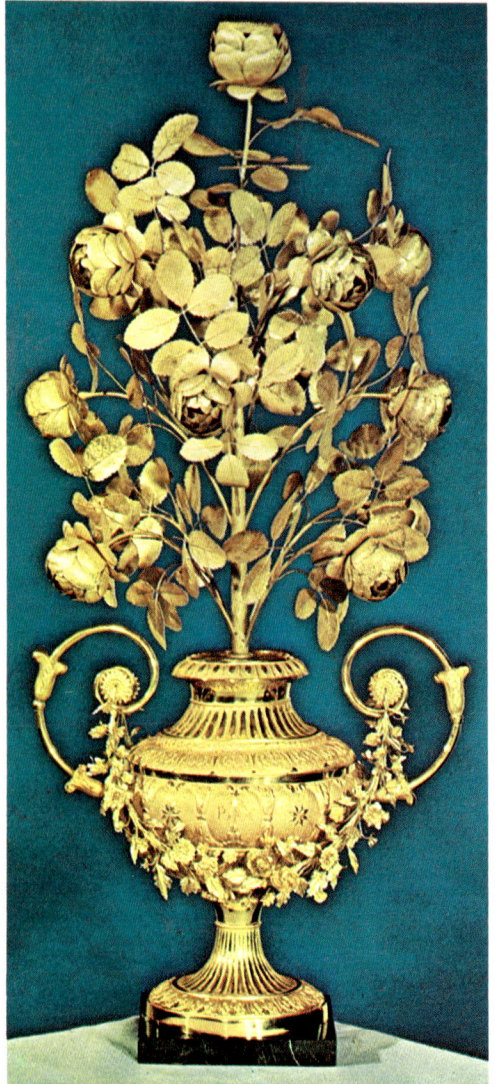

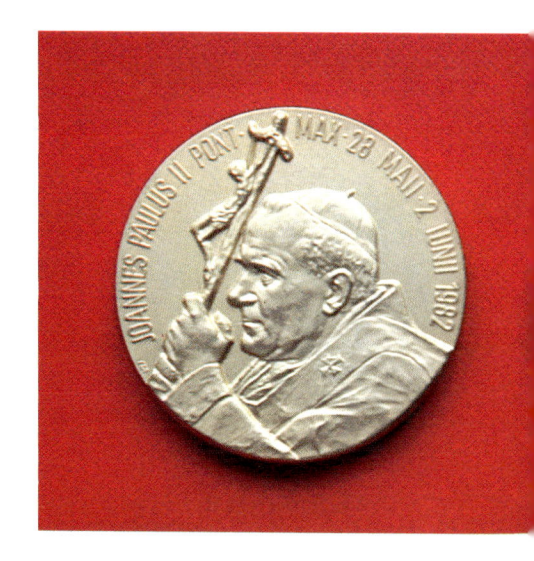

Left column top: THE GOLDEN ROSE conferred by Pius VII, whose coat of arms it bears; bottom: The BENEMERENTI medal conferred by Pius XII in silver and bronze to mark the declaration of the Blessed Virgin Mary REGINA DEL CIELO E DELLA TERRA. Right column top: obverse of the Pontifical Medal on the occasion of the visit of John Paul II to England, Scotland and Wales in 1982; centre: the BENEMERENTI medal conferred by Pius XI in 1933, L'ANNO DELLA REDENZIONE; The Cross ADVOCATI DI SAN PIETRO (Leo XIII); bottom: the BENEMERENTI medals with military trophy of Pius XII and John XXIII.

Courtesy: Secretariat of State/Garrison Collection

XI

Left: The 78th Prince and Grand Master of the Sovereign Military Order of Malta, His Most Eminent Highness Frà Andrew Bertie, who was elected in 1988. Right: The Collar of the Prince and Grand Master.

Courtesy: Sovereign Council SMOM

H.M.E.H. Frà Andrew Bertie in Washington during his official visit to the U.S.A. in 1991 with Cardinal Hickey, members of the Sovereign Council and American prelates and confréres of the Sovereign Military Order of Malta.

Courtesy: Prior R. Barwig

XII

THE SOVEREIGN MILITARY ORDER OF MALTA. Top left: Insignia of a Professed Bailiff of Obedience and of Justice; Cross of a Knight of Justice, Donat and Conventual Chaplain. Top right: Bailiff Grand Cross of Obedience and of Honour and Devotion; Cross of Knight of Justice, of Obedience, of Honour and Devotion and of Grace and Devotion. Bottom left: Grand Cross of Grace and Devotion. Bottom right: Grand Cross of Magistral Grace; Chaplain *ad honorem*; Donats 1st – 3rd class and Chaplain of Magistral Grace.

Courtesy: Malteser Hilfsdienst, Köln

THE SOVEREIGN MILITARY ORDER OF MALTA – THE ORDER PRO MERITO MELITENSI. Top left: Collar and Star for Heads of State. Top right: Civil Class for Gentlemen: special class of Grand Cross; Grand Officer, Grand Cross; Officer; Commander; Cross of Merit. Bottom left: the same ranks of the Military Class (without special class of Grand Cross). Bottom right: Civil Class for Ladies: the same ranks but without special class of Grand Cross.

Courtesy: Malteser Hilfsdienst, Köln

Left: His Royal Highness Richard, Duke of Gloucester, Grand Prior of the Most Venerable Order of St. John, of which Her Majesty Queen Elizabeth II is the Sovereign.

Above right: THE PAPAL COPE OF RECONCILIATION that was presented to the Grand Priory of England after the visit of Pope John Paul II to England in 1982; it bears the embroidered coats of arms of the last five Popes, those of the Sees of Canterbury and York and the Cross of the Order of St. John on either side. Bottom left: The Cross of the Order of a Commander, suspended from a black ribbon. Bottom right: the Star of a sub-Prelate and of a Knight.

Courtesy: The Venerable Order of St. John

XV

Above left: His Eminence Giuseppe Cardinal Caprio, Grand Master of the Equestrian Order of the Holy Sepulchre; right: the Collar and Star of the Order of which only twelve are conferred.

Ancient insignia of the Order from the Neuville Collection dating from the 16th to 19th century. The Collection was a major exhibit in Lyon, organised jointly by the Musée de Fourvire in Lyon and the French Lieutenancy of the Order.

Courtesy: S.E. le Général d'Harcourt & M. Joseph Payen

XVI

Above: The showcase in one of the reception rooms of the Grand Magisterium of the Order of the Holy Sepulchre of Jerusalem, displaying the contemporary insignia of the Order, made by Giorgio Guccione; on the left side of the case are the insignia of members, on the right side, the Order of Merit. Below: Crosses and Stars of members of the various ranks. *Courtesy: Grand Magisterium & French Lieutenance*

patterns and designs given.

KNIGHTS OF THE MILITARY CLASS are professional soldiers, either those who serve in the troops or guards of the Pope, or in the armed forces of any nation, but who for their outstanding service for God and the Supreme Pontiff, deserve to be specially honoured.

No special uniform is prescribed for Knights of the Military Class as they wear the uniforms of their own nations and regiments.

The Cross of the Order (Military Class) is an eight-pointed, gold-rimmed and ball-pointed Maltese cross in deep red enamel, with a blue medallion bearing the image of St. Gregory the Great in gold relief, and in a gold circle the inscription S. GREGORIUS MAGNUS. On the reverse side are the words PRO DEO ET PRINCIPE.

The Cross is surmounted by a gilded military trophy of the same depth and two thirds of the width of the Cross itself. It is for this reason that the Crosses in the respective ranks are smaller than in the equivalant ranks of the Civilian Class.

KNIGHTS GRAND CROSS OF THE MILITARY CLASS

Knights Grand Cross wear the Star of the Order, which is equivalent to that of the Civilian Class, on the left side of their breast. They have also the right to wear a Grand Cross, five centimetres in diameter, as a neck badge, suspended from a silk scarlet riband, five centimetres wide, with yellow borders.

KNIGHTS COMMANDER OF THE MILITARY CLASS

Knights Commander are entitled to wear the Cross, five centimetres in diameter, as a neck badge, suspended from a scarlet silk riband, five centimetres wide, with yellow borders.

Knights Commander *con placca* wear the identical star to that worn in the Civil Class on their left breast.

KNIGHTS OF THE MILITARY CLASS

Knights wear their Cross, three and a half centimetres in diameter, on the left side of their breast, suspended from a silk scarlet ribbon, three and a half centimetres wide, with yellow borders.

The Crosses, according to size and shape, and the riband and ribbon as to colour and width should not differ from the designs laid down.

LUIGI CARD. MACCHI
Grand Chancellor of the Pontifical Equestrian Orders

114 ORDERS OF KNIGHTHOOD AND OF MERIT

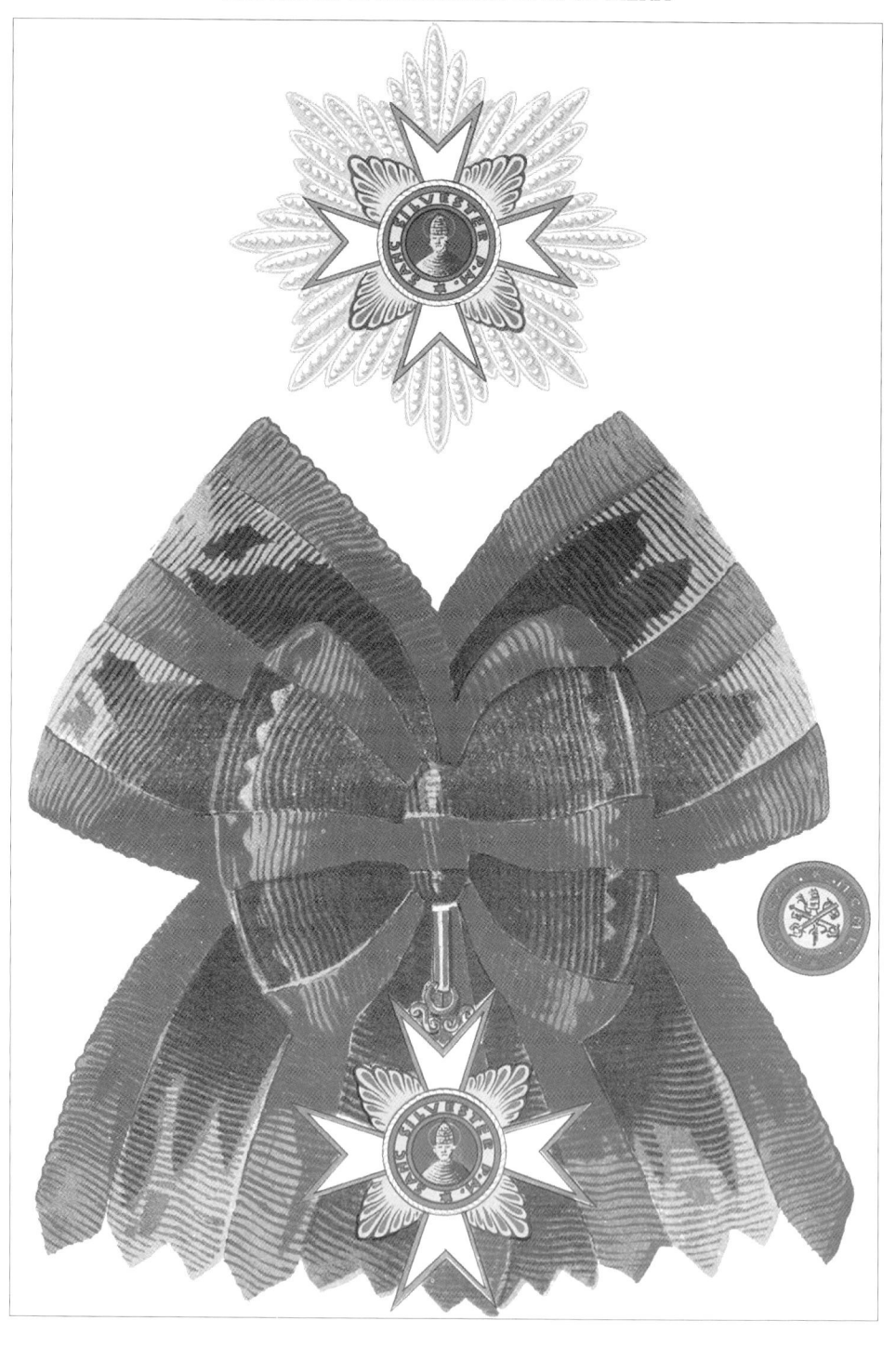

THE ORDER OF POPE SAINT SYLVESTER
(Ordo Sancti Silvestri Papae)

The Order was instituted by Pope Gregory XVI on 31 October 1841 in his Papal Brief *Cum honinum mentes*. It was Pope Gregory's intention that the Order of St. Sylvester should absorb the Order of the Golden Spur. Because of strong opposition to the Pope's intentions, especially from those who feared the loss of their title 'Papal Count Palatine' which was to be abolished immediately, Gregory XVI did not force the issue; instead the Order of St. Sylvester simply remained adjoined to the Order of the Golden Spur and was theoretically dormant from the moment it was instituted until Pope St. Pius X detached it from the Order of the Golden Spur, gave the Order its own statutes and independence in his Papal Brief *Multum ad excitandos* of 7 February 1905.

The Order of Pope St. Sylvester ranks fifth among the Pontifical Orders of Knighthood (though it is now listed sixth because of the creation of the Golden Collar of the Pian Order as a separate Order in 1957). It was created to reward laymen who are active in the apostolate in particular in the exercise of their professional duties and masters of the different arts. It has always been open to well-deserving non-Catholics and it comprises, like the Pian Order and the Order of St. Gregory the Great, three classes: Knight Grand Cross, Knight Commander (also awarded with Star) and Knight. The Order has only a civil division.

The question has frequently been raised why, for example, in some countries very few Knights of St. Sylvester are created, and in other ecclesiastical jurisdictions mainly Knights of St. Sylvester while few Knights of St. Gregory the Great are appointed. The Polish Church, especially in the diaspora, is a typical example; several eminent members of the Polish community in Great Britain have been appointed Knights and Knights Commander of the Order of St. Sylvester. All of them are active in the apostolate of the Church in a professional, though voluntary capacity. For example, Commendatori A.M.A. Sczaniecki and R.J. Gabrielczyk have been for many years Chairman and Secretary of the Polish Benevolent Fund, the economic division of the Polish Catholic Mission, as such they are responsible for the administration of properties for the Polish Housing Association, which in turn has branches responsible for homes for the elderly, the handicapped and the sick. After the Second World War, hundreds of thousands of Polish ex-servicemen and women and their families settled in Great Britain, the United States, Canada and many other English-speaking countries. The Polish Catholic

During his frequent visits to England, the late Cardinal Wladyslaw Rubin, (left centre), was always attended by two Polish Knights of the Order of Pope St. Sylvester, Mr. A. M. A. Sczaniecki, KCSS, and Mr. R. J. Gabrielczyck, KSS. (Right) The Knights in attendance on the late Bishop Mateusz of the Polish Orthodox Church at the service commemorating the victims of the Katyn massacre.

Mission and especially the Polish Benevolent Fund were not only close links with the homeland they had to leave behind, but they helped the Polish settlers to integrate into the societies of their new homelands. They sponsor schools in which the Polish language, Polish history and culture are taught, but most of all, they take care of those who have lost the ability to care for themselves. The administration of such enormous and costly projects can only be carried out by highly professional people. On this basis most Knights of the Order of St. Sylvester in Great Britain are members of the Polish Catholic Church.

There is no more apt example of the criteria laid down for admission to the Order of St. Sylvester: laymen who are active in the apostolate, particularly in the exercise of their professional duties.

One of the outstanding artists who have ben honoured with a knighthood of St. Sylvester is the Flemish painter Felix de Boeck. Among his best known paintings are the portraits of Popes John XXIII, Paul VI, and John Paul II; the latter was the last portrait he painted before his eyesight failed him. He had endowed many Belgian churches and institutions with his paintings. Being a Protestant, he was honoured by the Pontiff at the instigation of the Apostolic Nuncio to Belgium.

The insignia and uniform for all classes of the Order of Pope St. Sylvester are described in detail in the statutes of the Order which is appended here in translation in the English language; the original Latin text is to be found in Appendix 1.

The two Polish Knights of Pope St. Sylvester attended on Cardinal Josef Glemp of Warsaw during a Pontifical High Mass in 1992. On the left of the Cardinal sits the Right Reverend Rector of the Polish Mission in England and Wales, Mons. Stanislaw Swierczynski, an Ecclesiastical Knight of Grace of the S.M. Constantinian Order of St. George.

THE PONTIFICAL EQUESTRIAN ORDER OF POPE ST. SYLVESTER

FROM THE CHANCERY OF THE PONTIFICAL EQUESTRIAN ORDERS

7 February 1905

HIS HOLINESS POPE PIUS X, having given consideration to all the mandates of the Holy See promulgated to encourage virtue and to reward good conduct, wishing such rewards to be fitting and proper and, indeed, honour the Holy See itself, has on this occasion turned His attention to the Orders of Knighthood.

Hence, having discussed the matter with the undersigned Cardinal Secretary of Briefs, the Grand Chancellor of the Pontifical Orders of Knighthood, He has ordered, to the greater honour and memory of Pope St. Sylvester I, that the Pontifical Order of the Golden Militia and St. Sylvester, according to the Apostolic Brief of His Predecessor the late Pope Gregory XVI, dated 31 October 1841, shall change its name henceforth, and no longer join it to another Order of Knighthood, but that the Order shall be known only by the name of His Holy Predecessor, Pope St. Sylvester, the first patron of Christian Chivalry; and He decrees further that like the other Pontifical Equestrian Orders, it shall not only comprise Knights and Knights Commander but also Knights Grand Cross. He has ordered in an Apostolic Letter which bears today's date, that matters pertaining to the honours, privileges, uniform and head-dress be precisely defined according to the following regulations: —

KNIGHTS GRAND CROSS OF THE ORDER OF POPE ST. SYLVESTER

Their uniform should be of black cloth with coat-tails.

The collar and cuffs should be of black velvet.

The embroidery, all in gold thread, should be a row of laurel leaves on the collar, on the cuffs and on the pockets. There should be a double row of laurel leaves on the chest, and also a narrow gilt border, decorated with laurel leaves, along the top edge and front of the collar, surround the pocket flaps and run along the edge and side of the cuffs.

THE PONTIFICAL ORDERS OF KNIGHTHOOD

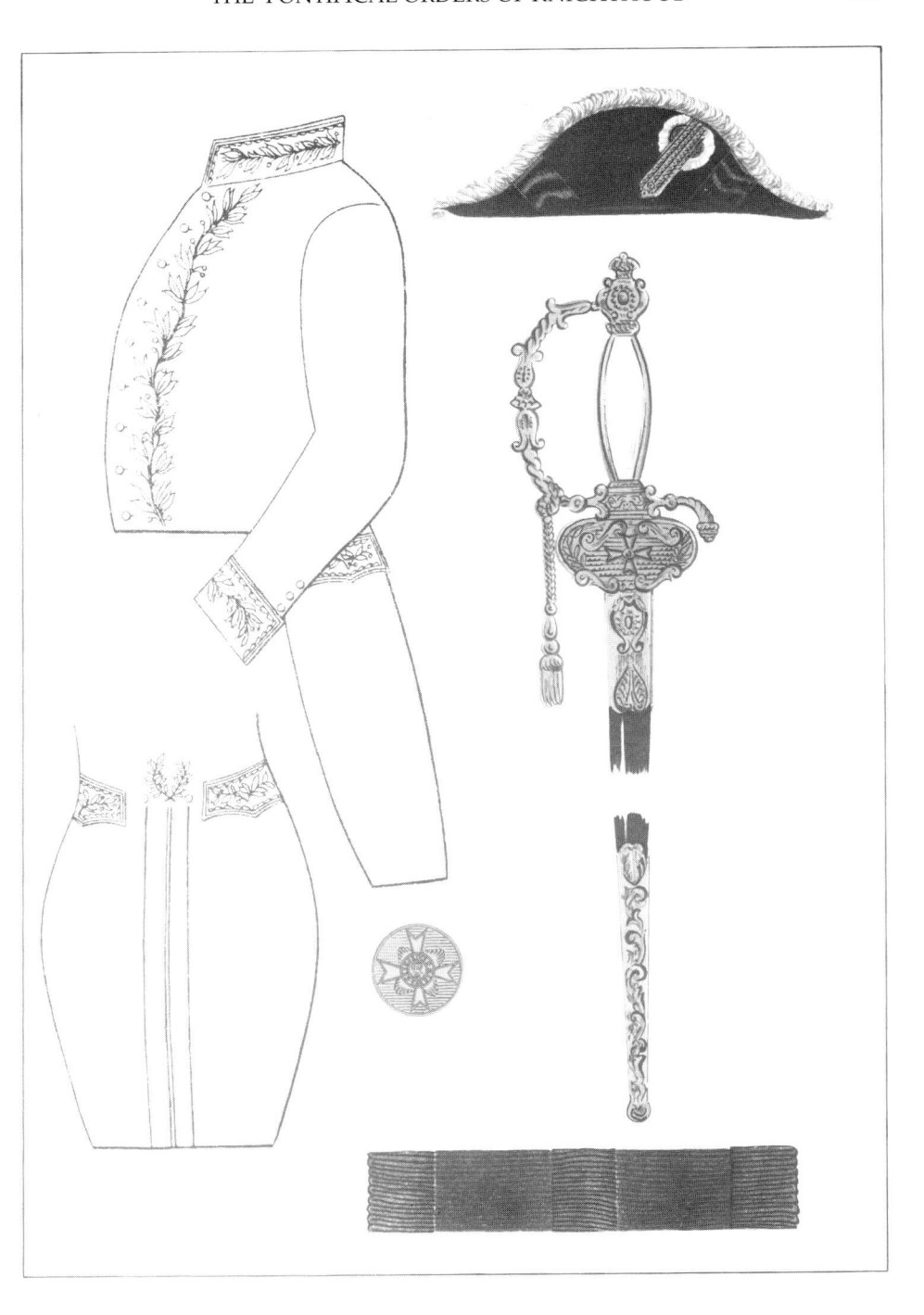

There should be nine buttons on the chest and three smaller buttons on each sleeve. The tail of the coat which borders on the pocket flaps should be adorned with two larger buttons, and in the centre, above the buttons, should be two embroidered sprays of laurel leaves arranged in an oval circlet.

On both shoulders should be a twisted gilt cord, fastened near the collar with a button.

The trousers should be long and of black cloth. A gold stripe, four centimetres wide, decorated with laurel leaves, should run down the outer sides of the trousers.

The cocked hat should be of black heavy silk, adorned with two black bands running diagonally at either end and on both sides from the upper rim of the hat to the lower part, and a small gilt tassel should be at either end of the hat which is to be surmounted by a white plume to which the Pontifical Cockade is attached on the right side, held by four strands of intertwined gilded cord and fastened at the lower end with a gilded button.

The buttons, all gilded, should be embossed with the Cross of the Order. The court sword should be worn in a sword frog made of gold braid decorated with laurel leaves. The sword should bear on the hilt the Cross of the Order. The handle should be of mother of pearl with gilded mounts and with a gilt sword-knot hanging from it. The scabbard should be of black leather with gilt boss an ferrule.

The Cross of the Order is a gold-rimmed, eight-pointed, white enamel Maltese cross with four shorter clusters of eight gilded rays protruding between the arms of the Cross. In the centre of the Cross is a blue medallion with a silver-rimmed yellow border, bearing in gilt relief the image of Pope St. Sylvester wearing a tiara, and in the yellow border the words: SANC SILVESTER P.M.

The Knight Grand Cross wears the Cross, five centimetres in diameter, from a sash ten centimetres wide, which is of black moiré with three red stripes, one in the centre and one along each border.

The Star of a Knight Grand Cross is the Cross of the above size, superimposed on an eight-pointed silver star, eight centimetres in diameter, which is worn on the left side of the breast.

The Cross, Star and buttons, according to their shape and sizes, and the sash, bands and stripes, according to colour and width should not vary from the patterns and designs given.

KNIGHTS COMMANDER OF THE ORDER OF POPE ST. SYLVESTER

Their uniform should be of black cloth with coat-tails.

The collar and cuffs should be of black velvet.

The embroidery, all in gold thread, should be a row of laurel leaves on the collar, on the cuffs and on the pockets, and a narrow gilt border, should run along the top edge and front of the collar, the top and on the side of the cuffs and surround the pocket flaps.

There should be nine buttons on the chest and three smaller buttons on each sleeve. The tail of the coat which borders on the pocket flaps should be adorned with two larger buttons, and in the centre, above the buttons, should be two embroidered sprays of laurel leaves arranged in an oval circlet.

The trousers should be long and of black cloth. A gold stripe, four centimetres wide, decorated with laurel leaves should run down the sides of the trousers.

The cocked hat should be of black thick silk, adorned with two black bands running diagonally at either end and on both sides from the upper rim of the hat to the lower part, with a small gold tassel at either end. The hat should be surmounted by a black plume to which the Pontifical Cockade is attached on the right side, held by four intertwined strands of gilded cord and fastened at the lower end with a gilded button.

The buttons, all gilded, should be embossed with the Cross of the Order. The court sword should be worn in a sword frog made of gilded braid decorated with laurel leaves. The sword should bear on the hilt the Cross of the Order. The handle should be of mother of pearl with gilded mounts and with a gilt sword-knot hanging from it. The scabbard should be of black leather with gilt boss an ferrule.

The Cross of the Order is a silver-rimmed, eight-pointed, white enamel Maltese cross with four clusters of eight shorter gilded rays protruding between the arms of the Cross. In the centre of the Cross is a blue medallion with a silver-rimmed yellow border, bearing in gilt relief the image of Pope St. Sylvester wearing a tiara, and in the yellow border the words: SANC SILVESTER P.M.

A Knight Commander wears his Cross, five centimetres in diameter, on a neck riband, five centimetres wide, of black moiré with three red stripes, one in the centre and one on each border.

A Knight Commander *con placca* wears in addition a smaller eight-pointed silver star, seven centimetres in diameter, on which a Cross, four

ORDERS OF KNIGHTHOOD AND OF MERIT

and a half centimetres in diameter is superimposed, and it is worn on the left side of the breast.

The Cross, Star and buttons, according to their shape and sizes, and the riband, bands and stripes, according to colour and width, should not vary from the patterns and designs given.

KNIGHTS OF THE ORDER OF POPE ST. SYLVESTER

Their uniform should be of black cloth with coat-tails.

The collar and cuffs should be of black velvet.

A narrow gilt border, decorated with laurel leaves, runs along the top edge and front of the collar, along the top and the side of the cuffs and surrounds the pocket flaps.

There should be nine buttons on the chest and three smaller buttons on each sleeve. The tail of the coat, which borders on the pocket flaps should be adorned with two larger buttons, and in the centre, above the buttons should be two embroidered sprays of laurel leaves in gold thread, arranged in an oval circlet.

The trousers should be long and of black cloth. A gold stripe, decorated with laurel leaves, three centimetres wide, should run down the outer sides of the trousers.

The cocked hat should be of black thick silk. Along the upper rim runs a black silk band to which the Pontifical Cockade is attached on the right side, held by four strands of intertwined gilded cord and fastened at the lower end with a gilded button. A small gold tassel decorates the hat at either end.

The buttons, all gilded, should be embossed with the Cross of the Order. The court sword should be worn in a sword frog, made of gold braid decorated with laurel leaves. The sword should bear on the hilt the Cross of the Order. The handle should be of mother of pearl with gilded mounts and with a gilt sword-knot hanging from it. The scabbard should be of black leather with a gilt boss and ferrule.

The Cross of the Order is an eight-pointed, silver-rimmed white enamel Maltese cross with four clusters of eight shorter gilded rays protruding between the arms of the Cross. In the centre of the Cross is a blue medallion with a silver-rimmed yellow border, bearing in gilt relief the image of Pope St. Sylvester wearing a tiara, and in the yellow border the words SANC SILVESTER P.M.

A Knight of the Order wears the Cross, four centimetres in diameter, on a ribbon, three and a half centimetres wide, of black moiré with three red

ORDERS OF KNIGHTHOOD AND OF MERIT

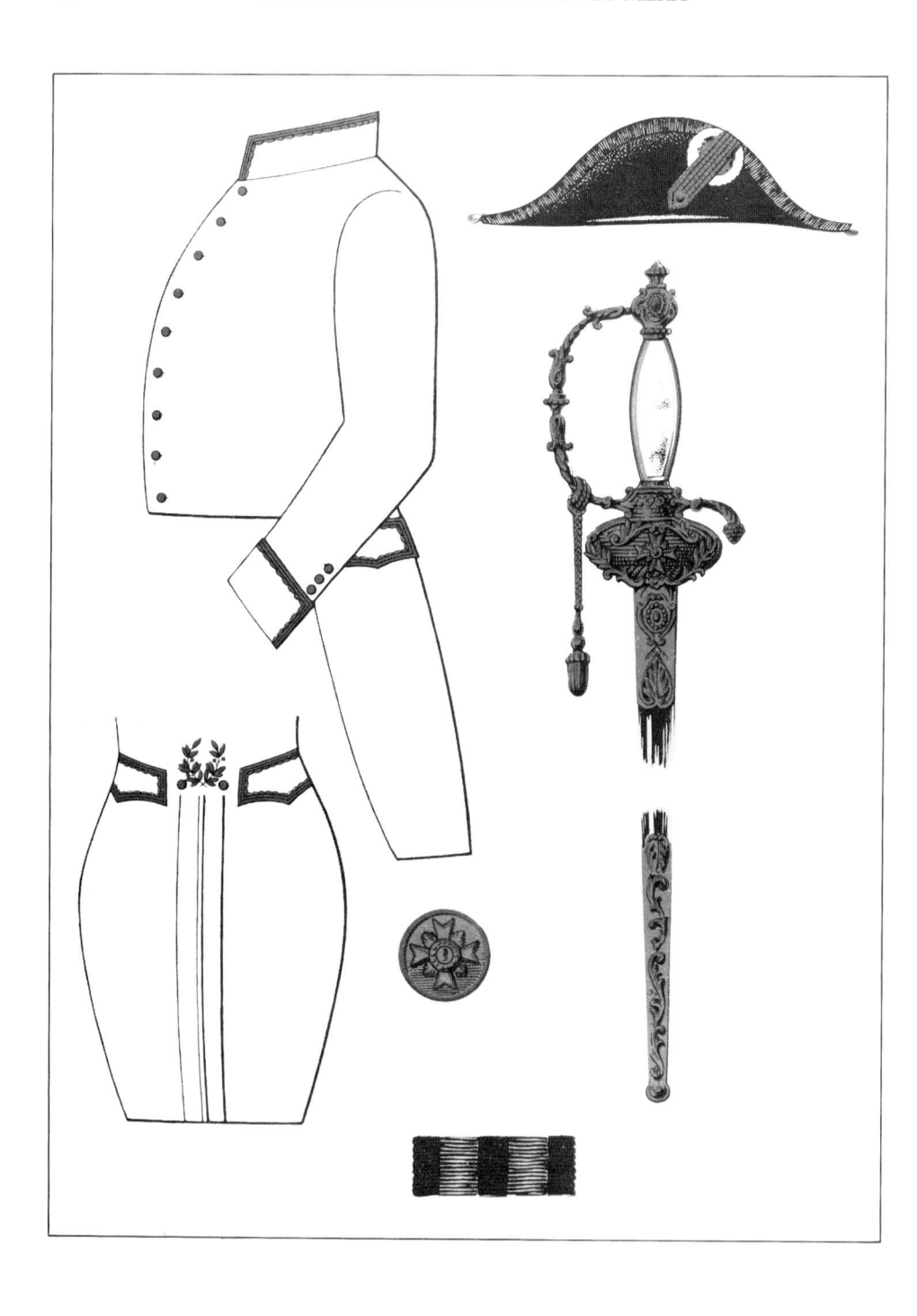

stripes, one in the centre and one at each border, on the left side of his breast.

The Cross and buttons, according to their shape and sizes, and the ribbon, bands and stripes, according to their colour and width, should not vary from the patterns and designs given.

LUIGI CARD. MACCHI
Grand Master of the Pontifical Equestrian Orders

VIII

COROLLARY ON NON-CATHOLIC KNIGHTS OF THE PONTIFICAL EQUESTRIAN ORDER OF ST. GREGORY THE GREAT

Following the publication of *The Cross on the Sword* in 1987, a fundamental and central question was raised, both in Rome and abroad, concerning the appointments of non-Catholics, and even some non-Christians to the Order of St. Gregory the Great. It would be wrong not to address this question, because closing one's eyes to problems that arise and pretend that they do not exist always proves counterproductive.

In *The Cross on the Sword* I dealt with this question in two chapters. In retrospect, I understand the criticism levelled against me for drawing so much attention to the appointment of non-Christians to the Order of St. Gregory the Great; it would probably have been sufficient to restrict myself to two points which put the matter in perspective. First, the conferment of a papal knighthood is in the gift of the reigning Supreme Pontiff. He alone is the *fons honorum* and can change a tradition which is not incorporated in the existing statutes of the Order simply by changing the statutes. Although the tenor of the Papal Briefs of Foundation of the Orders implies or presupposes that the recipients of the Order of St. Gregory the Great are Roman Catholics, there is no actual statement to that effect. Consequently, there was legally no need to change the statutes, when the Supreme Pontiff gave the Order to a meritorious non-Catholic gentleman[1].

Secondly, non-Catholic and non-Christian gentlemen upon whom the Supreme Pontiff bestowed the honour of a knighthood because of their meritorious services to the Church and the Pontiff, were expressly not requested – as are the newly appointed Catholic Knights in the recently-devised guidelines to a ceremony of investiture – to promise unswerving and continued obedience to the Holy Father, the Apostolic See and the Catholic Church, and the defence of Catholic doctrine.

One assumes that a non-Catholic or non-Christian Papal Knight would at all times act prudently and make no hostile statements and say or do anything detrimental to the Order and especially the Catholic Church and the Supreme Pontiff who offered them this honour which they accepted, well knowing that, on occasion, they might find themselves in a conflict of conscience. Whilst the defence of Catholic doctrine is enshrined in the statutes of the Order of St. Gregory the Great, it is rather a matter of

---

[1]The admission of ladies to the Pontifical Equestrian Orders would require a change in the statutes because they speak throughout only of 'meritorious gentlemen'.

common sense how non-Catholic Knights conduct themselves than a matter of law or rules.

In this context I go back to the example I chose in *The Cross on the Sword*: Sir Sigmund Sternberg, a leading member of the Jewish community, whom Pope John Paul II created a Knight Commander of the Order of St. Gregory. Since his investiture in 1986, there have been a number of disagreements between international groups of Jews and the administration of the Catholic Church. Unfortunately, such conflicts get easily polarised, and whilst militant Jewish groups are on the offensive, it is usually 'the Vatican' (a complete misnomer in the context), the Pope (who probably is the last person to learn of the issue), the Catholic Church (which with is 900 million members is most likely in total ignorance of the issue) and the Holy See (which does have the power and responsibility to deal with such matters, especially since it has established diplomatic relations with Israel), who have to defend themselves against all possible accusations.

Without wishing to go into details of these issues, they all were used to sour relations between Catholics and Jews and at times even endangered the enormous progress made since the publication of the document *Nostræ Ætate* during the Second Vatican Council in 1965.

Chapter Three

PAPAL KNIGHTS

The Cross on the Sword, the supplementary volume to Mons. Cardinale's revised edition of *Orders of Knighthood, Awards and the Holy See*, was chiefly written as a guide for members of Pontifical Equestrian Orders, though I was able to include in it some *addenda* and *corrigenda* to the main work.

It was mainly an endeavour to answer questions that were asked by Papal Knights and those who wanted information about procedure when becoming one. Late in 1985, Cardinal Hume, Archbishop of Westminster, asked me to devise a ceremony of investiture or conferment of the dignity of a Knight Commander of the Order of St. Gregory the Great, to which a prominent member of London's Jewish community had been appointed for his work in Catholic-Jewish relations. I was informed that it would be a public function attended by members of the Government, the upper and lower Houses of Parliament, ambassadors and public figures.

The investiture of Sir Sigmund Sternberg at Westminster Cathedral Hall in London; a special ceremony was devised for the occasion. Some forty Papal Knights had taken their seats in front of the stage; facing the Knights on the opposite side were ambassadors and members of both Houses of Parliament. Some 300 invited guests filled the Hall and balconies.

All ceremonial functions in the Church are based on precedent. Unfortunately, no official precedent for functions concerning the Pontifical Equestrian Orders existed, and new guidelines had to be established. With the assistance of the late Bishop Gerald Mahon, the representative of the Bishops Conference of England and Wales for interfaith relations, and by studying programmes of investitures of other Orders of Knighthood, especially the Religious Orders, I devised a ceremony of Induction and Investiture for this occasion, though I had to bear in mind that the Knight to be invested was not a Catholic, and the main feature of an investiture of a Catholic Knight, namely that the ceremony was an integral part of a Holy Mass, had to be left out. About fifty Knights of the Order of St. Gregory the Great and two of the Order of Pope St. Sylvester, all of whom would attend uniform, had accepted an invitation, as had a large delegation Knights and Dames of the Equestrian Order of the Holy Sepulchre of Jerusalem and of Knights of the S.M.Constantinian Order of George. Members of the Order of the Holy Sepulchre of Jerusalem were first scheduled to attend the function dressed in their robes, but were advised by ecclesiastical authority to wear civil formal dress, because the function was taking place in the large assembly hall adjacent to the Cathedral, but not in the Cathedral itself.

An exact timetable had to be worked out for the different processions of knights and dignitaries to enter the hall and take their seats, and for the procedure of the actual conferment of the insignia. At a given point, Sir Sigmund Sternberg, the recipient of the honour, would be presented to Cardinal Hume for the conferment of the Knight Commander's Cross by two Knights Commander, Brigadier Gordon Viner, CBE, MC, TD, of the Order of St. Gregory the Great, and Mr. A.M.A. Sczaniecki of the Order of Pope St. Sylvester. This was to be followed by five speeches, a short closing ceremony and the procession of dignitaries and Knights, in reverse order, to the Cardinal's Throne Room where a reception would take place. It is relevant to explain that Sir Sigmund Sternberg had already acquired a uniform of a Knight Commander of the Order of St. Gregory.

It is uncommon for newly created Papal Knights to possess a uniform for their investiture, however, this occasion was an unusual and very important one in which even the Holy See took a special interest. It was planned to take place shortly before the Pope's visit to Rome's Synagogue, and Sir Sigmund Sternberg was a leading world figure in establishing Catholic-Jewish relations. The civil guest list, headed by the Lord High Chancellor of the United Kingdom, leading politicians and diplomats from many countries, notably Israel, the ecclesiastical list of representatives of the Holy See, the Episcopate, the Chief Rabbi and the members of the Jewish Board of Deputies, Archbishop Lord Coggan and other high dignitaries, demanded a ceremony more like a state occasion

His Eminence Cardinal Basil Hume conducted the investiture; seated in the front row on the stage, left of the Cardinal's throne were S. E. R. Mons. Rino Passigato, the Chargé d'Affaires of the Apostolic Nunciature, the Lord High Chancellor, the Lord Hailsham, Mons. Kieran Conry of the Apostolic Nunciature and the Speaker of the House of Commons, The Rt Hon. Bernard Weatherill.

than a spiritual ceremony. There was wide international press and television coverage, and apart from organising the seating for hundreds of invited guests, the question of security posed additional problems.

It would therefore be wrong to regard this event as a typical investiture ceremony for a Papal Knight, however, because of the wide national and international press and television coverage, within days I found myself inundated with letters from all over the British Isles as well as the continent of Europe. Papal Knights wanted to know why there had been an investiture ceremony for a Jew, while none of the Catholic Knights had ever been invested, the papal knighthood having simply been conferred upon them at a private ceremony, either in the Bishop's House or after a Mass in Church.

It is fair to say that considerable resentment was expressed that Catholic Knights should have been deprived of such a ceremony when they had become members of a Papal Equestrian Order. Why, I was asked, had no bishop ever used the investiture ceremony for Catholic Papal Knights, and where could a book that gave such guidelines about the ceremony be found? I replied to all enquirers that this investiture ceremony had been specially devised for the occasion and that no investiture guidelines for Papal Knights existed, but that I would take up the matter with the appropriate authorities in Rome and, hopefully, be able to publish general guidelines for the investiture of a Papal Knight in due course.

I also received many letters asking for information how a gentleman could receive a papal knighthood. Although there has been a standard procedure for the admission to the Pontifical Equestrian Orders since the Orders were founded, very little appeared to be known about it as it was published in Latin, the language in which Papal Decrees and also the official bulletin of the Holy See, *Acta Apostolicae Sedis*, are published. Not only in the British Isles and, perhaps more relevant, not just to laymen, rules and regulations concerning Pontifical Equestrian Orders, especially any new arrangements, remain largely unknown.

It was therefore relatively easy to compile the regulations concerning admission to Pontifical Equestrian Orders, the prerequisites and administrative work involved, from the application for a knighthood to having the eventual conferment gazetted in the *Acta Apostolica Sedis*, which verifies a knight's status, and without which a Papal Knight has no evidence of registration of his knighthood.

However, regulations alone are not enough, especially when trying to solve problems that arise out of the apparent contradiction of rules, the lack of specific criteria dealing with unusual situations, and attempting to integrate those already existing practices that had developed over decades during different pontificates and in different countries and ecclesiastical jurisdictions.

As to the task of devising a ceremony of investiture for Catholic Papal Knights, I fortunately had the assistance of His Eminence Cardinal Jacques Martin, whose vast experience in matters of protocol and ceremonies proved invaluable. However, I very soon realised that any guidelines for services or ceremonies of investitures would only be practical if they allowed national and provincial practices to be added to them. With this in mind, Cardinal Martin suggested I first consult experts who would be able to change the basic infrastructure of an investiture ceremony into a service worthy of the great dignity the Pontiff had bestowed on the new member of one of his Pontifical Equestrian Orders.

With regard to compiling rules and regulations for admission to a Pontifical Order of Knighthood, I am deeply indebted to the late Archbishop Cesare Zacchi, formerly an Apostolic Nuncio, then President of the Pontifical Ecclesiastical Academy for diplomats in the service of the Holy See, and Canon of St. Peter's Basilica in Rome. He organised for my benefit several informal lunches and dinners to which he invited important members of the Curia, all of whom were experienced in such matters and contributed their expert opinions, especially on controversial subjects. The eminent prelates knew the juridical position, but the majority of them felt that, for example, the exclusive Catholic character of the Order of St. Gregory the Great should have been retained. This, however, would obviously require another papal encyclical, similar to *Equestres Ordines* by Paul VI in 1966, which reserved the Supreme Order of Christ to Christian Sovereigns and Heads of State.

Cardinal Martin attended all the meetings because it was important for him to gauge the consensus of opinion of his colleagues which, in turn, could be incorporated in his suggestions for the guidelines of an investiture ceremony. It is important to place on record here that the general consensus was that it should be optional as to whether there should be a service of investiture or a simple ceremony of conferment of the insignia for a newly appointed knight.

Any guidelines had to originate from the *fons honorum*, and before even attempting to compile them, the Apostolic Palace had to give the lead in this endeavour. Both Cardinal Casaroli, the Secretary of State and Grand Chancellor of all Pontifical Equestrian Orders, and Cardinal Martin gave me their unstinting help.

Cardinal Martin wrote the introduction to the section on the Pontifical Equestrian Orders in *The Cross on the Sword*, and it was the foundation on which I could build a general structure of guidelines, protocol and etiquette for Papal Knights. His Eminence also furnished me with invaluable information, particularly with instructions and directives jotted down by several Pontiffs (three of whom he had served for seventeen years as Prefetto della Casa Pontificia) concerning Papal Knights contained in memoranda to their Prefect of the Papal Court or their Master of Ceremonies.

Nothing could be more relevant at this point than some extracts from Cardinal Martin's introduction:

'There is in the idea and in the word 'decoration', in the titles 'Knight', 'Knight Commander' and 'Grand Officer', in all insignia – civil and military conferred in recognition of merits, real or supposed, something temporal and secular that seems to go against the idea that a spiritual power like the Holy See should make use of them.

'Nevertheless, this book attests to the fact that there is nothing more ancient, more venerable, more diversified than the Orders of Chivalry that have existed or still exist, and none are more desired, more sought after by certain people, than a papal decoration.

'If the Holy See seems thus to be aligned with the secular states over their use, students of history perceive that the contrary is sometimes true. In every case, it is always necessary to underline the essential differences between the temporal decorations and those that are conferred by the Sovereign Pontiff.

'The nature of the originating principle is in having the power to decorate someone. It is not 'The Vatican' that creates Knights and Knights

His Eminence Jacques Cardinal Martin, who sadly died in 1992 before he could see the publication of this book, was material in laying the foundations for the ceremonial of the investitures for Papal Knights.

Courtesy: *L'Oservatore Romano*

Commander: it is the Sovereign Pontiff. There are no orders or decorations of the Vatican. All those extant are the gifts of the Pope. They receive their status from the sovereignty of the Supreme Pontiff.

'Furthermore, they are not to be viewed solely as honours, as rewards; they also incorporate a duty and a mission, that of serving and protecting the person of the Vicar of Christ.

'Those with pontifical decorations form a sort of army, on the devotion of which the Pope must be able to rely. They have promised 'fidelity to God, to the Sovereign Pontiff and to the Church'. There is a ceremony of investiture by which the insignia are conferred, which appoints them with their allotted tasks and obligations. It is not the honour that matters, but one's obligations and service.

'This was made quite clear by Pope St. Pius X when in 1905 he reconstituted three Pontifical Equestrian Orders and confirmed two others, and when, for the first time, he established the regulations concerning the uniform and the wearing of decorations.

'Particularly significant was the date chosen by the Pontiff to bring about the revisions – fifty years after the definition of the dogma of the Immaculate Conception. He wished to give 'the Virgin Mother of God, fearsome as an army ranged for battle, as a celestial patroness to the carefully chosen men who belong to the Pontifical Equestrian Orders'.

'What he expected of them can be deduced from the qualities that he required of those honoured by one of the principal Orders, that of the Golden Spur. 'They are uniquely', he wrote, 'eminent men who, by their use of arms, by their writings, or by their achievements, contribute to the progress of the Catholic cause, defend the Church by their courage or have improved it by their their thought'. And fearing that quantity might harm quality, he established that 'for the entire Catholic universe, the Knights of the Golden Spur shall not exceed one hundred in number'.[1]

'The author's task' of dealing 'with matters of etiquette and ceremonials for Papal Knights has been a very difficult task, and because so much of Church ceremonial is based on tradition and precedent, he found himself on occasion at the disadvantage of not having any precedents to guide him.

'As Prefect of the Papal Court under three successive Pontiffs, from April 1969 until December 1986, I occasionally had to deal with problems of protocol and ceremonial, especially when receiving important guests, and introducing them to the Holy Father, and when organising special occasions in Rome or abroad. I know from personal experience that occasions can arise for which there is no precedent.

'As far as Papal Knights are concerned, Peter Bander-van Duren, the author of this book... had to rely on Papal Briefs, usually by the Founders of the Pontifical Equestrian Orders. Pope St. Pius X has made several provisions for Papal Knights,[2] most of which were contained in personal directives and memoranda. However, it was left to Dr. Bander-van Duren to interpret these in the light of today's needs, as the Holy Father wrote them over eighty years ago:

'Those of us who have been in the service of the Supreme Pontiff – some for over half a century – are proud of our Papal Knights. We welcome, therefore, the fact that after so many years the guidelines for their duties have finally been worked out, collected and published.'

---

[1] Although the statutes of St.Pius X have never been changed, later Popes gave this Order to several Muslims and non-Christians. Paul VI issued a decree in 1966, reserving the Supreme Order of Christ and the Order of the Golden Spur for Christian Heads of State, the question as to whether recipients of certain Orders have to embrace the Catholic or a Christian religion has never been answered permanantly. Because of the juridical status of Papal Knights – and incidentally that of the Orders to which they have been appointed – any answer will always be arbitrary and can change from pontificate to pontificate.
[2] Cardinal Martin had originally mentioned only the Order of St.Gregory the Great; but this was later changed to 'Papal Knights' to involve the members of other Pontifical Orders in the ceremonial duties.

I
THE ROLE AND FUNCTION OF THE PONTIFICAL EQUESTRIAN ORDERS

The involvement of the Apostolic See in the field of chivalry and the history of the Pontifical Equestrian Orders have been extensively described. However, it has only been since, and as a result of, the publication of the revised edition of *Orders of Knighthood, Awards and the Holy See* that many questions were raised. For example, nobody had before enquired about a Grand Chancellor or other Officers of the Pontifical Orders of Knighthood, until by comparing them with other Orders, there appeared to be no hierarchical structure or centrally coordinated administration for them. The most recently published decrees of a Grand Chancellor of the Pontifical Equestrian Orders are also the first, being dated 7 February 1905. Although the Papal Constitution *Regimini Ecclesiae Universae*, issued on 15 August 1967 by Paul VI mentioned the Grand Chancellery of the Pontifical Equestrian Orders for the first time in sixty-two years, almost nobody had noticed it.

The definition of the duties of a Christian Knight by His Eminence Agostino Cardinal Casaroli in 1984 was the first published statement by the dignitary in whom the powers of the former Grand Chancellor of the Pontifical Equestrian Orders had been vested since February 1905.

When devising procedures for the investiture of a Papal Knight, the late Bishop Gerald Mahon, (Auxiliary Bishop of Westminster), Canon Adrian Arrowsmith (Westminster Cathedral) and myself used Cardinal Casaroli's definition and the information furnished by Cardinal Jacques Martin as a basis for defining the role and function of those Pontifical Equestrian Orders that were to be involved in the ceremonial of the Church on a national, diocesan and also parochial level. Cardinal Martin also gave me invaluable help when compiling the basic structure of a service of investiture for Catholic Papal Knights.

Cardinal Casaroli's main concern, however, was to stem the never-ending flow of letters from individual Papal Knights, but especially Knights of the Sovereign Military Order of Malta, complaining about each other with regard to precedence in processions and seating arrangements at religious functions. Within the framework of the Pontifical Orders of Knighthood, successive Pontiffs had laid down an order of precedence, and at public functions in countries where all the Orders were recognised and their members allowed to wear their insignia publicly, that question never arose because precedence among all Orders of Knighthood was strictly governed by the date of their foundation.

PAPAL KNIGHTS

The late Bishop Gerald Mahon, Auxiliary of Westminster, and Canon Adrian Arrowsmith of Westminster Cathedral, attended by a Papal Knight enter the church for a service of investiture.

This problem had its origin in the dispute between the Holy See, the Sovereign Military Order of Malta and the Equestrian Order of the Holy Sepulchre of Jerusalem shortly after the Second World War. Archbishop Cardinale who was as a young Monsignor on the staff of Assistants to Pope Pius XII under Cardinal Nicola Canali, had always kept a diary from the day he entered the service of the Holy See. When I joined him as one of his three research assistants in 1979, he gave me to read those diaries that dealt with the period from 1950 to 1963. The French writer Roger Peyrefitte, who had already stirred up a hornets' nest with his book *Les Clefs de St. Pierre* (*The Keys of St. Peter*), added to the unhappy state of affairs in 1957 with his *Chevaliers de Malte* (*The Knights of Malta*), both of which deepened the rift. There were major issues at stake which were finally settled after twelve years of arguments. What apparently was never settled was the question of precedence.

Cardinal Casaroli, though a high dignitary in the Order of Malta, was scrupulously fair in settling the matter and in advising me. In his considered judgement, Knights of the Pontifical Equestrian Orders should not be part of this 'hangover' from the past. He was delighted that Cardinal Martin had discovered that the Knights of St. Gregory the Great had been assigned a place in the ceremonial by Pope St. Pius X, and he suggested that it would be reasonable and fair if that privilege to serve upon the Supreme Pontiff and have a place by right in the papal cortege, should be extended to the Orders of Pius IX and of Pope St. Sylvester.

ORDERS OF KNIGHTHOOD AND OF MERIT

His Eminence Cardinal Agostino Casaroli, Secretary of State from 1979 until 1990, was *ex officio* Grand Chancellor of all Pontifical Orders of Knighthood.

The function of Papal Knights would be to serve upon the Supreme Pontiff the Vicar of Christ on Earth – and upon Cardinals, Patriarchs, Archbishops, Bishops and Prelates – the successors of the Apostles and Disciples. During the ceremonial in cathedrals and churches and in processions Papal Knights would be part of the episcopal curia or sacerdotal entourage. There was unanimous consensus of opinion among all the dignitaries that it would be alien to the eminent position the Supreme Pontiff had conferred on them if they allowed themselves to get involved in such temporal matters as precedence of Orders of Knighthood.

In order to give pragmatic advice, an arbitrary number of Papal Knights was chosen to attend on certain dignitaries, provided that a sufficient number of Knights in uniform attended the function. It was, however, left to the discretion of the Masters of Ceremonies at religious functions to deploy them in a practical way.

Such was the enthusiasm among Papal Knights that in retrospect I believe I overgilded the proverbial lily when I devised the services of investiture for Catholic Papal Knights, as in *The Cross on the Sword* I provided different guidelines for investitures in Cathedrals, Parish Churches, and Church Halls. I also think I was probably too rigid in the assignment of certain tasks.

Much credit and appreciation must go to the Knights of St.

Columbanus in Ireland, especially their Supreme Secretary, Mr. Peter Durnin. Together with their Supreme Chaplain, Mons. Stephen Green, he has produced a complete liturgy for a Mass of Investiture for every member of the Knights of St. Columbanus who was honoured with a papal knighthood. Mr. Durnin always sent me a number of copies, which in turn have found their way into many European countries from which I had requests for more detailed assistance.

Because of the nature of this book, and because unlike the Religious and secularised Catholic-founded Orders that publish their own statutes and guidelines for members, this book affords the only opportunity of publishing guidelines for Papal Knights.

One Knight Commander and two Knights of the Order of St. Sylvester and a Knight of the Order of St. Gregory, all members of the Knights of St. Columbanus, who were honoured for their services to Church and community in the Irish Republic.

Courtesy: *Knights of St. Columbanus, Ireland*

S.E.R. the Metropolitan of Gniezno and Counsellor of the World Synod of Bishops, Archbishop Henryk Josef Muszynski, attended by two Papal Knights of the Order of St. Gregory the Great, was received outside the church by Mons. Stanislas Swierczynski, the Rector of the Polish Mission in England and Wales and Mons. Wladislaw Wyszowadski, Metropolitan Canon of Warsaw, who first offered to the Archbishop the *aspergillum* and Holy

Water and then greeted him with incense. After processing into the church, the Archbishop and Prelates kneel before the Altar; the two Knights in attendance have taken up their position behind the Archbishop. During Holy Mass, the Knights in attendance took their seats in the choir stalls on the side of the Altar where they remained until they followed the Archbishop, who was flanked by his concelebrants, in procession after the service.

II

THE PROCEDURE FOR ADMISSION TO THE PONTIFICAL ORDERS OF KNIGHTHOOD

Admission to a Pontifical Order of Knighthood can never be achieved through personal application; it is always the result of presentation. A candidate is presented or sponsored for admission by a responsible authority, unless the conferment is made directly by the Sovereign Pontiff at his own initiative and by his own choice (*motu proprio*), as is always the case for the Supreme Order of Christ.

Priests and members of Religious Orders cannot become papal Knights, and until November 1993 the Pontifical Orders of Knighthood were not open to ladies.

The Order of Pius IX, the Pian Order, is usually granted on presentation by the Secretariat of State or senior Curia Cardinals. The Equestrian Orders of St. Gregory the Great and of Pope St. Sylvester, as well as the two Pontifical Religious Awards, the Cross 'Pro Ecclesia et Pontifice' and the Medal 'Benemerenti', both of which are open to ladies and members of Religious Orders, are officially requested by the Bishop in whose diocese the candidate is resident. A petition to grant a papal knighthood to a person may be presented to the Diocesan Bishop by responsible bodies or eminent persons in the diocese.

The Bishop's proposal is first sent to the Apostolic Nuncio of the country for his *Nihil Obstat*. An application by someone other than the Diocesan Bishop, however exalted he may be, does not suffice. The petition must state the name, place and date of birth, address and brief life of the candidate, bringing out his special merits and the service it is intended to reward, so as to justify the conferment of the requested papal distinction. Decorations already held by the candidate must also be listed, so as to assist the Papal Secretary of State deciding on the rank and to which Pontifical Order the candidate should be appointed.

If the application is approved by the Cardinal Secretary of State, he will inform the Diocesan Bishop through the Apostolic Nuncio, and in due course he will send the Papal Brief of appointment through the usual diplomatic channels.

Papal Briefs for the Supreme Order of Christ, the Order of the Golden Spur and the Collar of the Pian Order are signed by the Supreme Pontiff personally. On occasion he may also sign the Papal Brief for a Knight Grand Cross of an Order. Since the publication of the Papal Constitution *Regimini Ecclesiae Universae* Papal Briefs for Knights Grand Cross, Knights

Commander and Knights are signed by the Cardinal Secretary of State *non de mandato*.

Depending on the Pontifical Order of Knighthood to which the candidate has been appointed and the rank (granted or promotion), the Papal Secretariat of State, exercising its function as successor to the Chancery of the Pontifical Equestrian Orders, levies a tax on the Papal Brief. This tax, which is payable by the original applicant and not by the newly appointed knight, contributes to the administrative costs involved in the procedure. If the application has been made, for example, by a parish priest, he will be informed by the Local Bishop of the charges due. He is asked to pay the tax to the diocesan treasury, which in turn pays these taxes half-yearly to the Apostolic Nunciature, which forwards them to the Secretariat of State with the general accounts. Changes in the tax levied on a Papal Brief are always announced in the *Acta Apostolicae Sedis*.

The responsibility for providing the decoration, the miniature, rosette or the uniform does not rest with the Secretariat of State or the applicant, though the Local Bishop or the applicant often acquires the decoration for presentation.

A papal knighthood which is conferred *motu proprio* is not subject to any tax, and the insignia are presented as a gift from the Supreme Pontiff by the Secretariat of State.

It is a personal matter for the applicant or the local bishop to decide whether to bear the cost of the decoration as well as the tax for the Papal Brief, or to advise the newly appointed or promoted knight to acquire the decoration personally.

To ensure that the correct insignia are obtained, it is strongly recommended that the decorations are bought from a reputable dealer or manufacturer. In recent years a number of firms have entered the 'order business', offering cut-price decorations. Often the Crosses bear little likeness to the correct decoration as described in the statutes of the various Orders. Decorations conferred *motu proprio* and presented by the Secretariat of State are usually acquired from Ditta Cravanzola, Via del Corso, 340-341, Rome, or directly from the manufacturer, who also makes the Collars and Stars for the three principal Orders, Studio Giorgio Guccione, Via dell'Orso,17-18, Rome. (See: Appendix II)

Details concerning uniforms for Papal Knights are in the statutes of the Order, a copy of which, in the Latin and Italian languages, is always given to the candidate together with the Papal Brief, and which for the Orders of Pius IX, of St. Gregory the Great and of Pope St. Sylvester have been appended in English to the separate chapters on the individual Orders in this work. It is recommended that Papal Knights who wish to acquire a dress uniform should do so from the Pontifical Tailors, Ditta Annibale Gammarelli, Via Santa Chiara, 34, Rome. There is no need to go to Rome for a fitting, a diagram with the correct measurements sent to Ditta

Annibale Gammarelli is sufficient. The uniform with court sword and bi-cornered hat are not inexpensive but, as in the case of the decorations, quality and the correct style are important factors to consider.

There remains one more important administrative matter: the bestowal of a papal knighthood only takes effect after it has been gazetted in the *Acta Apostolica Sedis*. The gazetting takes place at the discretion of the Papal Secretariat of State after all the other administrative requirements, such as the payment of the tax on the Papal Brief, have been fulfilled.

The *Acta Apostolicae Sedis* in its present form dates from the decree by Pope St. Pius X of 29 June 1908. From 1865 until 1908 a periodical with the title *Acta Sanctae Sedis* published the main Papal Briefs, but it lacked centralised control and frequent omissions occurred. Omissions of names of newly appointed Papal Knights in the *Acta Apostolica Sedis* still occur on occasion, however there is usually a simple administrative reason for this: a papal knighthood will only be gazetted after all the above mentioned requirements have been met and the tax for the Papal Brief has been received by the Vatican. This process can take up to eighteen months and a two year's delay in publishing the knight's appointment in the *Acta Apostolicae Sedis* can occur.

In almost all countries Papal Knights can apply to their Head of State through their Ministry of Foreign Affairs for permission to wear the insignia at public and state functions.

Since *The Cross on the Sword* was published in 1987, but more markedly since 1990, the usually tranquil world of the Pontifical Orders of Knighthood and other papal honours appear to have undergone a metamorphosis. Rumours seem to have become the currency of communication. What Cardinal Martin described in 1987 as the most 'sought after honours', are in danger of becoming devalued by rumours of people buying papal knighthoods from a high dignitary, bypassing the diocesan bishop and flouting the rules laid down in the statutes. I have always refused to take any notice of such rumours.

There has been righteous indignation among Papal Knights who have really been honoured by the Supreme Pontiff. Their main grievance is that it is impossible to nail those rumours or to do something about the relatively few who abuse or corrupt the system. We must bear in mind that the practice of buying honours is as old as the honours themselves, and not a single country can claim to have devised an honours system that cannot be corrupted by those who are determined to do so. Cardinal Martin may have had this in mind when he opened his statement about the temporal and secular practices of conferring decorations: 'it seems to go against the idea that a spiritual power like the Holy See should make use of them'.

III

THE IMPLICATIONS OF THE SUPREME PONTIFF BEING THE *FONS HONORUM* OF PONTIFICAL KNIGHTHOODS

In March 1992, a national Italian newspaper carried a headline which suggested that the Holy See had broken yet another taboo; the article named the five Swedish ladies whom Pope John Paul II had created Papal Knights, although the statutes of the Pontifical Equestrian Orders state explicitly that the Orders are only open to men.[1]

As mentioned earlier, I received much criticism after explaining in *The Cross on the Sword* that a special ceremony of investiture had been devised for a Jewish gentleman whom John Paul II had created a Papal Knight.

There was worldwide criticism in the press, on radio and television when John Paul II conferred the Collar of the Order of Pope Pius IX on Jean Claude Duvalier, then President of Haiti, in 1984.

It is neither my brief, nor would it be appropriate for me, to defend the Supreme Pontiff's actions. Juridically he is the *fons honorum*, the ultimate authority whence all papal honours come, and as the Sovereign of all Pontifical Orders, Awards and Honours, he can do whatever he wants. Besides, as explained earlier, the Order to which the recipient is appointed expresses the Pope's or the Cardinal Secretary of State's[2] degree of appreciation of the recipient's merit.

With regard to the conferment of Papal Knighthoods on five Swedish ladies, the Papal Secretariat of State refused to give any official comment to the press. Actually, there is a precedent for the Pope's action: in the 1983 edition of *Orders of Knighthood, Awards and the Holy See* Mons. Cardinale made mention of an incident when in 1981 Pope John Paul II gave the Grand Cross of the Order of Pius IX to Ambassador Chibesakunda of Zambia on leaving the ambassadorial position to the Holy See, and that Ambassador was a lady. I was asked to delete the reference to this incident in subsequent editions as it might give rise to other ladies claiming similar honours, and it was once again reiterated that the Pontifical Orders of Knighthood were open to gentlemen only, and that meritorious ladies would receive the Cross 'Pro Ecclesia et Pontifice' or the Medal 'Benemerenti'.

---

[1] The five ladies were part of the entourage of the King of Sweden who had paid a State Visit to the Vatican. They received decorations on a reciprocal basis appropriate to their rank and status.
[2] The Papal Constitution *Regimini Ecclesiae Universae* (15 August 1967) gave to the Cardinal Secretary of State the right to make appointments to Pontifical Orders of Knighthood and sign the Papal
[3] Briefs *non de mandato*, without a specific mandate.

Following many enquiries to me after the incident concerning the five ladies in 1992, I was informed that this was a delicate matter which had arisen as a result of the preparations for the State Visit of the King of Sweden to the Vatican. According to diplomatic practice, advance arrangements had been made with the protocol department of the Swedish government which prepared the State Visit, which dignitaries in the Vatican (i.e. the Cardinal Secretary of State, the Prefect of the Pontifical Court etc.) would receive a decoration from the King of Sweden, and which member of the Royal entourage would receive a decoration from the Pope (i.e. ministers, chief of protocol etc. who were accompanying the King on his official visit). As it turned out, five of the officials due to receive a reciprocal decoration from the Pope were ladies.

This immediately raised the perennial question from certain quarters as to whether the Holy See should open Orders of Knighthood to women. The Secretariat of State has been inundated with such requests for years, and two possibilities have been under consideration since the pontificate of Paul VI: to open the Order of Pope St. Sylvester to women or to institute an Order for women, creating the ranks of Dame, Dame Commander and Dame Grand Cross with the possibility of adding a Collar of the Order as an additional rank for female Heads of State. This was always considered a matter for the Supreme Pontiff to decide.

As far as the conferment of a Papal Knighthood on a non-Catholic and a non-Christian is concerned, the Order of Pius IX has always been bestowed on, for example, diplomats who have been accredited to the Holy See, regardless of their religion. Similarly, the Order of the Golden Spur was given to non-Christians until Paul VI decreed that the Golden Spur, dedicated to the Blessed Virgin Mary, should henceforth be given to Christian Heads of State only.

The Collar of the Order of Pius IX has always been open to both Christian and non-Christian Heads of State. The Order of Pope St. Sylvester has frequently been given to non-Catholics and non-Christians since its foundation in 1905. The strict Catholicity of the Pontifical Equestrian Order of St. Gregory the Great has been adhered to until fairly recently; conferments of this Order on non-Catholics have always been extremely rare.

As I explained before, the question of whether or not a non-Christian should be given the Order of St. Gregory the Great was prompted by a specific precedent which was set on 4 March 1986, when Sir Sigmund Sternberg, a prominent Jew, was created a Knight Commander of the Order of St. Gregory the Great.

Because of the importance of this precedent, which could serve as a guideline for the future, it is important not to be ambiguous in dealing with this matter. It would be wrong to assume that questions about the wisdom of perpetuating such a precedent by publishing details about it were first asked in London. It was far more widely discussed in R̶ where high dignitaries held very strong, and often opposing, views on the subject. They spoke to me very frankly but without ethnic prejudice. In their opinion it concerned a matter which they considered could weaken fundamental principles of Roman Catholic tradition. The subject matter raised was specific and concerned only the Order of St. Gregory the Great, though the question of the Order of the Golden Spur and its original criteria for conferment were also raised several times. Without exception, those who raised the matter always added that an honour for Sir Sigmund Sternberg was well deserved but expressed the opinion that even a higher rank in the Order of Pope St. Sylvester would have been more appropriate.

It is easy to sweep delicate matters which might cause embarrassment under the proverbial carpet, but this helps nobody in the long run and will only create confusion in the future.

An important question which was raised several times after the publication of *The Cross on the Sword* concerned the commitment which was asked for during the investiture of a Catholic Papal Knight. It referred to the 'fidelity to God, the Supreme Pontiff, the Holy See and the Church' which Knights are asked to promise the Bishop who invests them. Such a commitment is not asked for when the insignia are conferred on a newly created Papal Knight outside a ceremony of investiture, and no Papal Brief exists which places any obligation to promise anything on a recipient of a Papal Knighthood. In the final analysis, therefore, such a commitment is voluntary, but if a Papal Knight chooses to be invested during Holy Mass, he knows that this commitment is part of the ceremony.

Nothing a reigning pope does with regard to awarding honours can be criticised on a juridical question or precedent. Even when a Pope promulgates new statutes or changes rules laid down by one of his predecessors, they are only guidelines for the remaining years of his pontificate or until they are changed by one of his successors. If it is his wish, he can change the statutes of the Pontifical Orders, expand them, or open them to women. In fact, Pope St. Pius X states quite clearly in the seminal Apostolic Brief *Multum ad excitandos* that the Pontifical Equestrian Orders do not have 'the capacity of perpetual succession' – a Pope can abolish any one or all the Orders of Knighthood if he so wishes – and that remains the juridical position, as no pope is bound by tradition or precedent.

The Apostolic Constitution *Regimini Ecclesiae Universae* left one question unanswered: how extensive are the powers that were vested in the Cardinal Secretary of State when he received the right to sign Papal Briefs concerning Pontifical Orders of Knighthood *non de mandato*? Is this power restricted to appointments or can a Cardinal Secretary of State

...ne statutes of an Order or revoke rules about an a previous Pope?

the statutes of Pontifical Equestrian Orders and the ...y the Chancery of the Orders are dealt with in the *Codex* ... in Book I.III, under the heading 'General Decrees and ...'. My book is not a legal thesis and it would be presumptuous ... examine all the Papal Briefs that deal with Pontifical Orders and int... ...et them according to Canon Law. However, some Canons are self-explanatory and the reader can draw his own conclusions.

Canon 30: 'A general Decree, as in can.29, cannot be made by one who has only executive power, unless in particular cases this has been expressly authorised by the competent legislator in accordance with the law, and provided the conditions prescribed in the act of authorisation are observed.'

Canon 33 Para.2 'These Decrees cease to have force by explicit or implicit revocation by the competent authority, and by the cessation of the law for whose execution they were issued. They do not cease on the expiry of the authority of the person who issued them, unless the contrary is expressly provided.'

It would be naive to believe that these two Canons answer the many open questions that remain. Book I.IV of the *Codex Iuris Canonici* deals with privileges, and several Canons can be applied to the privilege of a Papal Knighthood.

I believe that many questions and much criticism has arisen as a result of the different values individuals attribute to Pontifical Orders of Knighthood. If we look on them as Orders of Merit and as gifts the Supreme Pontiff – or his appointed executor – bestows on those who are recommended to him as deserving recognition, it removes the need to search for theological reasons or divine justice when either justifying or criticising an honour that has been given.

Cardinal Jacques Martin put it so simply and yet so very succinctly when he said that the nature of the originating principle of creating someone a knight is in having the power to decorate someone, and all the extant pontifical knighthoods are a gift of the Pope.

Chapter Four

PONTIFICAL RELIGIOUS AWARDS OF MERIT

Pontifical Religious Awards of Merit, as distinct from Pontifical Orders of Knighthood, are also conferred by the Supreme Pontiff as a reward for services rendered to the Church and society, especially in the direct exercise of a lay apostolate. These decorations are not normally awarded to members of the clergy, but only to the laity. They may, however, be given to religious sisters and brothers, who like priests are never given Pontifical Orders of Knighthood, whose members are exclusively laymen.

The main Awards of Merit are The Golden Rose, the Cross 'Pro Ecclesia et Pontifice' (for the Church and the Pontiff), and the Medal 'Benemerenti' (for a well-deserving person).

Both these latter honours owe their permanent character (which was retained until 1972) to Pope Leo XIII, Vincenzo Gioaccino Pecci, (1878-1903) who came from a patrician family. Born in 1810, he was educated by the Jesuits, and gained his doctorate in theology in Rome. There he entered the Accademia dei Nobili Ecclesiastici at Rome where the diplomats of the Holy See are trained. The Academy was founded in 1701 by Pope Clement XI, and only ecclesiastics from noble families qualified for the training as diplomats. Although Pope Leo XIII reformed the Academy one year after ascending to the See of St. Peter, it was Pope Pius XI who changed its name to Pontificia Academia Ecclesiastica, removing the aristocratic connotation.

In 1983, Archbishop Cesare Zacchi, then President of the Academy discussed with me the complex personality of Pope Leo XIII and told me that as an applicant he was determined to join the Academy and become a diplomat of the Holy See; he spent some time proving noble descent to qualify for entry, and contemporary records show him to have been very able in promoting his own case.

After several diplomatic appointments and having been consecrated a bishop, Pope Gregory XVI sent him to Brussels as Apostolic Nuncio. There he was confronted with the dispute then raging between the Jesuits and the Catholic University of Louvain.

Whilst in Belgium, he became a close friend of King Leopold I of the Belgians (1831-1865), a Protestant, and the favourite uncle of Queen Victoria of Great Britain. King Leopold used to invite his Nuncio to travel with him, and he took Mons. Pecci with him to London, where he stayed at Buckingham Palace and was warmly received by Queen Victoria. During his pontificate which lasted twenty-five years, Leo XIII became one of the great reformers of the Church. Several of his encyclicals, such

The coronation of Pope Leo XIII on 3 March 1878 in the Sistine Chapel. Although he did not add to or make any changes to the Pontifical Equestrian Orders, more awards and decorations were instituted during his pontificate than any other. Most have fallen into disuse, but two, the Cross 'Pro Ecclesia et Pontifice' and the Medal 'Benemerenti' are still extant.

Courtesy: *Biblioteca Apostolica Vaticana*

as *Rerum Novarum*, are still relevant social documents more than a century later. There is, however, a mystery, if not paradox, about his Papal Brief addressed *Ad Anglos* (1895), which concerned itself with bringing the Anglican Church into Communion with Rome and caused much consternation in England. The encyclical *Ad Anglos* may be the reason why historians have concentrated on this contentious issue instead of probing deeper into the relationship between Leo XIII and Queen Victoria. When John Paul II visited Great Britain in 1982, all commentators on television, radio and in the press stated categorically that never before had a pope or bishop destined to become pope set foot in Buckingham Palace. I have never seen a reference to the not infrequent correspondence between Queen Victoria and Pope Leo XIII. In the context of this book I will restrict myself to one exchange of letters concerning a subject relevant to Orders. In 1896, on the eve of her diamond jubilee, Queen Victoria founded the Royal Victorian Order, an Order of Knighthood and Merit, ranking fifth among the six British Orders of Chivalry then extant. I owe it to Cardinal Martin that I saw the letter Queen Victoria wrote to Pope Leo in 1895, when, in her own words, her new Prime Minister, the Marquess of Salisbury, put every obstacle possible in her path when she had decided to institute the Royal Victorian Order, initially to reward those who had been meritorious in their personal service to the Queen. In fact, she attached to her letter a copy of the letter the Marquess of Salisbury had sent to her, asking for an undertaking that the Monarch would always pay all and every expense arising out of that Order. This means that the Queen had to pay for the manufacture of the insignia, the Order's Chancellery, all costs involved in investitures, services, etc. Queen Victoria asked Pope Leo whether he had to suffer as much from the obstinacy of his Cardinals as she had from her Ministers.[1] I was not shown Pope Leo's reply, but it goes without saying that the Queen would not discuss such a sensitive matter with a total stranger. It is also reasonable to assume that Her Majesty was not as infuriated with the Pope about the encyclical *Ad Anglos* as some historians try to make out, especially as they continued to exchange presents on special occasions.

Leo XIII took a particular interest in honours for meritorious services; he instituted and sanctioned many decorations, crosses and medals for all manner of rewards; few survived his pontificate, and only two are extant, though reformed, today. It is fair to say that Leo XIII (unlike his successor Pope St. Pius X) showed a far greater interest in this form of recognition than in that of Pontifical Knighthoods, especially those conferring nobility.

[1] Although the historian Kenneth Rose states categorically that Britain only has Orders awarded with or without ministerial approval but no dynastic Orders, it appears that the RVO was founded as a Family Order.

I
THE GOLDEN ROSE

The Golden Rose is a distinction of the highest class. It is now conferred by the Supreme Pontiff on female Catholic Sovereigns and must be regarded as equivalent to the Supreme Order of Christ, which is reserved for male Catholic Sovereigns and Heads of State. The Golden Rose is also given to shrines, especially those dedicated to the Blessed Virgin Mary.

In the past, prior to St. Pius X's 1905 encyclical *Multum ad excitandos*, the Golden Rose took probably precedence over the Order of Christ; It was also bestowed on very eminent men, mostly of imperial, royal and princely rank, as well as on important Catholic cities on the occasion of historical events with a special religious significance.

The origin of the blessing and bestowal of the Golden Rose is lost in history and shrouded in mystery. The earliest verifiable reference to it is in a document of Pope Leo IX (1049-1054). It is dated 1049 and refers to a commitment taken upon themselves by the nuns of the Convent of the Holy Cross in Tulle, Alsace, to present to the Pope every year a Golden Rose in gratitude for having been exempt from the jurisdiction of the local bishop. The document alludes to the fact that the Golden Rose is well known.

The first verifiable document concerning a Golden Rose conferred by a reigning Pontiff, Urban II (1088-1099) is dated 1096, when the Pope, travelling through Angers where he preached in favour of the First Crusade, bestowed the Golden Rose on Count Fulco d'Angiò. Many records of a bestowal of the Golden Rose exist for the period during and after the Popes' residence in Avignon. The recipients were royal and princely men and women, basilicas, cathedrals and cities.

Among the male Sovereigns who received the Golden Rose are various Emperors who were crowned in the Church of Santa Maria in Cosmedin, Rome, as well as several Kings and leaders of high noble rank.

Dom Manuel I, King of Portugal (1495-1521), received the Golden Rose in 1513 for having paved the way for the propagation of the Faith in the Indies; Alfonso, King of Naples and of Aragon, received it in 1451 for his victory over the Turks; and John of Austria was honoured with the Golden Rose for his famous part in the victory of Lepanto in 1567.

The last man to receive the Golden Rose was the Doge of Venice, Francesco Loredan, upon whom it was bestowed by Clement VIII (1758-1769) in 1759.

From then on, the Golden Rose was reserved exclusively for Catholic

Queens and Princesses. Among the first Queens to receive it was Casimira of Poland in 1684 for the Victory of Vienna. Moving into the nineteenth century, among the recipients were Queen Maria Teresa of Sardinia in 1825; Isabella II in 1868 and Maria Christina in 1886, both Queens of Spain; to Princess Maria Pia di Savoia in 1848; on Maria Grazia Pia, Royal Princess of the Kingdom of the Two Sicilies, on the occasion of her baptism in 1849, at which Pope Pius IX acted as Godfather. (The Pope had taken refuge in Gaeta under the protection of King Ferdinand II of the Two Sicilies from 1848 to 1850). The Empress Eugénie of France received the Golden Rose in 1856; (parts of the Golden Rose given to the Empress are preserved in Farnborough Abbey, England, but the major part was stolen). The Empress Elizabeth of Brazil received the Golden Rose in 1888; and Queen Amelia of Portugal in 1892; Queen Marie Henriette of the Belgians received it in 1893.

In the twentieth century, the Golden Rose was sent in 1925 to Queen Elizabeth of the Belgians; Queen Elena di Savoia of Italy received it in 1937 (this was the fifth Golden Rose bestowed on a member of the House of Savoy); and in 1956 Pope Pius XII sent it to the sovereign Grand Duchess Charlotte of Luxembourg.

The presentation of the Golden Rose is performed with great pomp and ceremony. The ornament itself has varied in appearance. The design finally adopted by Sixtus IV (1471-1484) is a thorny branch with several leaves and flowers, the petals of which are adorned with precious stones, usually sapphires. It is surmounted by the main rose, which contains a repository into which balsam and musk are poured. The entire ornament is made of solid gold.

The Golden Rose is blessed by the Pope in the Vatican during a special solemn service, usually on *Laetare* Sunday (the fourth Sunday in Lent). If the recipient is in Rome, it is customary for the Pope personally to bestow it on the recipient in the Sistine Chapel. If the recipient is elsewhere, a Special Mission is entrusted with the presentation of the Rose and the Apostolic Brief which announces the bestowal, gives the reason for the conferment, and mentions the merits and virtues of the recipient.

As an example of the pomp and ceremony of the bestowal of the Golden Rose, the event in 1956 in Luxembourg gives a picture of the solemnity of the occasion. The Apostolic Nuncio to Luxembourg was named Papal Legate for the occasion, representing the Supreme Pontiff in person, and the Delegation included four high prelates and four high lay dignitaries. The presentation took place in the Cathedral of Luxembourg, in the presence of the entire Grand Ducal Family, all the members of the Government of Luxembourg and the Ambassadors of the Diplomatic Corps accredited to the Grand Duchy.

The Papal Legate celebrated Pontifical High Mass, which was followed by his formal presentation of the Golden Rose to the Grand Duchess, and

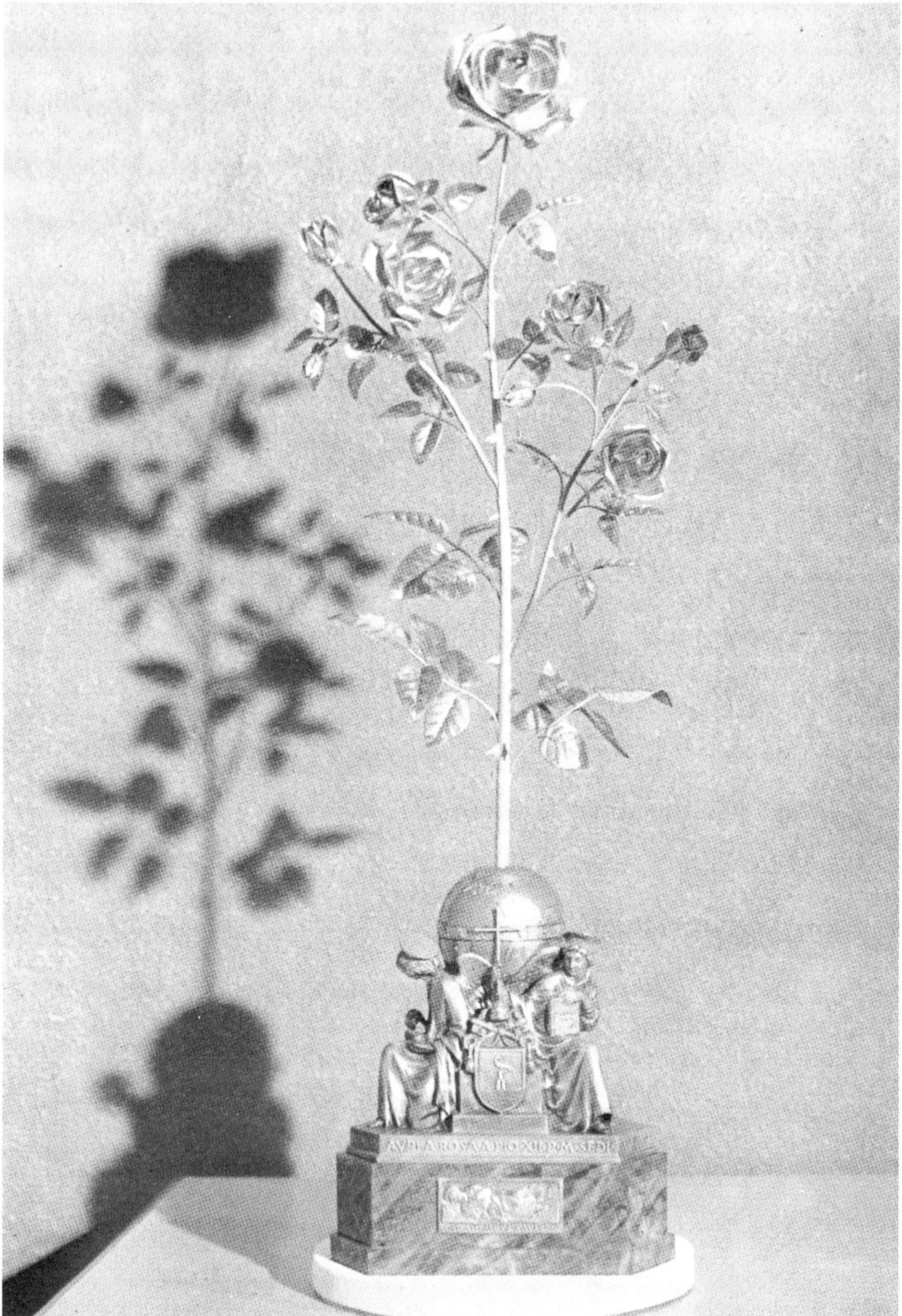

Opposite: A Golden Rose conferred by Pius XII. Above, a Golden Rose bestowed on the Shrine of Our Lady of Fatima by Paul VI. According to Innocent III (1198-1216), the Golden Rose is meant to express Christian love, exhaling the fragrance of all virtues (hence the expression 'the odour of sanctity'). After its blessing by the Pope at the Lateran Basilica, the Rose is carried in procession to the nearby Basilica of the Holy Cross in Jerusalem, which had been built to hold the relics of the True Cross the Empress Helena is said to have brought back from the Holy Land.

Courtesy: Felici

Pope Pius XII bestowed a Golden Rose on H.R.H. the Grand Duchess Charlotte of Luxembourg in 1956. The occasion was celebrated in Luxembourg and is remembered as one of the greatest festive occasions in the Grand Duchy. The Apostolic Nuncio was appointed Papal Legate for the occasion and presented the Golden Rose to the Grand Duchess.

the announcement that the Sovereign Pontiff had granted a plenary indulgence, in the normal terms, to all those present at the ceremony. Afterwards the Golden Rose was exposed at the Cathedral for the rest of the day.

It is expected that the presentation ceremony will be much simplified if the Golden Rose is ever again conferred, and the ornament itself will not be as elaborate.

Among the most important churches and shrines to receive the Golden Rose are the Basilica of St. Peter in Rome (five times); the Basilica of St. John Lateran (four times); the Basilica of St. Mary Major in Rome (twice); the Marian Shrines of Our Lady of Loreto; Santa Maria del Fiore in Florence; Our Lady of Lourdes; Our Lady of Fatima; Our Lady of Guadalupe, Mexico; Our Lady of Aparecida, Brazil; and the Shrines of the Image of the Holy Infant, Bethlehem, and of St. Francis Xavier in Goa.

The cities that received the Golden Rose are Venice, Bologna, Siena, Savona and Lucca.

II

THE CROSS 'PRO ECCLESIA ET PONTIFICE'

The Cross 'Pro Ecclesia et Pontifice' (For Church and Pontiff) was instituted by Pope Leo XIII on 17 July 1888 with his Papal Brief *Quod singulari Dei concessu* (reproduced in Appendix 1), to mark the occasion of his golden jubilee as a priest. It was initially intended to be conferred on those who had contributed significantly to the success of the jubilee celebrations and of the Vatican Exhibition that was organised for this occasion. The Cross continued to be awarded as a sign of the Pontiff's recognition of the recipients' distinguished service to the Church and to the Papacy.

It was also decreed to be the highest honour that could be bestowed on women. In the case of queens, consorts of heads of state, female ministers of state, female diplomats or high female politicians who made official visits to the Vatican, the Cross was conferred in solid gold. Originally, the Cross was for a while also conferred in silver and in bronze, but later the metal for the usual presentations was changed to *ormolu* (gilt bronze),[1] and until the pontificate of John XXIII, it was conferred with great parsimony.

The Cross, the images engraved on it and the ribbon were completely changed by Paul VI. The original Cross had been made a permanent decoration in October 1898, and was a large octangular cross *fleury* with four large *fleurs-de-lis* being placed between the arms of the cross, and the extremities of the cross were flory triparted. On the obverse, in the centre of the cross was a medal with an image of the founder in relief, facing left, that was encircled by a band bearing the words LEO XIII P.M. ANNO X. On each of the four arms of the cross was a comet, facing outwards, which with a *fleur-de-lis* formed the armorial charges of the Pecci family's arms. The medal in the centre on the reverse bore the papal insignia, the tiara and the crossed keys, and the band surrounding the medal had the inscription PRO ECCLESIA ET PONTIFICE.[2] The Cross was suspended from a deep red ribbon with delicate borders in the papal colours.

During the eighth year of his pontificate (June 1970 to June 1971), Pope Paul VI (1963-1978) changed both the 'Pro Ecclesia et Pontifice' Cross and the 'Benemerenti' Medal. The authoritative record of all medals struck from 1929, when the Vatican City State came into being, to 1972, the tenth year of the Pontificate of Paul VI, *Le Medaglie del Vaticano 1929-1972*, has

---

[1]See colour plate on Pontifical Awards.
[2]*Ibid.*

The Cross *Pro Ecclesia et Pontifice* (left) which was awarded in gold, silver and bronze since its institution in 1888 by Leo XIII, until Paul VI changed it to a simple gilt Greekshaped cross, more in keeping with the Pope's liking for modern art forms. A special cross in gilded Italian silver, hallmarked '800' was struck for Queens and female Heads of State.

an appendix which shows in monochrome the original 'Benemerenti' Medal bearing the image of Paul VI under the heading: 'Medaglie senza riferimento ad una data precisa' (Medals without reference to a specific date). The Cross 'Pro Ecclesia et Pontifice', continued to be conferred for a short while in its original form, bearing the image of Leo XIII. It was changed between 1971 and 1973, although initially it was conferred in its new design only on the occasion of the dissolution of the Pontifical Gendarmerie.

The traditional 'Benemerenti' Medal, with the head of the reigning Pontiff on the obverse, was conferred by Paul VI from 1963 until 1971 when the new design was introduced.

The same reference book lists the last two medals (crosses) struck in the

H.M. Queen Sophia of Spain on her way to an audience with Pope John Paul II wearing the silver gilt Cross 'Pro Ecclesia et Pontifice' next to the Star of the Spanish Order of Carlos III.

Courtesy: *L'Osservatore Romano*

eighth year of the Pope Paul VI's pontificate as 'Medaglie distribuite quale premio di fedeltà per i Gendarmi Pontifici all'atto dello scioglimento del Corpo' (Medals for conferment on members of the Corps of the Pontifical Gendarmerie for their outstanding loyalty on the occasion of the dissolution of the Corps).

The description of the two crosses is that of the new 'Pro Ecclesia et Pontifice' Cross and the new 'Benemerenti' Medal as they were changed by Paul VI and slowly phased in to replace the original insignia described in 1972 as 'sensa riferimento ad una data precisa' (without any reference to a specific date).

The shape of the 'Pro Ecclesia et Pontifice' Cross as officially introduced by Paul VI after 1972 is difficult to describe. It is more of a squarish diamond-shaped plaque with four small triangular notches than a Greek-shaped, four-pointed cross, which it is said to represent. In its centre are two arches in relief next to each other with the images of the Apostles St. Peter and St. Paul. Under the both arches is the inscription PAULUS VI PP, and centrally at the bottom of the Cross a small cross *pattée*. Centrally above the arches in the upper points of the Cross is a modern version of the coat of arms of Paul VI. On the left arm of the cross, facing inwards, are the words PRO ECCLESIA, and at the extreme point of the arm another small cross pattée; on the right arm of the cross, facing inwards, are the words ET PONTIFICE, and again at the extreme point of the arm a small cross *pattée*. The metal is gold plated bronze with a matt finish.[1] The Cross is suspended from a ribbon in the papal colours yellow and white but reversed to white and yellow.[2] John Paul II, who succeeded as Pope in 1978, retained Pope Paul's modern innovation of the Cross 'Pro Ecclesia et Pontifice'. He changed the name under the arches to JOANNES PAULUS II, and the coat of arms above the arches to his own. He also changed the ribbon to the correct papal colours yellow and white.[3]

III

THE MEDAL 'BENEMERENTI'

The first 'Benemerenti' Medal was awarded by Pope Pius IV (1555-1565) as a military decoration, recognising valour on the field of battle. Similar

The obverse of a 'Benemerenti' Medal struck for Pope Pius IX. The Pope used to reward his corps of guards and fighting troops with such a medal after a battle. The reverse of the medals vary and usually have the occasion for which it was awarded and the date impressed on them.

Courtesy: Garrison Collection

---

[1]There were gilded examples of the Cross that had the Italian silver mark 800 stamped on the obverse, but none in solid gold. The reference book does not mention the silver-gilt version for special recipients.
[1]Renato Calò, *Le Medaglie del Vaticano 1929-1972* (Rome, 1973).
[2]Renato Calò, *ibid*.

medals were bestowed by subsequent Pontiffs on men who had distinguished themselves by special service to the Pontiff or, if the men belonged to a papal militia, on the battle field. In 1831, Pope Gregory XVI had a special 'Benemerenti' Medal struck to reward those who had fought with distinction and valour in the papal army at Ferrara, Bologna and Vienna, while Pope Pius IX had various Benemerenti Medals struck to be conferred on soldiers who had remained loyal to the Papacy during the difficult years for the Papal States (1848-1877), among them the Medal 'Pro Petri Sede' (For the See of Peter) with which the Pope honoured the veterans of the battle of Castelfodardo in 1860, and the Medal 'Fidei et Virtuti' (For Faith and Valour) to reward the veterans of the battle of Mentana in 1867. To King Ferdinand II of the Two Sicilies, whose daughter had been given a Golden Rose during the Pope's refuge in Gaeta in the Kingdom of the Two Sicilies, he presented two *ormulu* statuettes, replicas of the statues of Saints Peter and Paul which he had erected in front of St. Peter's Basilica. Although his popularity among the Romans was not very high during the latter part of his pontificate, Pius IX always showed himself appreciative and generous towards those who had remained loyal to him.

Pope Pius XI instituted two special 'Benemerenti' Medals in 1925 in recognition of distinguished service to the Holy See on the occasions of the celebration of the Holy Year and the opening of the Missionary Exhibition organised by the Vatican.

Because of the great number of semi-official and privately struck medals and commemorative crosses, celebrating all major events, especially after the inauguration of the Vatican City State, I must restrict myself to official issues of the 'Benemerenti' Medal, though several of the privately struck medals were given *motu proprio* the status of a 'Benemerenti' Medal by the Pontiff.

As is explained in Appendix V, from the eighth year of his pontificate onwards, Paul VI dissolved all the various Corps of Papal Guards, with the exception of the Corps of the Swiss Guard. The first Corps to be dissolved was the Corpo della Gendarmeria Pontificia, already mentioned above, for which Paul VI instituted the two medals that he subsequently adopted as the 'Pro Ecclesia et Pontifice' Cross and the 'Benemerenti' Medal. He also ordered special 'Benemerenti' Medals to be struck when he dissolved the Corps of the Pontifical Noble Guard, and the Corps of the Pontifical Palatine Guard of Honour.

In 1966, Paul VI had a special 'Benemerenti' Medal 'Concilium Oecumenicum Vaticanum II' struck in gold, silver and bronze, of which the silver and bronze versions were suspended from a ribbon in the papal colours, yellow and white. The medal is superimposed on the Greek

[1] Benemerenti Medals conferred on special occasions are only awarded for a limited period of time, usually one year.

Left: the medal for meritorious services struck for Pius IX in 1847, one year before the Pope had to flee to the Kingdom of the Two Sicilies and seek refuge from the revolutionaries. Throughout his pontificate he continued to confer this medal for civil merit to the Pontiff and the Church. Right: The Medal 'Benemerenti' conferred by Pius XII at the end of the Holy Year 1950. It is a white-enamelled, gold-rimmed cross (*Fusil* at each end) superimposed on a green- and gold-enamelled laurel wreath, surmounted by the pontifical insignia, the tiara and the crossed keys, and suspended from a green ribbon. The centre medallion on the obverse contains the Greek letters Chi (X) and Rho (P) and in a circle the inscription ANNO IUBILAEI MCML. On the reverse is the word 'Benemerenti'.

letters *Chi Rho* and bears an engraving of St. Peter's Basilica in Rome. Fathers of the Council received the gold or silver medal without the ribbon. In 1975, to mark the closing of the Holy Year, Paul VI had another special 'Benemerenti' Medal struck in silver and bronze. It was issued by the Vatican City State (the Papal Brief of Conferment, signed by Cardinal Villot as Secretary of State, being dated Christmas 1975, and was conferred on members of the Roman Curia, members of the administration of the Vatican City State and those who have rendered outstanding meritorious service to the Holy See or the Vatican State. The obverse bears the image of Paul VI, wearing a mitre and holding his pontifical crozier, and the inscription PAULUS VI PONT. MAX. On the

The *Benemerenti* Medal in the traditional form has been awarded since 1891 by successive pontiffs. Having used this traditional design for some years, Paul VI changed it to a modern cross composed of losenges.

reverse the medal bears an engraving of the major Basilicas in Rome and the inscription ANNO IUBILAEI ROMAE MCMLXXV.[1]

In 1983, Pope John Paul II raised the Pontifical Medal *Anno VI* (see Appendix on Pontifical Medals) to the status of a 'Benemerenti' Medal for the Corps of the Swiss Guards who wear the medal suspended from a ribbon in the papal colours, yellow and white.

The original 'Benemerenti' Medal which Pope Leo XIII instituted in 1891 was designed to be of a permanent kind, and was confirmed as such by his successors, including Paul VI, who later changed it to its present form. It was always struck in *ormolu*, but in 1912, Pope St. Pius X had it also struck in silver as a special medal. The medal always bore the image

[1] Both are reproduced in this volume in colour and monochrome.

Left: a silver *Benemerenti* Medal conferred by Paul VI at the end of the Holy Year 1975 in silver or bronze on members of the Roman Curia, members of the administration of the Vatican City State, those having given meritorious service to the Holy See and members of the Swiss Guard. Right: the special 'Benemerenti Medal' *Concilium Oecumenicum Vaticanum II*, struck in gold, silver and bronze. Both medals are suspended from a ribbon in the papal colours yellow and white.

in relief of the reigning Pontiff who had made the award, surrounded by his name; the medal was encircled by a gilt laurel wreath and was suspended from the papal insignia, also in gilt, the tiara and the crossed keys, the whole being awarded suspended from a ribbon in the papal colours, yellow with white border stripes.

However, since the Vatican City State came into being in 1929, the 'Benemerenti' Medal has also been struck in gilt bronze and in silver, suspended from a military trophy instead of the papal insignia, and awarded as a military medal to members of the corps of guards, and was last awarded in the pontificate of Pope John XXIII.

The 'Benemerenti' Medal introduced by Paul VI and gradually phased

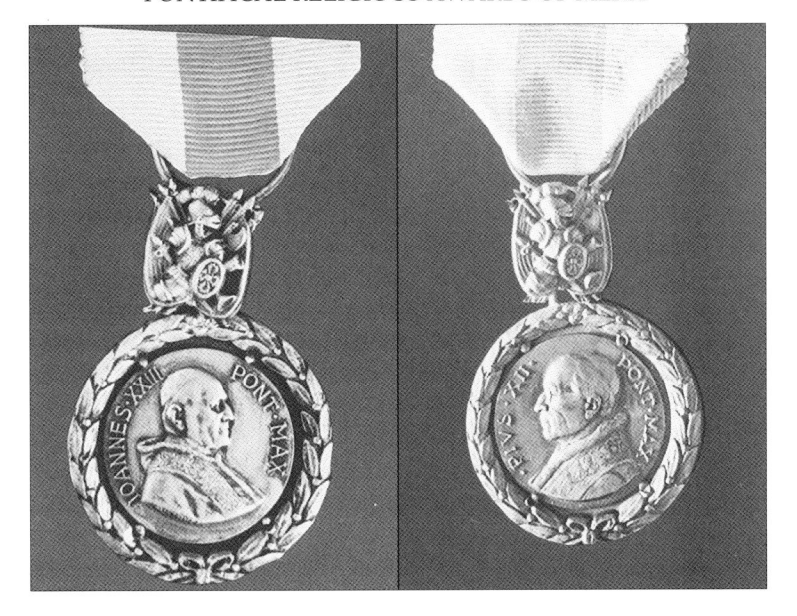

Left: the 'Benemerenti' Medal in silver, surmounted by a military trophy and suspended from a ribbon of the papal colours, conferred on members of the corps of guards by John XXIII. Right: the *Benemerenti* Medal in gold, surmounted by a military trophy and suspended from a ribbon of the papal colours, conferred on members of the corps of guards by Pius XII.

in after 1972, is not dissimilar to the 'Pro Ecclesia et Pontifice' Cross, though more clearly recognisable as a cross composed of one large and four smaller squares.[1] Superimposed on the cross is a large figure of Christ with his right hand raised in blessing; on the left arm are the papal insignia, the tiara and crossed keys and on the right the coat of arms of Pope Paul VI. On the reverse is the word 'Benemerenti'. Pope John Paul II only changed the Montini arms for his own, the reverse remaining unchanged.

Those 'Benemerenti' Medals conferred by Popes on special occasions were only awarded for a limited period of time, usually one year.

---

[1] It is reproduced in this volume both in colour and in monochrome.

CHAPTER FIVE

RELIGIOUS BUT NON-PONTIFICAL ORDERS OF KNIGHTHOOD

There are only two Religious Orders of Knighthood that are recognised as such by the Holy See: The Sovereign Military Hospitaller Order of St.John of Jerusalem, of Rhodes and of Malta, which for practical purposes is referred to as 'The Sovereign Military Order of Malta', SMOM, or simply as 'the Order of Malta', and the Equestrian Order of the Holy Sepulchre of Jerusalem, which for practical purposes is referred to as 'the Order of the Holy Sepulchre' or 'EOHS'.

As I mentioned before, during the period from 1951 to 1958, Monsignor Hyginus Eugene Cardinale was attached to the staff of His Holiness Pope Pius XII as an Assistant, working directly under Cardinal Nicola Canali; in 1958 he became *Assessore* of the Secretariat of State of His Holiness Pope John XXIII and in 1959 Chief of Protocol of the Supreme Pontiff, positions he held until he was consecrated Archbishop in 1963 by the new Pope Paul VI.

The reason I make special mention of these facts is that this coincided with the eleven-year period from the death of H.M.E.H. the 76th Prince and Grand Master of the Order of Malta, Frà Ludovico Chigi Albani della Rovere (1931-1951), until the appointment of his successor, the 77th Prince and Grand Master, Frà Angelo de Mojana di Cologna (1962-1988), during which time, often referred to as the interregnum, the Order of Malta was governed by Lieutenants because no Prince and Grand Master was confirmed by Pope Pius XII, and John XXIII confirmed the 77th Prince and Grand Master in the last year of his pontificate.

As I mentioned in an earlier chapter, Archbishop Cardinale allowed me to read the entries in his diaries which dealt with that period. From them I learned how directly and closely he was involved in the politics of this period, when he acted for the Holy See under instructions of Cardinal Nicola Canali.

Without wishing to discuss the different points of view held at that time by either side, and while endeavouring to be scrupulously impartial in presenting the section on the Order of Malta, I am using the section concerning juridical matter in the chapter which I revised for the 1985 edition of Archbishop Cardinale's work. When I undertook the task of revising the book in 1983, Cardinal Agostino Casaroli informed me that the Sovereign Council of the Order of Malta had objected to many statements that had been made in the first edition, and he counselled me

In 1948, His Eminence Nicola Cardinal Canali was installed as Grand Prior of Rome of the Sovereign Military Order of Malta. Cardinal Canali had been appointed Grand Master of the Equestrian Order of the Holy Sepulchre of Jerusalem in 1940 by Pope Pius XII. After the death of the 76th Prince and Grand Master, Frà Ludovico Chigi Albani della Rovere in 1951, Cardinal Canali advised Pope Pius XII not to confirm a new Grand Master to the Order, and an interregnum followed that lasted eleven years.

to take the advice of the Sovereign Council when revising that section, which I did.

I wish to state that I have always been warmly received at the Order's Headquarters, by H.M.E.H. the Prince and Grand Master Frà Angelo de Mojana di Cologna, and those members of the Sovereign Council who have given me their unstinting assistance at all times, notably H.E. Frà Oberto, the Venerable Marchese Pallavicini, and H.E. Frà Cyril, the Prince Toumanoff. No pressure was brought to bear on how I should change what Archbishop Cardinale had said, but I was given objective historical and juridical explanations, that I was happy to accept, and I therefore included them in my revisions for the 1985 revised edition to the full satisfaction of the Order.

It is for this reason that I hesitated to rewrite the juridical sections dealing with the Order of Malta and concentrated on revising and bringing up to date the history of the Order. The juridical sections and the comments arising from them which refer to the Court of Cassation of Italy (1935), the judgement of the Tribunal of Cardinals set up by Pope Pius XII (1953), the assertions of the legal department of the U. S. Government (1959), and the extracts from the Constitutional Charter approved by John XXIII (1961) are in content and presentation as Archbishop Cardinale wrote them, unless they had been changed in the revised edition on the advice of the Sovereign Council of the Order of Malta.

I recall with personal sadness that whilst Archbishop Cardinale was in a coma for several weeks prior to his death, I had to take the

RELIGIOUS BUT NON-PONTIFICAL ORDERS OF KNIGHTHOOD

responsibility for reprinting two sections of the first edition which had already been printed in order to omit and amend certain passages, because I was informed that some statements might cause unnecessary aggravation and only reopen long healed wounds.

Because of their common roots and origin, I placed the Most Venerable Order of the Hospital of St. John of Jerusalem (Great Britain), better known as the Venerable Order of St. John, immediately after the Sovereign Military Order of Malta. It is a common error to refer to the Venerable Order of St. John as 'the Protestant counterpart of the Order of Malta'. It is an Order of the British Crown, the Sovereign of which is the Monarch of the United Kingdom, and only subjects of Her or His Britannic Majesty who confess the Christian Faith (of whatever denomination) can be appointed full members. The Order has Sub-Prelates of several major Christian denominations, including Roman Catholic bishops. British subjects who are non-Christians and foreign citizens can be appointed associate members. After the section of the

H.E. Archbishop Bruno B. Heim, Apostolic Delegate in Great Britain and later Pro-Nuncio to the Court of St. James, wore on the occasion of presenting his credentials to the Queen, the Grand Cross of Magistral Grace of the Sovereign Military Order as a neck badge and the Cross of the Venerable Order of St. John, of which the British Monarch is the Sovereign, as the principal Star.

Venerable Order of St. John, I briefly make reference to the various 'Johanniter Orden' that also have a common origin with the Sovereign Military Order of Malta, however, they are expressly Protestant Orders.

The Equestrian Order of the Holy Sepulchre of Jerusalem played an important part during the period of the Interregnum in the Order of Malta from 1951-1962. Cardinal Nicola Canali had been appointed the Order's first Cardinal Grand Master in 1949, but he had also been the Grand Prior of the Rome Grand Priory of the Sovereign Military Order of Malta since the previous year. In that year also, Mons. Cardinale became an assistant in Cardinal Canali's department, his special task being to liaise between the Holy See (represented by the Cardinal) and the Sovereign Order. As I learned from his diaries, he unreservedly agreed with the policies of the Holy See, although he commented on occasion that he would have preferred it not to have compromised to the extent the Holy See appeared to do from time to time; he was also psychologically much more in sympathy with the aims of the Equestrian Order, with which he had established close links. The same could not be said of his relations with the Sovereign Order; all this was reflected in the early drafts of the relevant chapter of his book. He himself made changes, as he tried very hard to be impartial, and not to influence me, beyond showing me those of his diaries that covered the Interregnum. He insisted on retaining in the first edition of the book his interpretation of certain matters and told me not to worry about this as he would, should it become necessary, take up the matter himself and defend his interpretations. His death in March 1983 left me with the responsibility of dealing with this chapter in as detached and unprejudiced a manner as possible, so I gladly took Cardinal Casaroli's advice and consulted the Sovereign Order.

I have revised the original chapter, adding some important historical details, and brought the Order's history up to date in text and illustrations. Originally I also prepared a brief memorandum on the Equestrian Order's status for the late Maximilien Cardinal de Fürstenberg, Grand Master of the Order of the Holy Sepulchre from 1973 until his death in 1988. It was done on my own initiative after several meetings with the Cardinal, when we discussed certain matters informally and in a wider context, including the practice of the Knights of the Order in the United States of America styling themselves 'Sir'. Because the use of the title 'Sir' is a prerogative of those knighted by the British Crown and Baronets, and as formal protests had been lodged with Archbishop Cardinale about the use of this title by Knights of a Religious Order, I suggested to the Cardinal that it might be possible to persuade the American Knights of the Order to change the style 'Sir' to an appellation that both of his and my ancestors had used in Flanders in the fifteenth and sixteenth centuries: 'Sieur'. Cardinal de Fürstenberg agreed in principle, but explained that the practical aspects might prove too complicated, and enforcing such a change could be counter-productive.

In 1987, I gave him a copy of my memorandum on the Equestrian Order, especially as in spite of frequent reminders by the Cardinal Grand Master and others, many privately published histories of the Order also stated that the Order of the Holy Sepulchre was a Pontifical Order of Knighthood. Sadly, His Eminence died shortly afterwards, before he could give me his reaction to my memorandum.

Since Pope John Paul II appointed Giuseppe Cardinal Caprio successor to Cardinal de Fürstenberg as Grand Master of the Order of the Holy Sepulchre in 1989, His Eminence, and separately, Vice-Governor General Dr. Russell Kendall in the U.S.A., an eminent lawyer, have both written to the Knights and Dames of the Order, stating categorically that the Order is not a Pontifical Equestrian Order, but an Order under the Protection of the Holy See.

I

THE SOVEREIGN MILITARY HOSPITALLER ORDER OF ST. JOHN OF JERUSALEM, OF RHODES AND OF MALTA

This is the most ancient religious Order of Chivalry in Christendom; it is composed of not only professed but also of secular knights and other associates.

It is a religious Order, whose membership is made up of lay brothers and of chaplains, the aims of which are the glorification of God through the sanctification of its members, service to the Faith and to the Holy See, and welfare work in the whole world. As a religious Order, it follows the principles of the Gospel and Canon Law, and the teaching of the *Magisterium* of the Church, which inspire its constitutional charter. Its professed members, its churches, chapels and conventual institutions are exempt from the jurisdiction of local Ordinaries and are placed under the authority of their own Prelate.

Furthermore, it is a sovereign international entity and thus subject to international law, being governed in accordance with its own Code of Laws, but with the approval of the Supreme Pontiff. The Order's sovereignty, not only resulting from initial official recognition by the Holy See but also by other subjects of international law, including numerous sovereign states, does not depend on territory, although the Order did once hold land, as described in its official appellation, in sovereign possession. This sovereignty however is not to be taken in a plenary sense, in that in practice the Order does not at present exercise all the attributes of sovereignty.

On 11 April 1988, His Most Eminent Highness, Frà Andrew Bertie, was elected the 78th Prince and Grand Master of the Sovereign Military Order of Malta.

The religious and sovereign aspects of the Order are integrally related and connected. As a result of its sovereign, but also supranational character, it is able to pursue its religious and charitable mission on a worldwide scale. It dedicates itself especially to aiding the sick, among whom the victims of leprosy have pride of place, emigrants, refugees and exiles, abandoned children and the destitute, those stricken by natural disasters and war casualties, and it also ministers to the spiritual development of all these needy people.

Traditionally the Order is a nobiliary body, and one of the conditions for admission is nobility of sixteen quarterings. Nowadays, because the rank of Knight of Magistral Grace was introduced to which novices could be appointed, the Order's membership is open in some measure to self-deserving Catholics of a respectable status and position, especially in those countries where nobility no longer exists as an institution.

The uninterrupted history of the Order goes back to the first Crusade. It began in 1070 as a hospice-infirmary for pilgrims travelling to the Holy Land from Amalfi, *sacra domus hospitalis*, from which the Order took the appellation 'hospitaller' in the official title. The construction of the hospital was authorised by the Fatimid Caliphs, masters of Palestine. Its founder and first head was the Blessed Gerard (+1120) who gave the hospice the name of St. John the Baptist. The rule of the confraternity in charge was a variant of that of St. Augustine. On 15 February 1113, in a Papal Bull addressed to Gerard, Pope Paschal II (1099-1118) approved the new institution and placed it under the protection of the Holy See. It also had the support and approval of many Christian rulers. In 1126 this religious confraternity also took on military-chivalric functions, with the aim of protecting the sick and the pilgrims, and of defending the Christian nations in the Levant and especially the Holy Places against Muslim attacks. Indeed, the chief strength of the Christian Kingdom of Jerusalem lay in the support it received from the Hospitallers and the Templars.

In 1120 Frà Raymond du Puy succeeded the Blessed Gerard as the Order's second head (and the first to be called Master). Under his guidance it became a Religious Military Order with its members being divided into Knights, Chaplains and Serving Brothers, all of whom on entering took the three religious Vows of Obedience, Chastity and Poverty. With its first known rules, Master Raymond du Puy introduced the white eight-pointed cross – the Maltese Cross – which has remained the Order's emblem ever since. In 1158 Frà Raymond was succeeded as Master by Frà Auger de Balben.

In 1291, as a result of the fall of the last Christian stronghold in the Holy Land, St. Jean d'Acre (now known as Acre) the Order, under Master Frà Jean de Villiers, was forced to leave Palestine and moved to Cyprus, establishing its headquarters at Limasol under the protection of the

Lusignan Kings. In 1310, under Grand Master Frà Foulques de Villaret, the Order completed the occupation of the Island of Rhodes, thus acquiring territorial sovereignty and ensuring its independence from other political rulers. The 'Knights of Rhodes', as the Order's members became known, became an important international naval Power and took part in several crusading campaigns for the defence of Christendom.

From the beginning of the fourteenth century, the members of the Order who came to Rhodes from all over Europe were separated into groups according to their native language. There were originally seven independent national branches or *Langues*, each headed by a Bailiff: Provence, Auvergne, France, Italy, Aragon (-Navarra), England (with Scotland and Ireland), and Germany, but in 1462 Portugal separated from Aragon as the eighth *Langue*.

The Order was ruled by a Grand Master and a Sovereign Council, minting its own money, and maintaining diplomatic relations with other European States. The high offices of the Order were shared among the different *Langues*, and the headquarters of the Order consisted of a series of national religious houses.

Expelled by the Muslims from Rhodes in 1522, the Order was homeless for four years before it received the Islands of Malta, Gozo and Comino and the stronghold of Tripoli in Africa as a feudal grant from the Emperor Charles V in his capacity as King of Sicily. The Order took up residence on, and the possession of the Maltese Islands in 1530 with the approval of Pope Clement VII (1523-1534). It was stipulated that the Order was to remain neutral in any war fought among Christian nations.

In the Great Siege of Malta from 18 May to 8 September 1565, the Turks were finally defeated by the Knights lead by their Grand Master Frà Jean de La Valette after whom the island's capital, Valletta, is named. The defeat of the Turks at Malta ended Muslim sea power. The navy of the Order of St. John, or of Malta, as the Order had now become known, played a decisive part in the defeat of the Turks at the naval battle of Lepanto in 1571.

Because of its vigilant presence in Malta the Order halted the advance of Islam towards the heart of Christendom. In 1575 the Order built a hospital in Valletta, consisting of eleven wards for 500 patients, with Schools of Anatomy, Surgery, and Pharmacy, and it had established an eminent medical team. It was a remarkable enterprise of worldwide renown, and the first international hospital in history.

In 1607 and again in 1620, the Grand Masters of the Order of Malta were created Princes of the Holy Roman Empire, and in 1630 Pope Urban VIII accorded them a rank equal to that of a Cardinal of the Holy Roman Church and the style of 'His Most Eminent Highness'. Since 1581 the Grand Masters had worn a special crown.

In 1798 Malta capitulated to the French invaders lead by Napoleon

Bonaparte, on their way to Egypt. After Nelson destroyed the French fleet in Aboukir Bay in 1801, British forces occupied Malta, and although the Treaty of Amiens in 1802 recognised the Order's sovereignty over the island, it has never been restored to it.

After temporary seats in Russia, at the invitation of Czar Paul I,[1] in Messina, Catania and Ferrara, Pope Gregory XVI welcomed the Order in Rome in 1834, where it established its headquarters and continues to exist and holds extraterritorial rights over the Palace in the Via Condotti and the Villa on the Aventine.

Though twice in imminent danger of collapse, and even without territorial power, the Order retained the title and status of sovereign in, and is therefore subject of, international law, and this was upheld by the Italian Court of Cassation in a decision given in 1935.

In 1959, however, the Office of the Legal Adviser of the U.S. Government asserted that 'the United States, on its part, does not recognise the Order as a State', but it is obvious that he was confusing the concept of State with that of a subject of international law. The Order does not presume to be a State, but it is a fully-fledged subject of international law, enjoying and exercising the pertinent prerogatives in all normality. This is recognised not only by the States entertaining diplomatic relations with the Order, but also by international organisations and agencies such as the United Nations, UNESCO and the Council of Europe.

'Sovereignty' as the Italian Court of Cassation put it, 'is a complex notion, which international law, from the external standpoint, contemplates, so to speak, negatively, having only in view independence *vis-à-vis* other States. . . . It is impossible to deny to other international collective units a limited capacity of acting internationally within the ambit and the actual exercise of their own functions, with the resulting international juridical personality and capacity which is its necessary and natural corollary' (cf. Nanni and Others, v. Pace and the S.O. of M., Court of Cassation of Italy, Mar. 13, 1935 [1935-1937] Ann.Deg. 2, 4-6 [no.2]).

The position of the Order with regard to the Holy See is defined by the judgement of the Tribunal of Cardinals, instituted by Pius XII in 1951, which was promulgated on 24 January 1953. According to the Tribunal's decision,

> 1) the sovereign quality of the Order, repeatedly recognised by the Holy See, consists in the enjoyment of certain prerogatives inherent in the Order itself as a subject of international law. Said prerogatives are proper to sovereignty, in harmony with international law and have been recognised by a number of States, following the example of the Holy See. They do not, how ever, constitute in the Order the ensemble of powers and prerogatives which belong to sovereign

---

[1] See the corollary on the Imitation Orders of the Order of Malta and the the Russian Government's statement in *The Orders of Russia* (Moscow, 1993) regarding the 1817 law about the Order of St. John.

bodies in the full sense of the word; and
2) it is also a religious Order, approved by the Holy See, pursuing the sanctification of its members and other religious and charitable ends (cf. *Acta Apostolica Sedis*, vol.XX, 1953, pp. 765-767).

All this shows that the Order of Malta is indeed a unique subject of international law, and is, in fact, the second oldest in existence after the Holy See.

At the time of writing the Order now has more than 10,000 members, located in six Grand Priories, three sub-Priories, and forty-one National Associations throughout the world. The Sovereign Order has sixty-five ambassadors and delegates accredited to sovereign States, including to the Holy See and a special Mission to the Russian Federation at ambassadorial level, and the same number of ambassadors and delegates accredited on a reciprocal basis to the Order. In addition, the Order has accredited several Observers to international organisations such as the United Nations Organisation, the Council of Europe, Unesco and others.

According to its constitutional charter of 24 June 1961, approved by Pope John XXIII, the members of the Sovereign Military Hospitaller Order of Malta, who must belong to the Catholic Faith, are divided into the following classes:

Knights of Justice and the professed Conventual Chaplains;
Knights of Obedience and the Donats;
lay members and Honorary Chaplains (*ad honorem*);
Knights and Dames of Honour and Devotion;
Knights and Dames of Grace and Devotion;[1]
Magistral Chaplains;
Knights and Dames of Magistral Grace;
Donats of Devotion.

There is also an Order of Merit, with both a civil and military division, attached to the Order of Malta. It is destined for persons who have acquired special merit in the affairs of the Order. It decorations are conferred on meritorious persons, independently of their origin, as a recognition of conspicuous merit or works of charity. They do not require a profession of faith and they do not imply membership of the Order as such. The recipients must be persons of flawless integrity. If they do not belong to the Catholic Faith, it is up to the Sovereign Council whether the conferment is appropriate.

---

[1]This is a relatively newly created class which requires less rigorous proof of nobility and which has been introduced in several Grand Prio ries and Associations.

Frà Andrew Bertie was the first Professed Knight of Justice of the Sovereign Military Order of Malta in England since the Reformation.

In 1994, Frà Matthew Festing was elected the 55th Grand Prior of the Sovereign Military Order of Malta in England, the first since the Reformation.

Frà Matthew Festing was installed as Grand Prior of England by the Apostolic Nuncio to the Court of St. James, Archbishop Luigi Barbarito, in the Order's Chapel in London.

Courtesy: Grand Priory England SMOM

Above: The newly elected Prince and Grand Master, Frà Andrew Bertie, is congratulated by the Cardinal Patronus of the Order, the late Sebastiano Cardinal Baggio, who died in 1993. Below. Below: Frà Andrew accepts the homage of the Venerable Bali Frà Giancarlo Pallavicini, who as Interim Lieutenant had been in charge of the Order's affairs during the *Sede Vacante*.

RELIGIOUS BUT NON-PONTIFICAL ORDERS OF KNIGHTHOOD

Above: The Venerable Frà Cyril Prince Toumanoff, High Historical Consultant to the Order's Sovereign Council, greets the new Prince and Grand Master. Below: After the election, His Most Eminent Highness The Prince and Grand Master Frà Andrew Bertie, accompanied by Cardinal Baggio, steps out into the courtyard of the Villa S. Maria in Anventino.

Courtesy: *L'Osservatore Romano* and Prior Regis Barwig.

SEGRETERIA DI STATO

N.201.767

DAL VATICANO, 9 Aprile 1988

Signor Cardinale,

Mi è gradito comunicare a Vostra Eminenza Reverendissima che il Santo Padre, al Quale ho riferito in merito, approva l'elezione del Gran Maestro del Sovrano Militare Ordine di Malta nella persona di S.E. il Cavaliere Frà Andrew W.N. Bertie e m'incarica di far pervenire all'eletto i Suoi cordiali voti.

Il Sommo Pontefice Si compiace del confortante sviluppo delle attività dell'Ordine, e rileva con soddisfazione come i Cavalieri di Malta, nella loro azione, si studino di orientarsi secondo le linee da Lui tracciate in ripetuti interventi e, da ultimo, nell'Enciclica "Sollicitudo rei socialis", valendosi, per tale singolare e qualificata collaborazione con l'impegno caritativo della Chiesa, delle peculiari possibilità che la prerogativa sovrana conferisce all'Ordine.

Nell'auspicare che l'opera del nuovo Gran Maestro valga a rendere sempre più fruttuoso il carisma di fondazione dell'Ordine Ospedaliero di San Giovanni, Sua Santità sprona tutti i Membri ad onorare con rinnovato slancio le finalità della "tuitio fidei" e dell'"obsequium pauperum", che da secoli distinguono persone e attività della nobile Istituzione.

Con tali sentimenti il Vicario di Cristo volentieri imparte al neo eletto ed a tutto il Sovrano Ordine la Sua propiziatrice Benedizione Apostolica.

Profitto della circostanza per confermarmi con sensi di profonda venerazione

dell'Eminenza Vostra Rev.ma
Dev.mo in Domino

A Sua Eminenza Reverendissima
il Sig. Card. SEBASTIANO BAGGIO
"Cardinalis Patronus"
del Sovrano Militare Ordine di Malta

After his confirmation by the Pope as Prince and Grand Master, Frà Andrew Bertie paid his first official visit to His Holiness.

After the Investiture of the new Prince and Grand Master of the Sovereign Military Order of Malta, Frà Andrew Bertie (left), was invested with the Grand Collar of the Sacred Military Constantinian Order by its Grand Master, H.R.H. don Ferdinando Maria Bourbon delle Due Sicilie, Duke of Castro (centre) and the Order's Grand Chancellor, Bali don Achille di Lorenzo, who hands the insignia to Frà Andrew. The previous Grand Master of the Order of Malta, Frà Angelo di Mojana di Cologna, had been invested with the Constantinian Grand Collar by the late Prince don Ranieri, Duke of Castro, who was also accompanied by the Order's Grand Chancellor, don Achille di Lorenzo.

At solemn ceremony in the Palazzo di Malta, Frà Andrew Bertie, Prince and Grand Master of the Sovereign Military Order, received the Collar of the Most Holy Order of the Annunziata from an envoy of H.R.H. Prince Victor Emmanuel, Duke of Savoy, Head of the Royal House of Italy, Grand Master of the Orders of the Annunziata and of SS. Maurice and Lazarus. Because of political complications in Italy, not least the fact that there have been over fifty governments, more than there have been years, since King Umberto II and his family left their homeland in 1946, the Duke of Savoy and his son and heir, Prince Filiberto Emmanuel (born in 1972), are still prevented from setting foot on Italian soil because of a Communist-instigated law that was passed after the Second World War. Frà Andrew Bertie (right) wearing the Collar of the Annunziata, is accompanied by the Chief of Protocol and Master of Ceremonies of the Sovereign Council, the Venerable Frà Oberto The Marchese Pallavicini, who wears the Grand Cross of the Order of SS. Maurice and Lazarus.

THE ORDER OF MERIT
(Ordo pro Merito Melitensi)

The Order comprises three ranks: the Collar, consisting of one class, generally reserved for Heads of State; the Cross, with civil and military divisions (the latter with swords), consisting of five ranks: Grand Cross of Merit, Grand Officer, Commander, Officer and Cross of Merit. All have equivalent ranks for ladies; the Grand Cross *pro piis meritis*; the Cros *pro piis meritis*. (The latter two are reserved for the clergy.

There is also a special Medal, divided into three ranks: gold, silver and bronze. Other medals struck to mark important historical events in which the Order was able to play a significant charitable rôle; these are conferred upon benefactors.

THE INSIGNIA OF THE SOVEREIGN MILITARY ORDER OF MALTA[1]

The Badge of the Order is an eight-pointed white enamelled cross, known as the Maltese cross, with the extremity of each arm having a V-shaped indentation. The arms are narrow where they meet and gradually expand. The emblem placed between the arms of the cross varies according to the *Langue* or national branch to which the recipients belongs. Several countries follow the Maltese pattern of having slightly different versions of fleurs-de-lis, as one can see, for example, in the French, the Spanish and the British branches among others. The English *Langue* ranked sixth in the order of seniority when it was abolished by Henry VIII in 1534. Many of the 500 Knights belonging to the *Langue* at that time died on the scaffold, having refused to give up the Catholic religion.

When the *Langues* were formed all the Knights retained their original insignia, the eight-pointed white enamelled Maltese cross, but in the centre of the Cross those of the German *Langue* had a golden crown and a black eagle, whereas those of the French *Langue* had a golden fleur-de-lis. Later the national differences became more prominent; the German *Langue*, for example, adopted a double-headed crowned eagle between the arms of the Cross instead of the fleur-de-lis.

The Cross is surmounted by a crown, suspended from a shield with a Latin cross in the centre and a military trophy of flags and arms for Knights of Justice and Knights of Honour and Devotion, while Knights of Grace have a gold bow.

The Star consists of an eight-pointed, white enamelled cross, and the

[1] See: Colour Plates on which all decorations of the Sovereign Military Order of Malta are reproduced.

ribbon is of black watered silk. The Badge and Star for the Order of Merit are somewhat different in form and the ribbon is of white watered silk with two bordering red stripes; the colours are reversed for the military division.

Although there are traditional national variations, both in the uniform and the cowl which is worn for religious functions and in the embroidered crosses on mantle and cowl according to tongue and rank, the dress uniform only varies in the richness of embroidery with gold braid and gold lace on collar, lapels and cuffs according to the respective classes the knights have been appointed to and the ranks they hold.

The uniform of a Knight of Magistral Grace consists of a red cloth jacket, with cuffs, lapels and collar of black velvet, closed in front by twelve gilded buttons with the Cross of the Order embossed on them, and gold, fringed epaulettes on the shoulders. The trousers are dark blue with gold braid and red stripes down the sides. A gold embroidered black belt with a similarly embroidered frog from which the sword is suspended, spurs and a bi-cornered cocked hat complete the uniform. A Knight Grand Cross of Magistral Grace has the same uniform, but with gold embroidered cuffs, lapels and collar.

Knights of Grace and Devotion and of Honour and Devotion wear a similar uniform, but with the facings of the cuffs, the lapels and collar embroidered with gold lace and a different motif and more elaborate embroidery for higher ranks. They also have a plumed bi-cornered cocked hat, and the higher ranks wear white plumes.

Knights of Justice wear white lapels, collar and cuffs, which are embroidered according to rank.

The mantle for all Knights is a long black cloak reaching below the knee, with silk lapels, velvet collar, and a golden chain fastening in the middle.

The cowl is a black tunic of light woollen fabric, with white silk cuffs and the Cross of the Order, according to *Langue* and rank embroidered in white in front or on the left side of the tunic. As mentioned above, there are several national variations.

The seat of the Government of the Order is in Rome. The Prince and Grand Master is elected by the Council and accedes to his most eminent position on receiving the confirmation of his election from the Supreme Pontiff, which is sent by the Cardinal Secretary of State to the Cardinal Patron of the Order, who immediately takes the oath of the new Prince and Grand Master.

Since the publication of the revised edition of Archbishop Cardinale's book in 1985, there have been important developments, and some projects are about to be realised.

On 3 July 1897, the occasion of the twenty-fifth anniversary of his election as Prince and Grand Master of the Sovereign Military Order of

Malta, His Most Eminent Highness Frà Angelo de Mojana di Cologna was honoured by the His Holiness Pope John Paul II with the dignity of a Knight of the Supreme Order of Christ, an honour he then shared with His Majesty King Baudouin of the Belgians. Sadly, H.M.E.H. Frà Angelo, the 77th Prince and Grand Master of the Order, died on 18 January 1988.

On 8 April 1988, the Council of the Sovereign Military Order of Malta elected H.M.E.H. Frà Andrew Bertie as its 78th Prince and Grand Master. The approval of the election of the new Grand Master by the Supreme Pontiff was sent by messenger the following day. On 14 April, the Cardinal Patron of the Order, Cardinal Sebastiano Baggio, celebrated the Pontifical High Mass of Thanksgiving for the election of the new Prince and Grand Master at the Chiesa di Santa Maria all'Aventino in the presence of the Sovereign Council and dignitaries of the Order, the members of the diplomatic corps accredited to the Order, members of the Italian Government and invited guests who had come from all over the world. Frà Andrew had always maintained personal and special relations with the Island of Malta, and the Sovereign Council of the Order has announced that the Sovereign Military Order of Malta will soon return to its former domicile in Malta, though the Headquarters of the Order in the Via Condotti in Rome will be retained.

II

THE MOST VENERABLE ORDER OF THE HOSPITAL OF ST. JOHN OF JERUSALEM

As already explained in the introduction to this chapter, the Most Venerable Order the Hospital of St. John of Jerusalem, known as the Venerable Order of St. John, is not, as often stated in books dealing with European Orders of Knighthood, a 'Protestant counterpart' of the Sovereign Military Order of Malta, but a British Order of Chivalry under the Crown, established in 1888 by Royal Charter, open to all British Christians as Members and foreigners and non-Christians as Associates.

Since the Royal Charter of 1888, the Monarch has been the Sovereign of the Order, and the Grand Priors have always been Royal Princes, H.R.H. Albert Edward, Prince of Wales, (subsequently King Edward VII), (1888-1901); H.R.H. George, Prince of Wales, (subsequently King George V) (1901-1910); H.R.H. The Duke of Connaught (1910-1939); H.R.H. Prince Henry, Duke of Gloucester (1939-1974); and presently H.R.H. Prince Richard, Duke of Gloucester in 1974.

The principal officers of the Order after the Grand Prior are the Lord Prior, the Prelate, the Chancellor and the Bailiff of Eagle.

The Order of Malta became the victim of the Reformation in several countries. Following the principle adopted by some European rulers, *cuius regio, illius religio*, one must recall that during the Reformation a Protestant group at Brandenburg – where a Bailiwick of the Sovereign Military Order of Malta had existed since 1350 – constituted itself into a chivalric body resembling that of the Sovereign Order. Immediately after the treaty of Westphalia in 1648 seven commanderies of the Brandenburg Bailiwick who now embraced the Lutheran faith, formed the Protestant Order 'Balley Brandenburg des Ritterlichen Ordens St. Johannis vom Spital zu Jerusalem' but continued to use almost identical insignia to those of the Sovereign Order. This group was closely associated with the Royal House of Hohenzollern, which ruled Prussia. In 1812 King Friedrich Wilhelm III of Prussia, after suppressing the Protestant Bailiwick of Brandenburg, founded the Royal Prussian Order of St. John, which in 1852 was abolished by King Friedrich Wilhelm IV of Prussia, who created an Order of St. John along the lines of the former Protestant Bailiwick of Brandenburg; he appointed Prince Karl of Hohenzollern Grand Master. The Protestant Bailiwick of Brandenburg continued to exist under the name of 'Johanniter Orden' with associations affiliated to it in Germany, Switzerland, Finland, Hungary and France.

In 1920, a Swedish Order of St. John with the King of Sweden as its Patron came into being, and after the second World War the Netherlands

Her Majesty Queen Elizabeth II, Sovereign of the Venerable Order of the Hospital of St. John of Jerusalem.

Courtesy: The Venerable Order of St. John

RELIGIOUS BUT NON-PONTIFICAL ORDERS OF KNIGHTHOOD

King Edward VII of Great Britain during his visit to Malta in 1907, wearing the Cross of Honour and Devotion of the Sovereign Military Order of Malta

Courtesy: Kenneth Rose, London

The Insignia of the Balley Brandenburg des Ritterlichen Ordens St. Johannis vom Spital zu Jerusalem.

Courtesy: Garrison Collection

and Norway followed suit, each establishing a Protestant Johanniter Order under royal patronage.

In England, the original Priory of the Order was founded at Clerkenwell, London, in about 1144; the buildings of which were burnt down during the Wat Tyler's Rebellion in 1381. The Grand Prior Thomas Docwra completed the rebuilding of the great Gatehouse at Clerkenwell in 1504, but in 1540 the Order was dissolved in England by Henry VIII, who ordered the confiscation of all its estates and, although re-established under Royal Letters Patent of 1557 by Queen Mary, it was suppressed by Queen Elizabeth I and so fell in abeyance.

After the Order's suppression by Henry VIII, the Royal Letters Patent reconstituting the Sovereign Military Order of Malta were signed by Queen Mary in 1557. The illuminated document consists of twenty-five folios, and it was presented to the Order by a member in 1986. The first letter, P, is illuminated with minature portraits of Queen Mary and her husband King Philip of Spain. The Royal Letters Patent are on permanent exhibition in the Order's Museum at St. John's Gate London.

Courtesy: The Curator of the Museum of the Order

The Order was revived in England in 1831 through an initiative by members of the Sovereign Military Order of Malta in France, but it was eventually disowned by the Grand Magistry, and no official status was granted at that time.

Eventually St. John's Gate was restored to the ownership of the British Order of St. John and its headquarters were established there through the generosity of a member of the Order in 1874. Later the original Grand Priory Church was also given to the Order.

The members of the Order elected to dedicate themselves to do good works and were so successful in their efforts that members of the Royal Family were, early on, attracted to support its charitable endeavours and it was granted its Royal Charter in 1888 because of its outstanding work. They established two foundations which operate worldwide, St. John Ambulance (and the St. John Ambulance Brigade) and the St. John Ophthalmic Hospital in Jerusalem. A historic photograph, taken on the

The Great Gatehouse, headquarters of the Order since 1144; it was burnt down during Wat Tyler's Rebellion in 1381 and rebuilt by Grand Prior Thomas Dowcra in 1504. After the suppression of the Order by Queen Elizabeth I, St. John's Gate was given to the Venerable Order of St. John in 1874 in the reign of Queen Victoria.

Courtesy: The Curator of the Museum of the Order -

occasion of Queen Victoria's golden jubilee, shows the St. John Ambulance on its first public duty. Both foundations have been greatly expanded since they were established.

The Order has a Prelate, Sub-Prelates and Chaplains. The Prelate is according to the statutes 'a Brother of the Order of episcopal rank in the Church of England as by law established and shall be appointed by the Grand Prior to hold office during his pleasure or resignation'. Sub-Prelates are appointed from other major Christian denominations.

In 1963 a Concordat was signed between the Venerable Order of St. John and the Sovereign Military Order of Malta. Many members of the Sovereign Order are also members of the Venerable Order.

The Sovereign Military Order of Malta's newly appointed 55th Grand Prior of England (the first since the Reformation) Frà Matthew Festing, was a member of the Venerable Order before joining the Sovereign Order, and he still is.

The Venerable Order is also in alliance with the Protestant Orders of

H.R.H. The Duke of Gloucester, Grand Prior of the Venerable Order of St. John (left), on the occasion of The Lord Vestey being installed as Lord Prior of the Order.

Courtesy: The Venerable Order of St. John

northern Europe stemming from the Bailiwick of Brandenburg and the Johanniter Orden.

During his visit to Great Britain in 1982, Pope John Paul II blessed and took possession of a 'Cope of Reconciliation'. It is embroidered with the armorial bearings of five Pontiffs and the Sees of Canterbury and York. His Holiness specifically asked the donor to place the cope with an Order or organisation where the spirit of oecumenism was practised. Two

RELIGIOUS BUT NON-PONTIFICAL ORDERS OF KNIGHTHOOD

The Order's foundation, St. John Ambulance (see also Chapter Eleven), on its first duty on the occasion of Queen Victoria's Golden Jubilee in 1888.

Courtesy: The Curator of the Museum of the Order

The Cross of a Knight and a Commander, worn as a neck badge, and the Star of a sub-Prelate and Knight of the Order.

embroideries of the Cross of the Venerable Order were added by the donor and the cope was presented as a gift to the Venerable Order on the occasion of the centenary of its foundation of St. John Ambulance, and it was worn for the first time since the Supreme Pontiff's visit by the Prelate of the Order, The Rt.Rev. and Rt.Hon. The Lord Coggan of Canterbury, in the presence of the Order's Sovereign, H.M. Queen Elizabeth II, the Duke of Edinburgh, the Grand Prior and the Lord Prior. It is frequently used and exhibited in the Order's Museum at St. John's Gate when it is not used during functions outside London or abroad.

III

THE EQUESTRIAN ORDER OF THE HOLY SEPULCHRE OF JERUSALEM

The origin of this Order, as we know it today, can be traced back to Godefroy de Bouillon, leader of the first Crusade, who captured Jerusalem from the Saracens in 1099. From its beginnings, the aim of the Order was the protection of the Holy Places and of pilgrims, and to start with its history coincided with that of the Crusader Kingdom of Jerusalem until the loss of St. John of Acre in 1291 when 60,000 Christians perished.

Godefroy de Bouillon founded the Order with a body a Crusader knights for the purpose of assisting the Chapter of Canons who watched over the Holy Sepulchre under the direction of a Guardian and the authority of the Patriarch of Jerusalem. For their emblem, these knights adopted the coat of arms of the other Crusaders, but in red rather than gold. The foundation of the Order received the approval of Callistus II (1119-1124) in 1122, and its main aim was to defend the Church Universal,[1] protect the city of Jerusalem, guard the Basilica of the Holy Sepulchre, look after the pilgrims and fight the Muslims. After incessant battles the knights were compelled to withdraw from Jerusalem completely in 1244 and take refuge at St. John of Acre, until this fortress town also capitulated in 1291, which brought to a close the first period in its long and chequered history.

The second period of the Order's history lasts from 1291 to 1847. During this time the Franciscan Custody of Mount Sion was established in Jerusalem. The Guardian, also known as the Custodian, was the only authority representing the Apostolic See in the Holy Land (1333), and he had been given the apostolic authority to dub knights in the Basilica of the Holy Sepulchre. Meanwhile, the knights themselves had joined the many priories of the Order in Europe, and only the Franciscans remained in the Holy Land.

After twice overcoming pontifical threats of suppression, the Order of the Holy Sepulchre, which had been provisionally made part of the Order of St. John of Jerusalem and of Rhodes (the Order of Malta) by Innocent VIII (1484-1492) in 1489, was re-established as an independent Order by Alexander VI (1492-1503) in 1496, but as the Sovereign Pontiff was now the Grand Master under the Order's new statutes, it had juridically become a Pontifical Equestrian Hospitaller Order. The papal Grand Master confirmed the prerogative of the Custodian in Jerusalem of

---

[1] Considering the turbulent events in Rome, the struggle between popes and anti-popes, there was little the Order could do for the Church in Europe while it was locked in combat with the Muslims in the Holy Land.

His Holiness Pope John Paul II addresses Knights and Dames of the Equestrian Order of the Holy Sepulchre of Jerusalem.

Courtesy: EOHS (France) & Musée de Fourvière, Lyon

dubbing knights, and renewed the conditions required for investitures. The Order's position and privileges were approved by subsequent Pontiffs, but during the following centuries the Order was the victim of many vicissitudes without, however, breaking down under the weight of events. In 1516 Pope Leo X confirmed the right of the Franciscan Custodian to dub knights, and in 1527, in order to maintain the good reputation of the Order, Pope Clement VII added instructions that only candidates of the required standing should be invested.

It is important to pay particular attention to the kind of privileges granted to the Order of the Holy Sepulchre; these may account for the hostility the Order encountered from other Orders, notably the Order of St. John of Jerusalem and of Rhodes and (since 1522) of Malta.

These privileges were recorded by the Guardian of the Order in 1553, and they gave the Knights of the Holy Sepulchre of Jerusalem:

1) powers to legitimize bastards;
2) to change a name given in baptism;
3) to pardon prisoners they might meet on the way to the scaffold;
4) to possess goods belonging to the Church even though they were laymen;
5) to be exempt from all taxes;
6) to cut down a man found hanging on a gallows and order him to be given a Christian burial;
7) to wear brocaded silk garments reserved for knights and doctors;
8) to enter a church on horseback;
9) to fight against the Infidel.

These privileges were approved by successive popes. Pope Benedict XIV (1740-1758) approved all but the last, which he abolished for political reasons. However, in the same document, the Pontiff states that the Order of the Holy Sepulchre should enjoy precedence over all Orders except over the Order of the Golden Fleece. Both the privileges granted to the Order and that it had been given, by implication, precedence over the Order of St. John of Jerusalem were the seeds from which grew centuries of disharmony between the two Orders.

The third period of the Order's history began in 1847, when Pope Pius IX reinstated the Latin Patriarch of Jerusalem, and appointed him the 'ecclesiastical authority' of the Order and Grand Master.[1]

This was a shrewd political move on the part of Pius IX as, having successfully completed a treaty with the Sublime Porte, the Pope was thus able to counterbalance the influence the Greek Orthodox Church had been gaining in Jerusalem. The Patriarch of Jerusalem encouraged the

---

[1] By this act the Order again lost its status as a Pontifical Order, but not its links with the Apostolic See. Pius IX not only appointed the Patriarch Grand Master of the Order but also gave him sovereignty over the Order by appointing him the 'ecclesiastical authority', thus abdicating ecclesiastical sovereignty in favour of the Latin Patriarch of Jerusalem.

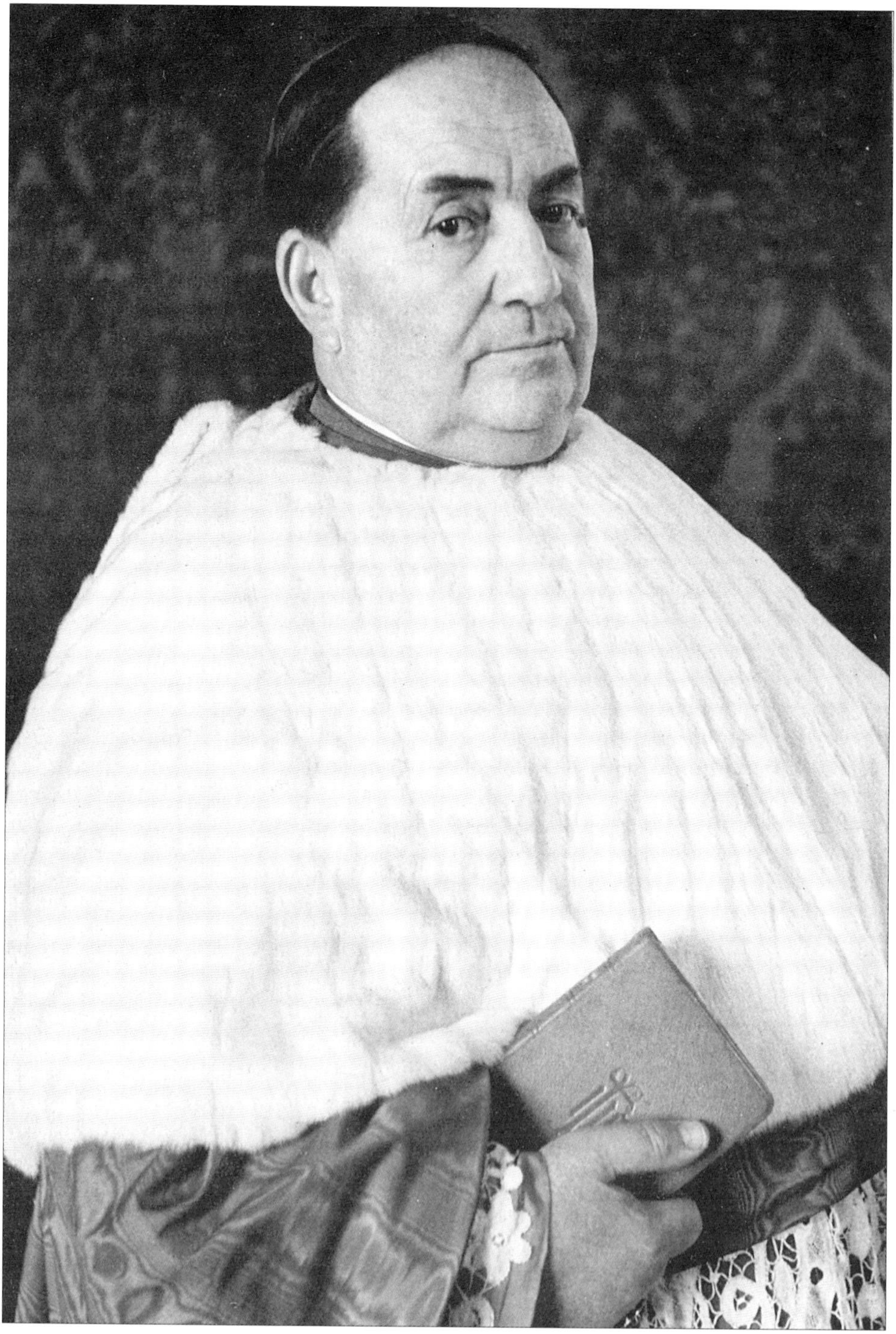

Right: Pope Benedict XV (1914-1922) was the last Pontiff to exercise the Office of Grand Master of the Holy Sepulchre of Jerusalem. Below left: Eugene Cardinal Tisserant, Dean of the Sacred College of Cardinals, succeeded Nicola Cardinal Canali (opposite) as Grand Master. Below right: Maximilien Cardinal de Fürstenberg became Grand Master in 1973.

In 1945, Pope Pius XII placed the Order under the patronage of the Holy See and gave to the Order the Church and Monastery of St. Onofrio (opposite).

Courtesy: Secretariat of State

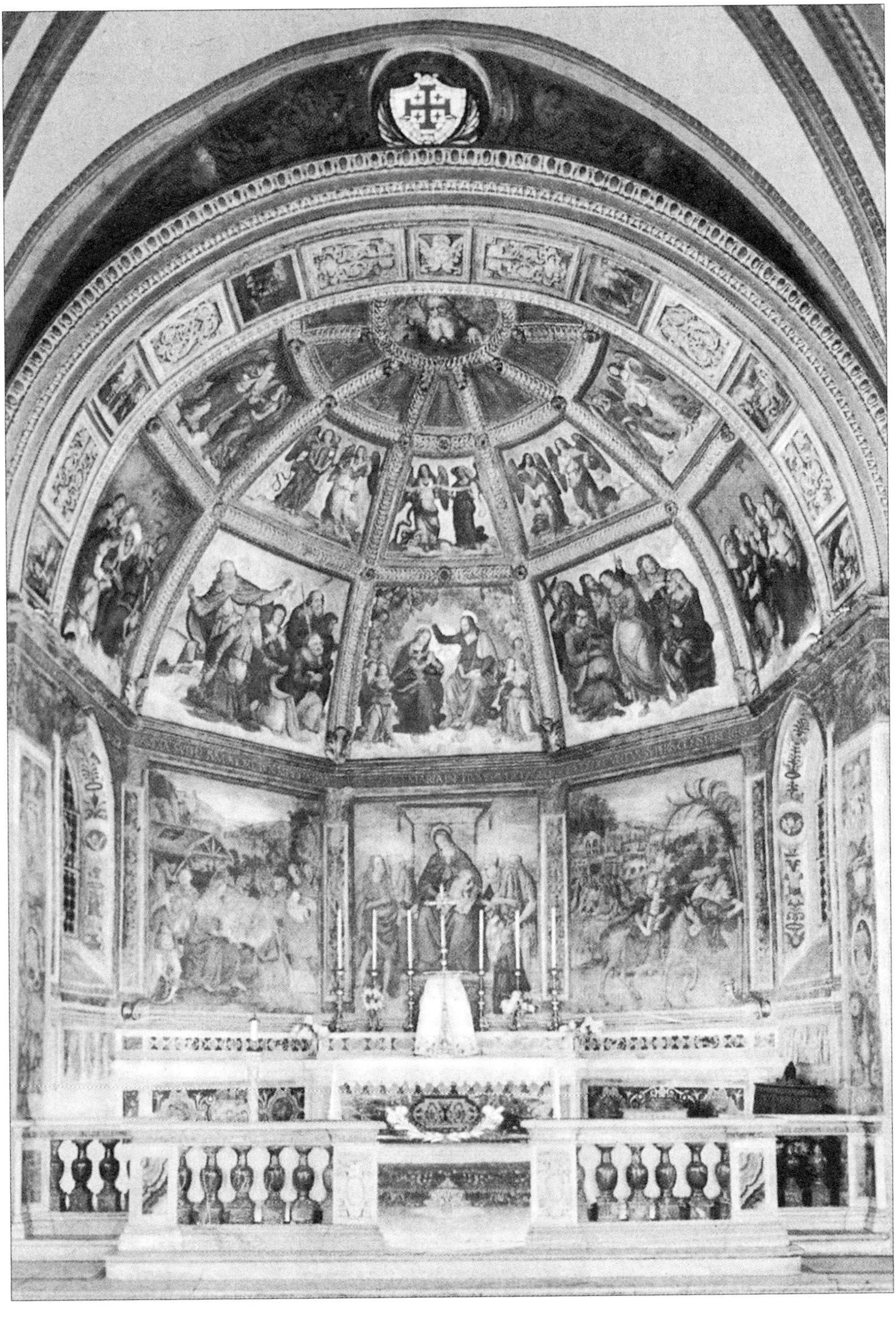

In 1989, Giuseppe Cardinal Caprio succeeded Cardinal de Fürstenberg as Grand Master of the Equestrian Order of the Holy Sepulchre of Jerusalem.

Courtesy: EOHSJ (Rome)

Order of the Holy Sepulchre to expand throughout the whole world by authorising certain knights to dub other knights outside the Basilica of the Holy Sepulchre in whatever country they were.

In 1868 Pius IX approved three classes of knights: Grand Cross, Commander and Knight, and in 1871 the Countess Mary Frances Lomas was the first woman received into the Order, but it was only in 1888 that Leo XIII formally approved the admission of women in the same three classes as existed for men, with grades equivalent to those of the knights.

In 1907 Pope St. Pius X again reserved for the Supreme Pontiff the Office of Grand Master of the Order of the Holy Sepulchre of Jerusalem to which he added 'Protector of the Order',[1] and granted to the knights the right to wear the insignia suspended from a military trophy; he also instituted a fourth grade, that of Grand Officer (Commander with Star).

Pope Benedict XV (1914-1922) retained the offices of Grand Master and Protector of the Order but in 1928 Pius XI relinquished these offices in favour of the Patriarch of Jerusalem. It is not known for certain what were the reasons that moved the Pope to instruct the Holy See to ask the Order of the Holy Sepulchre to change its appellations 'Sacred' and 'Military' and replace them with 'Equestrian', but suffice it to say that another serious dispute had arisen between the Order of Malta and the Order of the Holy Sepulchre, as a result of which in 1930 Pius XI ordered a Commission of Cardinals to adjudicate on the case. The Grand Master and spiritual head of the Order was now the Patriarch of Jerusalem, Monsignor Barlassina, and his representatives in other countries were no longer to be called Bailiff but Lieutenant.[2]

Foreseeing the outbreak of the Second World War, Monsignor Barlassina pleaded with Pope Pius XII (1939-1958) to appoint another Protector and place a high Roman Prelate in charge of the affairs of the Order. By Papal Brief of 16 July 1940 Pope Pius XII nominated a senior member of the Roman Curia, Cardinal Nicola Canali, as Protector of the Order of the Holy Sepulchre of Jerusalem.

In 1945 Pius XII decreed that the seat of government of the Order be transferred to the Vatican, and he gave the Church and Monastery of St. Onofrio to the Order as its headquarters, and the Order was placed officially under the protection of the Holy See where it has remained since.

In September 1949 Pope Pius XII approved new statutes for the Order: the office of Grand Master was transferred to a Cardinal of the Holy Roman Church, and the Latin Patriarch of Jerusalem was given the office of Grand Prior of the Order. The Order was also given the former palace of the confessors of the Basilica of St. Peter in the Via della Conciliatione

---

[1] St.Pius X restored the Order's status to that of a Pontifical Order of Knighthood. The Pope was once again Sovereign and Grand Master of the Order.
[2] The Order had not only lost its status as a Pontifical Equestrian Order, but it had been publicly degraded.

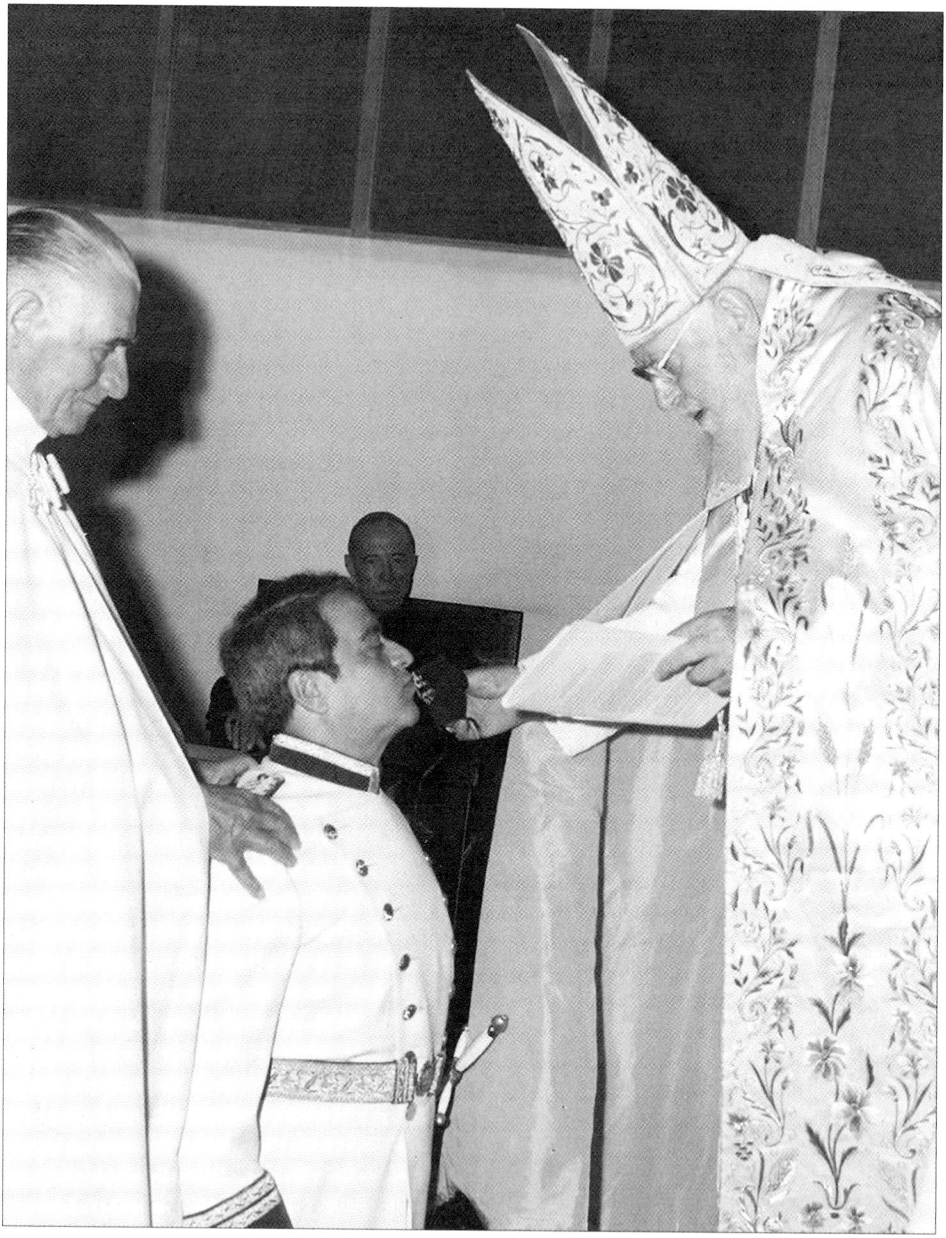

Opposite: Cardinal Tisserant investing Chev. Anthony DeSantis in Rome. Above: The Order of the Holy Sepulchre has retained the ancient custom of investing the knights by dubbing them. Left: Bishop Michael F. McAuliffe of Jefferson City, Grand Prior of the Northern Lieutenancy of the Order in the USA, dubbing Chev. Thomas E. McKiernan.

Courtesy: Grand Magisterium Rome, North Central Lieutenancy, USA.

near the Vatican for offices. Part of that palace was developed as a hotel to provide an income for the Grand Magisterium of the Order and to meet the cost of the Order's administration.[1]

The first Cardinal Grand Master to be appointed was Cardinal Canali, and he was followed by Cardinal Tisserant, who was responsible for the new statutes that were approved by Pope John XXIII in 1962. In 1973 Cardinal Maximilien de Fürstenberg became Cardinal Grand Master, and under his authority Pope Paul VI approved further new statutes in 1973. Cardinal Giuseppe Caprio succeeded Cardinal de Fürstenberg in 1989.

Since the end of the second World War the largest expansion of the Order has taken place in the United States of America.

---

[1]This unique status of the Order, being under the protection of the Holy See, a sovereign Power, and having a Cardinal as Grand Master, has given rise to some fundamental juridical questions. Because of the statutes of the Order, it can be stated categorically that the Order is not the property of the Holy See, yet being under its protection and having a Cardinal of the Holy Roman Church as its Grand Master, the Order has been set aside as something special and unique. If the Holy See's protection over the Order were to be juridically interpreted as sovereignty, the Order would have to be restructured, and its Grand Magisterium could no longer make appointments to the Order in its own right but only if given a special mandate to do so by the Holy See. In any event, such a change would not make the Order a pontifical one, but change it to an Order of the Holy See.

Knights of the Holy Sepulchre in their dress uniform and the white-plumed, black bi-cornered hat, which were substituted in 1977 with the white woollen mantle introduced by St. Pius X and a black beret-type head-dress. The mantle is only worn for religious services and for processions.

The two American members of the Grand Magisterium in Rome. Left: Vice-Governor General of Honour Alfred Blasco; right: Vice-Governor General Dr. Russell Kendall. Both are wearing the mantle and the head-dress with the embroidered rank of a Vice-Governor General and are among the twelve recipients of the Order's Grand Collar.

RELIGIOUS BUT NON-PONTIFICAL ORDERS OF KNIGHTHOOD

The Badge and Silver Star of a Grand Officer of the Order of Merit of the Equestrian Order of the Holy Sepulchre of Jerusalem.

Courtesy: Guccione, Rome

The Order is recognised in Italy and some other countries by governmental decree; however, it is not a subject of international law (as is the Sovereign Military Order of Malta), although in many countries it has the status of a legal entity in public law.

The motto of the Order is 'Deus lo vult', that given to the first Crusaders by Urban II (1088-1099). The Order now comprises five classes: Knight of the Collar, a rank established by Pius XII in 1949, and of whom there are twelve in number; Knight Grand Cross; Grand Officer (Knight Commander with Star, an honour given for special merit); Knight Commander and Knight. All these classes are also given to women in separate divisions: Dame of the Collar; Dame Grand Cross; Dame Commander with Star; Dame Commander and Dame. Some countries prefer the title Lady to Dame. Only Roman Catholics can belong to these classes, since the investiture ceremony includes a profession of faith, a pledge of exemplary Catholic life and loyalty to the Pope. The members of the Order do not take vows.

The Knights of the Order of the Holy Sepulchre have a uniform, but the revised statutes of the Order (1977) state that the wearing of the uniform is no longer obligatory; indeed, one might say it is discouraged. The uniform consists of a white dress coat with collar, cuffs and breast facing of black velvet with gold embroideries; epaulettes of twisted gold cord, white trousers with gold stripes on the sides, a sword and a bi-cornered black hat with white plumes.

To this, Pope St. Pius X added a large woollen mantle with the Jerusalem Cross of the Order in red fabric on the left side, and this mantle is now worn by the Knights of the Order by itself without the uniform,

Members of the Lieutenancy of England and Wales on pilgrimage to the Holy Land. In the first row centre, the Grand Prior, Archbishop Michael Bowen of Southwark, and on his right, wearing the beret, the former Lieutenant and Knight of the Collar Douglas Jenkins, also a member of the Grand Magisterium in Rome. The English Lieutenancy has founded several independent Lieutenancies in other English-speaking countries.

although its wearing is restricted to religious functions. A black beret-type head-dress with insignia of rank embroidered on it has taken the place of the bi-cornered plumed hat.

Dames of the Order wear a long cloak of black cloth, lined with facings of black silk, and the Cross of the Order in red fabric on the left side outlined in gold.

The Equestrian Order of the Holy Sepulchre has its own Order of Merit, that can be conferred on non-Catholics and does not imply membership of the Order. Instituted by Pius XII in 1949, it had originally five classes: Knight or Dame of the Collar; Knight or Dame Grand Cross; Knight or Dame Commander with Star; Knight or Dame Commander and Knight or Dame.

In accordance with the revised statutes, the Order of Merit now has only three classes: Grand Cross (Cross of Merit with gold Star); Grand Officer (Cross of Merit with silver Star) and Cross of Merit, which is worn as a neck badge. The Cross differs from that of the Order; it is a gold-rimmed, red-enamelled Cross *Potence*, resting on a gold crown of thorns. The Star, gold or silver, is eight-pointed, faceted, and has the red-enamelled Cross *Potence* resting on a gold crown of thorns superimposed on it. The Order confers also two special Awards:

THE PALM OF JERUSALEM
(Palma di Gerusalemme)

This Award is conferred in gold, silver and bronze by the Grand Master to those who have given special service to the Order or to the charitable work of the Order in the Holy Land. The decoration is worn on the left breast, suspended from a ribbon of black watered silk.

Permanent residents in the Holy Land and in exceptional circumstances pilgrims, may receive the Award from the Latin Patriarch of Jerusalem and Grand Prior of the Order, who will confer it only on behalf of the Cardinal Grand Master.

THE PILGRIM'S SHELL
(Conchiglia del Pellegrino)

The Pilgrim's Shell can only be awarded to members of the Order on a pilgrimage to Jerusalem by the Latin Patriarch of Jerusalem and Grand Prior of the Order on behalf of the Cardinal Grand Master. Knights and Dames wear it in the centre of the embroidered cross on their mantles.

Chapter Six

A TRANSFORMED RELIGIOUS ORDER OF KNIGHTHOOD: THE TEUTONIC ORDER

On 11 February 1991, at the conclusion of the ceremony that celebrated the 800th anniversary of the Teutonic Order receiving apostolic approval, the High Master, Priests, Brothers, Sisters and Familiars of the Order were received in audience by Pope John Paul II, who addressed them as follows:

'On 6 February 1191, my predecessor, Clement III promulgated the Papal Brief *Quotiens postulatur* and placed the Teutonic Brothers of the Church of St. Mary in Jerusalem under his papal protection. During the following centuries, including our own, several of my predecessors have

The insignia of Knights (left) and Knights of Honour of the Teutonic Order. Both Badges are still conferred.

repeatedly shown the benevolence of the Apostolic See towards the Teutonic Order.

'In 1929, the Apostolic See completed the transformation of the Teutonic Order of Knighthood into a Religious Order. At the same time the Institute of the Sisters was placed under the leadership of the High Master. Finally, in 1965, the revived Institute of Familiars was juridically recognised and subordinated to the Religious Order. Without being incorporated into the Order as Professed Members, the Familiars make an important contribution towards the good works of the Order and they contribute towards realising the ideals of the Order in today's society.'

Theoretically, the Teutonic Order (*Fratres Domus Hospitalis Sanctae Mariae Teutonicorum in Jerusalem*) belongs in the chapter dealing with long-lived Orders of Knighthood, because it ceased to be a Chivalric Order in 1929, when Pope Pius XI ratified its new constitution. However, unlike all the others, it did not become extinct, but was transformed, together with its associate organisations, the Priests (known as the Clerical Brothers), and the Sisters of the German Hospital of St. Mary in Jerusalem, into a Religious Order under the Sacred Congregation for the Religious in Rome. The Clerical Brothers make solemn perpetual vows, and the Sisters simple vows. The Familiars, mainly lay people or secular priests, make no vows but must profess the creed of the Roman Catholic Church and guarantee that because of their position in public life they will further the aims of the Order.

The Teutonic Knights were one of the three great military and religious Orders that had been founded in the Holy Land at the time of the Crusades. Their beginnings go back to the third Crusade, when in 1190 pilgrims from Bremen and Lübeck under the Duke of Holstein established a hospital for the sick of their country. There had been a German hospital in the Latin Kingdom of Jerusalem, dedicated to the Blessed Virgin Mary which had been dissolved when Jerusalem was captured by Saladin in 1187. The new hospital adopted the same name, and the son of Emperor Friedrich I Barbarossa, Friedrich Duke of Swabia, the new leader of the Crusade, appointed religious knights to protect the sick pilgrims, and the Order of the Teutonic Knights of St. Mary's Hospital in Jerusalem was founded. In 1191, the Teutonic Knights adopted the hospital rule from the Order of St. John of Jerusalem, and the military organisation from the Order of the Templars.

During the fourth Crusade the Order took possession of its first house in Jerusalem, St. Mary of the Germans (1229), but the Teutonic Knights left Palestine in 1291 when it finally fell to Islam.

A second career for their belligerent and religious zeal was opened in Eastern Europe in the Baltic region against the pagans of Prussia, who had hitherto resisted the efforts of missionaries, many of whom had been killed in their endeavours. Because the Military Order of the Sword

Bearers, which had been founded with the object of avenging the murdered missionaries, had failed, the Polish Duke Conrad of Massovia asked the Teutonic Knights to assist him in defeating the Prussian pagans and promised the Order the territory of Culm, plus whatever territory they could conquer from the infidels. The struggle lasted twenty-five years, and owing to special privileges granted to the Teutonic colonists, the entire country belonging to the Letto-Slavic race was Germanized, and the subsequent history of this military principality is identified with that of Prussia.

After the Lithuanians had also been defeated by the Teutonic Knights, and after the Lithuanian Grand Duke Jagellon, who embraced Christianity, had married the heiress to the Kingdom of Poland in 1386, paganism ended in Europe, and the Teutonic Knights had lost their *raison d'être*, so that from then on, their history consisted of incessant conflicts with the Kings of Poland, until they were finally defeated and lost more than half of their territory, but they were allowed to hold the rest under the suzerainty of the Polish King.

The Grand Master's residence was moved from Marienburg to Königsberg in Germany, and the Knights offered the grand-mastership to German Princes in order to strengthen their security against the Kings of Poland. However, the second of the German Grand Masters, Albert von Brandenburg, embraced Lutheranism, secularised Prussia and made it an hereditary Duchy under the suzerainty of the Polish Crown.

Those Knights who broke with the apostate chose a new Grand Master who moved his residence to Franconia in 1526, but these Teutonic Knights lost their remaining twelve Bailiwicks in Germany one by one, and when in 1809 Napoleon abandoned the possessions belonging to the Teutonic Knights to the Confederation of the Rhine, the Knights retained only their Bailiwicks in Tyrol and Austria.

The Teutonic Order thus became purely Austrian under the supreme authority of the Emperor of Austria, who reserved the grand-mastership for an archduke of his house. Archduke Eugene of Austria, who became Grand Master in 1894, resigned his grand-mastership in 1923 when, after the fall of the Austrian Empire, allegations were made that the property of the Teutonic Order really belonged to the House of Habsburg. Pope Pius XI accepted the Archduke's resignation, and during the next six years the Order of the Teutonic Knights changed its character and constitution and became a religious Order.

The members of the Brotherhood of the German Hospital in Jerusalem suffered badly under the rule of the Third Reich; unfortunately the persecution of the religious Teutonic Order coincided with the phenomenon of a mystical and historically indefensible glorification of the ancient Knights of Prussia which had begun to spread throughout Germany just before Hitler came to power. When the Nazis established an

H.R.H. Archduke Eugen of Austria resigned as High Master of the Teutonic Order in 1923 rather than allow malicious rumours that the property of the Teutonic Order belonged to the Imperial and Royal House of Habsburg to damage the Order.

Order which they called the 'Teutonic Order', they also fabricated a complete mythology for the Prussian Teutonic Knights who, so it was claimed, had been the forerunners of the Third Reich. Sadly, the history of the real Teutonic Order became confused in the minds of many, especially in Germany, Austria and German-speaking regions in Eastern Europe, and even after the second World War, when the religious Teutonic Order, had its property restored by the new Austrian Government, it still suffered from the effects of Nazi propaganda, although it had been the first Order to have lost all its property and been dissolved.

The Order is active in parish work, hospitals, old people's homes, schools and training colleges. The High Master has the same powers and authority as the Superior General of other religious Orders, the Order has its own ProcuratorGeneral at the Holy See, and a General Chapter meets every six years at which are elected the higher officers of the Order, including an Assistant-General for the religious Sisters. The Provinces are administered by Priors, and every convent has its own Father or Mother Superior. In 1983 the Order had thirty clerical and ten lay Brothers, 500 religious Sisters and about 400 Familiars, of whom twelve were Knights of Honour. Although the Order is very active today in the true hospitaller spirit of chivalry, it is no longer an Order of Knighthood.

The habits of the clerical and lay Brothers, the mantles of the Familiars and the insignia, the Teutonic Cross, are reminiscent of the dress and insignia worn by the Teutonic Knights. It is remarkable that in spite of its

Two senior Officers of the Teutonic Order escort the Grand Prior of Austria of the Sovereign Military Order of Malta, senior Knights of Malta and Pontifical Knights in a religious procession prior to 1929.

turbulent history the Teutonic Order survived so long as an Order of Knighthood, and although it belongs theoretically among the extinct Orders of Knighthood, its tenacity to survive, both as an Order of Knighthood and under the Nazi persecution as a religious Order, justifies a chapter of its own in this work.

Chapter Seven

DYNASTIC ORDERS OF KNIGHTHOOD

Every dynastic Order belongs to a sovereign Royal House and remain its property even if the Dynasty is non-regnant. They are often called 'House Orders' or 'Family Orders', and the Grand Master is usually the Head of the Royal House, although the headship of a dynasty and the grand-mastership of a dynastic Order of Knighthood need not necessarily be held by the same person.

Dynastic Orders of a reigning Royal House do not belong to the Crown as head of State, and a monarch who is forced into exile can take the dynastic Orders with him or her and continue to bestow them, because they were originally instituted to reward personal services to the Head of Dynasty or Royal House. On his death, the grand-mastership normally passes to the heir. Archbishop H.E. Cardinale, a foremost international and canon lawyer, to name but one of many who have written books on this subject, always maintained and counselled the Holy See that a monarch, although he may abdicate as Sovereign of his country, does not renounce the grand-mastership or sovereignty over the dynastic Orders of Knighthood, and his possible renunciation of a grand-mastership is not binding on his legitimate heirs who have inherent rights of which they cannot be deprived. However, a renunciation is valid when made in accordance with family or dynastic laws if there is no heir living who would otherwise have inherent rights.

Mons. Cardinale's counsel was sought by Pius XII in the 1950s, when the Pontiff prepared his official position with regard to the Italian Republican Government and its relations with King Umberto of Italy and his infant son Prince Victor Emmanuel, now the Duke of Savoy and Head of the Royal House of Savoy of Italy.

Opposite: A decorative shield depicting a knight in prayer before a statue of the Blessed Virgin in the upper half, and St. George slaying the dragon in the lower half. In the bordure above are the words 'REGINA EQUITUM CHRISTIANORUM O.P.N.' – 'Queen of Christian Knights, pray for us' –. The border is decorated with Pontifical, Religious and Dynastic Orders of Knighthood which are (clockwise starting on the right): the Supreme Order of Christ, (Holy See); the Order of Pius IX, (Holy See); the Order of St. Gregory the Great, (Holy See); the Order of Pope St. Sylvester, (Holy See); the Order of the Holy Sepulchre; The Sacred and Military Constantinian Order of St. George (Two Sicilies); the Sovereign Military Order of Malta; [the Papal Insignia]; the Order of St. Hubert (Bavaria); the Royal Order of St. Januarius, (Two Sicilies); The Noble Order of the Golden Fleece (Austria and Spain); the Monastic Military Order of Alcantara and Calatrava, (Spain); the Monastic Military Order of Santiago, (Spain); the Order of SS. Maurice and Lazarus, (Savoy); the Order of the Golden Spur, (Holy See). *[W.E. Maitre Sculp. – Valdausa Invent.]*

Courtesy: Bali Achille di Lorenzo

A Sovereign in exile, and after him his legitimate heirs and successors as Head of the Dynasty or Grand Master, continue to enjoy the *Ius Collationis*, the right to confer honours, and therefore continue lawfully to bestow honours, provided the Order itself is extant. Unless the Order was given in perpetual trusteeship to the Dynasty by the Apostolic See, no authority can deprive them of the right to confer honours, since this prerogative belongs to them as a lawful personal property by *iure sanguinis* – right of blood and both its possession and exercise are inviolable.

These rules have always been applicable when the Orders in question have at one time been solemnly recognised by the Supreme Authority of the Apostolic See and therefore fall into the category of Catholic-founded Orders of Knighthood. No secular or political authority has the right to suppress this recognition when it has been established in official documents, such as Papal Bulls, by merely issuing unilateral decrees of suppression or abolition. So long as the recognition has not been revoked by the Apostolic See itself, canonically the Order must be considered extant. However, even if the Apostolic See withdraws its recognition and the Order becomes secularised, the rights of Heads of Dynasties and Grand Masters remain inviolate under international law, unless the Order is the property of the Apostolic See, when withdrawal of recognition means the abolition or temporary placement in abeyance of an Order. However, every legitimate political authority is entitled to forbid the wearing of such Orders and insignia within its territory according to its own rules concerning the wearing of decorations.

A sovereign Monarch can give or surrender a dynastic Order to the Crown, which is a separate legal entity, and with this act it belongs to the State, and then becomes a State Order in the sole possession of that State.

There exists a widely-held misconception about one particular matter which is alleged to disqualify a legitimate heir from inheriting either the headship of a Dynasty or the grand-mastership of a Catholic-founded Order of Knighthood. Some people maintain that the Holy See would not recognise the Head of a non-regnant royal house or Grand Master of a Catholic-founded Order if he has entered into a morganatic marriage or is the offspring of a morganatic marriage. However, if the person has entered into a canonically valid Catholic marriage, the Holy See will recognise that union and its legitimate issue. The Holy See is not concerned with the secular issues of morganatic marriages, if they exist in a Dynasty, and only a breach of the laws of marriage laid down in the *Codex Iuris Canonici* would have a bearing on the Holy See's recognition of the marriage or the legitimacy of the issue of such a marriage under canon law, as the Church applies these laws to all the faithful, disregarding their social standing.

It is necessary to explain first the use of the term 'Catholic' as applied in this chapter to dynasties and dynastic Orders of Knighthood, because the criterion for inclusion in this section is the Roman Catholic character of legitimate dynastic Orders of Knighthood conferred by legitimate heads of dynasties.

The *Codex Iuris Canonici* (28 January 1983), Book II, Title V, deals with 'Associations of Christ's Faithful' and the right to use the appellation 'Catholic'.

Dynasties no longer use the appellation 'Catholic'. Even countries with large Roman Catholic populations, such as Italy, Spain and Portugal, no longer accept the Roman Catholic Faith as their state religion. King Juan Carlos I of Spain gave up using the title 'Most Catholic Majesty' which had been bestowed upon one of his ancestors, and expressly asked for it to be removed from the caption under his portrait in the 1985 edition of Archbishop Cardinale's work. His Majesty felt that the use of this ancient title could be interpreted as prejudicial to other religious denominations in Spain. There were expressly Catholic dynasties in the past, and today the principle *cuius regio, illius religio* (religion goes with the land), an outgrowth of the Reformation, has been universally abolished.

The term 'Catholic' is therefore applied to dynasties in a descriptive rather than legal term; it implies no more than that the head and members of the royal family embrace the Roman Catholic religion. It must be stressed that the Catholicity of a royal house, regnant or non-regnant, is a matter of tradition and not law.

The position with regard to Catholic and Catholic-founded Orders of Knighthood is different, although the purpose of defining whether an Order is Catholic or Catholic-founded is merely to establish the criterion for the Order's inclusion in this section. As well as the laws and rules imposed on dynastic Orders of Knighthood by the civil authorities of the respective countries where the Orders are domiciled, those using the appellation 'Catholic' in their letters patent, in their statutes, or in the description of the Order's character, are subject to the codes of canon law which govern the right of private associations to use the appellation or description 'Catholic', even by implication. No dynastic Order of Knighthood uses the appellation 'Catholic' in its name. There can, however, be little doubt that Orders with names like 'of the Most Holy Annunciation' or 'of Our Lady of the Conception of Vila Viçosa' have a profoundly Catholic character.

Although knighthoods of Pontifical Equestrian Orders have on occasion been conferred on non-Catholics and even non-Christians, full membership of the Sovereign Military Order of Malta, the Equestrian Order of the Holy Sepulchre of Jerusalem, The Order of the Golden Fleece of Austria (House of Habsburg) and the dynastic Sacred Military Constantinian Order of St. George of the Two Sicilies, has hitherto been restricted to Roman Catholics.

The legal position of the Pontifical Orders of Knighthood and that of the two Religious but not Pontifical Orders – the Equestrian Order of the Holy Sepulchre of Jerusalem and the Sovereign Military Order of Malta – have already been defined in the respective chapters. The criterion upon which Orders of Knighthood have been classified in this work as Catholic-founded dynastic Orders is that they must have fulfilled at the time of their foundation the conditions laid down in the code of canon law as stated in the 1983 edition of the *Codex Iuris Canonici* in canon 298, 1; canon 299, 1-3 and canon 300.

Canon 313 regards by implication the juridical definition of dynastic Orders of Knighthood as *'private* associations' because it states that a *public* association 'receives its mission to pursue, in the name of the Church, those ends which it proposes for itself'. No Order of Knighthood has the power or right to speak 'in the name of the Church'.

The definition 'Catholic-founded Orders of Knighthood' has been applied to Orders that were bilaterally founded by a sovereign head of state and the Supreme Pontiff who issued a bull confirming the foundation or granting special privileges to the Order. Often, successive Pontiffs endorsed an Order's statutes and added more privileges with further bulls or papal briefs. Sometimes Catholic-founded Orders were founded by the sovereign head of state and subsequently received pontifical approval of the Order's aims by papal bull or papal brief. A Catholic-founded Order can be secularised with papal approval, or unilaterally suppressed, become dormant, but subsequently be revived as a secular Order of Merit. This does not alter the historical fact that it was Catholic-founded.

The appellation 'Catholic-founded' has also been applied to dynastic Orders that have been expressly placed, with the approval of the appropriate apostolic authority, under the patronage of a Roman Catholic Saint in order to extol virtues associated with the Saint. Examples are the Order of St. Charles of Monaco which was placed under the protection of St. Charles Borromeo; the Spanish Order of Carlos III which was placed under the protection of the Immaculate Conception of the Virgin, as its aim was to defend the Catholic religion and extol that mystery; and the Spanish Order of Isabel la Catolica which was given special papal approval by Pius VII in 1816. The operative criterion is not the name of the Saint that is given to the Order but the apostolic approval. This is the reason why, for example, the Russian Orders prior to the 1917 Revolution, all of which were given the name of a Saint, do not qualify for inclusion in this book. St. Andrew, St. Anne and St. George, to name but three, are also Saints in the Orthodox Church, and Orders named after them did not receive the approval of the Apostolic See.

It cannot be stressed too strongly that if a Cardinal, a Patriarch, an Archbishop or a Bishop accepts membership of, or decorations from, a

self-styled Order of Knighthood, this act does not constitute recognı
or approval of that organisation by the Apostolic See.[1]

It can be argued that some organisations operate under canon 312 1 /2°
or 3° on a national or diocesan basis and call themselves a 'Catholic Order
of Knighthood'. It is quite legal for a private Catholic charitable
association to do so; however, this does not confer chivalric status upon
an organisation.

The criteria for possessing chivalric status, or dynastic matters
appertaining to an Order of Knighthood, are laid down by temporal
international law, unless a Supreme Pontiff has placed an Order into the
perpetual trusteeship of a reigning Dynasty but reserved to the Apostolic
See the prerogative of ultimate sovereignty. In such cases those rules
apply that were laid down in the statutes promulgated by the Supreme
Pontiff who placed the Order into the trusteeship of a Royal Dynasty.
Whenever certain prerogatives in an Order of Knighthood have been
reserved to the Apostolic See, the Supreme Pontiff *pro tempore* is the
Supreme Sovereign of that Order, in spite of the fact that the Order has
been placed into the perpetual trusteeship of a Dynasty. The dynastic
character of the Order is in no way affected by such a provision; it was
merely designed to ensure that the Grand Master of the Order, who is
usually also the Head of the Dynasty, does not abuse or neglect the
obligations placed upon him by his high office.

Since the reign of Paul VI, the Holy See has been reluctant to comment
on, or intervene in, matters concerning the non-regnant Catholic
Dynasties that bestow Catholic-founded Orders of Knighthood,
notwithstanding any prerogatives retained in those Orders by the
Apostolic See as a result of the papal bulls of earlier pontiffs. As a matter
of principle, the Secretariat of State of His Holiness has restricted itself to
stating publicly that the only Roman Catholic Orders officially endorsed
by the Holy See are the five Pontifical Orders of Knighthood: the Supreme
Order of Christ, the Order of the Golden Spur, the Order of Pius IX (also
known as the Pian Order), the Order of St. Gregory the Great, and the
Order of Pope St. Sylvester.

The Holy See expressly recognises as Roman Catholic Orders only the
Equestrian Order of the Holy Sepulchre of Jerusalem, which Pius XII
placed under the direct patronage of the Holy See and to which the
Supreme Pontiff appoints a Cardinal Grand Master, and the Sovereign
Military Order of Malta which, although a sovereign entity, is also a
Religious Order of Knighthood, the Grand Master of which must be
approved after his election by the Supreme Pontiff.

In cases where the Holy See used to appoint Cardinal Patrons or
Protectors, no objection is raised when Cardinals and other high

---

[1] See: Chapter Thirteen: 'Unrecognised Organisations styling Themselves Orders of Knighthood'.

dignitaries accept the position of Prior or Spiritual Counsellor. This applies mainly to dynastic Orders, especially those whose link with the Papacy has remained strong.

The Apostolic See recognises all Orders of Knighthood and Awards of Merit conferred by sovereign States. Several senior Catholic dynastic Orders of Knighthood of non-regnant Royal Houses have always been held in high esteem by, and enjoyed a close relationship with, the Apostolic See because of their traditional loyalty to the Papacy. Among them are the Order of the Golden Fleece of the Imperial and Royal House of Habsburg, the Sacred Military Constantinian Order of St. George of the Royal House of Bourbon Two Sicilies, the Order of Our Lady of the Conception of Vila Viçosa of the Royal House of Portugal, and the Orders of the Most Holy Annunciation and of SS. Maurice and Lazarus of the Royal House of Savoy – Italy.

The esteem these dynastic Orders enjoy with the Apostolic See is solely due to their strong Catholic character which is enshrined in the statutes of these Orders. If a strictly Catholic dynastic Order of Knighthood of a non-regnant royal house were to be secularised or the Order's statutes fundamentally changed after they had been originally endorsed by a Supreme Pontiff when the Order belonged to a regnant royal house, the Order could not automatically claim to be 'an Order recognised by the Holy See'. It would be illogical for such an Order to claim recognition by the Apostolic See because of its former Catholic character.

An Order of Knighthood that has been placed in the perpetual trusteeship of a Royal Dynasty that has since become non-regnant, but the ultimate spiritual sovereignty of which had technically belonged to the Apostolic See (as explained above), cannot by the sole volition of its Grand Master *pro tempore* or a Council of its Officers secularise itself and retain at the same time its Catholic status.

It is doubtful that the Apostolic See would oppose a Grand Master or Head of a non-regnant Dynasty if he unilaterally secularised a dynastic Order, but that Order would obviously lose its Catholic character and could no longer lay claim to a special relationship with, or recognition based on tradition by, the Apostolic See. Legally, it would have placed itself in the category of secular dynastic Orders, although is was Catholic-founded.

A non-regnant head of a dynasty cannot found a new Order or revive an old Order that was formally abolished by a reigning head of the dynasty. That is not permitted under international law, even if he were to use the name and statutes of a former Catholic Order, and these criteria have been applied in this book. A newly founded Order, established by a non-regnant head of a dynasty, would have to be placed among the self-styled orders that enjoy no recognition.

We are entering here a grey area as far as dormant dynastic Orders are concerned:[1] if a dormant Order is revived by a non-regnant head of a dynasty, unforeseen problems can arise which may lead to complications which could also compromise the legitimate dynastic Orders of the royal house. In this context I must put the record straight concerning one such dormant Order which in 1986 I accepted as being a lawful revival of the Order that was founded in 1171. Without wishing to cast any aspersions on the Order of St. Michael of the Wing (founded in 1171 by Dom Alfonso I, King of Portugal, I acted prematurely when I included the revived, dormant Order among the Dynastic Catholic Orders of Knighthood in *The Cross on the Sword* in 1987.

There is no doubt about the Order's origin and history up to the beginning of the nineteenth century. Although I was familiar with the Order's subsequent history including its political underground activities, especially after 1834, I did not fully appreciate the implications of two important developments which strongly militated against the revival of that Order as a dynastic Order of Knighthood. After *The Cross on the Sword* had been published, a leading expert on Iberian history and constitutional jurist explained to me the difficulties that would arise if the former 'Secret Society of St. Michael of the Wing' were to be revived as a dynastic Order of Knighthood.

The original Order became a 'Secret Society' after the King, Dom Miguel I, was forced to go into exile, and while the religious aims of the Secret Society were firmly based on traditional Catholic ideology, its political aims were partisan and against the constitutional Sovereigns. These political objectives remained the same after 1910, though the constitutional Monarch (Dom Manuel II) had gone into exile and Portugal had become a Republic. The second development that deprived the 'Secret Society of St. Michael of the Wing' of its *raison d'être* was the Pact of Paris, signed in 1922 by H.M. King Dom Manuel II and H.R.H. Dom Duarte Nuno, Duke of Bragança, in which the King agreed that Dom Duarte Nuno, as the lineal successor of King Miguel I, would become Head of the Royal House of Bragança of Portugal if King Manuel II should die without issue, which he did. Before rectifying the section on 'St. Michael of the Wing' for this book, I have taken counsel from experts and discussed the problem with H.R.H. Dom Duarte Pio, Duke of Bragança, who immediately accepted the advice of the experts, agreed to the change of status and signed the documents containing the alterations.

In 1992, H.R.H. Dom Duarte Pio, the Duke of Bragança redefined the status and style of 'St. Michael of the Wing' as 'a knightly order, open to men and women dedicated to charitable works in education and support of Portuguese citizens abroad and in Portugal'. He also opened the

---

[1]The three dynastic Orders of the Royal House of Bourbon-Orléans are an example. They have not been conferred for many decades but have not been abolished.

knightly order to Christians of other than the Catholic religion and to foreigners as associate members.

It is important to clarify the question of reviving dormant Orders and leave no ambiguity which could be wrongly interpreted. Three questions cannot be answered: when does an Order become officially dormant? Does a dormant Order cease to exist after a specified period of time? If an Order has not been placed in abeyance but is not conferred, is it dormant?

I doubt that an arbitrary period of time would satisfy jurists with regard to considering such an Order legally extinct if the legitimate successor to the last reigning Head of the Dynasty were to revive it. Whether or not the House of Bourbon-Orléans will once again confer its dynastic Orders in the near future remains to be seen. I personally believe it is reasonable to assume that if four generations of heads of dynasties do not confer an Order, that Order should be regarded as extinct, but I would prefer one of them to issue an official document to that effect.

There is, however, no firm rule on the question of time. As can be seen in the case of the four Monastic-Military Orders of Alcantara, of Calatrava, of Montesa, and of Santiago, they were suppressed by the Spanish Republic in 1931, abolished by law passed in the Cortes in 1934, and Generalisimo Franco did not revive them after he had become the Head of State of Spain. Almost half a century after their abolition, H.R.H. Don Juan, Count of Barcelona, the father of King Juan Carlos of Spain, who also inherited the appellation of 'Grand Master and Perpetual Administrator by Apostolic Authority of the Monastic Military Orders', was given the title 'Dean President' of the four Orders which he built up again. He was succeeded in 1993 by H.R.H. Don Carlos, now Infante of Spain, as 'Dean President'. All the information I had received from the Holy See until 1990, pointed to the four Orders being extinct since 1934, However, Guy Stair Sainty repudiates this viewpoint in his latest book and states that the Holy See did not recognise laws passed by the Cortes in 1934.

The secular rules universally applied to dynastic Orders of Knighthood are very strict. As a matter of principle, many sovereign countries only recognise honours and decorations bestowed by reigning sovereigns or sovereign states to whom they accord diplomatic recognition. This can, on occasion, create paradoxical situations. For example H.M. Constantine II, King of the Hellenes, went into voluntary exile in 1967 without actually abdicating. The constitutional position of King Constantine remained unsettled until 1974 when Greece became a Republic. Although His Majesty was diplomatically represented abroad only until 1967, he never abdicated his status as *fons honorum* of the dynastic Orders of Knighthood and Merit.

As soon the new Greek government was recognised by the governments of foreign countries, including Great Britain, where King

Constantine took up residence, the dynastic Orders of the Greek Royal Family, the House of Schleswig-Holstein-Sonderburg-Glücksburg, were no longer granted recognition when subsequently conferred by the King. Only requests for permission to wear decorations conferred by the Head of new Government were submitted to the Heads of State that had recognised the new regime in Greece.

The secular dynastic Orders of many European royal houses that became non-regnant after the World Wars I and II became part of history, although some dynasties continue to bestow their House Orders on members of their family. In this context special mention should be made of the secular dynastic Order of the Royal House of Savoy, Ordine Al Merito Civile di Savoia. Prior to dealing with the Order – quite peripherally, because it does not fall within the scope of this work not being a Catholic-founded Order – I corresponded with representatives of H.R.H. Victor Emmanuel, Duke of Savoy, son of the late King Umberto II, and Head of the Royal House of Savoy. I received the assurance that this was not a new Order, instituted by the Head of a non-regnant Royal House, but a change of statutes of an existing, legitimate Order, that had been brought up to date. Because circumstances had changed, and the criteria of conferment of the existing Order – the Ordine Civile di Savoia, which had been founded in 1831 by H.R.H. Carlo Alberto, King of Sardinia and Duke of Savoy – had become impractical, the hereditary Grand Master legitimately changed the relevant statutes. Originally, the intended recipients were mainly subjects of his kingdom and servants of the State, and although the Duke of Savoy sanctioned some revisions to the statutes in 1985, they were obviously not expanded sufficiently to fulfil the contemporary requirements of a secular Order of Merit of the House of Savoy in exile. Most of the recipients would inevitably be foreigners and not Italians, and even the latter were *de jure* and *de facto* no longer subjects of the Royal House but citizens of the Italian Republic.

I was assured that the Duke of Savoy, in his capacity as Head of the Royal House and hereditary Grand Master of the Ordine Civile di Savoia, had changed its title to Ordine Al Merito Civile di Savoia, with modified statutes, in 1988. Nevertheless, there are critics who maintain that the Duke of Savoy has instituted a new Order; they may have been misled by a booklet published by the Cancelleria degli Ordini Dinastici della Real Casa di Savoia, which, apart from giving the statutes of the 1831 Ordine di Civile di Savoia, gave separately those of the Ordine Al Merito Civile di Savoia.

It can be argued that the fortune of Catholic dynastic Orders has always been inextricably linked to the lay apostolate which membership of these Orders entails. The Apostolic See as *Mater et Magistra* of all Catholic-founded Orders of Knighthood continued to give spiritual guidance and comfort to the members of those dynastic Orders that continued in the lay

Top left: the red robe of the Savoyan Order of SS. Maurice and Lazarus. The Cross of the Order is displayed on the front. Above: the blue cape of the S.M. Constantinian Order of St. George of the House of the Two Sicilies; The Cross of the Order is worn on the left side, and the red collar is embroidered with laurel leaves according to the rank. Left: the white robe of the Portuguese Order of Our Lady of the Conception of Vila Viçosa of the Royal House of Bragança. It has a royal blue velvet collar and two broad velvet stripes along the front. The large gold tinsel star is on the left breast.

apostolate of the Church. Several of them are still participating actively in the ceremonial and liturgical life of the Church, and their knights walk in procession, wearing their distinctive church robes, such as the red robe of the Order of SS. Maurice and Lazarus (Savoy), the white mantle of the Order of the Conception of Our Lady of Vila Viçosa, and the blue mantle of the S.M.Constantinian Order of St. George (Two Sicilies).

It is the continued active lay apostolate of the Catholic dynastic Orders, that gives them not only their purpose but justifies and ensures their continuity of existence.

The position of the Holy See with regard to Catholic non-regnant Royal Dynasties is a delicate one. The main problem arises from the Holy See's commitment under international law to honour its obligations towards *de jure* and *de facto* governments of sovereign states. Many monarchies have become republics, and whilst not necessarily rejecting old friends and centuries of close collaboration with reigning dynasties, the Holy See cannot support royalist movements in republics, as this would be interpreted as unacceptable interference in internal national affairs. The relationship of the Apostolic See with heads of non-regnant royal dynasties is entirely based on the personal esteem in which the Supreme Pontiff holds the individual head and members of such royal families.

The present pragmatic approach of the Holy See in its role as a sovereign power means that it is no longer possible to speak of it having a special relationship with any of the Catholic-founded Orders: all three editions of Archbishop Cardinale's book refer to relationships that no longer exist. On the other hand, the quite different function of the Apostolic See allows it to maintain relations with heads of dynasties and extant Catholic-founded Orders of Knighthood.

Almost all reigning monarchs and their successors, who became non-regnant heads of royal houses, were initially forced to live in exile. In 1861 King Francis II of the Two Sicilies was given refuge by Pope Pius IX, who thus reciprocated the asylum given to the Pontiff himself in Naples a few years earlier. When, almost a century later the Savoyan King Umberto II left Italy after a referendum on the monarchy in 1946, the republican government of Italy passed a law exiling the King and his direct male descendants, prohibiting their setting foot on Italian soil. Before leaving Italy, King Umberto took leave of Pope Pius XII in the Vatican, and the Pontiff assured him that the Holy See would always respect the Catholic dynastic character of the Orders of SS. Annunziata and SS. Maurice and Lazarus.

In most cases laws exiling descendants or successors of former reigning monarchs have been relaxed after some decades. For example, in 1950 the National Assembly of the Republic of Portugal invited the Head of the Royal House of Bragança and his family to return to Portugal, the last King of Portugal and his legitimate successors having lived abroad since

1910. The first official visit the then Head of the Royal House, Dom Duarte Nuno, Duke of Bragança, paid after his return from exile was to the Supreme Pontiff, so that his son, the present Duke of Bragança, Dom Duarte Pio, could pay homage to his Godfather, Pope Pius XII.

Another serious problem facing many non-regnant royal dynasties since the end of the Second World War, are the self-styled, spurious pretenders to several dynasties that have appeared in drove, and on occasion they have caused acute embarrassment to the Apostolic See. The problem is aggravated by people who for their own social advancement, ingratiate and attach themselves to the courts of non-regnant royal houses or, failing to gain the expected advancement there, to self-styled pretenders. These social climbers can often be found attached to more than one dynasty or dynastic Order of Knighthood, usually looking for an office to give them a power base from which to plan their intrigues. They are like malignant growths: by the time they are recognised for what they are, the cancer has usually grown beyond the chance of a simple cure.

This is an appropriate place to expose the outrageous claims made by some of these self-styled pretenders to dynasties or grand-masterships to Orders of Knighthood, who have had photographs of themselves published in their publicity brochures, showing them with Pope John Paul II and claiming that this constitutes *ipso facto* recognition of their status. It is a well known fact that the Pope walks along the barriers behind which thousands of people stand, attending one of the public audiences. It is also known that the Pope greets personally hundreds of pilgrims who have come to see him. Many of them offer gifts to the Holy Father, and he always makes a point of establishing as much personal contact as possible.

On several occasions people have been seen to divest themselves of their overcoat or cloak on the approach of the Holy Father. Under their plain coat or cloak they wore a fantasy uniform or formal evening dress and all possible orders and decorations. They usually offered a gift to the Holy Father, such as a book, and the papal photographers, who after the audiences sell large colour prints of the Pope with groups or individuals, have obligingly taken pictures of these imposters in their fantasy uniforms. What has happened in some cases is not difficult to discern. Cutting off the lower part of the picture which shows the person actually standing behind a barrier and further trimming the photograph, they now have a picture showing the Holy Father with men in uniform or formal dress, profusely decorated with decorations, handing the pope a book. These pictures are then reproduced as proof of a private audience with the Pope.

In 1990 a photograph was published that showed the Papal Secretary of State, Cardinal Agostino Casaroli, in full mass vestments, surrounded by members of a self-styled chivalric order. It so happens that this order is frowned upon by the Holy See in general and by Cardinal Casaroli in particular, because it is one of the imitation orders of the Sovereign Military Order of Malta. Cardinal Casaroli was not aware that such a photograph had been published, claiming recognition of the order by the Holy See and stating that the Cardinal had celebrated Mass for the members of that self-styled order. Immediate enquiries revealed that after celebrating a Mass, Cardinal Casaroli found himself suddenly surrounded by a group of black-clad men and women, claiming to be from the Order of Malta, and somebody took a photograph. He never knew who they were until he was shown the published photograph in a book publicising that spurious organisation which used both a photograph with His Holiness and the one with the Cardinal Secretary of State to give credence to their self-styled order of chivalry and the spurious decorations.

Countless spurious dukes and princes, dressed up and covered in all manner of decorations and claiming to be heads of royal, ducal and princely dynasties, have had their picture taken with the Holy Father; hundreds of these misleading pictures have been distributed, sometimes to magazines that have published them with invented stories about somebody's claims to a title. It is particularly deplorable that such ambitious social climbers use elderly and infirm cardinals or ecclesiastical dignitaries in their schemes for deceiving the general public. This is a facet of these spurious organisations which has rarely been published, and it would be naive to believe that all elderly cardinals and ecclesiastical dignitaries retain their unimpaired powers of judgement and reasoning until they die. They are human beings like everyone else, and in old age and a few, most sadly, suffer a deterioration of their faculty, and are unable to distinguish a genuine prince from a theatrical imposter, especially if the latter wears a magnificent uniform and the real prince a lounge suit.

I do not blame the popular press for making the most of such imaginative stories; they appeal to a certain type of readership and are usually accompanied by marvellous photographs. However, in a serious appraisal of Catholic-founded dynastic Orders of Knighthood it is important to draw reader's attention to this unwelcome phenomenon which has grown considerably since the end of the Second World War.

His Holiness regularly receives Heads of Catholic Dynasties in private audience, such visits taking place in the Pope's library or private apartments.

The High Historical Consultant of the Sovereign Military Order of Malta, H.E. Frà Cyril, the Prince Toumanoff, is a well-known historian and expert on self-styled pretenders, princes, orders and the entourage of *arrampicatori sociali* that can be found everywhere. In various publications, Frà Cyril has highlighted many of the abuses committed by such people,

H.R.H. Dom Duarte Pio, Duke of Bragança, Head of the Royal House of Portugal, in private audience with Pope John Paul II in the Pontiff's library.

Courtesy: *L'Osservatore Romano*

especially abuses against the Supreme Pontiff, the Apostolic See and the Sovereign Military Order of Malta. In an appendix of the 1985 edition of Archbishop Cardinale's book, Frà Cyril Toumanoff listed nineteen self-styled orders, all imitating the Sovereign Military Order of Malta. He also published a book *Les Dynasties de la Caucasie Chrétienne* (Rome 1990), which contains well-researched genealogical tables that have made it more difficult for these self-styled princes, dukes and grand-masters of fantasy orders from far-off countries to keep up their pretence.

The third, but perhaps most serious, threat to the continuity of several non-regnant dynasties lies within the royal families themselves. Because the legitimacy of their titles is not in question, the criterion *noblesse oblige* is sometimes not adhered to by some members of the family, who look upon their titles as a commercial asset or commodity which provides them with a comfortable income.

It follows that grand-masterships to dynastic Orders of Knighthood must undergo the same scrutiny with regard to their legitimacy as do the heads of dynasties.

A new argument has recently been introduced in the debate concerning non-regnant dynasties and their dynastic Orders. In a debate concerning spurious orders, especially the imitation orders of the Order of Malta, it was suggested that a solution could be found in an international ruling that as a matter of principle the recognition of a *fons honorum* should expressly exclude heads of dynasties who abuse their position by aiding self-styled orders.

Whilst the majority in the Roman Curia feel that the authenticity of a dynastic Order does not depend on the quality of some of the participants in it, some want the Holy See to go further and terminate its relationship with all dynastic Orders of Knighthood, in order to protect from exploitation those elderly retired cardinals who fall victim to imposters. It is sad to think that imposters and social climbers have created an atmosphere of distrust and deep concern which is not improved by inter-family quarrels and feuds in some legitimate non-regnant royal houses.

The most far-reaching change in the section of Catholic-founded dynastic Orders has been made with regard to the Most Noble Order of the Golden Fleece of Spain. This has not been an arbitrary and sudden decision but was the result of consultation and an objective assessment of the Order's evolution over many decades, culminating in the wish of His Majesty King Juan Carlos of Spain to see the Order's position once again on a par with the principal Orders of other countries.

Both the Catholicity and in some respects the dynastic character of the Spanish Order of the Golden Fleece have undergone a metamorphosis since H.M. King Juan Carlos ascended the throne and two years later became the grand-mastership of the Order. In the 1985 edition of Archbishop Cardinale's work the Order was listed as a Catholic dynastic Order of Knighthood conferred by a reigning Monarch, although Mons. Cardinale had stated in his 1983 edition: 'The Order no longer possesses an aristocratic and religious character, but is more of a Royal Order with a civil character. . . . Nominations are made with the previous agreement of the Council of Ministers; it is therefore no longer subject to the exclusive authority of the Sovereign.'

At the suggestion of His Majesty, I changed this phrase in the 1985 edition to: 'The Spanish Golden Fleece is granted by the King in his capacity as Head of State with the previous knowledge of the Council of Ministers.'

In *The Cross on the Sword* (1987), I reproduced two recent Royal Warrants conferring the Order of the Golden Fleece; the wording used in the Warrants stated that 'His Majesty has heard the advice of the Council of Ministers, before the Warrants were issued'.

As far back as 1983, it was the King's wish to give to the Spanish Order of the Golden Fleece a status similar to that enjoyed by the Most Noble

JEFATURA DEL ESTADO

REAL DECRETO 1818/1985 concediendo el Collar de la Insigne Orden del Toisón de Oro a Su Majestad la Reina Beatrix de los Países Bajos.

Queriendo dar un relevante testimonio de mi Real aprecio a Su Majestad la Reina Beatrix de los Países Bajos y en muestra de la tradicional amistad entre los Países Bajos y España.

Oido el Consejo de Ministros.

Vengo en concederle el Collar de la Insigne Orden del Toisón de Oro.

Dado en el Palacio de la Zarzuela a ..7... de Octubre de 1985.

JEFATURA DEL ESTADO

REAL DECRETO ..1948./.1985. por el que se concede el Collar de la Insigne Orden del Toisón de Oro a Su Majestad Margarita II, Reina de Dinamarca.

Queriendo dar un relevante testimonio de mi Real - aprecio a Su Majestad Margarita II, Reina de Dinamarca, y en muestra de la tradicional amistad entre Dinamarca y España.

Oido el Consejo de Ministros.

Vengo en concederle el Collar de la Insigne Orden - del Toisón de Oro.

Dado en el Palacio de la Zarzuela a ..23. de ..Octubre.. de 1985

Order of the Garter in Great Britain. The Order of the Garter is an Order of the Crown and not a dynastic Order of the reigning Royal House.

The historian Kenneth Rose is an acknowledged authority on matters relating to British Orders of the Crown and the Sovereign as *fons honorum*, in whose name all British Orders are conferred. In the submission of Mr. Rose, there are no dynastic Orders in Great Britain; instead he distinguishes between Orders that are conferred with ministerial advice and those that are conferred without.

The Royal Victorian Order appears to be an exception because of the conditions attached to it at the time of its foundation in 1896 by Queen Victoria. It and the Order of Merit, founded in 1902 by King Edward VII, as well as the Royal Victorian Chain, founded in the same year, have always been conferred by the monarch without ministerial advice. (The Royal Victorian Chain is not an Order but a token of the Monarch's esteem; it confers neither title nor precedence, and unlike all the Orders, is not administered by the Chancellery of Knighthood). In 1946, after reaching agreement with the new postwar government, King George VI decreed that the Most Noble Order of the Garter, founded in 1348, and the Most Ancient and Most Noble Order of the Thistle, founded in 787, and reconstituted in 1540 and 1687, were henceforth to be conferred by the Monarch without ministerial advice.

The Most Noble Order of the Garter is often quoted as an example of a dynastic Order of Knighthood, but Mr. Rose has removed a serious misunderstanding in this regard. He explains that when the House of Stuart went into exile in 1688, James II and his descendants, who did not relinquish their claim either to the throne or to the Order, continued to bestow the Order of Garter abroad, while King William III and Queen Mary, the jointly reigning Sovereigns, continued to confer the Order legitimately in Great Britain. Mr. Rose suggests that had the Orders of the Garter and the Thistle been dynastic, they would have been divorced from the national life at that time and so lost the high esteem they presently enjoy throughout the world.

King Juan Carlos is a constitutional monarch and it is therefore more accurate, without prejudice to the prerogatives of His Majesty's headship of the Dynasty of Bourbon of Spain, to move the Spanish Order of the Golden Fleece from the category of 'Catholic dynastic Orders conferred by a reigning Monarch' to Chapter Eight, 'Secularised Catholic-founded Crown and State Orders'.

Also, the original criteria for the admission to, and objectives of the Order of the Golden Fleece are no longer the the present ones of the Most Noble Order of the Golden Fleece of Spain. In that respect its Catholicity must be called in question; it is, however, a Catholic-founded Order, and the esteem it enjoys will not be diminished by its secularisation.

The Golden Fleece of the Imperial and Royal House of Habsburg has retained its dynastic, Catholic and exclusive character since its separation from the Spanish branch. It is open only to members of royal families and to members of the higher nobility who profess the Catholic faith.

At this point, I should add that the best-known precedent for two branches of an ancient Order developing separately is that of the Order of Christ, which in 1515 became two separate Orders, one conferred by the Supreme Pontiff, the other by the King of Portugal, and today by the President of the Portuguese Republic. The Order of the Golden Fleece divided into two branches more than 200 years later when no decision could be reached at the Congress of Cambrai in 1724 to grant sovereignty to the Order.

Finally, with regard to the three major regnant Catholic dynasties, the Royal Houses of the Belgians (Saxe-Coburg-Gotha), Luxembourg (Nassau) and Liechtenstein, none of them have a dynastic Order of Knighthood that would qualify as 'Catholic' or 'Catholic-founded' according to the criteria laid down for inclusion in this work.

I

THE NOBLE ORDER OF THE GOLDEN FLEECE
OF
BURGUNDY
(From 1430 to 1724)

The non-territorial character of the Most Noble Order of the Golden Fleece always mitigated against the Order becoming a sovereign entity as is the Order of St. John of Jerusalem, of Rhodes and of Malta. Instead the Order was always considered to be the personal property of the heir to the Royal House of Burgundy, and from 1430 until 1700 it was shared – relatively harmoniously – between the Imperial and Royal House of Habsburg and the Royal House of Bourbon of Spain.

The Noble Order of the Golden Fleece was founded in Bruges on 10 January 1430 by Philip the Good, Duke of Burgundy (1396-1467), to mark the occasion of his marriage to Isabella, Infanta of Portugal. Its objects were:

'... the glory of God Almighty, the honour of his glorious Mother the Virgin Mary and of all the celestial Army, and the protection and defence of the Christian faith, especially by undertaking a Crusade to liberate the Holy Places in Jerusalem; to honour the Apostle St. Andrew, Patron of the House of Burgundy, and to promote the spirit and cause of Christian chivalry, to stimulate the practice of virtue and good behaviour, and to ensure the tranquillity of the Duchy of Burgundy.'

Philip the Good, Duke of Burgundy (1396-1467), founded the Noble Order of the Golden Fleece in 1430.

The founder reserved the 'extraterritorial sovereignty' of the Order for himself and his successors, in whose hands the Knights were to swear "total fidelity to the Christian faith and to the Sovereign of the Order". He assured himself of the absolute loyalty of the most influential feudal Lords by binding them to himself by means of a special oath.

The number of Knights was originally thirty-four, and later thirty-one, together with the Head and Sovereign of the Order. Emperor Charles V (1519-1556) raised the number to fifty-one, and King Philip IV of Spain (1605-1665) finally set the number at sixty-one. The Knights were to be 'Gentlemen-at-Arms', belonging to the most ancient nobility. In order to avoid conflicting loyalties, no knight (apart from fellow sovereigns) could be a member of other Orders, and if they already belonged to others, these had to be returned. For example, Prince Eugene of Savoy had to resign his family Order SS. Annunziata on being created a Knight of the Golden Fleece. Later, the High Masters of the Teutonic Order resigned the Order of the Golden Fleece so as to be able to wear the insignia of the Order of which they had become High Master.

The Knights of the Golden Fleece were to form 'a company of friends, owing each other love and brotherliness'. The Order itself was intended to 'outshine' the prestige of the Order of the Garter.

Charles the Bold, Duke of Burgundy and second Head and Sovereign of the Order (1433-1467-1477), included his brother-in-law, Edward IV, King of England (1461-1483), and the Kings Ferdinand I of Naples (1458-1494), and John II of Sicily (1458-1479), among the first fifteen Knights he nominated between 1468 and 1473.

When Charles the Bold died, the dignity of Head and Sovereign of the Order went to the Archduke Maximilian of Austria and later Emperor (1459-1519), who assumed the sovereign Mastership in place of his wife, Marie de Bourgogne, daughter of Charles the Bold because, according to the existing rules of chivalry, no women could be a Sovereign or Grand Master of an Order of Knighthood.

Maximilian was succeeded by Philip the Handsome as the second Head and Sovereign of the Order from the House of Habsburg (1478-1506), when he attained his majority in 1494. During his reign he proceeded to appoint thirty-one Knights, among whom were Henry VII, King of England (in 1491), and in 1505 his fourteen-year-old son Henry who became King Henry VIII in 1509[1].

Charles V, Holy Roman Emperor, King of Spain and Sovereign of the House of Habsburg (1500-1558), became the third Head and Sovereign of the Order from the House of Habsburg in 1516. He enriched the Order

---

[1] Henry VIII who had his portrait painted by Holbein in 1536, three years after his excommunication by Clement VII, still wore the Catholic Order of the Golden Fleece, but Holbein reversed the Fleece, to face right.

Chapter Meeting of the Knights of the Golden Fleece under Charles the Bold in 1473 when Edward IV, King of England, and the Kings of Naples and Sicily were among the first fifteen Knights Charles the Bold appointed to the Order.

Courtesy: Fitzwilliam Museum, Cambridge

with extraordinary privileges, making it the most important and prestigious Order of the time. This had the full approval of the Apostolic See which added special spiritual privileges to its temporal ones.

Charles V included among the Knights Francis I, King of France, and the Kings of Portugal, Hungary, Scotland, and Poland, together with the sovereign Dukes of Savoy, Florence, Bavaria, Saxony and Denmark. When Charles V abdicated in 1555, he was succeeded by his son Philip II, King of Spain, and fourth Head and Sovereign of the Order from the House of Habsburg (1527-1598). In 1577 Philip II obtained from Pope Gregory XIII (1572-1585) the exclusive rights to appoint Knights to vacancies, thus ending the practice of election by co-option, a practice introduced with pontifical encouragement by the Order's Chapter, which threatened to diminish the Order's prestige and standing because of the possibility of an unsuitable candidate becoming a member of the Order. He conferred the Order of the Golden Fleece on the Kings of France, Francis II and Charles IX, the future Emperors Rodolph, Mathias and Ferdinand, as well as on many Lords in the Lowlands, the Holy Roman Empire, Spain and Italy. Philip II retained the sovereign grand-mastership of the Order until 1598 when he passed the sovereignty of the seventeen Provinces to his daughter Isabella, and the dignity of Sovereign and Grand Master of the Order to Philip III, King of Spain and the fifth Head and Sovereign of the Order from the House of Habsburg (1578-1621). He was succeeded by King Philip IV (1605-1665) and King Carlos II (1661-1700) as Head and Sovereign of the Order of the Golden Fleece.

The death of Carlos II marked the end of the Spanish branch of the House of Habsburg. The sovereignty of the Crown of Spain was claimed by Louis XIV for a member of the House of Bourbon, Philip d'Anjou, while Emperor Leopold demanded the succession for a member of the House of Habsburg. In 1701 Philip d'Anjou became King of Spain and the first Head and Sovereign of the Order of the Golden Fleece from the House of Bourbon, while the new Emperor, Karl VI (1685-1740), claimed to be the eighth Head and Sovereign of the House of Habsburg. He received the Low Countries, Sardinia, Naples and Milan. Both Philip d'Anjou (Philip V of Spain) and Emperor Karl VI claimed to be Head and Sovereign of the Order of the Golden Fleece. Philip V based his claim on being the King of Spain, and Emperor Karl VI laid claim to the Order because, thanks to the treaty of Utrecht (1713), he had become ruler of the Low Countries, and he therefore regarded himself as the rightful successor to the Dukes of Burgundy.

The outcome of the dispute over the sovereignty of the Order polarised factions, and the dispute was submitted to the Congress of Cambrai in 1724. No decision was reached by the Congress, and all efforts to bring about a solution failed. The Houses of Habsburg and Bourbon therefore tacitly agreed to confer the Order independently in future.

Holbein's portrait of Henry VIII, King of England, wearing the Catholic Order of the Golden Fleece in 1536, three years after the King's excommunication by Clement VII. The Order was bestowed on Prince Henry in 1505, when he was fourteen years old. It is interesting to note that Holbein painted the Fleece in the reverse position.

Courtesy: National Portrait Gallery, London

XVII

His Royal Highness O Senhor Dom Duarte Pio, Duke of Bragança
Head of the Royal House of Portugal, Sovereign and Grand Master of the dynastic Order of Our Lady of the Conception of Vila Viçosa, Sovereign of the Order of St. Isabel.   Courtesy: Casa Real Portuguesa

Their Royal Highnesses Dom Miguel, Duke de Viseu, Chancellor, (left), Dom Duarte, Duke of Bragança, Grand Master (centre), and Dom Henrique, Duke of Coimbra (right), in their robes of the Order of Our Lady of the Conception of Vila Viçosa. Opposite top: Four members of the Order (from l. to r.) Dr. Manuel de Noronha e Andrade, Marquês de Arena; Prof.Arq. Marcello de Moraes Secretary of the Order; The Marquês de Santa Iria; Prof. de Sousa Lara, Conte di Guedes.

Left: the Star of the Order of Our Lady of the Conception of Vila Viçosa; right: the Badge of the Order. The positioning of the motto on the blue band surrounding the centre medallion has slightly changed since the Order was instituted.

XIX

The insignia of the Order of Our Lady of the Conception of Vila Viçosa in gold and enamel (actual size) of 1818/1820. Until 1823, the Order was only conferred in one class.

The Star of the Order of Our Lady of the Conception of Vila Viçosa made for King Dom João VI from Brazilian gold, is entirely covered in diamonds with a blue-enamelled band that bears the Order's motto.

Courtesy: Palácio Nacional da Ajuda, Lisboa

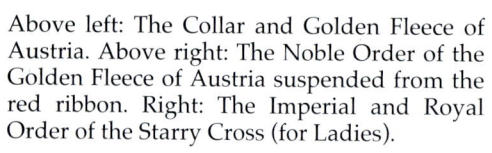

Above left: The Collar and Golden Fleece of Austria. Above right: The Noble Order of the Golden Fleece of Austria suspended from the red ribbon. Right: The Imperial and Royal Order of the Starry Cross (for Ladies).

Courtesy: HIRH Archduke Dr. Otto von Habsburg and Garrison Collection.

BAVARIA-WITTELSBACH – The Collar of the Order of St. Hubert.

Courtesy: Der Präsident der Verwaltung des Herzogs von Bayer

His Royal Highness the Prince Vittorio Emanuele
...ke of Savoy, Prince of Naples, Hereditary Head of the Royal House of Italy, Sovereign and
...and Master of the dynastic Orders of the Annunziata and SS. Maurice and Lazarus.

Courtesy: Real Casa di Savoia

XXII

XXIII

Above: Cardinal Ugo Poletti introducing Knights of SS. Maurice and Lazarus to Pope John Paul II.
Below: The 1991 annual Chapter of the Order held in Cascais, Portugal.

Facing page: clockwise from top left, H.R.H. The Prince Victor Emmanuel, Grand Master of the Order of SS. Maurice and Lazarus; Collar and Star of the Order of SS. Annunziata; Grand Cross and Star of the Order of SS. Maurice and SS. Lazarus; H.R.H. The Hereditary Prince Filiberto Emmanuel of Savoy, President of the Council of the Order of SS. Maurice and SS. Lazarus.

Courtesy: Real Casa di Savoia

XXIV

His Royal Highness don Ferdinando Maria di Borbone delle Due Sicilie, Duke of Castro, Head of the House of the Two Sicilies and Grand Master of the S.M. Constantinian Order of St. George and the Royal Order of St. Januarius.

Courtesy: Real Casa Borbone delle Due Sicilie

THE INSIGNIA OF THE ROYAL ORDER OF ST. JANUARIUS

Courtesy: Real Casa di Borbone delle Due Sicilie

Insignia of a Bailiff of Justice decorated with a Collar of the S.M. Constantinian Order of St. George. The Collar of the Grand Cross *Categoria Speziale* is reserved for Heads of State.

Courtesy: Real Casa di Borbone delle Due Sicilie

The Constantinian Cross of the category *di Merito* and *d'Ufficio* (left); the Cross of the category *di Grazia* and of the Grand Cross of the *Categoria Speziale* (right).

The silver Star of the category *di Grazia* and *di Merito*. (The category *di Justizia* and the Grand Cross of the *Categoria Speziale* have a gold Star).

The Ecclesiastical Star of the Grand Priors of the Constantinian Order from ca.1850 until 1959. Right: The Delegate for the USA, David L. Garrison wearing the *mantello* of the Order which is worn for religious services, and a Knight Grand Cross (*Categoria Speziale*) in court uniform.

XXVII

The Mini Orders (worn on the lapel) made by the papal engraver Prof. Rudolf Niedballa in gold and enamel (see Appendix X). Shown here are the Star of the Order of Our Lady of the Conception of Vila Viçosa, the Cross of the Order of St. Gregory the Great, and the insignia of the Order of St. Maurice and St. Lazarus.

The Spanish Golden Fleece made for King João of Portugal from Brazilian gold, diamonds, rubies and a large emerald.

Courtesy: Palácio Nacional da Ajuda, Lisboa

The Cross of the Order of St. George (Bavaria), made in 1729 in Paris; silver-gilt, enamel, emeralds, diamonds and rubies.

Courtesy: Der Präsident der Verwaltung des Herzogs von Bayern

A very rare 17th century 'Beaufort' Lesser George with five settings in gold for rubies and five in silver for diamonds.

Courtesy: Spink & Son Ltd., London

Her Majesty Queen Elizabeth II wearing the insignia of the Most Noble Order of the Garter and two House Orders of the House of Windsor, (the Garter itself on her left upper arm), is received in the Vatican by His Eminence Jacques Cardinal Martin, then *Prefetto della Casa Pontificia*, during her state visit to His Holiness Pope John Paul II in 1981.

Courtesy: *L'Osservatore Romano*

Her Majesty Queen Elizabeth the Queen Mother with the Prince of Wales by her side, and the Duke of Kent walking ahead of them during a Garter Procession.

Courtesy: The Ministry of Defence, London

XXIX

The Collar with the Greater George, Sash with the Lesser George and Star of the Most Noble Order of the Garter.
Courtesy: Spink & Son Ltd., London

The Collar with the Badge Appendant of St. Andrew, Sash with Badge & Star of the Most Ancient and Most Noble Order of the Thistle.
Courtesy: Spink & Son Ltd., London

The Collar with the Cross, Sash with the Badge and Star of the Military Division of the Most Honourable Order of the Bath.
Courtesy: Spink & Son Ltd., London

The Collar with the Badge, the Sash with the Badge and Star of the Civil Division of the Most Honourable Order of the Bath.
Courtesy: Spink & Son Ltd., London

The annual Garter Procession from Windsor Castle to St. George's Chapel.

Courtesy: The Ministry of Defence, London

Star, Lesser George and Garter of the Most Noble Order of the Garter.

Courtesy: Spink & Son Ltd., London

XXXI

The annual procession of the Knights of the Thistle from the Signet Library to the Kirk of St. Giles.

Courtesy: The Most Ancient and Most Noble Order of Thistle

Star and Badge of the Most Ancient and Most Noble Order of the Thistle.

Courtesy: Spink & Son Ltd., London

The 19th century jewel-encrusted Badge and Star of the Banda das Três Ordens with the image of the Sacred Heart superimposed on the insignia. The insigna were worn by the monarchs on special occasions.

Courtesy: Palácio Nacional da Ajuda, Lisbon

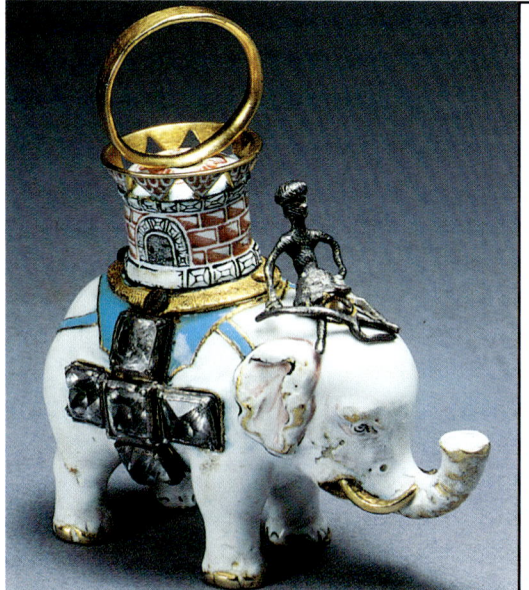

An 18th century Elephant Badge Appendant of the Danish Order of the Elephant in gold, enamel and set with diamonds.

Courtesy: Spink & Son Ltd., London

An early 19th century Cross of the S.M. Constantinian Order of St. George made of rubies and diamonds set in gold.

Courtesy: Bali Achille di Lorenzo

Although both dynasties agreed formally in 1724 to confer the Order of the Golden Fleece separately, the practice had begun in 1701 when Philip V of Spain, Head of the Dynasty of Bourbon of Spain, created five Knights of the Spanish Golden Fleece, apart from bestowing it on himself; Emperor Karl VI, Head and Sovereign of the House of Habsburg created twenty-two Knights in 1712.

At the signing of the treaty of Campoformio in 1797, following Napoleon's first Italian campaign, as a result of which Austria had to renounce its dominion over the Low Countries, no mention was made of the Order of the Golden Fleece, the implication being that the Order remained the property of the heir of the House of Burgundy as founder of the Order.

From the Order's foundation in 1430 until the year 1700, 618 Knights of the Order of the Golden Fleece had been created.

By the end of the First World War in 1918, when the Imperial and Royal House of Habsburg-Lorraine lost its sovereignty, the number of Knights of the Austrian Golden Fleece (including the 618 Knights appointed prior to 1700) had reached 1215, and the number of Knights registered then in Spain was 1147.

In 1962 the number of Knights of the Golden Fleece since the foundation of the Order in 1430 registered by the Imperial and Royal House of Habsburg-Lorraine was 1282, the last appointed Knight having been the first-born son of H.I. and R.H. Archduke Otto von Habsburg, Head of the Imperial and Royal House and Sovereign Grand Master of the Austrian Order of the Golden Fleece, Archduke Karl, Prince Imperial of Austria and Royal of Hungary and Bohemia, who was born in 1961.

Before the Revolution in 1931, the last King of Spain, Alfonso XIII, created four more Knights prior to going into exile, including Field Marshal Paul von Hindenburg, President of Germany. The Order of the Golden Fleece was not then conferred until 1941, when H.R.H. Don Juan, Count of Barcelona, as Head of the Royal House of Bourbon of Spain in exile, conferred the Order on his son Juan Carlos, who became King of Spain in 1975. By 1962, only H.M. King Baudouin of the Belgians (in 1960) and King Paul of the Hellenes (in 1962) had joined the ranks of Knights of the Golden Fleece created by the Royal House of Bourbon of Spain, who then numbered 1177.

The development of the two branches of the Order since 1700 has ben in several respects distinctly different. As I stated above, only the Habsburg branch of the Order retained its strictly Catholic and exclusively dynastic character.

H.I. and R.H. Archduke Otto von Habsburg, Head of the Imperial and Royal House of Habsburg Lorraine, Sovereign and Grand Master of the Austrian branch of the Noble Order of the Golden Fleece.

Courtesy: Archduke Otto von Habsburg

II

THE IMPERIAL AND ROYAL HOUSE OF HABSBURG-LORRAINE

THE NOBLE ORDER OF THE GOLDEN FLEECE

Emperor Karl VI was the first Sovereign and Grand Master of the Austrian Order of the Golden Fleece after the Order had separated into Austrian and Spanish branches. The latter is now listed in Chapter Eight 'Secularised Catholic-founded Orders of Knighthood conferred as Crown or State Orders', although I stress, without prejudice to the dynastic rights inherent in the Sovereign and Grand Master of the Order of the Golden Fleece as successor to the founder, the Duke of Burgundy.

Karl VI was succeeded by Emperor Franz I (1708-1765) who in 1740 became the ninth Head and Sovereign of the House of Habsburg-Lorraine. He was succeeded by the Emperors Josef II (1741-1790), Leopold II (1747-1792, Franz II (1768-1835), Ferdinand I (1793-1875), Franz-Josef I (1830-1916), and Karl I (1887-1922), father of the present, the sixteenth Sovereign and Grand Master of the Noble Order of the Golden Fleece, Archduke Otto of Habsburg-Lorraine (1912-), who, in turn, will be succeeded by his eldest son, Prince Imperial Karl of Austria and Prince Royal of Hungary and Bohemia.

A member of the European Parliament, H.I. and R.H. Archduke Otto von Habsburg-Lorraine (at his own request styled Dr. Otto Habsburg,) is the direct successor of a Sovereign who died in exile, being the first-born son of the Emperor Karl I who had been compelled to leave Austria after the proclamation of the Republic on 2 November 1918.

Following the abolition of the imperial monarchy in Austria, a group of notable Belgians attempted to persuade the Belgian Government to secure the inclusion of a special clause in the Treaty of Versailles (1919), ordering the return of the treasures of the Order of the Golden Fleece to Belgium. They also endeavoured to persuade King Albert of the Belgians to claim the sovereign grand-mastership of the Order on the basis that it was founded in what is now the Kingdom of Belgium. King Albert resisted these pressures as he considered the Order to belong irrevocably to the House of Habsburg-Lorraine, with whom his own House had always maintained friendly relations. The Belgian Government which had been also approached, rejected the suggestion because the treasure had been transferred to Vienna between 1794 and 1797 by the House of Habsburg-Lorraine itself when Franz II was the sovereign Grand Master of the Order. Assertions that the treasure had been looted from Belgium during the 1914-18 War were shown to be false.

In a Decree dated 16 September 1953, the Republic of Austria acknowledged that the Austrian branch of the Noble Order of the Golden Fleece belonged to the Head of the Imperial House of Habsburg-Lorraine, and recognised its independent juridical personality in international law as *Rechtspersînlichkeit Ausländischen Rechtes* (a juridical entity under foreign law) as appertaining to the Imperial House of Habsburg-Lorraine. This included the recognition of the property rights of the Noble Order of the Golden Fleece over its own archives and treasures which had been transferred from Brussels to Vienna while the French revolutionary army advanced through Burgundy after its victory at Fleurus in 1794. The Austrian Government has assumed the custody of these archives and treasures which are kept in the Weltliche Schatzkammer and in the Geistliche Schatzkammer (the secular treasury and the ecclesiastical treasury) at Hofburg. The Austrian Government allows the Order to make use of them freely for ceremonial and cultural purposes.

The badge of the Order consists of a golden fleece (sheepskin with head and feet attached) suspended from a blue-enamelled, white-dotted flintstone and emerging gold-rimmed red flame, all suspended from a gold crown-shaped plaque bearing the image of Jason slaying the dragon and the motto PRETIUM LABORUM NON VILE, (the reward of labour is not of little worth), and on the reverse: NON ALIUD, (No other), referring to the primacy of the Order among all other Orders of Knighthood. The Fleece is suspended from a gold chain, which constitutes the most important part of the insignia. The chain is composed of interlinking plaquettes representing a rifle and a flintstone in the shape of the letter 'B' (standing for Burgundy). The chain may be replaced by a ribbon of crimson moiré when necessary.

The rifle and flintstone are reminiscent of the motto of the Duchy of Burgundy, ANTE FERIT QUAM FLAMMA MICET (it hits its target before the flame blazes), very likely inspired by the invention of firearms in the fifteenth century.

The Fleece recalls the Greek legend of the Golden Fleece captured by Jason from the dragon, symbolising Jerusalem which, in the original Crusader spirit, the Order was to win back for Christendom from the Muslims.

Since the reign of Philip the Handsome, the symbolic interpretation of Jason was no longer used because of its Greek pagan connotations. Bishop Guillaume Filastre, Chancellor of the Order, gave six new references for the symbolic use of the fleece: Jason, Gideon, Jacob, Mesa, Job and David. Each of the fleeces represented one of the virtues with which a true knight should be endowed: magnanimity, justice, prudence, loyalty, patience and clemency.

As already noted, the Austrian branch of the Noble Order of the Golden Fleece has preserved its original aristocratic and religious character. It is therefore only conferred on members of royal families and high nobility who profess the Catholic religion.

DYNASTIC ORDERS OF KNIGHTHOOD

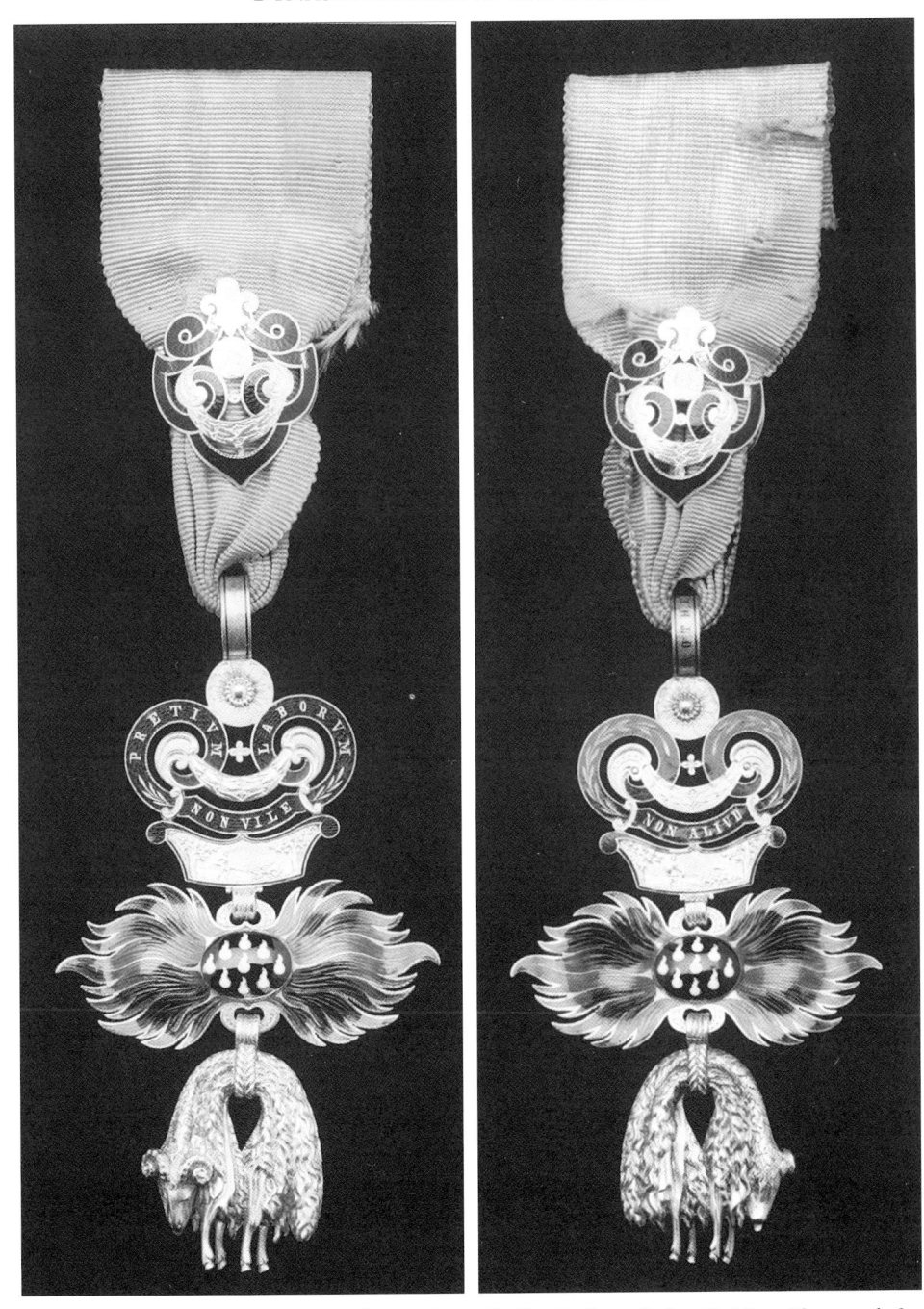

The obverse and reverse side of the Most Noble Order of the Golden Fleece of the Austrian branch.

Courtesy: Garrison Collection

THE ORDER OF THE DAMES OF THE STARRY CROSS

In 1662 the Dowager Empress Eleonore de Gonzaga had founded the first Order exclusively for ladies, 'The Order of the Slaves of Virtue' (Orden der Frauensklavinnen der Tugend), which was abolished six years later in 1668, when she founded a new and more important Order for Ladies, 'The Order of the Dames of the Starry Cross' (Ordo Stellatae Crucis). Eleonore de Gonzaga was the daughter of Charles II, Duke of Mantua, the widow of Emperor Ferdinand III (1608-1657), and stepmother of Emperor Leopold I (1658-1705).

The origin of the Order goes back to a priceless relic of the True Cross that had been in the possession of the House of Habsburg for many generations. It had been set into a golden cross, and the Emperor Leopold gave it to his stepmother as a present. She had a reliquary made for the cross which she venerated. In February 1668, a serious fire broke out in the imperial palace in Vienna which destroyed the wing the Empress Eleonore occupied. It was just possible to save the lives of the Empress and her staff and a very few items of jewellery. Unfortunately, the reliquary containing the gold cross with the fragment of the True Cross appeared to have perished in the fire. Eleonore ordered the ruins to be searched, and after five days one of the workers discovered something which could have been the reliquary; it had melted in the heat, and on examination it was discovered that the gold cross had also melted. However, the relic of the True Cross lodged undamaged in the molten gold, enamel and precious stones. The deeply religious Empress was convinced that she had witnessed a miracle, and she immediately asked the Cardinal Archbishop of Vienna to intercede for her with Pope Clement IX to sanction and approve a prestigious Order for ladies of the aristocracy. On 28 June 1668 Clement IX promulgated the Bull *Redemptoris et Domini Nostri*, approving the new Order of the Dames of the Starry Cross, founded in memory of the True Cross, and the Archbishop of Vienna added his own patronage to the planned Order; on 9 September, Emperor Leopold gave the Order his imperial approval, appointing his stepmother Protectoress of the Order, and on 18 September of the same year, Empress Eleonore de Gonzaga issued the proclamation of foundation of the Order. The number of members to be admitted was unlimited, though nobiliary proof was necessary. Also the ladies had to dedicate themselves to religious services and charitable works. The Head of the Imperial and Royal House of Habsburg-Lorraine is the Sovereign of the Order. Successive wives of Emperors as well as the Empress Maria Theresia, who was Sovereign of the Order, became Protectoress of the Order. After the death of Empress Zita, wife of the last Emperor, in 1991, the widow of H.I. and R.H. Archduke Otto von Habsburg-Lorraine, Archduchess Regina, became the present Protectoress.

The insignia of the Order, which are suspended from a black moiré bow, consist of a gold, blue-enamelled cross, with slightly elongated vertical arms, in the centre of which is a small red-enamelled cross, all superimposed on a gold, black-enamelled, double-headed Austrian Eagle without the crown. The Eagle with the cross is set in a gold, blue-enamelled and delicately decorated frame, which is surmounted by a white-enamelled scroll in three parts with the Order's motto SALUS ET GLORIA (Salvation and Fame).

The insignia of the Order of the Dames of the Starry Cross.

Courtesy: Garrison Collection

Courtesy: Palácio Nacional da Ajuda, Lisboa

III

THE ROYAL HOUSE OF BRAGANÇA OF PORTUGAL

The Royal Dynasty of Bragança which ruled Portugal from 1640 to 1910, was founded when Joâo, eighth Duke of Bragança, was acclaimed king. The revolt of the Portuguese nobility against the rule of King Philip IV of Spain and III of Portugal, placed the Duke on the throne as King Joâo IV on 1 December 1640.

The Duke was descended from the Kings of the Dynasty of Avis through two lines of male ancestry, his own and that of his paternal grandmother, the Infanta Catarina. His father, Teodosio II, was the son of the first Duke of Bragança, Alfonso, the son of King Joâo I, who founded the Dynasty of Avis which ruled Portugal from 1356 to 1580. Alfonso was created Count of Barcelos and later Duke of Bragança.

In November 1986 a document was published, the following translation of which was verified by the Portuguese Embassy in London as '...a correct translation of an original document, signed and sealed on 27 October 1986 in Lisbon by His Royal Highness O Senhor Dom Duarte Pio Joâo Miguel Henrique Pedro Gabrielo Rafael, Duke of Bragança'.

'I Dom Duarte, Duke of Bragança, by the Grace of God Head of the Royal House of Portugal, see fit to declare that the following Dynastic Orders belong to my House:

- The Order of the Conception of Our Lady of Vila Viçosa.
- The Order of Saint Isabel.
- The Order of St. Michael of the Wing[1].

Each of the Orders is self-governing by its own rules.

In order that this Act shall be known and appropriately recorded, I have ordered this document to be drawn up, signed it and sealed it with the seal bearing my arms.

(signed) Dom Duarte
Duke of Bragança'

The documents from the Portuguese Embassy in London also confirmed that none of the three above-mentioned Orders were on the list of Orders bestowed by the Republic of Portugal.

Residing in Portugal, His Royal Highness Dom Duarte Pio, Duke of Bragança, is universally recognised as the only legitimate Head of the Royal House of Portugal. The complex history of the House of Bragança is among the most complicated of all royal dynasties, and as far as the many genealogical intricacies of the Royal House are concerned, there are learned historians who are far more qualified that I to present, and elaborate on, the sometimes unconventional details.

Dom Duarte Pio, Duke of Bragança, inherited the positions of Sovereign and Grand Master of the Order of the Conception of Our Lady of Vila Viçosa, and Sovereign of the Order of Saint Isabel, when, on the death of his father, H.R.H. Dom Duarte Nuno, Duke of Bragança, he became the legitimate successor to the last reigning Sovereign of Portugal, King Manuel II.

[1] In May 1993, the Duke of Bragança confirmed a change in name and status of this organisation which he decreed should in future be known as 'The Knights and Dames of St. Michael of the Wing'. It has a lay apostolate of charitable works, benefitting Portuguese citizens in Por tugal and abroad in the field of education. The Duke of Bragança is now its Patron, not its Grand Master, and the organisation is centrally administered from Portugal by a Chancellor.

D. João VI (1767-1826) ‖ (1790)

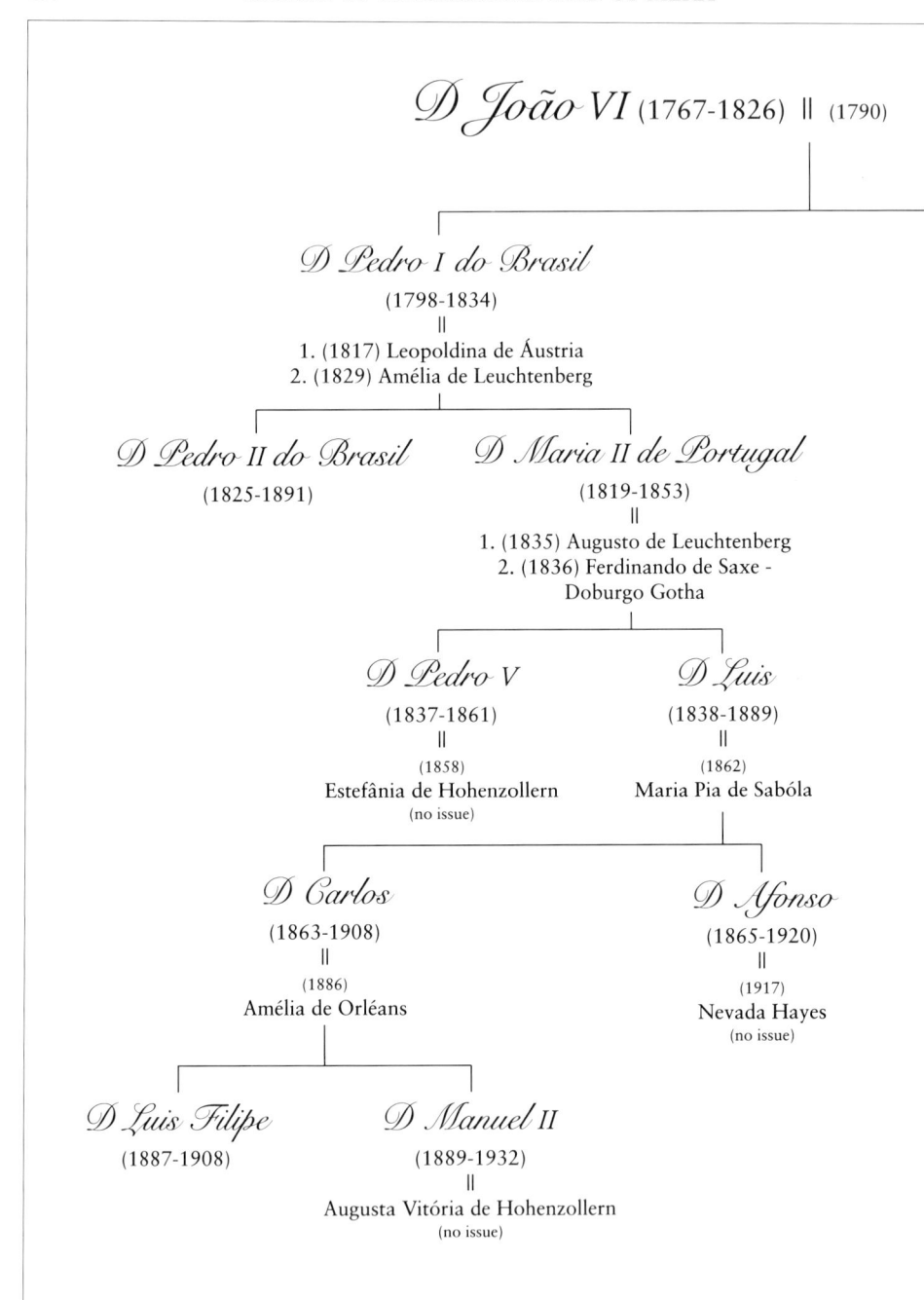

D. Pedro I do Brasil
(1798-1834)
‖
1. (1817) Leopoldina de Áustria
2. (1829) Amélia de Leuchtenberg

D. Pedro II do Brasil
(1825-1891)

D. Maria II de Portugal
(1819-1853)
‖
1. (1835) Augusto de Leuchtenberg
2. (1836) Ferdinando de Saxe - Doburgo Gotha

D. Pedro V
(1837-1861)
‖
(1858)
Estefânia de Hohenzollern
(no issue)

D. Luis
(1838-1889)
‖
(1862)
Maria Pia de Sabóla

D. Carlos
(1863-1908)
‖
(1886)
Amélia de Orléans

D. Afonso
(1865-1920)
‖
(1917)
Nevada Hayes
(no issue)

D. Luis Filipe
(1887-1908)

D. Manuel II
(1889-1932)
‖
Augusta Vitória de Hohenzollern
(no issue)

DYNASTIC ORDERS OF KNIGHTHOOD

Carlota Joaquina de Bourbon - Espanha

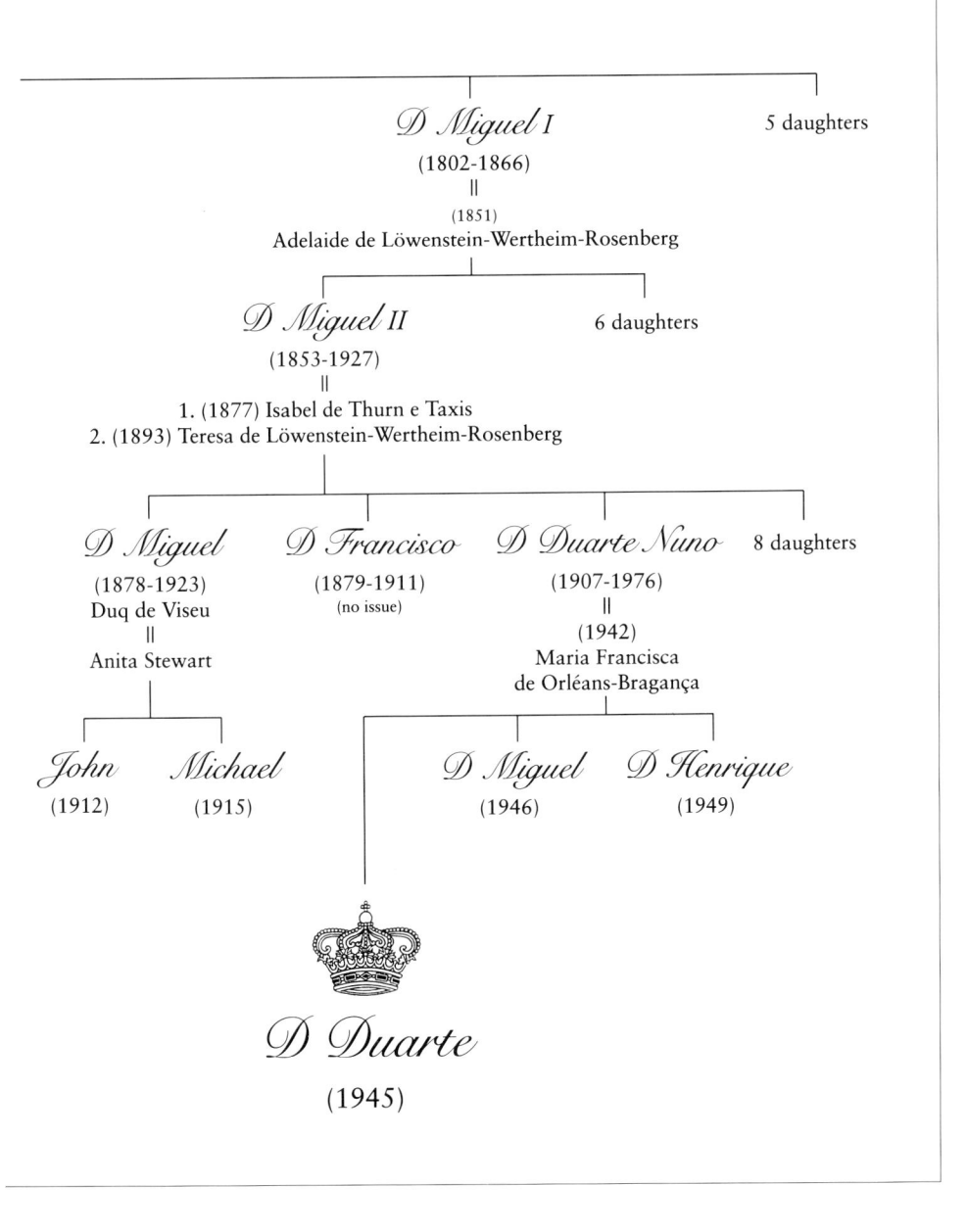

D Miguel I
(1802-1866)
=
(1851)
Adelaide de Löwenstein-Wertheim-Rosenberg

5 daughters

D Miguel II
(1853-1927)
=
1. (1877) Isabel de Thurn e Taxis
2. (1893) Teresa de Löwenstein-Wertheim-Rosenberg

6 daughters

D Miguel
(1878-1923)
Duq de Viseu
=
Anita Stewart

D Francisco
(1879-1911)
(no issue)

D Duarte Nuno
(1907-1976)
=
(1942)
Maria Francisca
de Orléans-Bragança

8 daughters

John
(1912)

Michael
(1915)

D Miguel
(1946)

D Henrique
(1949)

D Duarte
(1945)

Although no Portuguese monarch had admitted members to the Order of St. Michael of the Wing since Dom Miguel I had gone into exile in 1834, Dom Duarte Pio was advised to revive it as, apart from its political aims, it also had also a long tradition of charitable works, and he therefore agreed to assume sovereignty over it.

Because of the invasion of Portugal by Napoleon in 1807, the entire Portuguese Royal family was forced to flee to Brazil where they lived from 1808 until 1821. King Joâo VI, having returned to Portugal, left his eldest son, Dom Pedro, as Regent in Brazil. In 1822, Dom Pedro severed all ties with Portugal and declared himself Emperor of Brazil, effectively deposing his own father, King Joâo VI, who had been King of Portugal and Brazil but died as King of Portugal alone.

The death of King Joâo VI in 1826 led to a crisis in the succession and many upheavals, which eventually brought civil war to Portugal. The Regency Council which had governed the country during the last illness of Dom Joâo VI, recognised Dom Pedro as legitimate successor, however, Dom Pedro abdicated as King of Portugal in favour of his seven-year-old daughter Dona Maria da Glória, and he arranged the marriage of his daughter by proxy to his brother, Dom Miguel, believing this would solve the crisis of the succession. Dom Miguel was already Regent of the Realm, and he repudiated the marriage when he arrived in Lisbon in 1828. The Three Estates, Church, nobility and people, acclaimed him King, according to tradition, and he reigned as Dom Miguel I, the lawfully elected King of Portugal.

Dom Miguel's policies, personal attitudes and his reign as King were traditional; he was loyal to the Holy See and the Holy Roman Church and totally opposed to the liberalism and modernism of his brother, Dom Pedro, the Emperor of Brazil. He invited the Society of Jesus (Jesuits), which had been expelled by his predecessors, to return to Portugal, and he reinstituted the knightly Order of St. Michael of the Wing which soon became a powerful political movement in the King's fight against liberalism, modernism and other enemies of the Holy Roman Church.

By 1831, Dom Pedro had become so unpopular in Brazil, facing mass demonstrations against him, that he abdicated as Emperor in favour of his infant son Pedro, and left Brazil with his daughter Dona Maria da Glória, joining other liberal émigrés who had fled Portugal for England, France and other European countries, and became their leader.

He organised the overthrow of his brother Dom Miguel I, and in 1832 he sailed with fifty chartered ships and 7,500 mercenaries to Terceira in the Azores from where he launched a surprise attack on Oporto as well as other offensives. In 1834, King Dom Miguel I was forced to sign a peace treaty and go into exile. Dom Pedro immediately declared his daughter Dona Maria da Glória of age and placed her on the throne of Portugal as Queen Maria II, before dying in September that year.

King Dom João of Portugal who founded the principal Royal Order of the House of Bragança, De Nossa Senhora da Conceição de Vila Viçosa, in 1818.

Courtesy: Palácio Nacional da Ajuda, Lisboa

When Dom Miguel I went into exile he first paid a visit to the Supreme Pontiff, Gregory XVI, in Rome. Dom Miguel's marriage to his niece Dona Maria da Glória was declared null and void by the Patriarch of Lisbon on 1 December 1834, but It is extraordinary that Dona Maria da Glória's second betrothal, this time to Prince Auguste de Beauharnais, had already taken place, again by proxy, in Munich on 5 November 1834. Her second husband died on 28 March 1835, two months after they had entered another, this time canonically legal betrothal, in Lisbon.

King Dom Miguel I spent his exile in Genoa, marrying the Princess Adelaide Sophie zu Löwenstein-Wertheim-Rosenberg, and during his exile, he used the title Duke of Bragança. The Absolutists in Portugal and abroad continued to regard him as the lawful King and his children as Infantes of Portugal, and they continued to assert the legitimacy of his claim to the throne. When Miguel I died in 1866, his eldest son, Miguel II, was acknowledged as Duke of Bragança by the Portuguese Legitimists. Miguel's absence from Portugal did not settle the fundamental differences between the liberals and modernists on the one side, and Dom Miguel's loyal supporters on the other.

The Order of St. Michael of the Wing existed as a secret society from 1834 onwards: their acknowledged Grand Master was in exile, but they continued their fight against liberalism and modernism unabated. They refused to recognise King Dom Pedro and then Queen Maria II and continued to support Miguel I as King of Portugal. Because of its secret nature, none of the successors of King Dom Pedro IV was able to suppress it.

In January 1836, Dona Maria da Glória married for the third time by proxy, and in person in April of the same year in Lisbon. Her third husband, Prince Ferdinand of Saxe-Coburg-Gotha, was officially declared Prince Consort, and in 1837 was given the title 'His Most Faithful Majesty King Consort Ferdinand II of Portugal'. In 1853, Ferdinand II became Regent after the Queen's death, while their son Pedro was under age. Dom Pedro succeeded his mother to the throne of Portugal as King Dom Pedro V in 1853, but he soon died, in 1861, and his younger brother, Dom Louis, succeeded him. He married Princess Maria Pia of Savoy, Princess Royal of Italy, daughter of King Victor Emmanuel II, and reigned until 1889, when Dom Carlos was declared King on his father's death, and reigned as Carlos I. He and his eldest son, the Crown Prince Dom Louis Philip, were assassinated in Lisbon on 1 February 1908.

After the assassination of King Dom Carlos and the Crown Prince Dom Louis Philip, the younger son Manuel became King and reigned as Manuel II, but the activities of the various parties made his short reign a turbulent one. The proclamation of a republic on 5 October 1910 brought both his reign and the Portuguese monarchy to an end, and he went into exile to England, where he had been created a Knight of the Order of the

His Majesty King Dom Manuel II (1908-1910, dying in 1932 in England), whose father, King Dom Carlos I and elder brother, the Crown Prince, were assassinated in 1908.

Courtesy: Fundação da Casa de Bragança, Lisboa

Garter in April that year. He was a favourite at the English Court and a friend of H.R.H. the Prince of Wales (later King Edward VIII).

While in exile, both King Manuel II and H.R.H. Dom Miguel II, Duke of Bragança tried to achieve a reconciliation, and a meeting between them took place at Dover in 1912. On 31 July 1920, Dom Miguel II abdicated his rights in favour of his son Dom Duarte Nuno.

1922 was an important year for the Dynasty of Bragança. It was now certain that King Manuel II would have no issue, and his representatives and those of Dom Duarte Nuno, who succeeded his father as Duke of Bragança, signed and promulgated a pact on 17 April 1922 in Paris.

This pact formed the basis for the succession to the Headship of the Royal House of Bragança:

It has been declared:

A. By the first signatory (for His Majesty King Dom Manuel II) that His August Majesty in default of a direct heir will accept the

H.R.H. Edward, Prince of Wales (left), H.M.King Dom Manuel II, K.G., of Portugal (centre) and H.R.H. The Duke of Connaught in Garter robes outside St. George's Chapel, Windsor Castle, when the Prince of Wales was installed as a Knight of the Garter in 1911.

Courtesy: H.M.The Queen; Royal Archives, Windsor Castle

O Pacto de Paris

Bases do accordo firmado entre os Representantes de Sua Magestade El-Rei o Senhor D Manuel II; e de Sua Alteza Real o Senhor D. Duarte Nuno

declaram

O primeiro signatario al que o Seu Augusto Mandante, na falta de herdeiro directo,acceitará o Successor indicado pelas Côrtes Geraes da Nação Portugueza.

b) Egualmente acceitará as resoluções das mesmas Côrtes quanto á Constituição Política da Monarchia Restaurada

c) Que de accordo com a Santa Sé será resolvida a questão religiosa, mediante diploma a ser submettido ás Côrtes.

Pelo segundo signatario foi dito que perante as declarações anteriores o Seu Augusto Mandante pediria e recommendava a todos os seus partidarios que aceitem como Rei de Portugal o Senhor Dom Manuel II e que se unam realmente sob a mesma bandeira que abriga todos os Monarchicos, que é a Bandeira da Patria e a Bandeira que ha-de salvar Portugal.

Feito em Paris, aos 17 de abril de 1922

a) Ayres d'Ornellas
a) Conde d'Almeida e Avranches

S.M. El Rei D MANUEL II

S.A.R. D. DUARTE NUNO

In 1922 His Majesty King Dom Manuel II and His Royal Highness Dom Duarte Nuno signed the Pact of Paris in which the King acknowledged that the successor to the lineage of King Dom Miguel I would become the legitimate Head of the Royal House of Bragança of Portugal if he should die without issue.

successor indicated by the general Côrtes of the Portuguese Nation.

B. Equally he (H.M. King Dom Manuel II) will accept the resolution of the same Côrtes as to the political constitution of the restored Monarchy.

C. With the agreement concerning the Holy See the religious question[1] will be resolved by means of a Diploma which is to be submitted to the Côrtes.

By the second signatory (for H.R.H. Dom Duarte Nuno, Duke of Bragança), it was said before the preceding Declaration that His August Person, (Dom Duarte Nuno) would ask and recommend to all his supporters that they would accept as King of Portugal King Dom Manuel II, and that they would unite loyally under the same flag that shelters Monarchists. That is the Flag of the Motherland and the Flag that shall save Portugal.

---

[1] This refers to the property of the Church which had been confiscated under the liberal reign of the King's predecessors.

H.R.H. Dom Duarte Nuno, Duke of Bragança, wearing the insignia of the Order of the Golden Fleece, the Collar and Star of the Order of SS. Annunziata, The Star of the Order of Our Lady of the Conception of Vila Viçosa, the Star of the Grand Cross of the Pontifical Pian Order, and the uniform and insignia of a Bailiff Grand Cross of Honour and Devotion of the Sovereign Military Order of Malta.

Courtesy: The Duke of Bragança

H.R.H. Dom Miguel died on 11 October 1927, and H.M. King Dom Manuel II died in 1932 in England: thus the lineage of the male descendants of Queen Dona Maria II ended, and H.R.H. Dom Duarte Nuno, Duke of Bragança, became the legitimate Head of the Royal House of Portugal, and in 1942 he married his cousin H.R.H. Dona Marie Françoise de Orléans Bragança, a direct descendant of Dom Pedro, thus uniting the two branches of the Bragança family.

They had three sons: Dom Duarte Pio, born on 15 May 1945, whose Godfather was His Holiness Pope Pius XII; Dom Miguel, born on 3 December 1946; and Dom Henrique, born on 6 November 1949.

In 1950, by the unanimous decision of the National Assembly of the Republic of Portugal, the successor to the Côrtes, H.R.H. Dom Duarte Nuno, Duke of Bragança, was invited to return from exile to Portugal with his family.

H.R.H. Dom Duarte Nuno died on 24 December 1976 in Lisbon and was interred in the Pantheon of the Dukes of Bragança in Vila Viçosa.

He was succeeded by his eldest son, Dom Duarte Pio João Miguel Henrique Pedro Gabrielo Rafael, as Duke of Bragança, the new Head of the Royal House of Portugal.

When the Parliament of Portugal invited the Royal Family to return to their homeland, they accepted the legitimacy of the right to the headship

After his return from exile with his family, H.R.H. Dom Duarte Nuno, Duke of Bragança paid a visit to Rome, so that his son and heir, Dom Duarte Pio, the present Duke of Bragança, could pay homage to his Godfather, Pope Pius XII. From left to right: H.R.H. Dom Duarte Nuno, Duke of Bragança, the Infante Dom Miguel, His Holiness Pope Pius XII, the Pope's Godson, the Infante D. Duarte Pio, the Duke of Bragança's Principal Counsellor, Dom Antonio de Sousa Lara.

Courtesy: The Duke of Bragança

of the Royal House of Bragança of H.R.H. Dom Duarte Nuno. While the Assembleia da República can decide who – other than the Head of the Royal House, his spouse and children – belongs to the Royal Family and may use the title Infante and is in line to the succession, for example, the Duke of Bragança's brothers, neither Parliament nor the Council of Nobility of Portugal nor any political party can 'elect' the Head of the House of Bragança. He or she becomes the Head of the Royal House by the law of primogeniture, being first in line to the succession on the death of the last Head.

On the death of his father in 1976, Dom Duarte Pio inherited the *Ius Collationis*, the right to confer honours of the Royal House of Bragança, which became his personal property by *Iure Sanguinis* – the right of blood

H.R.H. The Duke of Bragança is one of the most photographed and written-about men in the world. Although he is on occasion decribed as 'a King without a throne', he has become known for his tireless service to the people of Portugal, especially its youth. Professionally he is among the foremost agronomists in Europe, and his advice is always available to Portuguese farmers. He has introduced the idea of the Duke of Edinburgh Award Scheme in Portugal and given it the name of 'Infante Dom Henrique' after Henry the Navigator. His work for peace and understanding is known from New York to Peking.

Courtesy: 'Royalty' Magazine, UK

DYNASTIC ORDERS OF KNIGHTHOOD

HRH The Duke of Braganza
PORTUGESE MAN-OF-PEACE

Portuguese monarchists regard him as the sole legitimate successor to the country's last monarch, King Manoel II.

ANOTHER *Royalty* EXCLUSIVE

– and both its possession and exercise are inviolable and vested solely in him.[1]

A Head of a Royal House, whether regnant or non-regnant, can abdicate, either in favour of the next person in line of succession or, by mutual agreement between the legitimate heir-apparent and heir-presumptives in favour of an heir-apparent who, however, must first be declared a member of the Royal Family by the Assembleia da República, the Parliament of Portugal, before such a transfer is possible. The lawful Head of the Royal House of Bragança cannot legitimately be removed from that position and a successor lawfully installed, unless the political forces trying to force such an issue resort to execution or assassination.

There have been the inevitable claimants to the headship of the House of Bragança just as there have been spurious claimants and imposters who have laid claim to almost every headship of regnant and non-regnant Royal Houses, and Portugal is no exception. I draw particular attention to those false claimants who by devious means published pictures of themselves with the Pope, thus pretending to have 'papal approval'. I have explained in the introduction to this chapter how these photographs are 'arranged' and subsequently exploited.

On 17 May 1982, by Royal Warrant, Dom Duarte, Duke of Bragança, conferred upon his brother and heir-apparent, H.R.H. the Infante Dom Miguel, the title of Duke of Viseu, and upon his youngest brother, the heir-presumptive, H.R.H. Dom Henrique, the dignity of Duke of Coimbra.

Unless H.R.H. Dom Duarte Pio, Duke of Bragança, whilst being without issue, proposes a person to the Portuguese Parliament to be named and approved as third in line to succession, so as to ensure the continuity of the Royal House, it is idle to speculate who might eventually succeed as Duke of Bragança.

The rôle and function of the Head of the Royal House of Portugal differs in many respects from those of other Heads of major Royal Dynasties, most of whom live outside their native lands. This is due to a

---

[1]In one important respect, the prerogatives of the Dukes of Bragança differ from those of all other legitimate successors to reigning monarchs: besides the royal prerogative of conferring the dynastic Orders of Knighthood, the Dukes of Bragança have always exercised and maintained, separately from their prerogatives as successors to the Monarchs of Portugal, the inherent rights and prerogatives of the Heads of the sovereign Ducal House of Bragança, the conferring of 'Foros', six titles of nobility. When Joâo, eighth Duke of Bragança, ascended the throne of Portugal as King in 1640, he did not surrender the ducal prerogative of conferring the six 'Foros' to the Crown. Instead, the Kings of Portugal conferred the 'Foros' as supplementary titles to the royal titles upon those whom they singled out for a personal honour. On occasion, a 'Foro' was conferred upon trusted friends of the Monarch – in his capacity as the Duke of Bragança – without a royal title. Because the Dukes of Bragança never surrendered the prerogative of conferring 'Foros' to the Crown, this prerogative continued to belong to them and did not pass to the State or Republic which became the heir to all other Crown privileges and prerogatives. The Duke of Bragança is therefore the only non-regnant Head of a Dynasty who has retained the right to confer titles of nobility. (See: Appendix VIII 'The Prerogatives of the Dukes of Brangança').

number of factors, foremost of which was the mutual respect between institutions of the Republic of Portugal and the Duke of Bragança, Dom Duarte Nuno.

His Royal Highness Dom Duarte Pio, the present Duke of Bragança, is advised by his own Counsellors. Affinity and support for the Duke of Bragança permeates not only all classes of society, but also the Assembleia da República, where he has friends in all political parties. He is not, for example, associated with political monarchist parties. There is no rivalry between the Head of the Republic and the Head of the non-regnant Royal House, but much mutual respect.

The reader might be tempted to draw a comparison with events in Spain prior to the accession of His Majesty King Juan Carlos of Spain, but such a comparison would be wrong. The Duke of Bragança is not a protégé of Portugal's Head of State (with the right of succession) as was the case in Spain; Dom Duarte Pio has only desired to serve Portugal in whatever capacity he can, and that wish is respected by the Government and the people of Portugal alike. His Royal Highness served for several years as a Pilot Officer in the Portuguese Air Force.

He has won the respect of the people, the Presidency of the Republic and the Government on his own merits, not on claims based on the deeds of his illustrious ancestors. Similarly, he has never tried to perpetuate

Eighty years after King Dom Manuel II had gone into exile to England and where he attended the Installation of Edward, Prince of Wales as a Knight of the Garter, H.R.H. Dom Duarte Pio, Duke of Bragança presents H.R.H. Charles, Prince of Wales, with a Polo Trophy.

Courtesy: Marquês de Arena

The Secretário Geral das Ordens Dinásticas da Casa Real Portuguesas and Secretário do Conselho da Ordem de N.S. da Conçeicâo de Vila Viçosa, Prof. Arq. Marcello de Moraes, who is directly accountable to the Sovereign of the Dynastic Orders, H.R.H. the Duke of Bragança, and also convenes the annual Chapter Meetings of the Order of Vila Viçosa.

Courtesy: Casa Real Portuguesa

spiritual values based on tradition alone. His Catholic faith and commitments to Catholic values are of paramount importance to him. This is reflected in the reaffirmation of the premier Catholic Dynastic Order of the Royal House of Bragança, the Ordem de Nossa Senhora da Conceição de Vila Viçosa.

Portugal can be cited as a society in which history has evolved without loss of respect for, or pride in, the past. The Chapter on the Catholic-founded Orders of the Republic of Portugal, the most ancient Orders of Chivalry and Merit that are still bestowed almost a millennium after their foundation, highlights that respect for past history and tradition that characterises the Portuguese people.

The prerogatives of the Dukes of Bragança are clearly defined and do not violate any democratic rights of the Republican Government or the people of Portugal. They complement the honours system of the Republic without infringing upon the prerogatives of the State. Like other Heads of Royal Houses, he has the right to confer the dynastic Orders; the Duke of Bragança is assisted in the administration of them by the Secretário das Ordens Real Portuguesas.

H.R.H. Dom Duarte Pio, Sovereign and Grand Master the Order of Our Lady of the Conception of Vila Viçosa.

THE ORDER OF OUR LADY OF THE CONCEPTION OF VILA VIÇOSA
(Ordem de Nossa Senhora da Conceiçâo de Vila Viçosa)

The Order of Our Lady of the Conception of Vila Viçosa is the senior Dynastic Order of Knighthood of the Royal House of Bragança of Portugal. It was founded by Dom Joâo VI, King of Portugal and Brazil (1816-1826) on 6 February 1818 in Brazil to honour its namesake, and placed under the protection of the Blessed Virgin Mary as Patroness of Portugal.

The Order was originally styled 'The Military Order of Our Lady of Vila Viçosa' and awarded for outstanding merit to Portuguese and foreign nationals. King Manuel II, when in exile, styled the dynastic Order 'Royal' instead of 'Military'. It is conferred in three classes, Grand Cross, Commander and Knight. When founded it was constituted to

Left: the Badge of the Order of Our Lady of the Conception of Vila Viçosa that is worn by all members of the Order either as a breast cross, a neck badge or suspended from a sash or grand cordon. Right the Star of the Order worn by Commanders and Knights Grand Cross.

Courtesy: Casa Real Portuguesa

consist of twelve Knights Grand Cross and supernumerary Grand Crosses, forty Commanders and one hundred Knights.

The Order has always been conferred with great parsimony and was last conferred by a King of Portugal in September 1910. Since the return of the Royal Family of Bragança to Portugal in 1950, conferment of the Order by the Head of the Royal House has been very rare. It is regarded as one of the most prestigious Catholic-founded dynastic Orders of Knighthood in Europe which is reflected in its membership.

The Badge of the Order, which is surmounted by a gold crown, is a nine-pointed, gold-rimmed, white-enamelled star with nine clusters of gold rays between the arms of the star, and a small white five-pointed mullet superimposed on the clusters of the rays; the initials 'AM' in the centre of the golden medallion stands for 'Ave Maria', The inscription in the blue-enamelled, gold-bordered surround reads PADROEIRA DO REINO (Patroness of the Kingdom).

The Star of the Order is similar though larger than the Badge, and the crown, which is embellished with three red and four green jewels, is set lower upon the badge, slightly covering the centre arm of the nine-pointed white-enamelled star. The Star is conferred on Knights Grand Cross and Commanders.

The riband and sash of the Order are pale blue moiré with a narrow white stripe on either side.

The gold-embroidered Tinsel Star of the Order. It is worn on the white robe of the members, but old paintings exist that show the star embroidered on uniforms and court dress.

Courtesy: Prof. Marcello de Moraes

On his official visit to Portugal Pope John Paul II went to Vila Viçosa to pray at the shrine of Our Lady of the Conception of Vila Viçosa. H.R.H. The Duke of Bragança welcomed His Holiness to the Order's Chapel which is the spiritual home of the Knights.

Courtesy: The Order of Vila Viçosa

In May 1983 the Prince and Grand Master of the Sovereign Military Order of Malta, Frà Angelo de Mojana di Cologna, paid a visit to the Shrine. H.R.H. the Duke of Bragança invested Frà Angelo with the Grand Cross of the Order.

Courtesy: The Order of Vila Viçosa

As a result of his desire to mark the 350th anniversary of Portugal's independence in an appropriate manner while maintaining the status and rarity of the principal Order of the Royal House, the Duke of Bragança issued a decree in Council, which added to the Order a medal of merit to be conferred on suitable recipients. It is worn on the left breast, pending from the ribbon of the Order.

The patronal feastday of the Order of the Conception of Our Lady of Vila Viçosa is the Feast of the Immaculate Conception on 8 December

H.R.H. The Duke of Bragança and his cousin, H.I. and R.H. Archduke Joseph Arpád of Austria, in the robes of the Order of Our Lady of the Conception of Vila Viçosa.

when, in alternate years, the Grand Master leads the Knights of the Order in prayer at the Shrine of Our Lady of the Immaculate Conception in Vila Viçosa or convenes a Chapter of the members in the Chapel of his residence. On this and special ecclesiastical occasions, the Knights wear their white robes with the insignia of the Order embroidered on the left side.

The Royal Chapel of the Order, where the image of Our Lady of the Immaculate Conception is revered, is in Vila Viçosa. It was visited by Pope John Paul II on 15 May 1982, when the Duke of Bragança welcomed His Holiness to this much venerated Portuguese shrine of the Blessed Virgin Mary.

In 1955, the Fundaçâo da Casa de Bragança, Lisbon, published *A Ordem Militar de Nossa Senhora da Conceiçâo de Vila Viçosa*, which contains the statutes of the Order, a list of all appointments from the date of its foundation in 1818 to September 1910 when King Manuel II went into exile, an extensive bibliography, Decrees and Royal Directives, and illustrations of the decorations and relevant documents. It is the most authoritative work on the Order for that period.

THE ROYAL ORDER OF SAINT ISABEL
(Real Ordem de Santa Isabel)

The Order of Saint Isabel was established in 1801 by the Prince Regent, the future King of Portugal, Dom Joâo VI, inspired by his wife the Princess Carlota Joaquina of Spain, as an award to Catholic ladies of noble birth for conspicuous deeds of charity and service to the Royal House of Bragança.

The Order is awarded in one class only and the statutes limit membership to twenty-six ladies of noble birth. The spouse of the Duke of Bragança is the Grand Master, though the Duke of Bragança as Head of the Royal House is the Sovereign of the Order and can confer the Order.

The obverse of the Badge is an oval enamelled medallion portraying Saint Isabel helping the poor, surrounded by a green-enamelled laurel wreath set in a gold garland of roses, surmounted by a gold-winged angel. The Badge is surmounted by the gold crown of Portugal. The inscription on a blue-enamelled scroll reads PAUPERUM SOLATIO (Comfort of the Poor).

The reverse of the Badge is a white-enamelled medallion with the Queen's initials 'CJ' intertwined, surmounted by a small laurel wreath. The medallion is surrounded by a blue-enamelled circlet with the inscription REAL ORDEM DE SANTA ISABEL, and on a scroll is its date of the foundation. The Order is worn on a pink riband with four narrow white stripes, tied in a bow.

On the occasion of the 350th Anniversary of the independence of Portugal on 1 December 1990, the Duke of Bragança issued a Decree in

The Badge of the Order of St. Isabel.

Council adding a Medal of Merit to the Order. This will enable the Sovereign and the Grand Master to honour more meritorious ladies. Nobility is not a prerequisite for receiving the Medal.

IV
THE ROYAL HOUSE OF BOURBON-TWO SICILIES

The Royal House of Bourbon-Two Sicilies is inextricably linked to the history of one the most ancient Catholic Orders of Knighthood, the Sacred Military Constantinian Order of St. George.

Although there have been numerous Papal Bulls concerning the Sacred Military Constantinian Order of St. George since the 12th century, that promulgated by Pope Clement XI in 1718 which laid down the statutes of the Order is the most important. *Militantis Ecclesiae* has been confirmed, unchanged, by almost every successive Pontiff and many additional favours were granted to the Order.

The forty-four page Papal Bull of Clement XI differs in some respects from those granted by popes to other reigning dynasties concerning their dynastic Orders: it places the Constantinian Order in the permanent trusteeship of The Royal House of Parma (it became the dynastic Order of the Kingdom of the Two Sicilies in 1734), which provides the Order with its Grand Master. However, the Bull reserves to the Apostolic See the right to involve itself in the Order's affairs. It made provisions for a Cardinal Patron and Grand Prior, and the general tenor of the Bull conveys the clear impression that Clement XI considers the Constantinian Order to be held in trust for the Apostolic See. From letters written in 1924 to Pope Pius XI by the then Head of the Royal House and Grand Master of the Constantinian Order, H.R.H. the Count of Caserta, Duke of Castro, half-brother of the last King, Francis II, who had died in 1894, it is obvious that the Head of the House of the Two Sicilies accepted that the ultimate authority over the Order belonged to the reigning Pontiff.

Theoretically, therefore, the Bull of Clement XI could have far-reaching consequences even today. The Order has retained the appellation 'Sacred', a status that was only granted to Orders under the direct rule or protection of the Apostolic See. Juridically, the Sacred Military Constantinian Order of St. George has never ceased to be under the authority of the Apostolic See, and the prerogatives reserved by Clement XI to the Apostolic See have never been revoked. Because of changes in attitude, into which the Holy See was clearly coerced during the pontificate of Pius XI, largely due to the House of Savoy's initial hostility to Pope Pius IX (1846-1878) personally and to the House of the Two Sicilies, which was regarded as a strong ally of the papacy, the relationship between the Order and the Holy See, though remaining

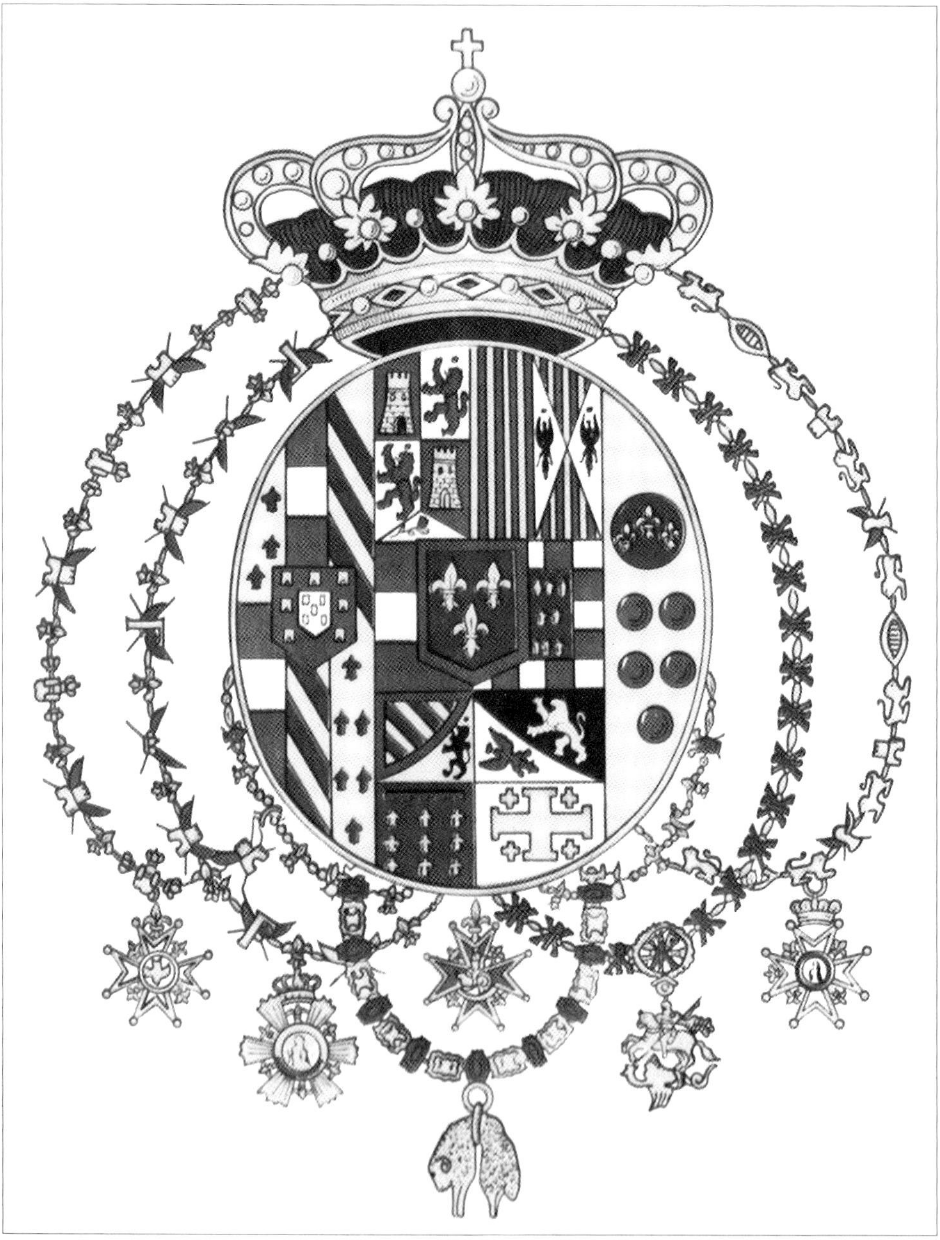

H.R.H. don Alfonso, Count of Caserta, Duke of Castro, (1892-1934), was the half-brother of the last King of the Two Sicilies and became Head of the Dynasty when the King died in 1894. He wrote on 27 December 1931 to his son don Ferdinando Pio and conferred the dignity of Grand Master of the S.M. Constantinian Order of St. George on him.

Courtesy: Bali don Achille di Lorenzo

friendly, had changed irrevocably. It is unlikely that the Apostolic See would nowadays lay claim to the Order or involve itself in its affairs, because Pope Pius XI (through Cardinal Gasparri) expressly declined to accept sovereignty of the Order when in 1924, in the letter mentioned above, the Count of Caserta offered it to the Apostolic See and suggested a transformation of the Constantinian Order from one of Chivalry to a Religious Order with professed ecclesiastics and lay knights, similar to proposals for the Teutonic Order, that were being discussed in the Vatican at that time.

Secular historical developments during the *Risorgimento* in the 19th century, and again at the beginning and in the middle of the 20th century have obscured the strong link that the Sacred Military Constantinian Order of St. George has always had with the Apostolic See. It was because of these strong links that its material fortunes and that of the Royal House of the Two Sicilies were similar to those the papacy endured after the loss of the papal states in the mid-nineteenth century.

Whereas the papacy regained sovereignty in 1929, though greatly diminished as far as territorial boundaries were concerned, the Constantinian Order of St. George of the House of the Two Sicilies had to wait another thirty years before the beginning of its renaissance.

After the death of the Head of the House of the Two Sicilies, H.R.H.

Sacro Militare Ordine Costantiniano di S. Giorgio

Gran Magistero

Carissimo mio figlio Ferdinando

La grave età che pesa su di me mi fa pensare alla successione nel Gran Magistero dell'Ordine Costantiniano di San Giorgio.

A norma degli Statuti redatti dal nostro antichissimo predecessore Francesco I° Farnese ed approvati dalla Venerata memoria di Papa Clemente XI con la Bolla Militantis Ecclesiae i quali regolano tutto il Governo dell'Ordine, tu come primogenito mio, e non facendo io altra designazione, sarai il mio successore nel Gran Magistero dell'Ordine.

Vi è però una circostanza alla quale tu dovrai rivolgere tutta la tua attenzione ed eliminare gl'inconvenienti che ne potrebbero derivare in discordo con gli statuti dell'Ordine. L'Ordine dopo il suo trasferimento dall'Oriente è diventato per volontà della Santa Sede Latino. Questa è dove restare Latino. Questa è la mia ferma volontà in armonia con gli statuti e con la volontà del Sacro Romano Pontefice.

Tu quindi dovrai usare tutta la tua doverosa attività a beneficio dell'Ordine secondo sempre di mira la latinità di esso. E per ciò ottenere desidero e voglio che la Sede dell'Ordine sia sempre in paese Latino. Sicuro che seguirai questa mia volontà di tutto cuore ti abbraccio e ti benedico e sono, Il tuo aff.mo padre

Cannes 27 Dicembre 1931. *Alfonso*

The translation of the first two paragraphs: 27 December 1931

My dearest Son Ferdinand, My age which weighs me down makes me think of the succession of the Grand Magistry of the Constantinian Order of St. George. According to the statutes compiled by our old predecessor Francisco Farnese and approved by the venerated memory of Pope Clement XI with the Bull "Militantis Ecclesiae" which regulates all the government of the Order, you as my first born and myself not making any other designation you will be my successor in the Grand Magistry of the Order.

H.R.H. don Ferdinando Pio, Duke of Castro (1934-1960), succeeded his father as Grand Master of the S.M.Constantinian Order of St. George in 1931, four years before the Count of Caserta died. On 8 December 1955, he wrote to his brother don Ranieri stating that Ranieri should succeed him as Head of the Dynasty and Grand Master of the Royal Orders but NEVER the Infante Don Alfonso, son of the Infante Don Carlos.

Courtesy: Bali don Achille di Lorenzo

Prince don Ferdinando Pio, Duke of Castro (1934-1960), he was succeeded by his younger brother, H.R.H. Prince don Ranieri, Duke of Castro (1960-1973); this was done according to arrangements which had been made with the full approval of H.R.H. Don Carlos, the first brother in line of succession, who had renounced all claims to the throne of the Kingdom of the Two Sicilies and to the headship of the Royal House. He considered himself ineligible for the headship of the House of Bourbon-Two Sicilies because he was an Infante of Spain, and declined to accept the Grand Mastership of the S.M.Constantinian Order because of his commitments as Captain-General of the Spanish army.

1960 marked the beginning of a period of strife and acrimony within the family of Bourbon Two Sicilies, that the Royal House had not encountered even in the darkest days of despair one hundred years earlier. This rift caused the Spanish Infante Don Alfonso to claim the headship of the House and the grand-mastership of the Order, as well as the grand-mastership of the Royal dynastic Order of St. Januarius. He also took the name Duke of Calabria.

Both parties sought the approval of the Supreme Pontiff, John XXIII who, in consultation with his Head of Protocol and *Assessore* of his Secretariat of State, Mons. Hyginus Eugene Cardinale, and others decided for reasons given below to favour don Ranieri Maria, third son of the late

Lindau 8-12-55

Carissimo Ranieri,

Rispondo subito alla tua lettera del 5 corrente. Ti prego di far sapere al Conte Raoul de Warren che il mio successore presuntivo sei te e dopo di te Ferdinando, ma mai Alfonso, figlio di Nino, essendoci la rinuncia di Nino per sé ed i suoi figli ed eredi. Penso che l'autore non stia al corrente dei fatti non posso credere che ci sia una coincidenza con la lettera che Alfonso mi scrisse il 13 maggio 1950; alla quale, come ti dissi a Lindau, non ho risposto.

Spero che stiate tutti bene e che abbiate bel tempo e con tutti i miei vi anticipo i nostri auguri per Natale e Capo d'Anno a Voi tutti e ringrazio per i Vostri.

Abbraccio te ed i tuoi e sono

il tuo affmo fratello

Ferdinando

My dearest Ranieri, I reply immediately to your letter of the 5th instant. Please let Count Raoul de Warren know that you are my presumptive successor and after you Ferdinand, but never Alfonso, son of Nino, as Nino's renunciation exists for himself and for his children and heirs. I think the author is not aware of the facts. I cannot believe that there is a coincidence with the letter that Alfonso wrote to me on the 13th May 1950, to which, as I told you in Lindau, I did not reply. I hope that you are well and that you are having good weather, and with all mine I take this opportunity of sending our greetings for Christmas and New Year to you all and thank you for yours. I embrace you and yours and I am your affectionate brother. Ferdinando.   Lindau 8.12.55

The Spanish Infante Don Carlos (1870–1949) who in 9101 married Mercedes, Princess of the Asturias, and renounced all claims to the Kingdom of the Two Sicilies and its dynastic Orders. He became Captain General of the Spanish Army.

Courtesy: don Achille di Lorenzo

don Alfonso Count of Caserta, Duke of Castro, and declined to consider the claim of the Spanish Infante Don Alfonso.

Don Alfonso refused to accept the provisions that had been made by the Count of Caserta and by his eldest son and heir don Ferdinando Pio. He took particular umbrage at the written instructions don Ferdinando Pio had sent to his younger brother, don Ranieri, which specifically refer to him, and he refused to acknowledge their validity. Similarly, he refused to accept as valid previous treaties which excluded him because he was a Spanish Infante. As far as Pope John XXIII and the Holy See were concerned, H.R.H. don Ranieri, who had inherited the title Duke of Castro on the death of his eldest brother, don Ferdinando Pio, became the new Head of the House of the Two Sicilies and Grand Master of the two dynastic Orders of Knighthood. When don Ranieri, Duke of Castro, became the Head of the Royal House of the Two Sicilies in 1960, he appointed Bailiff don Achille di Lorenzo *Maggiordomo Maggiore* of the Royal House and Grand Chancellor of the S.M. Constantinian Order of St. George.

The succession of don Ranieri to the headship of the House of Bourbon Two Sicilies was based on conditions concerning the succession laid down in the Act signed in Cannes on 14 December 1900 and the interpretation of that Act. It was never questioned by the Infante Don Carlos, nor did he place any conditions on his younger brother, Ranieri, succeeding to the headship of the House.

Left: H.R.H. don Ranieri Maria, Duke of Castro, Head of the Royal House of Sicilies and Grand Master of the Royal Orders, who succeeded his elder brother H.R.H. don Ferdinando Pio in 1960. Right: The Duke of Castro with his Maggiordomo Maggiore of the Royal House and Grand Chancellor of the S.M. Constantinian Order, Bali don Achille di Lorenzo.

Courtesy: Bali don Achille di Lorenzo

Some changes concerning the right of succession to the grand-mastership were later claimed to have been contained in letters exchanged between the Count of Caserta and his three sons, don Ferdinando Pio, don Carlos and don Ranieri. It is unfortunate that only part of the correspondence has survived. None of it is in any way conclusive.

The Count of Caserta had already expressed great concern about the future of the Constantinian Order, when the heir presumptive, the only son of the heir apparent, don Ferdinando Pio, died in 1914. The Count of Caserta's anxiety was aggravated in 1924, when Minister Boselli, Chancellor of the Order of SS. Maurice and Lazarus of the reigning House of Savoy of Italy, launched an unprecedented attack against the Constantinian Order which Pius IX had protected at the time of the *Risorgimento* from being annexed by the Order of SS. Maurice and Lazarus, claiming that the Constantinian Order had been abolished in 1861.

H.R.H. the Infante Don Alfonso, son of the Infante H.R.H. Prince Don Carlos, and father of the Infante H.R.H. Don Carlos. Both took the title Duke of Calabria on the death of their fathers.

Courtesy: Guy Stair Sainty

By 1924 the delicate negotiations concerning compensation to be paid to the Papacy for the loss of the Papal States and the establishment of a sovereign state for the Holy See, between Prime Minister Benito Mussolini for the Kingdom of Italy and Cardinal Gasparri, Papal Secretary of State, had begun. Although the Concordat between Italy and the Holy See, which became known as the Lateran Treaty, was not signed until 1929, Cardinal Gasparri, anxious not to jeopardize the delicate negotiations, yielded to the pressure of the King's Minister and wrote to the Count of Caserta that 'the Sacred Congregation has decided to suspend temporarily the functions assigned to the Cardinal Protector of the Constantinian Order until the Order's legitimacy has been recognised by the Italian Government'. The reason for the hostility shown by the Savoyan Order of SS. Maurice and Lazarus may have been an act of revenge for the harsh criticism against that Order by Pope Pius IX on 22 January 1855, and because the Pope had defended the Constantinian Order against the attempts of the House of Savoy to annex the Order after 1861.

As far as Cardinal Gasparri (himself a Bailiff Grand Cross of Justice of the Order) was concerned, temporarily withdrawing the Cardinal Patron from the Constantinian Order seemed a small price to pay if it pleased the Italian Minister and assured the continuation of the negotiations towards

H.R.H. Don Carlos de Bórbon Dos Sicilias e de Bórbon Parma was created an Infante of Spain by H.M. Juan Carlos I of Spain on 16 December 1994.

Courtesy: Guy Stair Sainty

a treaty. A farcical and pathetic sequel to the Lateran Treaty of 1929 is referred to in the Chapter on the Order of the Golden Spur, which Cardinal Gasparri conferred on Benito Mussolini in 1932 on behalf of Pope Pius XI for his help in finalising the Concordat.

Deeply grieved by Cardinal Gasparri's letter suspending the Cardinal Patron of the Constantinian Order, the Count of Caserta addressed himself to Pope Pius XI, asking His Holiness to take full possession of the Sacred Military Constantinian Order of St. George for the Apostolic See, so that it could be transformed into a Religious Order of Knighthood.

There is sufficient circumstantial evidence to suggest that this letter was intercepted by sympathisers of the Italian Minister inside the Holy See, and that Pius XI never saw it or learned of its existence. No reply was received by the Count of Caserta, which was out of character with the meticulous manner in which Pius XI always dealt with his correspondence.

Don Alfonso, an Infante of Spain and the son of the Infante Don Carlos, (who died in 1949), claimed the headship of the Royal House of Bourbon Two Sicilies and the grand-mastership of the Constantinian Order in 1960 when don Ferdinando Pio, Duke of Castro, had died. He put his claim directly to the Pope, though, according to the diary notes of an eye-witness, Mons. Cardinale, without producing any evidence which might have persuaded John XXIII to accept his claim that his father, the Infante Don Carlos, had only renounced the position of Head of the House of the Two Sicilies and the grand-masterships of the dynastic Orders of Knighthood for himself but not for his heirs and descendants. No written evidence exists that this had been the wish of the Infante Don Carlos.

Don Ranieri Maria, Duke of Castro, younger brother of the late Infante Don Carlos, on succeeding don Ferdinando Pio in 1960, was entirely guided in all his decisions by his *Maggiordomo Maggiore* and Grand Chancellor, don Achille di Lorenzo, who proved don Ranieri Maria's legitimacy as Head of the House of Bourbon Two Sicilies and Grand Master of the S.M.Constantinian Order of St. George to the satisfaction of the Holy See and the Italian Government.

Pope John XXIII would not be persuaded to lend his support to Don Alfonso because he was an Infante of Spain, and His Holiness was adamant that as an Infante of Spain Don Alfonso could not be at the same time Head of another Royal House that was sovereign and independent from Spain.

After a less than harmonious retirement from his office as Grand Chancellor, two written statements by don Achille di Lorenzo of 10 April and 23 April 1993 suggest that the Infante Don Alfonso, who had assumed the title Duke of Calabria, could possibly have claimed the grand-mastership of the Constantinian Order because changes to the rules of succession to the grand-mastership of the Order, had been discussed by the Count of Caserta. Don Achille also believes that the Count of Caserta might have been under the impression these changes had been made when he asked his eldest son, the Infante don Carlos, to accept the grand-mastership of the Constantinian Order, though no such changes were ever made in the statutes, nor were they mentioned in the Last Will and Testament of the Count of Caserta.

In any case, this argument was not put forward by the Infante don Alfonso when making his claims in Rome. Everything points to the fact that neither the Spanish Infante H.R.H. Don Alfonso who died in 1964, nor his son, Don Carlos de Bórbon y Bórbon (Dos Sicilias), who was not an Infante of Spain in 1964, knew anything of the Count of Caserta's idea to separate the sovereignty of the House of the Two Sicilies from that of the Constantinian Order, or they would have put forward this argument to support their claim.

In fact, the first time that this issue was mentioned was in 1993 when don Achille di Lorenzo sent me two affidavits to that effect.

In 1966, at the instigation of don Achille di Lorenzo, don Ranieri Maria, Duke of Castro, handed over the office of Grand Master of the S.M.Constantinian Order of St. George to his son don Ferdinando Maria, Duke of Calabria, who succeeded as the Head of the Royal House of the Two Sicilies in 1973, on his father's death.

Prince ALFONSO, Count of Caserta (Duke of Castro) =
1841-1934

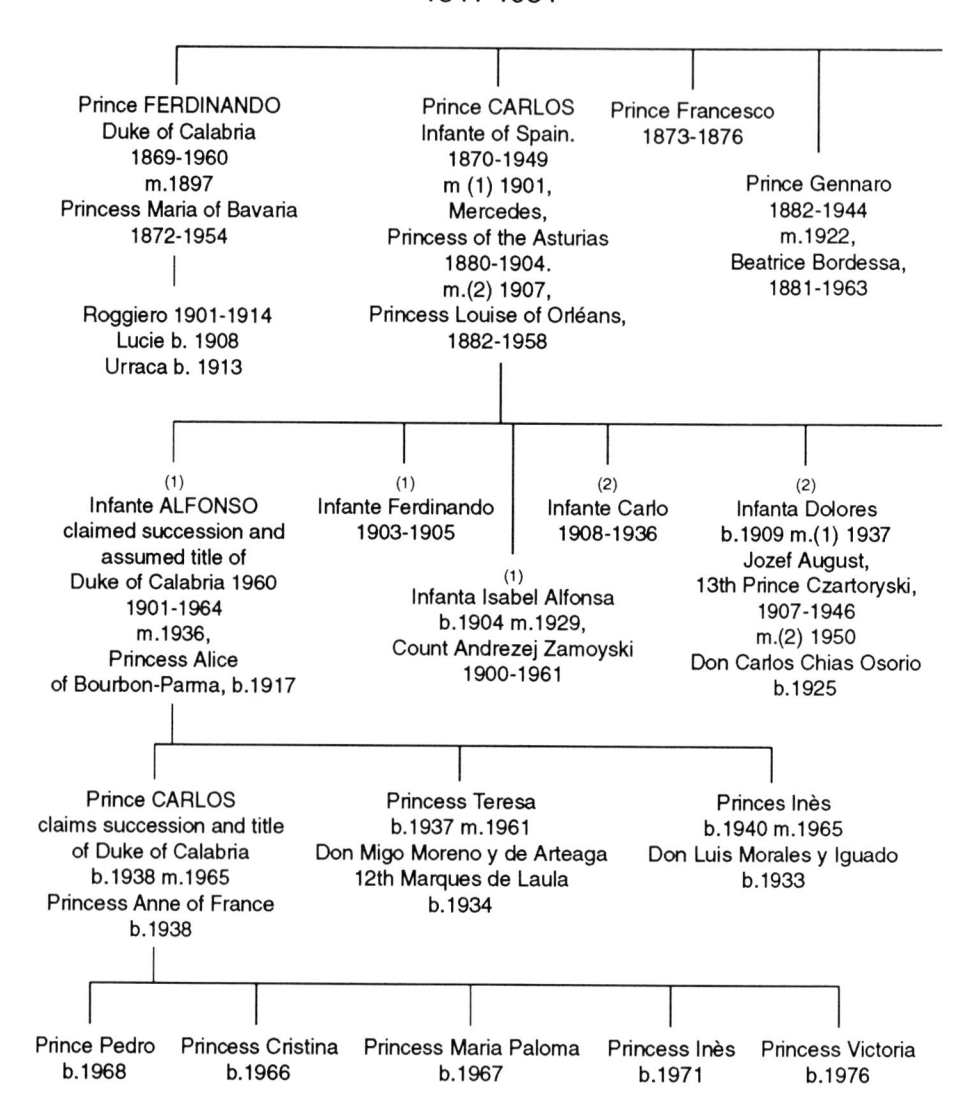

Prince FERDINANDO
Duke of Calabria
1869-1960
m.1897
Princess Maria of Bavaria
1872-1954

Roggiero 1901-1914
Lucie b. 1908
Urraca b. 1913

Prince CARLOS
Infante of Spain.
1870-1949
m (1) 1901,
Mercedes,
Princess of the Asturias
1880-1904.
m.(2) 1907,
Princess Louise of Orléans,
1882-1958

Prince Francesco
1873-1876

Prince Gennaro
1882-1944
m.1922,
Beatrice Bordessa,
1881-1963

(1)
Infante ALFONSO
claimed succession and
assumed title of
Duke of Calabria 1960
1901-1964
m.1936,
Princess Alice
of Bourbon-Parma, b.1917

(1)
Infante Ferdinando
1903-1905

(1)
Infanta Isabel Alfonsa
b.1904 m.1929,
Count Andrezej Zamoyski
1900-1961

(2)
Infante Carlo
1908-1936

(2)
Infanta Dolores
b.1909 m.(1) 1937
Jozef August,
13th Prince Czartoryski,
1907-1946
m.(2) 1950
Don Carlos Chias Osorio
b.1925

Prince CARLOS
claims succession and title
of Duke of Calabria
b.1938 m.1965
Princess Anne of France
b.1938

Princess Teresa
b.1937 m.1961
Don Migo Moreno y de Arteaga
12th Marques de Laula
b.1934

Princes Inès
b.1940 m.1965
Don Luis Morales y Iguado
b.1933

Prince Pedro
b.1968

Princess Cristina
b.1966

Princess Maria Paloma
b.1967

Princess Inès
b.1971

Princess Victoria
b.1976

1868 Princess Antonietta of Bourbon-Two Sicilies
1851-1938

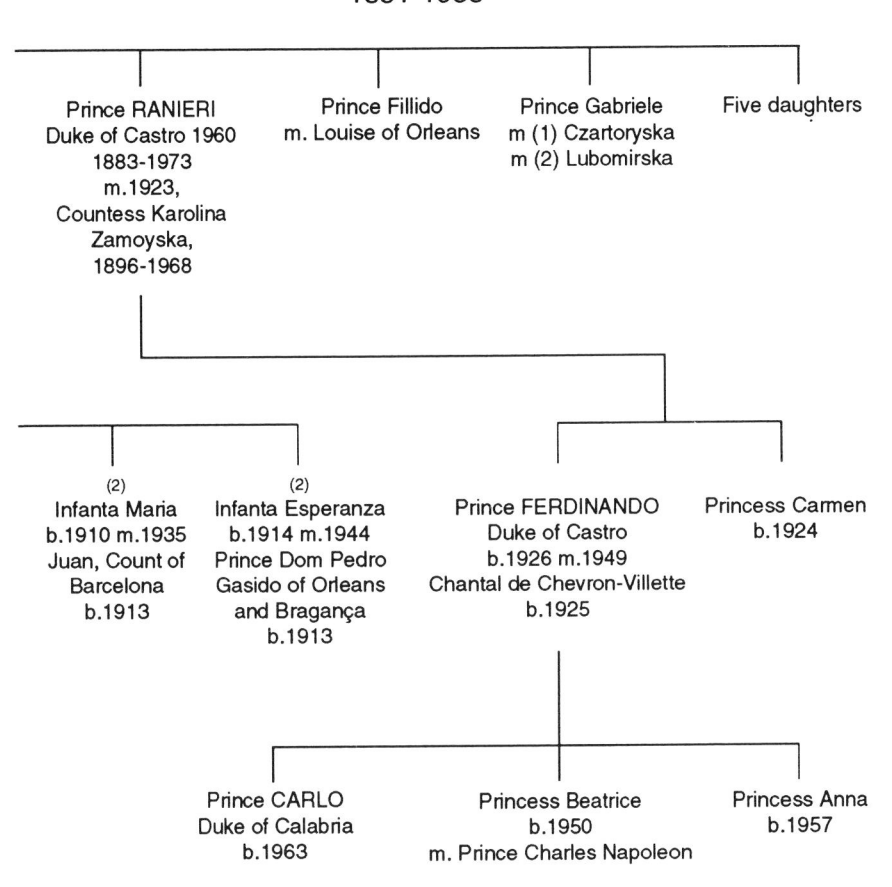

- **Prince RANIERI**
  Duke of Castro 1960
  1883-1973
  m.1923,
  Countess Karolina
  Zamoyska,
  1896-1968
- **Prince Fillido**
  m. Louise of Orleans
- **Prince Gabriele**
  m (1) Czartoryska
  m (2) Lubomirska
- Five daughters

Children of Prince Ranieri:

- (2) **Infanta Maria**
  b.1910 m.1935
  Juan, Count of
  Barcelona
  b.1913
- (2) **Infanta Esperanza**
  b.1914 m.1944
  Prince Dom Pedro
  Gasido of Orleans
  and Bragança
  b.1913
- **Prince FERDINANDO**
  Duke of Castro
  b.1926 m.1949
  Chantal de Chevron-Villette
  b.1925
- **Princess Carmen**
  b.1924

Children of Prince Ferdinando:

- **Prince CARLO**
  Duke of Calabria
  b.1963
- **Princess Beatrice**
  b.1950
  m. Prince Charles Napoleon
- **Princess Anna**
  b.1957

H.E. Bali don Achille di Lorenzo, Maggiordomo Maggiore of the Royal House of the Two Sicilies from 1960 until 1991, first under H.R.H. don Ranieri, then under don Ferdinando Maria. A Knight of Justice of the S.M.Constantinian Order of St. George created by the Count of Caserta in 1931, Grand Chancellor of the Order under don Ranieri Maria and don Ferdinando Maria until 23 April 1991, Minister Secretary of the Royal Order of St. Januarius until 23 April 1991.

Courtesy: Grand Chancery, S.M.C.O., Naples

DYNASTIC ORDERS OF KNIGHTHOOD

Interment of the last King of the Two Sicilies, Francesco II, his consort, Queen Maria Sophia, and their daughter the Princess Maria Christina in the Basilica de S. Chiara in 1984. Left: H.R.H. don Ferdinando Maria Head of the Royal House of the Two Sicilies (right) and his Maggiordomo Maggiore and Grand Chancellor, Bali Achille di Lorenzo.

The Duke of Castro's transfer of the grand-mastership of the Constantinian Order to his son don Ferdinando Maria in 1966 has always been judged by observers as a brilliant ploy by don Achille di Lorenzo, as it prevented any possible renewed claim to the grand-mastership of the Constantinian Order by Don Carlos de Bórbon y Bórbon after the eventual death of the Duke of Castro. Don Achille surmised that because Don Carlos was not then – unlike his grandfather and father – an Infante of Spain, his claim might find perhaps a more sympathetic hearing from Pope Paul VI, especially if he was able to produce relevant letters written by the Count of Caserta to his son the Infante don Carlos, urging him to accept the grand-mastership of the Constantinian Order. However, apart from don Achille di Lorenzo nobody knew that such letters had actually been written, and if they had been written what had happened to them in the course of time.

It was well known in the Roman Curia and in royal and princely circles of Europe that the affairs of the Neapolitan House of the Two Sicilies, the administration of the S.M. Constantinian Order of St. George, and the Royal Order of St. Januarius were in the hands of Bali don Achille di Lorenzo. There is no doubt that the renaissance of the Neapolitan Constantinian Order and, indeed of the Dynasty of Bourbon Two Sicilies (Naples), from 1960 onwards owes don Achille a large debt. H.R.H. don Ranieri lived in Damaine de St. Sauveur, France, and the residence of his son, H.R.H. don Ferdinando Maria, is in St. Aygulf, France. The Grand Chancery of the Constantinian Order between 1960 and 1991 was in the Villa di Lorenzo in Naples where its traditional domicile had been since the seventeenth century. Since 1992, the offices of the Grand Chancellery are divided between Naples and Rome.

Don Achille di Lorenzo's first achievement was the settlement of the dispute the Order had had with the Italian Government since the fall of the Kingdom of the Two Sicilies in 1861 until the end of the Second World War, when the subject matter was no longer relevant to the republican Government. In 1963, the President of the Republic of Italy, Signor Antonio Segni, recognised and authorised the S.M. Constantinian Order as a dynastic Order of Knighthood of the Royal House of Bourbon-Two Sicilies, and he was subsequently appointed a Bailiff Grand Cross of Justice of the Order. This was consolidated when in 1985 the Italian President, The Hon. Francesco Cossiga, showed great admiration for the important social work undertaken by the Sacred Order and was invested with the Collar and Grand Cross (*categoria speziale*) of the Constantinian Order.

The House of the Two Sicilies (Naples) was not spared continued disputes concerning the headship of the Royal House and the grand-mastership of the Constantinian Order of St. George. Don Carlos de Bórbon y Bórbon Dos Sicilias whose position was backed by the then

Head of the Royal House of Bórbon of Spain, H.R.H. Don Juan, Count of Barcelona, (the son-in-law of the late Spanish Infante Don Carlos and father of H.R.H. Juan Carlos, Prince of the Asturias, continued to confer the Constantinian Order, the Order of St. Januarius and some other former Orders of the Kingdom of the Two Sicilies. All attempts at bringing about a compromise between the two branches in the House of the Two Sicilies have failed.

As a result of Archbishop Cardinale's former position as the Chief of Protocol of Pope John XXIII and *Assessore* of the papal Secretariat of State, he was well aware of the situation; his close work with the Spanish episcopate and his strong Italian connections created a genuine dilemma for him. It was for this reason that in 1980 he asked me to take charge of the chapter in *Orders of Knighthood, Awards and the Holy See* on the House of the Two Sicilies and the Constantinian Order, though he personally continued to work on it. However it freed him from having to listen to the claims of either side which caused serious embarrassment to him and to his diplomatic mission. My nominal charge of that chapter made it possible for him to divert some of the pressure on him by telling enquirers that he was not dealing with that section. Mons. Cardinale continued to view the situation concerning the Constantinian Order pragmatically and he personally wrote every word in the chapter that

H.R.H. don Ferdinando Maria, Duke of Castro, Head of the Royal House of the Two Sicilies and Grand Master of the Royal Orders of the Dynasty. He became Grand Master of the S.M. Constantinian Order of St George in 1964 as Duke of Calabria and succeeded his father, don Ranieri Maria as Duke of Castro in 1973.

Courtesy: Grand Chancery, S.M.C.O., Rome

appeared in 1983. While he was in a coma during the weeks before his death, several factual errors of dates and names in that chapter were drawn to my attention by Count Andrzej Ciechanowiecki, and they were corrected before publication.

Archbishop Cardinale told me several times that he was probably not in possession of all the historical facts. As it happened, statements that cast some doubt on what had been hitherto accepted as a *fait accompli* only emerged between 1991 and 1993. With hindsight I believe that he suspected that whatever secrets might be hidden from him, their eventual revelation would cause even more upheaval and damage to the Constantinian Order, which he held in the highest esteem.

From 1960 onwards, Bali don Achille di Lorenzo had expanded the Constantinian Order of St. George and established the National Association of the Knights of the Constantinian Order in Italy (Ente Morale) and Associations and Delegations of Knights throughout the Western world. He appointed a new Delegate in the United States of America and a Chargé d'Affaires for Great Britain.

Loyalty to the Supreme Pontiff and to the Holy See was a prerequisite he demanded from those who were admitted to the Order. Don Achille was, in the words of Mons. Cardinale, 'the only guarantor of a continued Catholic Constantinian tradition', and it was for this reason that he always encouraged the Holy See to support the Order under don Achille's grand-chancellorship.

As mentioned above, after Pope John XXIII had decided not to support

His Holiness Pope John XXIII (1958-1963) who in 1960 refused to support the claims of the Spanish Infante Don Alfonso.

H.R.H. don Carlo di Borbone, Duke of Calabria and heir to the Duke of Castro. He succeeded don Achille di Lorenzo as Grand Chancellor of the S.M. Constantinian Order of St. George in 1992.

Courtesy: Grand Chancery, S.M.C.O., Rome

the claims of the Spanish Infante Don Alfonso, it appeared for a while that the dispute between the two branches of the Bourbons of the Two Sicilies had died down, but a growing undercurrent of querulous and contentious charges and countercharges continued to dominate the relationship between them.

Archbishop Cardinale was very conscious of the enormous damage done to the Constantinian Order by these quarrels that were aggravated and fanned by outsiders, several of whom he named and described in letters to me in 1981 as 'notorious peripatetic social climbers and trouble makers, who drift from Order to Order, always leaving destruction behind them and a stench of treachery'. Right to the end of his life he felt that only a reconciliation between the members of the family of Bourbon Two Sicilies in Naples and in Spain could bring about a satisfactory solution, but he was firm in his view, which he had always shared with Pope John XXIII, that the Order's future as a Catholic Order of Knighthood could under present circumstances only be guaranteed if it was organised from its traditional Grand Chancellery in Naples, and he always stressed that because of that, the grand-chancellorship of don Achille di Lorenzo was a pivotal factor in such a guarantee.

In November 1982, Mons. Cardinale informed me of his decision to force the pace of a reconciliation by attributing in the heading of the chapter the Constantinian Order both to the Two Sicilies and to Spain. He was well aware that the Constantinian Order had never belonged to the House of Bourbon of Spain, but he thought it was worth trying to provoke the House of Bourbon Two Sicilies into reaching a settlement. Unfortunately, events were overtaken by his death on 24 March 1983.

After my visit later that year to Cardinal Casaroli, the Secretary of State who, with the Holy Father, had encouraged Mons. Cardinale to write this book, and before I was asked to take on the task of revising and editing the book, I paid a visit to King Juan Carlos of Spain, and later to don Achille di Lorenzo in Naples.

Although this was not the purpose of my visit, I asked the King whether the Head of the House of Bourbon of Spain laid claim to the Sacred Military Constantinian Order of St. George. King Juan Carlos made it absolutely clear that the Order had nothing whatsoever to do with Spain and had always belonged to the Kingdom of the Two Sicilies; he also thought that Mons. Cardinale's attribution of the Order both to the Two Sicilies and to Spain had been a grave error, which should be corrected as soon as possible. Both His Excellency Joaquîn Martinez-Correcher, Count de la Sierragorda (the Chief of Protocol of the Spanish State), during his earlier diplomatic mission in Brussels, and I had assisted Mons. Cardinale for some years and we both had asked him not to make this attribution as it would further complicate the situation. However, the Archbishop was adamant and insisted on it because he believed that King Juan Carlos, as Head of the senior Bourbon branch, would actively intervene in this matter and bring it to a satisfactory conclusion.[1]

In the revised edition of 1985, the Constantinian Order was attributed to the House of the Two Sicilies, but at that time nothing had changed with regard to the Neapolitan Order's position *vis-a-vis* the Holy See. The main aim of don Achille di Lorenzo had been to strengthen the Order's obligations as a 'Sacred' Order of Knighthood, which he considered synonymous with its strict Catholic principles and being a lay apostolate in the Catholic Church; the Order's money was being used for charitable works and donations to the Holy Father for his charities. He associated the Order's works with the appellation 'Sacred', which the Order has borne for centuries, and he always expressed his fear that any change in its policies would endanger that.

The two written statements by don Achille di Lorenzo, who was close to four Grand Masters, the Count of Caserta (since 1930), don Ferdinando Pio, don Ranieri and don Ferdinando Maria (until 1991), inevitably raise many more questions, if not about the Constantinian Order *per se*, then about the House of the Two Sicilies.

The strong position of the Order in Italy was consolidated when don Achille di Lorenzo blocked any attempt by don Carlos de Bórbon y Bórbon (Dos Sicilias) to represent claims to a reigning Pontiff. No illegal act was committed in 1966 when don Ranieri Maria, Duke of Castro, followed the advice given him by don Achille di Lorenzo to transfer the grand-mastership of the Constantinian Order to his son don Ferdinando Maria, Duke of Calabria, without delay. According to don Achille's statements, one powerful consideration persuaded the Duke of Castro, following his initial unwillingness: the Infante Don Alfonso, the son of don Ranieri's elder brother, the Infante Don Carlos, and don Ranieri's nephew, had died in 1964; Don Alfonso's son, Don Carlos, who had taken his father's name Duke of Calabria after his father's death, was then not an Infante of Spain.

Mons. Cardinale discussed the matter with Pope Paul VI several times and he counselled the Holy See not to involve itself in the internal dynastic politics of the Two Sicilies and maintain the support for the Neapolitan branch under the stewardship of don Achille di Lorenzo.

In both his written statements, don Achille di Lorenzo gives a verbatim account, as he remembers it, of don Ranieri's opposition to the transfer of the grand-mastership of the Constantinian Order to his son don Ferdinando Maria, to which he agreed only when don Achille used the argument that the Kingdom of the Two Sicilies was in Italy, and the

---

[1] See Appendix XII. On 16 December 1994, H.M.King Juan Carlos I conferred upon S.A.R. Don Carlos de Bórbon Dos Sicilias y Borbón Parma the appellation 'Infante of Spain' and declared him to be representative of a Spanish Bourbon branch linked to the senior Spanish Crown.

undesirability of letting the Sacred Constantinian Order of Naples go to Spain by default.

Don Achille di Lorenzo, who states that he was with the Count of Caserta at the time, recalls that in 1931, the Count of Caserta discussed changing the statutes of the Constantinian Order with regard to the succession to the grand-mastership. It appears that details of the envisaged changes were known only to the Count of Caserta and don Achille, who feared that in 1931 the Count of Caserta might have decided:

> 1) that the Mastership of the Constantinian Order could pass from a Prince of Bourbon Two Sicilies to a Prince of Bourbon of Spain and continue through that line of descent;
>
> 2) that an Infante of Spain *could* become the Grand Master of the Neapolitan Constantinian Order of St. George;
>
> 3) might have created documentary evidence that he (the Count of Caserta) did not consider that his son Carlo's renunciation of the eventual succession to the throne of Naples also included the renunciation to the grand-mastership of the Sacred Military Constantinian Order of St. George for his heirs.

As history has shown, neither the Count of Caserta nor his eldest son, Don Ferdinando Pio, who succeeded him, made any such changes.

Don Achille di Lorenzo then put forward one further argument which finally persuaded don Ranieri Maria to transfer the grand-mastership of the Constantinian Order to don Ferdinando Maria in 1966: by the time of don Ranieri Maria's death, don Ferdinando Maria would had served several years as Grand Master of the Constantinian Order, and the Holy See would never disturb the equilibrium and peace that had been so difficult to establish.

In the absence of written and verified documentation proving that the Count of Caserta wanted to change the statutes with regard to the succession to the grand-mastership of the Constantinian Order, there was no case to be put to Paul VI; also the right of the Don Carlos de Bórbon y Bórbon (Dos Sicilias) to the title 'Duke of Calabria' was strongly refuted in the two statements of don Achille di Lorenzo, because Don Carlos' father, the Spanish Infante Don Alfonso had claimed that title in 1960 on the death of his uncle Prince Ferdinando Pio, and on his death it was claimed by his son Don Carlos.

Legally, the wishes of a Grand Master are not binding on his successors and any possible obligation to the successors of the Infante Don Carlos, the son of the Count of Caserta, regarding the succession to the grand-mastership of the Constantinian Order are outweighed by the legality of the succession as it took place; masterminded, as it was, by don Achille di Lorenzo.

Between 1986 and 1992, both branches of the House of the Two Sicilies presented their arguments to the public at large. First, the historian and writer on chivalric subjects, Desmond Seward, published his *Italy's Knights of St. George, The Constantinian Order* (Gerrards Cross, 1986), which firmly placed the headship of the House of the Two Sicilies and the grand-mastership of the Constantinian Order with H.R.H. don Ferdinando Maria, Duke of Castro. The views expounded by Desmond Seward were endorsed by the Sovereign Military Order of Malta, twenty-three Cardinals, and favourably discussed in the *Journal of the Orders and Medals Research Society*, which exercises extreme caution when giving an opinion on foreign orders and decorations. Three years later, Guy Stair Sainty, also a noted writer on chivalric subjects, published *The Orders of Chivalry and Merit of the Bourbon Two Sicilies Dynasty – A Historical Survey with the Statutes and Recent Documents* (Madrid, 1989), and placed the headship of the Dynasty and grand-mastership of the Constantinian Order with H.R.H. Don Carlos de Bórbon y Bórbon, Duke of Calabria.

In January 1990, a booklet appeared (without any imprint), containing a legal Opinion by The Right Honourable the Lord Rawlinson of Ewel PC QC, an eminent lawyer, following the submission of certain documents to him by Prince Rupert zu Loewenstein, Delegate of the Constantinian Order under Don Carlos (Spain), who commissioned a legal Opinion on three questions: 1) the legal status of the S.M. Constantinian Order of St. George; 2) who was the legitimate successor to the grand-mastership of the Order after the death of don Ferdinando Pio in 1960; 3) who was the legitimate successor to the headship of the Dynasty of the Two Sicilies after the death of don Ferdinando Pio in 1960.

On the basis of the documents shown him, Lord Rawlinson found in favour of Don Carlos de Bórbon y Bórbon, Duke of Calabria.

Don Achille di Lorenzo issued a rebuttal of Lord Rawlinson's Opinion using documents that had not been available to Lord Rawlinson. The entire October 1990 issue of *The Constantinian Chronicler* and thirty-two pages of the January 1992 issue are devoted to this rebuttal, reproducing facsimiles of twenty-five relevant documents.[1]

To the Sovereign Military Order of Malta and several members of the Roman Curia who gave me their opinion, it was not only the rebuttal by don Achille, but the publication of the documents that appears to have weighed the argument in favour of the Neapolitan cause.

The statutes promulgated and given to the Order by Clement XI in 1718, request the Knights and Dames to be faithful to the fundamental principles of the Catholic religion and to be loyal to the Supreme Pontiff. The Order's task is to help and assist those who have been given a chivalric dignity in achieving that aim.

---

[1] *The Constantinian Chronicler* (Colin Smythe, 1990-1992). Interested scholars should write to the publishers for further information.

Both sides of the divide have always agreed that there can only be one Sacred and Military Constantinian Order of St. George, one Grand Master and, in fact, one Head of the Dynasty. However unpalatable the family dispute has been to the Knights and Dames of the Order, it in no way affects or infringes upon their legitimate chivalric status.

The Sacred Military Constantinian Order of St. George is the major factor for the continued importance of the House of the Two Sicilies. The Head of the Dynasty is the Sovereign of the Constantinian Order even if he were not also the Grand Master. The only two occasions when the positions have been separated have been when three years before his death Alfonso, Count of Caserta, Duke of Castro, passed on the Grand Mastership to his eldest son, don Ferdinando Pio, Duke of Calabria, and secondly when don Ranieri, Duke of Castro passed it to his son don Ferdinando Maria at don Achille di Lorenzo's instigation. Both succeeded to the Headship of the House and the title Duke of Castro on the death of their fathers.

As a matter of principle, the Apostolic See now refuses sit in judgement on matters of succession that are subject to secular laws, such as the headship of a dynasty. Its interests are spiritual and only concern the Constantinian Order inasmuch as Pope Clement XI promulgated its statutes and its religious or 'sacred' aims. By the same token, the Apostolic See will not take sides in this dispute although it has never expressly abdicated its spiritual responsibility or influence over the Order.

The statutes of the Constantinian Constitution state that the succession to the grand-mastership of the Order is by male primogeniture, although a sovereign Grand Master of the Order possesses the power to change this if circumstances make it necessary. Charles III, for example, changed the succession by transferring the grand-mastership to his third son. During the Kingdom of the Two Sicilies, the succession returned to succession by primogeniture. The Count of Caserta may have considered separating the two sovereignties again by transferring the Order's grand-mastership to his second son and the headship of the house to his third son, but he did not do so.

THE SACRED MILITARY CONSTANTINIAN ORDER OF ST GEORGE
(Sacro Miltare Ordine Costantiniano di San Giorgio)

Tradition has it that the Sacred Military Constantinian Order of St George is the descendant of the Golden Militia probably formed by the Emperor Constantine as the guard for his standard of the Labarum, the model of the cross he saw in the sky with the words 'In Hoc Signo Vinces' prior to

H.R.H. don Ferdinando Maria, Duke of Castro, Grand Master of the S.M. Constantinian Order of St. George, in audience with Pope John Paul II.

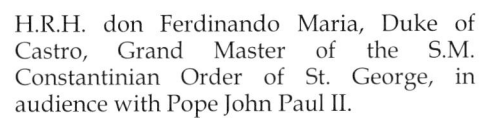

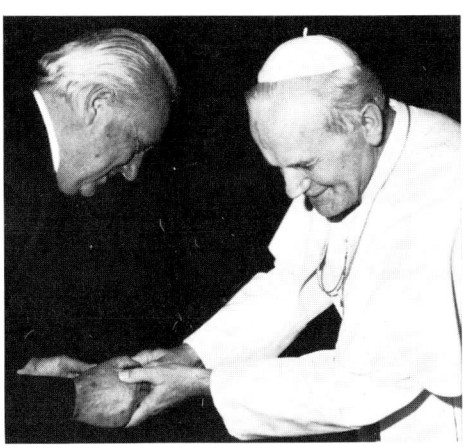

the battle of the Milvian Bridge in AD 312 against his rival Maxentius, whom he decisively defeated. Eusebius, writing prior to AD 340 described it as 'a long spear, overlaid with gold, formed the figure of the cross by means of a piece laid over it transversely. On top there was a crown composed of gold and precious stones, and on this two letters indicating the name of Christ represented the Saviour's title by using its initial letters, P crossing the centre of X'. Of a square form, the standard was carried at the head of the army, and after this success, whenever it was taken into battle, the enemy fled. All this information was given Eusebius by Constantine himself.[1]

The date given for the foundation of the Sacred Military Constantian Order of St George by the Byzantine Emperor Isaac II Comnenus is 1190, and early histories state that after the fall of the Eastern Empire, the Angeli descendants of the imperial family came to Italy, and with them came the Grand Mastership of the Order. But the first verifiable documents that mention it at all are Papal Bulls of the mid 16th century, and the first documented Grand Master was Hieronimo Angelo (1505-91) who was joined in a triple Magistry with his two obscure brothers. It would appear that the Holy See felt it politically advisable to have the family seen to be the internationally recognised pretenders to the throne of the Eastern Empire, one Papal Bull going so far as to threaten anyone who questioned their imperial ancestry with excommunication.

The first printed statutes of the Order were published in Venice in 1573, and six editions appeared in the next fifteen years, published at Padua, Rome, Ravenna, Milan, Bologna and Madrid. In 1623 the then Grand Master Giovanni Angelo ceded the Grand Magistry to Don Marino Caracciolo, Prince of Avellino and Grand Chancellor of the Kingdom of

---

[1]For fuller details I refer the reader to Desmond Seward's seminal work *Italy's Knights of St George: The Constantinian Order* (Gerrards Cross, 1986).

During a pastoral visit to the Archdiocese of Naples on 13 November 1990, Pope John Paul II had a private meeting with representatives of the Constantinian Order. The Grand Chancellor, don Achille di Lorenzo, presented to the Pope a cheque for US25,000, a gift from the American Knights, and introduced His Holiness to the members of the Constantinian delegation.

Courtesy: Bali don Achille di Lorenzo

the Two Sicilies, and his heirs, but the following year Giovanni's son Angelo Maria claimed to be the lawful Grand Master, and in spite of Pope Urban VIII's acknowledgement of the transfer to Don Marino, the Sacred Rota found for the Angeli, and Urban confirmed this decision, so the Caraccioli had to accept the judgement. By 1697 the last of the Angeli line, Gian Andrea, was living in poverty, and it was arranged for the Grand Magistry to be transferred to Duke Francesco Farnese of Parma (who was technically *ex officio* Commander-in-Chief of the Armies of the Church), Gian Andrea living the rest of his life in comfort, dying in 1702.

The Order having won high esteem in European countries and especially in the Vatican, Pope Clement XI (1700-1721) approved the Order once again and promulgated the Orders statutes on 6 June 1718. He also made the Order directly dependent on the Apostolic See, enriching it with many privileges. As I explained in the introduction to the section the Dynasty of the Two Sicilies, these statutes have been confirmed by many successive Popes and have never been revoked, thus ensuring the Order's continued dependency on the Apostolic See, up to the present day.

S.A.R. don Carlo di Borbone, Duke of Calabria, who in 1992 succeeded don Achille as Grand Chancellor of the Order, presented the Pope with a medal that was struck in 1848 for King Ferdinand II of the Two Sicilies; it showed Pope Pius IX who had found refuge in the Kingdom for two years during the rebellion in Rome.

Courtesy: Bali Don Achille di Lorenzo

The Farnese period lasted until 1731, with only two Grand Masters, Francesco and his brother, neither of whom produced heirs, but through their niece Elizabeth, who was now Queen of Spain, her fifteen-year-old son, the Infante Carlos de Borbon was recognised as Duke of Parma on Antonio's death in 1731, and he also succeeded as Grand Master of the Order. War broke out between Spain and Austria over the Polish succession in 1733 and in 1734, leading a large Spanish and Italian army, Carlos entered Naples to become King of the Two Sicilies, being crowned the following year as King Carlos VII. In 1738 he had his Grand Magistry confirmed by a Bull of Pope Clement XII (and that year also founded the Order of St Januarius for the greatest Neapolitan families), but he still considered the Constantinian Order to belong to Parma, and very few of the Knights he appointed were Neapolitan. However, when by the Treaty of Aix-la-Chapelle his younger brother Filipe of Bourbon became Duke of Parma, Piacenza and Castro, Carlos nevertheless retained the Grand Magistry for himself. When Ferdinando VI of Spain died in August 1759 he succeeded as King Carlos III, and on 6 October by Royal Decree, known as the 'Prammatica', he separated the throne of Spain from that of the Two Sicilies, abdicating the latter in favour of his third son who was eight years old and thus became Ferdinando IV of the Two Sicilies. On 16 October Carlos also renounced the Grand Magistry of the Order in favour of his son as 'the eldest Farnese by rank, title and right, although third-

Bali don Achille di Lorenzo (centre) introduces to the President of the Republic of Italy, Sig. Francesco Cossiga (right), S.A.R. don Carlo, Duke of Calabria, (left), during the President's official visit to Naples.

Courtesy: Bali don Achille di Lorenzo

born' – his eldest son being a lunatic, and his second son was sailing with him to Spain as heir to that throne.

Ferdinando was Grand Master of the Order until his death in 1825, and both Pope Clement XIII, by his Admonition in 1763 and Pope Pius VI, by his Bull in 1777 supported the Order and added to its wealth and privileges.

Under the Treaty of Vienna (1815) the wife of the Emperor Napoleon, Marie Louise, received for life the sovereignty of the Duchies of Parma, Piacenza and Guastalla which after her death were to be returned to the House of Bourbon of Parma. The following year she established a Constantinian Order of St. George for the Duchies of Parma and Piacenza, and she assumed the grand-mastership.

After her death a dispute arose between the Bourbons of Naples and the Bourbons of Parma over the possession of the original Constantinian Order, and to avoid open conflict, the two branches of the Royal House of Bourbon tacitly agreed to confer the Order independently, which their Heads did as reigning Sovereign until the annexation of Parma in 1859 and Naples in 1861 to the newly founded Kingdom of Italy. Although both Heads of the Borbon branches continued to confer the Order, the Holy See gave its support and approval only to the Head of the Royal House of the Two Sicilies, which continued to confer it as the only legitimate Sacred Military Constantinian Order of St. George.

As mentioned, don Achille di Lorenzo worked towards a settlement of the dispute between the Sacred Military Constantinian Order of St. George and the Republic of Italy. On 20 July 1963 the Presidency of the Italian Republic officially declared that:

> The National Association of the Knights of the Sacred Military Constantinian Order of St. George is an *ente morale* [a moral/legal entity under the law of the country] recognised and authorised in Italy as a legitimate dynastic Order of the Royal House of Bourbon of the Two Sicilies, of which the Head now is H.R.H. the Prince Ranieri Maria of Bourbon Duke of Castro.[1]

Italian citizens were henceforth permitted to accept and wear the insignia and decorations of the Order in Italy, as were visiting foreign members of the Order.

In 1983 a Spanish Commission issued a document, which was submitted to the Spanish Ministry of Justice, stating that the Infante Don Alfonso, the son of the Infante Don Carlos, automatically succeeded both to the headship of the House of the Two Sicilies and the Grand Mastership of the Constantinian Order on the death of don Ferdinando Pio, Duke of Castro, though it does not refer to or explain the objections of Pope John XXIII in 1960.

In 1993 the Grand Master of the Sovereign Military Order of Malta who, upon becoming the 78th Prince and Grand Master of the Sovereign Order, had already accepted the Collar of the Constantinian Order from don Ferdinando Maria, Duke of the Castro, attended the Order's functions in Naples a year later, and also accepted the Royal Order of St. Januarius from the Duke of Castro.

The insignia of the S.M.Constantinian Order of St. George is a red-enamelled, gold-rimmed, cross *fleury*, the arms of which bear at the extremes the letters I. H. S. V. in gold, (standing for the Order's motto IN HOC SIGNO VINCES (By this sign conquer), which recalls the vision of the Emperor Constantine before the battle of the Milvian Bridge in 312. The letters Alpha and Omega are inscribed in gold on the horizontal arms of the cross near the centre. The Greek letter Chi (X) on the letter Rho (P) (standing for Christos), both in gold metal, are superimposed on the cross.

The Star of the Order is an eight-pointed, faceted star in silver or gold,

---

[1] In 1981 the President of the Italian Republic confirmed the decree of 1963, appertaining to all members of the Order, and confirming H.R.H. don Ferdinando Maria as Head of the Dynasty and Grand Master.

Cross of the category *di Grazia* and the Grand Cross *Categoria Speziale*.

Star of the Order; in gold: category *di Justizia* and Grand Cross *Categoria Speciale*; in silver: categories *di Grazia* and *di Merito*.

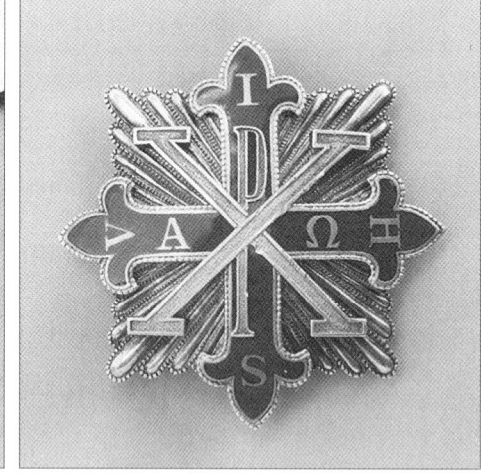

Cross of the categories *d'Ufficio* and *di Merito*.

Ecclesiastical Star of the Order. This is the original Star of the Order's Grand Priors from 1840 to 1959; (see also colour section and Appendix X).

Prof. Dr. M. Sas-Skowronski, Rector of the Polish University Abroad, has been one of only three recipients of the special Medal *Benemerenti Pro Christiana Cultura* in gold which is worn as a neck badge from a light blue ribbon.

depending of the class, with the Cross of the Order superimposed on it. The Star of Ecclesiastical Knights, Knights Commander and Knights Grand Cross are also eight-pointed and faceted, but square in appearance because the upper and lower right and left arms are more prominent. The ribbon and sash of the Order are of celeste blue watered silk.

There are four classes, Justice, Grace, Merit and Office, as well as several ranks within the classes, Grand Cross, Commander and Knight/Dame. In addition, the Order has a Grand Cross (*categoria speziale*) with gold Star, which is conferred very rarely and on Heads of State with a special collar.

The Cross is worn by Knights and Dames of Office as a breast badge, and by Knights, Knights Commander and Grand Officers of the Merit class as a neck badge. Knights and Dames Grand Cross of Merit wear the Cross on a sash. Knights with Star, Grand Officers and Knights/Dames Grand Cross wear a silver Star on their left breast; Grand Officers and Knights Commander also wear an identical cross to their neck badge on their breast.

The Cross of the class of Grace is surmounted by the gold crown of the Kingdom of the Two Sicilies. All ranks wear a silver Star.

The Cross of the Justice Class is suspended from a military trophy, and the Star is gold. Bailiffs Grand Cross have an image of St. George slaying a dragon pending from the Cross. A Constantinian Collar is also conferred.[2]

The Order has a 'Benemerenza' Medal in gold, silver and bronze which is also available to non-Catholics. A special Medal 'Benemerenti Pro Christiana Cultura' in gold was instituted which has only been awarded three times, to the late Cardinal Siri, to Cardinal Ratzinger and to Professor M. Sas-Skowronski, Rector of Polski Universitet Na Obczysnie.

The Order's Feastdays are St. George's Day, 23 April, and the Feast of the Exaltation of the Cross, 14 September.

Some of the Constantinian Knights in Houston, Texas, wearing the blue *mantello* with the Constantinian Cross on the left side. On the left of the Order's Priest in Houston, stands the Delegate for the United States of America (with embroidered collar), The Hon. David Garrison Jr.

Courtesy: USA Delegation, SMCO -

THE ROYAL ORDER OF ST JANUARIUS
(Insigne Reale Ordine di San Gennaro)

This dynastic Order was founded on 3 July 1738 by Carlos, Infante of Spain, ninth Duke of Parma, King of Naples and of Sicily (the Two Sicilies), before he became King Carlos III of Spain. His aims for the foundation were to honour St. Januarius, the Patron Saint of Naples, who had died a martyr in AD 305. The occasion of its foundation was his marriage to Princess Amalia Walburga of Saxony, daughter of Frederick Augustus II, Elector of Saxony and King of Poland.

Pope Benedict XIV gave the Order his approval in 1741, the first year of his pontificate. The aim of Carlos VII was to create an Order that would be equal in prestige to the Orders of the Golden Fleece and of the Garter. He restricted the number of Knights to twenty, who came from the most noble families of the Two Sicilies.

When he became King of Spain, he took the Royal Order of Januarius with him and retained the grand-mastership until 1766. Only then did he hand it over to his son Ferdinand IV of the Two Sicilies, who meanwhile had come of age. Ferdinand IV was already a Knight of the Order since 1759 before becoming its Grand Master in 1766.

In 1771 Carlos III of Spain used the statutes of the Order of St. Januarius as a pattern for the Order of Carlos III when he founded it in gratitude for his prayers having been answered for a grandson, who was born on the Feastday of St. Januarius, 19 September.

The Most distinguished Order of Charles III remained the principal Order of the Spanish State until recently, when King Juan Carlos restored the Noble Order of the Golden Fleece (Spanish branch) once more to its traditional position.

The Order of St. Januarius continued to prosper. Even after King Francis II went into exile in 1861, he continued to bestow it, as have all his successors to the present day. As with the Constantinian Order, the Order of St. Januarius has been the subject of disputed ownership within the Royal Family of the Two Sicilies. It is interesting to consider why the Sacred Military Constantinian Order of St. George and not the Royal Order of St. Januarius, which was founded to be the equal of the Golden Fleece and the Order of the Garter, is in the forefront of the dispute. I believe the reason lies in the fact that the Constantinian Order became ultimately far more influential because it had no numerical limitations.

In 1827, King Francis I of the Two Sicilies appointed several Officers to

[2]See Colour Plates on the S.M.Constantinian Order.

The insignia of a Knight of the Royal Order of Januarius

Courtesy: Real Casa di Borbone delle Due Sicilie

the Order of St. Januarius, and on 19 September 1983 H.R.H. don Ferdinando Maria, Duke of Castro, changed Article IV of the original statutes of King Carlos VII of 1738, raising the number of members to be appointed to the Order to sixty Knights.[1]

The Order is conferred in one class; its Badge consists of an eight-pointed, gold-rimmed, red-enamelled and white-bordered cross with gold balls at the eight points and four gold *fleurs-de-lis* between the arms of the cross. The profusely coloured enamelled red robed and mitred figure of St. Januarius, holding two vials filled with his miraculous blood in his left hand on a book of the gospels in gold, pressing his crozier to his body, and blessing with the right hand, is portrayed in the centre above a blue-enamelled scroll with the gold inscription IN SANGUINE FOEDUS (the covenant is sealed by the blood). The Badge is suspended from a gold Collar consisting of eighteen alternating religious emblems and military trophies, some enamelled. A similar Badge, but without St. Januarius holding the crozier, is suspended from a deep red sash.

The Star of the Order is similar in form to the Cross, but silver and faceted with four faceted *fleurs-de-lis* between the arms of the cross-shaped, eight-pointed star, on which the profusely enamelled figure of St. Januarius is superimposed.

The Star of the High Officers of the Order is also silver, but is slightly smaller and not as ornately faceted as that of the Knights, and the figure of St. Januarius is sculpted in silver with a white-enamelled alb and a gold choir cope and gold crozier. The motto is engraved on a silver scroll.

The Feastday of the Order is 19 September.

The Star of a Knight of the Royal Order of St. Januarius.

---

[1] Dr. Antonio Spada and Desmond Seward set the original number of Knights at twenty and mention the enlargement of the Order to sixty in 1983. Gritzner and Guy Stair Sainty state that the origial number was sixty.

V

THE ROYAL HOUSE OF SAVOY – ITALY

When His Majesty King Umberto II, who had left Italy after a referendum on the Monarchy in 1946, died on 18 March 1983, six days before Archbishop H.E. Cardinale, the category 'Catholic Dynastic Orders bestowed by a Sovereign in Exile' ceased to exist, as King Umberto had been the last living Catholic Monarch in exile.

His Majesty was succeeded by his son, His Royal Highness Victor Emmanuel as Duke of Savoy, Prince of Naples and hereditary Head of the Royal House of Savoy, Sovereign and Grand Master of the dynastic Orders of the Royal House.

Before leaving Italy in 1946, King Umberto had taken leave of Pope Pius XII, who assured him that the Holy See would always honour the dynastic status of the Orders of SS. Annunziata and of SS. Maurice and Lazarus, both of which the King took with him into exile.

On 3 March 1951 the Italian Republic instituted the Order 'Al Merito della Repubblica Italiana' and specified that this new Order took the place of the Order of SS. Maurice and Lazarus which had been suppressed, and the wearing of its insignia outlawed in Italy. The Republic justified this decision by declaring that the Order of SS. Maurice and Lazarus had been an Order of the Crown and therefore of the State, and that the Republic of Italy could abolish it. In the article of law No. 178 of 30 March 1951, the republican Government also declared the Order of SS. Annunziata and its decorations suppressed.

There is no argument that the law suppressing the Order of SS. Annunziata and the decree abolishing the Order of SS. Maurice and Lazarus were based on grave historical and legal errors, and that the Italian Republic had no jurisdiction over either Order.

Although the Italian Republic did not deny the dynastic character of the Order of SS. Annunziata, it was not prepared to give a dynastic status to the Order of SS. Maurice and Lazarus. The historical and legal errors with regard to the latter are obvious: in 1572, Pope Gregory XIII granted by Papal Bull the grand-mastership of the Order of SS. Maurice and Lazarus 'for ever to the Duke of Savoy for himself and his Royal Successors', and thus it became irrevocably a dynastic Order of the Royal House of Savoy.

Having democratically voted – disregarding the regional difference between the northern and southern regions and the narrow overall margin in favour of a republic – Italy was governed by a republican government which would have acted within its rights forbidding the public wearing of insignia of dynastic Orders of Knighthood and Merit in Italy, but overstepped its competence when it first suppressed the Order of SS. Maurice and Lazarus and then the SS. Annunziata. In any event, the Italian Government could not forbid the wearing of the Orders' insignia outside Italian territory. Furthermore, as the King had not abdicated, he was fully entitled to continue conferring the dynastic Orders and create titles, though titles claimed by some petitioners are suspect.

As to the wearing of the insignia of the allegedly suppressed dynastic Orders, it is interesting to note that, for example, General Anders, the Commander in Chief of the Polish Armed Forces during the Second Word War and afterwards with the Polish Government-in-exile, who had been decorated by the King of Italy with the Grand Cross of the Order of SS. Maurice and Lazarus, continued to wear the green sash from which the Cross was suspended and the Star every year when he made his annual pilgrimage with the former Polish combatants to Monte Cassino.

The relationship between the Royal House of Savoy and the Republic of Italy was further strained by laws passed after King Umberto II left Italy. These laws prohibited the King and his direct male descendants from setting foot on Italian soil. The King's request to die in his homeland was not granted, though the republican government would not have opposed the King being interred in Italy. This, however, was complicated as far as the actual place of interment was concerned because of disagreements with regard to the ownership of the rightful resting place for a King of Italy.

As with other former monarchies, Italian laws restricting the descendants of the last monarch from entering their homeland are reviewed periodically and are likely to be revoked by the republican parliament in due course.

During much of his exile King Umberto II lived in Portugal. His Royal Highness Prince Victor Emmanuel, Duke of Savoy, who inherited the grand-mastership of the Orders of SS. Annunziata and SS. Maurice and Lazarus, resides with the Royal Family in Geneva, Switzerland, where the Private Office of the Head of the House of Savoy is temporarily situated, as is the Chancellery of the dynastic Orders. The Duke's heir apparent is his don, H.R.H. Prince Emanuele Filiberto.

With regard to the question of *fons honorum*, King Umberto II of Italy did not abdicate; he left his homeland without signing any document of abdication or transfer of power. His Majesty was, in fact, strongly advised at the time not to leave Italy but to establish himself in the central and southern regions where the vote in the referendum had been markedly for retaining the monarchy, whereas the northern region, especially the

H.R.H. Victor Emmanuel, Duke of Savoy, Prince of Naples and Head of the Royal House of Savoy, Sovereign and Grand Master of the Dynastic Orders of Knighthood.

Courtesy: Real Casa di Savoia

strongly Communist controlled cities and towns had voted for a republican government.

It is idle to speculate what might have happened if the King had taken the advice to stay in the southern regions; His Majesty chose to leave Italy and not to divide his country. Nevertheless, the King-in-exile retained, and made extensive use of, his prerogative of *fons honorum*, which in 1983 passed to his legitimate heir and successor H.R.H. Prince Victor Emmanuel, Duke of Savoy.

The history of the House of Savoy begins with Umberto I (1003-1048), Count of Savoy; existing in relative obscurity until the Emperor Sigismund (1410-1438), King of Hungary and of Bohemia, created Count Amadeus VIII Duke of Savoy in 1416. During the pontificates of Pope Eugene IV (1431-1447) and Pope Nicholas V (1447-1455), Amadeus of Savoy in 1439 became one of the five fifteenth century antipopes. The Council of Basel (the conclave consisting of only one cardinal and thirty-two electors) deposed Pope Eugene and choose Duke Amadeus to demonstrate the Council's resolve to elect someone of wealth and international standing to the See of St. Peter. As Pope, he assumed the name Felix V. The Council of Basel lasted from 1431 to 1449. Pope Felix V abdicated his pontificate in 1449 and died in 1451.

The first Duke of Savoy to achieve royal status was Victor Amadeus II, who became King of Sicily in 1713 and was King of Sardinia from 1720 to 1730 when he abdicated in favour of his son Carlo Emmanuel.

Perhaps the most famous member of the family was Prince Eugene of Savoy (1663-1736), great-grandson of Carlo Emmanuel I, Duke of Savoy. Prince Eugene, whose noble chivalry is recalled in ballads throughout Europe, was one of the most celebrated generals and military strategists of the late sixteenth and early seventeenth centuries.

The Dynasty of Savoy continued, though with some vicissitudes: Carlo Felix, King of Sardinia (1821-1831), was the last of the lineage of the Dukes of Savoy, of which Victor Amadeus II had become the first King of Sardinia in 1720. King Carlo Felix was succeeded by his cousin Carlo Alberto, a Prince of the Carignano lineage, who traced his direct descent to the Dukes of Savoy to the same ancestor as Prince Eugene of Savoy, Duke Carlo Emmanuel I.

Carlo Alberto, King of Sardinia (1831-1849) abdicated in favour of his son, Victor Emmanuel II, King of Sardinia (1849-1861), who became the first King of Italy in 1861 and ruled until his death in 1878, aged fifty-seven years. In his reign the *Risorgimento* drew to its conclusion, but so had the Papal States, and he had found formidable enemies in Pope Pius IX and the entire Roman Curia who had fiercely opposed the arrival of the Savoyards. King Victor Emmanuel II was succeeded by Umberto I, who reigned as King of Italy until 1900, and he was succeeded by Victor Emmanuel III. The tragic end for the Kings of Italy began in 1943, when

Prince Eugene of Savoy, a brilliant general and strategist, and one of the most famous members of the Savoyan family.

the King Victor Emmanuel first tried to dismiss the fascist leader Benito Mussolini when he called on the King at the Villa Alada for the last time to give him the report of the Grand Council, and have him arrested. The Queen disapproved because she believed firmly that Savoyan hospitality should never be used for setting a trap to arrest somebody. Even his staunchest supporters and loyal monarchists advised King Victor Emmanuel to abdicate in favour of his son Umberto, but the King refused to do so after the war was over. Finally he agreed to abdicate in Rome, but was not allowed to enter the city to do so. He resigned on 9 May 1946 and fled to Egypt where King Farouk gave him refuge. He died in December 1947 in Alexandria. His son Umberto, who had already been made Lieutenant General of the Kingdom of Italy on 5 June 1944, wanted to fight on the side of the allies and go to Rome, but King Victor Emmanuel did not allow it. Umberto II became King upon his father's abdication, less than one month before the referendum on 2 June 1946 ended the reign of the House of Savoy as Kings of Italy. He left Italy on 13 June 1946.

His Majesty King Umberto II, the last King of Italy.

THE SUPREME ORDER OF THE MOST HOLY ANNUNCIATION
(Ordine Supremo della SS. Annunziata)

Instituted in 1362 by Amadeus VI, Count of Savoy (1343-1383), under the title of the Order of the Collar, its origin has clearly religious connotations. As the name given to it at a later date implies, it was dedicated to the Blessed Virgin Mary, Our Lady of the Annunciation, portrayed on the gold medallion, which is suspended from a gold chain made up of love-knots and roses in memory of the fifteen mysteries in the life of Our Lady, with the letters F.E.R.T. interwoven, referring probably to the victory at Rhodes by Count Amadeus V in 1310. The letters have later been interpreted as the initials of FORTITUDO EIUS RHODUM TULIT (by his bravery he conquered Rhodes), an allusion to the help Savoy rendered to Rhodes in 1310, but is has been suggested that they merely stand for the third person singular of the present indicative tense of the Latin verb ferre. In this case it could imply that the member of the Order is supported by the bond of faith he swore to Mary, or even that he puts up with all for the love of Mary. The letters may also refer to the motto FOEDERE ET RELIGIONE TENEMUR (We are held by Pact and Religion) found on the gold doubloon of Victor Amadeus I (1718-1730), or they could be the initials of FORTITUDO EIUS REPUBLICAM TENET (his strength defends the State). All these interpretations, and others, have been put forward over the centuries. Pope Pius IX (1846-1878), who had frequently protested to Victor Emmanuel II, and who sent a diplomatic note strongly protesting against the "iniquitous despoliation" of the Church to Umberto I when he succeeded to the throne of Italy in 1878, interpreted the motto F.E.R.T. to mean FRAPPEZ, ENTREZ, ROMPEZ TOUT! (Knock, enter, break everything!).

The number fifteen became symbolic of the number of Knights forming the Order, the number of the Chaplains celebrating the fifteen daily masses, and that of the clauses of the original statutes which under Amadeus VIII (1391-1451) added five more in 1434. It was given its present name by Duke Charles III (1504-1553) in 1518, when the image of Our Lady of the Annunciation and the Angel, surmounted by the Holy Spirit, was represented on the medallion. He also added five Officers to the Order.

The Order, which has only one class, and soon enjoyed the greatest prestige, ranking with the Orders of the Golden Fleece and the Garter. Though mainly open to Catholics who had rendered outstanding services, non-Catholics were on rare occasions admitted as honorary members, such as the Duke of Wellington in 1815, and Edward, Prince of Wales, in 1915. Recipients of this Order are required to have already been awarded the Order of SS. Maurice and Lazarus.

DYNASTIC ORDERS OF KNIGHTHOOD

The Badge and Star of the Order of SS. Annunziata. Courtesy: Real Casa di Savoia

The Order has two sets of insignia. The *Piccola Collana* consists of a solid gold filigree pendant in the centre of which the Annunciation of the Blessed Virgin by the Archangel Gabriel is sculpted. The filigree medallion is surrounded by three intertwined Savoyan knots, decorated with small crosses *fleury*, and in the upper centre, between two of the Savoyan knots is a sculpted image of a dove, representing the Holy Ghost, in a cluster of gold rays. The Badge is suspended from a gold Collar consisting of fifteen ornate filigree sections each of which is linked by a filigree Savoyan knot.

The gold Star, which was introduced in 1680, also has a representation of the Annunciation in a medallion in the centre, heraldically similar to a cross of four pommels, and is surrounded by a cluster of rays. In four faceted fields, between the arms of the cross of four pommels of the centre medallion, are the letters F.E.R.T.

The *Grande Collana* is also of gold and worn only on special occasions. It consist of fourteen profusely ornate sections, each of which is made up of the letters F.E.R.T. in gold, intertwined with a white- and red-enamelled Savoyan knot. The sections are interlinked with fourteen roses, alternately enamelled red and white. The gold filigree pendant is slightly smaller and consists of a number of gold Savoyan knots surrounding the Annunciation which is enamelled white, red and blue.

The Grand Collar of the Order of SS. Annunziata which is worn on special occasions.

THE ORDER OF SS. MAURICE AND LAZARUS
(Ordine dei Santi Maurizio e Lazzaro)

Amadeus VIII, Count of Savoy (1391-1416), first Duke of Savoy (1416-1440) – as well as being Antipope Felix V from 1439-1449 – founded the Order of St. Maurice in 1434. The Order's aims were to serve God, to lead a monastic life and to assist the Dukedom of Savoy in its needs.

Pope Gregory XIII recognised the Order of St. Maurice as a Military Religious Order of Knighthood in 1572, and in the following year he sanctioned the annexation by the Order of the Italian Commanderies of the Military Hospitaller Order of St. Lazarus of Jerusalem, founded as an Order of Hospitallers in Palestine in ca. 1070, fusing the Italian Knights of St. Lazarus with the Order of St. Maurice. The new Order of SS. Maurice and Lazarus adopted the rule of St. Augustine, already adopted by the Order of St. Maurice, and added to its aims the defence of the Papacy.

The combined Order prospered from the support it was given by the House of Savoy and the Papacy, and it soon was regarded with such high esteem that many European Sovereigns would recommend their most illustrious Knights for admission to it. After 1861, against the protests of

H.R.H. Victor Emmanuel, Duke of Savoy and Grand Master of the Order of SS. Maurice and Lazarus in the robes of the Order.

Courtesy: Real Casa di Savoia

Pope Pius IX, who had severely admonished and criticised the Order of SS. Maurice and Lazarus on 22 January 1855, the Order annexed the estates belonging to the S.M. Constantinian Order of St. George. In 1868 King Victor Emmanuel II reformed the Order of St. Maurice and Lazarus more on the lines of an Order of Merit.

As has already been noted, on his departure from Italy in 1946, King Umberto II of Italy took with him both Catholic-founded dynastic Orders of the House of Savoy, the Order of the Most Holy Annunziata and the Order of SS. Maurice and Lazarus.

During his exile, King Umberto conferred the Order of SS. Maurice and Lazarus upon cardinals, sovereigns, heads of state and also some high Italian officials even though the Italian government tried to replace it with its own State Order of Merit. In Italy itself, those dependant upon the State for their livelihood were careful when they wore the insignia, but many Italians had no such worries and wore them were they could,

Knights of the Order of SS. Maurice and Lazarus in procession.

Courtesy: Real Casa di Savoia

DYNASTIC ORDERS OF KNIGHTHOOD 317

The Cross of the Order of SS. Maurice and Lazarus (I – IV class, though different in size).

The Star of a Grand Officer of the Order of SS. Maurice and Lazarus.

Duke Karl Albrecht of Wittelsbach-Bavaria (1726-1745) who founded the Bavarian Order of St. George in 1729.

Courtesy: Der Präsident der Verwaltung des Herzogs von Bayern

though technically this was an imprisonable offence. Foreign dignitaries, too, wore the Order of SS. Maurice and Lazarus when in Italy; as mentioned above, General Anders, the Commander-in-Chief of the Polish Armed Forces during the Second World War, and several high-ranking Officers, veterans of the Italian campaign, always wore the insignia when annually attending the Monte Cassino commemorations.

The Order has five classes, Grand Cross, Grand Officer, Commander, Officer and Knight. The Order's Cross consists of its original white-enamelled cross *botonnée* superimposed on the green Maltese Cross of St. Lazarus of Jerusalem.

The Cross for classes I – IV is surmounted by a gold crown and varies in size according to the rank. A Grand Officer wears a four-pointed faceted silver star, the Grand Cross an eight-pointed faceted silver Star, with the Cross of the Order superimposed on them. The ribbon and sash of the Order are green.

VI

THE ROYAL HOUSE OF BAVARIA WITTELSBACH

The Catholic Royal House of Bavaria (Wittelsbach) which celebrated its eighth centenary in 1980, is probably best known for its Monarch, King Ludwig II, who ruled from 1864 until his suicide in 1886. In many respects with the tragic death of Ludwig II, an important era of the formerly proud sovereign Royal House ended. His brother Otto I, who was insane and ruled in name only until his death in 1916, and his cousin Ludwig, son of the Regent Luitpold, who died in 1912, and who declared himself King in 1913, and legitimately became King Ludwig III in 1916, only to be deposed in 1918, never achieved the greatness of their predecessors. Ludwig III died in 1921 and was succeded by Prince Ruprecht (1869-1955), who became the first of the legitimate successors to a former King of Bavaria (Wittelsbach). Prince Albrecht, Duke of Bavaria (1905-), is the present Head of the Royal House, Crown Prince Franz (1933-) is the heir apparent.

The Dynasty of the sovereign Dukes of Bavaria Wittelsbach traces its origins to 1180 when the Emperor Frederick I granted Bavaria to Otto von Wittelsbach, and this first native Bavarian ruler laid the foundations of the future Bavaria. The Emperor Napoleon, made the Dukedom of Bavaria a Kingdom in 1806. The history of Bavaria became closely associated with that of Bismarck's creation of the German Reich; after supporting Austria in its contest with Prussia in June 1866, it made peace with Prussia in August the same year. In 1870, Ludwig II declared his intention to join Prussia in its war with France, and in 1871 he proposed in a letter to the King of Saxony that the King of Prussia should be made Emperor of the Great German Reich.

The pro-German sympathies of Ludwig II secured Bavaria a special status in the confederation of the Greater German Reich. Ludwig's rebellion against Papal Infallibility must be seen in context with the *Kulturkampf* Bismarck waged against the Papacy and the Holy See, and in retrospect much of what then seemed to bear the mark of finality, was merely a passing phase.

The dynastic Orders of Knighthood of the Royal House of Bavaria (Wittelsbach) were originally endowed with special papal favours and retained a strong Catholic character, though their active life in the ceremonial of the Church diminished after Ludwig II backed his former teacher in his fight against Papal Infallibility and in 1871 expelled the Jesuits from Bavaria.

Although the Kingdom of Bavaria had three dynastic Orders, the Royal Bavarian Dynastic Order of St. George has remained the principal Order of the House of Bavaria Wittelsbach and plays still an important part in the chivalric life of Bavaria.

The reason for the continued influence of the House of Wittelsbach in Bavarian affairs after the First World War is largely due to a factor which, in the context of the upheavals in the next few decades, is often overlooked by historians. In April 1917, Pope Benedict XV created the young Monsignor Eugenio Pacelli (later Pope Pus XII) titular Archbishop of Sardes and appointed him as Apostolic Nuncio to Bavaria. Although Archbishop Pacelli was transferred in 1920 as Nuncio to the new Republic of Germany, he laid the foundation of a very favourable Concordat between the Holy See and Bavaria as soon as he arrived there, and he personally brought the Concordat to a successful conclusion in 1924[1]. Archbishop Pacelli was also largely responsible for reestablishing the previously cordial relations between the House of Bavaria Wittelsbach and the Holy See.

Besides the Order of St. George, the dynastic Orders of St. Hubert and of St. Michael also belong to the Royal House of Bavaria Wittelsbach. Because of political developments and the role Bavarian Dukes have always played in a wider territorial context, these Orders were definitely confirmed and annexed by the Royal House of Wittelsbach, though unlike the Order of St. George, their purpose and criteria for conferment differed, and their importance in Bavarian chivalric life is no longer as important and prominent as that of the Order of St. George.

---

[1] The Concordat he completed with Prussia in 1929 was far less advantageous. Archbishop Eugenio Pacelli was created a cardinal in 1929 and succeeded Cardinal Gasparri as Papal Secretary of State.

Dubbing of the new Knights by the Grand Master, King Ludwig II, on St. George's Day 1880 in the Old Chapel Royal.

Courtesy: Der Präsident der Verwaltung des Herzogs von Bayern

THE ORDER OF ST. GEORGE, DEFENDER OF THE FAITH IN THE IMMACULATE CONCEPTION

In 1979, the Royal House of Bavaria Wittelsbach celebrated the 250th anniversary of the revival of the ancient and highly esteemed Catholic-founded Order of St. George. The Order is active in the field of charitable works and participates in the ceremonial of the Bavarian Church. On St. George's Day 1994 three candidates were invested with the Order.

Tradition has it that the Order's origin goes back to the Crusades, and historical records show that members of the House of Wittelsbach participated in all of them. It is also a historical fact that Orders and Fraternities under the patronage of St. George were fighting in the Crusades, and the Bavarian Order of St. George links itself to these.

The statutes in the Decree of Foundation of Duke Karl Albrecht of Wittelsbach, Elector of Bavaria, promulgated in 1729, lay down what is expected of members of the Order: 'You must honour God above all things. You must be firm in your faith in Our Lord Jesus Christ. You must honour your King and Lord, love him and respect his prerogatives, and as much as is in your power to do so, defend them. You must protect virgins, widows and orphans, and where you can prevent oppression of the weak, you must do so.'

The Papal Bull of 15 March 1728, confirming the foundation of the Order of St. George, issued by Pope Benedict XIII, draws a comparison with the Teutonic Order. In it, Pope Benedict states: 'We furthermore endow the Order of St. George with all titles of honour, prerogatives, privileges, powers and favours, which, through the benevolence of the Apostolic See have been granted in great abundance to, and which are enjoyed by, the Teutonic Order of the Blessed Virgin Mary, which has served as a role model in the foundation of the Order of St. George.'

The Order was also given the ceremonial of investiture used by the Teutonic Order, and some obligations placed upon the Knights of the Order of St. George had been increased. The draft for the final statutes and the Royal Decree of Foundation of the Order were completed in 1728, and the Order officially instituted by Duke Karl Albrecht, *Fundator Ordinis*, Grand Master, on 28 March 1729.

The Royal Decree consists of a comprehensive historical account of the Order prior to its revival; the Decree of Foundation of Duke Karl Albrecht; the statutes comprising forty paragraphs; *addenda (articuli additionales et separati)*; the oath to be taken by the knights; the ceremony of the dubbing, and directives concerning proof of nobility.

The most important decree of the statutes concerns the interpretation of

The Badge and the Star of the Order of St. George of Bavaria.

Courtesy: Garrison Collection

the letters V I B I – Virgini Immaculatae Bavaria Immaculata (dedicated to the Virgin of the Immaculate Conception of Bavaria which is immaculate in its faith) – and the letters I V P F – Iustus Ut Palma Florebit (the righteous will flourish like the palm tree).

THE ORDER OF ST. HUBERT

The Order was founded in 1444 by Gerhard V, Duke of Jülich-Berg to commemorate his victory over Arnold of Egmont at Ravensburg on St. Hubert's Day. It received its statutes in 1476 from Duke Wilhelm of Jülich-Berg. When the male lineage of the ducal Dynasty became extinct in 1609, it became part of the Dynasty of Palatine-Neuburg, of the Palatinate of the Rhine, one of the seven ancient electorates of Germany, but the Order of St. Hubert lay dormant until it was revived in 1708 by Duke Johann Wilhelm of Neuburg, Elector of the Palatinate.

The Order was confirmed in 1718 by Duke Karl Philip, and in 1744 and 1760 by the Elector of the Palatinate of the Rhine, Duke Karl Theodor, who in 1777, after the younger line of Wittelsbach had come to an end, also became Duke of Bavaria-Wittelsbach and Head of the ducal Dynasty of Wittelsbach. The Elector Duke Maximilian Josef of Bavaria Wittelsbach, who became King of Bavaria in 1806, confirmed the Order in 1800, and later decreed that it should rank as the senior Order of the Bavarian Crown, reserved for members of the Royal Family of Bavaria Wittelsbach, some foreign princes and twelve counts and barons.

The Badge of the Order is an eight-pointed, gold-rimmed Maltese cross, tipped with gold balls, white-enamelled and *guttée d'or*. Superimposed in the centre is a gold medallion depicting the legend of St. Hubert. The medallion is encircled by a gold-rimmed, re-enamelled band with the Order's motto IN TRAU VAST (steadfast in loyalty) in white letters. The cross has three gold rays between each arm and is surmounted by the crown of Bavaria. On the reverse the red-enamelled medallion shows a gold imperial orb surrounded by a white band with the inscription IN MEMORIAM RECUPERATAE DIGNITATIS AVITAE 1708. The ribbon of the Order is red with a light green border on either side.

The eight-pointed faceted silver Star has white-enamelled, *guttée d'or*, gold-bordered cross *formàe* superimposed on it; in the centre is a red-enamelled medallion with the motto of the Order in gold letters IN TRAU VAST, surrounded by a white-enamelled circle with gold borders and a gold ornate ring in the centre.

The Collar of the Order consists of forty-two alternating links: twenty-one gold plaquettes depicting the legend of St. Hubert and twenty-one devices with the letters T and V red- and green-enamelled and decorated with gold.

The dynastic Order of St. Hubert remains extant; it is still conferred on members of the family and other royal princes. H.R.H. Duke Albrecht of

Bavaria conferred the Order in 1991 on H.R.H. the Duke of Württemberg and in 1993 on the reigning Prince of Liechtenstein.

The Badge and the Star of the Order of St. Hubert which H.R.H. Duke Abrecht of Bavaria conferred on the Duke of Württemberg in 1991 and on the reigning Prince of Liechtenstein in 1993.

Courtesy: Garrison Collection

THE ORDER OF ST. MICHAEL

The Order was founded as a Catholic Religious Order of Knighthood by Josef Clemens, Duke of Bavaria-Wittelsbach, Archbishop and Elector of Cologne, Bishop of Liege, of Regensburg and of Hildesheim, in 1693. Josef Clemens was the fourth of five Dukes of Bavaria-Wittelsbach who held the office of Archbishop and Elector of Cologne between 1583 until 1761.

Maximilian Theodor, Duke of Bavaria-Wittelsbach and Elector of the Palatinate of the Rhine, Head of the House of Wittelsbach from 1777-1799, annexed the Order to the Bavarian Orders of Chivalry, adding to its tasks the defence of the Ducal House.

Duke Maximilian Josef (Head of the Dynasty of Bavaria-Wittelsbach from 1799 until 1825), confirmed the Order in 1812 after he had become King of Bavaria in 1806, and he added to the Order's tasks that of helping the poor and sick soldiers. The Church of St. Michael in Munich became the Order's chapel.

King Ludwig I of Bavaria (1825 until his abdication in 1848) secularised and reconfirmed the Order in 1837 and changed it into an Order of Merit. He made further changes to the statutes in 1844. Since 1846 the Order has had three classes: Knight Grand Cross, Knight Commander and Knight. His son and successor, King Maximilian II Josef (1848-1864), added in 1855 two further classes to the Order: Grand Officer (after Grand Cross and before Knight Commander) and a Knight of the second class. The Order is still listed by Maximilian Gritzner in his comprehensive work *Handbuch der Ritter- und Verdienstorden* (Leipzig, 1893), as active and flourishing, though it has been dormant during the twentieth century.

The Badge of the Order is a dark blue-enamelled, gold-rimmed cross *formée* (larger for the first three classes). The Badge of the Grand Cross, Grand Officer and Knight Commander has in the centre a gold or silver oval medallion, emanating from it are rays of gold. It depicts in relief the figure of St. Michael slaying a dragon, holding on the left a shield with the Order's motto on it QUIS UT DEUS?. On the arms of the cross of first four classes are the letters in gold P[RINCIPI] F[IDELIS] F[AVERE] P[ATRIAE]. The Badge is surmounted by a crown and is suspended from a dark blue ribbon with a pink-red border on each side. The (smaller) cross of a Knight of the first class has on the obverse a round blue-enamelled medallion with golden rays emanating from it and the Order's motto. The medallion on the reverse bears for all classes the inscription VIRTUTI. The Badge of Knights of the first class has rays emanating from the round medallion and the cross is surmounted by a crown. The Badge of Knights of the second class is in plain silver, has no letters on the arms of the cross, no rays emanating from the centre medallion, and is not surmounted by a crown.

The eight-pointed Star of silver rays has in its centre a gold cross *formée*,

The insignia of the Order of St. Michael of Bavaria which has been dormant during the twentieth century.

Courtesy: Garrison Collection

rimmed with silver beads, and the letters P.F.F.P. in silver on the arms of the cross. In the centre of the cross is a round, blue-enamelled medallion surrounded by white pearls and the motto in gold letters. The Star of a Knight Grand Cross is larger than that of a Grand Officer, who wears his Star on the right breast.

VII

THE ROYAL HOUSE OF BOURBON OF FRANCE
The Royal House of Bourbon Orléans

The direct line of the Royal House of Bourbon of France ended with the death of the Count of Chambord in 1883, and the Royal House of Bourbon Orléans became the senior branch of the Bourbons in France. They represent the continuity of a great dynasty that took control of France in 1589 at a time of ill fortune for the nation and led France through over two hundred years of greatness and international prestige.

The Royal House has three Catholic-founded dynastic Orders, none of which has been conferred since H.R.H. Prince Henri, Count of Paris,

The Count of Chambord was the last member of the House of Bourbon of France. The French Parliament had voted him King of France, but he refused the office because he would not tolerate the tricolour which he demanded be replaced with the Bourbon flag. His dynasty ended in 1883 and the junior branch, the House of Bourbon Orléans became the senior Bourbon branch in France.

became Head of the House of Bourbon-Orléans. There have been four claimants to the Royal House of Bourbon of France. Some of them awarded the Order of the Holy Ghost and of St. Michael (but not the Order of St. Louis) as late as the early 1970s. As explained above, H.R.H. the Count of Paris, who has been universally recognised as the legitimate Head of the Royal House of Bourbon-Orléans, always expressed the view that the three Orders of the House of Bourbon-Orléans should only be conferred by a ruling Sovereign of France. However, the Orders were never officially placed in abeyance but merely considered dormant, and the legitimate successors of the Count of Paris to the headship of the Royal House would be within their right to confer the Orders again in their capacity as legitimate successors of a sovereign Monarch, though it is doubtful that any of the Orders will regain a link with the Apostolic See because its principal dynastic Order of the Holy Ghost had already lost its Catholic character during the life time of its founder. The Order of St. Michael, ranking second in precedence, was amalgamated with the Order of the Holy Ghost and only independently revived in 1816, being restricted initially to Catholics of noble birth. The third dynastic Order, The Royal and Military Order of St. Louis was reformed in 1693, and although initially reserved for Catholic subjects as a long service award, the Order was secularised in 1759 and revived after the Revolution in 1816 by Louis XVIII as a secularised, Military Order of Knighthood, is open to all religions, although it appears never to have been conferred by the House of Bourbon-Orléans, nor, for that matter, by any of the other three pretenders to the throne of France.

There is a similarity between the uncompromising view of H.R.H. the Count of Paris of the House of Bourbon-Orléans and the last member of the Royal House of Bourbon of France, H.R.H. the Count of Chambord. After the fall of the Empire, the parliamentary Chamber, which was elected on 8 February 1871, had a two-thirds majority of royalists who aimed to restore the monarchy with the Count of Chambord reigning as King Henry V. In July 1871 the Count refused to accept the Crown of France unless it was accompanied by the white flag of the Bourbons of France and the tricolour abolished as the national flag. The Count's demand was considered so reactionary, even by the royalists in the parliamentary Chamber, that the monarchist cause was abandoned and lost.

THE ORDER OF THE HOLY GHOST

The Order was founded in 1578 by Henri III, King of France (1574-1589) to mark his election to the throne of Poland and to the Presidency of the Catholic League. Its main tasks were therefore to defend the Catholic religion and to uphold the dignity of the Catholic nobility.

The tinsel Star of the Order of the Holy Ghost. Founded in 1578, it immediately became one of the most prestigious Order in the late sixteenth century.

Courtesy: Garrison Collection

Some historians maintain that another Order of the same name had been founded in France in 1352 which became better known as the Order of the Knot because of the Badge worn by the Knights, but there was no connection between the former, ancient Order, if it was indeed founded in France and not in the Two Sicilies, and the Order of the Holy Ghost which immediately became one of the prestigious Orders of the late sixteenth century, the number of knights being restricted to 100.

As a result of the Order's prestige, that of the Order of St. Michael appeared to decline, and for a while many Knights of the Order of St. Michael appear to have been absorbed into the Order of the Holy Ghost.

The Order has one class, and its Badge is an eight-pointed, gold-rimmed and ball-tipped Maltese cross, enamelled white with green-enamelled foliage in the center upon which is superimposed a white enamelled dove, head downwards, symbolising the Holy Ghost. Between the arms of the cross are four gold fleurs-de-lis. In the centre on the reverse of the cross is the figure of St. Michael slaying a dragon. This appears to have been a concession made to the Knights of St. Michael who had been absorbed into the Order of the Holy Ghost, and encouraged to join the new Order by King Henry III himself.

The Badge was suspended from a *celeste* blue riband which was worn over the right shoulder.

The insignia were complemented by a large embroidered silver Star in the form of the cross with the dove in the centre. Many members of the Order, French and foreign sovereigns, had themselves painted in the magnificent gold embroidered velvet robes of the Order. Above an equally richly embroidered velvet mantle they wore the badge on a collar very similar to the Collar of the Order of St. Michael.

The foundation of the Order of the Holy Ghost was undoubtedly politically motivated. It took place in a period of universal unrest throughout Europe during which France suffered terribly from the religious wars of the Reformation and Counter-Reformation. The Catholic League was a powerful force on the Continent of Europe, and Henry III, being politically in a most precarious position, applied the basis of a science that was not to be invented for another 300 years to demonstrate his purported aims and zeal: psychology. Among the politically planned Orders, the Order of the Holy Ghost was the first one to adopt a cross as its Badge instead of just an emblematic figure.

The Order survived the assassination of its founder in 1589, and flourished again under the Bourbons of France, beginning with Henri IV, until the Order of the Holy Ghost fell into abeyance from 1791 to 1814 because of the French Revolution. Louis XVIII (1814-1815 and 1815-1824) re-established the Order as a dynastic Order of the House of Bourbon of France, and after the death of the Count of Chambord, in 1883, the Order became a dynastic Order of the House of Bourbon-Orléans.

THE ROYAL AND MILITARY ORDER OF ST. LOUIS

Founded by Louis XIV, King of France (1643-1715), in 1693 as a civil and military award for Catholics, it was the first of the knightly Orders of Merit, awarded in three Classes, Grand Cross, Knight Commander and Knight, to Catholics who had rendered at least twenty-eight years service to the crown. In 1759, King Louis XV confirmed the Military Order of St. Louis and supplemented it with the Military Order of Merit which was founded on the same principles for protestant Officers in the French army, who could not be decorated with the Order of St. Louis.

However, the Order of St. Louis had always mainted a Chapter of an Order of Knighthood and the character of a corporate Order, wheras the newly added Military Order of Merit was *de jure* and *de facto* an Award or Decoration, though Protestant Officers thus honoured were officially 'appointed to the Order'.

The insignia of the three French Orders are not dissimilar in design. The Badge of the Royal and Military Order of St. Louis is an eight-

The Badge and the Star of the French Royal and Military Order of St. Louis. A similar Order was subsequently founded for non-Catholics.

Courtesy: Garrison Collection

pointed, gold and ball-tipped Maltese cross with a white-enamelled border with gold fleurs-de-lis between the arms. In the centre was a oval red-enamelled medallion, with the figure of St. Louis in his royal mantle, holding in his right hand a wreath of laurels and in his left hand a wreath of thorns, all in gold. The medallion was surrounded by a blue-enamelled circlet with the inscription in gold letters LUDOVICUS MAGNUS INSTITUIT 1693. On the reverse was a similar medallion with a flaming sword piercing a laurel wreath and in the surround the Order's motto BELL[ICAE] VIRTUTIS PRAEM[IUM].

The Star of the Order was a silver embroidered enlargement of the Badge, but the medallion in the centre was round, and the ribbon of the Order was crimson.

The added Military Order of Merit, open to non-Catholics, was almost identical; the medallion on the obverse of the Badge and in the embroidered Star showed a raised sword and had the inscription PRO VIRTUTE BELLICA; the medallion on the reverse of the Badge showed a laurel wreath and had the inscription LUDOVICUS XV INSTITUIT 1759. The ribbon was dark blue.

The Royal Military Order of St. Louis and the added Military Order of Merit were suppressed in 1789 but revived by King Louis XVIII in 1816.[1]

Like several other French Royal Orders that had been revived, it appears to have fallen dormant after King Charles X went into exile in 1830.

Neither Louis Philippe, a member of the younger Bourbon branch of Orléans, separated for more than a century from the lienage of Bourbon of France, who however disavowed his family connection and accepted an elected Crown, being voted King in the French Assembly, and taking the name King Louis Philippe I, nor his successor, the grandson of King Charles X of the House of Bourbon of France, the Count de Chambord, conferred the Royal and Military Order of St. Louis. Although generally assumed to be a dynastic Order of the Bourbons of France which was subsequently inherited by the younger Branch of the Bourbon family, the Bourbons of Orléans, the Order appears to have remained dormant; however, it was not juridically abolished and therefore remains extant.

THE ORDER OF ST. MICHAEL OF FRANCE

Louis XI, King of France (1461-1483), founded the Order of St. Michael in 1469 to commemorate the heroic defence of the isle Mont St. Michele (Brittany), restricting the number of Knights to thirty-six. The original badge of the Order was a gold oval medallion bearing the figure of St.

Although a Royal Order, Louis XVIII delegated the administration and conferment of the Order of St.Louis to the French Ministry of War and a list of equivalency between it and the Légion d'Honneur was published.

The gold medallion of the Order of St. Michael of France that was conferred until 1563.

Courtesy: Garrison Collection

Michael, with a slightly trapezoid surround of a gold twisted cord. It was suspended with two small chains from a gold collar consisting of twenty-three shells, linked by a gold twisted cord. The motto of the Order was IMMENSI TREMOR OCEANI (The Fear of the Mighty Ocean). This medallion[1] appears to have been conferred until 1563, when King Charles IX increased the number of Knights to fifty.

The insignia of the Order were changed sometime after 1563 when the number of admissions to the Order was also greatly exceeded. The oval medallion of St. Michael, enamelled in colour, was superimposed in the centre of an eight-pointed, ball-tipped gold Maltese cross with white enamelled borders and gold fleurs-de-lis between the arms of the cross; the medallion was encircled by an oval gold band with a green-enamelled twisted cord. The Badge was suspended from a black neck ribbon.

During the reign of King Louis XIV, (1643-1715), the Order was bestowed so lavishly that it soon lost its prestige. However, it is very doubtful that the actual Order was amalgamated with the Order of the Holy Ghost in 1578 because the Order of St. Michael of France was still bestowed as a separate entity in 1650, as is shown by the insignia and the Royal Letters Patent, signed by King Louis XIV for Jonkheer Johann Huydecoper of the Dutch East India Company, who in 1660 travelled with a deputation to England to congratulate Charles II on his restoration to the throne.

Scholars of phaleristics differ substantially in their accounts of the Order's history. However, the above-mentioned Royal Letters Patent, which were auctioned in 1986 by Sotheby's in London, photographs of which were kindly placed at my disposal, contradict the scholars who

[1]The medallion reproduced here is very rare because the original insignia were conferred with great parsimony before the number of knights was increased and the badge changed.

The Order of St. Michael of France conferred on Johann Huydecoper in 1650 by King Louis XIV of France. The Royal Letters Patent (on the next page) are signed by Louis XIV. Johann Huydecoper was a director of the Dutch East India Company and a prominent merchant in Amsterdam. He was ennobled and accorded the title of Jonkheer by Queen Christina of Sweden. Shortly before his death he travelled to England with a deputation to congratulate Charles II on his restoration to the throne.

Courtesy: Coins & Medal Department, Sotheby's, London.

maintain that the Order was absorbed into the Order of the Holy Ghost in 1578. Archbishop Cardinale refers to radical reforms of the Order by Louis XIV between 1661 and 1665,[2] though there is no reason to assume that the Order lost its independent existence. It is more likely that the Order was subordinated to the Order of the Holy Ghost and that eminent members joined that new Order.

As with the other Orders, it was suppressed during the French Revolution in 1789 and revived by Louis XVIII as an independent Order in 1816. He limited the number of knights to 100 and reserved it as an award for outstanding scientific and artistic merits.

The Royal House of Bourbon Orléans inherited the Order of St. Michael as a dynastic Order[1].

[1] A.M.Perrot, *Collection des Ordres de Chevalerie* (Paris, 1820), lists the Order of St. Michael as extant and refers to Louis XIV having enlarged the number of knights to 100, and changed the Order's statutes

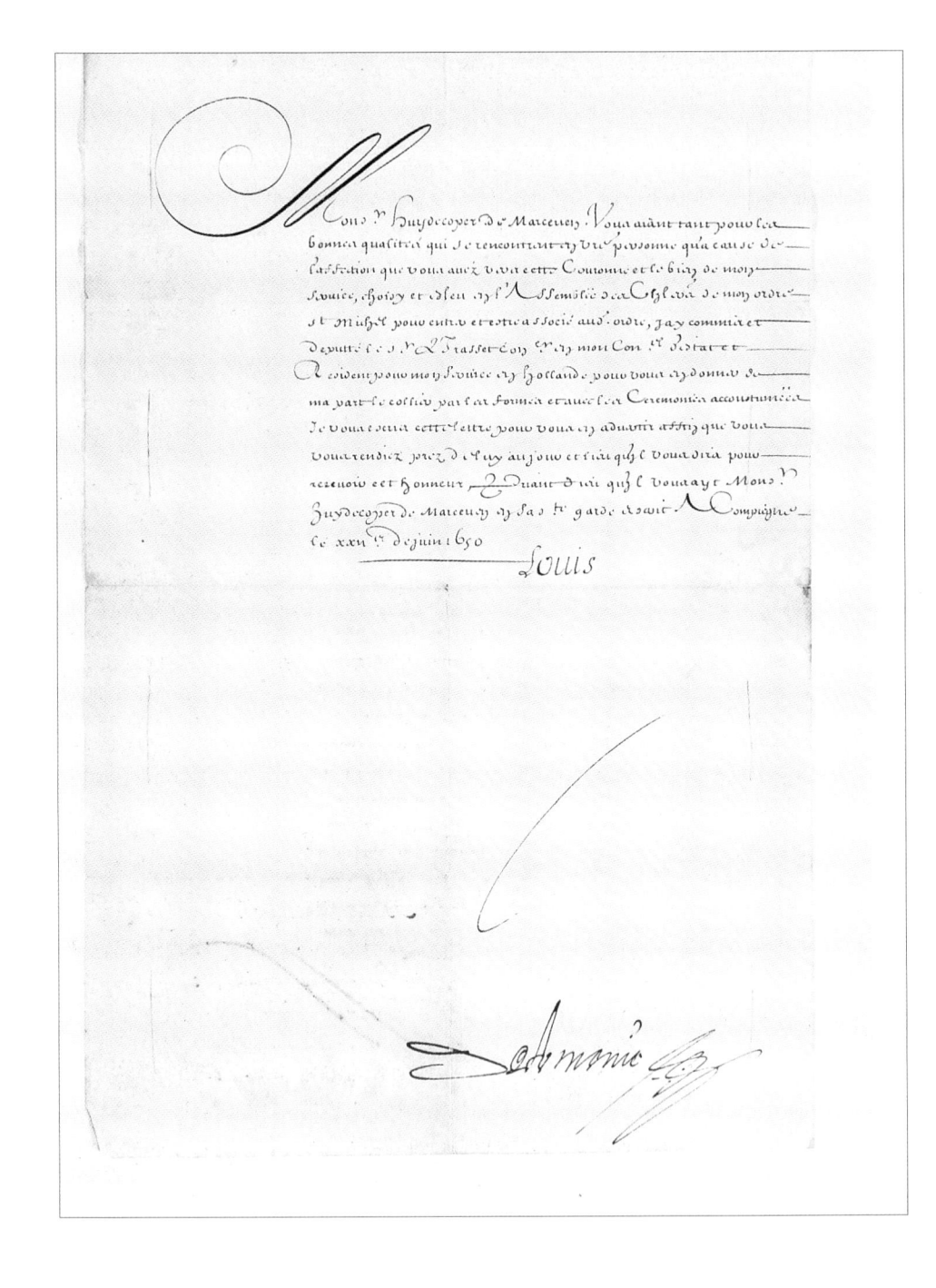

Mons.r Huydecoper d.e Marcenes, Vous aiant tant pour les bonnes qualitez qui se rencontrent en v.re personne qu'a cause de la ffection que vous avez v.rs cette Couronne et le bien de mon Service, choisy et esleu en l'Assemblée des Chl.rs de mon ordre s.t Michel pour entrer et estre associé aud.t ordre, J'ay commis et Deputté le S.r L.t Frasser, l'on d'eux mon Con.er d'estat et Resident pour moy S.ruice en Hollande pour vous en donner de ma part le collier par la forme et avec les ceremonies accoustumées. Je vous escris cette lettre pour vous en advertir aff.in que vous vous rendiez prez de luy au jour et lieu qu'il vous dira pour recevoir cet honneur. Quant à moi qu'il vous aye, Mons.r Huydecoper de Marcenez en sa s.te garde. Escrit A Compiegne ce xxv.e de juin 1650

Louis

De Lomenie

THE DUCAL HOUSE OF HABSBURG-TUSCANY
(The Grand Duchy of Tuscany)

The history of the Grand Duchy of Tuscany has been a varied and turbulant one. From the twelfth century onwards serious conflicts arose between Tuscany and the Papacy over the land that was claimed by the Pope. In 1523, Allessandro Medici became the ruler of Tuscany, but it was not until 1569 that Pope St. Pius V created Cosimo d'Medici Grand Duke of Tuscany.

In accordance with the treaty of Vienna of 1735, Francis, Duke of Habsburg-Lorraine became Grand Duke of Tuscany. There soon followed further disputes with the Papacy because the Dukes of Tuscany supported the Jansenists, closed numerous monasteries and, much to the annoyance and anger of Popes Clement XII and Benedict XIV, interfered in internal theological matters. In 1807, Napoleon annexed Tuscany and made it part of his Empire; he created his sister Grand Duchess of Tuscany. The House of Habsburg-Lorraine ruled with some difficulty after the fall of Napoleon, and after 1860 Tuscany became part of the Italian Kingdom under the Royal House of Savoy and the Grand Duke and his family went into exile to Austria from where he continued to claim the Grand Duchy.

The two Catholic-founded Orders of Knighthood of the Grand Duchy of Tuscany are well known. Letters of protest were sent to the Holy See in the 1960s, claiming that some distant members of the ducal family were selling the Orders in Europe and in the United States of America, whilst the Archdukes of Habsburg-Tuscany, legitimate successors to the rulers of the Grand Duchy of Tuscany, lived in exile, and continued to confer the two Orders as Dynastic Orders of the Grand Ducal House of Tuscany. They also created titles of nobility such as Duke and Count, a prerogative which belongs exclusively to a sovereign. In the 1970s letters in the form of affidavits, signed by well-known members of ducal and princely families, petitioned the Holy See through Archbishop H.E. Cardinale, in his capacity as the Apostolic Nuncio to the European Community, to act on the wish of Archduke Gottfried of Habsburg-Lorraine who in their presence, whilst physically unable to sign a document, had expressed the

---

[1] I mentioned in the introduction to the House of Borbon Orléans that there are four pretenders to the throne of France; R.E.Prosser, in his *The Royal Prerogative* (Iowa 1981), lists conferments of French Royal Orders by some of the Pretenders, among whom the Duke of Anjou and Segovia appears to have awarded the Orders of the Holy Ghost and of St. Michael as late as 1973. Mr. Prosser clearly champions the claim of the Dukes of Anjou and Segovia, who added the dukedoms of Burgundy and Bourbon to their titles as well as the appellation 'Head of the House of Bourbon'.

fervent wish that the Holy See should abolish both Catholic-founded dynastic Orders of the Archduchy of Tuscany, the Order of St. Stephen and the Order of St. Joseph.

Archbishop Cardinale wrote to the signatories of the letter that after the annexation of the Grand Duchy of Tuscany by the House of Savoy in 1866, the Orders had been declared abolished by the Governor of Florence, acting on behalf of the King of Italy, but that the last reigning Archduke had not recognised his authority and retained the Orders as dynastic property. Whilst sympathising with the wish of Archduke Gottfried, the Apostolic Nuncio was unable to forward the request to the competent authority which might have been able to formalise the abolition, the Royal House of Savoy, as the King of Italy was himself in exile and no longer had the *de jure* and *de facto* authority to act in this matter. The Republic of Italy was not interested, and the Holy See considered the Orders outside its sphere of interests to express an opinion. The Apostolic See declined to comment on any relations between the Dynasty and its Orders.

The juridical position of both Orders is therefore difficult to define: the last legitimate reigning Grand Duke had retained the Orders for the House of Habsburg-Lorrain-Tuscany and claimed dynastic status for them. The then sovereign Monarch of the Grand Duchy, the King of Italy, had abolished the Orders, which was not accepted by the Grand Duke in exile, and the sovereign Head of the Grand Duchy of Tuscany since 1946, the President of the Republic of Italy does not recognise the Orders or their *fons honorum*.

Taking into account all circumstances, I have no choice but come to the following conclusion: as Pope Pius IX condoned the abolition of the two Orders by the King of Italy in 1866 and did not intercede on behalf of the Grand Duke of Tuscany, both Orders might be better placed in a different chapter of this book, probably 'Extinct Catholic-founded Orders of Knighthood'. Had it been the wish of the Apostolic See to see the two Orders retained as Catholic dynastic Orders, it would either have intervened by protesting against their abolition by the House of Savoy as it did in the case of the Constantinian Order of the House of the Two Sicilies, or indicated to the last reigning Grand Duke that it would continue to respect their dynastic status, as Pius XII did when King Umberto left Italy in 1946 with regard to the Orders of the SS. Annunziata and of SS. Maurice and Lazarus.

However, as there has been no papal interdict against the Orders, nor has any Pontiff actively dealt with the two Orders, which were originally Catholic-founded, I have retained them in the section of Catholic-founded dynastic Orders, though I stress that a justification to do so leaves much to be desired.

THE ORDER OF ST. STEPHEN

This was the more illustrious of the two Tuscan Orders. It was founded in 1562 by Cosimo de'Medici, Duke of Florence. Its members were of noble

The Badge and the Star of the Order of St. Stephen of Habsburg Tuscany.

birth and had to belong to the Catholic religion. The Order was committed to fighting pirates, defending the Catholic Faith, and liberating slaves. The Order was also involved in successful attacks against the Turks. Abolished during the French Revolution, Ferdinand III, Grand Duke of Tuscany revived the Order in 1817.

The Order was abolished in 1866 when the Grand Duchy of Tuscany became part of the Italian Kingdom, but the Grand Duke continued to award it because he considered the Order to be dynastic and belonging to the House of Habsburg-Tuscany.

The Badge consists of a gold-rimmed, red-enamelled Maltese Cross with gold fleurs-de-lis between the arms, surmounted by a crown and pending from a military trophy, on a red ribbon. The Star used to be an enlarged Cross of the Badge, superimposed on a round cluster of gilded rays; these were later abolished and only the enlarged cross of the Badge remained as the Star.

THE ORDER OF ST. JOSEPH

Although the Order claims 1514 as its year of foundation, it remained completely dormant until Ferdinand III, Archduke of Austria revived it in 1807 when he became Grand Duke of Tuscany. In 1817 he divided the Order into three grades with a limited number of members, who originally had to be Catholics. The Order was later opened to members of other religions.

The Badge is a six-pointed, white-enamelled Star, tipped with gilded balls at the cleft points and with gilded rays between the arms of the Star. An ovel gold medallion with the figure of St. Joseph is in the centre, and the medallion is surrounded by a red-enamelled band with the insciption UBIQUE SIMILIS. The Badge is surmounted by a crown, suspended from a red ribbon with white stripes near the borders. On a medallion in the centre of the reverse is the inscription: S.J.F. 1807 [Sancto Josefo Ferdinandus 1807].

The Star of the Grand Cross is a much enlarged version of the badge, all in silver and without the surmounting crown.

The Collar consists of white-enamelled medallions alternating with red flames and gilded roses.

The Star and Badge of the Order of St. Joseph of Tuscany.

NOTA BENE

Archbishop Cardinale listed the Catholic-founded dynastic Orders of Knighthood in two categories, the second being referred to as 'No longer as exalted[1] Orders which are juridically still extant'.

Though this was not an arbitrary decision by Mons. Cardinale, who based the classification on the Orders's activities in charitable works and their participation in the ceremonial of the national or universal Church, the information available to him was based on information received from

---

[1] The description "less exalted" was first used by Pope St. Pius XI in a list of precedence he prepared for his Masters of Ceremonies in 1911. Mons. Cardinale listed the Orders of the Houses of Bourbon-Orléans and of Habsburg-Tuscany in that category.

sources outside the administration of the Apostolic See, and he included the Orders because they had originally some historical link with the Apostolic See, had never been officially abolished or a pontifical interdict placed on them.

Because of the charitable and ceremonial activities in the Bavarian Catholic Church of the Order of St. George of Bavaria of the Royal House of Wittelsbach, and also the close cooperation between the Royal House and the national Church and the State of Bavaria, I have moved the Dynasty and its Orders out of the former category of 'less exalted Orders'.

The reason why the dynastic Orders of the Royal House of Bourbon-Orléans were placed there was indirectly at the request of H.R.H. Henri, Count of Paris, who informed Mons. Cardinale that the Orders should only be conferred by a reigning Sovereign of France and that he refused to confer any of the Orders. He had effectively placed them in abeyance and still considers them dormant. Their link with the Apostolic See is only historical, and to find any influence of the Apostolic See on the Orders, historians have to go back to the seventeenth century. All three dynastic Orders of the Royal House of Bourbon of France have a strong Catholic and religious origin, but they had gradually evolved into secularised Orders since the reign of King Louis XV (1715-1774).

The turbulent history of the Royal House of Habsburg-Tuscany and its involvement in politics, often hostile to the Apostolic See and the Papacy, was one of the factors why the claim to any Catholicity of the two dynastic Orders soon became farcical. In addition, Mons. Cardinale received letters from one of the Heads of the Dynasty and later affidavits from Heads of other dynasties who stated that it had been the wish of the Archduke that both the Order of St. Joseph and the Order of St. Stephen should be abolished and considered by the Holy See as extinct Catholic-founded Orders of Knighthood. Archbishop Cardinale believed that such a draconian measure could only be taken by the Pope himself, and he listed the two Orders in the section of 'no longer as exalted Orders'.

I have seen reproductions of documents, however, dated as late as 1970, and purportedly signed and sealed by the then Head of the House of Habsburg-Tuscany, conferring the Order of St. Joseph. There is no way of stating categorically whether or not the two Orders of the House of Habsburg-Tuscany are dormant or extinct. It is possible that the Orders of that name which are offered for sale probably qualify for the category of self-styled orders, using the names of extinct Catholic-founded Orders. The Royal House of Savoy which took over the Duchy of Tuscany after 1860, neither annexed these Orders to the list of Italian chivalric Orders nor recognised them as extant.

In any case, though Catholic-founded, neither of the two Orders has any official link with the Apostolic See.

CHAPTER EIGHT

SECULARISED CATHOLIC ORDERS OF KNIGHTHOOD ST CROWN OR STATE O..

As explained in Chapter One, the Apostolic See has always be active in the field of chivalry. One might well ask why the Papacy, although always ready to encourage and approve Orders of Knighthood founded by others, and often juridically joining in their foundation or endowing the Orders with favours and privileges, appears to have been somewhat wary about establishing Orders of its own. Apart from its initial close involvement with, and claim to, the Supreme Order of Christ, which the Apostolic See eventually ceded to the Crown of Portugal, because it was originally a Monastic-Military Order fighting the Moors on the Iberian Peninsula, and strictly controlled by the Papacy, most of the Orders founded by the Apostolic See were short-lived Militias. Those Orders founded in the nineteenth century, the Pontifical Equestrian Orders of St. Gregory the Great and of Pius IX, and the Order of Pope St. Sylvester, reconstituted in 1905, belonged in the category of Orders of Merit, even before many other Catholic-founded Orders of Knighthood became Orders of Merit and features of the honours system of modern States.

The reason for the Holy See's reluctant and cautious procedure is twofold. On the one hand, the Apostolic See had no desire to become involved in all the complexities of military aspects of institutions as they were constituted in the Middle Ages. On the other hand, it felt no special need to establish Orders of Knighthood directly dependent on itself, but could as the *Mater et Magistra* of Chivalry intervene in the life of chivalric Orders established by others when it came to approving or disapproving religious aspects, and on occasion act as arbiter in political disputes. The degree of the Papacy's involvement varied from Order to Order.

The original object of the majority of these Orders of Knighthood was the defence of Catholic beliefs and ideals, which were the universal heritage of all the members of the *Res Publica Christiana*. The Apostolic See could rely entirely on the loyalty of Catholics in the chivalrous society of Western Europe when it proved necessary to defend these ideals and beliefs, even when the founding Sovereigns were moved by their own political aims.

During the thirteenth and fourteenth centuries, several Orders of Knighthood were established in the Iberian peninsula on the model of the

...stic-Military Orders. Their main objective was to drive out the ...who were putting Portugal and Spain to a very difficult test in a ...struggle which lasted several centuries. The repulse of Islam in ...ircumstances also meant the restitution of the Catholic religion to ...ands that had been invaded by Islamic forces.

One must not overlook certain material aspects concerning the relationship between the Orders and the Apostolic See. Almost all these Orders were first given the Rules of one of the great Religious Orders, for example, St. Benedict, St. Augustine, St. Basil, or the Rule of the Cistercians. Their Grand Masters were often appointed by the Church, but if the pressure from the Monarch of the country where the Order had its seat or from the Knights themselves, became too strong, the Order was usually ceded to the Monarch. However, successive Popes continued to grant many privileges to the individual Orders, particularly those that were active in the Age of Discovery. The material benefits to the Papacy and the Church as a result of the privileges granted to those Orders were substantial. On other occasions individual Popes participated in the dissolution of Orders and the reallocation of the Orders's properties and wealth.

Such a society, however, was subject to historical evolution. Three main factors eventually intervened to hasten its transformation: the rise of absolute monarchies claiming the undivided allegiance of their subjects; the decline of the feudal nobility that had formed a military aristocracy over which the Church had exercised a particularly strong influence; and at a later date, the upsurge of secular political republicanism, which severed all links with religious institutions.

Nevertheless, the spirit of chivalry continued to exist even when the deliverance of the Holy Places or the restoration of the Catholic religion to the invaded lands was no longer a determining factor of Catholic Knighthood, and when the unity of the *Res Publica Christiana* was broken up by the all-pervading principles of Protestantism, and when secularism became more and more the basis of the whole social structure of the Christian world.

Catholic Sovereigns appreciated the importance of the spirit of chivalry for the cohesion of the social body and the defence of the State against the invasion of Europe by Islamic armies from the East and the South, especially in the more exposed Mediterranean countries. This explains why most of the Orders of Knighthood which appeared on the European scene after the loss of the Holy Places, were founded in Portugal and Spain.

Some of these Orders still exist with their original statutes approved by the Apostolic See still in tact. Most of the Orders of Knighthood that were Catholic-founded eventually lost their Catholic character and had their constitutions and statutes changed, being broadened into Christian

SECULARISED CATHOLIC-FOUNDED ORDERS OF KNIGHTHOOD

Orders, free from any particular Christian denomination, or completely secularised, and are still bestowed by Sovereigns and Heads of State in several Western European countries. Some of these Orders are among the most ancient and illustrious of Europe, as well as ranking among the highest in their own countries. The most prestigious of these secularised Orders are the English Orders of the Garter, of the Thistle and of the Bath, the Danish Orders of the Elephant and of the Dannebrog, the Portuguese Orders of Christ, of Avis and of St. James of the Sword and the Spanish Order of the Golden Fleece.

All of these Orders have retained some vestiges of their Catholic past either in their insignia or in their statutes or traditions. Thus 'Collar Days', when Collars are worn by Knights and Dames of the Garter, the Thistle, the Bath and the Golden Fleece and the Knights and Dames Grand Cross or Grand Commanders of the various Orders, comprise religious feast days, especially those dedicated to Our Lady and the Saints under whose protection the Orders were originally placed.

The secularisation of most Orders came about in perfect agreement with the Apostolic See when, for instance, it was a question of transforming an ancient Monastic-Military Order into an Order of Merit. Some were transformed unilaterally, at the time of the Reformation, others when a republican regime came to power in place of a monarchy. In the last two instances, Catholic-founded Orders of Knighthood sometimes abolished but usually suppressed and being temporarily left dormant, were later revived by the Crown or the State because the new Powers realised the vital place these Orders had occupied in the history and culture of the country. Though there is at present no direct relationship between them and the Apostolic See, they are fully recognised and held in high esteem by the Holy See.

There is another category of Orders of Knighthood and of Merit, founded at a much later date by Catholic Sovereigns, who gave the Orders a clearly Catholic character by basing their statutes on Catholic principles or placing the Orders under the protection of the Blessed Virgin Mary or a Catholic Saint. This is particularly the case with dynastic Orders of Knighthood that did not belong the Crown but to a particular Royal Family. Thus we find that the Royal House of Bragança of Portugal retained two dynastic Orders that were suppressed by the Republic in 1910 and the Royal House of Savoy of Italy retained three dynastic Orders, two of which were ancient Catholic-founded and one a 19th century civil Order.

If we study the origin and development of the more important Orders of Knighthood that were either originally Catholic-founded or founded later on Catholic principles, and which are still bestowed by Sovereigns and sovereign States, we see immediately the important part played by the Apostolic See and the Catholic Church in the history of the different

...omposed the *Res Publica Christiana* and are still ...ur present Christian civilisation.
...vo Religious Orders of Knighthood and two dynastic ...thood, the Austrian Order of the Golden Fleece, and to ... S.M. Constantinian Order of St. George (Two Sicilies), have become secularised. Of the five Pontifical Equestrian Orders of Knighthood only the Supreme Order of Christ has had its Catholic character restored in 1966 though Paul VI reserved it to be conferred on Christian Monarchs and Heads of State.[1] In the same Papal Brief *Ad perpetuam rei memoriam* of 25 April 1966, Paul VI also restricted the Order of the Golden Spur to Christian Heads of State, (although only after he had conferred it in 1964 on the Mohammedan King Hussein I of Jordan). The Collar of the Pian Order is open to all Heads of State regardless of their religion.

The Pontifical Equestrian Orders of Pius IX, of St. Gregory the Great and of Pope St. Sylvester have also become secularised, although the Order of St. Gregory the Great was reserved to meritorious Catholic gentlemen until Paul VI conferred it occasionally on non-Catholic and even non-Christians.

There is some obvious disagreement among scholars about the definition 'Catholic-founded' (or approved or sanctioned by a Pope) of some of the Orders listed in this chapter. Whilst the date of foundation of most Orders of Knighthood presupposes some degree of involvement by the Papacy, the origin of a few is shrouded in mystery. For example, I received angry protests from Protestant sources in Denmark because the Apostolic See has always maintained that the Order of the Dannebrog was founded by Waldemar II (1202-41) in close collaboration between the King, the aristocracy and the Papacy, but that the Order had remained dormant for several centuries and was revived by a Protestant King after the Reformation, though with no reference to its previous existence. The Chancery of the Royal Orders of Denmark gives 1671 as the date of foundation by King Christian V and 1693 as the date when the Order received its statutes. One learned correspondent, who is involved in the administration of the Royal Danish Orders, most strongly objected to any mention of the Order prior to the Reformation, and insisted that the date of foundation should be given as 1671, but the Cross of the Order bears the crowned initials of King Waldemar II, who is traditionally accepted as the founder of the Order in 1219.

Although I received a few letters criticising Archbishop Cardinale's

---

[1] Although it has been the practice of the Supreme Pontiff to confer the Supreme Order of Christ only upon Catholic Heads of State, the Papal Brief by Paul VI mentions both the Supreme Order of Christ and the Order of the Golden Spur in the same section, requiring the recipient's adherence to the Christian faith. Juridically, the Order of Christ is therefore open to a non-Catholic but Christian Head of State.

SECULARISED CATHOLIC-FOUNDED ORDERS ...

account of the Catholic origin of the Order of the Thistle,
the eighth century, Charles Burnett, Ross Herald of Arms, of the
the Lord Lyon of Scotland and a foremost authority on the Most Ancient
and Most Noble Order of the Thistle, who has given me his help and
assistance in my endeavour to put the record straight and rewrite the
Order's history for this book, is more tolerant of the period prior to the
official date of foundation of the Order in 1687 by James VII of Scotland.
He points to heraldic evidence which supports the theory that there
existed a Collar of the Thistle, dating back to the reign of James III of
Scotland (1460-88), possibly as a dynastic Order of the Catholic Monarchs
of Scotland.

More serious – as far as errors are concerned – has been the treatment
of Portugal's premier Military Order of the Tower and the Sword, of
Valour, Loyalty and Merit. Historians dealing with chivalric Orders,
beginning with A.M. Perrot (Paris, 1820), claim that the Prince Regent,
later King Joâo VI of Portugal, 'revived' the Order which had been
established in 1459 by King Alfonso V of Portugal, and the Holy See's
record has always listed the Order as one of the four Catholic-founded
Military Orders of Portugal.[1] The Order of the Tower and the Sword, of
Valour, Loyalty and Merit was one Order, the history of which needed
revision because, after careful study of the evidence, there remained no
doubt in my mind that the Order was a new foundation, the purpose of
which was based on different criteria to those of Catholic-founded
Orders. I am particularly grateful for having had made available to me
photocopies of Papal Bulls from the archives of the Presidency of the
Portuguese Republic, the contents of which contrast with interpretations
by many of the Orders's chroniclers. It is more likely that these self-
perpetuating errors are the result of one chronicler simply copying what
another had written.

Such a prejudiced account of an Order's history can have different
reasons. For example, where a revival of a dormant Order is claimed
instead of a new foundation, the founder usually intends to add antiquity
to the new Order, thus also gaining precedence over other Orders, as the
date of the original foundation of a dormant Order decides not just its age
but also its precedence.

No serious historian can deny the important rôle the Papacy and the
Apostolic See have played in the foundation and evolution of almost all
the Orders of Knighthood in this chapter, nor is there any reason to doubt
that much of the Orders' character or tradition have their origin in the
practices and criteria of the *Res Publica Christiana*. It is, however, a matter
of academic integrity to put errors right, because it will enhance, not

---

[1] Dr. José Vicente de Bragança, Secretary General of Portugal's Orders, corrected several errors about the Portuguese Orders which have become self-perpetuating over the centuries. He made available to me information that was available from the Portuguese State Archives but not from Vatican sources.

...gistra of Chivalry that the Apostolic See
...es.
... to this book, the rôle of *Mater et Magistra* is
... anachronism, most certainly by those Orders that
...ring or after the Reformation. The description
indicates that at one time in the Order's history there
... the Papacy or the Apostolic See. Only for the Religious
...nighthood and several of the Catholic-founded dynastic
...as the Apostolic See retained a purposeful rôle as *Mater et Mag...ra*. This rôle is exercised through the appointment of a Cardinal Patron or Cardinal Grand Master to the Religious Orders, and the tacit permission granted for dynastic Orders to have ecclesiastical Priors or Spiritual Advisors, sometimes Cardinals, and the participation of the robed Knights of these Orders in the ceremonial of the national or international Church.

There is no longer any direct link between the secularised Crown or State Orders belonging to different sovereignties nor is there an overriding supranational authority or arbiter in cases of disputes. The rôle of arbiter in disputes between Orders of Knighthood or within an Order belonged to the Apostolic See for many centuries, but secularisation of the Orders and absolute sovereignty over the Orders by their Grand Masters has made this rôle obsolete. I am not aware of any sovereign Crown or State Order having asked the Holy See to act as arbitrator in any internal disagreement for several centuries.

What the Orders in this chapter have in common is that their founders, not necessarily those who revived an Order after it had been dormant for some centuries, dedicated the Order to some Catholic aim, and in many cases were supported in their foundation by the Papacy.

DENMARK

THE ORDER OF THE ELEPHANT

This is Denmark's highest ranking Order of Knighthood, and it has retained its eminent position among the European Orders for many centuries. Tradition links the Order's origin to the Society of the Mother of God, mentioned by King Christian I in a Charter of 1464. Although this Catholic Brotherhood was revived by Christian I in 1462, legend attributes the foundation of such a Brotherhood to Knut IV, King of Denmark (1182-1202).

King Christian I (1448-81) gave to the Order a Badge, consisting of a medallion depicting the Virgin Mary, and a smaller medallion showing three nails of the cross suspended from it. Tradition has it that the Knights, whose numbers were limited to fifty, wore a Collar with

H.M. Queen Margrethe II of Denmark, Sovereign and Grand Master of of the Order of the Elephant and the Order of the Dannebrog, Lady of the Most Noble Order of the Garter, Lady of the Noble Order of the Golden Fleece (Spain).

Courtesy: Royal Danish Embassy, London

alternating elephants and spurs, from which the medallion was suspended. However, an association between the symbol of the elephant and the Brotherhood of Mary can only be traced to 1508. The Order was still active under Christian II (1513-23), who was dethroned, but it fell into abeyance because of the Reformation; Christian III (1533-59), son of Frederick I, a younger son of Christian I, established the Lutheran religion in Denmark.

The Order of the Elephant was again conferred at the coronation of Frederick II in 1559, and the effigy of the Elephant appeared as the new insignia, initially as a gold elephant with a tower on its back, worn from a golden collar.

There was a brief and not very widely known period during the reign of King Christian IV (1588-1648), when the Order of the Elephant was combined with the Order of the Mailed Arm (also referred to by some scholars of phaleristics as the Order of the Arm in Armour, 'Vae Bnede Arms Orden'), which had been instituted in 1616 and ceased to exist in 1634. Christian IV had a Badge made for himself which shows the Mailed Arm, holding a sword in the hand which is covered by a gauntlet, suspended from a white enamelled elephant, bearing an ornate gold, jewel-encrusted and enamelled tower, with a Moor sitting in front of the tower. Both the gold, blue-enamelled Mailed Arm and the Elephant are profusely encrusted with jewels. On the upper arm is a crown made of precious stones surmounting the red-enamelled letter 'C' with the white enamelled figure 4 inside. This, probably unique, Badge of a short-lived Order can be seen in the Rosenborg Castle, Copenhagen. After this short period the Order was conferred with the Elephant as a Badge.

The statutes of the Order were revised in 1693 by King Christian V (1670-99), and membership was limited to the Monarch, princes of royal blood and thirty knights. The Order has always been bestowed on sovereigns, Danish and foreign. Since 1850 the Order became even more exclusive and was – with a few exceptions – only conferred on Danish and foreign royalty and Heads of State. After the Second World War, four notable commoners were decorated with the Order: Sir Winston Churchill KG, Fieldmarshal The Viscount Montgomery of Alamein KG, General Dwight D. Eisenhower and General Charles de Gaulle.

The Badge of the Order is a white-enamelled Elephant with a blue cover, bearing on the obverse a cross of five diamonds and on the reverse the initials of the reigning Monarch. On its back the Elephant carries a battle tower, and a Moor carrying a spear. The entire Badge is richly encrusted with precious stones.

The gold Collar consists of alternating enamelled elephants and towers. On less festive occasions the Badge in worn suspended from a celeste moiré sash.

The Star of the Order is eight-pointed with silver rays emanating from

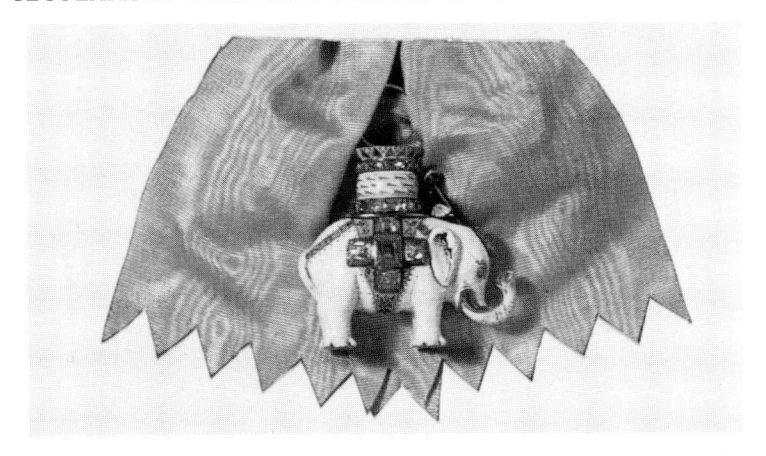

The Badge of the Order of the Elephant which is worn from a light blue watered silk sash and on festive occasions from the gold Collar.

Courtesy: Royal Danish Embassy, London

the centre medallion which is red-enamelled and has at its centre a Latin cross formed of six pearls, surrounded by a silver laurel wreath.

The reigning Monarch is the Grand Master of the Order, and its Feast Day is New Year's Day.

THE ORDER OF THE DANNEBROG
(or The Order of the Flag of the Danes)

This Order ranks after the Order of the Elephant and counts as one of the most illustrious Orders of Knighthood in Europe. It is traditionally believed that it has its origin in the Order which was instituted in 1219 by Waldemar II (1202-41) at a time of close collaboration between the Danish Crown, the Apostolic See and the Danish nobility.

The Order soon became dormant for some centuries and was restored after the Reformation by King Christian V (1670-99) in 1671 on the occasion of the birth of his first son Frederick.

The Order of the Dannebrog takes its name from a red flag (*brog* flag or cloth) with a white cross that was probably a present of Pope Honorius III (1216-27) to King Waldemar II for the Crusade of the Catholic Danes against the pagan Livonians and Estonians. The first authenticated record of the name Dannebrog dates from Swedish accounts of the fifteenth century.

King Christian V gave new statutes to the Order in 1693, and it was reserved for princes of royal blood and fifty knights who were the highest dignitaries of the Court. Prior membership of the Order of the Dannebrog was required for admission to the Order of the Elephant.

In 1808 King Frederick VI changed the statutes and extended the Order, making it an Order of Merit and opening it to all meritorious subjects irrespective of their social status. He also enlarged the Order from one class into four: Grand Commander, Knight Grand Cross, Commander and Knight. In 1842 King Christian VIII (1839-48) decreed that only Danish and foreign royalty should be admitted to the class of Grand Commander. Royal Decrees of 1864 and 1952 extended the Order further by dividing the Commander and Knight Class into two grades, and in 1951 the Order was opened to women.

The Order also includes the Cross of Honour of the Men of the Dannebrog; this was changed in 1952 into the Silver Cross of the Order of the Dannebrog and it can only be conferred on Danish subjects who have already been awarded the Order.

The reigning Monarch is the Grand Master of the Order.

The Cross of a Commander 1st class and a Commander, worn as a neck badge suspended from a white watered silk ribbon with red side stripes.

Courtesy: Royal Danish Embassy, London

The Badge of the Order is a white-enamelled Latin cross *pattée*, in gold (in silver for knights), the periphery of the cross being slightly convex, with a red enamelled border. In the centre of the Badge is the letter 'C' with the figure 5 inside (for Christian V), surmounted by a crown; the motto GUD OG KON GEN (God and the King) is displayed on the arms of the cross, clockwise, beginning on the left arm of the cross. On the reverse is the letter W (for Waldemar) in the centre. At the end of the arms are the dates 1219, 1671 and 1808. Surmounting the Badge is the letter R (Rex or Regina) combined with the initial of the reigning Monarch. Above the two initials is a Crown, and gold royal crowns are between the arms of the cross. The cross of a Grand Commander has on the obverse fourteen cut diamonds, arranged in the form of a Latin cross and diamonds in the other ornamentations of the cross. On the white-enamelled reverse are the crowned initials of Waldemar II, Christian V and Frederick VI and the motto of the Order.

The Star Grand Cross is an eight-pointed faceted silver star superimposed with the Badge of the Order, the lower arm of the cross covering the lowest point of the star, and there are no crowns between the arms of the cross. In the centre of the cross is the crowned letter W (Waldemar). When the Order is awarded with diamonds, the badge is ornamented with cut stones.[1] The Breast Cross for a Commander of the first class is the large Badge of the Order faceted silver instead of being white-enamelled; the Breast Star also has the letter W in the centre, surmounted by a crown, and the motto of the Order is displayed on the arms of the cross.

The Collar of the Order is gold and consists of alternating links, the crowned initials of Kings Waldemar II and Christian V and red-bordered, white-enamelled Latin crosses.

The ribbon of the Order is white with red border stripes.

Commanders I class
Courtesy: Royal Danish Embassy, London

---

[1] It is not unusual that a sovereign confers the Badge of a Grand Cross encrusted with diamonds or precious stones as a special favour to the recipient.

Above: In 1961, H.M. Queen Elizabeth II and H.R.H. Prince Philip, Duke of Edinburgh, during their official visit to Pope John XXIII in the Vatican. Below: Twenty years later, in 1981, they paid a visit to Pope John Paul II, who reciprocated the courtesy with a visit to Buckingham Palace in 1982.

Courtesy: Felici

THE UNITED KINGDOM OF GREAT BRITAIN AND NORTHERN IRELAND

THE MOST NOBLE ORDER OF THE GARTER

The highest Order of English Knighthood and one of the most important of all Knighthoods throughout the world, The Most Noble Order of the Garter is, in fact, the only one, to have preserved its ancient feudal character. There are different legends about its origin. Some believe it was

The Collar with the Great George suspended from it, the sash with the badge (the Lesser George), and the Star of the Most Noble Order of the Garter.

Courtesy: Spink & Son Ltd., London

founded by King Richard I (1189-99) during the siege of Acre in the Holy Land in 1191, where he distributed garters to the main officers so that they could be recognised. Others maintain the Order was instituted by King Edward III (1327-77) at a Court ball in 1344, when the King picked up the blue garter that had fallen off from his lover Joan, Countess of Salisbury, with whom he was dancing. He then diverted the attention of the guests by binding the garter round his own leg and exclaiming HONI SOIT QUI MAL Y PENSE (Shame on him who thinks evil of it).

The generally accepted date of the Foundation of the Order is 1348 when in August of that year Edward III issued Royal Letters Patent for the Foundation of its parallel and supportive body, the College of St. George within Windsor Castle, which was to be the spiritual home of the Order. The first Bull relating to the College was issued on 30 November 1350 by Pope Clement VI (1342-52), authorising the institution of the College and the promulgation of the Statutes. In 1351 Clement VI issued a further Bull, granting exemption from ordinary jurisdiction and took the College under the jurisdiction of the Pope as Bishop of Rome.[1]

Over the years the Most Noble Order of the Garter has undergone a number of revisions, notably in 1522, 1557 and 1636, whilst the membership was extended in 1786, 1805 and 1831.

Edward III also prescribed that Knights were required to have Holy Masses celebrated for the repose of deceased members. They were also required to refrain from making war upon one another, but this was later qualified, allowing them to wage war upon one another if commanded to do so by their Liege Lord. It is interesting to note that until the First World War and the degrading of Kaiser Wilhelm II of Germany, no foreign

[1] In April 1984, S.E.R. Archbishop Cesare Zacchi, President of the Pont ifical Ecclesiastical Academy for Diplomats (Vatican), paid several visits to Windsor Castle where he studied with the Very Rev.D.I.T. Eastman, Canon of St. George's Chapel, Windsor Castle, the question of the jurisdiction of the College. They agreed that it had passed to the Bishop of Rome with whom it technically remained because the Bull of Clement VI of 1351 had never been revoked or expressly declared void by the Monarch. Mr Peter Begent, Chronicler of the College of St. George, St. George's Chapel, Windsor Castle and the Most Noble Order of the Garter, disagrees and feels that Canon Eastman's opinion was liable to misunderstanding because the Bull concerning the exemption of the College of St. George from ordinary jurisdiction was irrelevant as far as historical development was concerned. In the case of Canons, appointments were made by the Monarch and installations by the Dean of St. George's Chapel, who was himself installed by the Senior Dean of the Chapels Royal. No Dean was ever assigned to the College. Under the Statutes, completed in 1352, there was to be a Warden, but soon the titles of Dean and Warden became interchangeable. Both Richard Kingston (in 1412) and John Arundel (in 1417) were appointed Dean, not Warden. On 22 September 1429 the King, by Royal Letters Patent, decreed that in future the title should be Dean. Jurisdiction over and supervision of the Monarch's Free Chapels was always and still is exercised by the Lord High Chancellor of England, who at that time was usually a high ranking ecclesiastic. The Dean was never subject to the jurisdiction of the Bishop of Salisbury as such. This confusion arose out of the fact that Edward IV annexed the chancellorship of the Order to the bishops of this See in about 1475, but while the Chancellors were (with some exceptions) the Bishops of Salisbury during the next few decades, this right was abolished by Henry VIII. The Dean was subject to the Chancellor of the Order who for a period was usually the Bishop of Salisbury then in office; but that is very different from claiming that the Dean was subject to the direct jurisdiction of the Bishop of Salisbury.

sovereign was ever removed from the roll of the Order for conducting war against the King of England; not even Philip of Spain or the Emperor Hirohito of Japan in the Second World War.

A more visible religious symbolism of the Order was laid down by the Founder who decreed in the Order's statutes that a Knight Companion was required to set his helmet with his heraldic achievements and his sword above his Stall in St. George's Chapel to demonstrate that he bore them in defence of the Holy Church.[1]

In 1522, Henry VIII set out in the new statutes three 'points of reproach', requiring the Knights Companion to refrain from heresy, treason and flight from battle, to which was later added a requirement that a Companion would be degraded from the Order if he indulged in 'wasteful living' so as to be unable to maintain his station in life.

For many years membership of the Order was strictly limited to the reigning Monarch as Sovereign of the Order and twenty-five Knights Companion. Since the early years of the nineteenth century the extension of the membership has allowed the appointment of lineal descendants of George I to be appointed as Extra Knights, whilst from 1987 Ladies have been eligible for admission to be numbered among the twenty-five Companions.

Special statutes have since, at different times, been promulgated for the admission of Extra Knights and Extra Ladies, who are foreign Sovereigns. In the twentieth century there have been three Ladies of the Garter who were consorts of reigning Monarchs: Queen Alexandra, consort of Edward VII (1902), Queen Mary, consort of George V (1911), and Queen Elizabeth, consort of George VI (1936).

The Officers of the Order are: the Prelate, an office held by the Bishop of Winchester; the Chancellor, who is a Knight Companion; the Register of the Order, who is also Dean of Windsor; Garter Principal King of Arms; the Gentleman Usher of the Black Rod, (so called because of his staff of office); and the Secretary to the Order.

Princess Elizabeth, the eldest daughter of King George VI, was admitted as a Lady of the Garter in 1947. Foreign sovereign Queens are admitted as Extra Ladies of the Garter. Among those honoured were H.R.H. Princess Juliana of the Netherlands, who was admitted as Queen Juliana in 1958 and who abdicated in favour of her daughter the Crown Princess Beatrix in 1980, H.M. Margrethe II, Queen of Denmark, who was

---

[1] As part of the original establishment of the College of St. George, twenty-six Poor Knights were required to pray daily for the Sovereign and the Knights Companion during life and for their souls after death: in return they received lodgings in the Castle and maintainance. They wore a red cloak with a shield of the arms of St. George on the left shoulder. During the early years of the nineteenth century, the Poor Knights who were all retired army officers objected to being termed 'poor' and petitioned to King William IV to be allowed to change the name and to wear a uniform. In 1834 the name was changed to Military Knights and the members were allowed to wear the uniform of Unattached Officers which is worn still.

A mid-nineteenth century breast star and a privately made Lesser George badge.

Courtesy: Spink & Son Ltd., London

Right: A Lesser George in gold and enamel, privately made before 1820.

Photograph: Sotheby's

Her Majesty Queen Elizabeth the Queen Mother and His Majesty King Juan Carlos I of Spain in procession on Garter Day.

Courtesy: The Ministry of Defence, London

In 1990, Her Grace Lavinia, Duchess of Norfolk, widow of the 16th Duke of Norfolk, was the first Lady of the Garter to be admitted to the Order who was not a member of a Royal Family.

Courtesy: The Ministry of Defence, London

created an Extra Lady of the Garter in 1979, and H.M. Queen Beatrix of the Netherlands, who was admitted to the Order in 1989.

The first commoner for many years to be made a member of the Order was Sir Edward Grey, later The Viscount Grey, in 1912. The Prime Minister during the Second World War, Winston Churchill, the most famous commoner who had steadfastly refused all honours of a peerage, even a Dukedom, accepted the Order of the Garter in 1953 when Queen Elizabeth II offered him the honour on behalf of the peoples of Great Britain and the Commonwealth for his services to the country. He wore the Garter robes for the first time at the coronation of Queen Elizabeth II, who had invested him with the dignity. When the Queen honoured Sir Winston Churchill by making an official call on him at his residence on the occasion of his retirement, the Prime Minister received her wearing levee dress with the Garter on his left leg, the Star of the Order, and the Lesser George pending from the broad, dark blue riband. Other distinguished commoners admitted to the Order were the Prime Ministers Anthony Eden (Earl of Avon), James Callaghan (Lord Callaghan of Cardiff), Harold Wilson (Lord Wilson of Rievaulx), and Edward Heath (Sir Edward Heath, KG, MBE, PC, MP).

In 1990 Her Grace Lavinia, Duchess of Norfolk, was the first Lady of the Garter to be admitted who was not a member of the Royal Family and on St. George's Day 1995, the Queen announced that she had created Margaret Thatcher, the country's first ever woman Prime Minister (now Baroness Thatcher of Grantham) a Lady of the Garter.

There are two Badges of the Order: 'The Greater George', as it is known, consists of a multicoloured enamel figure of St. George slaying a dragon, and is suspended from a Collar of gold medallions on which are portrayed red-enamelled roses surrounded by blue-enamelled garters bearing the Order's motto HONI SOIT QUI MAL Y PENSE. The medallions are linked with gold knots.

The second Badge, also known as 'The Lesser George', is a gold oval medallion, also showing St. George and the dragon, which is surrounded by a band on which the motto of the Order is inscribed. It rests on the right hip from a dark blue riband which is worn over the left shoulder.

The Star of the Order is an eight-pointed, silver faceted star, with the red cross of St. George, surrounded by the dark blue Garter with the motto of the Order inscribed on it.

The Garter itself is a ribbon of dark blue velvet, edged and buckled with gold on which the motto HONI SOIT QUI MAL Y PENSE is set in letters of gold. Some Knights Companion may have what are usually called 'informal Garters' made for them on which the letters are embroidered in solid gold.

The official and full dress worn in precession, consists of the Garter, the Mantle, Hat and Hood. The surcoat has not been worn in procession since

In the procession Her Majesty Queen Elizabeth the Queen Mother and His Royal Highness the Duke of Kent are followed by the Officers of the Order in their scarlet mantles.

Courtesy: The Ministry of Defence, London

1911 (see the photograph in the chapter on Dynastic Orders, The Royal House of Bragança, of the Prince of Wales and King Manuel II in the Garter procession of that year). The full ceremonial dress as worn by Prince Edward in 1911 was only worn once again in 1953 by the four Knights Companion of the Order who bore Her Majesty's canopy at the coronation. The Order has still its ceremonial dress, but it has been slightly simplified, and the dress worn in the processional photographs shows the simplified version.

The Garter is worn by the Knights Companion under the knee on the left leg; Ladies of the Order of the Garter and Ladies Companion wear the Garter on the left arm above the elbow.

Knights and Ladies Companion are required to wear the Collar on Collar Days (certain religious festivals and secular anniversaries) and on such occasions when commanded by the Sovereign. The Collar is worn

Above the stall in St. George's Chapel, Windsor Castle, each Knight of the Garter has the sword, his helmet and crest displayed with decorative mantling hanging on either side. The Knight's banner hangs overhead. On the death of a Knight his banner and the other insignia are removed after being offered at the altar. The first banner on the left is that of the Duke of Norfolk, Earl Marshal of England and principal Roman Catholic Peer of the Realm.

Courtesy: The Dean and Chapter of St. George's Chapel, Windsor Castle

outside the Mantle and fastened to the shoulders with white satin bows.

Knights of the Garter are entitled to add the letters K.G. after their name and use the title 'Sir' unless they use their title of nobility; Ladies of the Garter are entitled to the postnominal letters D.G. and the title 'Dame'.

The armorial banners of the Knights and Ladies hang over their stalls in St. George's Chapel, and a three-dimensional representation of the Knight's and Ladies' crest is also placed above the stall. These are taken down when a Knight or Lady dies. The stall plate with the Knight's or Lady's coat of arms,[1], name and titles remains at the back of the stall in perpetuity.

The patronal feastday of the Order is St. George's Day, 23 April, when the names of the new Knights and Ladies Companion are usually announced. The Investiture and Installation of new members of the Order takes place on Garter Day in June.

THE MOST ANCIENT AND MOST NOBLE ORDER OF THE THISTLE

This is a uniquely Scottish Order of Knighthood, ranking second to the Most Noble Order of the Garter in the list of precedence of British Orders of Knighthood. The Order is also known as the Order of St. Andrew and the Order of the Burr, but although the statutes of the Order, promulgated in 1687 by King James VII of Scotland (King James II of England), speak of the Order being revived, Charles Burnett, Ross Herald of Arms, one of the foremost authorities on the Order of the Thistle, has found little authentic proof that the Order as we know it today, existed in Scotland before that date.

There is no evidence at all for the often repeated legend that the Order traces its origin back to the eighth century. However, Ross Herald presents two compelling arguments why one should include the Order of the Thistle in this chapter: first, for heraldic reasons. There is evidence that a Collar of Thistles existed during the reign of James III of Scotland (1460-88), and it can be assumed that the Collar was a dynastic Order. From the reign of his son, James IV of Scotland, onwards, there exist many pictorial heraldic representations showing the royal arms surrounded by the Collar of the Thistles; the arms of James IV in the Vienna Book of Hours also shows the figure of St. Andrew pending from the Collar.

Secondly, according to the extensive research by Ross Herald, there is a dichotomy between what King James VII intended the Order to become and its ultimate development. Quite apart from the King wanting to honour Scotland with its own principal and unique Order, the King intended it to further the Catholic faith.

[1]Legend will have it that in the past foreign ladies had been received into the Order, and the name of Laura Bacio Terracina, a Neapolitan poetess, is sometimes mentioned, who is said to have been made a Lady of the Garter by King Edward VI (1547-1553). However, her name does not appear in any records of elections in the reign of Edward VI nor in any list of Companions. There is no evidence that would suggest that Ladies were admitted to the Order before 1901. In medieval times some ladies received robes but they were never given the Mantle, the most important item of the robes, and they never had stalls allocated to them.

The Collar of the Order of the Thistle with the Badge Appendant, the sash with the Badge, and the Star.

Courtesy: Spink & Son, Ltd., London

Circumstantial evidence is put forward by several historians that James V (1513-42) may have founded the Order in 1540 and that it was suppressed following the execution in England of Queen Mary in 1587 but *revived* by James VII. Ross Herald maintains that if such an Order was founded by James V in 1540, it must have ceased to exist when he died in 1542, because there is no mention of any knights until James VII's promulgation of the statutes in 1687. Another well-known expert on the Order of the Thistle, Russell J. Malloch, in 'Register of Knighthood, Part III',[1] also gives a comprehensive account of the Order, its officers, ceremonial and insignia, and places the foundation firmly in 1687. Ross

[1] In *The Despatch*, IV, 3, 1981, pp. 269-301.

The Star and the Badge of the Most Noble and Most Ancient Order of the Thistle.

Courtesy: Spink & Son

Herald, apart from producing with Helen Bennett a seminal work on the Order[2], published a thesis in *The Double Tressure*, No.5, 1983, in which he draws special attention to the research and works of the late Lord Lyon King of Arms, Thomas Innes of Learney, who presented evidence that James III founded the Order of the Thistle.

Ross Herald also related some other interesting facts about James III: in 1486 he received the Golden Rose from Pope Sixtus IV; from France he received the Order of St. Michael, and from Denmark the Order of the Elephant. James III was responsible for the change of royal symbolism and for the introduction of the thistle as an heraldic emblem.

The insignia of the Order of the Thistle consist of the Badge Appendant, the St. Andrew Jewel, depicting the image of St. Andrew in a green mantle over a purple garment, holding before him a white-enamelled Cross of St. Andrew, the Saint being surrounded by golden rays. The other insignia are the Collar, which is of gold and consists of

---

[2]'THE GREEN MANTLE – A Celebration of the Revival in 1687 of the Most Ancient and Most Noble Order of the Thistle', Edinburgh, 1987.

Ross Herald of Arms wears the Badge of an Officer of the Order of the Thistle and takes part in the Order's ceremonial. He also wears his Chain of Office as a Herald of Arms and the insignia of a Knight of the Venerable Order of St. John.

Courtesy: The Lyon Court, Edinburgh

alternate green-enamelled sprigs of pine and thistles, enamelled in natural colours; a four-pointed silver Star with the silver Cross of St. Andrew superimposed, and in the centre, on a gold medallion a green-enamelled thistle, surrounded by a green enamelled band which bears in gold letters the Order's motto: NEMO ME IMPUNE LACESSET; both the Star and the Cross are faceted. A green Sash, which is worn over the left shoulder, resting on the right hip with, suspended from it a gold oval-shaped Badge which has in the centre the figure of St. Andrew holding the Cross, and the motto of the Order on the surrounding band.

The Monarch is the Sovereign Head of the Order which has a Chancellor, a Secretary and King of Arms, two positions presently combined in the Lord Lyon, a Gentleman Usher and a Dean. All Scottish Officers of Arms are also Officers of the Order of the Thistle and they wear their distinctive Badge, a gold oval-shaped medallion with St. Andrew, wearing his purple garment and holding the Cross, superimposed on it; the Badge is surmounted by the Royal Crown of Scotland. The Order of the Thistle is the only British Order of Knighthood to have its Chancery outside London, in Edinburgh at the Court of the Lord Lyon.

The banners of the Knights of the Thistle are displayed in the Order's Chapel in St. Giles' Kirk, Edinburgh. The Mantle of the Order, which is worn on Collar days and on special occasions commanded by the Sovereign Head of the Order, is made of green velvet, bearing an embroidered Star on the left shoulder. The Collar is worn outside the Mantle, fastened to the shoulders by white satin bows. Members of the Order are entitled to the post-nominal letters K.T.

The patronal feastday of the Order is St. Andrew's Day, 30 November.

Finally, I refer the reader to the explanations given by the historian

The Insignia of the Dean of the Order of the Thistle, the Lord Lyon King of Arms, who is also King of Arms of the Order, and the Scottish Officers of Arms who are Officers of the Order.

Courtsey: The Most Ancient and Most Noble Order of the Thistle

Kenneth Rose about the Order of the Garter and the episode of James VII of Scotland (James II of England) taking the Order of the Garter with him into exile to France; similarly, he also took the Order of the Thistle with him as a dynastic Order, and he considered himself to be the *fons honorum* of these two Orders.

Whilst the Old and the Young Pretenders created Catholic Knights abroad, both the legitimate Orders of the Garter and of the Thistle were expanded in the United Kingdom, first by Queen Anne and after her by the three Hanoverian Kings, George I, George II and George III.

In 1821 George IV increased the number of Knights from twelve to sixteen. Members of the British Royal Family are known as Royal Knights; Her Majesty Queen Elizabeth the Queen Mother is the only woman to have been admitted to the Order as a Lady of the Thistle since 1687. In 1962 His Majesty King Olav V of Norway was the first Extra Knight to be admitted for over 200 years in 1962.

The Prince of Wales, although he holds the hereditary title of Duke of Rothesay, is not a constituent part of the Order of the Thistle as he is of the Order of the Garter.

THE MOST HONOURABLE ORDER OF THE BATH

The Order of the Bath ranks third among the British Orders of Knighthood. The name of this ancient Order is derived from the

His Majesty King Juan Carlos I of Spain wearing the Jewel of the Spanish Noble Order of the Golden Fleece, the Riband and Star of the Royal and Most Distinguished Order of Charles III, and the Stars of the Grand Cross of the Military, Naval and Air Force Orders of Merit. He is also the Sovereign of the Order of Isabella the Catholic (next page) and all other Spanish Orders of Knighthood and of Merit. King Juan Carlos has restored the Spanish Noble Order of the Golden Fleece to its former pre-eminent position among all Spanish Orders.

Courtesy: The Count de la Sierragorda with special permission of the King

XXXIV

Top left: His Majesty's Collar and Fleece of the Noble Order of the Golden Fleece. Top right: The insignia of the Spanish Golden Fleece and (smaller) His Majesty's Jewel of the Golden Fleece. Above: the Star of the Grand Cross of Order of Isabella the Catholic

Courtesy: The Count de la Sierragorda with special permission of the King (All photographs on this pla

The insignia of the Grand Cross of the Royal and Most Distinguished Order of Charles III.

XXXV

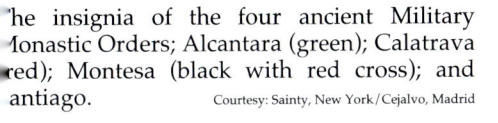

The insignia of the four ancient Military Monastic Orders; Alcantara (green); Calatrava (red); Montesa (black with red cross); and Santiago.
Courtesy: Sainty, New York/Cejalvo, Madrid

H.R.H. Don Carlos de Borbón Dos Sicilias y Borbón Parma, Infante of Spain, Dean President of the Council and Tribunal of the Military Monastic Orders as successor to the Count of Barcelona, the King's father.
Courtesy: Sainty, New York

MONACO – Left: The Collar of the Sovereign Grand Master of the Order of St. Charles; right: the Grand Cross and the Star of the Order of St. Charles.
Courtesy: The Palace Archives, Principality of Monaco

His Serene Highness Rainier III, Sovereign Prince of Monaco, and his son, the Hereditary Prince of Monaco, H.S.H. Prince Albert.

Courtesy: Foto Sygma; Mrs. Paul Gallico; The Palace Archives, Mona-

XXXVII

His Excellency Dr. Mário Soares, President of the Republic of Portugal (1986-), Grand Master of all Portuguese Orders of Knighthood and of Merit, wearing the Banda das Três Ordens, the insignia of the President of Portugal.

Courtesy: The Secretary General of the Presidency (This and the following plates on Portuguese Orders)

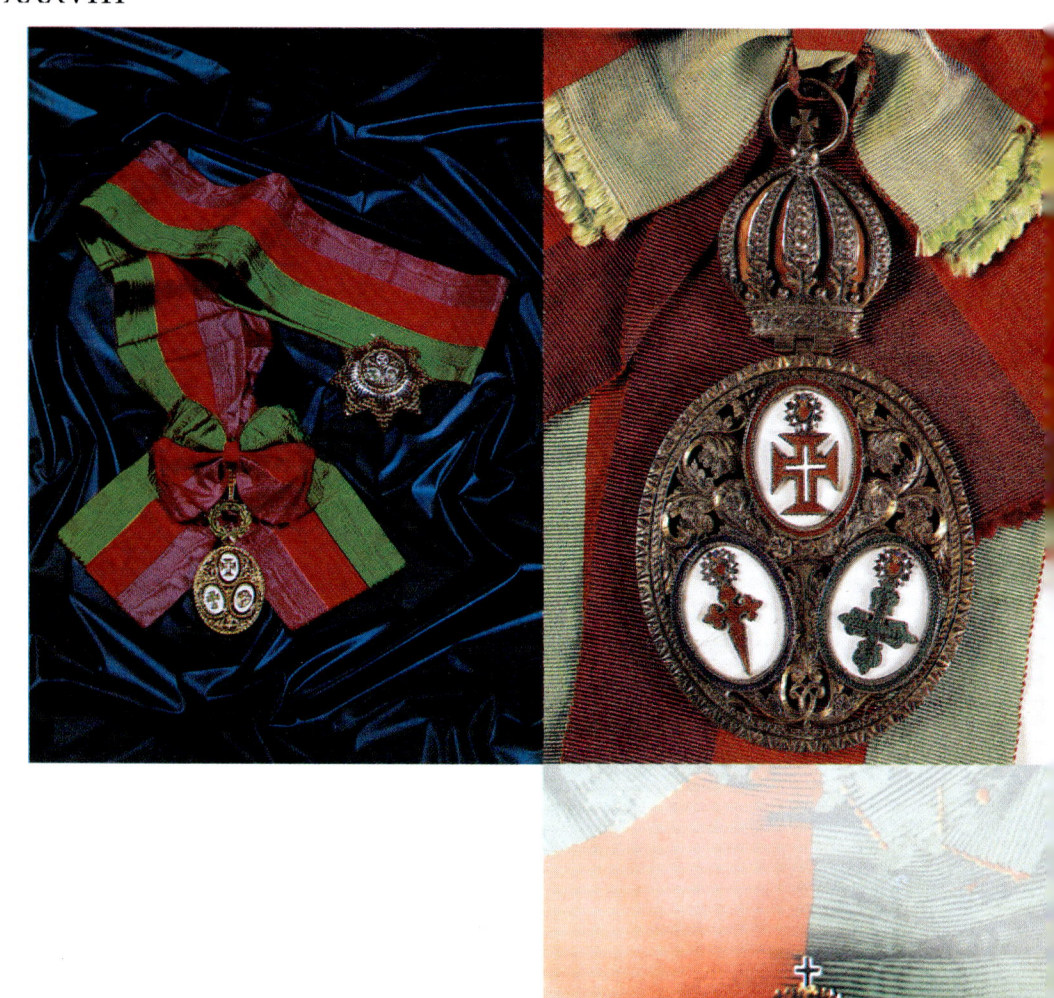

Above left: The Presidential Insignia of the Banda das Três Ordens. Top right: A rare Badge of the Banda das Três Ordens, made in Brazil in 1826, the year of King João's death. The Royal Crown of Portugal has been substituted with the Imperial Crown of Brazil. Right: A rare example of the Star of the Riband of the Two Orders (Christ and Avis), surmounted by the emblem of the Sacred Heart. Though not official but with royal approval, this star dates from the mid-19th century.

Courtesy: Secretary General of the Presidency of the Republic; and Paulo Morais-Alexandre

XXXIX

The Stars of a Commander of the Order of the Tower and the Sword, of Valour, Loyalty and Merit, and of the Order of Christ.

The Crosses of an Officer of the Orders of Avis, of Christ and of Santiago.

During his state visit to Great Britain, President Dr. Mário Soares (right), who wears the Grand Cross of the Most Honourable Order of the Bath, bestowed on H.M. The Queen the Grand Collar of the Order of the Tower and the Sword (below). H.R.H. The Prince Philip, Duke of Edinburgh, next to Mme Soares, wears the Grand Cross of the Order of Christ.

SECULARISED CATHOLIC-FOUNDED ORDERS OF KNIGHTHOOD 369

The Collar with the Badge Appendant, sash with Badge and the Star of a Knight Grand Cross of the Military Division of the Most Honourable Order of the Bath.

Courtesy: Spink & Son, Ltd., London

ceremony of taking a ritual bath which was part of the ceremony performed at the inauguration of a knight, symbolic of the purity henceforth required of him by the laws of chivalry. The ritual bath was followed by a night in prayer, ending with attendance at the Mass that was celebrated in the chapel.

The generally accepted date of foundation is 1399, when at his coronation Henry IV of England (1399-1413) created forty-six Esquires Knights of the Bath. Tradition also gives 1377 as a possible date of foundation of the Order by King Richard II of England (1377-99 dethroned; murdered 1400) during his conquest of Ireland.

The Collar with the Badge Appendant, sash with Badge and the Star of a Knight Grand Cross of the Civil Division of the Most Honourable Order of the Bath. Collars are worn with the ceremonial mantle of the Order on Collar Days and special occasions commanded by the Sovereign.

Courtesy: Spink & Son, Ltd., London

This English custom of a ritual bath before being invested a knight spread to several European countries, notably France and Italy. In England, knighthood to the Order of the Bath was afterwards conferred on occasion of great national ceremonials. King Charles II (1660-85) created sixty-eight Knights of the Bath at his coronation, after which the Order went into abeyance until it was revived by King George I (1714-27) in 1725 as a Military Order , consisting of the Sovereign, a Great Master, who had to be a Prince of the blood royal, and thirty-six, later forty-five knights. Prince George, eldest son of King George III, who had become Prince Regent in 1811, later King George IV (1820-30), used the Order to reward many distinguished officers, both in the Army and the Navy. Queen Victoria finally gave the Order a new constitution in 1847, decreeing that though once and primarily a Military Order of Knighthood, it would henceforth be conferred for military and civil merit, and promulgated the ranks of civil Knight Commander and Companion. The Order was further enlarged in 1865, and the statutes revised in 1925 and 1936. Ladies were first admitted to the Order by Queen Elizabeth II (1952-) in 1971.

The Queen is the Sovereign of the Most Honourable Order of the Bath, and The Prince of Wales is the Order's Great Master and Principal Knight Grand Cross. The Dean of Westminster Abbey is the Dean of the Order, and Bath King of Arms, who in that capacity is not a member of H.M. College of Arms, though the position can be held by one of Her Majesty's Officers of Arms, is the heraldic authority; the Order has also a Registrar, a Secretary, and a Gentleman Usher of the Scarlet Rod.

As already stated, the Order has a Military and a Civil Division and comprises three ranks with a limited number of members in each of the Divisions and classes: Knight or Dame Grand Cross (G.C.B.), Knight or Dame Commander (K.C.B. or D.C.B., and Companion (C.B.).

The insignia belonging to the Grand Cross are the Collar, the Badge of the appropriate Division, the Ribbon of plain crimson silk, the Star, and a Mantle of rich crimson satin, lined with white taffeta, with the Star of the appropriate Division embroidered on the left shoulder. Thirty-four Knights Grand Cross (twenty-two Military and twelve Civil) are allotted Stalls in the Chapel of the Order, where they are entitled to have their Banners, Crests and Stall Plates affixed to their Stalls.

The insignia belonging to a Knight/Dame Commander of the Order are the Badge pending from a crimson ribbon and the Commander's Star; and the insignia of a Companion is the Badge of the appropriate Division pending from a crimson ribbon.

The Most Honourable Order of the Bath is the highest Order of Knighthood to be conferred on foreign Heads of State, though foreign sovereigns often receive the dignity of an Extra Knight of the Order of the Garter. It is also – in the Military Division – the highest Order of Knighthood conferred for military merit.

The Collar of the Order is of gold, composed of nine imperial crowns and eight roses, thistles, and shamrocks, issuing from a sceptre and enamelled of their proper colours, all united together by seventeen white-enamelled knots. The Collar is the same for the Military and the Civil Divisions. The appropriate Badge is suspended from the imperial crown in the centre of the Collar.

The Badge of the Military Division is a gold Maltese cross enamelled

The insignia of a Knight Commander of the Civil Division of the Order of the Bath (left), and of the Military Division (right). Companions of the Order only wear the neck badge.

Courtesy: Spink & Son, Ltd., London

white, each of its points terminating in gold balls; in each of the four angles is a old lion of England rampant. The white-enamelled centre medallion bears a rose, a thistle and a shamrock radiating from a sceptre between three gold imperial crowns, surrounded first by a gold-rimmed, red-enamelled band bearing in gold letters the Order's motto, TRIA JUNCTA IN UNO (Three United in One), all within two gold-rimmed, green enamelled laurel wreaths, fruited red. Beneath the medallion is a gold-rimmed blue enamelled scroll with the inscription ICH DIEN in gold letters.

The Badge of the Civil Division is oval and entirely of gold, the external fillet containing the motto of the Order, encircling the device of a rose, thistle, shamrock, sceptre and three imperial crowns.

The Star of the Grand Cross, Military Division, is a silver faceted eight-pointed star with a gold Maltese cross superimposed, in the centre of which is a white-enamelled medallion, bearing three imperial crowns in relief, encircled by a red-enamelled band with TRIA JUNCTA IN UNO in gold letters. The band is surrounded by a wreath of green-enamelled laurels, the stems of which issue from a blue-enamelled scroll with ICH DIEN in gold letters.

The Star of the Grand Cross, Civil Division, is similar to the Star of the Military Division, but without the superimposed Maltese cross, laurel wreath and scroll.

The Star of a Knight/Dame Commander, Military Division, is a silver faceted Cross PATTÉE with five graduated short rays issuing between the arms. The centre medallion, with the three imperial crowns in relief, the band, motto, scroll and laurel wreath are the same as on the Grand Cross.

The Star of a Knight/Dame Commander, Civil Division, is similar to that of the Military Division but without the laurel wreath and scroll.

The motto of the Order has been interpreted differently by different chroniclers: some refer to the three theological virtues faith, hope and charity; others see in it a reference to the Holy Trinity under Whose protection the Order was said to have been placed; a third, post-Reformation and secular interpretation is a reference to the three Kingdoms of Great Britain.

KNIGHTS BACHELOR

'He that receiveth the Dignity of a Knight kneeleth down, and then the King lightly striketh him upon his shoulder and saith to him these words in French,'Sois Chivaler au nom de Dieu'; and afterwards saith moreover, 'Advance Chivaler'. [This] is meant of Knight Bachelors, which is the lowest, but most ancient Order of Knighthood.'

Thus Giles Jacob describes the ceremony of dubbing a Knight in 1762, and it has changed little to the present day. Sir Colin Cole K.C.V.O.,

The Breast Badge of a Knight Bachelor (centre) which is worn as an Order Star, the miniature of the insignia (left) and the Ladies' Brooch (right) which may be worn by wives and daughters of Knights Bachelor.

Courtesy: The Imperial Society of Knights Bachelor

former Garter King of Arms and Knight Principal of the Imperial Society of Knights Bachelor, extensively researched the evolution of Knighthood and published his findings in *The Roll of Knights Bachelor* (London, 1981). Besides the above quotation from Giles Jacob, Sir Colin cites the *Anglo-Saxon Chronicle* of 1086. Although the actual ceremony of dubbing was then not known to, or practised by, the English, there is a reference to such a ceremony where William the Norman 'dubbade his sun Henrie to ridere thaere' – 'there he dubbed his son Henry a Knight'. The word *riddere* is still used in its Germanic form in Germany where a Knight is called *Ritter*, and in the Netherlands where that title is called *Ridder*.

Knights Bachelor do not constitute a Royal Order of Chivalry; however, they date back to early Christian times, preceding the Crusades, and embrace Catholic customs. They recall the early history of Knighthood which under the influence of the Church was inspired by Christian principles. The word 'knight', as defined in the *Oxford English Dictionary*, is derived from the Old English *cnight, cnecht*, signifying a boy, youth or lad, as the German derivative of the word *Knecht* still does.

At an early date it also came to mean a young attendant or follower of the King or another personage of high rank, and later someone devoted to the service of a lady as her attendant or champion in war or at a tournament. Later still, the title came to mean a feudal tenant holding land from a superior on condition of serving in the field as a mounted and well-armed man. Gradually it took on the meaning of one raised to the honourable military rank of a Knight by the King or other competent Noble.

A Knight was usually a person of noble birth who had served a regular apprenticeship as page or squire to the profession of arms. This was the usual progression, even for those of the highest rank.

A Knight Bachelor was a young knight who was either not old enough or who had too few or no vassals to bring into the field under his own banner. Not being a 'banneret', therefore he followed the banner of another knight as a novice in arms.

The term is used in this sense in the Prologue to the *Canterbury Tales* by Chaucer (c.1345-1400). Hence it is conjecturally suggested that 'bachelor' is derived from the French *bas chevalier*, in the sense of being lower than a Knight of an Order.

The Latin adjective *baccalarius*, however, applied to farm labourers, those who worked for the tenant of the land, which itself is called *baccalaria*, – division of land. If we look for an equivalent rank to Knight in the French or Italian tongues, the reference to the fighter on horseback is obvious: *chevalier* and *cavaliere*. The German *Ritter* (and the Dutch *Ridder*) are also fighters who ride on horses.

The rank of a Knight Bachelor is a dignity conferred by the British Sovereign on commoners. It is a personal and non-hereditary honour and carries with it the appellation 'Sir', unlike baronets who are also known by the same honorific title. E.C.Joslin, of Spink & Son Ltd. of St. James's, London, which has been publishing the annual *Catalogue of British Orders, Decorations and Medals* for many years, attributes the introduction of the title 'Knight Bachelor' to King Henry III (1216-72), who wished to signify that the title was not to be hereditary. Unlike Knights belonging to prestigious Orders of Knighthood, Knights Bachelor, who do not belong to any particular Order, were with justification referred to by Giles Jacob in 1762 as 'the most ancient Order of Knighthood'. Here, the word 'Order' should be interpreted as a fraternity or society. It was not until 1908 that the late Sir William Bull convened a meeting of Knights in the House of Commons and formed a Society of Knights that in 1910 gave itself statutes 'to continue and complete to the date of the constitution the lapsed Roll instituted by the Warrant of His Majesty King Charles I regarding the creation of Knights Bachelor, to bring into existence and continuously keep up to date a properly authenticated Roll of Knights Bachelor, to uphold the status, maintain the rights of precedence and generally to protect the interests of Knights Bachelor'.

In 1912, King George V (1910-36) commanded that the Society be henceforth known as 'The Imperial Society of Knights Bachelor', granting

Neck Badge of a Knight Bachelor.

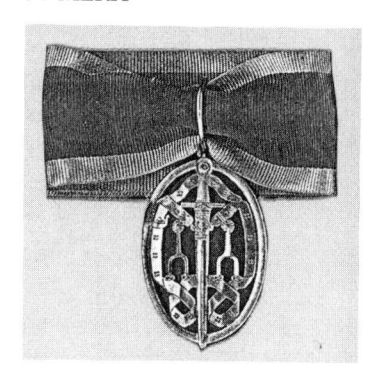

Knights Bachelor in 1926 the right to wear a Breast Badge. In 1973, Queen Elizabeth II authorised Knights Bachelor to wear a neck badge, suspended from a ribbon, red with yellow borders. In the list of precedence, Knights Bachelor take their place after Knight Commanders of the Most Excellent Order of the British Empire (which was founded in 1917) and before the Companions of all other Orders of Knighthood.

The Badge of a Knight Bachelor is officially described as:

> Upon an oval medallion of vermillion, enclosed by a scroll, a cross-hilted sword, belted and sheathed, pommel upwards, between two spurs, rowels upwards, the whole set about with the sword-belt, all gilt.

Knights Bachelor use the post-nominal letters Kt. after their surname. They are addressed as 'Sir', followed by their Christian name or forename. The wife of a Knight Bachelor is given the courtesy title 'Lady' which is followed by her husband's surname; she may not use her Christian name after the title 'Lady' unless they are Peeresses or daughters of certain Peers of the Realm[1]. The title 'Dame' is now reserved to ladies who have received an honour equivalent to that of a Knight Commander or Knight Grand Cross in an Order of Knighthood.

THE PRINCIPALITY OF MONACO
The Sovereign Princely House of Grimaldi

The Rock of Monaco has been occupied since ancient times by many conquerors. In 1197 the Genoese took possession of the territory, but ownership changed frequently until 1419 between the Ghibellines, vassals of the Emperor Frederick Barbarossa, and the Guelphs who were loyal to

---

[1] Prior to the promulgation of statutes in 1910, some wives of Knights appear on official Letters Patent with their Christian names, followed by the surname of the husband, for example Lady Gregory (widow of Sir William Gregory, KCMG, appears as 'Dame Augusta Gregory' on the Letters Patent for the Abbey Theatre, Dublin, dated 20 August 1904.

SECULARISED CATHOLIC-FOUNDED ORDERS OF KNIGHTHOOD 377

His Most Serene Highness Rainier III, Prince Sovereign of Monaco, wearing the Collar of the Grand Master of the Order of St. Charles. The Star nearest to the Badge Appendant of the Collar is the Grand Cross of the Légion d'Honneur, and on the right the Star of the Pontifical Order of the Golden Spur with which Prince Rainier was invested by Pope Pius XII in 1957.

Courtesy: The Embassy of the Principality of Monaco, Brussels

the Pope; the Grimaldi family belonged to the latter. Rainier I, a Grimaldi, and Jean II, son of Rainier II, established the authority of the Grimaldi family over Monaco.

In 1499, Louis XII of France assumed the rôle of protecting power over Monaco, but recognised Monaco's independence in 1515. There followed a number of unwelcome 'protectors', Spain, France and Sardinia, but Monaco's total independence was finally established in 1861.

Prince Albert I, a scientist who founded the Institute for Oceanography, succeeded to the throne in 1889. His son Louis II succeeded as Sovereign Prince in 1922. In 1924, Charlotte, the only child of Louis II, married the Count Pierre de Polignac, who took the name Grimaldi and substituted it for his own. On the birth of their son Rainier, his mother abdicated her right to the throne in his favour.

Because of its geographical position, during World War II Prince Louis joined the French army and was appointed General; his heir and grandson, Rainier, also became an officer in the French army. In 1945, Monaco was once again restored to full independence. Prince Louis II died in 1949, and his grandson became the Sovereign Prince of Monaco and reigns as Rainier III. His heir and successor, Prince Albert Alexandre Louis Pierre, was born in 1958.

Largely through the efforts of Prince Rainier III and his wife, the late Princess Grace, Monaco has become one of the major cultural centres in Europe.

THE ORDER OF ST. CHARLES
(L'Ordre de Saint-Charles)

The Order of St. Charles was instituted on 15 March 1858 by the Sovereign Prince Charles III as an award for outstanding services to the Sovereign Prince and the Principality of Monaco. The Order was given its name in honour of the Founder's Patron Saint, the sixteenth century St. Charles Borromeo. The reigning Prince is the Grand Master of the Order, which can be conferred on citizens of Monaco and on foreigners.

All reigning Princes since the foundation of the Order, Charles III, Albert I, Louis II and Rainier III, have signed Royal Ordinances in 1863, 1905, 1923, 1953 and 1973 respectively, making minor changes to the statutes of the Order.

The Badge of the Order is an eight-pointed, gold-rimmed and ball-tipped white-enamelled Maltese cross with a red border and a gold, green-enamelled laurel wreath between the arms of the cross, pending from a princely crown. In the centre of the cross is a red-enamelled medallion with the monogram C counter-couchant, for Charles, surmounted by a princely crown. The medallion has a white-enamelled,

The insignia of a Knight Commander of the Order of St. Charles (centre), a Knight Officer (left), and the reverse of the insignia of a Knight (right).

Courtesy: The Royal Palace Archives, Monaco

gold-rimmed surround bearing in gold the motto PRINCEPS ET PATRIA (Prince and Country). On the reverse the Badge has a medallion which bears the red and white lozenges of the Grimaldi arms, and in the white-enamelled surround the words DEO JUVANTE (With God's Help).

The Star of the Order is an eight-pointed, faceted silver star with the Badge of the Order in the centre, but without the surmounting crown.

The ribbon of the Order is red with a broad white centre stripe and a thin white border on either side.

The Grand Master wears a Collar consisting of sixteen alternating oval medallions, eight red enamelled with the monogram C counter-couchant in gold and a gold, green-enamelled wreath of laurels surrounding the medallion; the other eight, surrounded with a similar laurel wreath, bear the red and white lozenges of the Grimaldi arms. The Badge, surmounted by the crown, is suspended from the Collar.

The Order is awarded in five classes:

The Knight Grand Cross wears the Badge of the Order suspended from a sash and the Star of the Order on his left breast.

Grand Officers wear the Commander's neck badge on a ribbon and the Star of the Order on their right breast.

Commanders wear the neck badge of the Order suspended from a ribbon.

Officers and Knights wear a smaller Badge pending from a chest ribbon; Officers have the ribbon adorned with a rosette.

THE REPUBLIC OF POLAND

Mons. Cardinale's first edition of *Orders of Knighthood, Awards and the Holy See* made only a fleeting reference to the Order of the White Eagle in the section of the extinct Catholic-founded Orders of Knighthood, and the illustration that accompanied the brief notice showed the Order as an Imperial Russian Order, mounted on the black-enamelled double-headed Russian Eagle. Archbishop Cardinale, had received from the Ambassador of the Polish People's Republic in Bruxelles a curt reply to his enquiry about the Order, informing him that the Order had been abolished by the Polish People's Republic.

During my visit in 1983 to the Papal Secretariat of State, the opinion of the Holy Father was conveyed to me that further enquiries about this ancient Catholic-founded Polish Order should be made before publishing a revised edition of *Orders of Knighthood, Awards and the Holy See*, though I was expressly asked to conduct any future enquiries privately and, if I discovered that the Order should not have been listed as extinct, restore the Order of the White Eagle to its proper place among the Catholic-founded Orders of Knighthood.

Poland was under Communist domination, and although 95% of the population belong to the Roman Catholic Church, which even, and especially, during the most oppressive years of Communist dictatorship, never yielded to the pressures of the regime, heavily guarded frontiers and total censorship of information made it difficult to make further enquiries in Poland about the Order.

The legitimate Polish Government had gone into exile in 1939. The Polish Constitution of 1935 had provided for the continuity of a legal government in case of war, when the democratically elected Parliament and the State would not be able to function normally. On the strength of the Polish Constitution, in September 1939 President Moscicki (1926-39) appointed Mr. Wladislaw Raczkiewicz, who was already in Paris, as his successor. In 1940 President Raczkiewicz was recognised by all foreign Governments while he was still in France and thereafter in London. Both he and his Prime Minister, General Sikorski, were also recognised by the Soviet Union after Hitler invaded Russia in 1941.

On the strength of this constitutional rule, the office and the legal title of President of Poland was preserved until Poland became free again, and a President could be democratically elected in the normal constitutional manner.

The grand-mastership of the Polish Orders of Knighthood rested constitutionally with the Presidents of Poland, and the *de jure* President of

Poland in 1983 was Count Edward Raczynski. Nevertheless, I first approached the Government of the Polish People's Republic through their London Embassy, and on 21 December 1983 I received a reply from the Ministry of Foreign Affairs of the Polish People's Republic:

'A bill passed by our Parliament on 17th February 1960 (Dziennik Ustaw No poz 66 of 1960) lists all orders and medals which can be awarded in Poland including those which were given before World War II and which are continued to be awarded now. The Order of the White Eagle is not included on this list. At the same time Article 29 of the said Bill provides that all previous bills and laws which constituted the bases for awarding orders and medals cease to be legally binding. In view of the above, the Order of the White Eagle formally ceased to exist.'

International Jurists who were consulted after I received this reply, rejected the conclusion of the writer that Article 29 of that Bill had abolished anything, let alone the Order of the White Eagle, since the jurisdiction over the Order, as well as the other Polish Orders of Knighthood and Merit, rested solely with the Polish President-in-Exile. The office of Head of State of the Polish People's Republic was held by the First Secretary of the Central Committee of the Communist Party. Curiously, the Communist Government decided not to have a President in Poland to rival the Polish President-in-Exile.

Technically and under international law, the First Secretary, holding *de facto* the office of Head of State, was entitled to suppress the Order of the White Eagle within the territory he governed. This in no way infringed on the Order's continued lawful existence or the Order's lawful Grand Master, the President of Poland-in-Exile. The Grand Master was within his rights to continue to bestow the Order if he so wished. Besides the Presidents-in-Exile, who were entitled *ex officio* to wear the Order of the White Eagle and the Grand Cross of the Order of 'Polonia Restituta'.

This highest Polish honour was conferred by Presidents-in-Exile in 1941 on Dr. Henryk Liberman, posthumously in 1943 on General Wladislaw Sikorski, posthumously in 1950 on Tadeusz Tomaszewski, in 1959 on Eustachy Sapieha, posthumously in 1964 on General Michael Tokarzewski-Karaszewicz, and posthumously in 1990 on Wladyslaw Cardinal Rubin.

On 22 December 1990, Mr. Lech Walesa was sworn in as the first democratically elected President of the new Republic of Poland. Although this book is merely concerned with Catholic-founded Orders of Knighthood and cannot by its very nature give detailed political histories of countries, the unusual circumstances of the total change of fortune of Poland, and also the juridical issues governing the Order of the White Eagle and the Order of 'Polonia Restituta', justify to place on record, both in words and pictures, the momentous event which took place on 22 December 1990 when President Walesa took over the title of President of Poland from the last President-in-Exile, Mr. Ryszard Kaczorowski, thus becoming the eleventh President of the Republic of Poland and Grand Master of the Polish Orders of Knighthood. Since its foundation as a Republic in 1918 Poland had the following Presidents: Josef Pilsudski,

The Requiem Mass in London of Count Edward Raczynski, President-in-Exile from 1979 to 1986, was held in the Brompton Oratory. Senior Officers of the Polish Army, Navy and Air Force carried the principal insignia of Orders of Knighthood that had been bestowed upon Count Raczynski: the Order of the White Eagle; the Grand Cross of the Order of 'Polonia Restituta'; the Order of Merit of the Polish Republic; the Grand Cross of the Most Excellent Order of the British Empire; and the Grand Cross of the Pontifical Order of Pius IX. The Master of Ceremonies, Chev. Barbarski, Polish Pontifical Knights and Military Attachés from the Embassy of the Polish Republic awaited the arrival of the coffin and accompanied it into the church. After the Requiem, the remains of Count Raczynski were flown to Poland.

Courtesy: J.Englert

though his title was Chief of State, 1918-22; Gabriel Narutowicz, (1922); Stanislaw Wojciechowski, (1922-26); Ignacy Moscicki, (1926-39); Wladyslaw Raczkiewicz, (1939-47); August Zaleski (1947-72); Stanislaw Ostrowski, (1972-79); Edward Raczynski, (1979-86); Kazimierz Sabbat, (1986-89); Ryszard Kaczorowski, (1989-90); Lech Walesa, (1990-). No other people are recognised by the present Polish Government as having been Presidents of Poland.[1]

On 30 July 1992, *Polska Zbrojna*, the armed forces daily newspaper (Warsaw), published an article which reported the debate in the Sejm on the previous Wednesday (29 July 1992) concerning the law President Walesa had placed before the Polish Parliament concerning the restoration, retention and precedence of the four Polish Orders of Chivalry, four Crosses and two Medals[2].

[1] See Appendix XI which deals with which conferments of Orders and Awards between the end of the second World War and 1990 are recognised and which are not. The final decision was not published until 1994.
[2] Mr. Krzysztof Barbarski, the Curator of the Sikorski Museum in London and foremost expert on Polish Orders and Decorations, supplied me with the information and tranlated it for this book.

SECULARISED CATHOLIC-FOUNDED ORDERS OF KNIGHTHOOD 385

President-in-Exile Kazimierz Sabbat (1986-1989) decorated the Portuguese Minister of State for Culture, Prof. de Sousa Lara with the insignia of an Officer of the Order of 'Polonia Restituta'.

The last investiture of President Sabbat before his sudden death in 1989. He decorated Mr. Richard Model (second from right) with the Cross of Merit in Gold. Prof. Edward Szcepanik, Prime Minister-in-exile (left) and the Foreign Minister, Prof. Zygmunt Szkopiak, also attended the investiture.

The order of precedence proposed was:
 – The Order of the White Eagle
 – The Order of 'Virtuti Militari'
 – The Order of 'Polonia Restituta'
 – The Order of Merit of the Polish Republic
(ex-Communist Order instituted in 1974)

The Crosses of Merit are listed in the following order of precedence:
- The Cross of Valour
- The Cross of Merit with Sword, (gold silver and bronze)
- The Cross of Merit (gold, silver and bronze)
- The Cross of Merit for Bravery

To remove any conflict and embarrassment to some active politicians, the Sejm passed a law to clarify the position of those who received any of the above-listed Orders and Decorations between 1 September 1939 and 22 December 1990. The most important decision taken by the Sejm was that Orders and Awards conferred by the Presidents-in-Exile (who are listed above), the Polish Government-in-Exile in London, and those awarded by the Communist Heads of State of the Polish People's Republic need not be verified again and are recognised as legitimately conferred Orders and Awards of the Republic of Poland.

THE ORDER OF THE WHITE EAGLE
(Order Orla Bialego)

The origin of the Order is shrouded in legend; some stories try to link the Order's foundation to Lech I, a Prince of Poland in the sixth century. Even the generally accepted foundation date of 1325 is not absolutely certain because the statutes of the Order which are said to date from the early fourteenth century no longer exist. It is assumed, but there is no documentary evidence to substantiate it, that the Order of the White Eagle was founded when Casimir of the Piast Dynasty married Anna, Princess of Lithuania.

The Order as we know it, however, was established in the eighteenth century, though the precise date has never been established. One source suggests the meeting between King Frederick Augustus I and Czar Peter I ('The Great') of Russia on 1 November 1705. On this occasion Augustus I issued a gold medal, suspended from a sky-blue ribbon, bearing the White Eagle of Poland and the motto PRO FIDE, REGE ET LEGE. Another source points to 1709, the occasion of Augustus I's ascent of the throne for the second time, and it is suggested that he introduced the Order on that occasion in the form of a cross.

The Badge of 1709 was a gold Maltese Cross with ball tips, red enamelled arms edged white, and gold rays set with diamonds filling the spaces between them. A white enamelled eagle, surmounted by a gold crown, was mounted in the centre of the cross, which was worn on a white ribbon with a red stripe near the edges.

In 1713 the crown was removed and the rays redesigned. The reverse

SECULARISED CATHOLIC-FOUNDED ORDERS OF KNIGHTHOOD

The Order of the White Eagle, the principle Order of Knighthood of the Polish Republic.

carried a shield showing a cross with Saxon swords and the royal monogram with the above-mentioned motto. The Badge was worn with a sky-blue sash over the left shoulder to the right side. In the same year, an embroidered Star was added to the Order. The Star was made of gold and silver bullion thread and worn on the left breast.

During the reign of Stanislaus Augustus Poniatowski (1764 – resigned his sovereignty in 1795 and died at St. Petersburg, a state prisoner in 1798), the insignia of the Order were again changed, the reverse of the Badge now carrying the name of the Virgin Mary, MARIA, arranged in a stylised monogram.

Following the third partition of Poland in 1795, the Order fell into abeyance, but it was revived on 22 July 1807 by a Decree of the Duchy of Warsaw. The Badge of the Order was redesigned; the rays were altered and an emblem, similar to the earlier Saxon one replaced the MARIA monogram. It was at this time that metal Stars were first introduced, replacing the embroidered ones.

Following the creation of the Kingdom of Poland in 1815 (the so-called Congress Kingdom), the Order of the White Eagle was retained in a similar form to that adopted by the Duchy of Warsaw.

After the November Insurrection of 1830-31, the Order of the White Eagle, together with other Orders, was incorporated into the Russian Orders system to emphasize the fact that Poland was now an integral part of the Russian Empire. The Polish Badge of the Order of the White Eagle was mounted on a black enamelled Imperial Russian Eagle, the design of the Star was changed and the colour of the sash was altered to a dark royal blue.

On 4 February 1921, the elected Parliament of the Republic of Poland, the Sejm, restored the Order of the White Eagle as the highest Polish award. The new design was based on the nineteenth century version, with a sky-blue sash worn over the left shoulder, and the Star was worn on the left breast. In the Polish table of precedence the Order ranked above all other Polish and foreign Orders. The motto on the reverse of the Badge and on the obverse of the Star was changed to ZA OJCZYZNE I NAROD (For Fatherland and Nation), and the centre of the Star was replaced with the monogram RP within a green wreath.

The Collar of the Grand Master dates from the reign of King Stanislaus Augustus and is preserved in the Royal Castle in Warsaw. It consists of twenty-four links of three recurring motifs: the white enamelled eagle, an oval blue enamelled medallion edged with gold rays and bearing the images of the Virgin and Child, and a similar medallion with the name MARIA in stylised form.

According to the 1921 statutes, the Order of the White Eagle is an award recognising significant civilian or military service performed in time of peace or war, for the honour and benefit of the Polish Republic.

The first Grand Master of the restored Order was Marshal of Poland Józef Pilsudski in his capacity as Poland's Head of State. Subsequently the position of Grand Master has been held by successive Presidents of Poland.

The Order continued to be awarded with great parsimony by the Allied Polish Government during the second World War and, indeed, by the legal successors of that government.

THE ORDER OF 'POLONIA RESTITUTA'
(Order Odrodzenia Polski)
(successor to the Catholic-founded Order of St. Stanislaus)

After the establishment of an independent Poland in 1918, the Order of 'Polonia Restituta' (Order of the Rebirth of Poland) was instituted by the Sejm, the Parliament of the Republic of Poland, on 4th July 1921.

There have been many arguments since 1944, when Poland came under Soviet rule and a Communist regime ruled the Polish People's Republic, as to whether or not the Order of 'Polonia Restituta' was the successor of the former Catholic-founded Order of St. Stanislaus, which had been founded by Stanislaus Augustus Poniatowski, the last King of Poland (1764-95), in 1765 on the eve of the Feast of St. Stanislaus, Bishop, Martyr and Patron Saint of Poland.

The Communist Regime instituted its own version of the Cross and Star of the Order of 'Polonia Restituta' on 22 December 1944 by removing the gold crown from the Polish Eagle in the centre medallion of the cross and replacing on the reverse of the Cross the date 1918 with 1944. On the Star of the Order they placed a medallion with the letters PRL, standing for 'Polish People's Republic'.

The reason for the institution of the Order of 'Polonia Restituta' in 1921 instead of restoring the Order of St. Stanislaus has its roots in 1830. After the Insurrection of 1830 and the suppression of the Kingdom of Poland, Czar Nicholas I incorporated the Order among the Russian Orders of Chivalry in 1831, and he changed the insignia by substituting the double-headed eagle of Russia for the Polish Eagle in 1832. The Order of St. Stanislaus remained in the hands of the Russian Czars until 1917 and was lavishly bestowed on Russians and foreigners who actively worked against the interest of the Polish people.

Originally, the Order of St. Stanislaus had one class and the number of Knights was restricted to one hundred; additional foreign Knights were admitted; the Order ranked second only to the Order of the White Eagle. The Order's Badge was an eight-pointed, red-enamelled and gold bordered cross with gold balls on the points, and in the white enamelled

During his state visit to Great Britain in 1992, President Walesa gave a reception for H.M.The Queen and H.R.H.The Duke of Edinburgh, The Polish President had been invested by the Queen with the Grand Cross of the Order of the Bath, and Her Majesty had received the Grand Cross of the Order of Merit of the Polish Republic from President Walesa.

Courtesy: J. Englert

centre, surrounded by a gold and green laurel wreath, the figure of St. Stanislaus. On the reverse, also white enamelled, the cypher SS (Sanctus Stanislaus). Between the arms of the cross the golden-crowned, white Polish Eagle with its wings spread. The Motto on the green and gold enamelled wreath was PRAEMIANDO INCITAT.

The Order was suspended from a red sash with one white stripe on either side of the sash and was worn from the right shoulder to the left hip, but Knights who also had the Order of the White Eagle wore the insignia on a narrower ribbon around the neck.

In 1815, Czar Alexander I, as King of Poland, slightly changed the design of the insignia and divided the Order into four classes.

In 1989, when there was still a Polish President- and Government-in-Exile, Mr. Krzysztof Barbarski wrote a treatise on Polish Orders and decorations for the *Golden Jubilee Book* of Polski Uniwersytet Na Obczyznie, the Polish University Abroad in London. I have once again drawn upon Mr. Barbarski's expertise in this section on The Order of 'Polonia Restituta'. In my Editor's Foreword for the University's book, I

SECULARISED CATHOLIC-FOUNDED ORDERS OF KNIGHTHOOD 391

The Cross of a Commander suspended from a red ribbon with white side stripes and the Star of the Grand Cross and of a Grand Officer.

mentioned the arguments which had been put to me for and against the assumption that the Order of 'Polonia Restituta' was the successor of the Order of St. Stanislaus. In October 1992 I received from Mr. Barbarski the official Polish publication *The Orders of the Kings and Presidents of Poland in the Orders Room of the Royal Castle in Warsaw, (1991/92)*, the Polish text of which is by Tadeusz Jeziorowski. On page 16 the author deals with the Order of Polonia Restituta, and I quote verbatim Mr. Barbarski's translation of the first paragraph:

'The Order of the Rebirth of Poland was instituted by the Sejm on 4th July 1921, together with the restoration of the Order of the White Eagle. The Order is commonly known as the 'Polonia Restituta' from its motto, meaning Poland Reborn. Although the Order of St. Stanislaus was not restored, both the Order's statutes and its ribbon, which were in the colours of the Polish Republic, were drawn upon. The beautifully proportioned white cross of Maltese style is a testimony to its designer Mieczyslaw Kotarbinski (executed by the Germans in 1943). Kotarbinski was also the designer of the restored Order of the White Eagle.'

Although the Order of 'Polonia Restituta' was originally conceived as an Order with four classes, it was extended to five classes: Grand Cross, Grand Officer (or Commander's Cross with Star), Commander, Officer and Knight.

The Badge of the Order is a gilt Maltese Cross with ball tips at the end of the arms; the obverse is enamelled white, with a central circular enamelled medallion bearing the crowned white eagle on a red background and a blue surround bearing the motto POLONIA RESTITUTA. The reverse of the Cross is gilt and on a red enamelled central medallion is the date 1918 in gilt.

The Badge of the first and second class is worn with a silver Star, consisting of eight clusters of rays which has a circular white enamelled medallion in the centre, bearing the gilt monogram RP (Republic of Poland) and has a gilt bordered blue enamelled surround with the motto POLONIA RESTITUTA.

The Grand Cross is worn on a red sash with white stripes near the edges, on the right shoulder to the left side. Grand Officers and Commanders wear their Crosses as a neck badge suspended from a ribbon. Grand Officers also wear the Star of the Order. Officers and Knights wear their Crosses on the left breast, suspended from a ribbon. Superimposed on the ribbon of an Officer is a rosette.

The Chapter of the Order is presided over by the Grand Master.

THE REPUBLIC OF PORTUGAL

The Republic of Portugal's extant Military Orders are among the most ancient, famous and illustrious Orders of Knighthood in the world. The country has always had a turbulent history, and it adopted a republican government as early as 1910. However, it has never ceased to take pride in its traditions, as is reflected by its retention of its Orders of Knighthood and awarding them as Orders of Merit.

The three Catholic-founded Military Orders of Knighthood, The Order of Christ, The Order of Avis, and The Order of St. James of the Sword, share a long and important link with the Apostolic See, although they lost their religious aspects in 1789 when with papal approval Queen Maria I had the Orders secularised, and they became aristocratic Orders of Merit, rewarding services to the Crown[1]. In 1917/18 they became Military Orders of Merit when the Republican Government that had come to power in 1910 and initially had placed all Orders in abeyance, reconstituted them.

Because of their long and proud history and their involvement with the Apostolic See during the many centuries of their existence, their secular status and their full integration in the honours system of the State of Portugal were often misunderstood. I recall Archbishop Cardinale's impatience when listing the Portuguese Orders, especially The Riband of the Three Orders. He referred to it as 'a peculiar insignia of the "First Magistrate of Portugal" during his term of office and a Grand Collar of the insignia reserved for foreign Heads of State'. On several occasions he received information from the Portuguese Ambassador in Belgium that was contradictory; his description of the Riband of the Three Orders, especially his reference to 'the First Magistrate of Portugal', caused understandable resentment, as there had never been a First Magistrate of Portugal.

The President of the Republic is *ex-officio* the Grand Master of all State Orders, and in this capacity wears as his official insignia the 'Riband of the Three Orders'. The Riband is given precedence in the list of Catholic-founded Orders, as it combines the insignia of the three ancient Military Orders of Knighthood – of Christ, of St. Benedict of Avis, and of St. James of the Sword.

The precedence of the Military Orders of Knighthood is given in the *Diário da República* (published by the Government) and in the *Anuátrio das Ordens Honoríficas Portuguesas*, (published by the Presidency of the Republic).

---

[1] After secularisation in 1789, the prerequisites for membership in the three Orders remained those of nobility and belonging to the Catholic religion.

Portugal, more than any other European country – in spite of its sometimes turbulent history – has always demonstrated the value of continuity and change without destructive forces of modernism destroying the country's heritage. Thus we often find that descendants of illustrious noble families, whilst adopting different values and ideologies, are members of Parliament, belonging to different parties or work in leading positions of the Republic.

Unlike some European countries that underwent a painful metamorphosis from monarchy to republic, banning, for example, hereditary titles of nobility and even parts of names in an endeavour to erase past history, the Portuguese people are proud of their ancestors and continue, if they so wish, to bear all the names and titles which are rightfully theirs.

As I explained in Chapter Seven, Portugal was the first Republic that invited the descendants of the former reigning Royal Family to return from exile to their homeland, because there was on the part of the Royal Family no conflict of loyalty and devotion to their country and its democratic Constitution.

Because of constitutional principles, monarchism and republicanism are inevitably at opposite ends of the political spectrum. It would therefore be wrong to give the impression that the two chapters in this book, on the Republic of Portugal and on the Royal House of Portugal, represent a composite political whole: Republicans do not wish to have a Monarchy ruling the country, and Monarchists do not like the political concept of a Republic.

In spite of this, and the fact that Portuguese republicanism has at times also embraced extreme political opposites, right-wing dictatorship, socialism and communism, the strength of the country lies in the fact that the people have never tried to erase the past from the history of Portugal, but viewed it as part of the country's evolution.

Following the Revolution of 25 April 1974, the Orders were temporarily placed in abeyance until 1986, the Chancellors of the Orders being dismissed from office and the Councils dissolved. However, the Constitution of the Republic approved by Parliament in 1976 had declared the President of Portugal to be the Grand Master of all Portuguese Orders and gave him the power to confer decorations *motu proprio*.

The statutes of the Orders that had been promulgated in 1962 and that gave power to propose conferment of an Order to the Government and to the Councils of the Orders was suspended.

Dr. Mário Soares was elected as President of the Republic in March 1986, and in December he gave presidential assent to a Decree of the Council of Ministers, regulating the criteria of conferment, insignia and all other matters relating to Orders of Knighthood and Merit in the Republic of

Dr. Mário Soares, President of the Portuguese Republic (1986–).

Courtesy: The Secretary General of the Presidency of the Republic of Portugal

Portugal.[1] These Decrees re-established the offices of Chancellors and the Councils of the Orders. With regard to the precedence of Orders, the traditional precedence of the Order of Christ over the Military Order of Avis was legally re-established, after a brief period when the Order of Avis had claimed precedence over the Order of Christ.

The President of the Republic, in his capacity as Grand Master of the Portuguese Orders, is assisted by a Secretary-General of the Portuguese Orders and by three Chancellors with their respective Councils, for the Military Orders, for the National Orders, and for the Orders of Civil Merit.

As mentioned above, the insignia of the President, the 'Banda das Três Ordens', takes precedence over all other insignia. The Orders of Knighthood follow as Military Orders ('Antigas Ordens Militares') in the order of precedence given in this chapter, and they, in turn are followed by two National Orders of Merit ('Ordens Nacionais'), The Order of the Infante Dom Henrique ('Ordem do Infante Dom Henrique') and The Order of Liberty ('Ordem da Liberdade'); and in the third category by the Orders of Civil Merit ('Ordens de Mérito Civil'), The Order of Merit (Ordem do Mérito), The Order for Public Education ('Ordem da Instruçao Publica'), and the Order of Merit in Agriculture, Commerce and Industry ('Ordem de Mérito Agrícola, Comércio e Industrial').

THE RIBAND OF THE THREE ORDERS
(Banda das Três Ordens)

Today, these are the unique insignia of the President of the Portuguese Republic which he wears *ex officio* as Head of State and Grand Master of all state Orders of Knighthood and of Merit. It combines in its insignia the Grand Crosses of the Military Orders of Knighthood, the Order of Christ, the Order of St. Benedict of Avis and the Order of St. James of the Sword.

The origin of the insignia of the Riband of the Three Orders can be traced to 1551, when Pope Julius III promulgated the Bull *Praeclara Clarissimi* in which he gave to the Crown of Portugal in perpetuity the grand-mastership of the three ancient Military Orders of Knighthood.[2]

Until then the administration of the Orders was in the hands of elected Grand Masters who needed confirmation of their election by the Apostolic See; the grand-masterships of the three Military Orders with their properties and wealth had been passed, to the reigning Royal House of Portugal. Only the Portuguese Priory of the Sovereign Military Order of Malta in Portugal continued to be a Religious Order.[3]

---

[1] Decreto-Lei n° 414-A/86 de 15 Dezembro de 1986, and Decreto-Lei n° 71-A de 15 Dezembro 1986.
[2] 'The Portuguese Orders of Merit – A Brief Account' by Dr. José Vicente de Bragança, Secretary General of the Orders, Lisbon.
[3] The Prince and Grand Master of the Sovereign Military Order of Malta is elected, but must be confirmed by the reigning Pontiff before he can exercise his office. See: Chapter Five, I.

Members of the Portuguese Royal Family continued to be the Grand Masters of the Military Orders; King Joâo I (1356-1433), became the Grand Master of the Military Order of St. Benedict of Avis in 1385 before he was proclaimed King. The Infante Dom Henrique (1394-1460) – Prince Henry the Navigator – one of King Joâo's sons, was Governor or Grand Master of the Military Order of Christ; another, Dom Joâo, became Grand Master of the Order of St. Benedict of Avis, and a third, Dom Fernando, was appointed Grand Master of the Order of St. James of the Sword.

The Badge and the Star of the Riband of the Three Orders. Insignia dating from different historical periods are reproduced in colour in this book.

Courtesy: Presidência da República

Queen Maria I (1734-1816) secularised the three ancient Military Orders with the approval of Pope Pius VI in 1789. However, she surmounted the insignia with the image of the Sacred Heart and retained the Catholic Faith and nobility as a prerequisite for conferment of the Orders, thus giving rise to the erroneous assumption that secularisation of the three Military Orders had been unilaterally introduced when the Republican Government revived the Orders in 1918 and at the same time restored the insignia of the three Orders to their original simplicity by removing the Sacred Heart which had been added to them in 1789 by Maria I, who had thereby given the impression that the Orders were as a result even more 'Catholic' than before.

At the same time as Sovereign and Grand Master of the three Military Orders, she introduced the riband and the insignia of the Three Orders. From then until 1962, except for the first years of the Republic, The Riband of The Three Orders was conferred by Portuguese Heads of State, both Monarchs and Presidents, on foreign Heads of State.

398　　　　　　　　ORDERS OF KNIGHTHOOD AND OF MERIT

A Star dating after 1789 and prior to 1910, worn with a red and green sash, combining the Orders of Christ and of Avis.

Private collection

Among the recipients were three British Monarchs, George V, George VI and Elizabeth II. A lesser known fact is that between 1931 and 1962 a second multiple Order was conferred on a very few eminent foreigners by Presidents of the Portuguese Republic: The Riband of the Two Orders, comprising the Grand Cross of the Military Orders of Christ and of Avis.[1]

The future King Edward VIII (The Duke of Windsor) was the first recipient of this Order in 1931.[2]

The present insignia of the Riband of the Three Orders[3] consist of a Badge suspended from a laurel wreath; it is a large oval gold filigree medallion on a blue-enamelled background with three small white-enamelled oval medallions inside which are, in red the emblem of the Order of Christ, in green that of the Order of Avis, and in purple that of the Order of St. James of the Sword, resting on two green laurel branches. The Badge is suspended from a sash of red, green and purple stripes, all of equal width.

A Star was also instituted: it is an eight-pointed, faceted gold star upon

---

[1] Examples of the Orders of Christ and of Avis being worn jointly on a Grand Cordon (red and green) after 1789 are known, though the 'Riband of the Two Orders' was only instituted in 1931 and abolished in 1962.

[2] Dr. J.V. de Bragança gives the complete list of all recipients with the dates of conferment of both multiple Orders. Examples of the Riband of the Two Orders (Christ and Avis) after 1789 but before 1910 can be found in some private and national collections in Europe. The Double Order must have been sanctioned by the Monarch, but was never instituted as a separate Order. The insignia were obviously privately made.

[3] Among the colour plates of Portuguese Orders, The Riband of the Three Orders is shown as worn by the President of the Republic and the insignia of the Order made for João VI as Emperor of Brazil; the Imperial Crown of Brazil has been substituted for the Royal Crown of Portugal.

which an eight-pointed silver star is superimposed. In its centre is a round gold filigree medallion on a blue enamelled background of the Badge with a red-enamelled circle inside a gold one. Within the medallion are three small white oval medallions with the emblems of the three Military Orders.

THE MILITARY ORDER OF THE TOWER AND THE SWORD OF VALOUR, LOYALTY AND MERIT
(Ordem Militar da Torre e Espada do Valor, Lealdade e Mérito)

Although the Order is said by some chroniclers to have been instituted as the Military Order of the Sword and placed under the protection of Sant'Iago in 1459 by King Alfonso V (1438-81), as an award for the Knights who had conquered Fez in Morocco and other African territories, there is no reliable evidence that this Order was ever founded.

Because of lack of concrete evidence for the Order's existence, most historians today agree that the Order of the Sword was perhaps an unrealised project of Alfonso V or the Order ceased to exist after his death in 1481 without leaving a trace of evidence for its existence.

In the Vatican archives are records about the strained relations between the Apostolic See and Portugal between 1438 and 1451, due to the mother of the young Alfonso, Queen Leonor, being refused the Regency of the country during his childhood. After relations had been restored in 1452, Pope Nicholas V issued a Bull on 8 January 1454, in which the Apostolic See ceded to Alfonso V all the conquests in Africa from Cape Non to Guinea, and the government over all his conquests; the Bull also prohibited any vessel from sailing to those parts without express leave from the King of Portugal. A second Bull, also dated 8 January 1454, extended Portuguese dominion over all the seas from Africa to India. There is also a mention of an undated and unspecified Bull about the

Order of Christ granting that Order authority over the peoples subdued by the Portuguese as far as India, and provided that no one but the King of Portugal should be entitled to send expeditions of discovery to those parts. In 1481, Pope Sixtus IV (1471-84) confirmed to the Kings of Portugal all territories and islands discovered prior to the date of the Papal Brief and in the future.

There is in the historical chronology of the Vatican Archives no reference to the foundation of a Portuguese Order called 'of the Tower and the Sword'. Nevertheless, ecclesiastical and secular lists of Orders of Knighthood published after 1808 refer to the date of foundation for the Order of the Tower and the Sword as 1459 and give Dom Alfonso V as the founder. An ecclesiastical list refers to the Order having been placed under the patronage of Sant'Iago, and A.M.Perrot (Paris, 1820), mentions the 'Ordre de la Tour et de l'Epée' stating: 'Cet ordre fut institué en 1459, par Alphonse V, qui eu vingt-sept chevaliers: tel était le nombre d'années qu'il avait lorsqu'il s'empera de Fez sur les Maures' – the Order had twenty-seven Knights because that was the number of years it had taken to conquer the Moors at Fez. This is, in this author's opinion, another case of overgilding the lily.

The corroborated facts are that the Order was 'renewed' in 1808 in the reign of the ailing Queen Maria I by the Prince Regent João, the future King João VI.[1] Because the Order was soon given precedence over the Ancient Military Orders of Christ, of St. Benedict of Avis and of St. James of the Sword, and because antiquity added to the kudos of an Order, it is reasonable to assume that the 'renewal' was based on a less than solid foundation, and bearing in mind that it was the expressed wish of the Prince Regent João to establish an Order that had no Catholic links, it is erroneous to place it among the Catholic-founded Orders. It found its place there on the false assumption that it was founded in 1459, had remained dormant and had been revived.

Today it is (and has been officially since 1832) the principal Military Order among the 'Antigas Ordens Militares' of Portugal. Its inclusion in this chapter of secularised Catholic-founded Orders of Knighthood is not designed to perpetuate the legend of its origin, but merely to comply with the word meaning 'renewed' or 'reconstituted' that was used in the Royal Letters Patent of Foundation in 1808.

It can therefore be said authoritatively that the Order of the Tower and the Sword was founded rather than renewed by the Prince Regent João (1792-1816), the future King João VI of Portugal (1816-26), by Royal Decree given at Rio de Janeiro, Brazil, on 29 November 1808, in

---

[1] The Royal Charter of Foundation ('revival') of the Order, 'Carta-de-Lei of 29 November 1808', states categorically that the Order is to be considered the only Portuguese Order of Knighthood without any religious origin or link, being a secular, strictly dynastic Order of the Royal House of Bragança.

commemoration of the save arrival of the Royal Family in Brazil, after they had to flee Portugal because of Napoleon's invasion. The Letters Patent give as the criteria of conferment military and political merit and services to the Crown by Portuguese and foreigners. They also expressly state that it is the wish of the Prince Regent to reward subjects of His Majesty the King of Great Britain who had escorted him to Brazil and facilitated the safe arrival of the Royal Family, and who for reasons of their religion could not receive any of the extant Military Orders which, even after Queen Maria I had the Orders secularised in 1789, could only be conferred on Catholics.

In 1832 and 1833 the Prince Regent Dom Pedro, Duke of Bragança, and former King of Portugal and Emperor of Brazil (1828-34), reformed and re-established the Order again and gave it the name 'The Ancient and Most Noble Order of The Tower and The Sword, of Valour, Loyalty and Merit', with precedence over the other Orders of Knighthood.

The Badge and Star of the Order of the Tower and the Sword, of Valour, Loyalty and Merit.

Courtesy: Presidência da República

The reformed Order had four classes: Grand Cross, Commander, Officer and Knight. In 1896, as a result of the reform of the Military Order of St. Benedict of Avis, a fifth class was added to the Military Order of the Tower and the Sword: Grand Officer, ranking immediately below the Grand Cross.

In 1910, the Government of the Republic suspended all Military Orders of Knighthood without expressly suspending the Military Order of the

Tower and the Sword.[1] Nevertheless on 26 September 1917, the Order officially was re-established, under the name of 'Order of the Tower and the Sword, of Valour, Loyalty and Merit' with four classes, the highest class, the Grand Cross, belonging *ex officio* to the President of the Republic. The rank of Grand Officer having been abolished.

In 1918, the former five classes were restored to the Order, and the President of the Republic was named the Grand Master and *ex officio* a Knight Grand Cross.

The Grand Collar of the Order was created in 1939[2] to be conferred upon Heads of State who had outstanding military merits. The first Head of State upon whom the Grand Collar was conferred was Generalissimo Francisco Franco, Head of the Spanish State.

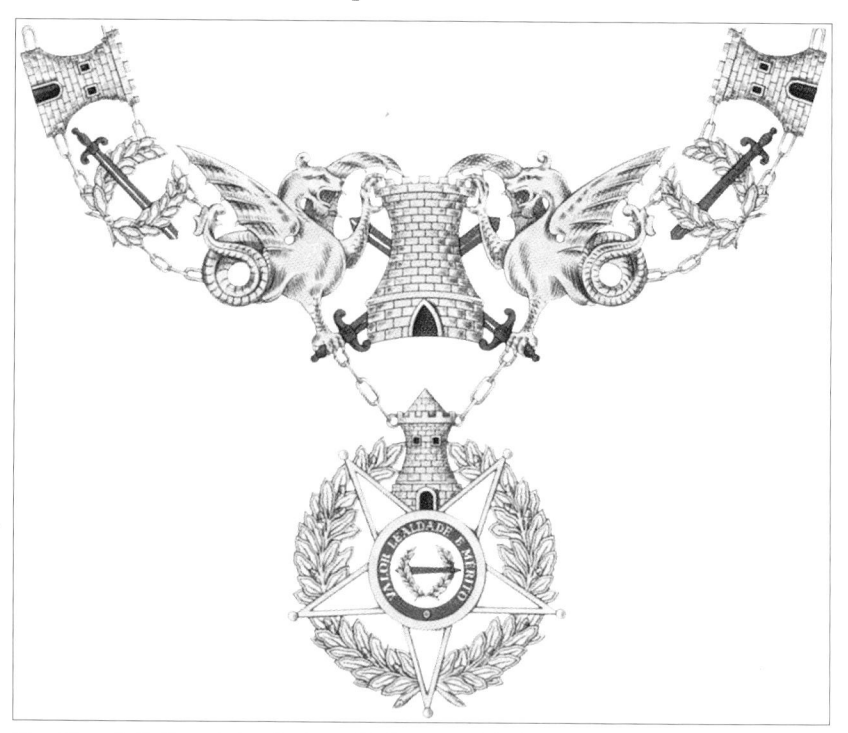

The Grand Collar of the Order which was added in 1986. The President of the Republic automatically receives this highest decoration, and it is given to foreign Heads of State in exceptional circumstances.

Courtesy: Presidência da República

---

[1] By 1918 the republican government had restored all the Military Orders of Knighthood; whilst the three Military Orders had belonged to the Crown of Portugal and therefore became automatically the property of the State, the Order of the Tower and the Sword was founded as a dynastic Order. Nevertheless, the Republic took over this Order and the only two dynastic Orders that remained the property of the Royal House of Bragança were the Order of the Conception of Vila Viçosa and the Order of St. Isabel.

[2] Decreto-Lei n° 29.567 de 2 Maio de 1939.

The revised Statutes of 1962-63 provided that the Grand Collar was also conferred on those who had been Presidents of the Republic.

The Statutes of 15 December 1986 retained the earlier rulings, but added that Presidents of the Portuguese Republic automatically receive the Grand Collar of the Order on leaving office, reiterating the fact that the President of the Republic is the Grand Master of the Order.

Apart from Generalisimo Franco, Head of State of Spain, the Grand Collar was conferred by special decree upon the President of Brazil, Sr. Emílio Garastazu Médici, in 1973, and in 1993 on Queen Elizabeth II during the state visit to the United Kingdom by the President of the Republic of Portugal, Dr. Mário Soares.[1]

The Badge of the Order consists of a gold-rimmed, five-pointed, white-enamelled and ball-tipped star, the centre medallion having a green-enamelled, gold-fruited oak wreath, upon which rests a blue-enamelled sword, surrounded by a blue enamelled, gold-rimmed band bearing in gold letters the inscription VALOR LEALDADE E MÉRITO – Valour, Loyalty and Merit. A golden tower rests on top of the star between the two upper arms, and a green-and-gold-enamelled, gold-fruited oak wreath surrounds the star, finishing just below the turret of the tower. The centre medallion on the reverse is enamelled blue and shows the armorial bearings of the State of Portugal, and on the surround in gold letters *República Portuguesa*.

The Star of the Order is a pentagonal faceted plaque, in silver for Commander, gold for Grand Officer and Grand Cross, with a tower, also silver or gold, resting on the superimposed white-enamelled star badge of the Order, but without the surrounding oak wreath.

The Grand Collar of the Order is gold, made up alternately of gold and blue-enamelled towers and blue enamelled swords that rest horizontally on gold-rimmed, gold-fruited, green-enamelled oak wreaths, linked together with golden double chains. In the centre of the Grand Collar is a gold and blue-enamelled tower superimposed on two blue-enamelled crossed swords, supported on each side by a gold dragon rampant, the Badge being suspended from the tower by a chain.

The Collar of the Order for the other ranks is gold (silver for the knight class) and made up alternately of gold/silver blue-enamelled towers and green-enamelled oak wreaths with a blue-enamelled sword resting on them. Suspended from the Collar is the Badge with the towers enamelled gold and silver for the knights class. On special ceremonial occasions all classes were their Collar.

The ribbon of the Order is blue.

The Grand Collar is worn together with the insignia of the Grand Cross, the Badge of the Order is suspended from a sash and the Star of the Order is gold.

[1] See Colour Plates on the Orders of the Republic of Portugal.

The Grand Cross wears the Badge of the Order suspended from a sash and the Star of the Order in gold. The Grand Officer wears the Badge of the Order pending from a necklace and the Star of the Order in gold. The Commander wears the Badge of the Order pending from a necklace, and the Star of the Order in silver. The Officer wears the Badge of the Order on a chest ribbon with a rosette. The Knight wears the Badge of the Order on a chest ribbon.

This is the only Portuguese Order where the recipient in case of promotion to a higher class within the Order may continue to wear the insignia of the former, lower class as well as the insignia of the new class.[1]

Foreigners receiving the Order become Honorary Members. There is no obligation to return the insignia to the Chancery after the recipient's death, though the Chancery of the Order should be informed.

THE MILITARY ORDER OF CHRIST
(Ordem Militar de Cristo)

The Military Order of Christ traces its origin back to the Religious Military Order of Jesus Christ which was founded by Dinis I, King of Portugal (1279-1325), and confirmed in 1319 by Pope John XXII (1316-34) in the Papal Bull *Ad ea ex quibus*[2] to replace the Order of the Knights Templars which had been suppressed in 1312 by Pope Clement V (1305-14). This Bull granted the new Order, originally called the Militia of Jesus Christ, a name also used by the Knights Templars, all the Templars' estates in Portugal.

In founding the Order, Dinis I was prompted by the need for a military body capable of defending the Kingdom of Portugal against the Moors as

---

[1]'The Portuguese Orders of Merit' – Dr.J.V.de Bragança. Although some historians place the papal confirmation in 1318, John XXII signed the Bull in the third year of his pontificate which is 1319.
[2]In Spain the Monastic Military Order of Montesa absorbed many Knights Templars and was given their properties there.

efficiently as the Knights Templars had done. Referring to the section on the Knights Templars in the chapter on extinct Catholic-founded Orders, it is important and relevant to draw special attention to the Bull of Foundation by John XXII, because of all the Christian Orders of Knighthood, only the Military Order of Christ can truly claim to be the legitimate successor to the Order of the Knights Templars.

The Papacy was the high protecting power of the Order, which had become a Monastic Military Order, the Knights being obliged to make the vows of poverty, chastity and obedience. Its original seat was at the medieval town of Castro Marim in the Algarve. In 1357, during the reign of King Dom Pedro I, the Order moved under Grand Master Dom Nuno Rodrigues to the town of Tomar, the former seat of the Knights Templars.

The Order's last elected Grand Master, Dom Lopo Dias de Sousa, died in 1417. King João I (1385-33), who had married Philippa of Lancaster, requested on behalf of his son, Infante Dom Henrique – Prince Henry the Navigator – the office of Grand Master of the Order of Christ; the Infante assumed the office in 1420. It is unfortunate that the Bull issued by Pope Martin V (1417-31) granting this request, has been lost. However, although the Bull itself cannot be found, contemporary records in the Vatican Archives do refer to it. A glorious period in the history of Portugal commenced which has permanently linked the Order of Christ with the Age of Discoveries.

In 1449 the Order was reformed by João, Bishop of Lamego, with the approval of Pope Eugene IV (1431-47), obtained prior to the Pontiff's death. The years between 1348 to 1415 had been a turbulent era for the Papacy, as there had been numerous anti-popes, sometimes more than one at the same time.

In 1492, a Papal Brief issued by Pope Alexander VI (1492-1503) freed the Knights of the Order of Christ from their obligations to take solemn vows, and this was confirmed by Pope Julius II (1503-13). All subsequent Kings were confirmed by the reigning Pontiffs in their office as Grand Master of the Order of Christ.

The year 1516 was an important year for the Order of Christ, the Order of St. Benedict of Avis and the Order of St. James of the Sword, as in that year they became the sole prerogative of the Crown of Portugal. In spite of this, and of the increasing secularisation of the Order of Christ, Pope Leo X continued to influence affairs in the Order until his death in 1521. King João III, confirmed as Grand Master by Adrian VI in 1522, instituted a special council, the 'Mesa das Ordens', for the government of the three Military Orders in the King's name.

In 1523, the King held a Chapter of the Order of Christ at Tomar, the seat of the Order since 1357, and he charged Frei António de Lisboa to reform it. In 1529, new statutes were approved and adopted which, among other changes, separated the Friars of the Order from the Knights and regarded the Order of the Friars as a Regular Religious Order. Joâo III ordered the building of a convent, the Convento de Cristo at Tomar, into which the Friars moved to exercise their chosen religious life.

Following the death in 1550 of Dom Jorge de Lancastre, Duke of Coimbra, Grand Master of the Military Orders of St. Benedict of Avis and St. James of the Sword, in 1551 Pope Julius III (1550-55) ceded by Papal Brief the grand-masterships of the three Military Orders in perpetuity to the Crown of Portugal.

After King Sebastiâo died in 1578, the crown passed to his great-uncle, Cardinal Dom Henrique and on his death in 1580 to the Cardinal's brother, Dom Antonio, Prior of Crato. King Philip II of Spain deposed him later that year and annexed Portugal. Portugal was under Spanish domination during the reigns of Philip II, Philip III, and Philip IV, until Joâo, Duke of Bragança liberated Portugal from the Spanish occupation in a bloodless revolution and was proclaimed King of Portugal as Joâo IV.[1] Thereafter the Portuguese Military Order of Christ continued as an Order of the Crown, and it, together with the Military Orders of Avis and of St. James of the Sword, was secularised in 1789 by Queen Maria I with the full approval of Pope Pius VI.

As to the widespread misconceptions about the Military Order of Christ, the reason would appear to be that historians and chroniclers of Orders of Knighthood and Merit have not only frequently copied each other's mistakes, but have tended to give credence to certain sources without double-checking the facts.

Apart from the figure of the Sacred Heart with which Queen Maria surmounted the insignia below the Portuguese Crown, the Badge was an oval, white-enamelled, gold-rimmed medallion with a red-enamelled, gold-rimmed Latin cross *pattée*, containing a smaller, white-enamelled Latin cross in the centre.

[1] For historical dates I have made much use of *Haydn's Dictionary of Dates* (London 1910, twenty-fifth edition); this reference work has also been very useful during the compilation of extant and extinct Orders of Knighthood and Merit. Dr. J.V.de Bragança, Secretary General of the Presidency of Portugal and of all Orders of the Republic, has made available to me Papal Bulls and documents, particularly those concerning the Military Orders, from the Presidential Archives of the Republic, because it had proved virtually impossible to trace many of these relevant documents in the Vatican Archives. Some historians appear to have camouflaged and even distorted some facts, which is the reason why other chroniclers have perpetuated different and incorrect accounts of the Portuguese Military Orders. After the publication of the Papal Brief *Multum ad excitandos* by St. Pius X in 1905, which lays down the statutes of the Pontifical Supreme Order of Christ, two prominent ecclesiastical historians wrote in the authoritative *Catholic Encyclopedia* (1910) – though without citing any evidence – that the Apostolic See had retained the right to appoint knights to the Portuguese Order of Christ, justifying their erroneous claim thus: 'The son of King Joâo III, Sebastiâo, intended to reverse the decision of Popes Leo X and Adrian VI but was prevented from doing so by his untimely death. His successor as King, Cardinal D. Henrique, also attempted a reversal of the statutes; he died in 1580 before he could realise his wish. Finally, King Philip IV (the last Spanish King to dominate Portugal), promulgated such a revision in 1627, thus restoring the status quo of the Portuguese Military Order of Christ prior to 1516 which exists to this day.'

The Cross of the Portuguese Order of Christ as conferred in Brazil. It is suspended from a star bearing the image of the Sacred Heart and is surmounted by the Imperial Crown of Brazil which has been exchanged for the Royal Crown of Portugal.

Courtesy: Paul Morais Alexandre

In Portugal, the Order was temporarily suppressed by the republican government in 1910, but was revived with new statutes in 1918, the number of classes having been extended to five and the President of the Republic became its Grand Master. The Order had its statutes revised on several occasions: during the First Republic (1910-26), in 1962 and again in 1986.

The Badge of the Order, which varies in size according to class, is a red-enamelled, gold-rimmed Latin cross *pattée*, bearing a smaller white-enamelled Latin cross in the centre, similar in form to the corresponding papal decoration; both obverse and reverse of the Badge are the same. The ribbon of the decoration is red moiré.

The Star of the Order is a multi-pointed, asymmetrically-rayed plaque with a round white-enamelled medallion in the centre bearing the Cross of the Order.

The holder of the Grand Cross wears a large Badge of the Order on a sash and the Star in gold; the Grand Officer wears the Cross of the Order on a neck ribbon and the Star in gold; the Commander wears the Cross of the Order on a neck ribbon and the Star in silver; the Officer wears a smaller Cross of the Order on a chest ribbon with a rosette; and a Knight wears a smaller Cross of the Order on a chest ribbon. Chest ribbons are worn with a silver-gilt bar.

On ceremonial occasions Officers and Knights may wear the Cross of the Order in the Commander's size, suspended from a ribbon as a neck badge. There are no special rules for Ladies, though they are advised to wear the Cross suspended from a ribbon in form of a bow on the left side of their coat or dress.

The Order of Christ: the Officer's Cross and the Star after 1917.

Courtesy: Presidência da República

The Military Order of Christ can be conferred on civilians as well as members of the armed forces, for outstanding services to the Republic whether or not they are Portuguese citizens, but foreigners who had the insignia of the Order of Christ conferred upon them are Honorary Members of the Order; it ranks in precedence after the Military Order of the Tower and the Sword, of Valour, Loyalty and Merit, and takes precedence over the Military Order of Avis.

In the event of a promotion to a higher class within the Order the person so honoured loses the right to wear the insignia of the former lower class.

There is no obligation to return the insignia upon the death of the holder. However, the Chancery of the Orders, Palácio de Belém, Lisboa, should be informed of the holder's death, and in case of foreigners the Portuguese Embassy or Consulate should be informed.

THE MILITARY ORDER OF AVIS
(Ordem Militar de Avis)

The Military Order of Avis is the most ancient of the Portuguese Orders of Knighthood, and its origins may be traced back to 1166, when some members of the Order of Calatrava who had established themselves at Coimbra transferred to Évora. Other chroniclers place the origin of the Order in 1140, when Portuguese noblemen established themselves as 'The New Militia', which was affirmed in 1166 by King Alfonso Henriques and converted in 1187 into a Religious Monastic Order of Knighthood and adopted the rules of the Order of Calatrava. It followed the Rules of St. Benedict until 1187, when it adopted those of the Cistercians. Their main task was the defence of the city of Évora and they also became known as the 'Évora Militia of Calatrava'. Pope Celestine II (1191-98) confirmed the Order in 1192.

Dom Sancho I, King of Portugal (1185-1211), was the Commander of the Order, and he charged the Knights to defend the castle of Alcanede and the city of Alpedriz (today called Estremadura). He also promised them the Fort of Juromenha if they won the war against the Moors.

Pope Innocent III (1198-1216) took the Order under the personal protection of the Papacy, confirming in his Bull *Religiosis vitam eligentibus*, promulgated in 1201, the Order's property rights over a large territory stretching from Évora to Panoias. He also granted many privileges to the Order, including immunities and indulgences already enjoyed by the Order of Calatrava. The Knights were given the town of Avis in 1211 by King Dom Alfonso II, on condition that they built a castle there and protected the population of the area. The Order rendered many important services to the Realm whilst fighting the Moors. The Order, known as The Friars of Évora, moved its seat to Avis between 1223 and 1224 and became henceforth known as the Friars of Avis; it acquired many estates in Portugal and became one of the wealthiest Orders.

Pope Gregory VIII (1187) in his Bull *Quoties a nobis*, and Pope Innocent III in three Bulls, dated 1199, 1201 and 1214, refer to the possessions of the Order of Calatrava in Portugal; they regarded the Militia of Évora as a branch of the Order of Calatrava[1].

King Dom Dinis (1279-1325) asked the Apostolic See to grant independence to the Orders of Avis (and also to the Order of St. James of the Sword). Although the Order of Avis was formally dependent on the Grand Master in Castille, who had the prerogative of visitation and

---

[1] The Bull *Religiosis vitam eligentibus* of 1201 concedes to the Friars of Évora the same privileges and immunities as had been granted to the Spanish Order of Calatrava. Dr. J.V. de Bragança concludes that this implied that the Friars of Évora had a separate national identity.

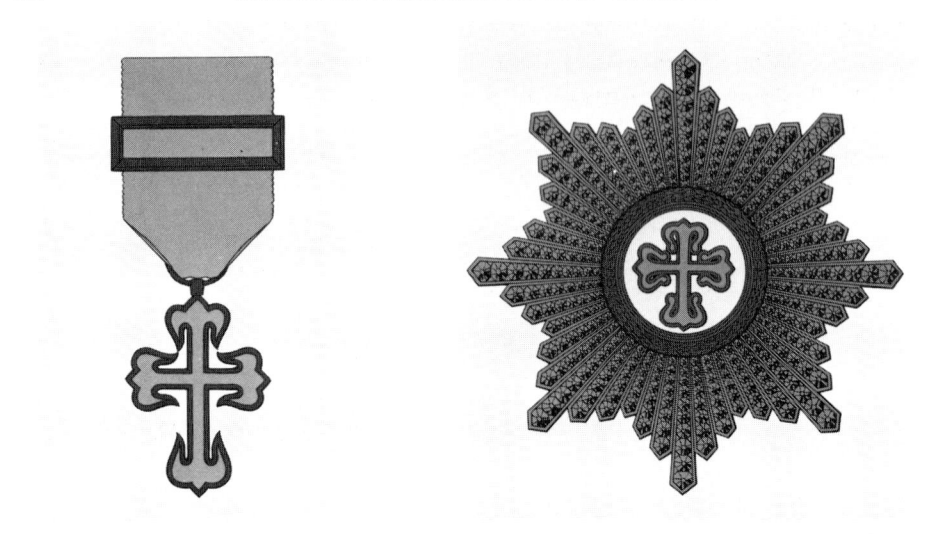

The Officer's Badge and the Star of the Order of Avis after 1917. The insignia have been restored to their original simplicity.

Courtesy: Presidência da República

confirming the election of the provincial Masters of Portugal, from the beginning the Order there had assumed a distinct national identity and depended politically only on the Kings of Portugal, who gave to the Order the land reconquered from the Moors. From the beginning of the 12th century, the Knights of Avis elected their own Master. The tension between the Crown of Castile and the Crown of Portugal made the dependence of the Order of Avis on a Castilian Grand Master untenable.

There followed a century of bitter disputes that are reflected in the contradictory Papal Bulls that were issued by successive Popes. Shortly after his election, Nicholas IV (1288-92) promulgated the Bull *Pastoralis officii* which gave to the Portuguese Knights the right to elect their own Grand Master for Portugal, but as a token of reconciliation granted to the Spanish Grand Master of the Order of Calatrava the right of Visitation (as mentioned above). The King of Castile protested, and Popes Celestine V (who only reigned for less than four months in 1294 and promulgated a modification prior to his death that was published in 1295) and Boniface VIII (1294-1304) in 1295 modified the Bull of Nicholas IV in favour of Spain. Prior to the election of Pope John XXII, the Portuguese Knights elected their own Grand Master, whereupon the Castilian Grand Master declared the Portuguese Friars of Évora excommunicated and demanded from Pope John XXII (1316-34) that he should revoke the original Papal Bull *Pastoralis officii* of Nicholas IV forthwith. The modification of that Bull by Boniface VIII, *Inter caetera*, ordered the submission of the Portuguese Friars of Évora to the Castilian Grand Master. King Dinis of

Portugal appealed to the Pope and demanded that the Bull *Inter caetera* be revoked. In 1319 John XXII instituted an enquiry to be held under the Archbishops of Compostella and Braga, though the dispute remained unresolved.

Without renouncing its identity, the Order of Avis continued formally to submit to the grand-mastership of the Order of Calatrava, until in 1385, Joâo, Grand Master of the Order of Avis, on becoming King of Portugal (1385-1433), openly rebelled against the authority of Calatrava and foreign domination over the Order of Avis. A serious dispute arose and continued for many years, being finally referred to the Council of Basel in 1436 for a solution. The Council approved and confirmed the reunion of the two Orders, but the Order of Avis refused to accept this decision.

In 1440, the Bull of Pope Eugene IV (1431-47) granted total independence from Castile to both the Order of Avis and the Order of St. James of the Sword. The century of disputes between the Spanish Grand Master of the Order of Calatrava and the Portuguese Master of the Portuguese Order of Avis was one of great upheaval in the Church, when six anti-popes were elected as well as those canonically recognised. At one time, the Spanish Grand Master of the Order of Calatrava actually sided with the anti-pope.

The Order of Avis remained independent of Calatrava, even when Philip II, King of Spain, became King of Portugal (1580-98).

During the reign of King Dom Duarte I (1433-38), the grand-mastership of the Order of Avis became the prerogative of the Royal Family, and for a time the Order took on a dynastic character, until in 1551 Pope Julius III (1550-55) granted the grand-mastership to the Crown of Portugal.

Queen Maria of Portugal (1777-1816) reformed the Order in 1789, after obtaining permission for its secularisation from Pope Pius VI, and transformed the Order into a Military Order of Knighthood and an Order of Merit but, as with the Military Orders of Christ and of St. James of the Sword, the Order was only conferred on members of the nobility who belonged to the Catholic religion.

When Portugal was invaded by Napoleon's army King Joâo VI of Portugal (1816-26), was compelled to take refuge in Brazil in 1807 while he was still Regent for the ailing Queen Maria (1792-1816); he took the Order with him to Brazil, where he also conferred it on his colonial subjects. On his return to Europe as King Joâo VI in 1816, the Order continued also to be conferred in Brazil as an independent Order. It kept the same decoration as the Portuguese Order, with a variant only in the ribbon to which a pink border was added. The Order of Avis of Brazil was abolished by the Brazilian Republic in 1891.

In 1894, the Order of Avis was reformed, given the name 'The Royal Military Order of St. Benedict of Avis' and received three classes: Grand Cross, Grand Officer and Knight. The office of Grand Master was

The Badge of the Grand Cross of the Order of Avis surmounted by the emblem of the Sacred Heart on a white-enamelled plaque.

Courtesy: Spink & Son Ltd., London

reserved to the King, and that of Grand Commander to the Crown Prince of Portugal. The Order of Avis was from then on only conferred on members of the Portuguese and foreign armed forces.

The Order was placed in abeyance by the Republic in 1910, but re-established in 1918 under the name 'The Military Order of Avis' with five classes, and with the President of the Republic as Grand Master.

The Military Order of Avis had its statutes revised under the First Republic (1910-26), in 1962 and in 1986. The Order can still only be conferred on officers of the Portuguese or foreign Armed Forces, or on military units for outstanding military services. It ranks after the Military Order of Christ, and the five classes are Grand Cross, Grand Officer, Commander, Officer and Knight.

Between 1789 and 1910 the Badge of the Order was a gold-rimmed, green-enamelled cross fleury, resembling that of the Order of Calatrava, suspended from a white-enamelled, seven-pointed star with gold rays between its arms and the figure of the Sacred Heart in its centre, which Queen Maria I had added in 1789.

As with the other Orders, in 1918, the Republic restored the insignia of the Order to their former simplicity. The Badge of the Order, which varies in size according to the class, is a gold-rimmed, green-enamelled cross fleury.

The Star of the Order is an eight-pointed faceted golden star (silver for

Commanders); in the centre is a silver medallion with the green-enamelled Cross of the Order, surrounded by a golden laurel wreath.

The ribbon of the Order is green.

The Grand Cross has the Cross of the Order suspended from a sash, and the Star in gold. Grand Officers wear the Cross of the Order pending from a neck ribbon and the Star in gold. Commanders wear the Cross of the Order suspended from a neck ribbon and the Star in silver. Officers wear the Cross of the Order on a chest ribbon with a rosette while Knights wear the Cross on a chest ribbon.

On ceremonial occasions, Officers and Knights may also wear the Cross of the Order suspended from a neck ribbon.

Foreigners who are awarded the Order become Honorary Members. In case of promotion to a higher class within the Order, the promoted recipient may no longer wear the Cross of the former, lower class. There is no obligation to return the insignia on the death of a member of the Order, though the Chancery of Orders should be notified.

THE MILITARY ORDER OF ST. JAMES OF THE SWORD
(Ordem Militar de Sant'Iago da Espada)

The Order was founded in 1170 by Ferdinand II, King of León and Galicia (1157-88) and it shares its early history with that of the Military Order of Santiago of Spain. In fact, it was a Spanish Order with a branch of Knights in Portugal, where the Order appears for the first time in the country's annals in 1172. It had successfully helped the first Kings of Portugal to reconquer Portuguese land from the Moors and fight the Islamic invasion which had also threatened Spain. The first grant of land in Portugal to the Order is recorded in 1172.

The Spanish Grand Master of the Order had his seat at Uclés in the Kingdom of Castile; the Order adopted the rule of St. Augustine, and the Knights took vows of poverty, chastity and obedience.

Pope Alexander III (1159-81) was the first Pontiff to confirm the Order, in 1175. Pope Innocent III (1198-1216) approved the statutes in 1215 at the Fourth Lateran Council.

Although the Order was under the jurisdiction of the Grand Master in Castile, from the beginning the branch in Portugal assumed a national character, similar to the other Monastic Military Orders, and it depended politically on the Kings of Portugal, who endowed the Order with vast territories reconquered from the Moors. In 1194 the Order was endowed with the Convent of Santos near Lisbon, and in 1217 the recently reconquered town of Alcácer do Sal was given to it, as were Almada and Palmela. That same year the Order moved its seat to Alcácer do Sal.

The Order of St. James of the Sword played a pivotal rôle in the reconquest and liberation of the Algarve from the Moors in the first half of the thirteenth century. Because of the state of war that existed over a long period of time between the Crown of Castile and the Crown of Portugal, the formal dependence of the Order on a Grand Master in Castile was not in the interests of Portugal, and successive Kings of Portugal petitioned the Apostolic See to grant full autonomy of the Order in Portugal.

The Portuguese Order of St. James of the Sword finally gained its independence from Castile in the Apostolic Constitution *Pastoralis officii*, given by Pope Nicholas IV (1288-92) and by a second Papal Brief in 1290 in the reign of King Dinis I of Portugal (1279-1325).

The histories of the Order of St. James of the Sword and of St. Benedict of Avis run almost parallel; and the same Papal Bulls, from Nicholas IV (1288-92) to Eugene IV (1431-37) concerned both the Order of Avis and the Order of St. James of the Sword. As in the case of the Order of Avis, this was the beginning of a long dispute between the Portuguese Knights of the Order of St. James of the Sword and a Grand Master of the Spanish Order in Castile, who appealed against the Apostolic Constitution and Papal Briefs by Popes Nicholas IV, Boniface VIII, Pope Clement V and John XXII. Although John XXII (1316-34) endorsed the Apostolic Constitution of Nicholas IV, the Order gained its final independence from Castile only in 1440 when Pope Eugene IV (1431-47) granted full autonomy to the Orders of St. James of the Sword and of Avis in the reign of King Dom Alfonso V, during the regency of his uncle, Dom Pedro, Duke of Coimbra.

In 1415, during the reign of King João I, one of his sons, Prince João, was appointed Grand Master of the Order of St. James of the Sword with papal approval. Pope Gregory VII (1406-15) died in 1415, and although several anti-popes claimed the See of St. Peter at that time, an interregnum began in Rome that continued until Pope Martin V ascended the See of St. Peter two years later.

In 1482, Prince Dom João transferred the seat of the Order from Alcácer do Sal to Palmela, where he had a convent built to house the Knights. From 1415 onwards the grand-mastership of the Order had remained in the Royal Family, until in 1551, during the reign of King Dom Joâo III of Portugal (1521-57), Pope Julius III (1550-55) granted the grand-mastership to the Crown of Portugal in perpetuity. Ecclesiastical archives refer to a Papal Brief, given in 1556 by Pope Paul IV (1555-59), confirming this grant.

Nobility and adherence to the Catholic religion remained the conditions for admission to the Order.

In 1789, when Queen Maria I secularised the Order with the approval of Pope Pius VI and changed it into a Military Order of Merit, it had three ranks, with three Knights Grand Cross, apart from the Infantes of the Kingdom, who were born members of the Grand Cross; fifty Commanders, and an unlimited number of Knights. Although secularised, the Order remained still only open to Catholics and nobility was a prerequisite for membership.

By a Royal Decree of 1862 the Order was completely reorganised under King Louis I (1886-89), and reformed under the name 'The Ancient, Noble Order of St. James for Scientific, Literary and Artistic Merit' and conferred upon meritorious persons in those disciplines.

The Order was suppressed by the Republic in 1910 but re-established and reformed under the name 'Military Order of St. James of the Sword' with five classes in 1918. Further reforms of the Order took place during the First Republic (1910-26), in 1962 and in 1986. The President of the

The Officer's Badge and the Star of the Order of St. James of the Sword after 1917.

Courtesy: Presidência da República

The Grand Collar of the Order of St. James of the Sword is reserved to foreign Heads of State.

Courtesy: Presidência da República

Republic is the Order's Grand Master. The Military Order of St. James of the Sword can be conferred upon Portuguese citizens and foreigners, both civilians and military, for outstanding services rendered to Literature, Science and Art.

The Badge of the Order is suspended from a green and gold laurel wreath and consists of a red-enamelled Latin cross fleury, also known as the St. James's Cross, the lower arm of the cross ending in a sharp point

The Collar or Chain of the Order.

Courtesy: Presidência da República

resembling a sword. Gold and green-enamelled palm branches surround the arms of the cross, and a gold-rimmed, white-enamelled scroll adorns the base with the inscription SCIENCIAS, LETRAS E ARTES in gold letters.

The Star of the Order is a multi-rayed plaque, in gold for Knights Grand Cross and Grand Officers, in silver for Commanders, with asymmetrical rays. In the centre is a round silver medallion with the red cross of the Order set in two laurel branches. The medallion is surrounded by a red-enamelled border with the same inscription as on the scroll of the Badge. The entire centre medallion is surrounded by a heavy gold ring with three rings of small laurel leaves. The ribbon of the Order is lilac.

The Sacred Heart had been introduced into the design of the Grand Cross and Commander's Cross by Queen Maria I in 1789, but the insignia were restored to their original simplicity in 1918.

The Order ranks after the Military Order of Avis and now has now six classes:

The Grand Collar, which is reserved for foreign Heads of State, has the Cross of the Order suspended from a laurel wreath and garlanded with a laurel wreath, worn on the Grand Collar which consist of a gold double chain which holds golden Vanets reversed. In the centre of the Grand Collar is a large Escalope reversed, with two Dolphins 'naiant embowed' as supporters, all gold. It is worn with the insignia of the Grand Cross, but the Cross, suspended from the sash is surrounded by a garland of laurels in gold and surmounted by a laurel wreath, also gold.

The holders of the Grand Cross wear the Badge of the Order suspended from a sash and the Star of the Order in gold. Grand Officers also wear the Star in gold, Commanders in silver. Officers wear the Badge of the Order, but smaller, on a chest ribbon with a rosette; Knights wear the smaller Badge hanging from a chest ribbon.

The Collar or Chain of the Order, which is gold for the Grand Cross, Grand Officer and Commander, and silver for Officer and Knight/Dame, is composed of alternate enamelled Badges of the Order and gold- or silver-rimmed, green-enamelled laurel wreaths. The Collar is worn by all members of the Order at special ceremonial occasions designated by the Order's Grand Master.

Foreigners honoured with the Order become Honorary Members. In the event of promotion within the Order, the newly promoted recipient loses the right to wear the insignia of the former, lower class.

THE REPUBLIC OF SAN MARINO
(La Serinissima Repubblica di San Marino)

San Marino is the smallest Republic in the world; although Monaco and the Vatican City State are smaller, they are a sovereign Principality and a sovereign Papal State respectively. San Marino is situated near the Adriatic between the Italian provinces of Forlç, Pesaro and Urbino.

The Apostolic See recognised the independence of San Marino in 1291, as did the Kingdom of Italy in 1862. There have been several attempts to invade or annex the small Republic but without much success.

The present constitution dates from the seventeenth century. The governing body is a Council from which every six months two Captains-Regent are elected who are both joint Heads of State and of the government.

San Marino is much favoured by philatelists for its abundance of postal stamps, but sadly also by those anxious to acquire an Order of Knighthood, of which San Marino has two, and certain minor titles of nobility. The Order of St. Agatha appears to be liberally given to foreigners.

Those who have acquired a Knighthood receive a Diploma signed by the Secretary of State for Internal Affairs of San Marino, and must subsequently apply to the Chief of Ceremonies of the Italian Foreign Ministry for a certificate giving the petitioners permission to wear the decoration in Italy.

THE EQUESTRIAN ORDER OF SAN MARINO
(Ordine Equestre di San Marino)

The Order was established in 1859 by the Grand- and General Council of the Republic of San Marino. The reason for the Order's foundation is given in the statutes: 'as a sign of gratitude towards Divine Providence and the Founder of San Marino'. The Founder was a certain Marinus, a stone-cutter from the island of Arbe, who had to flee the persecution of the Roman Emperor Diocletian (284-305). He took refuge, together with his associate Leo, on Mount Titano. The mountain range was later bequeathed to him by a noble lady from Rimini who he had converted to Christianity. St. Maurinus is the national Patron Saint.

The Order of San Marino ranks highest of the two Orders of the Republic; it is conferred in five classes, of which the first class, the Grand Cross, is reserved for Heads of State, members of Royal Families and high State Officials.

> IL CONSIGLIO GRANDE E GENERALE
> della Serenissima Repubblica di San Marino
>
> Nella tornata delli ....
>
> HA NOMINATO
>
> ....
>
> ....
>
> DELL'ORDINE EQUESTRE DI S. MARINO
>
> con facoltà di fregiarsi della decorazione stabilita
> per il grado conferitoGli
>
> NOI CAPITANI REGGENTI
>
> ORDINIAMO
>
> che in esecuzione alle soprascritte Disposizioni
> e in conformità agli Statuti dell'Ordine,
> sia al medesimo spedito il presente Documento
> munito del pubblico Sigillo e firmato di Nostra mano
>
> I CAPITANI REGGENTI
>
> Il Segretario di Stato per gli Affari Esteri
>
> Il Segretario di Stato per gli Affari Interni

Similar certificates are issued for both Orders of the Republic by the two Captain Regents. They are signed by the Secretaries of State for External and Internal Affaires.

The Captains Regent are *ex officio* the joint Grand Masters during their six months term of office.

The Badge of the Order is a gold-rimmed, white-enamelled cross *moline* with a gold ball in the centre at the end of each arm and a gold tower between the arms of the cross. In the centre is a medallion with the portrait of St. Marinus, encircled by a gold-rimmed, blue-enamelled band with the inscription SAN MARINO PROTETTORE (St. Marinus Protector). On the reverse of the Badge is a medallion with the armorial bearings of San

> *MINISTRO DEGLI AFFARI ESTERI*
> *Cerimoniale*
>
> Roma, ...
>
> N. .... *del Registro*
>
> *Il Ministro Segretario di Stato per gli Affari Esteri*
>
> ....
>
> CERTIFICA
>
> *che in data* ....
>
> *Il Signor* ....
>
> *è stato autorizzato a fregiarsi della Onorificenza di*
>
> ....
>
> *dell'Ordine Equestre di* ....
>
> *conferitoGli dal Governo della Repubblica di San Marino.*
>
> *d'ordine*
> *Il Capo del Cerimoniale*
>
> (*Timbro*: *Ministero degli Affari Esteri della*
> REPUBBLICA ITALIANA)

A second certificate is issued to a recipient of a decoration from the Republic of San Marino; it is signed by the Head of the Department for Ceremonies of the Italian Foreign Ministry. The certificate gives permission to wear the decoration in Italy.

Marino; the blue-enamelled band has the inscription MERITO CIVILE E MILITARE (For Civil and Military Merit). Although San Marino has always been a Republic, the Badge of the principal Order is suspended from a royal crown.

The ribbon of the Order is striped in the Republic's colours, blue and white.

The Star of the Order is an eight-pointed, faceted silver star with the gold-rimmed, white-enamelled cross MOLINE in the centre. Between the arms of the Cross on the sinister side are branches of fruited olive leaves and on the dexter side branches of oak leaves. The blue-enamelled round medallion, which has a gold corded surround, has the inscription RELINQUO VOS AB UTROQUE HOMINE (I leave you freed of any man), a

The Badge of the Order of San Marino

Courtesy: The Government of San Marino

The Star of the Order of St. Agatha.

Courtesy: The Government of San Marino

reference at earlier attempts of submission by external powers, both temporal and spiritual.

The Order has five classes: Grand Cross, Grand Officer, Commander, Officer and Knight.

THE EQUESTRIAN ORDER OF ST. AGATHA
(Ordine Equestre di S. Agata)

The Order was founded in 1923 by the Captains Regent of the Republic as a mark of gratitude to St. Agatha for having, as a co-Patron of San Marino, protected the Republic against the many attempts of the invading armies to deprive the country of its independence.

The Order is reserved for foreigners who 'through initiative, work or charity towards the pious foundations of the country, have earned the gratitude of the Republic'. In fairness to those who may wonder what initiative or charity are required of them to obtain such a decoration, it may help to explain that the Order of St. Agatha of St. Marino ranks among the leading export commodities of this small Republic.

The Order has five ranks: Grand Cross, Grand Officer, Commander, Officer and Knight. The Badge of the Order is a white-enamelled, gold-rimmed cross *pattée* between the arms on the sinister side of which are branches of fruited olive leaves, on the dexter side branches of oak leaves. The figure of St. Agatha with a gold halo is portrayed in colour on the centre medallion. On the white-enamelled, gold-rimmed band surrounding the medallion is the inscription SANT.AGATA PROTETTRICE (St. Agatha Protectress). On the reverse are the armorial bearings of the Republic and in the surrounding band is the inscription BENE MERENTI (well deserved).

The Star of the Order is an eight-pointed faceted silver star with the obverse of the Badge superimposed on it.

The ribbon of the Order is deep purple red with a white and gold stripe on each side.

H.M. King Juan Carlos I of Spain, Sovereign and Grand Master of the Noble Order of the Golden Fleece and all Orders of the Kingdom of Spain.

Courtesy: The Royal Spanish Embassy, London

THE KINGDOM OF SPAIN

King Juan Carlos ascended the throne of Spain in 1975 after the upheavals of a change of government from monarchy to republic in 1931, a civil war lasting from 1936 until 1939, followed by the rule of Generalissimo Don Francisco Franco Bahamonde which ended in 1975. He is the grandson of Spain's last King, Alfonso XIII, who went into exile, without abdicating, in 1931.

In 1947, Generalissimo Franco announced the Law of Succession, declaring that Spain was traditionally a Kingdom. Juan Carlos had been the likely successor to Generalissimo Franco since 1947, but because of political strife in the country and also disagreements concerning the succession within the Royal House of Bourbon of Spain, his status was only consolidated when in 1969 Generalissimo Franco announced that Juan Carlos was to be his successor as Head of State, and the Prince took the oath as the future King of Spain.

The Dynasty of Bourbon of Spain has over the years been plagued by no less heated arguments about the succession than have the Bourbons of the Two Sicilies and the Bourbons of France. There has been a long list of claimants to the Spanish throne and the headship of the Royal House of Bourbon of Spain since King Ferdinand VII revoked the Salic Law in the 'Pragmatica' of 1830 and Isabella II became Queen in 1833.

Under the Law of Succession the throne of Spain should have passed to H.R.H. Don Juan de Bourbon y Battenberg, Count of Barcelona, the father of King Juan Carlos, following the renunciation of the throne by the elder brother of Don Juan, H.R.H. Don Jaime , Duke of Segovia, in 1933 for medical reasons, but the Duke complicated matters by withdrawing his renunciation in 1939.

Thus, although Prince Juan Carlos became King Juan Carlos I of Spain in 1975, the Head of the Royal House of Bourbon of Spain was H.R.H. Don Juan, Count of Barcelona, who only abdicated his dynastic right to the headship of the Royal House in favour of his son, King Juan Carlos, in 1977.

As a matter of historical record it is important to explain that during the Carlist wars of the previous century both the Carlist and the reigning lines conferred the Order of the Golden Fleece, but by 1900 the Order was generally regarded as an Order of the Crown. King Alfonso XIII did not confer it while he was in exile. Generalissimo Franco held the Order in such high esteem that he believed only a rightful King of Spain could confer it. He did, however assume the grand-mastership of the Most Distinguished Order of Carlos III, then Spain's premier Order of

Knighthood. Following the death of King Alfonso in 1941, H.R.H. Don Juan, Count of Barcelona, assumed the grand-mastership of the Order and conferred it immediately on his son, the future King Juan Carlos I, some other royal Heads of State and members of his family.

As late as 1963, a further division in the House of Bourbon of Spain occurred; H.R.H. Don Jaime, Duke of Segovia, claimed the sovereignty and grand-mastership of the Spanish Order of the Golden Fleece because he regarded it as a strictly dynastic Order of Knighthood which in no way was dependent on the Monarchy of Spain. Furthermore, the Duke of Segovia claimed that his renunciation of 1933 had neither included the title 'Duke of Burgundy' nor made any reference to the sovereignty and grand-mastership of the Golden Fleece. The Duke of Segovia awarded the Order to several persons, among them King Peter II of Yugoslavia and the Prince de Polignac.

It is not part of my remit to untangle the web of claimants and counterclaimants to the Dynasties of the Bourbons. The only reason for my mentioning the question of the dynastic succession in the House of Bourbon of Spain is the Spanish branch of the Order of the Golden Fleece. There is no doubt that the Order was instituted as a non-territorial dynastic Order that belongs to the legitimate successors of Philip the Good, Duke of Burgundy, who founded the Order in Bruges on 10 January 1430. The Order's history until the Treaty of Utrecht in 1713, and its continued history under the Sovereign Master of the Austrian branch until the present day, have been given in the section of the Catholic-founded Dynastic Orders.

Spain has the largest number of Catholic-founded Orders of any country in the world. Even Generalissimo Franco instituted two expressly Catholic-orientated Orders, the Order of Cisneros in 1944 and the Order of the Cross of St. Raymond de Peñafort in 1945.

The four ancient Monastic Military Orders of Santiago, Calatrava, Alcantara and Montesa had been suppressed by the Republican Government of Spain in 1931, abolished by the Cortes in 1934 and ignored by Generalissimo Franco, and it was not known until the early 1980s that King Juan Carlos confirmed their revival by the Count of Barcelona. After the Count had abdicated as Head of the Royal House of Bourbon of Spain and Grand Master of the Noble Order of the Golden Fleece in favour of his son, King Juan Carlos I assumed the sovereign's traditional title of 'Grand Master and Perpetual Administrator of the four Orders by Apostolic Authority', and the Count of Barcelona was appointed their Dean President of the Council and Tribunal.

After the death of the Count of Barcelona in 1993, the former Minister Counsellor of the four Orders, H.R.H. Don Carlos de Bórbon y Bórbon, was nominated by the King to the positions held by his late father. On 16 December 1994, he was created an Infante of Spain as representative of a dynastic line linked to the Spanish Crown. (See Appendix XII regarding this appointment.)

As to precedence among the other Spanish Orders of Knighthood and Merit, I have placed the Monastic Military Orders after the Noble Order of the Golden Fleece and before the Orders of Knighthood and Merit because of their antiquity. I have also retained their original description as 'Monastic Military Orders', because they distinguish themselves from all other Spanish Orders by their retention of the original criteria for membership: adherence to the Catholic religion and proof of nobility for several generations.

Numerically, the four Orders do not have a large membership; however, they claim superiority over the Order of St. John of Jerusalem (The Sovereign Military Order of Malta).[1]

According to their latest chronicler, the first novices to the four Orders were admitted in 1982, and in 1983 the first professions were permitted, some of the new professed Knights having been novices over sixty years ago. At the time of writing (1994) the number of Knights and Novices in the four Orders totals about one hundred and fifty.

THE NOBLE ORDER OF THE GOLDEN FLEECE
(SPANISH BRANCH)
(Orden del Toisón de Oro)

There are several reasons why the Spanish branch of the Noble Order of the Golden Fleece has been placed in the section of Catholic-founded Orders conferred by a sovereign Head of State and removed from the section on Catholic-founded dynastic Orders:

Archbishop Cardinale had already voiced a consensus of opinion on the character of the Order in 1983. He wrote about the Spanish Order of the Golden Fleece:

'It no longer possesses an aristocratic and religious character but is more of a Royal Order with a Civil character, remaining however, in the dynastic category. Nominations are made with the previous agreement of the Spanish Council of Ministers. It is therefore no longer subject to the exclusive authority of the Sovereign. Non-Catholics and even non-Christians have been awarded the Order since 1812 when the National Junta of Cádiz (the General Cortes, the sovereign Parliament of Spain from 1810-14) conferred it upon Arthur Wellesley, First Duke of Wellington and Duke of Ciudad Rodrigo, as a token of gratitude for the help Spain had received from him during her struggle with Napoleon. The bestowal was later confirmed by Ferdinand VII, King of Spain and

---

[1] Guy Stair Sainty, *The Orders of St. John*, New York, 1996.

The insignia of the Order of the Golden Fleece conferred in 1812 by the National Junta of Cádiz upon Arthur Wellesley, first Duke of Wellington, Duke of Ciudad Rodrigo and a Grandee of Spain, Duke of Vittoria, Marquis of Torres Vedras and a Fidalgo da Casa Real of Portugal.

Courtesy: The Royal Spanish Embassy in Brussels

sixth Head and Sovereign of the House of Bourbon (1784-1833) who, among many others, made George Frederick, Prince of Wales (later King George IV) a member of the Order. Furthermore, King Ferdinand VII abolished the Salic Law, and female Sovereigns, starting with Isabella II, were henceforth allowed to assume sovereign mastership over the Order, and an Italian King, Amadeo of Savoy, duly elected by the Cortes in 1870, became the Order's Grand Master during an interregnum (1870-73).'

At this point the reader should be reminded that only a legitimate successor of the Duke of Burgundy can be the Grand Master of the dynastic Order of the Golden Fleece, so that King Amadeo (the son of King Victor Emmanuel II of Italy, and at the time of his election Duke of Aosta) was acting beyond his powers in assuming the grand-mastership of the Spanish branch of the Order, provided it had remained strictly dynastic. Technically, therefore, the period 1870-73 can be considered an interregnum. During this 'interregnum', however, Amadeo conferred the Golden Fleece on nine recipients, including the Kings of Greece and Sweden, and the President of France. Between his abdication and the decision of the two chambers of the Cortes to become a republic on 11 February 1873 and the proclamation of Isabella II's son Alphonso XII as King of Spain on 30 December 1874, there truly was an interregnum in every sense of the word.

From 1980 onwards, and especially after the death of Archbishop Cardinale in 1983, I continued to enjoy the same counsel and assistance of His Excellency Ambassador Joaquin Martinez-Correcher, Count de La Sierragorda, that he had given to the Archbishop. He became Chief of Protocol of the State of Spain, and after my return from Rome, following the death of Mons. Cardinale, he arranged my visit to His Majesty King Juan Carlos at the Palacio de la Zarzuela. The main subject of discussion was the Noble Order of the Golden Fleece, its status among the other leading Orders of Knighthood and technical questions concerning the conferment of the Order.

His Majesty the King explained clearly his assessment of the status and rôle of the Order. This question was topical because he intended to bestow the Spanish Order of the Golden Fleece upon His Royal Highness the Grand Duke Jean of Luxembourg who had already received the Austrian Order of the Golden Fleece from H.I. and R.H. Archduke Otto von Habsburg. As there had never been a double conferment before, the question arose as to whether it might cause offence.

The Count de La Sierragorda stressed that the Spanish Order was fundamentally different from the Austrian Order and was awarded by the King as Head of State, with the previous agreement of the Spanish Council of Ministers, as the highest Order Spain could bestow, and as an Order of Merit, also on non-Catholics, unlike the Austrian Golden Fleece which had retained its strict Catholic dynastic character and can only be

Besides the Duke of Wellington, other non-Catholic Knights of the Spanish Golden Fleece have included H.R.H. Prince Albert, Consort to Queen Victoria; H.M. King George V; and H.R.H. the Duke of Windsor. King George and the Duke of Windsor received the honour from King Alfonso of Spain. Recent non-Catholic appointments to the Order included H.I.M. the Emperor of Japan; H.M. Queen Margrethe II of Denmark, and H.M. Queen Beatrix of the Netherlands.

Courtesy: The Count de La Sierragorda

conferred on members of royal families and the highest nobility who profess the Roman Catholic faith. The Archduke Jean of Luxembourg had on a previous State Visit received the Collar of the Most Distinguished Order of Carlos III, which was then still regarded as Spain's premier State Order.

At His Majesty's request, in the revised edition of 1985 I changed Archbishop Cardinale's 'Nominations are made with the previous agreement of the Spanish Council of Ministers' to 'The Spanish Golden Fleece is granted by the King in his capacity as Head of State, with the previous *knowledge* of the Council of Ministers'.

In his appraisal of the Order's status, His Majesty desired that the Spanish Order of the Golden Fleece should once again take its place among the highest Orders of Chivalry and hoped to see it on a par with the Most Noble Order of the Garter.

In October 1985, the Count de La Sierragorda sent me, with other documentation, photocopies of Royal Decrees conferring for the first time the Order of the Golden Fleece on Ladies, Her Majesty Queen Beatrix of the Netherlands and Her Majesty Queen Margrethe II of Denmark.

Another reason for placing the Spanish Order of the Golden Fleece as the principal Spanish Order of Knighthood in this section and not in the section of dynastic Orders is the actual procedure of conferment of the

Order. The Royal Decrees N° 1818/1985 and N° 1948/1985, conferring the Order of the Golden Fleece, are expressly issued by the Head of State of Spain and say 'Oido el Consejo de Minstros' – His Majesty has heard the advice of the Ministers before the Royal Decree was issued.

In the introduction to the Chapter on dynastic Orders of Knighthood, I have quoted above the considered appraisal of Orders of Knighthood by the historian Kenneth Rose, an acknowledged authority on the question of the Crown, the State or the Sovereign as *fons honorum* of Orders of Knighthood and of Merit.

He distinguishes strictly between Orders that are conferred with ministerial advice and those that are conferred without it. The same advantages cited by him with regard to the ownership of the Order of the Garter not being available to possible claimants to sovereignty over the Order if it divorced that sovereignty from that of Great Britain, apply also to the Order of the Golden Fleece of Spain. Raising its status to the position of the highest Order of the Kingdom of Spain, eliminates those who claim ownership of a purely dynastic Order because of family connections and descent from the Duke of Burgundy alone.

In 1946 King George VI decreed that henceforth the Orders of the Garter and of the Thistle would be conferred by the Monarch without ministerial advice, but that was a concession made by Parliament because of the high esteem in which it held the King.

However, George VI did not divorce either Order from the national life of the United Kingdom by a decree that the two principal Orders were now dynastic Orders of the House of Windsor. Nobody who might make some hypothetical claim to the throne of the United Kingdom would be taken seriously if he tried to confer either the Order of the Garter or the Thistle.

Similarly, by expressing his wish to make the Noble Order of the Golden Fleece the premier Order of Spain, King Juan Carlos' prerogatives as successor of the Order's founder, the Duke of Burgundy, are in no way infringed. All he has done is to safeguard the sovereignty over the Order against usurpers and false or misguided claimants.

The original criteria for the conferment of the Order of the Golden Fleece, cited in Chapter Seven, no longer apply to the Spanish branch. The move of the Spanish Golden Fleece from the chapter on dynastic Orders to that of Secularised Catholic-founded Orders conferred by a Head of State is designed to clarify the position of the Spanish Order of the Golden Fleece among the other leading Orders of Knighthood in Europe.

The Badge of the Spanish Golden Fleece differs slightly from the Austrian. The lamb's fleece with flintstone and flames is surmounted by an ornamental clasp with stylised leaves and flowers in gold and enamel. The colour of the ribbon is the same, bright red.

The insignia of the Spanish Golden Fleece, encrusted with diamonds, rubies and sapphires conferred upon King Joâo of Portugal. This gold jewel was made for the King in Brazil.

Courtesy: Palálico Nacional da Ajuda, Lisboa

As with other important Orders, the insignia of the Golden Fleece has to be returned to the Chancery on the death of the recipient.

Many privately manufactured copies of the Order, encrusted with diamonds and precious stones, exist and can be seen in family collections. Both the Austrian and the Spanish Golden Fleece therefore exist in a variety shapes and forms, depending of the wealth of the person who commissioned a famous goldsmith to fashion the objet d'art, and that craftsman's sense of style.

THE FOUR MONASTIC MILITARY ORDERS

The four Orders were suppressed during the Napoleonic era from 1808 until 1814, again from 1869-76 and by the republican government in 1931. The Cortes abolished them by law in 1934. As mentioned above, they owe

H.R.H. Don Carlos de Borbón-Dos Sicilias y Bórbon-Parma, Infante of Spain, (above, in white robes, next to H.R.H. the Countess of Barcelona), succeeded in 1993 H.R.H. Don Juan de Borbón, Count of Barcelona, father of H.M. King Juan Carlos I of Spain, as President and Dean of the Tribunal of the four Monastic Military Orders of Spain. He was created an Infante of Spain on 16 December 1994.

Courtesy: G.Stair Sainty

their revival in or about 1978 to Don Juan, Count of Barcelona, the father of King Juan Carlos.[1]

The Orders are not listed among the Orders of the Spanish State, nor as dynastic Orders of the Royal House of Bourbon of Spain. Their structure is not unlike that of the Sovereign Order of Malta, though the King is their Grand Master.[2]

[1] In 1981 Mons. Cardinale was merely informed that the King did not recognise the suppresion in 1931 and abolition in 1934 of the Orders by the Republic. The Orders were therefore listed as extant, although their existence was considered to be *de jure* rather than *de facto*.
[2] Guy Stair Sainty gives a detailed account of the Orders' endeavour to have the role of 'Grand Master and Perpetual Administrator with Apostolic Authority' confirmed by the Apostolic See. A reply was received from the Holy See which neither commented on the revival of the Orders nor any appointment, but merely stated that the Holy See had not recognised decrees of the Communist government in Spain in 1934.

I

THE MILITARY ORDER OF ALCANTARA

Originating as a religious military fraternity established by two brothers, Don Suero and Don Gómez Fernandez Barrientos in 1156, in 1175 Ferdinand II, King of León and Galacia (1157-88) gave it the status of an Order of Knighthood under the name of Knights of St. Julian Pereiro.

The Order's aim was halt the invasion of Islam and drive back the Moors to Africa. The Order was approved by Pope Alexander III (1159-81) in 1177 under the rule of St. Benedict and it received the support of many later popes.

In 1212 the Order assumed the name of 'Alcantara'. Its members continued to follow the rule of St. Benedict, took vows of chastity and swore to defend the Catholic faith and in particular the Immaculate Conception of the Blessed Virgin.

The badge of the Order is a rhomb-shaped, white-enamelled, gold-rimmed medallion, bearing four stylized fleurs-de-lis in the form of a green-enamelled cross. The badge is suspended from a plumed helmet and a trophy of flags. The breast cross is green-enamelled and consists of four stylized fleurs-de-lis. It is similar to that of the Order of Calatrava, with which it was closely connected for several centuries.

Admission to the Order of Alcantara is restricted to Catholic gentlemen who can prove four noble quarters.

II

THE MILITARY ORDER OF CALATRAVA

The Order was founded by Don Sancho III, King of Castile (1157-58), in 1158 under the rule of St. Benedict and the constitution of St. Bernard. Pope Alexander III approved it in 1164, and subsequent Pontiffs renewed the papal approval. In 1523 Pope Adrian VI (1522-23) granted the Order's grand-mastership to Emperor Charles V as King of Spain.

The aim of the Order was to defend the Catholic faith and the kingdom, fighting Islam and driving back the invading Moors to Africa. Membership of the Order of Calatrava was restricted to Catholic noblemen who could prove that they had no Moorish or Jewish ancestry. A parallel Order for noble ladies was founded by Doña Gazelas Maria Yonnes in 1219.

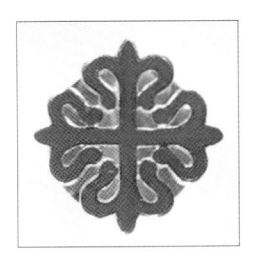

The Order's badge and cross are similar to those of the Order of Alcantara but red-enamelled.

The rules of admission to the Order have been changed and are now identical to those of the Order of Santiago.

III

THE MILITARY ORDER OF MONTESA

This Order was instituted in 1312 by James II, King of Aragon (1291-1327), as a result of the annihilation of the Knights Templars in 1312. The King of Portugal had already refused to persecute the Knights Templars and objected to the annexation of their properties and wealth by the Hospitaller Order of St. John in Jerusalem. James II, King of Aragon, obtained the Pope's approval that whilst the Portuguese Order of Christ was to be the lawful successor of the Order of the Knights Templars, the Order of Montesa could absorb Knight Templars and take possession of their properties in Aragon.

After Portugal's Order of Christ, the Order of Montesa was the second Order to receive papal permission to absorb local Knights Templars and their properties. Unlike the Papal Bull *Ad ea ex quibus*, promulgated by Pope John XXII in 1319 at the request of King Dom Dinis of Portugal, expressly naming the Order of Christ successor to the Order of the

Knights Templars, John XXII's approval did not make the Order of Montesa a successor of the Order of the Knights Templars.

The principal aim of the Order of Montesa was to defend Aragon against the Moors, although they were only marginally involved in that Crusade because the Islamic invaders seldom threatened the security of Aragon. Its membership was restricted to members of the Catholic nobility.

In 1399, Pietro de Luna, the anti-pope Benedict XIII from Aragon (1394-1423) united the Monastic and Military Order of St. George of Alfama with that of Montesa, since their aims were identical.

The Order of Montesa had its independent Grand Masters until Pope Sixtus V decreed in a Bull of 1587 that the Order was to belong to the Crown of Aragon. It remained an independent Order until 1739, when it was united with the other three Monastic Military Orders of Spain.

Admission to the Order requires that the families of the paternal and maternal grandparents must be noble, legitimate and neither family may be descended from non-Christians.

The decoration of the Order is a black-enamelled badge, similar in shape to that of the Order of Calatrava with a red-enamelled Latin Cross cross in the centre.

IV

THE MILITARY ORDER OF SANTIAGO

The Order of Santiago or St. James of the Sword, traces its origins as a fraternity to 1070, and Ferdinand II, King of León and Galicia, gave the fraternity a charter as an Order of Knighthood one hundred years later. Pope Alexander III (1159-81) approved the Order in 1175, and Innocent III and the Fourth Lateran Council confirmed it again in 1215.

The Order's original task was to guard the roads leading to the shrine of St. James of Compostella and defend the pilgrims to the shrine. The members of the Order shared community life with the Canons of the monastery of St. Eligius (Eloi) in Galicia, which was situated near the shrine. The Knights also adopted the rules of St. Augustine confessed by the Canons. The combined Order consisted of Catholic knights and dames, of fully noble birth, canons and nuns, all of whom took the vows of poverty, obedience and chastity. Alexander III (1159–81) dispensed those Knights of the Order who wished to marry from their vow of chastity, but the same dispensation did not extend to Dames of the Order.

Eventually the Order became so wealthy, powerful and influential that their Grand Master, who had been given episcopal dignity and sole authority over the Order of Santiago, ranked second only to the King. The Portuguese Commandery, established in 1172, had always retained a strong national identity and finally gained independence from the Spanish Grand Master in a Papal Brief of 1288.[1] Alexander VI (1492-1503)) transferred the Office of Grand Master to the Crown of Castile under King Ferdinand II of Aragon (1479-1512), who had married Isabella of Castile and united the two Kingdoms. Pope Adrian VI granted to Carlos I, the first Habsburg King of Spain, then already Emperor Charles V, the perpetual grand-mastership of the Order. Condition of admission to the Order was that the candidate could prove four noble quarterings. These strict conditions were later modified to 'ancient nobility of the paternal line', and today the conditions for admission are that the Novice Knight can prove the nobility of each of his four grandparents, that he and his parents and grand parents are legitimate and not descended from non-Christians, and he must produce proof that he himself is a Roman Catholic of good standing.

Since 1655 the Order's objects include the defence of the belief in the Immaculate Conception of the Blessed Virgin.

The Cross of the Order is a red cross fleury which has a longer lower arm , shaped like a sword, while the upper arm ends in the shape of an overturned heart. Knights wear the Cross sewn on their white habits; the gold badge with the red-enamelled cross is worn suspended from a red ribbon, either as a neck badge or on the left breast.

---

[1] See: The Portuguese Military Order of Santiago.

THE MOST DISTINGUISHED ORDER OF CARLOS III
(Muy Distinguida Orden de Carlos III)

Until His Majesty King Juan Carlos I of Spain raised the Noble Order of the Golden Fleece to its eminent position, the Most Distinguished Order of Carlos III was the principal Order of the State of Spain. It was founded in 1771 by Carlos III of Bourbon, King of Spain and the Indies (1759-88), the former King Carlo di Borbone, King of the Two Sicilies (1734-59), as a token of thanks to God for giving him a grandson to secure the succession of the Dynasty. The Order was approved and granted special privileges by Clement XIV (1769-72) in 1772, and by Pius VI (1775-99) in 1783.

King Carlos III placed the Order under the protection of the Immaculate Conception of the Blessed Virgin, and proclaimed her the Patroness of Spain. The statutes of the Order are based on the statutes of the Order of St. Januarius (of the Kingdom of the Two Sicilies).

The aim of the Order was to defend the Catholic religion and particularly the mystery of the Immaculate Conception, and to serve faithfully the Kingdom of Spain and His Most Catholic Majesty. The Patriarch of the Indies was *ex officio* the Chancellor of the Order.

Suppressed in 1808 during the Napoleonic occupation of Spain, the Order was restored in 1814 by King Ferdinand VII, (1784-1808 and 1814-33). The republican government abolished the Order in 1931; it was revived and restored as Spain's highest Order of Knighthood and Merit in 1942 by Generalissimo Franco.

The Badge of the Order is a gold-rimmed, ball-tipped, blue enamelled Maltese cross with a broad white-enamelled border, with gold fleurs-de-lis (the emblem of the House of Bourbon) between its arms. In the centre of the cross is an oval medallion which bears a picture in colour of the Blessed Virgin Mary on a silver cloud (after the painting of the Virgin Mary by Murillo), set in a gold radiance, surrounded by a gold-corded blue band. The badge is suspended from a gold laurel wreath. The blue medallion on the reverse of the badge bears the initial C combined with the Roman III, and in the centre is a white-enamelled, gold-rimmed circlet with the motto VIRTUTI ET MERITO (For Bravery and Merit).

SECULARISED CATHOLIC-FOUNDED ORDERS OF KNIGHTHOOD

The Badge suspended from a sash of a Knight Grand Cross of the Most Distinguished Order of Carlos III.

Courtesy: The Count de La Sierragorda

The Star of the Grand Cross.

Courtesy: The Count de La Sierragorda

The ribbon of the Order is bright blue with a wide white centre stripe.

The Star of the Order for the first and second class is a silver faceted Maltese cross. The fleurs-de-lis between the arms of the cross for the first class are gold, for the second class, silver. The gold centre medallion bears the same image of the Blessed Virgin Mary as the Badge of the Order. The motto of the Order is on a white scroll, and the mirrored monogram of the founder with the Roman III in the centre is in a shield under the medallion. The Star of the Order for the third class is a blue-enamelled, silver faceted Maltese cross. The medallion in the centre bears the mirrored initial C with the Roman III in the centre, surrounded by a gold, green-enamelled laurel wreath.

The Collar of the Order is gold and consists of alternating links of a lion rampant regardant next to a tower, the monogram of the founder and a trophy. The Badge is suspended from a neck link which is composed of the initial C and a laurel wreath with the Roman III in the centre.

The Order has five classes: Grand Cross with Collar, Grand Cross, Commander by Number, Commander and Knight.

THE ORDER OF ISABELLA THE CATHOLIC
(Orden de Isabel la Catolica)

The Order of Isabella the Catholic was founded by Ferdinand VII, King of Spain (1808 and 1814-15) in 1815 to honour the memory of Isabella, Queen of Castile and wife of King Ferdinand II of Aragon (1451-1504). Both Ferdinand II and Isabella have the appellation 'the Catholic'. The Order was much favoured and approved by Pope Pius VII in 1816. Originally the Order was awarded for distinguished diplomatic, civil and military merit, but thereafter it had rather a chequered history and underwent various reforms.

Abolished in 1873 by the first Spanish Republic, it was restored shortly afterwards when the King returned to power. The republican government of 1931 abolished the Order, but in 1938 Generalissimo Franco restored it to its original splendour and status, making it a high-ranking Order of Merit. The Decree of that year confirms the object of its original foundation, namely to honour Queen Isabella 'who opened the gates of Catholicity of an Empire with a never-setting sun'.

The Order is now conferred, often on foreigners, for services of a civil nature for the benefit of the country. It has five classes: Grand Cross with Collar, Grand Cross, Commander by Number, Commander and Knight.

The Badge of the Order is a gold-rimmed and ball-tipped, red-enamelled Maltese cross *fitchée* of five at each end with rays between the arms. The medallion of the cross has a white ring with the inscription A LA LEALTAD ACRISOLADA (For well-tested loyalty); it depicts in the centre

SECULARISED CATHOLIC-FOUNDED ORDERS OF KNIGHTHOOD

The Order of Isabella the Catholic. Left: the Cross of an Officer; right: the Star of a Knight and Dame Grand Cross.

Courtesy: The Count de La Sierragorda

two world globes capped with a crown, next to two gold pillars of Hercules with a white banner bearing the inscription PLUS ULTRA (More beyond). The reverse medallion bears on a blue enamelled background the initials FY (Ferdinand and Isabella) surmounted by a crown, and on a white-enamelled background the inscription POR ISABEL LA CATOLICA (For Isabel the Catholic). The Badge is suspended from a green-enamelled laurel wreath.

The Star of the Order, which varies in size according to class, is similar to the cross. For the first and second class the medallion in the centre is identical to that of the Badge, surrounded by a green-enamelled laurel wreath with a white scroll which bears the inscriptions A LA LEALTAD ACRISOLADA in the upper part and POR ISABEL LA CATOLICA in the lower part. The surround of the medallion culminates in a shield with the initials FY, surmounted by a crown. The Star of the third class shows the two pillars of Hercules with a scroll and the inscription PLUS ULTRA and an imperial crown.

The Collar of the Order consists of alternate links, a yoke with five arrows penetrating it, with the initials F and Y on either side, and identical medallions of the obverse of the Badge, surrounded by a laurel wreath.

The ribbon of the Order is yellow with a narrow white border stripe.

The last four Spanish Orders in this chapter owe their survival or foundation to Generalissimo Francisco Franco, who became Head of the Spanish State in 1936 after the start of the Civil War. None of the Orders ever received official papal approval, although the Civil Orders of Cisneros and of The Cross of St. Raymond of Peñafort, which were founded by Generalissimo Franco, enjoyed the highest regard of the Papacy and the Holy See.

Both Orders have a distinct Roman Catholic character, and those under whose patronage they were placed symbolise Catholic virtues in the fields for which the Orders were created. It can be said with reasonable certainty that both Orders would have received official papal approval, had not Pope Pius XII (1939-58) in the first year of his pontificate begun to curtail the Papacy's involvement in secular chivalric orders and titles.

Contrary to an inaccurate but widely held view, Pius XII was not only not interested in but, as he often told those who were near him, disliked triumphalism and papal involvement in secular 'theatricals'. Archbishop Cardinale, who for periods of time worked in the Pope's private office, told me of his deep spirituality and abhorrence of secular practices, such as the papal granting of titles of nobility or giving spiritual approval to secular Orders of Knighthood and Merit.

This is particularly relevant in the context of the Orders founded by Generalissimo Franco and his personal character. Knowing Mons. Cardinale to have been extremely anti-fascist in his outlook[1], I questioned his favourable references to the Generalissimo in his book. He explained that Franco was first and foremost a devout Catholic, who placed his faith above everything. He had never made a secret of being a monarchist and only regarded himself a caretaker Head of State until a King could be restored to the Spanish throne.

Pius XII admired Franco's religious zeal and in 1953 conferred on him the Supreme Order of Christ, the highest honour a Pope can confer on a Head of State.

---

[1]Towards the end of World War II, he was condemned to be executed by the Fascists and only escaped death by a miracle.

THE MILITARY ORDER OF ST. FERDINAND

Founded in 1811 by the General Cortes, the Parliament of Spain, it was placed under the patronage of the saintly King Ferdinand III of Castile and León (1217-52), whose mortal remains rest in the royal chapel of the Cathedral of Seville.

The Order was confirmed in 1815 by King Ferdinand VII who had been restored to the throne of Spain the previous year. Abolished by the republican government in 1931, it was restored as a Military Order by Generalissimo Franco in 1940. The Order's character is exclusively military, and the five classes in which it is conferred correspond to the ranks the generals and officers hold in the armed forces, and all classes carry a substantial life pension.

The Badge of the Order is a gold- or silver-rimmed, ball-tipped, white enamelled Maltese cross, with the figure of St. Ferdinand in regal robes in the centre medallion, which is surrounded by a blue enamelled band with the gold inscription AL MERITO MILITAR (For Military Merit). The Badge is superimposed on a gold, green-enamelled laurel wreath, and suspended from a similar but smaller laurel wreath.

The ribbon of the Order is scarlet with yellow border stripes.

THE ROYAL AND MILITARY ORDER OF ST. HERMENEGILDUS

Founded in 1814 by Ferdinand VII, King of Spain (1808 and 1814-33), the Order was dedicated to a famous Spanish Saint, Hermenegildo, who was taken prisoner when leading a military insurrection. In AD 585 at Tarragona he chose to suffer martyrdom rather than abjure his Catholic faith, and Pope Sixtus V canonised him on the thousandth anniversary of his death.

It is interesting to note that several European scholars of phaleristics refer to the 'Order of St. Hermenegilda', obviously mixing up their Saints. One presumes they confuse him with St. Ermenhilda (Hermynhild), Queen of Mercia and Abbess of Ely (England), who is better known in countries outside Spain.

Conferred in three classes, the criteria for conferment are the same as those of the Order of St. Ferdinand, although the Order can in exceptional circumstances be conferred for outstanding bravery in battle regardless of the actual rank or age of the officer. The general rule has been that officers become entitled to a particular class at a certain age and after specified years of long service in the armed forces. Those who hold the Order for ten years become entitled to a special pension whilst in active service.

The Badge of the Order is a white-enamelled, gold-rimmed cross *pattée* with a blue enamelled centre medallion showing in gold relief St. Hermenegildus riding on horseback (heraldically facing to the dexter side); the medallion is surrounded by a blue-enamelled, gold-bordered band with the inscription Premio A La Constancia Militar (For Military Perseverence). The cross is suspended from a royal crown.

The Star of the Grand Cross is gold-faceted, ball-pointed Maltese cross with nine faceted silver rays between the arms of the cross, which are in special cases encrusted with diamonds. The central medallion shows in gold relief the Saint on horseback, and the blue-enamelled, gold-bordered band with the motto is surrounded by a green-enamelled laurel wreath.

The ribbon of the Order is white with a deep-red stripe in the centre.

THE ORDER OF CISNEROS

Generalissimo Franco founded this Order in 1944 in honour of Cardinal Francisco Jiménez de Cisneros (1436-1517), who after joining the Franciscan Order became Confessor to Queen Isabella. In 1495 he became Archbishop of Toledo and Primate of Spain, Chancellor of the Realm and Principal Advisor to King Ferdinand and Queen Isabella. He founded the University of Alcalá and procured the most eminent scholars from many European universities. In 1506 he was appointed Viceroy of the Kingdom and later Grand Inquisitor of Castile and León, though he did not bring the Inquisition to Spain.

As a public servant of the Kingdom he was sternly conscientious and always fearless of the consequences to himself in the performance of what he knew to be his duty. His private life was austere and that of a simple Franciscan Friar. In morals he was above reproach and most exact in the observance of his religious state.

To Generalissimo Franco, Cardinal Cisneros was the ideal servant of the State, and with the foundation of the Order, which was conferred on outstanding Spaniards who served their country selflessly and conscientiously, the Founder stressed that the Government of Spain must rest on a solid, honest and fair basis and always serve the Catholic cause.

The Badge of the Order consists of a gold-rimmed and ball-tipped, red-enamelled Maltese cross with a black eagle in its centre, superimposed on a gold star with ten golden arrows as rays.

THE ORDER OF THE CROSS OF ST. RAYMOND OF PEÑAFORT
(Orden de la Cruz de San Raimundo de Peñafort)

Founded in 1945 by Generalissimo Franco, the Order was placed under the protection of the great Spanish canonist (1180-1275) whose name it bears. St. Raymond was canonised in 1601 and he is the Patron Saint of lawyers.

The Order was established to honour outstanding jurists, judges, civil servants in the administration of justice, civil and canon lawyers, and those who have contributed to the promotion of the law, the study of canon law and the legislative work of the State. The Order, which has five classes, is open to men and women. The classes are: Grand Cross, Cross of Honour, Cross of Distinction 1st class, Cross of distinction 2nd class, and Cross.

The Badge of the Order consists of a gold- or silver-rimmed, white-enamelled Maltese cross with ornate gold or silver loops in the form of the figure 8 between the arms. In the centre of the cross is the figure of St. Raymond with a halo, and beneath the figure is a gold-rimmed, blue-enamelled scroll with the gold inscription IN IURE MERITA (In law is merit). The vertical arms have the inscription S. RAYMUNDUS PENNAFORTI (St. Raymond of Peñafort).

The Star of the Order is similar to the Badge. For the 1st and 2nd classes the Stars have laurel branches between the arms instead of loops. The Star for the Grand Cross is gold, while those for the 2nd and 3rd classes are silver. The ribbon of the Order is crimson with narrow blue edges.

A Medal of Merit is attached to the Order; it has four classes: gold with enamel, silver with enamel, bronze with silver and bronze. The Medal is worn on the chest ribbon of the Order.

The Collar of Knights 2nd class of the Order of the Cross of St. Raymond of Peñafort.

Courtesy: The Count de La Sierragorda

H.M. King Carl Gustav XVI of Sweden, Sovereign and Grand Master of the Royal Swedish Orders of Knighthood and Merit, and his Consort, H.M. Queen Silvia.

Courtesy: The Royal Swedish Embassy, London

THE KINGDOM OF SWEDEN

Although a predominantly Protestant country, the two principal Orders of the Kingdom, The Most Noble Order of the Seraphim and the Royal Order of the Sword, are both believed to be Catholic-founded, to have fallen dormant or been placed in abeyance, and reconstituted as secular Orders of Merit.

Technically, they are on the periphery of those Orders qualifying for inclusion in this chapter, but Mons. Cardinale believed them to have their roots in Catholic tradition.

As early as 1983, I received protests from Norway whose Order of St. Olaf had been placed under the patronage of the country's Patron Saint, because it had not been included in the book. However, that Order is a relatively new creation, having only been founded in 1847 by King Oscar I, then falling dormant and being revived in 1906 by King Haakon VII. It was founded by a Protestant King in a predominantly Protestant country as a secular State Order of Merit, and the name given to the Order was incidental. Although at the time of the foundation of the Order of St. Olaf, Norway was a free, independent, indivisible and inalienable state, united to Sweden, the two Swedish Orders definitely belong in a different category. If, as most historians state, particularly in the eighteenth and nineteenth century, the Orders were revivals of older, Catholic-founded Orders, their place in this chapter is justified, especially if their original aim was to defend the Catholic faith. I have been criticised for including them in this chapter, but their inclusion is purely on the basis of their position in European history, although the Apostolic See never considered itself the *Mater et Magistra* of either. This was a role that was long past, belonging to the era of the 'Res Publica Christiana'.

THE ROYAL ORDER OF THE SWORD
or The Order of the Yellow Ribbon

Although presently published records of the Order begin on 23 February 1748 with the 'foundation' by King Frederik I, there is much contemporary evidence to show that the Royal Order of the Sword was founded in 1523 by King Gustavus I Wasa (1523-60) to strengthen the Catholic faction against the Lutherans during the internal struggle of the Reformation. Some writers on the subject try to explain the 'foundation' of 1748 as a revival of the long-extinct Livonian Order of the Knights of the Sword which existed in the thirteenth century and was absorbed by the Teutonic Knights, but I have found no historical basis for such an assumption.

The Order remained dormant after the Reformation until King Frederik I (1720-51) revived it in 1748 and gave it new statutes, which were reformed in 1772 by King Gustavus III who made it Sweden's principal Military Order. Since then, the statutes have been reformed on several occasions.

The Princes of the reigning House are born Commanders of the Order, which has three classes, the second and third classes being divided into two grades: Commander Grand Cross, Commander 1st class, Commander, Knight, and Knight (for clergy and Ladies who are called 'Member').

The Badge of the Order is a white-enamelled, gold-rimmed (silver-rimmed for knights of the second grade), Maltese cross, tilted at an angle of 45°, suspended from a royal crown, beneath which are two crossed swords, blades downwards. The cross for the first and second class has a sword, blade turned downwards, on the sides and crossed swords beneath the two lower arms. Between the arms of the cross are four golden crowns (silver for knights of the second grade). The blue-enamelled, gold-rimmed centre medallion shows an upright sword and the three golden crowns of Sweden, two in the upper part, one underneath the hilt of the sword. The reverse medallion shows an upright sword with a small laurel wreath around the point of the blade and the motto PRO PATRIA (For the Fatherland).

The Star of the Order is a silver Maltese cross with the same blue-enamelled centre medallion as the Badge of the Order. The Star for the Commander Grand Cross is filled in with a mitre-shaped point between the arms upon which golden crowns are superimposed. The Star for Commanders of the first class has only the golden crowns between the arms.

The Royal Order of the Sword. Star of a Knight Commander.

Courtesy: The Royal Swedish Embassy, London

The gold Collar of the Order is made up of alternating swords in blue-enamelled scabbards, entwined in a gold belt, and scallop-shaped gold emblems with a blue stone set in the centre.

There have been later additions to the ranks in the Order which can only be awarded when Sweden is at war: Knight of the Grand Cross of the Order of the Sword first class and Knight of the Grand Cross of the Order of the Sword were both added in 1788, and the War Cross of the Order of the Sword in gold, silver and bronze, instituted in 1952.

The Riband of the Order is yellow with blue-edged stripes.

Insignia that are awarded with diamonds or for valour in battle may also be worn if the recipient has received a higher class or grade of the Order. The sovereign Monarch is the Grand Master of the Order.

THE ROYAL ORDER OF THE SERAPHIM
(Kungliga Serafimerord)

The exact historical circumstances of the Order's foundation are uncertain, but it ranks as Sweden's highest Order of Knighthood and is restricted to thirty-two Swedish Knights, apart from Swedish Princes who are born Knights of the Order, foreign Sovereigns and Heads of State, and in exceptional circumstances foreigners who have rendered outstanding service to the Monarch and the country.

Most historians accept that the original Order was founded by King Magnus I Ladulæs (1275-90) between 1260 and 1285. Eighteenth and nineteenth century historians refer to documentary evidence that the Order was extant in 1336, after the hereditary crown of Sweden had been temporarily made elective, and Albert von Mecklenburg was king. His tyranny, however, caused the Swedes to revolt and they invited Queen Margrethe of Denmark to accept the throne.

Once again, ecclesiastical historical sources refer to King Gustavus I Wasa, who not only liberated Sweden from Danish domination, but in 1523 gave the Order the task of defending the Catholic faith against the Lutherans. (However, within four years he had decreed freedom of religion for all Swedes in 1527 and is credited with introducing Lutheranism into Sweden.) In 1544 he made the crown of Sweden hereditary once again.

The Order was placed in abeyance throughout the Reformation and remained dormant until 1748, when King Frederik I reconstituted the Royal Order of the Seraphim as a secular Order of the Crown.

King Charles VIII (1809-18) renewed and reformed the Order, making it Sweden's highest Order of Knighthood. There is some disagreement between scholars of phaleristics as to whether the Royal Order of the Seraphim is a dynastic Order of the Royal House (the Dynasty of

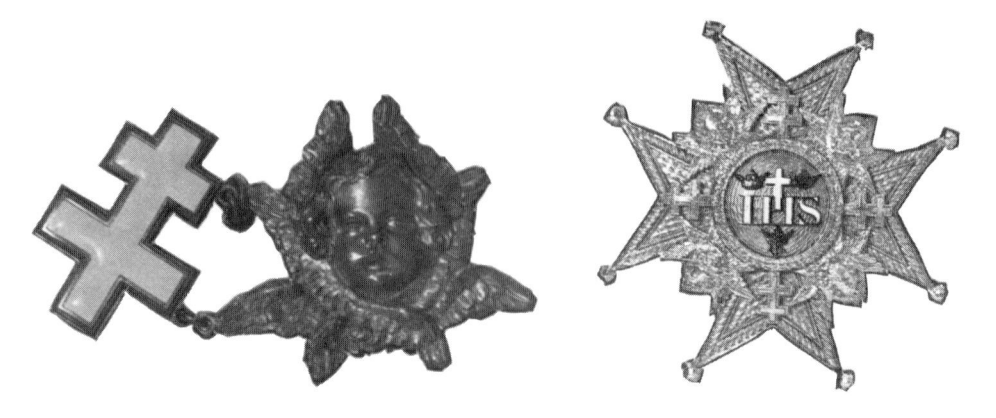

The Royal Order of the Seraphim. Left: two links from the ceremonial Collar; right: the Star of a Knight Grand Cross.

Courtesy: The Royal Swedish Embassy, London

Bernadotte since 1818) or an Order of the Crown of Sweden; all the evidence points to the latter view being correct.

The Order takes its name from the seraphic heads which adorn the Collar and are between the arms of the cross and the star, and has one class.

The Badge of the Order, which is suspended from the Royal Crown of Sweden, is a white-enamelled, gold-rimmed and ball-tipped Maltese cross. The blue-enamelled centre medallion bears the letters IHS ('Iesus Hominum Salvator' – Jesus, Saviour of Mankind), over the letter H a Latin cross, the three golden crowns of Sweden and three golden nails, symbolising the Nails of the Holy Cross. On the surround of the medallion, in the centre of the arms of the cross are double-traversed crosses, and between them the heads of Seraphim. The reverse medallion shows the initials FRS ('Fridericus Rex Sueciae') of Frederik I who revived the Order in 1748.

The Star of the Order is a faceted silver, ball-tipped Maltese cross, identical in design to the Badge of the Order but with mitre-shaped points between the arms with the heads of the Seraphim superimposed on the points in silver.

The gold Collar of the Order has twenty-two alternate links of golden heads of Seraphim and golden, blue enamelled double traversed crosses. The crown of the Badge is suspended from a Seraph's head.

Chapter Nine

EXTINCT CATHOLIC-FOUNDED ORDERS OF KNIGHTHOOD

I

When Archbishop Cardinale first prepared a chapter on extinct Orders of Knighthood in 1979, I could not foresee the acrimony and, in a few cases, justified grievance it would cause during the next decade.

Mons. Cardinale himself stated at the end of his introduction to the chapter that it was impossible to draw up a complete list of the Catholic Orders that have existed during the past millennium. He believed the reason for this was that their foundation and the *raison d'être* was no longer for military reasons, and that they were largely intended to provide Western society, whose mediaeval structure was officially Catholic, with pious organisations for lay men that were placed under the patronage of some favourite Saint, in which and through which the laity could attend to their own spiritual progress. Their diversified activity was all the more welcome because the State and society were not as yet sufficiently well organised to be able to attend to works of mercy and social welfare. This, as Archbishop Cardinale suggested, the State began to do in the latter part of the eighteenth century. The Orders of Merit which then took the place of the ancient monastic-military Orders were not invested with any special humanitarian activity because, as it evolved, the modern State gradually claimed for itself the right and duty to organise social welfare.

Mons. Cardinale continued to divide the extinct Catholic Orders into short and long-lived Orders, and appending a list of short-lived Orders which, he maintained, were of interest because they demonstrated the different facets of the spirit of chivalry as well as often providing names for many 'autonomous' and 'self-styled' Orders.

Before dealing with Mons. Cardinale's definition of extinct Catholic Orders of Knighthood, I must explain and take issue with several points that he also forcefully presented that are, however, misleading.

It would have been better if the word 'extinct' had been clearly defined, and the Orders had been described as Catholic-founded and not just Catholic. A great number of Catholic-founded Orders, such as the Orders of the Garter, the Thistle, the Dannebrog and others lost their link with the Papacy and the Catholic Church as a direct result of the Reformation when they were secularised. Even the strictly Catholic Religious Order of the Hospitallers of St. John of Jerusalem, of Rhodes and of Malta lost several of its major Bailiwicks in Central Europe, these becoming known as Johanniter Orden, adhering to the Protestant religion.

Unfortunately no distinct difference was made between an Order that had been abolished and one that was suppressed, yet in international law the difference between abolition and suppression in such cases is substantial. An Order that is legitimately abolished ceases to exist, but an Order that is suppressed can continue to exist under its legitimate *fons honorum*, even if that *fons honorum* resides abroad. Thus a monarch who leaves his country but does not abdicate and expressly give up his family's dynastic Orders takes them with him into exile, and they are inherited by legitimate heirs. In certain circumstances, when permitted by a country's constitution the same can apply to a President of a Republic, as is shown in the case of the Polish Orders of the White Eagle and 'Polonia Restituta'.

When the first edition of *Orders of Knighthood, Awards and the Holy See* was published to coincide with the opening of the extraordinary Holy Year of 1983 – the day after Archbishop Cardinale's death – I was immediately faced with an objection which emanated from the Apostolic Palace. Grave offence was taken at the highest level that the Polish Catholic-founded Order of the White Eagle had been consigned to the chapter on extinct Orders of Knighthood. As soon as I had taken on the responsibility for revising the book, the Order of the White Eagle therefore became my first priority, and today the Order of the White Eagle is once again Poland's highest Order of Knighthood.

Another example is the Portuguese Order of Our Lady of the Immaculate Conception of Vila Viçosa. Not only was it listed as suppressed but the wording carried the strong implication that the Order no longer existed, yet it had continued to exist as a dynastic Order of the Royal House of Portugal, first under the grand-mastership of H.M. King Dom Manuel II, who had gone into exile to England, and after his death, under the Head of the Royal House of Portugal, the Duke of Bragança.

In both cases, Archbishop Cardinale had taken the advice of members of the diplomatic corps accredited to Belgium who were unsympathetic to the questions under discussion, as their ideology influenced their reply. The Portuguese dynastic Orders have now been restored to their rightful positions.

A third case, although in a different category, is the Order of St. James of Holland (founded in 1290 with a strong political motivation), which remained strictly Roman Catholic until the Reformation. It appears to have become dormant, and remained so until it was resuscitated at the beginning of the 19th century. It never again became a Roman Catholic Order, although the Dutch Old Catholic Church has been involved in it for some time, and it never regained its former prominent position. It is

A Commander's Cross of the Order of St. James of Holland. Founded in 1290, it was suppressed during the Reformation. There is evidence that it was revived in the 19th century when the Dutch Old Catholic Church appears to have taken a special interest in it. It has never been again associated with the Roman Catholic Church.

Courtesy: Dr. E.A. Ates

not now listed among the Orders of State of the Netherlands, but several early nineteenth century portraits of Dutch generals clearly show them wearing it. It was not one of those of recent foundation that used the name on an ancient Order.

The latter case demonstrates the necessity for referring to the Orders as Catholic-founded (meaning co-founded, sanctioned or later approved by the Apostolic See) rather than as Catholic Orders, an appellation that should be reserved to the two extant Religious Orders of Knighthood.

Before returning to Archbishop Cardinale's definition as to what constitutes a Catholic Order of Knighthood, I must touch on the probably most contentious subject in this section: 'the Military Hospitaller Order of St. Lazarus of Jerusalem', but I shall be dealing with that Order in full in Chapter Ten. At the outset, it is important to state that there are about six organisations calling themselves 'Order of St. Lazarus', in the same way that there are more than twenty imitation Orders of the Sovereign Military Hospitaller Order of St. John of Jerusalem, of Rhodes and of Malta, the Venerable Order of St. John, of the Equestrian Order of the Holy Sepulchre of Jerusalem, of the Constantinian Order of St. George, and several others. The imitation orders are dealt with in Chapter Thirteen, 'Self-styled Orders of Knighthood', though most of those listed in that chapter are organisations that have adopted the name of an extinct or abolished Catholic-founded Order of Knighthood which they pretend still exists.

As far as the term 'extinct Catholic-founded Orders of Knighthood' is concerned, with a few exceptions Mons. Cardinale's lists were correct, especially with regard to the self-styled Orders of Knighthood. However, we must always bear in mind that only very few chivalric Orders have retained their strictly Catholic character.

In this context it must be said that the three Grand Priories of the Military Hospitaller Order of St. Lazarus of Jerusalem, the activities of which I was advised at the highest ecclesiastical level to acknowledge as chivalrous, and which are dealt with in the next chapter, are correctly described as 'formerly Catholic'. Although their origin is undoubtedly Catholic, and they stress their oecumenical character through their membership and activities they nevertheless have Cardinals, a Catholic Patriarch and many Catholic bishops as their spiritual leaders. Since the time I took over responsibility for revising this work, I am prepared to vouch for the resurrection of Lazarus from the dead, if only because he has haunted me for the last decade! Some groups that claim to be the Order of St. Lazarus first bombarded Archbishop Cardinale and later myself with letters and abuse. Those who are the subject of Chapter Ten worked without Archbishop Cardinale or I ever knowing of their existence: they were unique in that they never asked to be recognised or mentioned. I am in no way questioning or contradicting the rules observed by those purists who demand legitimate 'sovereignty', either regnant or non-regnant, as the prerequisite for the existence of an Order of Knighthood. However, if the *raison d'être* for the Order's continued existence is taken into account and is expressly cited as the reason why the chivalrous and hospitaller work of certain groups should be given recognition, it would be presumptuous of me to ignore such advice.

There is one more factor which must be taken into consideration when drawing a comparison between the straightforward, and sometimes dogmatic, presentation of this particular subject in Mons. Cardinale's revised editions and my present treatment of extinct Orders of Knighthood. Apart from the failure to distinguish between 'Catholic' and 'Catholic-founded' another matter must be taken into account. In the late 1950s and early 1960s when Archbishop Cardinale first laid the foundations for his work on Orders of Knighthood while writing *Le Saint-Siége et la Diplomatie*,[1] the Holy Father, the Holy See and the Roman Curia always spoke with one voice. Since then, individual members of the many departments which constitute the Holy See and members of the Roman Curia have changed their attitude to, and view of, many things and are

[1] Published as a much enlarged and revised edition in English under the title *The Holy See and the International Order*, Gerrards Cross, 1976.

prepared to voice them. In their interpretation of 'collegiality', one of the outcomes of the Second Vatican Council, they voice their individual opinions rather than a collective one, as was the practice prior to the Council. Then, Mons. Cardinale could justifiably use the apostolic 'We' when speaking with authority, because he knew that he spoke with the *Nihil Obstat* of the Supreme Pontiff and at the same time expressed the view of the Pope's Government, the Holy See.

Whilst in matters of Dogma the Church, through the voice of its Supreme Pastor, still speaks with one voice, attitudes towards secular matters – and that includes Orders of Knighthood to which the Pope has not expressly appointed a Cardinal Grand Master or Cardinal Patron to represent his Apostolic Authority – are no longer accordant. More than one voice can be discerned in the Vatican where it concerns, for example, the Holy See's attitude to dynastic Orders of Knighthood.

Relatively little has changed in principle, because in most of the cases previously dealt with, the principle has been logical and juridically correct under international law. However, there have been several errors of judgement and factual mistakes where certain Orders were concerned. I have endeavoured to correct these, as in the case of the Order of the White Eagle of Poland and the Portuguese Order of the Immaculate Conception of Our Lady of Vila Viçosa. In other cases, I have taken note of the opinions of senior members of the Roman Curia, although, as I explained, such opinions were not always unanimous and were in some cases strongly opposed by those who wished to see no changes made or in others, those who wanted to see the severance of the relationship between the Apostolic See and the Orders of Knighthood belonging to non-regnant dynasties, even though several take an active part in the ceremonial and liturgical life of the Church.

Archbishop Cardinale defined extinct Catholic-founded Orders of Knighthood as:

> those preponderantly but not exclusively medieval Orders which owed their existence to a Catholic initiative, were recognised and approved by the Holy See, but have ceased to exist. Attempts have been made from time to time to resurrect these Orders, but without success, especially because they had fulfilled the purpose for which they had been established and found it difficult to survive in a new political and social context. It is important to note here that many self-styled Orders with which We shall deal in another chapter, have called themselves after these ancient Orders but, as can be seen, they are not recognised by the Holy See nor by public law for that matter, because their attempted 're-establishment' is due to the efforts of private individuals or bodies and not to the initiative of a sovereign Power, who is the *fons honorum* (the source of honours).

This categorical opening statement of the chapter, which later listed these Orders, can be misleading. Much depends on how a particular Order ceased to exist, whether it was legitimately abolished and not just suppressed, and whether the 'resurrection' is really a new foundation. In my work since 1983, I have found it insufficient to give as a reason for an Order's suppression or abolition that 'it finds it difficult to survive in a new political and social context'. These were the sentiments expressed by the Communist Government of Poland in 1983 when it informed me that the Order of the White Eagle no longer existed.

As I have explained above, the Holy See, in which the sovereignty is vested, abides by internationally accepted laws and recognises – without necessarily approving of them – orders and decorations of all sovereign States with which it entertains diplomatic relations. In addition, the Apostolic See has continued to recognise and approve of those Catholic-founded Orders of Dynasties with which it had retained a close relationship, often for many centuries, good examples of which are the two Savoyan Orders of SS.Annunziata and of SS. Maurice and Lazarus. As I wrote earlier, when leaving Italy after the plebiscite in June 1946, King Umberto II of Italy took his leave of the Supreme Pontiff, Pope Pius XII, who assured him that the Apostolic See would always recognise and respect the two Savoyan Orders of Knighthood as dynastic Orders. Even after the King had left Italy, successive Cardinal Secretaries of State of His Holiness and other high dignitaries in the Roman Curia continued to be decorated with the insignia of the Most Holy Order of SS. Annunziata and the Order of SS. Maurice and Lazarus. To this day the Apostolic See has continued to extend that recognition to the major Catholic-founded dynastic Orders mentioned in Chapter Seven.

II

SHORT-LIVED ORDERS OF KNIGHTHOOD

For every extinct long-lived Order of Knighthood, there have probably been more than fifty short-lived ones, many of which did not survive their founders, and a great number ceased to exist even during their founder's lifetime.

Archbishop Cardinale listed only sixteen short-lived Orders of Knighthood, the last one being the Order of St. Bridget of Sweden (founded in 1814); however, many short-lived Orders and Awards of Merit, decorations and honours were approved and sanctioned as recently as during the pontificate of Pope Leo XIII (1878-1903), who had been one of Mons. Cardinale's predecessors as Nuncio to Belgium. Most of them were either placed in abeyance by his successors or just faded out of existence. Without being able to ascertain the exact number of orders, decorations and medals established or sanctioned by Leo XIII, I am reasonably certain that more honours were created during his than during any other pontificate.

All the editions of Mons. Cardinale's book had a special chapter entitled 'Religious but not Pontifical Awards' which listed three awards founded or approved by Leo XIII. As one edition reprinted a statement published in *L'Osservatore Romano* in 1954, in which the Pontiff and the Holy See dissociated themselves from the award, I consider it sufficiently important to list them all here: the first two were placed in abeyance and the third ceased to exist officially in 1977 under Paul VI. In spite of these facts, all three decorations still seem to be sold by unscrupulous purveyors of bogus orders to naive tourists in Rome who believe that pontifical honours are for sale in the market place.

The lavishness with which the three Crosses originally were awarded by those to whom they had been had been entrusted, caused considerable embarrassment to the Holy See and provoked several warnings. The publicity generated by some of the recipients that they had been decorated by the Pope or by the Vatican was unwelcome, because none of the awards was ever 'pontifical', and even the appellation 'religious' was a misnomer. These three decorations were founded with the sole purpose of rewarding benefactors for financial contributions to three religious buildings or institutions: the Lateran Cross supported the Archbasilica of St. John Lateran, the Lauretan Cross the Shrine of the Holy House of Loreto, and the Holy Land Pilgrim's Cross the Custodians of the Holy Land.

The reason the Holy See placed the first two in abeyance rather than abolish them was to gain time to examine the criteria applied to their conferment. For example, in the light of the terrorist attacks on the Archbasilica of St. John Lateran and the terrible damage inflicted on the Cathedral of the Bishop of Rome, it seems reasonable to reward generosity contributing to the restoration of this ancient and venerable building. However, the administration of such a reward must be organised, and administered centrally and according to strict guidelines. A similar case might be made for the upkeep of the Shrine of Loreto, but there is no need to consider reviving the abolished Holy Land Pilgrim's Cross: anyone wishing to contribute to the upkeep of the Holy Places can do so through the local lieutenancy of the Equestrian Order of the Holy Sepulchre of Jerusalem.

Nevertheless, the three Crosses in question have been widely circulated and can be found not only on the bars of medals worn by those who received or acquired them, but also as collectors items.

THE LATERAN CROSS

This Cross was approved by Leo XIII on 18 February 1903. The original intention had been to award it to benefactors who had contributed to the repairs of the roof of the Archbasilica of St. John Lateran, but it was later given as a mark of gratitude to anyone who rendered services to the Archbasilica, and the bestowal of the Cross was entrusted to the Chapter of Canons of the Basilica.

The Lateran Cross was awarded in gold, silver and bronze; it consisted of a bezant Cross which showed on the obverse, in medallions on the extremities of the arms the images of SS. Peter, Paul, John the Evangelist and John the Baptist, and in the centre the image of Christ the Redeemer. On the reverse of the Cross were the words SACROSANCTA LATERANENSIS ECCLESIA, OMNIUM URBIS ET ORBIS ECCLESIARUM MATER ET CAPUT (Most Holy Lateran Church, Mother and Head of all the churches in Rome and in the World). The Cross was suspended from a red ribbon with blue border stripes.

THE LAURETAN CROSS

Though originally planned by Paul III in 1547, it was Sixtus V who in 1587 instituted a Chivalric Order of Loreto with the purpose of watching over and preserving the Shrine, but it was short-lived and did not survive its founder who died in 1590.

In A. M. Perrot's *Tableau Chronologique Des Ordres Éteints* (Paris 1820), the author simply states: 'Après la mort de son fondateur, cet ordre tomba en décadence et disparut entièrement'.

To commemorate the third centenary of the Order's foundation, Leo XIII created the Lauretan Cross and authorised the Bishop of Loreto to bestow it on benefactors of the Holy House. The right of bestowal was subsequently transferred to the Father Guardian of the Holy House and Rector of its Universal Congregation.

The Lauretan Cross was given in gold, silver or bronze and was intended to reward them for their benefactions. Leo XIII enriched it with certain spiritual favours, and for a while it enjoyed prerogatives that had centuries earlier been granted to Orders of Knighthood.

Like the Lateran Cross, however, it was placed in abeyance, although no actual interdict appears to have been promulgated against it.

The Badge is a copy of the Medal of the ancient Knights, inset in an eight-pointed, blue-enamelled Cross, with the words in gold: BENEMERENTIBUS QUIBUS CORDI EST DECOR DOMUS LAURETANAE (To those who are meritorious, having at heart the beauty of the House of Loreto).

The Cross was worn on the left breast, suspended from a white ribbon with seven stripes, red-yellow-red-blue-red-yellow-red.

THE HOLY LAND PILGRIM'S CROSS

One of the more frequent enquiries I have received concern the Holy Land Pilgrim's Cross, instituted by Pope Leo XIII in 1900 to encourage pilgrimages to the Holy Land, its conferment being entrusted to the Father Custodian of the Holy Land. A metal Jerusalem Cross has existed since the sixteenth century, and Leo XIII retained the original form when he instituted the award, which was given in gold, silver and bronze. In the centre of the obverse it had the image of Pope and the words LEO XIII P.M. CREAVIT A.N. MCM (Established by Leo XIII Supreme Pontiff in the year 1900), and on the reverse are the words SIGNUM SACRI ITINERIS HIEROSOL (Memento of the holy pilgrimage to Jerusalem), with, on its arms AMOR – CRUCIFIXI – TRAXIT – NOS (The love of the crucified Lord has attracted us). It was given with a special diploma signed by the Father Custodian.

The Holy Land Pilgrim's Cross ceased to be awarded, and it was abolished in 1977 by Paul VI. Visitors to Rome in the pontificate of John Paul II have written to me enquiring about the status of the papal decoration they had been 'awarded' in Rome, including a photocopy of a certificate in Latin, bearing their name and a recent date, signed by someone claiming to be the Custodian of the Holy Land. They were also given 'statutes' (in Latin), signed in Rome on 11 May 1900 by Cardinal Ledochowski. Several visitors to Rome believed they had been created Knights of the Order of the Holy Sepulchre because they had purchased that cross.

THE CROSS OF THE ADVOCATES OF ST. PETER

In 1878 Leo XIII confirmed the statutes of the Advocates of St. Peter, a society which enrolled jurists as ordinary members, and as honorary members laymen who had made it a practice to defend Church interests, all of whom received a decoration in the form of a cross suspended from a ribbon, which I also reproduce in colour in this book because of its exquisite appearance. As to when it was withdrawn from circulation, I have been given a number of conflicting dates.

The Badge, worn on the left breast suspended from a purple ribbon with yellow borders, is a gilt eight-pointed, ball-tipped Maltese cross with the end of the arms couped *fitchée* and a burst of rays between the arms. Superimposed on it is a white-enamelled cross *pattée fitchée* at all points, and the gilded medallion in the centre shows a bust of the Apostle St. Peter in low relief, surrounded by a gold-rimmed, blue-enamelled band with the words ADVOCATI DI SAN PIETRO. The gilt cross is surmounted by a tiara and the keys of St. Peter, all gilt. The reverse of the Badge is similar but the centre medallion has in relief the tiara and the crossed keys of the

The obverse and reverse of the Cross of the Advocates of St. Peter which was founded by Leo XIII in 1878.

Courtesy: Garrison Collection

papal insignia encircled by the words FIDEI ET VIRTUTI and the inscription in the gold-rimmed, blue enamelled band which surrounds the medallion is TU ES CHRISTUS FILII DEI VIVI.

The names of some short-lived Orders of Knighthood seem to have survived considerably longer than the Orders themselves. Many attempts have been made to list all the Orders of Knighthood and Awards ever founded, but they have come to grief because too little is known about most of them. Some are merely remembered in legends and often involve a local connection with a Saint. The list of short-lived Orders of Knighthood published by Archbishop Cardinale in 1983 can easily be multiplied many times over without even remotely approaching the real number.

Some of the Orders that are supposed to have existed appear to have been the product of the over-fertile imagination of the compilers of reference books. Other Orders are known to have been planned but were never actually brought into existence: even Papal Briefs, consenting to the foundation of an Order of Knighthood, do not necessarily ensure that the Order was actually established. By far the largest group of extinct Orders comprises those that were founded and dissolved within a period of about thirty to sixty years of their foundation.

All lists of extinct Orders of Knighthood are arbitrary; it always depends on the compiler's set of criteria as to which Orders were included. The lists published in this work are incomplete and a comparison with other reference books will show that none has a list of extinct Orders that matches this list or any other. An important factor to consider is when these lists were published. One of the more comprehensive works on both extant and extinct Orders of Knighthood is A. M. Perrot's *Collection Historique des Ordres de Chevalerie, Suivie d'un Tableau Chronologique des Ordres Eteints* (Paris 1820), and I have included its list of extinct Orders and two pages of illustrations of their insignia in Appendix VI of this book. However, several Orders that are now extinct were then still bestowed legitimately, such as the French Order of St. George, (abolished by King Louis XVIII in 1824), the amalgamated Order of Our Lady of Mount Carmel and St. Lazarus (abolished in 1830), the Order of St. Ferdinand and of Merit (Two Sicilies) which ceased to be conferred after the death of the last King of the Two Sicilies in 1894.

Quite a number of extinct Orders of Knighthood were not even founded when Perrot published his list, for example the Orders of Our Lady of Guadalupe (Mexico, 1822), of St. Charles (Mexico, 1865), of St. Faustin (Haiti, 1849), of St. Louis (Parma, 1836), and of St. Rose (Honduras, 1868).

Haydn's Dictionary of Dates[1] appeared in twenty-five revised editions. The twenty-second edition published in 1898, lists an alphabetical register of 252 known Orders of Knighthood, but makes no distinction between extant and extinct Orders. Bearing in mind the politico-religious climate of the second half of the nineteenth century, it is perhaps not surprising that even such a work as this sometimes gives prejudiced information. For example, it merely gives three lines to the Holy Roman Empire, describing it as a renamed German Empire (which in fact only came into existence 900 years later), and therefore attributes its Orders to Germany. In spite of this Established Church British bias, the book is nevertheless an invaluable reference work.

All Orders of Knighthood with dates of foundation preceding the early Crusades should be viewed with caution. In order to gain precedence in ceremonial processions some legitimate Orders of Knighthood have often attempted to trace their origin to groups of soldiers, militias and guards that undoubtedly existed in earlier centuries. The concept of chivalry is inextricably linked to the Crusades, and thus to the creation of Orders of Knighthood.

The list of short-lived or ephemeral Orders which follows is, as I mentioned above, both arbitrary and incomplete; however, I print the Orders previously listed by Mons. Cardinale because he considered their

---

[1]See: Appendix VII.

influence during their short life to have been important, and I have moved some of those Orders which were in the list of the long-lived Orders to the short-lived section because of the brevity of their existence.

As I mentioned earlier, some Orders listed by Mons. Cardinale as extinct are still extant, and I have placed them in the appropriate chapters in this work.

With regard to two Orders, the Order of St. Ferdinand and of Merit (Two Sicilies) and the Order of St. George of the Reunion (Two Sicilies), the archives of the Royal House of the Two Sicilies show that they never received papal approval and should therefore not have been listed among the Catholic-founded Orders of Merit. Both Orders became legally extinct in 1894 with the death of Francis II, the last King of the Two Sicilies. In 1861 King Francis II took the two Military Orders of Merit with him into exile to Rome, where Pius IX reciprocated the hospitality for the refuge King Ferdinand II of the Two Sicilies had offered him in 1848. The King continued to award these two Orders whilst staying in Rome as the guest of Pius IX. I have therefore retained them in this book, but placed them in the short-lived Orders section.

Some Orders of which the date of foundation is known, suddenly seem to disappear from all records, and it has been impossible to trace the year they became extinct or, perhaps, amalgamated with another Order. As I mentioned earlier, the commercial practices of takeovers and asset-stripping are not twentieth century innovations. Even short-lived Orders of Knighthood were usually well endowed by their founders, and their possessions soon became the envy of larger and more powerful Orders which arranged matters so they could annex their victim's properties, take over its assets and either abolished the Order or absorbed its members. However, in some cases the date of an Order's extinction appears to coincide with the actual attainment of the aims and purposes for which it was founded.

Mons. Cardinale gave to all but one of those on his list of short-lived Orders their date of foundation, but not the year they ceased to exist. There is no doubt that there have been numerous foundations of Orders called 'of St. Mark', and many Orders were named after and dedicated to, the Immaculate Conception.

The chivalric Orders of St. John Lateran and of Our Lady of Loreto should not be confused with the Lateran and Lauretan Crosses, which I discussed at the beginning of this chapter.

Archbishop Cardinale's list comprised the following Orders, and their dates of foundation: The Order of St. Mark (early Middle Ages; no date available) The Order of St. Anthony of Vienna (1005); The Order of SS. John and Thomas (1205); The Order of the Militia of Jesus Christ, or of St. Dominic (1216); The Order of Mercy (1218); The Order of the Glorious St. Mary (1261); The Order of the Dove (1379); The Order of St. Anthony of

Hainault (1382); The Order of St. John Lateran (1560); The Order of Our Lady of Loreto (1587); The Order of Jesus and Mary (1615); The Order of the Immaculate Conception (1617); The Order of the Celestial Collar of the Holy Rosary (1645); The Order of Brotherly Love (1708); The Order of St. Bridget of Sweden (1814).

To this list I have added three more Orders which are often mentioned in reference books but about which almost nothing is known, other than that they did not exist for very long.

The Order of the Christian Militia, founded by Pope Paul V in 1615; The Order of Magdalen (or Mary Magdalen), founded for the suppression of duelling in 1614, although it is anybody's guess as to who qualified, why and how; and The Order of the Conception of Our Lady, founded by the Duke of Mantua and confirmed by Pope Urban VIII in 1623.

The following Orders are now moved here from the section on long-lived Orders of Knighthood because they only existed for less than a century.

THE ORDER OF THE FLEET
or
THE ORDER OF THE TWO MOONS
or
THE ORDER OF THE SHIP AND THE CRESCENT
(France)

In 1262 St. Louis, King of France, founded an Order which became known by the above-mentioned three names. Some reference books list the Order as three separate entities, and alternative foundation date is given as 1269. Its object was to encourage members of the nobility to go to the Middle East to fight the Muslims and defend the interests of the Church, but it appears that the Order did not survive its founder.

THE ORDER OF THE HATCHET
or HACHA
(Spain)

This Order was founded prior to 1149 by Raymond Berengarius, Count of Barcelona, as a female Order of Knighthood, to honour the women who fought for the liberation of Tortosa in Catalonia. The town was under siege by the Moors, and the women were a decisive influence in defeating them. The Dames admitted to the Order received many privileges from the Count of Barcelona and took precedence over men in public assemblies, although there is no record of how long the women enjoyed these privileges or of how long the Order continued to exist. Legends about the Lady Knights of the Hatchet have fired the imagination of many writers, but the historical accuracy in their accounts doubtless leaves much to be desired.

THE ORDER OF THE HOLY VIAL
(France)

Legend and some reference books have it that this is the most ancient of French Orders. Its foundation is attributed to Clovis I in 493, and it is said to have been reserved exclusively to members of the highest nobility. For many centuries nothing was known or heard of this Order until unsuccessful attempts were made in the 1800s to revive it.

The Order is sometimes referred to as the Order of Remi after the Apostle of the Franks, St. Remigius, who actually baptised Clovis in 496, (three years after he had allegedly founded this Christian Order of Knighthood). Others associate its foundation with the recovery, through the intercession of that Saint, of the Sacred Vessels stolen from Soissons. Another foundation date given is 499, which coincides with the establishment of bishoprics in Tornai and Cambrai. The Order's history is shrouded in legend and myth, and it quite possibly never existed, but used as an excuse to establish such an Order in the early nineteenth century.

THE ORDER OF THE MILITARY CINCTURE
(Sicily)

Founded by Roger I, Grand Count of Sicily (1072-1101) in the eleventh century, for the sole purpose of demonstrating rights and privileges undoubtedly gained for him by his powerful militia. The Order was reserved for members of the highest ranking families, and it would be premature to regard it as an Order of Knighthood in the accepted definition. Its Knights were known as the Torquati Aurati or Knights of the Golden Collar, a title reintroduced as late as Christmas Day 1957 when Pope Pius XII added the Golden Collar to the Order of Pius IX, which Paul VI in April 1966 reserved for Heads of State of all religions. The title Torquati Aurati was also used for the Knights of the S.M. Constantinian Order of St. George (Two Sicilies) prior to Prince Gian Angelo, the last Greek Grand Master of the Order, ceding the Grand Magistry to the Duke of Parma in 1697.

Little is known about the activities of the Order itself nor how long it existed. It is well documented that Roger I was granted extraordinary and

Her Majesty Queen Margrethe II of Denmark, Dame of the Garter, Dame of the Spanish Golden Fleece, her Consort, H.R.H. Prince Henrik of Denmark, H.R.H. Crown Prince Frederik and Prince Joachim. All members of the Royal Family wear the Collar of the Order of the Elephant and Prince Henrik also wears the Star of a Grand Commander of the Order of the Dannebrog.

Courtesy: Foto: Rigmor Mydtskov; Archives of the Royal Palace

XLII

Top left: The Elephant Badge suspended from the from the light blue, watered silk Sash; top right: The Star of the Order of the Elephant. Right: the Breast Cross of a Commander of the Order of the Dannebrog.

Courtesy: The Royal Danish Embassy, London

The Elephant Badge Appendant.
Courtesy: Spink & Son Ltd., London

The Star of a Grand Commander of the Order of the Dannebrog. Courtesy: The Royal Danish Embassy, London

The robe of a Knight of the Noble Order of the Golden Fleece.

The robe of a Knight of the Royal Order of St. Januarius.

The robe of a Knight Grand Cross of the Order of the Dannebrog.

The robe of a Knight of the Most Noble Order of the Garter.

22 December 1990. The first democratically elected President of Poland since 1939, Mr. Lech Walesa (centre), receives from the outgoing President-in-Exile, Mr. Ryszard Kaczorowski (right), the presidential insignia and the seals of the Grand Master of the Orders of the White Eagle and of Polonia Restituta.

Courtesy: H.E. Ambassador de Virion, Polish Republic

The Polish President-in-Exile, Mr. Kazimierz Sabbat (1986-1989), wearing the insignia of the Orders of the White Eagle and of Polonia Restituta.

Courtesy: Chancellery of the Polish Government-in-Exile

Queen Elizabeth II with President Lech Walesa during his state visit to Great Britain in 1991 when President Walesa was invested with the Grand Cross of the Most Honourable Order of the Bath.

Courtesy: Juliusz Englert

The presidential insignia of the Order of the White Eagle (left) and of the Order of *Polonia Restituta* (right). At the end of their term of office, past Presidents remain a member of the Order of the White Eagle and a Knight Grand Cross of Polonia Restituta.

Courtesy: Count Ciechanowiecki/P. Cumings Associates

Though a Pope never accepts decorations, John Paul II made an exception when he accepted the Medal (marked No. 1) which celebrated the help given to Poland during the years of its greatest need. The obverse of the silver medal shows below a relief sculpture of the Madonna of Czestochowa the presidential flags of the Republics of Germany and Poland and in the centre the eight-pointed Cross of the Order of St. Lazarus. The inscription above the Madonna reads Dank Für Polenhilfe. Among the other recipients were President Walesa of Poland, and the German President, Dr. Walter Scheel. The medal is suspended from a green ribbon with two stripes in the Polish national colours, red and white.

Courtesy: Lazarus Hilfswerk

His Holiness Pope John Paul II with the Patriarch Protector of the M.& H. Order of St. Lazarus of Jerusalem, His Beatitude Maximos V Hakim (centre) and the Grand Prior of America, H.E. Dr. Hans von Leden (left).
Courtesy: L'Osservatore Romano

H.S.H. François de Cossé, 18th Duc de Briss[ac], 48th Supreme Head and Grand Master of [the] Military and Hospitaller of St. Lazarus [of] Jerusalem.
Courtesy: Grand Priory of Am[erica]

Colonel Prof. Federsel of the Austrian Grand Priory during one of his regular reports to His Holiness on the progress of Hospice for the dying in Nova Huta (Poland).
Courtesy: Grand Priory of Austria

Chev. Klaus-Peter Pokolm, President of [the] Lazarus Hilfswerk which had by 19[..] undertaken nearly 300 trucking expeditio[ns] with food and medicine to Poland, gives [his] report to the Pope. President Pokolm, who [is] supported by several Grand Priories, notab[ly] the American and German, persona[lly] coordinates the relief programmes to Easte[rn] Europe, especially Poland, Russia, Hunga[ry] and the former Yugoslavia.
Courtesy: Lazarus Hil[fswerk]

XLVII

The Spiritual Counsellor of the American Grand Priory of the Order of St. Lazarus, His Eminence Ernesto Cardinal Corripio Ahumada (centre) with the Grand Prior of America H.E. Dr. Hans von Welden (right), and the Marshal and Aide-de-Camp of the Grand Prior, Chev. F. Miller McCahey (left).

Courtesy: Grand Priory of America

Cordon of a Knight Cross; Knights Commander and Knights wear the Badge suspended from a green neck ribbon; the Grand Collar (for exceptional meritorious services); Breast Star of a Dame Commander (left); Breast Star of a Knight Commander (right).

Courtesy: American Grand Priory

Cross of Justice of Knights Grand Cross and Knights Commander of Justice; Badge of an Officer (left); Badge of a Lady Commander (right); Cordon of a Knight Grand Cross of Merit; Breast Star of a Knight Grand Cross and a Knight Commander of Merit.

Courtesy: American Grand Priory

PRIMUS INTER PARES

The Supreme Knight of the Knights of Columbus, Mr. Virgil C. Dechant, is the most high[ly] decorated Catholic layman. In this painting he wears the Cordon and Star of the Grand Cross of t[he] Order of Pius IX, the Star of the Grand Cross of the Order of St. Gregory the Great, the Star of t[he] Grand Cross of the Holy Sepulchre of Jerusalem; his first neckbadge is the Jewel of the Supre[me] Knight of Columbus, below which he wears the Cross of the Sovereign Military Order of Malta a[nd] the multiple gold Chain with the papal tiara and crossed keys suspended from it are the insignia [of] a Chamberlain (Gentleman) of His Holiness. He is also an Honorary Cunsultor of the Pontifi[cal] Commission for the State of the Vatican City, Consultor to the Pontifical Council for Soc[ial] Communications and a Member of the Council of Superintendency of the Institute for the Works [of] Religion (Vatican Bank). Supreme Knight Dechant received the Grand Cross of Merit (EOHSJ) af[ter] the painting was completed.

Courtesy: The Supreme Council of the Knights of Colur[mbus]

unprecedented powers by Pope Urban II, and that he and his heirs held the *vicem legati*, the right to act as Papal Legate in the Two Sicilies, and later his family claimed full ecclesiastical authority in the kingdom.

THE ORDER OF MONTJOIE
THE ORDER OF MONTFRAC
THE ORDER OF TRUXILLO
(Spain)

Founded in Palestine in about 1180 for the protection of pilgrims to the Holy Land, it took its name from Mount Joie, after a fortress built by the Christians near Jerusalem. The Order was approved by Alexander III (1159-81), who put it under the rule of St. Basil. After the loss of the Holy Land, the Order returned to Spain to fight the Islamic invaders. It finally ceased to exist in 1221, after being divided into two different Orders, the Order of Montfrac and the Order of Truxillo; the members of the former eventually joined the Order of Calatrava, those of the latter the Order of Alcantara.

THE ORDER OF OUR LADY OF BETHLEHEM
(Papal States)

This Order was founded by Pius II (1458-64) in 1459 to defend the island of Lemnos against the onslaught of Islamic invaders. When the island fell, the Order collapsed and its estates were given to the Order of Malta by Innocent VIII (1484-92) in 1484.[1]

THE ORDER OF ST. GEORGE OF RAVENNA
(Papal States)

This was a military Order founded in 1534 by Pope Paul III (1534-49) for Ravenna to fight the Muslims off the Adriatic coast. The Order was abolished by Gregory XIII (1572-85) in 1574.

---

[1]This is now one of the best-known recently formed organisations that calls itself an Order of Knighthood and uses the name of an extinct Order of the Papal States. The magazine *Il Cavaliere* (N⁻10/93) featured an article and colour photographs about a recent investiture during which robed women were dubbed with a sword by a robed Grand Master, and the insignia of the organisation. In Chapter Thirteen, it is the first of the self-styled orders listed by the Holy See in its condemnation published in *L'Osservatore Romano* (1953, reprinted 1970).

THE SACRED AND MILITARY ORDER OF OUR LADY OF MERCY
or
THE ORDER OF OUR LADY OF RANSOM
(Spain)

This Order is listed in some reference books as two separate Orders. Founded in 1218 by St. Peter Nolascus under the rule of St. Augustine for the ransom of Christians captured by the Muslims, it immediately obtained the support of King James I of Aragon (1213-76), uncle of the founder, and the Order received the approval of Pope Gregory IX (1227-41) in 1235. During the first century of its existence it was an exclusively military Order of Knighthood, including priests among its members for spiritual administrations. The Order spread through Spain, Sicily and Southern France, and had a famous monastery in Paris. Its first eight Grand Masters were elected from among the Knights, but in 1317, Pope John XXII (1316-34) decreed that the office of Grand Master should be held by a priest appointed by him. The Knights protested, so the Pope changed the Order of Knighthood into a merely religious institution, when the Knights left the Order and joined the newly founded Order of Montesa.

THE ORDER OF THE SWORD-BEARERS
(Lithuania)

Instituted in 1202 by Albert of Apeldera, Bishop of Livonia, on the model of the Knights Templars, and recognised by Innocent III (1198-1216), the Order was incorporated into the Teutonic Order in 1237 by Gregory IX (1227-41), the Knights forming a branch of the Teutonic Order under a Provincial Master.

As Knights of the Teutonic Order (see Chapter Six: 'A Transformed Religious Order of Knighthood') their vast possessions, acquired by conquest, formed a principality under Charles V (1525). The last Provincial Master, Gothard Kettler, apostatized in 1562 and converted the principality into the hereditary Duchy of Courland under the suzerainty of the Kings of Poland.

THE ROYAL ORDER OF ST. FERDINAND AND OF MERIT
(Two Sicilies)

Established by King Ferdinand IV of Naples in 1800 to reward military

The Badge of a Knight Grand Cross of the Order of St. Ferdinand and of Merit. Although (with few exceptions) conferred only on Catholic recipients, the Order never received specific pontifical sanction and is not Catholic-founded.

Courtesy: don Achille di Lorenzo

and civil fidelity, the members of this Order were required to be Roman Catholic, preferably belonging to the Sicilian nobility. As mentioned above, the Order never received pontifical sanction or specific approval.

St. Ferdinand was portrayed on the centre gold medallion of the badge, superimposed upon a six-pointed gold star with a white enamelled fleur-de-lis between each ray, and in a circle surrounding the portrait of St. Ferdinand the inscription FIDEI ET MERITO (for loyalty and merit). The ribbon from which is was suspended was red with a dark blue edge.

The Order became extinct in 1894 on the death of Francis II, the last King of the Two Sicilies. This was, incidentally, one of the four favourite Orders of Admiral Lord Nelson, who had it embroidered on his uniform.

THE ROYAL AND MILITARY ORDER OF ST. GEORGE OF THE REUNION
(Two Sicilies)

Ferdinand I, King of the Two Sicilies, formerly Ferdinand IV, King of Naples, established this Order on 1 January 1819 in place of the Royal Order of the Two Sicilies which had been founded in 1808 by Joseph Bonaparte, King of Naples (1806-08), and which King Ferdinand I had abolished. His intention was to mark the reunion of Naples and Sicily and the creation of the Kingdom of the Two Sicilies. The Order was conferred

The Cross of a Knight Commander of the Order of St. George of the Reunion.

Courtesy: don Achille di Lorenzo

upon persons who had distinguished themselves by their loyalty and especially their valour on the battlefield.

The Order was first conferred in seven classes, then eight (1850). The badge of the Grand Cross had an image of St. George suspended from it. It consisted of a red enamel cross fleury superimposed on a green-enamelled laurel wreath with gold crossed swords between its arms. St. George slaying the dragon was portrayed in gold on the centre medallion, and the inscription was the motto of the Sacred Military Constantinian

The Star of a Knight Grand Cross of the Order of St. George of the Reunion. As with the Order of St. Ferdinand and of Merit, this Order received no specific pontifical sanction.

Courtesy: don Achille di Lorenzo

Order of St. George IN HOC SIGNO VINCES (in this sign you will conquer). The ribbon was sky blue with a yellow edge.

Because of its political connotations the new Kingdom of Italy suppressed the Order in 1860 when it absorbed the Kingdom of the Two Sicilies.

Pope Pius IX recognised this Order as belonging to the Crown of the Two Sicilies until the King's death would abolish it. The Order of St. George of the Reunion ended in two stages, becoming extinct *de jure* in 1894 after the death of Francis II, the last King of the Two Sicilies. However, H.R.H. Don Alfonso, Count of Caserta, Duke of Castro, the King's half-brother and the new Head of the Royal House of the Two Sicilies, fulfilling the wish of the late King, conferred the Order in 1895 on his two sons Ferdinando Pio and the Spanish Infante Don Carlos, as well as on Prince Antonio Statella, Prince of Cassero, after which the Order became extinct *de facto*.

THE ORDER OF ST. LOUIS
(Duchy of Lucca – Duchy of Parma)

The Order was founded in 1836 by Charles Louis of Bourbon, Duke of Lucca, as the Order of St. Louis for Civil Merit. In 1847, the Duchy of Parma, after various vicissitudes, passed to the House of Borbon of Lucca and in 1849 Duke Charles III transferred the Order to the Duchy of Parma and gave it new statutes. It was reserved for Catholics, but a few exceptions were made.

In 1848 Parma was occupied by Sardinians with Austrian support but in 1849, soon after Duke Charles II had abdicated in favour of his son Charles III they withdrew after the Battle of Novara. Charles was assassinated in 1854, his heir being his six-year-old son Roger I, and the Duchy was ruled by his widow as Duchess-regent who went to live in Switzerland in 1859 when a provisional government was established, which voted to be annexed to Sardinia. The following year, after a plebiscite, the Duchy was annexed to Italy and the Order was abolished.

The Badge of the Order was a cross Flory triparted around a cross degraded with, superimposed in the centre, a shield that, on the obverse contained a low relief image of St. Louis in gold, and on the reverse the gold fleurs-de-lis of the Bourbon Dynasty. Originally in three classes, the first class was in gold, the second class in silver with a blue-enamelled shield; the third class was in silver but lacking the enamel. After 1849, the new statutes extended the Order to five classes, adding a gold crown above the gold Badge for the first to third class, a silver crown to the silver Badge of fourth class, and only the fifth class remained in silver without a crown.

The five classes of the Order of St. Louis. The first three classes were surmounted by a gold crown after 1849. The Order was abolished by the House of Savoy in 1860.

Courtesy: Garrison Collection

THE ORDER OF THE SLAVES OF VIRTUE
(Austro-Hungarian Empire)

Founded in 1662 by Eleanor Gonzaga, mother of the Emperor Leopold I, to promote piety and virtue at the imperial court, the Order was reserved to Ladies of the highest nobility. In 1668 she abolished the Order and incorporated its members in the Order of the Starry Cross, which she had founded in that year and which became a dynastic Order of the Archducal House of Habsburg-Lorrain.[1]

[1] See: Chapter Seven.

THE IMPERIAL ORDER OF ST. ELIZABETH
(Austro-Hungarian Empire)

The Order was instituted by Emperor Franz Josef I in 1898 to honour St. Elizabeth of Thuringia (1207-31) who had been canonised in 1235. It was conferred on ladies for special religious and charitable.

The 1st and 2nd class of the Imperial Order of St. Elizabeth.

Courtesy: Garrison Collection

The arms of the Cross are composed of stylised fleurs-de-lis; the two outer leaves of the fleurs-de-lis are red enamelled, with a white-enamelled centred leaf. Between the arms of the Cross are stems of roses with green-enamelled leaves and red-enamelled flowers. In the centre of the Cross is a gold medallion with the sculpted bust of St. Elizabeth facing to the right. She wears a crown, above which is a small gold square with a white-enamelled cross. Her head is surrounded by a halo, and the entire medallion is surrounded by a pearl wreath.

The Order was conferred in three classes, the Grand Cross, first and second class. The Grand Cross was worn on a white sash with two red stripes, and the recipient also received an eight-pointed silver Star with the Cross superimposed in the centre. The Cross of the first class was identical to the Grand Cross, but was worn on a ribbon in a bow. The Cross of the second class was in silver and without the colourful enamel work.

The Grand Cross and the Order of the first class had to be returned to the Imperial Chancery on the recipient's death. As with the dynastic Order of the Golden Fleece and the Royal Hungarian Order of St. Stephen, the Emperor could give recipients permission to have private copies of the insignia made for themselves in solid gold with precious stones, which, of course, were not returned after the recipient's death.

The Emperor later enlarged the Order with a Medal of Merit. The Chancellor of the Order, which was abolished by the Austrian Republic in 1918, was always the Minister for Foreign Affairs, who also appointed the Officers of the Order.

THE ORDER OF MERIT FOR CATHOLIC PRIESTS IN MILITARY SERVICE
(Austro-Hungarian Empire)

The Order of Merit for Roman Catholic Priests attached to the Army was instituted by Emperor Francis II on 23 November 1801. It was awarded for exemplary bravery to those priests who ministered to soldiers on the battle field regardless of their own safety. It could also be awarded for acts of bravery in the face of the enemy and for personal participation in the battle.

The Badge of the Order, a cross Trefoil, was awarded in two classes. The Cross of the first class had a gold-rimmed, white-enamelled centre medallion with the gold inscription PIIS MERITIS (for pious services), and that of the second class had a silver-rimmed, blue-enamelled centre medallion with the same inscription in silver. The Cross was worn on the left breast, suspended from a white ribbon with three broad red stripes. The Order was abolished by the Austrian Republic in 1918.

The Cross 1st class of the Order of Merit for Catholic Priests in Military Service.
Courtesy: Garrison Collection

THE ORDER OF OUR LADY OF GUADALUPE
(Mexico)

This Order was founded in 1822 by the Emperor Agustin de Iturbide of Mexico to honour the Patron of Mexico, Our Lady of Guadalupe. It remained dormant after the Emperor's abdication in 1823[1] until President Antonio de Lopez y Santa Anna revived the Order in 1853. Abolished in 1855, Emperor Maximilian I of Mexico re-established it in 1864 when it became the principal Order of the Mexican Empire. Emperor Maximilian was executed in 1867, and the Order once more fell into disuse. Although

[1] He was killed soon after for attempting to regain his authority.

The Grand Cross, Commander's Cross and Knight's Cross of the Order of Our Lady of Guadalupe.

Courtesy: Garrison Collection

bad news is said to travel fast, news about the fate of Orders of Knighthood, especially their abolition or fall into disuse, seems to take a long time to filter through to the experts on the subject. Maximilian Gritzner, the foremost expert on nineteenth century Orders of Knighthood, who published his definitive *Orders of Knighthood and Merit* in 1893, only records a change of the statutes of the Order by President Santa Anna in 1853 but makes no mention of Emperor Maximilian of Mexico making it the highest honour in 1864, nor does he mention its fate in 1867. Some later reference books give 1867 as the date of the Emperor's execution but give no further information. It must have been generously conferred because decorations are not infrequently to be found in auctions.

The Order of Our Lady of Guadalupe is very colourful, but rather difficult to describe.

The Badge is a gold, red enamelled, and green-andwhite-edged cross Formy with slightly convex arms, tipped with gold balls. There are gold rays between the arms of the cross which are supported by gold half wreaths, on the sinister side laurels, and on the dexter, palm leaves. In the centre of the obverse is a gold oval medallion with a coloured representation of Our Lady of Guadalupe. The medallion is surrounded by a green-enamelled, gold-bordered riband with the gold-lettered motto RELIGION – INDEPENDENCIA – UNION (Religion – Independence – Unity). On the reverse the medallion is white-enamelled and the military award bears the legend AL PATRIOTISMO HEROICO (For heroic patriotism), for civilians AL MERITO Y VIRTUDES (For Merit and Virtue). The Badge is surmounted by a gold Mexican Eagle, crowned with the Imperial Crown, holding in its beak and with its left claw a snake and sitting on a rock surrounded by a cactus. Legend states that the Aztecs built their capital (now Mexico City) where they saw the eagle shown in this image.

The eight-pointed gold Star is diamond-cut with the Badge, without the Mexican Eagle, superimposed in the centre.

The sash and ribbon of the Order is dark blue with a violet stripe on the edge. The Order was conferred in five classes, Grand Cross, Grand Officer, Knight Commander, Officer and Knight.

THE ORDER OF ST. CHARLES
(Mexico)

This Order was named after St. Charles Borromeo, and established in 1865 by the Emperor Maximilian of Mexico for those who were meritorious in charitable work or civil service and displayed humility. Both the Emperor and the Empress Charlotte conferred the Order, bestowing it in two classes, the Grand Cross and the Cross second class. The sash for the Grand Cross and the ribbon in a bow for the second class are crimson moiré.

The white-enamelled Latin Cross fleury has in its centre a smaller, green-enamelled Latin Cross with the silver inscription HUMILITAS (the motto of St. Charles) on the obverse, and SAN CARLOS on the reverse.

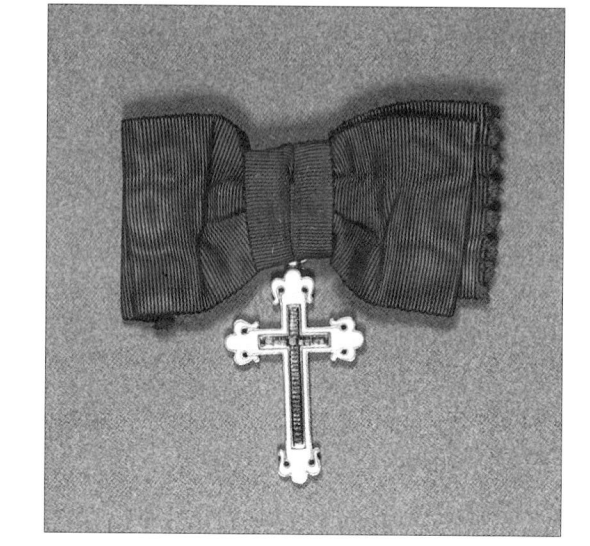

The Mexican Order of St. Charles, 2nd class.

Courtesy: Garrison Collection

THE ORDER OF ST. FAUSTIN
(Haiti)

Mons. Cardinale placed the Order among the extinct short-lived Catholic Orders of Knighthood as he accepted the widely held opinion that the Order of St. Faustin was established in 1849 by Faustin I, Emperor of Haiti, to honour the Saint and Martyr St. Faustinus. Historical records I have since studied contradict this. In 1849, the President of the Republic of Haiti, General Soulouque, issued an edict with the compliance of the Senate, changing the Republic into an Empire. The General ascended the imperial throne and assumed the name 'St. Faustin Soulouque', thus not only assuming the title of Emperor, but canonising himself at the same time. After his coronation in 1852 the Emperor Saint decreed the establishment of the Order of St. Faustin, but it ceased to exist with his overthrow in 1859. The sixteen-pointed Cross, the arms of which were alternately enamelled red and blue, and tipped with gold balls, was surmounted by the Imperial Crown of Haiti. The gold-bordered Cross was entwined with a gold laurel wreath and a gold bow ribbon at the lower part. In the centre of the Cross was a gold-bordered, red enamelled ring bearing the inscription FAUSTIN EMPEREUR D'HAITI surrounding a medallion with the profile of the Emperor Saint. The Cross was worn on a light blue sash. The Star of the Order was an eight-pointed silver plaque with a crowned eagle adorning the blue enamelled centre medallion with the inscription DIEU, MA PATRIE E MON EPÉE (God, my country and my sword) There was also a medallion on the reverse which bore the gold profile of the Emperor and the words FAUSTIN EMPEREUR D'HAITI.

Few examples of this Order seem to have been seen by writers of reference works as there are contradictions in the different descriptions of where the various emblems, the medallion, the Emperor's profile, the eagle and the inscriptions were placed, though all of them are mentioned.

III

SHORT-LIVED ORDERS FOUNDED BY PRIVATE INITIATIVE

In the eighteenth and nineteenth centuries there have been countless short-lived Orders with religious and secular aspects founded by private initiative, which is to say not by a sovereign power, but founded or subsequently approved by ecclesiastical authority and also acquiring secular patrons. Many of these were mixed Orders, and a great number were for women only, and as they were mainly designed to encourage charitable deeds, many were therefore dedicated to St. Anna or St. Elizabeth. Whilst their dates of foundation are known, few lasted longer than a century and most ceased to exist without the reason for their extinction being known. I give three examples of these.

Bishops, especially Prince-Archbishops with secular powers, also founded Orders; they were mostly of a commemorative character and restricted to members of the nobility. These Orders seem to have had no particular aim or purpose other than to commemorate an event. I give one example of this type.

Finally, I give an example of a knightly Order that was short-lived but seems to have served ever since as a rôle model for Orders or Associations of Ancient Nobility. Such Orders and Associations still exist today, especially in Spain and Portugal, where there are confraternities of members of the nobility in certain regions or countries. Although their statutes have never expressly mentioned the Catholic religion, they are strongly Catholic in their traditions and membership. Many of their members belong to one or more Catholic-founded Orders of Knighthood.

THE ORDER OF ST. ANNE
(München – Bavaria)

Founded in 1784 by Anna Maria Sophia, widow of the Elector Maximilian IV, for noble Catholic ladies, its founder decreed that the Order's abbess should always be a Princess of the House of Bavaria, and its object was to encourage charitable deeds. As is to be expected its badge bore the figure of St. Anne.

THE ORDER OF ST. ANNE
(Würzburg – Bavaria)

Established by the Countess Anna Maria von Dernbach in 1714 and approved by the Bishop of Würzburg, it was recognised by Ferdinand II, Grand Duke of Tuscany, when he also became Grand Duke of Würzburg in 1811. The Order was exclusively reserved for ladies of the Bavarian nobility, and its object was to help needy young women, its badge showing the figure of St. Anne.

THE ORDER OF ST. ELIZABETH
(Sultzbach – Bavaria)

Founded by the Countess Elisabeth Augusta, daughter of Joseph Charles, Count Palatine of Sultzbach, and first wife of the Elector Charles Theodor, in 1766, it was reserved exclusively for Catholic ladies of the nobility who had accomplished outstanding deeds of charity and to encourage further charitable works by its members. The Order received confirmation from Pope Clement XIII (1758-69), and its badge portrayed the figure of St. Elizabeth being visited by the Blessed Virgin Mary.

THE ORDER OF ST. RUPERT OF SALZBURG
(Austro-Hungarian Empire)

Prince Johannes Ernst von Thun, Prince Archbishop of Salzburg, created this Order in 1701 to honour St. Rupert, who had been the first Archbishop of Salzburg, and as a perpetual memorial to the Treaty of Carlowitz in 1699, when Prince Eugene forced the Turks to leave Austro-Hungarian soil after 150 years of occupation. Emperor Leopold I confirmed the Order which was reserved for gentlemen of the highest nobility.

The Order's Badge was a gold cross formy with slightly convex endings of the arms. In the centre is the portrait of St. Rupert; the ribbon is bright red with wide black stripes near the edges.

THE KNIGHTLY ORDER OF THE OLD NOBILITY
or
THE ORDER OF THE FOUR EMPERORS
(Limburg – Luxembourg)

Philip Ferdinand, Duke of Limburg, founded the Order of the Old Nobility, called also the Order of the Four Emperors, in 1768. The Order was founded in memory of four Emperors of the Holy Roman Empire who had belonged to the Luxembourg Dynasty, Henry VII, Charles IV, Wenzel I and Sigismund.

Attempts have been made to classify this Order among the long-lived Orders of Knighthood, attributing its foundation to the Emperor Henry VII himself in 1308 under the patronage of the Guardian Angel. It was then alleged to have become extinct in the seventeenth century, revived again and incorporated in the Order of the Lion of Holstein-Limburg under the patronage of St. Philip. It was supposed to have been given the somewhat ambiguous aim of 'the defence of the faith', but there is no foundation for assuming this to be anything but a legend, probably confusing the name of Philip, Duke of Limburg, with that of St. Philip.

The Badge of the 1768 Order was a white-enamelled, eight-pointed cross with gold flames between the arms, and a blue medallion in the centre that bore the inscription ILLUST. ET NOB., the inscription being surmounted either by a ducal hat or a count's coronet. On the surface of the white arms of the Cross were the initials of the names of the four Emperors, H.C.W.S. The badge was worn on various ribbons: German members wore it on a yellow one, the French on a light blue, the Spanish and Portuguese on a bright red, the Italians on a darker red, the English on a dark blue, and the Slavs on a green ribbon.

Later the Cross was slightly changed and the central medallion showed an angel with an infant; the badge was surmounted by a crown, and the ribbon was either red or blue with a yellow stripe near the edge.

The Order fell into disuse in 1818.

IV

LONG-LIVED ORDERS OF KNIGHTHOOD

It is surprising how few of the extinct Orders of Knighthood survived the first century of their existence. As mentioned above, for every extinct long-lived Order, there were at least fifty short-lived ones of which something is known, if only a legend.

The Reformation which swept through Europe, and later the period of Revolution that followed Absolutism and Feudalism, were major factors in the extinction of countless Orders of Knighthood, so it is surprising how many Catholic-founded Orders have actually survived, as is witnessed by this work.

There is also a large grey area where our knowledge of the fate of various Orders is very limited, and in the Chapter on self-styled Orders of Knighthood, I have shown that the Apostolic See is uncompromising when referring to some of the ancient extinct or suppressed Orders that were revived by private initiative in the last two centuries.

No historian will dispute that the Order of the Knights Templars was totally annihilated being abolished by two papal decrees in 1312 and had completely ceased to exist throughout Europe by 1350. There have subsequently been legitimate Orders founded on the Templars' model, notably the Portuguese Order of Christ, which was expressly founded and approved by Papal Bull as the successor to the Order of the Knights Templars. I do not wish to preempt the concise history of the Order of the Knights Templars which follows, but events which took place in the twelfth and thirteenth century have had a lasting effect on the entire history and development of the concept of chivalry. I therefore consider it necessary to separate these political undercurrents and events from the history of the Order of the Knights Templars, not only to simplify the narrative, but because the history of the Order is at the same time the history of Europe and the Middle East. Hundreds of learned books have been written about the Order which is still being passionately discussed by historians, often from extremely different viewpoints.

Mons. Cardinale, who during his term of office as Apostolic Delegate to Great Britain (1963-69) had taken a special interest in history of the Knights Templars in London, wrote a treatise on the Order long before he used it as a chapter in his book. He placed the blame for the Templars' annihilation firmly on Philip the Fair, King of France (1285-1314), but found mitigating circumstances for the French Pope Clement V, whom he considered to have been put under impossible pressure by the King.

Nobody who has studied the history of the Knights Templars can ever acquit the French Pope Clement V (1305-14) of the charge of callously sanctioning torture, unimaginably barbarous cruelty, and finally the foul murder of the Templars' senior members.

Many historians describe Philip the Fair as a completely unscrupulous king who covered himself with a thin veneer of piety. All the evidence points to the fact that he personally planned the kidnapping and murder of Pope Boniface VIII, and he is strongly suspected of having had the next Pope, Benedict XI, poisoned. By 1305 he had installed his own pawn, Bertrand de Goth, Archbishop of Bordeaux, on the papal throne as Clement V, and in 1309 Philip highjacked the Papacy itself, uprooting it from Rome and establishing the papal court on French soil, in Avignon, where it became an appendage of the French crown.

Although he was powerful enough to encroach upon the property of the Templars in France, he still needed the concurrence of the Pope to destroy them throughout Europe. To this effect he appointed ministers and members of the Inquisition that were his equal in unscrupulous machination. The King's disastrous Flemish wars had brought him into desperate financial difficulties, and his treasury was totally exhausted in spite of extortionate taxation, debasement of the currency and the merciless plunder of the Jews and the Lombard bankers. In the wealth of the Templars he saw a tempting prize, and his trail of treachery was soon complete.

Apologists of the Pope's rôle in the extermination of the Templars maintain that there had been two phases of the trials of the Templars. Philip the Fair had made 'preliminary enquiries', based on the false testimony of unworthy witnesses and submitting knights to horrible and pitiless torture. He conducted the persecution under the pretext of orthodoxy and the suppression of heresy, thus invoking and involving the Apostolic See in the action, by maintaining that he persecuted the Templars at the express request and under the orders of the Inquisition. Owing to the lack of evidence, the accused knights could be convicted only through their own confessions and, to obtain these, the use of the most ruthless and terrible torture was considered necessary and legitimate.

The second phase of the 'trials' is said to have been the process of a papal enquiry, which was not restricted to France, but extended to all Christian countries of Europe and even the Orient. In almost all other countries, for example, in Portugal, Spain, Germany, Cyprus and Italy, the Knights Templars were found innocent, but in France the episcopal Inquisition resumed its activities. With regard to the sentence on the Grand Master, the Pope reserved his judgement for a while, and to give this occasion more publicity, a platform was erected in front of Notre-Dame Cathedral in Paris for the reading of the sentence. The Grand Master, Jacques de Molay was burnt at the stake before the gates of the palace.

There is one more important factor which brought about the ultimate destruction of the Knights Templars: having been made independent of the jurisdiction of all regional bishops and placed directly under the Papacy by papal bull in 1172, while also enjoying exemption from all taxes and tithes, and from interdict, they were soon opposed by the Order of the Knights Hospitallers of St. John, which had become a Military Order of Knighthood, and was at first the imitator and later the rival of the Knights Templars. The latter's wealth, loyalty to the Pope and exceptional privileges made them the object of fear and hatred. The open quarrel between the two Orders which blazed into open warfare in Palestine in 1243, had shocked the moral sense of Christendom.

Mons. Cardinale mentions King Edward II of England (1307-27) as among the first of those who suppressed the Knights Templars, and also his son Edward III (1327-77) who gave their fortune to the Military and Hospitaller Order of St. John, but it is a historical fact that it was Philip the Fair, King of France, who destroyed the Order and, with Pope Clement V sanctioning his murderous campaign, had completed his gruesome task by 1314 – the year Clement V died – with the burning of Jacques de Moley. Edward II of England was just one of many sovereigns who tacitly condoned what was happening in France and suppressed the Knights Templars in his own country, though not threatening their lives.

To ensure that I leave no doubt as to whether any self-styled order can claim to be the true successor of the Order of the Knights Templars, calling itself by that name, I state here categorically and without any ambiguity that the Order was abolished in 1312 by two Papal Bulls: first, *Vox in excelso* (22 March 1312), followed six weeks later by *Ad providam* (2 May 1312).

As the legend of the Order will show, the spirit of the Knights Templars lived on and, many of the Knights continued their work as welcome members in several ancient and highly respected Orders of Knighthood.

Over the centuries no other Order has inspired authors and movements more than the Knights Templars. Many Orders endeavoured to emulate and perpetuate their example, but unfortunately many organisations that were founded by private initiative, especially in the nineteenth and twentieth centuries claimed to be the true successors of the Knights Templars, among them several Masonic societies in the United States of America. More unfortunate still, is the emergence of countless self-styled Orders calling themselves 'Knights Templars', whose claims to be the

The Temple Church in the City of London was consecrated in 1185; the choir was added in 1240. In 1312 the property of the Knights Templars, including the Temple Church, passed to the Knights of St. John (Order of Malta), who themselves were suppressed during the Reformation. The church became the property of the English Crown, and in 1608 King James I gave the freehold of the property to the Benchers of the Inner Temple and the Middle Temple, subject to the Inns of Court 'maintaining the Temple Church and its services for ever'.

Courtesy: The Master of the Temple, Canon J.Robinson

legitimate successors of the original Order lack any historical and juridical support. Some of them produce copies of ancient papal documents referring to the extinct Order as proof of their own legitimacy, but they are, of course, recognised neither by the Apostolic See nor by legitimate secular authorities. Others seek permission, which is officially refused, to use the old Temple Church off Fleet Street in London in order to establish some connection with the ancient Order and thereby attain some credibility. It is for this reason that the reprehensible behaviour of the many self-styled 'Orders of the Knights Templars' is constantly brought to the attention of the public in *L'Osservatore Romano*, and that they are frequently mentioned – by all possible names – in my chapter on self-styled Orders.

Since the eighteenth century, there have been three major historical epochs which had a far-reaching effect on many Orders of Knighthood: 1) the French Revolution and its aftermath which affected almost all Europe; 2) the Risorgimento of the mid-nineteenth century, which affected the Papal States, the Kingdom of the Two Sicilies, the Duchies of Parma, Tuscany and several sovereign principalities in Italy, most of which were linked to the Apostolic See and had Catholic Orders of Knighthood; 3) the revolutions between 1910 and 1931 on the Iberian peninsula ended the monarchies in Portugal and Spain, while the first World War brought about the end of many reigning European dynasties, notably that of the House of Habsburg Lorraine, (although, as we shall see, one of its principal Catholic-founded Orders of Knighthood, that of St. Stephen, appears to have continued to exist juridically until 1945). Finally, the aftermath of the second World War enforced the abdication of monarchs in the Balkans and Eastern European countries.

THE ORDER OF THE KNIGHTS TEMPLARS

The Knights Templars were the earliest founders of the military orders, and became the model on which most Orders of Knighthood were based. Their history falls into three epochs: their humble beginnings, their enormous growth and acquisition of great wealth, and their tragic end.

Immediately after the deliverance of Jerusalem, the Crusaders, considering their vow fulfilled, returned in a body to their homes, however the defence of this precarious conquest, surrounded as it was by Mohammedan forces, remained a necessity. In 1119, during the reign of Baldwin II, King of Jerusalem, Hugues de Payens, a knight of Champagne, and eight companions bound themselves by a perpetual vow, taken in the presence of the Patriarch of Jerusalem, to defend the

Christian Kingdom. Baldwin accepted their services and assigned them a portion of his palace that was built on the site of the ancient Temple; hence their title 'Pauvres Chevaliers du Temple' (Poor Knights of the Temple). They lived mainly on alms, and as long as there were only nine knights, they were hardly in a position to render important services to the King, and at this time they had neither a distinctive habit nor rule.

The Order's second epoch begins in 1128 when Hugues de Payens journeyed to the Council of Troyes to seek the approval of the Holy See and obtain recruits for his Order. At the Council the Templars adopted the Rule of St. Benedict, as recently reformed by the Cistercians; they accepted not only the three perpetual vows, as well as the Crusader's vow, but also the austere rules concerning the chapel, the refectory, and the dormitory. St. Bernard of Clairvaux drew up the Order's rule in seventy-two statutes and became the Order's Spiritual Advisor.[1]

The Order was sanctioned by the Council of Troyes in 1128 and was approved by Innocent II in 1139. Its members, consisting of Knights, Chaplains and Men-at-arms, owed obedience to their Grand Master and the Pope, and enjoyed absolute exemption from all other ecclesiastical jurisdiction. The Knights also adopted the white habit of the Cistercians to which they added a red cross *pattée* at the left shoulder. Notwithstanding the austerity of the monastic rule, recruits flocked to the new Order in great numbers.

Perhaps the best known representation of the Templars its seal, showing two knights riding one horse.

The Order owed its rapid growth in popularity to the fact that it combined the two highest mediaeval ideals, religious fervour and martial prowess. Men of great courage and pure devotion flocked to its ranks, often giving their personal wealth to the Order. Even before the Templars had proved their worth, ecclesiastical and lay authorities heaped on them

The seal of the Knights Templars showing two knights riding on one horse.

---

[1] St. Bernard's connection with the Order continued as its activities were not merely confined to the Holy Land: most of its manpower and wealth were in the various commanderies in western Europe. The thirteenth century was the age of the great Gothic cathedrals, almost all of which built on sites previously visited by St. Bernard and all, it has been argued, were funded by the Knights Templars, as at that time no one else, not even the Church had the necessary wealth and administrative ability to pay for and organise their construction.

favours of every kind. As mentioned above, they were exempt from all taxes, and successive popes took them under their personal protection. The benefits the Order received from all the sovereigns of Europe were no less important. By 1260 the Order is said to have numbered 20,000 knights, not counting the far more numerous serjeants and men-at-arms. By the year 1300 the Templars had lost their last battle in the defence of the Holy Land, and seven of their twenty-two Grand Masters had died in battle, so by any standard the Knights Templars hold a most glorious record of sacrificing their lives for their ideals. The Order had Commanderies in almost all European countries, and although still powerful and wealthy, the Templars had lost the main purpose for which they had been founded.

The third and tragic epoch of the Templars began in 1306 when Philip IV of France decided that with Pope Clement V under his control, there were no more obstacles in his way to capturing the 'Temple' in Paris and confiscating the treasures and properties of the Knights Templars in France. Although totally motivated by greed and vindictiveness against the Templars, Philip first claimed that the Order constituted a threat to his kingdom, because loss of the Latin Kingdom of Jerusalem left the Order of the Knights Templars, the most powerful fighting force in Europe, without a home, but then he changed the reason for persecuting the Templars to one of fighting heretics and enemies of the Church.

Philip the Fair then acted swiftly and without mercy: he sent out sealed orders stating that at dawn on Friday 13 October 1307 all Templars in France were to be arrested, their properties confiscated by the Crown and their goods to be delivered to the royal treasury. Historians have argued for hundreds of years as to whether Philip's objective of surprise was attained, as the most coveted prize of them all, the Order's legendary wealth, was never found. Some historians claim to have found evidence that the Templars received advance warning, and the Grand Master had time to ensure that all the Order's books were destroyed beforehand. Another mystery is the fleet of the Templars; not a single of the Order's ships was ever taken: they appear to have vanished along with their cargo. Historians have found it impossible to ascertain how many Templars were tortured, executed or burnt at the stake.

Philip's endeavour to win the support of his fellow monarchs in exterminating the Templars only met with a qualified success. In Lorraine the Templars were openly supported by the reigning Duke: a few knights were tried but immediately exonerated. In Germany, the Order was officially dissolved, but the German Knights Templars and their possessions were welcomed into the Order of St. John and the Teutonic Order. In Spain, the Templars resisted persecution and joined the Order of Calatrava, and the Military-Monastic Order of Montesa was specifically founded as a refuge for Knights Templars fleeing from persecution.

On 14 August 1318 Dom Dinis I, King of Portugal, founded the Order of Christ to replace the Order of the Knights Templars. The new Order was known as the Militia of Christ, a name which the Templars had used, and Pope John XXII ratified this Order in a Papal Bull, assigning all the Templars' estates to the Order of Christ.

While Philip found little support in Continental Europe for his attempt to exterminate the Templars, he expected greater cooperation from his son-in-law, King Edward II of England. However Edward was initially reluctant to act and wrote in his letters to Philip that he not only found the charges against the Templars incredible, but that he doubted the integrity of those who made them.

However, Edward II then received from Pope Clement V an official Bull sanctioning and ratifying the arrest of the English Templars: it obliged him to act, but he did so with marked reluctance, and it was only in February 1308 that thirty Templars were arrested in Ireland. There were no burnings and no executions, and the Order's Master of the Commandery of Ireland was released on bail.

With the exception of Portugal and Spain, where special provisions had been made with the Order of Christ and the Military-Monastic Orders of Calatrava and Montesa respectively, most Knights Templars joined the Knights of St. John of Jerusalem.

THE ORDER OF ST. JAMES OF ALTOPASCIO
(Tuscany)

Founded in Altopascio, Tuscany, in 952 with the object of helping pilgrims and ensuring the safety of the travellers, its members were originally religious brothers, who specialised in building bridges. This was the reason for their peculiar habit, a black mantle with a red hood, adorned with symbolic hammers. The Order had its Grand Magistry in Italy and a Commander General in France.

In 1459, Pius II suppressed it, commanding its members and applicants to join the Order of Our Lady of Bethlehem which he had recently founded. However the latter Order ceased to exist in 1484, and its estates, together with those of the Order of St. James of Altopascio, were given to the Order of St. John.

The Hospital of St. James of Altopascio near Lucca was eventually acquired by the Order of St. Stephen which had been founded in 1562 by the House of Tuscany.

The French branch of the Order of St. James of Altopascio under its Commander General appears to have survived the Tuscan branch by another two centuries; however, it was probably absorbed by one of the French Orders.

THE ORDER OF THE HOLY GHOST OF MONTPELLIER
(France)

The Order was established in 1195 as a confraternity at the service of the Hospital, and it was approved and transformed into a Religious Hospitaller Military Order in 1198 by Innocent III, its object being to care for the sick and to fight the Albigenses. The Order was suppressed by Louis XIV (1643-1715) in 1672, but revived in 1693.

It lost its military charter in 1708, and in 1711 Pope Clement XI (1700-21) amalgamated it with the already amalgamated Orders of Our Lady of Mount Carmel and of St. Lazarus of Jerusalem. Pope Clement XI certainly involved himself very actively in the lives of Religious and Sacred Orders of Knighthood.

THE ORDER OF ST. GEORGE OF ALFAMA
(Spain)

The Order was established in 1201 by Don Pedro II, King of Aragon (1196-1213), as a Religious Military Order in honour of St. Peter, and to fight the Moors and other Islamic invaders. In 1399, the anti-pope Benedict XIII (1394-1423) amalgamated it with the Monastic-Military Order of Montesa, which appears to have absorbed almost as many Orders as the Military Order of St. John.

THE ORDER OF ST. GEORGE IN CARINTHIA
(Holy Roman Empire)

This Order was established in 1273 by the Emperor-designate Rudolf I of Habsburg (1273-91) to continue the tradition of the Order of St. George of Austria. Although it appears to have fallen into abeyance, the Order was re-established in Rome on Christmas night 1468 by the Emperor Frederick III of Habsburg (1452-93). The Order was approved as a Military Religious and Civil dynastic Order of Knighthood first on 1 January 1469 by Paul II (1464-71), and again in 1472 by Sixtus IV (1471-84).

In 1493, the Order was enlarged by Emperor Maximilian I (1493-1519) and, together with the Confraternity of St. George in Carinthia, was approved in the same year by Alexander VI (1492-1503), who took the unique step of asking to be admitted to the Order, together with the members of the Sacred College of Cardinals. During the fifteenth and sixteenth centuries, the Order was regarded as one of the most important Orders of Knighthood in the Holy Roman Empire, but was first suppressed and then abolished in 1781 by Emperor Joseph II (1765-90), the abolition being sanctioned by Pius VI.

The Order's Badge consisted of a four-pointed Star with a red-enamelled Cross *Botonné* in the centre, surmounted by the Carinthian crown of the Holy Roman Empire.

The Order of St. George in Carinthia not only features prominently in the chapter on modern self-styled Orders that are in no way approved or recognised, but the Holy See draws particular attention to the fact that documents, whether ecclesiastical or pontifical, that were once granted for religious purposes to this Order before it was legitimately abolished, are neither acknowledged by the Holy See nor applicable with regard to a self-styled organisation, which is flourishing in the United States of America under this name. It is said to have a phenomenal income derived from the sale of fictitious chivalric diplomas, insignia and robes. The Head of the House of Habsburg-Lorraine, His Imperial and Royal Highness the Archduke Dr. Otto von Habsburg, is in full agreement with the Holy See that this self-styled organisation should not be allowed to flourish, even if distant relatives of his family are involved with this enterprise.

THE ORDER OF ST. GEORGE OF BURGUNDY
(Belgium)
(possibly Flanders under the rule of France or Burgundy)

Also known as the Order of Belgium or the Order of Miolans, this Order was founded in honour of St. George the Martyr in 1390 by Philibert of Miolans who is said to have brought back the relics of St. George from the Holy Land.

It began as a Confraternity and is said to have been reconstituted as a Religious Military Order in 1485 (when Flanders was under the rule of Austria, Belgium itself only gaining the status of an independent country in 1830). It is therefore more likely that the Order was founded in France and remained French.

In 1485 membership of the Order is said to have been restricted to the French speaking part of what became Belgium and dedicated to defending the purity of the faith, and obedience to the Sovereign. It is said to have gone into abeyance, but being revived by the Bourbons of France, it became dormant during the French Revolution and was finally abolished in 1824 by Louis XVIII, King of France, (1814-24).

THE ORDER OF THE SWAN
(Brandenburg)

Founded in 1440 by Friedrich II, Elector of Brandenburg (1440-70), and placed under the protection of the Blessed Virgin Mary, whose image with the child Jesus was portrayed on the Badge, the Order was conferred on men and women regardless of their religious beliefs. Having remained dormant for some centuries, King Friedrich Wilhelm IV (1840-61) revived the Order in 1843, but its revival was of short duration.

THE ORDER OF ST. HUBERT OF LORRAINE
or
THE ORDER OF THE BAR

(France) Founded in 1416 by Louis I, sovereign Duke of Bar, under the name 'Ordre de la Fidélité', the Order was placed under the patronage of St. Hubert and named after the Saint in 1423. It was awarded to members of ancient Orders of Knighthood for meritorious services to charitable causes. The Order was confirmed in 1605 by Duke Charles III, in 1661 by Duke Charles IV and in 1718 by Leopold, Duke of Lorraine and Bar. Gritzner and most other historians state that Louis XV, King of France, (1715-74), took the Order under his personal protection, and Perrot maintains that it had been a strictly Catholic Royal Order, reserved for the nobility, and endowed with special privileges by Louis XIV, Louis XV, and Louis XVI. It was suppressed by the French Revolution, revived in 1815 by King Louis XVIII and given new statutes in 1816, but finally abolished in 1824.

The Badge of the Order was a gold-rimmed, white-enamelled cross pattée with a blue-enamelled, medallion in the centre that bore the coat of arms of the Dukes of Bar, surrounded by a gold-rimmed, white enamelled band with he inscription ORDO NOB[ILIS] SANCTI HUBERTI INSTITUTUS ANNO 1416, and a silver Star, on which the cross was superimposed, with a green-enamelled medallion, bearing in gilded low relief a representation of the conversion of St. Hubert, with a white enamelled surround and the motto in gold VIRTUS ET HONOS.[1]

THE ORDER OF OUR LADY OF MOUNT CARMEL AND OF ST. LAZARUS OF JERUSALEM (amalgamated)

The Order of Our Lady of Mount Carmel was founded in 1607 by Henri IV, King of France (1589-1610), apparently to commemorate his conversion to the Catholic faith, but more like to facilitate the annexation of the substantial properties and wealth of the French Knights of the Order of St. Lazarus of Jerusalem. The Order added the name 'of St. Lazarus of Jerusalem' to its name a year later, following the merger with

[1] Spink & Son Ltd. of London received a commission for a Grand Cross of St. Hubert with precise instructions. It was ultimately sold at auction and must rank as one of the most interesting fatansy decorations. It is reproduced in Chapter Thirteen among the self-styled orders.

French Knights of the ancient Order of St. Lazarus of Jerusalem, which had been established in 1060. In 1711, at the instigation of Pope Clement XI (17001721) the Order of the Holy Ghost of Montpellier was also amalgamated with the Order. After being confirmed by the King's successors, the Order was suppressed in 1791 by the French Revolution, revived temporarily by Louis XVIII in 1814, but abolished in 1830.

The events of both the amalgamation in 1607 and what exactly happened in 1830, have been disputed by historians. The Sovereign Order of St. John maintains uncompromisingly that the abolition of the amalgamated Order in 1830 was the end of the Order of St. Lazarus, and refuses to recognise those who continued an independent existence under the name of Knights of St. Lazarus of Jerusalem either after the amalgamation in 1607, or after the abolition of the amalgamated Order in 1830.

The Virgin and Child were portrayed on a medallion in the centre of the Order's cross.

THE MILITARY ORDER OF ST. HENRY
(Saxony)

The Order was founded in 1736 by Frederick Augustus II, Elector of Saxony and King of Poland (1733-63), to mark his fortieth birthday and to honour the saintly Saxon Emperor Henry II, and was given for meritorious deeds, regardless of religion and class.

The Badge, an eight-pointed gilded cross with a white-enamelled border, surmounted by a royal crown, and a green-enamelled trefoil-shaped garland showing between the arms, had at its centre a gilded medallion bearing an image of St. Henry in imperial robes, surrounded by a dark blue gold-rimmed band with the inscription VIRTUTI IN BELLO. The medallion on the reverse of the Badge showed the coat of arms of Saxony.[1]

The eight-pointed, gilded Star of the Order had the medallion of the obverse of the Badge in the centre and was worn on the left breast by Knights Grand Cross and Knights Commander. The ribbon of the Order was light blue with two yellow stripes.

As to this Order ever having been Catholic-founded, I have been unable to find any evidence to support this theory other than that it had been placed under the patronage of a Catholic Saint. Originally it had one

---

[1]This Order was also mentioned to me in 1983 when I was asked to remove the Polish Order of the White Eagle from the list of extinct Orders. Mons. Cardinale had originally attributed the Order to Poland which caused offense and provoked protests. It was pointed out to me that the Order was never conferred on Poles by Augustus III, or his successors, and that the insignia only show Saxon emblems.

class but in 1807 the Order was extended to four classes and reserved for Army Officers for valour on the battle field.

THE ROYAL HUNGARIAN ORDER OF ST. STEPHEN THE APOSTOLIC KING
(Austro-Hungarian Empire)

This Order was founded by Maria Theresia of Austria, Hungary and Bohemia in 1764. It was placed under the patronage of St. Stephen, the Apostolic King of Hungary (969-1038), to whom Hungary owes its conversion to Christianity. The Order was expressly founded to reward extraordinary civilian merit.

The first article of the statutes *Constitutiones In Signis Ordines Equitum S. Stephani Regis Apostolici* state that it is an Order of Knighthood, of which the Grand Master is always the King of Hungary, but that **the Order belongs inextricably to the Hungarian Crown of St. Stephen**. The last stipulation is the reason why historians continue to disagree on the date of the Order's abolition.

The Order was divided into three classes, with twenty Grand Crosses, thirty Knights Commander and fifty Knights. Bishops and Priests were appointed in addition and only on the Grand Master's personal decision. The statutes continue to explain the civil and peaceful character of the Order and expressly forbid that it can be conferred 'with swords' for military merit or valour. The Badge of the Order is a dark-green enamelled, gold-rimmed cross *pattée* moline, not unlike that of the Order of Maria-Theresia, the centre of the Cross having on the obverse a medallion with the Hungarian armorial bearings in relief: on a green triple mount rests a golden crown from which rises a double-traversed patriarchal cross, on the left and right arms of the cross are the letters M and T (for Maria-Theresia). The medallion is encircled by a white-enamelled, gold-rimmed ring with, in gold, the motto of the Order: PUBLICUM MERITORUM PRAEMIUM (a reward for public merit), which is divided at the bottom centre by a five-pointed gold star. On the reverse the cross has at its centre a whiteenamelled, gold-rimmed medallion surrounded by a wreath of stylised oak leaves, with a three-line inscription: STO. | ST.RI. | AP. (Sancto Stephano, Regi Apostolico – St. Stephen, the Apostolic King). The ribbon and sash of the Order is crimson with broad dark green borders. The cross is surmounted by the Crown of St. Stephen.

Knights of the Grand Cross wear an eight-pointed, diamond cut, faceted silver Star. (The original Grand Cross had a larger embroidered gold tinsel star, and the medallion in the centre has the armorial bearings

The Royal Hungarian Order of St. Stephen the Apostolic King was considered not to have been abolished in 1918 when the Habsburg Dynasty came to an end. In 1920, the Head of State continued to confer the Order because, according to the statutes it belongs inextricably to the Hungarian Crown of St. Stephen and not to any Dynasty. The Order was suppressed under the Communist domination of Hungary in 1945.

Courtesy: Garrison Collection

of Hungary as in the cross, while the oak leaf circle, surrounding the medallion is bordered inside and out with small pearls.

On special festive occasions, the Grand Cross was worn on a golden collar, consisting of twenty-five Crowns of St. Stephen and thirteen monograms SS (Sanctus Stephanus) adorned at the top with a rose, and twelve monograms of the intertwined letters MT (Maria-Theresia), and the Knights Grand Cross wore their ceremonial robes.

The insignia of the Order had to be returned to the Grand Chancery on the death of a recipient.

Officially the Royal Hungarian Order of St. Stephen, the Apostolic King, ceased to exist with the end of the Habsburg monarchy in 1918, however, in 1920, Admiral Nicholas Vitéz Horthy de Nagybanjya became 'Reichsverweser' of the Kingdom of Hungary. This title is very difficult to translate, and the interpretation 'Regent of the Kingdom of Hungary', as it appears in some English reference books is wrong and misleading. A Regent reigns for a Monarch-in-waiting, either because the legitimate Monarch is under age or mentally incapacitated, and the Regent reigns until the next Monarch can take his rightful place. Admiral Horthy was not 'reigning' for anybody but in his own right as the 'Reichsverweser'. The word 'Reich' is more of an equivalent to a republican Realm; a 'Verweser' is a person who acts as chief-executive, with the full power of a Head of State.

On 20 August 1938, Admiral Horthy decreed that the Order of St. Stephen, the Apostolic King, was not to be regarded as having become extinct with the abolition of the Dynasty of Habsburg, but as all rights of and in the Order rested with the Hungarian Crown of St. Stephen according to the statutes of the Order, he assumed the title of Grand Master of the Order and continued to bestow it as the Head of State of Hungary.

Although he appears to have found a *modus vivendi* with Hitler during the second World War, he was arrested in 1944 and taken to Germany. After the war he spent his exile in Portugal, where he died in 1957. The Order was finally abolished by the Government of Hungary in 1945.

Chapter Ten

THE MILITARY AND HOSPITALLER ORDER OF ST. LAZARUS OF JERUSALEM

I

'Lazare, Veni Foras!'

This chapter may be contentious for some readers who will probably criticise me for including it. Such criticism may be to some degree justified, because I have previously been uncompromising in my refusal even to mention the subject matter.

Some critics have called me intransigent and blind to reality. I ignored them, because the criteria I used when revising Archbishop Cardinale's *Orders of Knighthood, Awards and the Holy See* in 1984 and 1985, and wrote relevant comments in *The Cross on the Sword* in 1987, had remained unchanged since Mons. Cardinale decided in 1981 that it would be in the interest of all concerned to declare the Order of St. Lazarus nonexistent. He was provoked into doing so by one person who claimed to be a leading figure in the Order, and whose conduct towards Archbishop Cardinale and the Holy See was objectionable.

In 1982 Archbishop Cardinale asked me to remove from the book a chapter which had in 1981 twice been drafted in collaboration with Lord Mowbray, Segrave and Stourton, Premier Baron of England, whose family links with the Order of St. Lazarus go back to the first Baron Mowbray who in 1283 founded a St. Lazarus Hospital for Lepers on his own land near Melton Mowbray.

Subsequent events did nothing to change my mind, until in 1987 as a result of a great number of enquiries I had received from members of the European Episcopate, I wrote formally to the Secretariat of State asking whether it might not be expedient to have the position of the Order of St. Lazarus reviewed by independent experts before further compounding the negative attitude I had to adopt in *The Cross on the Sword*. The then *Sostituto* of the Secretariat of State, Archbishop Eduardo Martinez Somalo, replied without delay and informed me that he saw no reason for the Holy See to do so.

During one of my stays in the Vatican with Archbishop Cesare Zacchi later in 1987, I was visited by a Bishop and a Prelate of the Roman Curia. They showed me several photographs and a report stating that Pope John Paul II had received members of the Order of St Lazarus of Jerusalem in private audience and had concelebrated Holy Mass with Cardinal

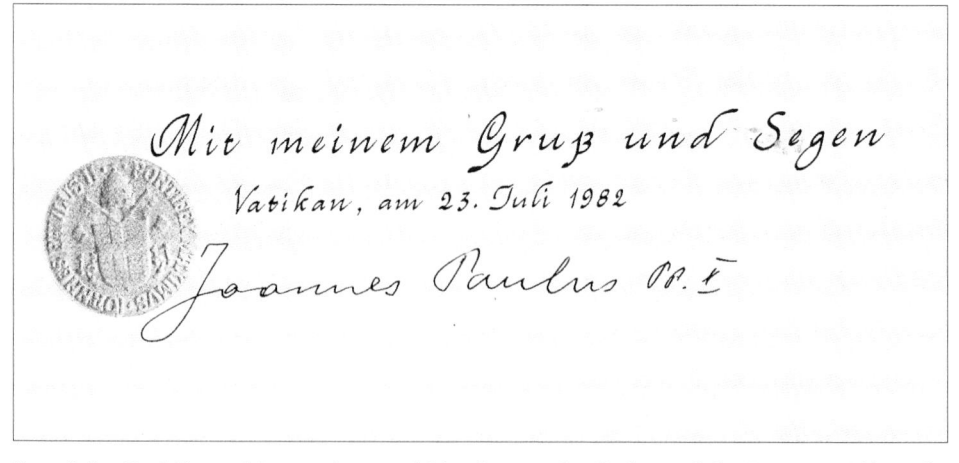

Mit meinem Gruß und Segen
Vatikan, am 23. Juli 1982
Joannes Paulus PP. II

Pope John Paul II sent his greetings and blessings to the Order and the Lazarus Hilfswerk.

Courtesy: Lazarus Hilfswerk, Deutschland

Macharski of Poland and Bishop Frotz, who represented the German Bishops Conference, as well as Prelates and Priests of the Order of St. Lazarus. During the private audience, His Holiness received a detailed report about the charitable contributions which had been placed at the disposal of the Holy Father and the Polish Bishops for the hungry and needy in Poland. By 1987, there had been over 300 trucking expeditions, and the cost of this particular Polish relief programme was in excess of twenty million US dollars. Pope John Paul II spent much time in conversation with the members of the St. Lazarus delegation, especially with Mr. Klaus-Peter Pokolm, the President of the Lazarus-Hilfswerk. Later the Pope accepted the first of the medals struck to commemorate the Relief Fund for Poland and arranged for photographs to be taken of the event.

I was informed that His Holiness had expressed his astonishment that these chivalrous benefactors had not received any recognition of their Order and indicated that he would make enquiries. This information was corroborated for me in 1987 and again in 1992 by His Eminence Cardinal Jacques Martin, who had been present at the discussions in his capacity as Prefetto della Casa Pontificia. The Bishop, who had followed up the

His Holiness Pope John Paul II concelebrated a Mass of thanks-giving in his private chapel for the help sent to Poland in his private chapel with Cardinal Macharski, Prelates and Chaplains of the Order for a delegation of the Order and the Lazarus Hilfswerk. In 1982 the Pope gave his Apostolic Blessing to the work done by the Order in Poland's greatest hour of need. By 1987, over 300 conveys with food and medicine had gone to Poland.

Courtesy: The American Grand Priory & Lazarus Hilfswerk

question about some form of recognition for the Order, had been given no direct reply by the Secretariat of State, but a senior member of the Secretariat suggested that the Bishop might consider private initiative. When he enquired what 'private initiative' implied, he was told to speak to me as I was in Rome. I visited the Secretariat of State twice with Cardinal Martin and Archbishop Zacchi between the visits of the two Prelates, but nothing was mentioned to me about the request which had been made to the Secretariat of State by them concerning the Order of St. Lazarus.

Several times during 1991 and 1992, I met Polish Bishops who conveyed to me the renewed and express wish of the Holy Father that I should try and acknowledge the work of those meritorious Grand Priories of the Military Hospitaller Order of St. Lazarus that had done so much for the hungry and needy in Poland and Eastern Europe, though His Holiness was aware that there were members of the Curia and other interested parties in Rome who opposed any form of recognition of the Order of St. Lazarus and the Lazarus-Hilfswerk or its work in Poland. I

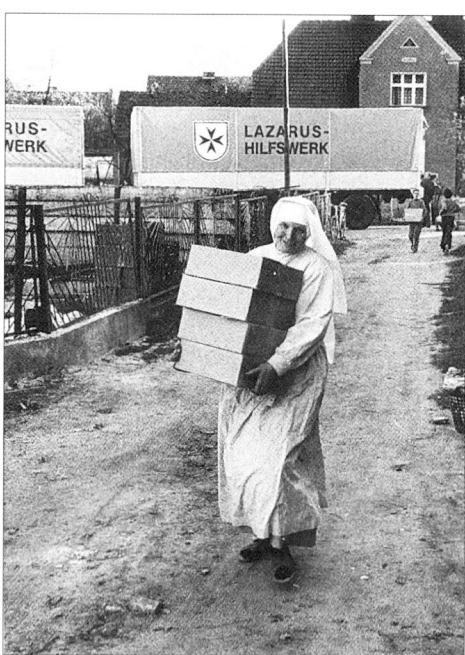

His Eminence Cardinal Macharski, Archbishop of Krakow, and Mons. Klaus Dick, Auxiliary Bishop of Cologne and Episcopal Vicar, in Düsseldorf when they blessed one of the convoys of trucks destined for Poland.

Courtesy: Lazarus Hilfswerk

The Polish Bishops planned and decided with Chev. Klaus Peter Pokolm, the President of the Lazarus Hilfswerk, where individual trucks were to be sent. Volunteers were then organised in Poland to await their arrival.

Courtesy: Lazarus Hilfswerk

agreed to abide by the personal wishes of the Holy Father, and this was much welcomed by some Cardinals and Bishops but, as I soon discovered, angrily denounced by other members of the Roman Curia. Although I made it clear from the outset that I had not yielded to any pressure from the Order of St. Lazarus, and, indeed, none of the above-mentioned Grand Priories had ever contacted me, I soon realised that the Pope's intervention did not change the attitude of those who were opposed to my even acknowledging the existence of that Order.

Towards the end of 1992, I received detailed reports of the work the Order of St. Lazarus in Eastern Europe. As much of this was said to have taken place under the auspices of the European Economic Community in Brussels, I asked for, and received, official reports about the outstanding charitable work undertaken in Eastern European countries by the German Grand Priory of the Order of St. Lazarus of Jerusalem under the tireless leadership of their late Grand Prior, the Prince von Metternich, the Princess von Metternich, who succeeded him as Grand Prior, and by the Lazarus-Hilfswerk (the President of which is Mr. Klaus-Peter Pokolm), by

Some trucks contained urgently needed medical equipment and medicines for the children's hospital in Wadowice, the birthplace of the Pope. This hospital was also built with the support of the Order and of the Lazarus Hilfswerk.

Courtesy: Lazarus Hilfswerk, Deutschland

the Grand Priory of America, under their Grand Prior, Dr. Hans von Leden, (who is also the Order's Grand Hospitaller), and members of the Order in Canada.

With the personal encouragement of Pope John Paul II and Cardinal Macharski of Krakow, the Grand Priory of Austria, under Archduke Leopold of Austria and Dr. Heinz Peter Baron von Slatin, and their Referendary Prof. Franz Josef Federsel, had constructed the first Hospice for the terminally ill in Poland, the St. Lazarus Hospice, in Nowa Huta, the American Grand Priory providing substantial financial assistance to this project.

The Grand Priory of France, under the late Pierre de Cossé, 12th Duc de Brissac, was particularly active in initiating the relief programmes of the Order in Croatia. The Chancellor, Chevalier Guy Coutant de Saisseval, strongly backed the relief missions of the Grand Hospitaller throughout Eastern Europe. The trucks, trailers, field kitchens and jeeps that were provided by the Order have continued to be used by the Order's members for humanitarian purposes only, and they remain the property of the Order.

Left: In October 1992, Pope John Paul II received Dr. Hans von Leden, Grand Prior of the Order in America and Grand Hospitaller for the entire Order, to thank him for the financial help he had organised and which had made the successful convoys possible. In the centre, between Dr.von Leden and the Holy Father stand Rt.Rev. Father V.A.McInnes, OP, the Senior Prelate of the Order in America. Right: After becoming the new Republic's first President, Mr. Lech Walesa paid a visit to the Headquarters of the Lazarus Hilfswerk in Cologne, Germany. Chev. Klaus Peter Pokolm, the President of the Lazarus Hilfswerk (right) presented President Walesa with two trucks and trailers laden with medicine; President Walesa is wearing the Medal 'Dank für Polenhilfe'. (See also: colour section on Poland).

Courtesy: Lazarus Hilfswerk, Deutschland

During the Winter of 1991/92, the European Community in Brussels earmarked US$125,000,000.00 worth of aid for food for the starving population in Russia. Transport and distribution were to be provided by organisations chosen by the European Community. Apart from the humanitarian aspects, it is a fact that this aid programme also prevented large scale social unrest and political instability in urban centres. Of this sum the European Community allocated half to the International Red Cross, and half to the Order of St. Lazarus of Jerusalem as represented by the Lazarus-Hilfswerk. For this purpose the Order set up three centres, in St. Petersburg, Moscow and Novgorad from which they operated their distribution system.

To satisfy myself about the correctness of the reports I had received, I also requested detailed information from the appropriate offices of the European Community, so I would have the evidence in my possession should there be claims that the reports were untrue. A letter from H.I.R.H. Archduke Dr. Otto von Habsburg, signed in his capacity as a Member of the European Parliament and addressed to the Grand Hospitaller of the Order of St. Lazarus of Jerusalem, Dr. Hans von Leden, Grand Prior of America, testifies to the high esteem in which the Grand Hospitaller and his work are held by the European Parliament.

For an Order the existence of which had so often been denied when I made official enquiries, and that I was obliged to consider extinct, the German, American, Austrian, some other Grand Priories and particularly their foundation, the Lazarus-Hilfswerk, have been remarkably active. These jurisdictions have also spent substantial amounts of their own money on charitable works and projects close to the heart of Pope John Paul II, the Polish and other Eastern European members of the College of Cardinals and the Polish and Eastern European Episcopate, as well as in other areas of activity.

For example, the Canadian Grand Priory works extensively in the field of Hansen's Disease (leprosy), both in the areas of research and of support services. In this and other fields, the Canadian Grand Priory has worked closely with the Venerable Order of St. John of Jerusalem, and many of the officers of the Grand Priory of the Order of St. Lazarus are also officers in the Venerable Order. Similarly, Grand Priories in New Zealand and Australia have been providing support for the victims of Hansen's Disease in their own countries and the islands of Oceania.

When faced with the task of assessing meritorious, chivalrous work on a vast scale instead of simply writing about a Catholic-founded Order of Knighthood in the context of other Orders, there is a danger of compiling an activity report rather than keeping strictly to the criteria upon which the book is based. However, very rarely something catches one's attention which seems to be so small, but in reality symbolises all that chivalry is about. I had learned incidentally that part of the contribution several

The construction of the hospice for the dying, built with the Order's support under the direction of Col. Prof. Franz Josef Federsel of the Austrian Grand Priory, who reports regularly to the Pope on the progress that is made.

Courtesy: Col.Prof. F.J.Federsel, Austria

Commanderies of the Order of St. Lazarus of Jerusalem expect their members to make are twelve full days a year given free of charge to work in hospitals and institutions which cater for the mentally or physically sick, the hungry and the needy, or do social work that benefits those who need help.

I was particularly impressed by the activities of the nine members of the Order in Liechtenstein: under their Commander, they set up in 1990 an emergency telephone helpline for the children of the Principality, 'Sorgen-Telefon für Kinder in Liechtenstein'. They give their time freely, answering calls in rotation twenty-four hours a day, seven days a week, throughout the year. Posters about this service are displayed in schools, and stickers are displayed in telephone booths and public places throughout the Principality. The members have been professionally trained as counsellors for this particular task, and they receive well over 300 calls from children every year out of a population of 30,000.

Other jurisdictions of the Order in Europe, South America and Africa are active in charitable activities, and the work of the Order in such countries as South Africa and Zimbabwe is remarkable, and some European Grand Priories still work as hospitallers in the way that members of the Order did in the early years of its existence, much of their work still concerned with fighting leprosy. Others, such as France, the Netherlands, Switzerland, and Bohemia, assist the Grand Hospitaller in relief work for the hungry and needy in several Eastern European countries.

Ancient insignia of the Order. Top and bottom row: three 18th century Badges cast in solid gold; centre left: 1788 tinsel Star of a Knight Grand Cross; centre right: a Badge dating from 1850.

Courtesy: Garrison Collection

This is an impressive list of charitable activities, and equally impressive are the official acknowledgements of gratitude from governments and especially the Headquarters of the European Community in Brussels.

There are several imitation orders which also use the name 'of St. Lazarus of Jerusalem' and certain individuals who claim to belong to, or to represent, 'The Military and Hospitaller Order of St. Lazarus'. They are at the root of much of the hostility which has been shown towards the Order, but their organisations have not demonstrated the same Spirit of Christian chivalry in this troubled world. As I mentioned earlier, there are at least eighteen very active imitation orders of the Sovereign Military Order of Malta and the Venerable Order of St. John of Jerusalem, all claiming to be the true Order of St. John of Jerusalem. All these imitation orders lay claim to chivalric privileges but show little or no inclination to take upon themselves the duties and responsibilities of true chivalry, and all of them hope to be mistaken for the genuine and legitimate Orders.

His Beatitude the Greek Melchite Catholic Patriarch Maximos V Hakim, the Spiritual Protector of the Order of St. Lazarus, and His Eminence Cardinal Ernesto Corripio, the Spiritual Counsellor of the Order's Grand Priory of America, with the enthusiastic support of several Cardinals, Archbishops, Bishops and Prelates from Poland, the U.S.A., Germany, Austria, Mexico and other Central and Eastern European countries, have often expressed their regret at the Holy See's policy of refusing to recognise officially the Order. The members of the hierarchy who actively support the Military and Hospitaller Order of St. Lazarus are members of the Roman Curia and the Cardinals and some of the Archbishops and Bishops are actually members the Holy See. They consider it unfair and against the principles of chivalry to withhold rightful recognition from the Order, and strongly reject the suggestion that the Military and Hospitaller Order of Saint Lazarus of Jerusalem should be merely accorded the status of a charitable society. They regard the Order as an Hospitaller Order of Knighthood, the 48th Grand Master of which is His Excellency François de Cossé, the 13th Duc de Brissac. As I have noted in earlier chapters, for reasons of international law, the Holy See cannot recognise any Order other than the Pontifical Orders, the Sovereign Military Order of Malta, the Order of the Holy Sepulchre, and those Orders granted by sovereign States with which it entertains diplomatic relations. However, the Apostolic See as represented by the Supreme Pontiff can express cognizance of the Order's status.

I am not introducing with this chapter a subject which might be seen by some as deliberately confrontational, but in the light of the express obligations which have been placed upon me since 1983, with particular reference to the Order of St. Lazarus – obligations I adhered to without reservation until I was informed of the Pope's wishes – I find it puzzling that eminent spiritual members of the Order should have been advised semi-officially to seek the help of the Sovereign Military Order of Malta to gain recognition as an Order of Knighthood from the Holy See.

It is a fallacy to believe that the Sovereign Military Order of Malta would or could obtain official recognition from the Holy See for the

The organisation of convoys carrying food and medicine to Eastern Europe is in the hands of Chev. Klaus Peter Pokolm, who arranges their destinations with the Commissioner of the European Union, the relevant authorities of the country where the convoy will go and, as often as possible with the Grand Hospitaller of the Order, Dr. Hans von Leden. The attendance of the high dignitaries at the departure of a convoy is designed to show that all members, from the most illustrious leaders of the order and of the Lazarus Hilfswerk to the hospitaller volunteers who load the trucks, are united in their work to alleviate hunger and need among their Eastern European neighbours.
H.S.H.the Duke de Brissac, Grand Master of the Order, and H.S.H.the Duchesse de Brissac (wearing the Order's mantle) and the Spiritual Protector of the Order, His Beatitude Patriarch Maximos V with the President of the Lazarus Hilfswerk, Chev. K.P.Pokolm (in uniform) watch the departure of a convoy carrying aid to Hungary.

Courtesy: Lazarus Hilfswerk, Deutschland

Military and Hospitaller Order of Saint Lazarus of Jerusalem through its intercession. In fact, whenever I have corresponded with the competent representative of the Sovereign Council of the Sovereign Order, I have always been informed that the Sovereign Order would never be prepared to give to the Military and Hospitaller Order of St. Lazarus of Jerusalem any form of confraternal recognition.

In fact, the Sovereign Military Order of Malta has published its view of, and attitude to, the Military and Hospitaller Order of St. Lazarus of Jerusalem in a joint declaration of the 'False Orders Committee' of the Federation of the Orders of St. John. Apart from the Sovereign Military Order of Malta, it is made up of internationally recognised Orders that have been incorporated in the list of Orders of Knighthood under the sovereignty of the respective heads of state, and is mainly concerned with imitation Orders of St. John, but it has always shown a special interest in the Order of St. Lazarus and its activities.

This and the repeated statements sent me by the representative of the Sovereign Council of the Sovereign Military Order of Malta, contradict all the vague promises which were made to a Spiritual Counsellor of the Order of St. Lazarus with regard to 'recognition by the Holy See'. As the criteria upon which the Holy See recognises Orders of Knighthood exist and are strictly adhered to, any special intercession would be totally useless.

This again raises the important question as to whether the criteria for recognition applied by the Holy See to Orders of Knighthood or Merit that do not form part of an honours system of sovereign States, and the decorations conferred by them, need reappraisal. Personally I doubt that the Holy See will change its practice.

In the past, it has not been unknown for some Popes to organise amalgamations of Orders. In today's terminology, such amalgamations would be considered 'take-overs', especially when the assets of an Order are absorbed by another. This has happened to the Order of St. Lazarus twice before: Pope Sixtus IV (1471-1484) tried unsuccessfully to have the Knights absorbed into the Order of St. John of Jerusalem, but in 1573 Pope Gregory XIII amalgamated the wealthy Italian Commanderies of St. Lazarus of Jerusalem with the Order of St. Maurice of the House of Savoy. Another, similar amalgamation took place in 1608 under Pope Paul V, when for political and economic reasons, he sanctioned the amalgamation of the Order's wealthy French Commanderies with the Order of Our Lady of Mount Carmel which had been founded by King Henri IV of France the year before.

The Order of St. Lazarus of Jerusalem was not the only Order of Knighthood to have been thus absorbed with its assets into another Order. The fate of the Knights Templars is well documented; in France many were arrested and subjected to mockeries of trials, some just

The label on all consignments sent by the Order under the auspices of the European Community to Eastern Europe.

Courtesy: Lazarus Hilfswerk, Deutschland

murdered, and the Order's great wealth divided up between interested parties. Having escaped such a fate, the Knights of St. Lazarus had much to be thankful for.

Assets of Orders are no longer only land and castles, but the money and assets of their individual members, especially when much of it has been converted into trucks, trailers, jeeps and field kitchens for the relief of the hungry and needy in the world. In addition, an Order's activities, and especially its reputation for efficiency in administering large charitable relief projects, are also tangible assets: indeed, in commercial terms, the good name of a company or business can be the greatest of them.

Why, one must ask, did the European Community ask the Order of St. Lazarus to distribute food and other aid worth 125 million US dollars? There were several organisations besides the International Red Cross and the Order of St. Lazarus in contention to carry out this enormous task, and I am sure that the Commissioners of the European Community who are responsible for allocating such vast sums of money, form their judgement and decision on very sound criteria.

However far-reaching such judgements and decisions have been, the criteria upon which they were based are not the criteria upon which 'purists', as they are styled, judge the status of chivalry.

If we ignore the splinter groups and separate, self-styled orders of St. Lazarus that abound in some countries, the question must be asked as to the juridical and chivalric status of The Military and Hospitaller Order of St. Lazarus of Jerusalem, with special reference to the Grand Priories of America, Canada, Germany and Austria whose work is so greatly appreciated by the Supreme Pontiff and the Most Eminent and Most Reverend Members of the Roman Curia, who have expressly asked that the Order to which the above-mentioned Grand Priories belong, should not be denied a chivalric-hospitaller status.

As I have emphasized time and again, my task is to chronicle the evolution of Catholic-founded Orders and their either continued or no longer existing relationship with the Apostolic See. I personally cannot grant recognition to anybody, and the whole concept of recognition is a very complex one. If the Holy Father, not as Sovereign Pontiff but as Supreme Pontiff and Pastor, recognises true chivalric works and merit, it is his prerogative to ask, indeed command me, to reflect his personal cognizance in a book that deals specifically with Catholic-founded Orders and the Holy See, the Apostolic See and the Papacy. Nobody can deny, regardless of the Order's evolution, that the Military Hospitaller Order of St. Lazarus of Jerusalem is a *Catholic-founded* Hospitaller Order of Knighthood.

Having endeavoured to present an objective record of the activities of the above-mentioned Grand Priories of The Military and Hospitaller Order of St. Lazarus of Jerusalem, as I was specifically asked to do, the reader may be tempted to think that these outstanding charitable accomplishments would be automatically reflected in the juridical status of the Order, its standing in the community of Catholic-founded Orders of Knighthood and its recognition. I consider the Supreme Pontiff's cognizance of the chivalric work of the Order on a par – if one speaks of justice rather than of law – with the Pope's continued cognizance of Orders of Knighthoood that have continued their loyal devotion to His Holiness and the Church in participating in the ceremonial and liturgy of the Church. I do not believe that His Holiness has ever given any consideration to the – sometimes very remote – possibility that some of the Orders of non-regnant dynasties may sooner or later become once again Orders of sovereign monarchs.

The statement published in *L'Osservatore Romano* on 22 March 1953 and again on 14 December 1970 lists the name 'St. Lazarus' among the 'deplorable phenomenon of the appearance of alleged Orders of Knighthood originating from private initiatives and aiming at replacing the legitimate forms of chivalric awards and not approved of or recognised by the Holy See'. In the same statement, the Holy See condemns Orders using the appellations: 'Military', 'Equestrian', 'Royal', 'Sovereign', 'Religious', 'Sacred' and similar titles. According to the statement such appellations belong exclusively to authentic Orders approved by the Holy See. There have been five pontificates since 1953, and if the Catholic-founded Orders of Knighthood of some non-regnant dynasties have a specific lay apostolate, then it may indeed be necessary for the Holy See to look at the subject again and, if necessary, introduce different levels or types of cognizance, if not full recognition in international law. I feel this is especially necessary if the definition in the *Codex Iuris Canonici* that equates the Holy See with the Apostolic See is to be realised without having constantly to refer to the opt-out clause about the *context* in which the names 'Holy See' and 'Apostolic See' are used.

However, there is the third factor which has to be consideration: the personal opinion and wishes of a Suprem Canon Law the personal opinions and wishes of a Pope fall i:

The hundreds of self-styled orders can find no comfort ⌐_ __, the Pope's wish to see the chivalrous work of the above-mentioned Grand Priories recognised. The self-styled Orders serve one purpose only: the vanity of men and women to enhance their appearance by decorating themselves with pieces of enamel and metal, the only value of which is what people are prepared to pay for them.

As far as the Military and Hospitaller Order of St. Lazarus of Jerusalem is concerned, the question of sovereignty, or the lack of it, is often raised by its critics. During the Crusade, in the 12th century, the city of Acre was temporarily placed under the sovereignty of the Order; this protection was later shared by other Orders that had been fighting in the Crusades. However, it would make nonsense of the ideals and principles governing these Orders to justify their existence on some very short-lived temporal power they enjoyed. Only the Order of St. John of Jerusalem, (now the Sovereign Military Order of Malta) continued to exercise sovereign power in different places.

This raises another important issue: following the independence of Croatia and its recognition by many States, including the Holy See, the Croatian Government promulgated and published on 6 May 1992 in Zagreb the *Projet de Décret de Reconnaissance* which recognises The Military and Hospitaller Order of St. Lazarus of Jerusalem, which had been largely responsible for the distribution of aid for the care and relief of refugees during its struggle for freedom, as an Order of Knighthood legitimately active in the sovereign territory of Croatia. The Decree has four Articles, three of which grant specific privileges to the Order, the fourth states the date of ratification of the Decree and declares the intent of the Croatian Government to inform other foreign powers that the decree had been lawfully signed on behalf of the Republic of Croatia.

The increasing hostility between Serbia, Bosnia and Croatia since that document was issued by the Croatian Government, and the fact that at the time of writing these words the territorial boundaries are changing almost daily, have no bearing on the legitimacy of the *Projet de Décret de Reconnaissance* which was issued by a member state of the United Nations. The Republic of Hungary and South Africa have followed with similar statements recognising the Order.

Has this in any way changed the Order's juridical or sovereign status? I

---

[1]Archbishop Cardinale's *The Holy See and the International Order*, Gerrards Cross, 1976, is the seminal work on the rôle of the Pope, the Holy See and the Apostolic See. In it he distinguishes between 'direct' power and 'indirect' power exercised by the Pope, especially when he neither pontificates on spiritual matters nor rules on matters inherent in the sovereignty of the Holy See or as Head of the Vatican City State. The wish of the Pope to see the chivalrous work of three Priories and the Lazarus Hilfswerk recognised must fall into a clearly defined category of the exercise of papal power.

know of no precedent where the recognition of an Order of Knighthood by a sovereign state has conferred a sovereign status on that Order, unless the Order were to establish its seat in that country and the State were to take the Order under its national sovereign protection.

The Knights of the Italian Commanderies of the Order of St. Lazarus, amalgamated in 1573 with the Savoyan Order of St. Maurice, have continued to exist in the Savoyan dynastic Order of St. Maurice and Lazarus. Many Knights of the French and other Commanderies were strongly opposed to an amalgamation with the Order of Our Lady of Mount Carmel under the protection of the King of France and refused to be absorbed by an Order that had only been founded the previous year, and they appear to have continued to exist independently.[1] After those Knights who had been amalgamated with the Order of Our Lady of Mount Carmel in 1608 had lost their temporal protection with the downfall of King Charles X in 1830, many joined the Commanderies that had refused to agree to the amalgamation of 1608. After that, the Knights of St. Lazarus were governed by a Council of Officers.

Eleven years later, in 1841, the Military and Hospitaller Order of St. Lazarus of Jerusalem requested the protection of the Greek Melchite Catholic Patriarch of Antioch, Maximos III Mazlûm, and petitioned that he become their Spiritual Protector; he accepted, both for himself and his successors.[2]

Eastern Patriarchs, whether autonomous or in union with the Roman Church, always refer to their patriarchate or religious jurisdiction as 'a nation'. Arab Sovereigns and Princes accord to them the status of a Head of State, though this must be seen in the light of political expediency, as an Islamic ruler cannot accord any honour to the leader of another religion.

On 19 January 1928, Pope Pius XI addressed a message through the papal Secretary of State, Cardinal Gasparri, to the Marquis Française de Saint-Lazare, the President of the French Association of the Knights of St. Lazarus:

'The Holy Father kindly accepts the filial homage.... offering in turn his best wishes for the prosperity of the Hospitallers of St. Lazarus of Jerusalem and their families, sends them all a special benediction.' (Reference 3511/27)

Whilst remaining under the spiritual protection of the Greek Melchite Catholic Patriarch, in 1935 the Chapter General of the Order elected as the new Grand Master Don Francisco de Bórbon y de la Torre, 3rd Duke of Seville.

---

[1] A private collector in the U.S.A. owns many examples of insignia of the Order dating from the 18th and 19th centuries that show beyond any doubt that an independent Order of St. Lazarus continued to exist.

[2] Catholic Eastern Patriarchs in Union with the Holy Roman Church have always retained a degree of autonomy, and only a papal interdict against the Order of St. Lazarus or the Patriarch could have prevented him from agreeing to become the Spiritual Protector of the Order.

Whilst the Order of St. Lazarus of Jerusalem requires that all its members are practising Christians, its statutes no longer make membership dependent upon membership of the Roman Catholic Church.

As the Supreme Pontiff, John Paul II, joined by members of the College of Cardinals, has on more than one occasion invited a group of people collectively as members of the Military and Hospitaller Order of St. Lazarus of Jerusalem to his private apartments in the Vatican, has celebrated Holy Mass with them in his private chapel, and continues to encourage them to undertake charitable projects which he monitors personally, can the recognition, trust and gratitude expressed by the Supreme Pontiff to those who have been directly involved in these projects, be without significance?

This will probably raise the perennial question of *ipso facto* recognition. However, I have always stressed in the past, and I do so now, that the neither the Apostolic See nor Holy See recognise anything or anybody *ipso facto*.

As far as I am concerned, a wish of the Supreme Pontiff, that has been conveyed to me on several occasions, is something I cannot ignore, regardless of who disagrees with the Holy Father's personal wishes and judgement in this matter. I reiterate, however, that in this case, as in several others, I am in no position to express the consensus of views held by all members of the Roman Curia.

For this reason I have focused my main attention on the Order's Grand Priories of America, Germany, and of Austria. For a number of years, these jurisdictions have been at the forefront of charitable and humanitarian projects supported by Pope John Paul II, and they were specifically singled out by him for their praiseworthy chivalric activities.

With the sole exception of the Sovereign Military Order of Malta, to whom the Supreme Pontiff appoints a Cardinal Patron, and the Equestrian Order of the Holy Sepulchre of Jerusalem, to whom the Pope appoints a Cardinal Grand Master, no other official appointments of Cardinals by the Supreme Pontiff are made, although individual Cardinals or high Prelates sometimes receive the Holy Father's express permission to act as Spiritual Counsellors to particular Orders of Knighthood. By the same token the Apostolic See has been known to expressly ask dignitaries of the Church to withdraw from any activities within some organisations. In such cases the Supreme Pontiff, acting through the Prefect of the Apostolic Court or the Papal Secretary of State, would as a matter of principle refuse to receive in private audience representatives of an Order or organisation of which he disapproves.

On 28 and 29 October 1992, members of the American, German, Austrian, and Canadian Grand Priories, with pilgrims from other jurisdictions of the Order of St. Lazarus of Jerusalem, under the leadership of the Order's Grand Hospitaller and Grand Prior of America, Dr. Hans von Leden, attended the celebrations of the silver jubilee of the Patriarchate of the Order's Spiritual Protector, His Beatitude Maximos V Hakim, in the Vatican. His Holiness Pope John Paul II made a special point of singling out and greeting the Grand Hospitaller from the tens of thousands who were present at the General Audience, and afterwards he invited Patriarch Maximos V Hakim to a special audience on the occasion of his jubilee, and Dr. Hans von Leden and the members of the Order to a private audience for the next day in the Sala Regia in the Apostolic Palace, where His Holiness spoke to every member individually, thanking them for the work they had done.

All the above-mentioned events, beginning with the continuation of activities of the Knights of the Military and Hospitaller Order of Saint Lazarus of Jerusalem before and after the dissolution of the Order of Our Lady of Mount Carmel and St. Lazarus of Jerusalem in 1830, to the present day, create a dilemma for me when assessing the Order's correct status and style. Before writing this chapter, I wrote to the two surviving Hospitaller Orders of Knighthood who with the Order of St. Lazarus share a common history in the early Crusades. The then Governor-General (now Lieutenant General) of the Equestrian Order of the Holy Sepulchre of Jerusalem, Prince Paolo Enrico Massimo Lancellotti, replied that as a matter of principle the Equestrian Order of the Holy Sepulchre of Jerusalem never comments on other Orders or organisations. The High Historical Consultant of the Sovereign Military Order of Malta, Frà Cyril, The Prince Toumanoff, stated unequivocally that the Sovereign Order would as a matter of principle never recognise the Military Hospitaller Order of St. Lazarus of Jerusalem.

As I said above, there are several self-styled organisations in existence that use the same name but have nothing to do with those who are the subject of this chapter. If we search for a *fons honorum* of the Order, there is no hereditary successor to a former reigning sovereign who claims the Order as a dynastic institution. The Duc de Brissac, a member of one of Europe's most ancient ducal houses, is the Order's Grand Master, and it should be noted that holders of this office are elected: it is not hereditary.

I mentioned at the beginning of the book that the criteria upon which chivalric orders are judged are being questioned inside the Roman Curia. The fact that the Military and Hospitaller Order of St. Lazarus of Jerusalem has members belonging to various Christian denominations, makes it impossible to judge it solely on Catholic criteria, in spite of the fact that the Order has had a Catholic Patriarch as its Spiritual Protector since 1841, and today a number of Cardinals and high dignitaries of the Roman Curia are Spiritual Counsellors to various Grand Priories.

There are two important issues raised in the previous paragraph: first, the Knights who in 1841 approached the Greek Catholic Melchite

Patriarch of Antioch and asked him to take the Order under his protection, did so because they felt that under the circumstances their most logical step was to go back to the Middle East where the Order had been founded and seek spiritual protection there. Secondly, whilst the Order's appellation 'Hospitaller' is self-evident by its activities, the Order defines its appellation 'Military' in terms that conform to fundamental principles of the Second Vatican Council. The Grand Hospitaller, Dr. Hans von Leden, said: 'We are a Military Order because we fight for Christian Unity. Much of our work is dedicated to that aim, and we endeavour to adhere to the fundamental Christian values.'

The Order does not style itself 'oecumenical' because it maintains that this term and 'oecumenism' have changed their original meaning: they used to imply Christian Unity, but over the last few decades they have no longer made fundamental Christian values a criterion, so that 'oecumenical' now means 'tolerance and coexistence between faiths of different cultures'. Whilst the Military Hospitaller Order of St. Lazarus of Jerusalem is committed to tolerance towards, and peaceful coexistence with, other faiths, it seeks to operate on strictly fundamental Christian values and principles on which the Order will not compromise.

Some insignia of the Military Hospitaller Order of St. Lazarus of Jerusalem are reproduced in the section of colour plates on the Order.

The National Shrine of the American Grand Priory in New Orleans.

Courtesy: The Grand Priory in America

The headquarters of the Knights of Columbus in New Haven, Connecticut.

Chapter Eleven

RECOGNIZED KNIGHTLY ORGANISATIONS

I am certain that more than two organisations could be placed in this category, but they are not listed because this chapter only appeared for the first time in the 1985, third edition of Archbishop Cardinale's book. The first two editions merely included a 'Corollary on the Association of the Knights of Columbus' at the end of the chapter dealing with self-styled and spurious Orders of Knighthood.

The then Cardinal Secretary of State and Grand Chancellor of all Pontifical Equestrian Orders, Agostino Cardinal Casaroli, objected to this and expressly asked that the Association should be given a separate chapter so as not to give the impression that it belonged to the category of self-styled Orders. He pointed out that the Association of the Knights of Columbus, founded in the USA in 1882, was now the world's largest organisation of Catholic men, and has always been engaged in charitable and chivalrous work. It had chosen the appellation 'knightly' association, but had never laid claim to being an Order of Knighthood, so the Cardinal considered it most unfortunate that it had been given such a short note positioned in such a way as to give the reader a totally incorrect impression about it.

In the 1985 edition of the book, therefore I gave the Knights of Columbus and its associated international fraternal organisations a short chapter to themselves, as I concurred with Cardinal Casaroli's view.

There was a second compelling reason for making the change: not only does the Association of the Knights of Columbus and its international associates, seen as a collective body, contain more Knights of Pontifical Equestrian Orders than any other organisation, but its Head, Supreme Knight Virgil C. Dechant, could be described as the most distinguished and decorated layman in the Catholic Church, the Curia and the Vatican City State. He holds the Grand Cross of the Pontifical Orders of Pius IX and of St. Gregory the Great, the highest class in the Orders of Merit of the Order of the Holy Sepulchre of Jerusalem and of the Sovereign Military Order of Malta, and he is also a Chamberlain of His Holiness, a Governor of the Vatican City State and a member of Pontifical Commissions and Tribunals. Many members of the Association have also been honoured with pontifical knighthoods for outstanding chivalrous work. However, the Association of the Knights of Columbus has never pretended to be an Order of Knighthood in its own right.

As to the other knightly organisation described in this chapter, when H.R.H. Dom Duarte Pio, Duke of Bragança and Head of the Royal House of Portugal, decided to change the status of the former Order of St. Michael of the Wing, which had been revived at the same time as the dynastic Royal Orders of The Conception of Our Lady of Vila Viçosa and of St. Isabel, calling it simply 'The Knights and Dames of St. Michael of the Wing', this chapter was the natural place for it.

Its lay apostolate was in charitable works; its original *raison d'être* as an Order of Knighthood no longer existed; it had been revived with entirely new aims; it would technically have had to be considered a new Order with an ancient name. Although members continue to be styled Knights or Dames of St. Michael of the Wing, its infrastructure is such that it is better described as a knightly association, with the Head of the Royal House as Patron rather than Grand Master, and a Chancellor who administers the international associated branches from headquarters in Portugal. This change of status and name in no way diminishes the role and function of the Knights and Dames of St. Michael of the Wing, it merely regularises the association's legal status. I must take responsibility for not recognising early enough several legal reasons why a revival of the Order could not be implemented as had initially been hoped.

When I was first asked to include in the book mention of Pope John Paul II's recognition of the chivalrous work of the three Grand Priories of the Military and Hospitaller Order of St. Lazarus[1], I suggested giving that Order a section in this chapter. Whilst the lack of sovereignty was frequently used by opponents who did not wish to see the Order being mentioned at all, let alone given a chapter to itself, protagonists of the Order in the Curia argued strongly that in both the chivalric and hospitaller fields, the Order of St. Lazarus of Jerusalem had continued to adhere to its founders' principles, and its *raison d'être* as an Hospitaller Order of Knighthood had remained the same, not only in the Commanderies that had been amalgamated with the Order of St. Maurice (House of Savoy) and later the Order of Our Lady of Mount Carmel (House of Bourbon of France), but in the independent groups which had placed themselves in 1841 under the patronage of the Greek Melchite Catholic Patriarch of Antioch.

As I have written in the Introduction to this work, and as has been publicly defined by Cardinal Casaroli in his address to the Association of the Knights of Columbus, the criteria for what constitutes a Christian Knight and Order of Knighthood have been undergoing a metamorphosis. There is no doubt that the Apostolic See, whilst meticulously observing the laws governing recognition of Orders of Knighthood and Merit under international law, also judges the *raison*

---

[1] See Chapter Ten.

d'être for continued existence of an Order and inherent but non-regnant sovereignty on merit.

After the publication of *The Cross on the Sword* in 1987, my attention was drawn by several independent sources to controversial legal issues that had arisen as a result of my inclusion of the Order of St. Michael of the Wing among the dynastic Orders of Portugal. I took counsel, especially of Cardinal Jacques Martin, who advised me to put this issue to the Duke of Bragança. His Royal Highness decided on a change in the status of the Knights and Dames of St. Michael of the Wing and the appellation of the association, relinquishing the position of Grand Master and taking on that of Patron.

Each step I took made me realise more and more how careful I had to be. As I have said repeatedly, I am in no position to grant recognition to any organisation. My brief has been to reflect the Apostolic See's view of, and attitude to, Catholic-founded Orders of Knighthood, extant and extinct. By the same token it has never been my brief to change the status of an Order of Knighthood unless an error had been made when including it in a particular category.

As I explain in Chapter Ten, there is no consensus of opinion in the Holy See or the Roman Curia about the Military and Hospitaller Order of St. Lazarus. On balance, I felt that the Pope's request to give full acknowledgement to their chivalrous work justified a separate chapter with special reference to those Grand Priories singled out by His Holiness.

I

THE ASSOCIATION OF THE KNIGHTS OF COLUMBUS

Several associations of Catholic men decribe their members as Knights but do not pretend to be an Order of Knighthood. It would therefore be unjust to confuse such associations with those self-styled and spurious orders described in Chapter Thirteen. They use the term 'knight' in the spirit it was used by the then Cardinal Secretary of State, Agostino Casaroli in 1982, when he attended the centenary celebrations of the Knights of Columbus in the USA as Papal Legate. In fact, speaking *ex officio* also as the Grand Chancellor of all Pontifical Orders, his definition of what constitutes the prerequisites of a Christian Knight, has been applied not only to the Pontifical Equestrian Orders, but also to the two Religious Orders of Knighthood and to those members of Catholic-founded dynastic Orders that continue to participate in the life of the Catholic Church.

There is little doubt that His Holiness, who was represented by Cardinal Casaroli as his personal envoy, embraced the Knights of

Columbus in the fraternity of Catholic Knights because His Eminence publicly articulated the definition during the centenary celebrations of the Association on 4 August 1982 at Hartford, Connecticut.[1]

The Association of the Knights of Columbus is the leading and largest Catholic laymen's organisation in the world, forming a fraternal society under a Supreme Knight[2] with the general objective of uniting Catholic laymen for religious and civic charitable work. Their specific objective is to be of unswerving service to the Church, loyalty to the Supreme Pontiff, service to society in various fields of their apostolate and to assist the Catholic Hierarchy in their service to the Universal Church under its Supreme Pastor.

Founded by Father Michael J. McGivney at New Haven, Connecticut, USA, and chartered by the General Assembly of Connecticut on 29 May 1882, the Association has used the description 'knight' for its members from the outset as a perfect description of the virtues which should inspire its members: rectitude and ready service.

The Knights of Columbus have associated councils in many countries besides the United States. When Cardinal Casaroli addressed the Knights as Papal Legate in 1982 he said that their name itself was meant to express a readiness to take inspiration, in a new form, from the ancient ideals of Knighthood into a modern and practical environment through the practice of 'Unity, Charity, Fraternity and Patriotism', which are the values contained in the motto of the Association[3].

Knights of Columbus in the Vatican Gardens with Pope Benedict XV in 1920.
Courtesy: Papal Secretariat of State

Supreme Knight Virgil C. Dechant and Supreme Chaplain Bishop Greco with Pope John Paul II.
Courtesy: Papal Secretariat of State

[1] Cf. *L'Osservatore Romano*, 5 August 1982.
[2] As mentioned above, presently Virgil C. Dechant.
[3] Cf. *L'Osservatore Romano*, 5 August 1982.

The Papal Brief appointing Cardinal Casaroli Papal Legate to the Centenary Celebrations in Hartford contained the Holy Father's personal message to the Knights of Columbus. After praising the members of the Association for their spirit of Christian chivalry, he exhorted them to keep 'Christian fraternity for their shield, truth for their sword, and for their banner peace springing from sacrifice'.[1]

The lofty principles with which the knights are imbued are demonstrated, illustrated and confirmed, His Holiness continued, by 'the boundless number and wonderful variety of their beneficent initiatives in aid of the Church's every need, the cause of justice as a whole, any human disaster whatever, and everything that is of true benefit to society'.[2]

A number of Catholic laymen's associations have formed themselves into the 'International Alliance of Catholic Knights'. Among them are The Association of the Knights of Columbus (USA) ; The Order of the Knights of St. Columbanus[3] (Ireland); The Knights of St. Columba (Great Britain); The Knights of the Southern Cross (Australia); The Knights of Da Gama; The Knights of the Southern Cross (New Zealand). Of these Associations the Knights of Columbus is by far the largest, with well over one million members in the USA, as well as organisations in Canada, Mexico, the Philippines, Puerto Rico and throughout South America.

All these Associations have the same aims and pursue the same charitable activities; they are, however, quite distinct and independent fraternal associations of Catholic men.

II

THE KNIGHTS AND DAMES OF ST MICHAEL OF THE WING
(Cavaleiros e Damas de S. Miguel da Ala)

The Order of St. Michael of the Wing was instituted in 1171 by Dom Alfonso I Henriques, the first King of Portugal. The original document of foundation of the Order was published in the *Chronicle* of the Cistercians; it also records the legend that the King founded the Order to

---

[1] *Ibid.*
[2] *Ibid.*
[3] The Irish Knights of St. Columbanus, acting on the inspiration of their Supreme Secretary, Peter F. Durnin, followed the suggestions in *The Cross on the Sword* and produced a Liturgy of an Investiture Service for their members who have been honoured with a Papal Knighthood. Masters of Ceremonies at such functions would be well advised to write to Chev. Durnin for a sample copy of an appropriate Liturgy for the Orders of St. Sylvester or St. Gregory the Great. Chev. Durnin also has available a complete list of Papal Knights in Ireland. Communications to him should be addressed to him at Rosaire, Moneymore, Drogheda, Co. Louth, Ireland.

Serie de' Maeſtri, ò Gran Maeſtri dell'Ordine di S. Michiele in Portogallo.

Numero de' Maeſtri.	Anni di Chriſto.		Anni do Magiſtrato
I.	1165 ò 1171	D. Alfonſo Henrico I. di Portogallo Fondatore dell' Ordine, Gran Maeſtro. Reſſe anni	20
II.	1185	D. Sancio I. il popolatore Rè figliuolo di Alfonſo.	27
III.	1212	D. Alfonſo II. Rè figliuolo di Sancio,	11
IV.	1223	D. Sancio II. Rè di lui figliuolo.	23
V.	1246	D. Alfonſo III. figliuolo di D. Alfonſo II.	33
VI.	1279	D. Dioniſio il Lauoratore figliuolo d'Alfonſo III.	46
VII.	1325	D, Alfonſo IV. chiamato il Brauo, figliuolo del Rè D. Dioniſio.	32
VIII.	1357	D. Pietro ſopranomato il Retto giudice, figliuolo del Rè D. Alfonſo IV.	10
IX.	1367	D. Ferdinando figliuolo del Rè D. Pietro.	16
X.	1383	D. Giouanni I. detto di buona memoria, già Maeſtro di Auis, figliuolo Naturale del Rè D. Pietro.	50
XI.	1433	D. Odoardo figliuolo di D. Giouanni I.	5
XII.	1438	D. Alfonſo V. nominato l'Africano figliuolo del Rè Odoardo.	43
XIII.	1481	D. Giouanni II. ſopranomato il Prencipe perfetto, figliuolo del Rè Alfonſo V.	14
XIV.	1495	D. Emanuele figliuolo dell'Infante D. Ferdinando, figliuolo del Rè D. Odoardo, ſucceſſe al di lui Cugino Rè D. Giouanni II.	26
XV.	1521	D. Giouanni III. figliuolo del Rè D. Emanuele.	35
XVI.	1557	D. Sebaſtiano I. nato poſtumo del Prencipe D. Giouanni figliuolo del Rè D. Giouanni III.	21
XVII.	1578	D. Henrico figliuolo del Rè D. Emanuele, fù Cardinale, indi Rè.	2
XVIII.	1580	D. Filippo II. Rè di Spagna, e Portogallo.	18
XIX.	1598	D. Filippo III. Rè di Spagna, e Portogallo.	23
XX.	1621	D. Filippo IV. Rè di Spagna, e Portogallo.	19
XXI.	1640	D. Giouanni IV. già Duca di Braganza acclamato Rè di Portogallo.	16
XXII.	1656	D. Alfonſo VI. Rè di Portogallo depoſto.	11
XXIII.	1667	D. Pietro II. Regnante.	

Così

Grand Masters of the Order from the foundation until the end of the seventeenth century.

A chronological list of Grand Masters of the Order of St. Michael of the Wing of Portugal from the foundation of the Order until the end of the seventeenth century.

Courtesy: M.Howe

commemorate the vision of the Archangel Michael's armed and winged arm that appeared in the sky during his victorious battle against the infidels at Santarém. The Order adopted the rule of St. Benedict, and the Abbot of the Cistercian Monastery of Alcobaça had jurisdiction over the Order.

A list of the Order's first twenty-three Grand Masters was published in 1672/1692 in the *Historie Cronologiche dell'Origine degl'Ordini Militari e di tutte le Religioni Cavalleresche* by Abbot Bernado Giustiani, and Prof. Manuel Borges Grainha covers in his *Historia da Franco – Maconaria em Portugal* the history of the Order from 1848 to 1910, the birth of the Portuguese Republic.

From the beginning of the nineteenth century onwards, the Order is referred to in contemporary writings as 'The Secret Society of St. Michael of the Wing', an appellation given to the Order by its own Grand Masters. Although not formally abolished by the Crown, the 'Secret Society' had to go underground because of its overt support and loyalty to its Grand Master, King Dom Miguel I. Throughout the civil unrest in the early years of the nineteenth century, after Dom Miguel had returned to Portugal in 1828, and especially after his expulsion in 1834, the Secret Society of St. Michael of the Wing fought the liberalism and modernism that were embraced by the new reigning royal party.

The sole *raison d'être* of the Secret Society of St. Michael of the Wing was to restore the successors of King Dom Miguel I to the throne of Portugal. After the advent of a Republic in 1910 and King Manuel II leaving Portugal for exile to England, small underground groups continued their work, hoping that if a King were to be restored, he should be a successor of King Dom Miguel I.

When on 12 April 1922 H.M. King Dom Manuel II and the successor of King Dom Miguel I, H.R.H. Dom Duarte Nuno, Duke of Bragança, father of Dom Duarte Pio, the present Duke of Bragança, signed the historic Pact of Paris which settled the succession, the Secret Society of St. Michael of the Wing lost its *raison d'être* for its continued existence for, as the nineteenth century statutes of the Order stated:

> 'This Order, following the 1st article of its statutes, is essentially secret, militant and political.
>
> 'It has as its ultimate objective (2nd article) to uphold the Roman Catholic Apostolic Religion and the restoration of the legitimate succession.
>
> 'One of its political methods of action is to resort to arms in extraordinary events (4th article).
>
> 'The grand-mastership of the Order is incumbant in the Kings of these realms (28th article) and belongs by right to King Dom Miguel I and, after him, to his legitimate successors to the Portuguese Crown.'

Following reaffirmation by H.R.H. Dom Duarte Pio, Duke of Bragança, of the extant Catholic Royal Dynastic Orders,[1] of which I received a certified translation from the Minister Counsellor at the Portuguese Embassy in London, I did not question in depth whether the original statutes of the ancient Order of St. Michael of the Wing, prior to becoming a Secret Society in the early nineteenth century, and especially after 1831, when the Order had been changed into a Secret Society, were still relevant at the end of the twentieth century, and whether the Order's *raison d'être* still existed . Canon lawyers in Rome drew my attention to the fact that insufficient consideration had been given to the possibility that membership of the Order by those professing a religion other than the Roman Catholic faith would contravene the fundamental statutes upon which the Order, and later the Secret Society, had been based.

I was greatly embarrassed by the injustice that had been done to the Royal House of Bragança in all the editions of *Orders of Knighthood, Awards and the Holy See* when I accepted the declaration and the facts as they were presented to me for publication in *The Cross on the Sword*.

The Duke of Bragança, whilst sanctioning *motu proprio* and as a temporary privilege for meritorious services the admittance of a limited number of Honorary Knights and Dames who belonged to a non-Roman Catholic denomination, has at all times been very conscious of the history of the Order of St. Michael of the Wing, the ultimate object of which had been to uphold the Holy Roman Catholic Apostolic Religion. In fact, he expressed to me his apprehension that the temporary privilege he had sanctioned might be in contradiction to the ancient Order's statutes as well as those of the Secret Society. He appointed his younger brother, Dom Miguel, Duke of Viseu, to the position of High Commander, and allocated to the Order a specific apostolate in the field of education.

In 1992, the Duke of Bragança, having taken advice, signed the draft I had prepared regularising the new status, name, statutes, membership and apostolate of this knightly association. His Royal Highness also abolished all regional and foreign Colleges of the former Order, and after taking further advice on the desirability of utilising the tradition of charitable works of the ancient Order of St. Michael of the Wing, redefined the style and status of the Order as 'The Knights and Dames of St. Michael of the Wing' ('Cavaleiros e Damas de S. Miguel da Ala'), open to men and women of all denominations who are dedicated to charitable works in education and support of Portuguese citizens in Portugal and abroad. Whilst being prepared to maintain the general structure which was adopted in 1986, the two fundamental changes introduced were, firstly that the Knights and Dames of St. Michael of the Wing would not to hold the status of a Catholic Order of Knighthood, but that of a

---

[1] The reaffirmation was signed in Lisbon on 25 October 1986, and it was published in November.

RECOGNIZED KNIGHTLY ORGANIZATIONS

The insignia worn by the Knights and Dames of St. Michael of the Wing: upper row: Esquire; Star of Grand Cross; and Novice; lower row: Honorary and Associate Knight; Knight; and Honorary and Associate Dame.

Courtesy: M.Howe

knightly order or association with a special apostolate, and secondly, that membership of that knightly order is not dependent on belonging to the Roman Catholic religion. Catholic Portuguese citizens can be full members, Portuguese and foreign citizens who belong to a Christian religion can be honorary members, and non-Christian applicants can be become associate members.

The Knights and Dames of St. Michael of the Wing will remain a dynastic institution of the Royal House of Bragança, though the Head of the Royal House, the Duke of Bragança, will be the Patron of this institution and not the Grand Master. The High Commander is the highest Officer, and the Chancellor the Chief Executive Officer for all members, Portuguese and foreign. No separate foundations bearing the name The Knights and Dames of St. Michael of the Wing may be instituted. Charitable functions under their auspices may not be organised without the express written permission of the Chancellor and Treasurer who, in turn, must first obtain the Patron's agreement to permit such a function or foundation.

It is expressly forbidden to use the name of H.R.H. the Duke of Bragança on writing paper or leaflets, as this might give the impression that he holds any responsibility for such functions.

The Knights and Dames of St. Michael of the Wing will be centrally administered for the Royal House of Bragança by a Chancellor in Portugal. All members come directly under his administration. The Chancellor will personally approve each individual candidate after consultation with the High Commander, the Treasurer and, as representative of the Patron, the Duke of Bragança, the Secretary of the Council of the Order of Our Lady of the Conception of Vila Viçosa. All financial matters concerning the administration of funds for supporting educational purposes that benefit Portuguese citizens in Portugal and abroad, are the responsibility of a Treasurer who will be elected by the above-mentioned Council for a period of three years.

The distinction as far as the badges are concerned between full members, who must be Catholic Portuguese citizens, and honorary and associate members will be maintained, and all members may, if they so wish, style themselves Knights or Dames of St. Michael of the Wing. Post-nominal letters denoting membership of the organisation of the Knights and Dames of St. Michael of the Wing are not permitted. While, as already stated, the Head of the Royal House of Bragança will be the Patron of the Knights and Dames of St. Michael of the Wing, the organisation's administration shall be self-governing under the Chancellor as Chief Executive Officer and accountable to the Head of the Royal House of Bragança.

Chapter Twelve

THE SPIRIT OF CHRISTIAN CHIVALRY TODAY

Just as we distinguish between the letter of the law and the spirit of the law, so chivalry as practised today and the true spirit of chivalry are not necessarily the same. Since the conception and evolution of the chivalric ideal almost a millennium ago, mankind's evolution and progress in science and technology have advanced beyond anything our ancestors could imagine in their wildest dreams. Yet human nature has changed very little.

Nothing would be easier than to write a chapter on the ideals of chivalry and pretend that these ideals are the focal point of chivalric life and activity today. Cardinal Casaroli was well aware of the danger of using platitudes when he defined the spirit of Christian Chivalry in 1982.[1] He spoke in the past tense, hoping that at least a few of his many knightly listeners and readers might feel inspired to revive those virtues and apply them in their daily lives as members of an Order of Knighthood. This is how he defined the original spirit of Christian Chivalry:

'A Knight was a man who intended to place himself completely at the service of a noble and difficult cause, a pure and arduous ideal. Fighting evil, promoting good, defending the weak and the oppressed against injustice. Bringing low the arrogance of the more powerful. Courage and unselfishness, generosity and readiness to make sacrifices: to the point of heroism, even to the point of death, if necessary. This is the picture, the *ideal* picture, let us say – of the Knight in the original accepted meaning of the term. Not for nothing was St. George the Martyr, who fought the dragon to protect the defenceless maiden, the prototype of the Knight; and he still is.

'In early times, becoming a knight did not merely mean receiving a title of honour, even though it was well deserved. It also demanded a vocation and a call, a preparation and a period of trial; it was an achievement and it presupposed a solemn commitment; and in its totality it was crowned by an austere and almost religious ceremonial.

'Becoming a Knight meant taking on a mission before God and man.'

It is important to distinguish between the individual knight and the Order of Knighthood to which he may belong. It is also necessary to clarify the legal position of the knight with regard to that Order. I have endeavoured to clarify that position in the various chapters of this book, though, unless that position is examined in the context of the Order's

---

[1] Cf.*L'Osservatore Romano*, 5 August 1982.

...titution, as well as the Order's purpose for its foundation ...uing *raison d'être*, ideals tend to become platitudes that bear ...n to an Order's activities or those of its individual knights.

... of Merit, whether or not they originated as Orders of ... ...ood with a specific purpose for their existence, are tokens of rew... .d. An honour is conferred on a recipient: it does not involve an obligation to the original aims and purposes for which an Order was founded, the essential feature of any Order of Knighthood. The best examples are the Pontifical Equestrian Orders themselves; they are in the gift of the Pope and conferred on individuals who legally are juridical entities neither represented by, nor under any particular obligation to the Order in which they have received their honour. While it was always assumed and usually practised that only Roman Catholic gentlemen were given a papal knighthood, a reigning Pope is not bound by practices of his predecessors and is at liberty to change the statutes and practices. The fact that some Popes changed practices without changing the statutes first only proves that they are not infallible in secular matters and can commit errors of omission. A Papal Knight of the Orders of Pius IX, St. Gregory the Great or of Pope St. Sylvester receives his knighthood *ad personam*, because the general criteria for conferment of this honour fall within a particular domain. Associations of Papal Knights are private institutions of those members who choose to join them; they do not represent the Knights unless they were all to request that it do so, and the separate Orders of Merit of the Religious Orders of Knighthood do not confer membership of the Order itself. State and Crown Orders belong in the same category as the Pontifical Equestrian Orders.

Of course, all members of Orders of Knighthood and Merit are honour-bound to live a life free from scandal and anti-social behaviour. Most Crown and State Orders are withdrawn from members who, for example, stand convicted of crimes, treason or unbefitting conduct.

As Archbishop Cardinale stressed: 'although chivalry was not originally founded by the Church but through the private initiative of individuals, it was the Church who, more than any other body, set about refining chivalry according to the spirit of the Gospel, spiritualised the military zeal and valour of the first Crusading Orders of Knighthood and granted them her approval and support. The Apostolic See inspired their 'chivalric system of virtues', all of which were based on ethico-aesthetic standards of a secular nature, and replaced these with high Christian ideals that transformed aggressive and violent mercenaries into disciplined, self-controlled, refined, gentle and strong defenders of the rights of God, of Christendom, of the Papacy, the Church and of society. The main aim of these new knights was consciously to bring the Catholic religion into their daily life with service to the less fortunate, and honour and courtesy to all.'

THE SPIRIT OF CHRISTIAN CHIVALRY TODAY

It is essential to remember that the constitutional code. Orders of Chivalry demanded of their members total su loving obedience to the authority of the Apostolic See and t obey the commandments and to protect the Church against 'Knights were encouraged to see in the Church the sweet Christ.' This explains why most of the ancient Orders of Knight were in fact also Monastic Orders, and why most Orders of Knighthood, even recent ones, claim some link with the Church or with religion in general. It also explains why the Apostolic See considered it expedient in the sixteenth century and again in the nineteenth and twentieth centuries to found, revise, suppress or re-establish her own Orders of Knighthood and Merit and why the Holy See gives public and official awards to meritorious persons, even of other religions, who have rendered conspicuous service to good causes.

It is, however, not enough to restrict this analysis to Military Orders of Knighthood as defenders of the Faith and militias founded to defend countries or defend pilgrims to Holy Shrines, because the most important attribute of some of them was that they were Hospitaller Orders, caring especially for the sick and infirm, while leaving the protection of pilgrims to their military knights, whose task also included fighting the Islamic invaders and trying to recapture Holy Places from the Infidel. There are few Hospitaller Orders left, but those that continue to serve in the same spirit of the ancient Hospitaller Orders, have certainly preserved the original *raison d'être* for their continued existence.

Throughout the centuries of Feudalism and the general upheaval that followed the Reformation, many Orders of Knighthood continued to do 'good works', endow hospitals, schools and generally contributed to charitable causes, in spite of the undoubted fact that after the breaking up of the *Res Publica Christiana* the Catholic inspiration and commitment had been drained out of the lifestream of many of the Orders of Knighthood that had contributed significantly to the strong foundation of Catholic Western Europe. This foundation was eroded when the bond of a Catholic commonwealth of nations collapsed, and the Catholic-founded Orders of Knighthood, the visible pillar of the *Res Publica Christiana*, had been overthrown.

Other symbols of chivalry, the armigerous knights, the hierarchy of a strongly defined class system, titles, with the corresponding badges, decorations, medallions and collars and the pageantry have survived up to this day, but so has the deeply ingrained spirit of the Hospitaller Orders: a different but essential spirit of chivalry.

Since the days of the Revolutions that caused upheavals not only in several countries but especially in the Church, once it had lost its Papal States, the question was asked more and more often whether it was not vain and futile to continue with conferring decorations and titles. In the

...urch the additional question arose as to whether accepting decorations for doing good works was not directly in conflict with the virtue of humility.

One can dismiss those who crave for any kind of distinction they can add to their personal collection, and the Church as a whole never overvalued the bestowal of titles, decorations and honours. In fact those who shunned such honours because they viewed them *sub specie aeternitatis* – in the light of eternity and heavenly reward – have always found praise and admiration in the Church.

On the other hand, the Apostolic See would have shown a singular ignorance of human nature had it turned its back on those who were happy to accept appreciation, acknowledgement and a reward for having striven towards goodness and their kindness to their Church, society and to mankind. The Apostolic See has never seen any wrong in those who in good conscience delighted in receiving a token of appreciation from the Supreme Pontiff or, indeed, from their sovereigns or countries, whenever these honours were well deserved.

Pope St. Pius X wrote in his encyclical *Multum ad excitandos* on 7 February 1905:

> 'Rewards that are given to honour valour and bravery are very useful to encourage men to accomplish praiseworthy deeds because, as they do credit to persons worthy of the grateful recognition of Church and society, they also stimulate others to follow their path leading to praise and honour. 'So it was that Our Predecessors, the Roman Pontiffs, turned their special attention to Orders of Knighthood, as a spur towards glory.'

Pope St. Pius X was well ahead of today's psychologists and psychiatrists who aim at creating role models for the younger generation to look up to and to follow their examples. He clearly expresses his approval of the joy and satisfaction that meritorious recipients of decorations receive, providing they enter into the true spirit of chivalry.

Psychologically the centuries in which Chivalry grew and flourished are immeasurably distant from our own age, and values have changed almost beyond recognition. The spirit of chivalry, however, which permeates the hearts of all good and upright men, has survived unscathed because it is based on fundamental Christian and spiritual values. I am not convinced that the spirit of chivalry is expressed only, if at all, in the codes of honour and conduct of the ancient Orders that merely aimed at rendering the upper classes worthy of the exceptional advantages knighthoods tend to bring with them. The true Christian Knight of the twentieth century and beyond, who has the great privilege of being associated with one of the lawful extant Orders of Knighthood, must endeavour to translate the ideals of the knights of old into the modern texture of present and future social life, especially where the need for that spirit of chivalry is sorely felt. They can still engage their efforts for the triumph of Christ's cause in this world.

It would be impossible to list the hundreds of good causes that have been supported by several of the extant Orders of Knighthood. However, I would fail in my task if I did not pay particular tribute to those have been in the forefront of such chivalrous and hospitaller work.

It would be unrealistic not to appreciate the value and importance of financial contributions and continued support given to hospitals, schools and other institutions by members of Orders of Knighthood. Some Orders diversify their hospitaller work, and national or regional jurisdictions direct their support to specific projects. The Knights of the Religious Orders of Knighthood, especially the Sovereign Military Order of Malta, made it an obligation upon their members to help the sick who travel to Holy Shrines like Lourdes, while the Equestrian Order of the Holy Sepulchre concentrates its hospitaller work in the Holy Land. The knights, who theoretically belong in the category of military knights, no longer engage in battles to defeat the Infidels who threaten to change the Christian religion and the moral values of a country and pose a genuine threat to western civilisation, a euphemism for our inheritance of what is left of the Christian countries. Sadly, where we see such practices as 'ethnic cleansing', for example in the former Yugoslavia, we not only condemn it as barbaric but, not unlike the sectarian murders in Northern Ireland, many mistakenly attribute a religious motivation to primitive tribal savagery – 'we kill all those who are not like us', and this covers religion as well as race.

There is, and there has been for many centuries, the deplorable phenomenon of religious fundamentalism, particularly in the Islamic faith; but there have also been such fanatics and irrational followers of fundamentalism in other religious faiths, including the Christian. With the age of 'enlightenment' and 'liberalism', humanitarianism and so-called tolerance, 'western civilisation' chose a policy of coexistence. Ethnic and racial divides have been made illegal, though no law can change what is in people's hearts: prejudices or hatred. Excesses of ethnic, racial or religious fights between countries and communities are disapproved of and, as far as wars between countries are concerned, they are usually fought for economic reasons or a mere craving for power and domination over weaker countries, while cloaked in the rhetoric of sanctimonious pretence or religious zeal. They are condemned by well-meaning humanitarian committees, unfortunately with very little power.

The second half of the twentieth century brought peacekeeping contingents of fighting soldiers from other countries to restore coexistence and tolerance, usually under the auspices of the United Nations

Organisation, but experience has shown these exercises to be token endeavours with little hope of success.

It is therefore wrong to draw a comparison between the Orders of Knighthood that successfully defended Christian Europe against the Islamic invaders whose aim it was to conquer Christian countries and defeat the Christian religion, or even with the Crusaders who wanted to liberate places that were religious shrines venerated by the Christians but had fallen under Islamic domination, and the hospitaller work done by several Orders of Knighthood today.

The balance of power has changed in the world and so have values and ideals, but most of all, the commitment to retain a Christian civilisation has been eroded over the last four centuries because of political changes and scientific evolution, which was hailed – in many respects with justification – as progress.

Perhaps the greatest 'progress' western civilisation has witnessed has been the general development of a sense of a responsibility for one's fellow man and the growth of a desire to alleviate the suffering of the needy and those struck by disasters. It was the ultimate metamorphosis of personal responsibility according to the Gospel to a mainly collective responsibility of the state towards fellow man and the creation of a philosophy and ideal of humanitarianism. Advances in science, technology and instant worldwide communication have had two contrary effects: the telegraph, telephone, radio and television enabled man to instantly learn, and later to actually witness the suffering of his fellow man as it takes place. The negative aspect has been the awareness of the multitude of disasters and the overwhelming numbers of those who suffer and needed help. Perhaps television more then any of the other media has gradually numbed human compassion.

Yet the tenacity of purpose among those who have continued to believe in, favour and harbour the true Christian chivalric and hospitaller spirit, have given a new *raison d'être* to several Orders of Knighthood.

As I said above, many of the Catholic-founded Orders of Knighthood, especially the Religious and dynastic ones, as well as the knightly organisations, support many good humanitarian and charitable causes. However, I must single out three Orders that established and maintain foundations that carry out true Christian hospitaller work on a worldwide basis and are recognised as international relief organisations. Each of these foundations has its own proud history, and although many of the hospitallers and workers in the field are members of the Order of Knighthood that established the foundation, not all of them are. Some of these foundations have become so much part of our daily life and, on an international scale, part of the fabric of our civilisation, that they are taken for granted, and even to single out any one of them, may suggest that it is more important than the others.

But can anybody imagine major national or regional events taking place in the British Commonwealth of Nations without hundreds of volunteer hospitallers of the St. John Ambulance being in attendance to care for casualties? It is difficult to think of disasters and the self-inflicted slaughter on roads as a result of careless drivers without the St. John ambulance in attendance to alleviate the suffering. It is a foundation of the Venerable Order of St. John in Great Britain and operates there and throughout the Commonwealth. I am delighted to be able to feature a photograph that was taken on the first occasion those truly venerable hospitallers went into action.[1] The other foundation of the Order of St. John, the world-famous Eye Hospital in Jerusalem (and the new one in Gaza), caters for all sufferers from widespread eye diseases in the Middle East. Without these hospitals and their ancillary mobile clinics, tens of thousands of human beings, regardless of race, colour or religion, would be blind and helpless today.

Is it not vividly brought home to us on television how on an international scene the rescue teams, including doctors and paramedics with jeeps, helicopters and ambulances, bearing the Cross of the Order of Malta, are usually the first on the scene of natural and man-made disasters? In this area of hospitaller work the Malteser Hilfsdienst has a record second to none.[2]

Have not the enormous trucks, laden with tents, blankets, food and medication, jeeps with soup kitchen trailers, bearing the Cross of St. Lazarus, become a familiar sight in Eastern Europe and on the battle fields of the Balkans? As a result of the tireless work of the Order and the Lazarus Hilfswerk in Eastern Europe, several of these countries have not only fully recognised the Military and Hospitaller Order of St. Lazarus of Jerusalem but actually had permanent representatives of the Order appointed, to whom they have given diplomatic status, and have themselves appointed a representative to the Order so that all future programmes can be coordinated.[3]

The three hospitaller branches of these ancient Orders are supported by their respective Orders of Knighthood, whose Crosses they bear. All of them work closely with the International Red Cross, Caritas and other international Aid Agencies and national Green Crescent Organisations, and they are welcome wherever they arrive to give comfort, help and aid to those who have fallen victim to man-made and natural disasters.

These are the Hospitallers of the twentieth and twenty-first centuries who keep the spirit of true Christian Chivalry alive in the spirit of the ancient Military Hospitaller Orders of Knighthood that were founded nearly a millennium ago.

[1] See Chapter Five, part III: The Venerable Order of St. John.
[2] See Chapter Five, part II: The Sovereign Military Order of Malta.
[3] See Chapter Ten: The Military Hospitaller Order of St. Lazarus of Jerusalem.

Above: St. John Ambulance volunteers are an integral part of the rescue and first aid services throughout Great Britain. After terrorist attacks in London, they were on the scene without delay. Below: After a particularly brutal massacre in South Africa, St. John Ambulance volunteers ferried the severely wounded to hospitals and gave on-the-spot first aid to hundreds of injured.

Courtesy: The Order of St. John

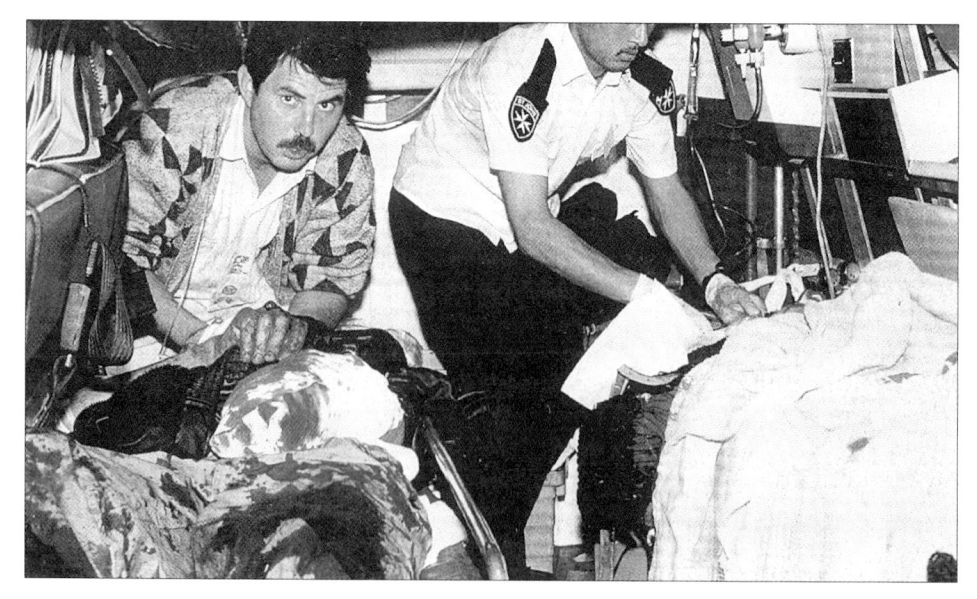

THE SPIRIT OF CHRISTIAN CHIVALRY TODAY

Above: St. John Ambulance looks after almost all sporting events in Britain, for example the London Marathon and all major football matches. Below: During the terrifying bushfires across New South Wales in Australia St. John Ambulance played a major part in the rescue services.

Courtesy: The Order of St. John

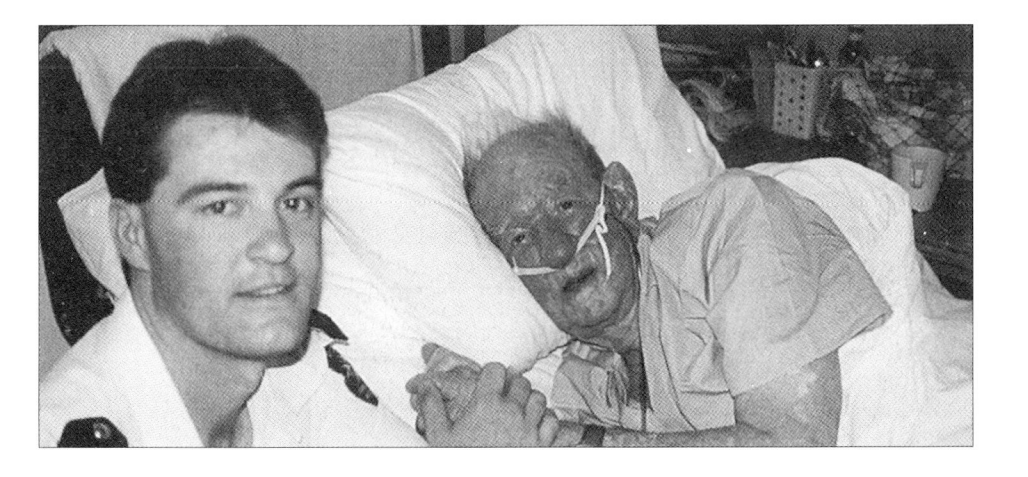

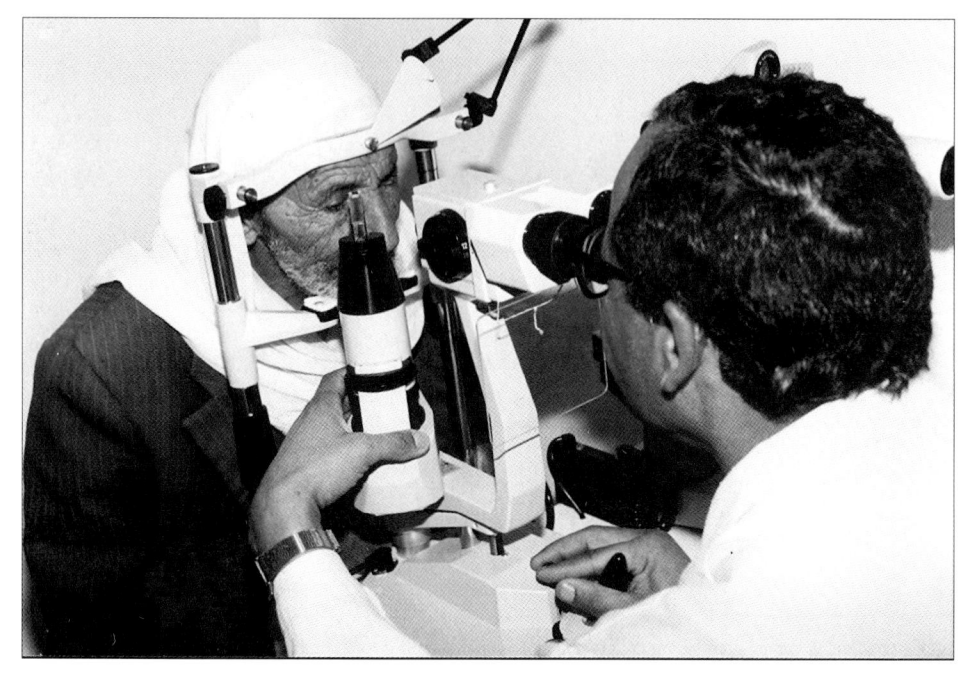

The Opthalmic Hospital in Jerusalem treats thousands of sufferers, regardless of the faith, colour or nationality of the patients. Its reputation for excellence is second to none. The Order of St. John has, apart from mobile units that visit remote areas, opened another eye clinic in Gaza (below).

Courtesy: The Order of St. John

Above: St.John Ambulance on the River Thames. Below: The Grand Prior of the Order of St. John, H.R.H. The Duke of Gloucester, greets St. John Cadets at St. Paul's Cathedral in London.

Courtesy: The Order of St. John

Knights Hospitallers of the twentieth century follow the same Christian principles as did their predecessors during the Crusades, 900 years ago. The Serious Accident Unit, equipped with the latest life-saving apparatus flies to the scene of the accident by helicopter. The Sovereign Military Order of Malta sponsors the Malteser Hilfsdienst in Germany which operates this and many other units.

Courtesy: Malteser Hilfsdienst, Deutschland

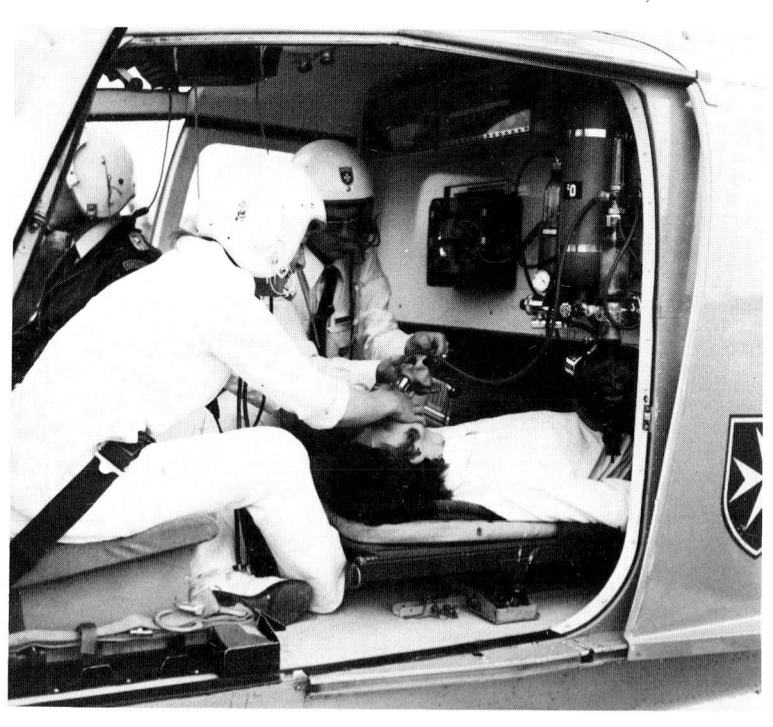

Above: Several serious Accident Units, operated by the Malteser Hilfsdienst, attend a massive motorway accident. Below: This impressive convoy of specialist rescue vehicles, supported by helicopters is always ready to relieve suffering from major disasters.

Courtesy: Malteser Hilfdienst, Deutschland

All Knights of Malta are obliged to attend pilgrimages to Lourdes where they assist and comfort the sick. Above left: H.M.E.H. the Prince and Grand Master of the Sovereign Military Order of Malta, Frà Andrew Bertie, and Prior Regis Barwig (USA) are two of the Knights on duty. Right: taking the disabled to the Shrine is one of the tasks undertaken by the Knights. Below: Knights and Sisters of the Order comfort the sick who are taken to the Shrine by stretcher.

Courtesy: Very Rev. Regis Barwig

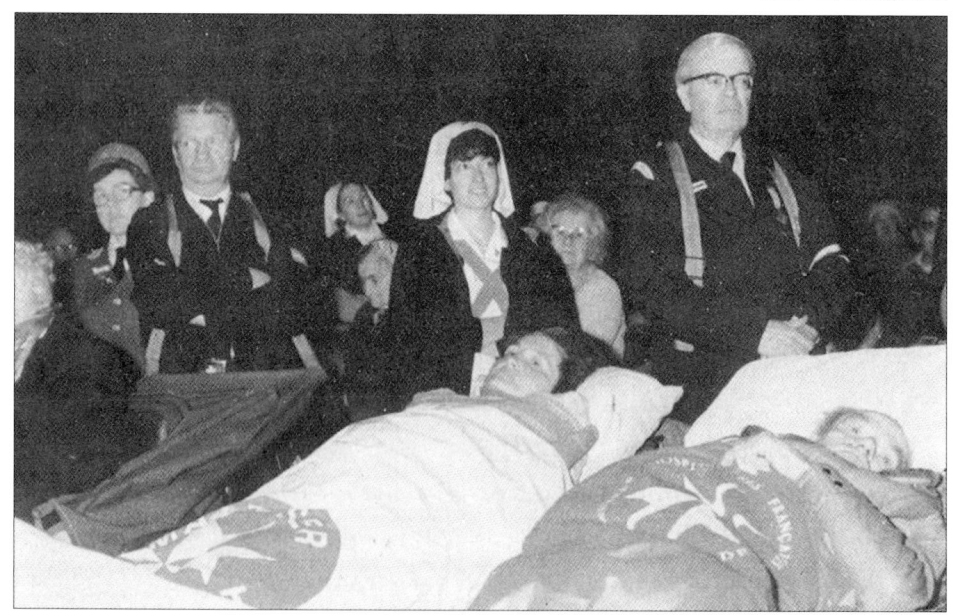

Above: Truck after truck is loaded by the volunteers of the Lazarus Hilfswerk for relief in Eastern Europe. Below: Many helping hands await the arrival of the trucks.

Courtesy: Lazarus Hilfswerk, Deutschland

Above: The Polish President Lech Walesa (left) during his state visit to the Federal Republic of Germany with the President of the Lazarus Hilfswerk, Chev. Klaus Peter Pokolm. Below: Cardinal Macharski, Archbishop of Krakow, visited the Headquarters of the Lazarus Hilfswerk to thank the Knights and Volunteers for their tireless help when Poland most needed it.

Courtesy: Lazarus Hilfswerk, Deutschland

THE SPIRIT OF CHRISTIAN CHIVALRY TODAY

Above: A large motor-pool is always ready to go into action. Below: The field kitchens were most effectively used on the streets and along the roads of the war-torn former Yugoslavia. Although local volunteers are helping with the field kitchens, the Lazarus Hilfswerk retains them as their property to ensure that they are not used for military purposes.

Courtesy: Lazarus Hilfswerk, Deutschland

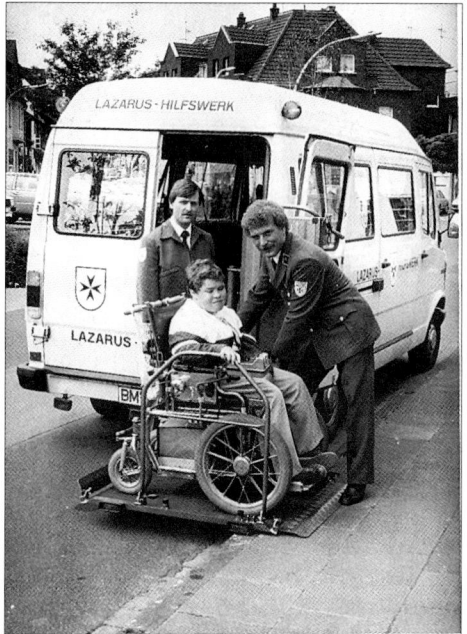

Above: Lazarus Hilfswerk Volunteers arrange for out-patient transport to hospitals (left) and a 'Meals on Wheels' service for the elderly. Below: specialist coaches with ramps for wheelchairs are available for the disabled who wish to attend special functions and events which they could otherwise not visit.

Courtesy: Lazarus Hilfswerk, Deutschland

Above: Catholic and Orthodox Bishops came to bless and see off the first convoy of trucks with food and medicine to Russia. On the extreme left is H.S.H. Princess Tatiana, Duchess von Metternich, who accompanied the convoy to Russia. Below: the convoy arriving at the Russian frontier in snow and freezing temperatures.

Courtesy: Lazarus Hilfswerk, Deutschland

CHAPTER THIRTEEN

UNRECOGNISED ORGANISATIONS STYLING THEMSELVES ORDERS OF KNIGHTHOOD

In the aftermath of the second World War a great number of organisations that styled themselves 'Orders of Knighthood' appeared many of which still exist and, undoubtedly, will continue in their pretence that they are the successors of many of the long-extinct ancient Orders of Knighthood. It is not the fact that they owe their foundation to a private initiative: as I mentioned in Chapter One, during the centuries when Orders of Knighthood flourished and were the guarantors of the *Res Publica Christiana*, they were all founded by private initiative. The Apostolic See as *Mater et Magistra* of the Orders of Knighthood encouraged such initiatives and gave to many of these Orders its blessing, privileges and dispensation from episcopal jurisdiction. Over the centuries that followed, hundreds of groups and organisations assumed chivalric status, and many of them had that status recognised by the Apostolic See. Being recognised by the Pontiff raised their status from a merely private enterprise to a Catholic Order of Knighthood, or, one should say, Catholic-*founded* Order, because of the recognition of the Order and its distinctly Catholic apostolate. Many of these Orders existed not only with the encouragement of the Apostolic See after their foundation by private initiative, but a great number were founded at the instigation of the Apostolic See, though always by members of the nobility or even sovereigns. Some flourished for several centuries, others were very short-lived. In Chapter Nine and Appendix VI, I give a rough idea of the vast number of these now extinct Orders of Knighthood.

The reason the Holy See and the Apostolic See alike unreservedly condemn the recently founded self-styled and imitation Orders is because, especially over the last few decades, they have tended to assume titles and names, and usually use photocopies of documents that emanated in centuries past from the Apostolic See or the Holy See or even from some State authorities, but have no juridical value when exploited by these entrepreneurs, who play at Knights in Orders in much the same way that children play Doctors and Nurses.

Because of these abuses, the Holy See found it necessary to state its position in this connection, by making it clear in *L'Osservatore Romano* that these organisations enjoy neither its recognition nor approval.

The claim to ancient titles is not new. For example, as I have mentioned elsewhere in this work, some legitimate and respected Orders of

Knighthood claim to be the successors of the ancient Order of the Knights Templars which was abolished in 1314, because when the possessions and wealth of that ill-fated Order were distributed by the reigning sovereigns in various countries, they received their share of the spoils. However, Pope John XXII (1316-34) issued his Bull *Ad ea ex quibus* in 1319, which confirmed only the Portuguese Order of Christ as replacing the Order of the Knights Templars. Members of the Order were initially called 'Militia of Jesus Christ', a title used by the Knights Templars themselves.

I first became involved in this minefield of chivalric Orders when assisting Archbishop Cardinale, especially with the chapter on those organisations that without justification claim chivalric status. Since the publication of the 1985 edition of Mons. Cardinale's work, I have been forced to study this particular matter again, because the metamorphosis both the Holy See and many legitimate Orders of Knighthood have undergone presented me with an entirely new situation, and as it had even then become obvious that any further revision would be unsatisfactory and inadequate patchwork, one change inevitably leading to another; the domino effect knocked down many of the previously-held views. I learned just how true is the saying 'ignorance is bliss': with every new reappraisal or investigation came new revelations, new evidence and sometimes even new guidelines on which I was to proceed, sometimes contradicting those I had received elsewhere.

I know from experience that most unfortunate mistakes are made or serious errors perpetuated because of simple language problems. One only has to look at the disastrous consequences that mistranslations of papal encyclicals have brought with them, only because the dictionaries translating Latin into other languages translate words which have a distinctly different meaning from language to language. Even papal constitutions translated from the Italian vernacular often need a footnote, explaining what is really meant by a word. The best example is the frequently quoted constitution *Regimini Ecclesiae Universiae*. The word 'suppressed' is used time and again in connection with departments, chancelleries and secretariats, yet its meaning in the context of the constitution is 'transferred' to another, larger department. There is a great difference between a translator and an interpreter or between a translation and interpretation; a translator usually prepares the draft of a document into another language whereas the interpreter's task is to ensure that it conveys the correct meaning. Archbishop Cardinale frequently complained that translations into the English language of important documents emanating from the Holy See appeared to have been left to translators with a mere smattering of school-English. He himself, though born in Rome, grew up in America, and he was fluent in Italian and English, both having been his mother tongues.

I am not digressing from the subject of Orders of Knighthood, real or imagined, but I endeavour to be fair to all when relying by necessity on translated documents. The days when the Apostolic and Holy See communicated worldwide in the universal language of the Church, Latin, vanished with the Second Vatican Council. Those who have studied Latin know it to be a language of precision that does not allow misconstruction or etymological inaccuracies. Those who are fanatics on the use of the vernacular argue that Latin is archaic, yet, if they are fair-minded, they will agree that combining authority and precision in a language with courtly flourishes of politeness and sometimes deliberate diplomatic understatement, creates an unique and accurate form of communication.

One used to speak of 'Vaticanese', often in jest, when some writers, not just in Latin but in other languages fashioned on the Latin idiom, wrote letters or articles in *L'Osservatore Romano* which became quite incomprehensible after the first three lines. Nevertheless, it is essential to overcome such linguistic difficulties if one sets out to express the Holy See's or the Apostolic See's view of, or attitude to important issues concerning Orders of Knighthood.

Since 1953, the Secretariat of State of His Holiness has issued three major statements in *L'Osservatore Romano* concerning organisations wrongly claiming to be Orders of Knighthood and enjoying the Holy See's recognition. The first one, parts of which are reproduced below, addresses the subject in a more general tone, and also mentions a number of these organisations.[1] The second statement concerns 'The Sovereign and Military Order of the Temple of Jerusalem'[2]. It is very inadequate and incomplete and does not highlight the numerous organisations calling themselves 'Knights Templars' and usually claiming to be their legitimate and true successors. I am somewhat surprised that the writer of the article on the so-called Knights Templars never referred to the Papal Bull *Ad ea ex quibus* issued in 1319 by Pope John XXII, and which settles all questions about the lawful successors the Knights Templars. The third statement, 'The Sovereign Order of St. John of Jerusalem',[3] only deals with one of the eighteen or more larger orders imitating the Sovereign Military Order of Malta or the Venerable Order of St. John (United Kingdom). The first official statement, written by a member of the Secretariat of State, reads as follows:

'Since some time one can observe the deplorable phenomenon of the appearance of alleged Orders of Knighthood originating from private initiatives and aiming at replacing the legitimate forms of chivalric awards.[4]

---

[1] For full text see *L'Osservatore Romano* of 22 March 1953, and reprinted on 14 December 1970.
[2] The full text can be found in *L'Osservatore Romano* of 24 July 1970.
[3] For the full text see *L'Osservatore Romano* of 1 December 1976.
[4] The word 'replacing' is a wrong translation. The writer means to say that those who join a self-styled Order might otherwise have joined a legitimate, recognised Order or may even be under the impression that they have done so.

have previously pointed out, these so-called Orders take their ⟨fr⟩om Orders which have in fact already existed but are now extinct ⟨for m⟩any centuries, or from Orders which had been planned but were neve⟨r⟩ realised or, finally, from Orders which are truly fictitious and have no historical precedent at all.

'To increase the confusion of those who are not aware of the true history of Orders of Knighthood and of the juridical condition, these private initiatives, which style themselves as autonomous, are qualified by appellations which had reason to exist in the past and which belong exclusively to authentic Orders duly approved by the Holy See.[1]

'Thus, with a terminology which is almost monotonous these alleged Orders claim for themselves – in differing degrees – such titles as "Sacred", "Military", "Equestrian", "Chivalric", "Constantinian", "Capitular", "Sovereign", "Nobiliary", "Religious", "Angelical", "Celestial", "Lascaris", "Imperial", "Royal", "Delcassian" etc.

'Among these private initiatives, which in no way are approved of or recognised by the Holy See, one can find alleged Orders such as the following:

St. Mary of Our Lady of Bethlehem;
St. John of Acre;
St. John the Baptist;
St. Thomas;
St. Lazarus;
St. George of Burgundy or of Belgium or of Miolans;
St. George of Carinthia;
Constantinian Lascaris Angelical Order of the Golden Militia;
The Crown of Thorns;
The Lion and the Black Cross;

---

[1] This was correct in 1953 and in 1970; since then, the Holy See (as an entity in international law) has, as I have already explained, gone on record and named the Orders it recognises. This is the reason why Archbishop Cardinale's book, which examines the relationship between the Catholic-founded Orders and the Holy See, is no longer correct and a new appraisal of the relationship between Orders and the Apostolic See had to be made. As to the appellations which belong to Orders 'duly approved' by the Holy See, some Orders are obviously not approved by it, but are looked upon with favour by the Apostolic See and are actively engaged in a chivalric, hospitaller or other lay apostolate of the Church and even take part in the ceremonial of services. Typical examples are the Sacred Military Constantinian Order of St. George (Two Sicilies), and the three Royal Orders of SS. Maurice and Lazarus (Savoy), of the Immaculate Conception of Our Lady of Vila Viçosa (Bragança), and St. George (Bavaria-Wittelsbach). All four dynastic Catholic-founded Orders are active in the lay apostolate of the Church. I must stress that the Holy See is not discriminating against these Orders by witholding recognition; it is merely exercising its special and particular function as a sovereign power. The Apostolic See, on the other hand, is not restricted in the exercise of its functions by rules of international law. Juridically, and under the Canons of the *Codex Iuris Canonici*(1983), many Orders dealt with in this book therefore come under the exclusion clause of Canon 361, which distinguishes between the Holy See and the Apostolic See because 'the contrary is clear from the nature of things or from the context'. I believe that as a loyal and devoted member of the Holy See, Archbishop Cardinale would not have accepted the task of writing *Orders of Knighthood, Awards and the Holy See* if the dichotomy between Holy See and Apostolic See had been known to him in 1983.

St. Hubert of Lorraine or of Bar;
The Concord;
Our Lady of Peace.

'To these allied Orders of Knighthood and similar ones, with the adjoining more or less international Gold, Silver and Blue Cross Associations, those Orders must certainly be added which, together with one of the names mentioned above, have taken the titles:

of Mercy;
of St. Bridget of Sweden;[1]
of St. Rita of Cascia;
of The Legion of Honour of the Immaculate;
of St. George of Antioch;
of St. Michael;
of St. Mark;

Left: the self-styled Order of the Lion and Black Cross; right: the self-styled Order (Grand Cross) of Signum Fidei. Both insignia were private commissions manufactured by Spink & Son Ltd. The Order of the Lion and Black Cross is mentioned on the list of non-recognised organisations published by the Holy See; there is no reference to the Order of Signum Fidei. Like the Star of St. Hubert and the Cross of the Order of the Temple, their manufacture is of the highest quality.

Courtesy: Spink & Son, Ltd.

[1]Not to be confused with the Order of Religious Sisters by that name.

A recently manufactured star of a spurious Order of St. Hubert. The centre medallion is identical to that of the 1824 abolished Royal Order of St. Hubert (which had been founded by the Duke of Bar). The motto is taken from the still extant Bavarian Order of St. Hubert: 'IN TRAU VAST'. A green coloured enamelled cross and crossed swords were added.

Courtesy: Spink & Son, Ltd.

of St. Sebastian,[1]
of St. William;
of the historical but extinct Order of the Temple;
of The Red Eagle;
of St. Cyril of Jerusalem.

'So as to avoid equivocations which are unhappily possible, also because of the abuse of pontifical and ecclesiastical documents, once granted for religious purposes or for merely Monastic Orders, and to put an end to the continuation of such abuses, entailing harmful consequences for people in good faith, we are authorized to declare that the Holy See does not recognise the value of the certificates and insignia conferred by the above-named alleged Orders.'

The subject of self-styled organisations who claim the status of an Order of Knighthood is an unsavoury one, the more so because innocent parties get hurt in the process of exposing the false and contentious. In Chapter Six of *The Cross on the Sword*, in which I tried to elaborate on the statements of the Secretariat of State published in *L'Osservatore Romano*, I did not question whether they were well researched because I had no reason to do so. At that time my own experience with self-styled Orders, but especially cantankerous and litigious persons who enjoyed nothing more than bringing a court action for libel against those calling their Order 'false', 'bogus', or 'fraudulent', was relatively limited. One of my tasks, therefore, was to have the chapters read by a libel lawyer who knew what phrases were actionable, and what were not, and when they

---

[1] Not to be confused with the traditional Riflemen's Societies in Belgium the western regions of Germany, Luxembourg and the Netherlands, all of which have adopted St. Sebastian as Patron Saint.

appeared in Archbishop Cardinale's text, have the former replaced by the latter.

Of course, no sooner did it become known that I had taken over the responsibilities for this work from the late Archbishop Cardinale, I began to receive the same sort of abusive letters, threats of legal action and all manner of unpleasant suggestions. For example, none of the people mentioned in Chapter Ten in this book were known to me, nor had I heard of them until my stay in the Vatican in 1987 after the publication of *The Cross on the Sword*. I had no contact whatever with them until 1990. Yet the name of 'St. Lazarus' featured prominently among those that were frowned upon and for which any reappraisal was refused. The entire acrimony that had built up over the Orders of St. Lazarus (or one of them, but universally applied at that time) was due to one man, whose rude and insulting comments to the Holy See only seemed to confirm that it was best simply to ignore the existence of anything with the name 'St.Lazarus'.

I remember that one of my first experiences of this nature involved a cardinal in Rome. Looking at Chapter Six of *The Cross on the Sword* six years later, I realised that I had been writing about 'defensive phaleristic studies' – much as American medical doctors practice 'defensive medicine' for fear of litigation by patients. I had generalised and referred to the cardinal 'unaware', 'elderly' and 'naive', because I wanted to avoid calling a cardinal 'feeble' or 'failing'. His Eminence, who had retired from active service some years before, had written a letter of introduction for someone claiming to be the illegitimate child of a reigning King who died before the first World War, and who had suddenly laid claim to the Crown of that Kingdom which by then had become a Republic. In this letter, addressed to an Apostolic Nuncio who was a long-standing friend of mine for many years, the Cardinal attributed to that person all the claimed titles. The Nuncio was so taken aback by the unexpected and unusual request that he should write on the letter (addressed to him) that he had read it, stamp it with the Nunciature's seal and then return it to the claimant, that he did so. After the person had left, the Nuncio realised that he probably had been tricked, so he immediately informed the Secretariat of State and explained the matter. However, the person lost no time in distributing photocopies of the letter in order to gain entry into society, and a book could be written on the consequences.

Whilst the person who initially and without any foundation had claimed the throne of a European country had subsequently – after conferring titles and selling decorations – sold the royal title to yet another foreigner, who then proceeded to add the decorations of the Republic to those he disposed of, court cases in the Republic not only proved the claims to be ludicrous and false, but both the original claimant ιe who purchased the 'claim' would face criminal charges y set foot in that country. The reason I have to be circumspect no names is again for legal reasons. Although another High a European country has found all these claims fraudulent and the practice of selling the Orders of Merit of the Republic a criminal act against the State, such a person, if named, could start legal procedures all over again in England if I mentioned a name. In spite of the fact that the publishers of this book and I would be able to prove – with the legal documentation from the competent European court – that it was in the public interest to expose such people, it would involve legal costs, and past experience has shown us that although the court may award costs to the winner of such a case, the loser only has to leave England for the court to be powerless to enforce its judgement.

In France the authors Arnaud Chaffanjon and Betrand Galimard Flavigny and their publishers Mercure de France were sued by one of the self-styled Orders for defamation in their book *Ordres & Contre-Ordres de Chevalerie* (Paris, 1982). The authors and publishers won the case and costs. [Judgement was given by the *Tribunal de Grand Instance de Paris – 1º Section* on 14 March 1984.]

Articles on self-styled Orders usually involve aggravation that is not worth the effort. It is also the reason why so many of the self-styled Orders flourish with impunity.

By 1987 I had learned much about that web of intrigue and threats of legal action that was being spun by these organisations; personal experience has made me immune to their antics. The fact that there is the next best thing to an 'Order of the Month Club' in the United States of America which sells all kinds of fake and imitation Orders, has become a source of amusement to me, though I feel sorry for its victims, as much as one can feel sorry for anyone who is prepared to pay for a piece of metal or enamel dangling from a ribbon and a worthless piece of paper purporting to be a document of conferment.

On 24 July 1970, *L'Osservatore Romano* published another official statement, written for the Holy See by the same author. It concerned 'The position of the Holy See with regard to 'Emissaries' of a certain 'knightly order' which gives itself the title of "Sovereign and Military Order of the Temple of Jerusalem".' There are several reference in this volume to Orders and Masonic organisations calling themselves 'of the Temple of Jerusalem'. This particular organisation appears to have aroused the Holy See's especial condemnation. The statement, to which I also refer above, reads in part:

'Their unqualified behaviour compels Us to put on their guard all the members of the Hierarchy in Italy and in other countries....; in the specific case at hand, the historical vicissitudes of the ancient Order of the Temple (the Knights Templars), suppressed (*sic*) by Pope Clement V

(1305-1314) and never again revived by any of his successors, are well known[1].

'It is hence obvious that its contemporary revival, aggravated by the pretended appellation of "Sovereign", appears to be an evident abuse and is therefore illegitimate.'

Archbishop Cardinale told me that Paul VI had personally ordered the author to write this condemnation for publication, though I never discovered the reason why Pope Paul VI felt so strongly about this particular organisation.

There is no doubt that the Orders most imitated and offended against are the Sovereign Military Order of Malta and the Venerable Order of St. John (United Kingdom). The above-mentioned book, *Ordres & Contre Ordres de Chevalerie*, lists sixteen of these imitation orders, all of which were founded between 1960 and 1975.

On 1 December 1976, *L'Osservatore Romano* published the above-mentioned statement concerning the 'Sovereign Order of St. John of Jerusalem' extracts of which follow:

A fantasy decoration – the Grand Cross of a self-styled Order of the Temple. It is silver-gilt, red-enamelled with the motto 'NON NOBIS SED OMNIBUS' in the band between the arms of the cross.

Courtesy: Spink & Son, Ltd.

---

[1] I have already referred to the Bull of 1319 by John XXII, a copy of which I received from the Secretary General of the Presidency of the Republic of Portugal.

.ries have been received from various parties asking for information regarding the "Sovereign Order of St. John of em" and in particular regarding how the Holy See looks on this

'We are authorised to repeat the clarification previously published in *L'Osservatore Romano* in this connexion. *The Holy See, in addition to its own Equestrian Orders, recognises only two Orders of Knighthood: The Sovereign Military Order of St. John of Jerusalem, called The Order of Malta, and The Equestrian Order of the Holy Sepulchre of Jerusalem* [italics added].

'No other Order, whether it be newly instituted or derived from a medieval Order having the same name, enjoys such recognition, as the Holy See is not in a position to guarantee its historical and juridical legitimacy. This is also the case with regard to the above-mentioned "Sovereign Order of St. John of Jerusalem" which assumes, in an almost identical form and in such a way as to cause ambiguity, the name of the Sovereign Military Order of Malta.'

The Grand Magistry of the Sovereign Military Order of Malta issued the following official statement in 1985 which I included in the 1985[1] edition of Mons. Cardinale's book:

'The Sovereign and Military Hospitaller Order of St. John of Jerusalem, of Rhodes and of Malta, currently known as the Order of Malta or the Sovereign Order, is the direct continuation of the Order of the Hospital of St. John founded in Jerusalem during the Crusades. Its governing monastic nucleus, springing directly from the religious community of the Hospital recognised by Pope Pascal II in 1113 as a Religious Order of the Church, which subsequently assumed a chivalric character; the uninterrupted recognition of its sovereign status and of its independence of any other State by the international community – it presently enjoys diplomatic relations with some forty-four States, are all proofs of its identity and authenticity.

'The Sovereign Order also maintains friendly relations with the other Orders of St. John, which are legitimate through their establishment by regnant Royal Houses, the Venerable Order of St. John in Great Britain and the Johanniter Orden in some North European countries. It collaborates with these Orders in the defence against unwarrantable usurpation of the names of the Order of St. John or of Malta by some private groups which pretend to be what they are not.

'There are in fact at present some twenty groups, mostly pretending to be the Sovereign Order, or 'branches' of it, as such assuming the appellation 'sovereign', selling 'diplomatic passports', endeavouring to

---

[1]Mons. Cardinale considered it inappropriate to include in his book any statement issued by the Sovereign Military Order of Malta; (see Chapter Five).

establish diplomatic relations with unsuspecting States and, of course, strenuously recruiting members.[1]

'So as to secure themselves against possible lawsuits, they use styles that are very similar to, but not identical with, the full style of the Sovereign Order, and these styles induce the gullible and the vain (many of whom ought to know better) into believing their pretensions. Some of these groups have registered themselves in various countries, especially in the United States, as charitable organisations.

'Needless to say, many perpetrators of these pretentious and false claims do not fail to attribute to themselves a variety of unauthentic names and titles.

'Appended here is a list of the twenty self-styled orders, compiled by a group of French researchers and leading experts in this field, with English translations of their various styles:

1) Sovereign Order of Saint John of Jerusalem, Knights of Malta; (1908?)
2) Sovereign Order of the Hospital of St. John of Jerusalem of Denmark (also called Autonomous Grand Priory of Dacia of the Maltese Order); (1934)
3) Sovereign Order of Jerusalem, Knights of Malta; (also known as The Knights Hospitaller O.S.J.) (1961/62)
4) Sovereign Order of St. John of Jerusalem, Knights Hospitallers; (1965)
5) French Fraternity of the Order of St. John of Jerusalem; (1965)
6) Military and Hospitaller Order of St. John of Jerusalem, Byzantine Protectorate; (1968)
7) Order of St. John of Jerusalem, Knights of Malta; (1968/69)
8) Sovereign Military and Hospitaller of John of Jerusalem, Knights of Malta, (also called Oecumenical Knights of Malta); (1970)
9) Grand Priory of Malta of the Sovereign Order of St. John of Jerusalem, Knights Hospitaller; (1970)
10) Sovereign Order of Hospitallers of St. John of Jerusalem, Knights of Malta; (1970/71)
11) Grand International Priory of the Sovereign Order of St. John of Jerusalem, Knights of Malta; (1971)

---

[1] The late Judge Caroline K. Simon of the New York Supreme Court mentioned four cases that had gone to appeal; from the charges it appears that Frà Cyril Prince Toumanoff credited the sale of these 'diplomatic passports' with too generous a purpose. Purchasers of these worthless documents acquired them not to establish diplomatic relations with gullible states, but merely to bluff country sheriffs and highway patrols to avoid speeding tickets. Many sheriffs appeared to have been sufficiently impressed to grant these 'diplomats' immunity and did not issue speeding tickets. The lengthy appeal proceedings in the U.S.A. often led attorneys for the defendants to demand the return of the 'diplomatic passport' whilst the next appeal was being prepared. Judge Simon believed that for every case coming to court, probably twenty escaped detection and prosecution. Speeding offences are not Federal cases, and an offender going to appeal and receiving his 'diplomatic passport' back until that appeal has been heard, can move to another State and continue to offend with impunity, unless he is caught by a not so gullible and observant sheriff.

12) The Sovereign Military Order of St. John of Jerusalem, Knights of Malta (1971)
13) Grand Priory of Russia of the O.S.J.; (1972/73)
14) Order of St. John of Jerusalem, Knights Hospitallers of Malta, Priory of the Holy Redeemer; (?)
15) Knights of Malta, Sovereign Order of St. John, Priory of the U.S.A. (1980/81)
16) American Grand Priory of the Sovereign Order of St. John Knights of Malta (1981)
17) The Orthodox Hospitallers; (of recent origin)[1]
18) Sovereign Order of the Orthodox Hospitallers of St. John; (of recent origin)
19) Orthodox Hospitallers of St. John; (of recent origin)
20) Ordre Souverain de St-Jean Baptiste, Milice des Hospitaliers; (of recent origin)

'Since all these groups have pretensions to claim for themselves the "Russian Tradition", a consequence of the Grand Mastership which Czar Paul (1799-1801) bestowed upon himself, it is proper to underline that His Imperial Highness the Grand Duke Wladimir, Head of the Imperial Russian House, Bailiff Grand Cross of the Sovereign Military Order of Malta, has, in January 1977, appointed to the aforesaid Sovereign Order a personal ambassador, authorized "to intervene in my name, to assist the Sovereign Military and Hospitaller Order of St. John of Jerusalem, of Rhodes and of Malta on every occasion which will present itself to act against the false associations, which usurping the titles belonging to the Sovereign Order, pretend to have their origin in Russia".'

On 14 August 1979, H.R.H. Prince Alexander, Head of the Royal House of Yugoslavia, son and heir of ex-King Peter II of Yugoslavia wrote a letter to the Prince and Grand Master of the Sovereign Military Order of Malta renouncing in clear terms any association of the Royal House of Yugoslavia with the self-styled Order 'La Orden de los Caballeros Hospitalarios de San Juan de Jerusalén' (The Order of the Knights

---

[1] On 2 December 1972, Archbishop Makarios III, Ethnarch and President of the Republic of Cyprus, founded the Order of the Orthodox Hospitallers and domiciled its headquarters in the Monastery of St. Barnabas, near Famagusta. In 1974, part of Cyprus was invaded, and the Monastery occupied by Turkish troops. After the death of Archbishop Makarios in 1977, his successor as Ethnarch of Cyprus, Archbishop Chrysostomos I, became the Order's new Grand Master, and Mr. Spyros Kyprianou, the new President of the Republic, its Temporal Protector. The administration of the Order was in the care of Baron von Bennigson in London. Many ecclesiastical dignitaries of other Churches and prominent lay persons were decorated with the Order's insignia. There appeared no doubt that the Orthodox Hospitallers was a legitimate Hospitaller Order. In 1988/89, the statutes and status of the Order were changed which consequently made it a new foundation. Juridically, conferments of insignia prior to 1988 are recognised, those after the change of status of the Order, must be regarded as having been given by a self-styled organisation. For this reason, I have reinstated the Orthodox Hospitallers in the list published by the Order of Malta.

Hospitallers of St. John of Jerusalem). His father, King Peter II of Yugoslavia had accepted in 1965 until his death in 1970 the position as Sovereign Protector of that organisation.

The question as to whether or not claims by self-styled Orders that they have a Russian tradition and are legitimate descendants of hereditary Russian Commanderies of the Sovereign Military Order of Malta are substantiated, was neither solved by the letters of His Imperial Highness the Grand Duke Wladimir, who distanced the Imperial Royal Family from the abuses going on, nor by the letter of H.R.H. Prince Alexander of Yugoslavia, severing his Dynasty's patronage over the above mentioned organisation. There always remained a lingering doubt that possibly some of these groups could have been descendants of hereditary Russian Commanderies which undoubtedly were in existence for a while. The generally used 'history' of these groups was always linked to the Russian Revolution in 1917 and the emigration of many noble Russian families to Western Europe and America.

In 1993, the Government of the Russian Federation, in collaboration with Russia's foremost experts on Russian Orders, published for the first time a statement,[1] giving exact details about the Czar's renunciation of his Grand Mastership and the legal act that followed, which sealed the fate of any pretensions by self-styled Orders to claim descent from a Russian Hereditary Commandery of the Sovereign Military Order of Malta. Following the history of the brief existence of the Order in Russia, the Government of the Russian Federation concludes:

'After the assassination of Czar Paul, his son and successor, Alexander I, declared himself the Order's Patron by a special Manifesto of April 16, 1801; but shortly afterwards the Maltese insignia were removed from the state emblem, and in 1803, Alexander I renounced the title of Patron and Protector of the Order.

'This was followed, on January 20, 1817, by a Legal Act under which heirs to family Commanders could no longer inherit the title after their death and had no right to wear the insignia of the Order of St. John of Jerusalem (alias of Malta) as the said Order did not exist in Russia any more.'

It would be stretching the imagination somewhat to think that a nobleman, well over 100 years old, emigrated from Russia in 1917 and founded a Commandery abroad. Even if such a miracle had occurred, the Legal Act of 1817 would have made it impossible for such a Commandery to be valid.

Archbishop Cardinale, who in 1979 had asked me to look after the chapter on self-styled orders, always expressed his distaste for these organisations, but it was not until after his death that I really appreciated

---

[1] *Voskresenie and the Government of the Russian Federation*, Moscow, 1993.

why he spoke of the embarrassment they caused him. Since 1983, I have been approached time and again, in writing and verbally at receptions and other functions, by members of self-styled orders, usually asking to be included in my book among the 'Orders recognised by the Vatican'. They were persistent in their demands even after I had explained that the Vatican did not recognise any Orders of Knighthood.

Decorations of every nature obviously fulfil a need in mankind's psyche – witness the satisfaction of those receiving awards from the Queen in the New Year's Honours List, for example – and it is therefore inaccurate to claim that they are an anachronism in this day and age. The strength of this urge in many people is so strong that they are prepared to go to almost any lengths to obtain some 'gong' or other decoration, and are therefore often prepared to put their common sense aside and accept the assurances given them by the purveyors of many unrecognised awards. However, I am always sorry for the individuals concerned if it is obvious that they have acquired their decorations in Rome and genuinely believe that the Pope or the Vatican has decorated them or made them knights. These are truly innocents abroad: they are exploited by those on the lookout for gullible people who feel that recognition of their services to the Church is long overdue, and are therefore psychologically in the right frame of mind to believe that such self-styled orders or individuals are the answer to their deepest desires.

APPENDICES

APPENDIX I

The original Papal Letters of Foundation, Papal Letters of Reconstitution, Papal Decrees, Apostolic Letters and Decrees issued by the Chancellery of the Pontifical Orders of Knighthood, Papal Letters concerning changes of the criteria of conferment of Honours, The Decree abolishing titles of nobility, Papal Decree of Foundation of the Pian Collar, The Letter of Foundation of the Cross 'Pro Ecclesia et Pontifice'.

DE SUPREMO EQUESTRI ORDINE MILITIAE D. N. IESU CHRISTI

Excerpta Brevi SS. D.N. Pii PP. X 'De Ordinibus Equestribus' pro Supremo Ordine Militiae D.N. Iesu Christi	563
Ex Cancellaria Ordinum Equestrium	564
Forma recipiende novos Milites ad habitum Supremi Ordinis Militiae D. N. Iesu Christi	566

DE EQUESTRI ORDINE MILITIAE AURATAE

Excerpta Brevi SS. D. N. Pii PP. X 'De Ordinibus Equestribus' pro Ordine Militiae Aurate	569
Ex Cancellaria Ordinum Equestrium	571

DE EQUESTRI ORDINE PIANO

Breve Pii PP. IX pro Equestris Piani Ordinis institutione	573
Breve Pii PP. IX de ratione gestandi Insignia Piani Ordinis propria	575
Decretum Pii PP. IX pro triplici Equitum classe in Piano Ordine constituenda	577
Ex Cancellaria Ordinum Equestrium (Pius PP. X, MDCCCCV)	578
Breve Pii PP. XII de nobilitatis privilegio iam Ordinis Piani proprio abolendo. (MCMXXXIX)	581

DE EQUESTRI ORDINE PIANO PRO EQUITIBUS TORQUATIS

Breve Pii PP. XII de institutione novi gradus, seu torquis aurei, in Ordine Piano. (Pius PP. XII, MDCCCCLVII)	582
Ex Cancellaria Ordinum Equestrium	583

DE EQUESTRI ORDINE S. GREGORII MAGNI

Breve Gregorii PP. XVI pro institutione Equestris Ordinis S. Gregorii Magni	584
Breve Gregorii PP. XVI pro tribus tantum gradibus in Equestri Gregoriano Ordine servandis et pro insignibus singulorum graduum propriis statuendis. (MDCCCXXXIV)	586
Ex Cancellaria Ordinum Equestrium. (Pius PP. X, MDCCCCV)	589

DE EQUESTRI ORDINE S. SILVESTRI PAPAE

Excerpta Brevi SS. D. N. Pii X 'De Ordinibus Equestribus' pro Ordine Sancti Silvestri Papae. (MDCCCCV)	594
Ex Cancellaria Ordinum Equestrium. (MDCCCCV)	597

LITTERAE APOSTOLICAE MOTU PROPRIO DE ORDINUM EQUESTRIUM DIGNITATE IIS DEFERENDA QUI CIVITATIBUS PRAESUNT PAULUS PP. VI (MCMLXVI) 600

LITTERAE APOSTOLICAE DE HONORIS SIGNO IIS TRIBUENDO QUI FAUSTUM EVENTUM SACERDOTALIS IUBILAEI SUMMI PONTIFICIS SINGULARI STUDIO SUNT PROSEQUUTI LEO PP. XIII. (MDCCCLXXXVIII) 602

Excerpta Brevi SS. D. N. Pii PP. X " De Ordinibus Equestribus "
pro Supremo Ordine Militiae D. N. Iesu Christi.

PIUS PP. X

Ad perpetuam rei memoriam. — Multum ad excitandos ad egregia facinora hominum animos praemia virtuti reddita valent, quae, dum ornant egregios bene de re sacra vel publica meritos viros, ceteros exemplo rapiunt ad idem laudis honorisque spatium decurrendum. Hoc quidem sapienti consilio Romani Pontifices Decessores Nostri Equestres Ordines, quasi gloriae stimulos, singulari studio prosequuti sunt, horumque alios instituere, alios iam institutos, vel pristino decori restituerunt, vel novis ac potioribus privilegiis ditarunt.

Nunc autem, cum peropportunum visum sit gravibus de causis quaedam immutare de nonnullis Equestribus Pontificiis Ordinibus, Nos collatis consiliis cum dilecto filio Nostro Aloisio S. R. Ecclesiae Diacono Cardinali Macchi, a Brevibus apostolicis Literis Secretario, et Pontificiae Sedis Equestrium Ordinum Magno Cancellario, omnibus rei momentis attente ac sedulo perpensis, ex certa scientia ac matura deliberatione Nostris haec quae infrascripta sunt decernenda existimavimus.

Oculos mentis Nostrae convertentes ad Militiae Iesu Christi nobilissimum Ordinem, quem anno MCCCXVIII post Ordinis Templi ruinam Dionysius I Portugalliae et Algarbiorum Rex auctore et auspice Ioanne PP. XXII rec. mem. Praedecessore Nostro instituit, hunc Equestrium Pontificiae Sedis Ordinum Supremum esse auctoritate Nostra per praesentes edicimus ac mandamus, quo non alter sit dignitate potior, sed ceteris amplitudine ac splendore supereminent. Una sit Equitum classis. Sed quo magis per Nos consultum sit huius Supremi Ordinis decori volumus ut posthac Crux, Ordinis propria, collo dependeat ex aureo torqui, qui constet alternis clypeolis Crucem Ordinis ac Pontificium Emblema enchausto referentibus, nodis aureis inter se iunctis. Traditum enim memoriae est, et ipsos veteres dictae Militiae Equites simili torqui iamdiu usos fuisse alternis ensibus ac tiaris caelato. Similiter volumus ut in magno Numismate corona laurea ex auro, parva taenia ex enchausto rubro inferius vincta, Crucem concludat; tandem ut femoralia alba e serico rasili genua vix praetergrediantur; caligae sint sericae, et item albae; aureae denique fibulae calceolos ornent. Quoad vestem, ensem et alia ornamenta nihil immutetur.

Verum tamen expresse mandamus, ne inter Equites eiusdem Militiae discrimen contingat, sed unusquisque Ordo stemmata, insignia, arma, atque ornamenta, a Sancta Sede praescripta servet integerrime, ut praefata insignia Cruces, Numismata, vestes, enses, opera phrygia, atque ornamenta, tum propria Supremi Ordinis Militiae Iesu Christi, cum ceterorum quos Apostolica Sedes conferre solet, sint adamussim confecta ad normam exemplarium et declarationum quas a Cancelleria Equestrium Ordinum edi et penes Nostram a Brevibus Apostolicis Literis Secretariam iussimus asservari; utque prae oculis habeantur apposita schemata, quae singulis vicibus cuilibet equestri dignitate aucto de more traduntur.

Haec statuimus, mandamus, praecipimus, decernentes praesentes Literas firmas, validas, atque efficaces semper fore et existere, suosque plenarios atque integros effectus sortiri atque obtinere, illisque, ad quos spectat et pro tempore spectabit, in omnibus et per omnia plenissime suffragari: sicque in praemissis per quoscumque iudices ordinarios et delegatos et alios quoslibet quacumque praeeminentia et potestate fungentes, sublata eis et eorum cuilibet quavis aliter iudicandi et interpretandi facultate et auctoritate, iudicari et definiri debere: irritumque et inane si secus quidquam super his a quocumque quavis auctoritate scienter vel ignoranter contigerit attentari. Non obstantibus Nostra et Cancellariae Apostolicae regula de iure quaesito non tollendo, aliisque Constitutionibus et Ordinationibus Apostolicis, nec non supradictorum et aliorum quorumcumque Equestrium Ordinum etiam iuramento, confirmatione Apostolica, vel quavis firmitate alia roboratis Statutis et consuetudinibus, ceterisque contrariis, licet speciali mentione dignis, quibuscumque, privilegiis quoque, indultis, et Literis Apostolicis, in contrarium praemissorum quomodolibet concessis, confirmatis et innovatis; quibus omnibus et singulis, illorum tenores praesentibus pro plene et sufficienter expressis ac de verbo ad verbum insertis habentes, illis alias in suo robore permansuris, ad praemissorum effectum hac vice dumtaxat specialiter et expresse derogamus. Datum Romae apud Sanctum Petrum sub Annulo Piscatoris die 7 Februarii anno MDCCCCV, Pontificatus Nostri anno secundo.

ALOISIUS Card. MACCHI.

Ex Cancellaria Ordinum Equestrium

Die 7 Februarii 1905.

SSmus Dominus Noster Pius Papa X, animo repetens omnia, quae ab Apostolica Sede sive ad homines virtute formandos sive ad praemia iisdem pro recte factis rependenda iugiter emanant, iis legibus servanda esse quibus et decori eiusdem Sedis et congrue rationi consultum sit, opportune mentem suam ad Equestres Ordines admovit.

Hinc est quod, re prius acta cum infrascripto Cardinali a Brevibus, magno Equestrium Ordinum Cancellario, sacrum et perillustrem illum Ordinem, ab eo appellatum Nomine in quo omnes genuflectantur oportet, Militiae nempe Domini Nostri Iesu Christi, iis praerogativis et insignibus commendatum voluit quibus, ut decet, ceteros Equestres Ordines antecellat.

Honorarias hasce praerogativas sartas tectasque praestitit per Breve hoc ipso die datum et specialia insignia adamussim statuta per leges quae hic sequuntur.

Pro Equitibus a Magno Torqui
Supremi Ordinis Militiae D. N. Iesu Christi.

Vestis e panno rubri coloris siet in longos post tergum producta limbos.

Circa collum atque ad extremas manicas sit e panno albo.

E panno item albo gestet pectorale.

Opera phrygia, omnia acu picta ex auro, circa collum, pectorale et extremas manicas taeniola dentata sint et laciniae laureas referentes; iuxta et supra peras pariter sint laureae acu pictae, quae inter utramque in sertum copulentur.

Posteriores vestis limbi ad quatuor extremas oras acu picto trophaeo Ordinis decorentur.

Duplex pectorali globulorum series, pro unoquoque latere novem; tres minoris moduli sive manicis sive circa peras, duo vero moduli maioris sub laurearum serto sint globuli.

Humeralia, aureo panno squamante prout in schemate contecta, superne globulo firmentur Crucemque Ordinis propriam acu pictam referant: aureis sint distincta circumdependentibus ut in schemate fimbriis exercituum Ducum propriis.

Femoralia, e serico rasili albo, brevia sunto: fibula et duobus parvis globulis sub genu nectantur.

Sint caligae e serico albo.

Calceoli nigri, lucidi, ornentur fibula aurea.

Galero nigro ex sericis coactilibus, aurea fascia praedivite circumornato, alba supereminaet pluma; eique Insigne Pontificium quatuor ex auro funiculis globulo coniunctis innexum sit.

Globuli, omnes ex auro, Crucem Ordinis caelato opere referant.

Item et ensis aurato cingulo suffultus, Crucem Ordinis prout a schemate apparet, in capulo caelatam referat; capulus ipse sit e concha albida ornatus auro, cum aureo dependente fimbriato funiculo; vagina ex corio nigro aureis fulcro et cuspide terminetur.

Torquis, Crux, Numisma, globuli quoad modulos et formam a schemate non differant.

ALOISIUS Card. MACCHI
MAGNUS CANCELLARIUS ORDINUM EQUESTRIUM.

NOTANDUM. - *Cum aliquem huius Supremi Ordinis Equitem ex hac vita migrare contingat, haeredibus curae sit huic Cancellariae decessum significare.*

Forma recipiendi novos Milites
ad habitum Supremi Ordinis Militiae D. N. Iesu Christi.

Novus Eques, Iesu Christi Militiam initurus, acceptis Apostolicis Litteris suae creationis, medius inter duos eiusdem militiae equites, uni ex Eminentissimis Cardinalibus sibi beneviso se sistat [1].

Emus Cardinalis, sedens vel apud altare in proprio Sacello vel in aula nobiliori sub baldachino, ad Novum Militem ante se genuflexum haec primo habet:

Quid petis?

Novus Miles respondet:

Eminentissime (*seu* Illustrissime) et Reverendissime Pater et Domine, peto me recipi ad habitum Militiae Domini Nostri Iesu Christi.

Tunc Emus Novum Militem interrogat:

Habes litteras Apostolicas?

Novus Miles exhibens Breve SSmi D. N. Papae respondet:

Habeo.

Emus tunc dicit:

Legantur.

Hic per caeremoniarum magistrum legitur Breve Apostolicum.

Post Brevis lectionem Emus iterum Novum Militem interrogat:

Promittis Deo, SSmo D. N. Papae; nec non Ordinario tuo pro tempore existenti reverentiam et obedientiam?

Novus Miles respondet:

Promitto.

Et Emus subdit:

Promittis ordinationes omnes Pontificias, leges, consuetudines approbatas, iura, honorem et decorem Supremi Ordinis Militiae D. N. Iesu Christi te pro viribus observaturum et defensurum?

Et Novus Miles respondet iterum:

Promitto.

Tunc Emus prosequitur:

Emitte iuramentum professionis fidei.

Novus Miles adhuc genuflexus legit clara voce fidei professionem, ut sequitur:

Ego _____ firma fide credo et profiteor omnia et singula, quae continentur in Symbolo fidei, quo Sancta Romana Ecclesia utitur, videlicet:

Credo in unum Deum, Patrem Omnipotentem: factorem coeli et terrae, visibilium omnium et invisibilium.

---

[1] *In locis ubi non adsit Emus Cardinalis, Novus Miles Episcopum suae dioecesis pro sui receptione ad habitum Militiae D. N. Iesu Christi adire debet. Ita etiam si inibi, ut plerumque, desint duo eiusdem praefatae Militiae Equites, eos in hoc sibi testes assumat viros, qui tali Equestris Ordinis, praesertim Pontificii, dignitatis gradu emineant, quo haud longe ab Iesu Christi Militibus differant.*

Et in unum Dominum Iesum Christum, filium Dei unigenitum: et ex Patre natum ante omnia saecula: Deum de Deo, Lumen de Lumine, Deum verum de Deo vero; Genitum non factum, Consubstantialem Patri, per quem omnia facta sunt; Qui propter nos homines, et propter nostram salutem descendit de coelis: et incarnatus est de Spiritu Sancto ex Maria Virgine, et homo factus est; crucifixus etiam pro nobis, sub Pontio Pilato passus, et sepultus est; et resurrexit tertia die secundum Scripturas; et ascendit in coelum: sedet ad dexteram Patris; et iterum venturus est cum gloria iudicare vivos et mortuos: cuius regni non erit finis.

Et in Spiritum Sanctum, Dominum et vivificantem, qui ex Patre Filioque procedit; qui cum Patre et Filio simul adoratur et conglorificatur; qui loquutus est per Prophetas.

Et Unam, Sanctam, Catholicam et Apostolicam Ecclesiam.

Confiteor unum baptisma in remissionem peccatorum.

Et expecto resurrectionem mortuorum, et vitam venturi saeculi. Amen.

Apostolicas et Ecclesiasticas traditiones, reliquasque eiusdem Ecclesiae observationes et constitutiones firmissime admitto et amplector.

Item Sacram Scripturam iuxta eum sensum, quem tenuit et tenet Sancta Mater Ecclesia, cuius est iudicare de vero sensu et interpretatione Sacrarum Scripturarum, admitto; nec eam unquam nisi iuxta unanimem consensum Patrum accipiam et interpretabor.

Profiteor quoque septem esse vere et proprie Sacramenta novae legis a Iesu Christo Domino Nostro instituta, atque ad salutem humani generis, licet non omnia singulis, necessaria; scilicet: Baptismum, Confirmationem, Eucharistiam, Poenitentiam, Extremam Unctionem, Ordinem et Matrimonium; illaque gratiam conferre, et ex his Baptismum, Confirmationem et Ordinem sine sacrilegio reiterari non posse. Receptos quoque et approbatos Ecclesiae Catholicae ritus in supradictorum sacramentorum solemni administratione recipio, et admitto.

Omnia et singula, quae de peccato originali et de iustificatione in Sacrosancta Tridentina Synodo definita et declarata fuerunt, amplector et recipio.

Profiteor pariter in Missa offerri Deo verum, proprium et propitiatorium sacrificium pro vivis et defunctis; atque in sanctissimo Eucharistiae Sacramento esse vere, realiter et substantialiter Corpus et Sanguinem una cum anima et divinitate Domini Nostri Iesu Christi: fierique conversionem totius substantiae panis in Corpus et totius substantiae vini in Sanguinem, quam conversionem Catholica Ecclesia Transubstantiationem appellat. Fateor etiam sub altera tantum specie totum atque integrum Christum, verumque Sacramentum sumi.

Constanter teneo Purgatorium esse, animasque ibi detentas Fidelium suffragiis iuvari. Similiter et Sanctos, una cum Christo regnantes, venerandos atque invocandos esse: eosque orationes Deo pro nobis offerre: atque eorum reliquias esse venerandas. Firmissime assero imagines Christi ac Deiparae semper Virginis, nec non aliorum Sanctorum habendas et retinendas esse, atque eis debitum honorem ac venerationem impertiendam.

Indulgentiarum etiam potestatem a Christo in Ecclesia relictam fuisse, illarumque usum Christiano populo maxime salutarem esse affirmo.

Sanctam, Catholicam, et Apostolicam Romanam Ecclesiam, omnium Ecclesiarum matrem et magistram agnosco; Romanoque Pontifici, Beati Petri Apostolorum Principis successori ac Iesu Christi Vicario, veram obedientiam spondeo ac iuro.

Caetera item omnia a Sacris Canonibus et Oecumenicis Conciliis, ac praecipue a Sacrosancta Tridentina Synodo et ab Oecumenico Concilio Vaticano tradita, definita et declarata, praesertim de Romani Pontificis Primatu et Infallibili Magisterio, indubitanter recipio atque profiteor; simulque contraria omnia atque haereses quascumque ab Ecclesia damnatas et reiectas et anathematizatas ego pariter damno, reiicio et anathematizo.

Hanc veram Catholicam Fidem, extra quam nemo salvus esse potest, quam in praesenti sponte confiteor et veraciter teneo, eamdem integram et inviolatam usque ad extremum vitae spiritum constantissime, Deo adiuvante, retinere et confiteri, atque a meis subditis vel illis, quorum cura ad me spectat seu spectare poterit, teneri et profiteri, quantum in me erit, pro meo munere curaturum spondeo, voveo et iuro.

Ego idem [1] .... denique promitto quoque et voveo Omnipotenti Deo, Sanctissimae Virgini Immaculatae Mariae et omnibus Sanctis me semper, divino fretum auxilio, uti bonum decet Militem Christi Iesu, spectatam virtutibus vitam in posterum traducturum.

Hic novus miles manu tangens Evangelium prosequitur:
Sic me Deus adiuvet et haec Sancta Dei Evangelia.
Postea osculatur imaginem Iesu Christi Crucifixi.
Tunc Emus surgens ad collum Novi Militis magnum Torquem aureum cum Cruce Ordinis imponit, dicens:

Accipe iugum Domini, quod leve et suave est; et hoc Redemptionis Nostrae Signum, quod tibi imponimus, cum honore et gaudio dignius quotidie perferas.

In Nomine Patris ✠ et Filii ✠ et Spiritus ✠ Sancti.
Omnes respondent:
Amen.

Datum et receptum iuramentum in aedibus nostris [2] ....

    die .... ✠ [3] ....

    Testes fuimus } [4]

---

[1] *Hic Novus Miles propria manu ponere debet suam signaturam per nomen et agnomen*
[2] *Hic indicetur locus.*
[3] *Hic manu propria signet Emus Cardinalis, vel Rmus Episcopus, prout contigerit.*
[4] *Hic signent manu propria duo Equites testes.*

Excerpta Brevi SS. D. N. Pii PP. X "De Ordinibus Equestribus"
pro Ordine Militiae Auratae.

PIUS PP. X

Ad perpetuam rei memoriam. – Multum ad excitandos ad egregia facinora hominum animos praemia virtuti reddita valent, quae dum ornant egregios bene de re sacra vel publica meritos viros, ceteros exemplo rapiunt ad idem laudis honorisque spatium decurrendum. Hoc quidem sapienti consilio Romani Pontifices Decessores Nostri Equestres Ordines, quasi gloriae stimulos, singulari studio prosequuti sunt, horumque alios instituere, alios iam institutos vel pristino decori restituerunt, vel novis ac potioribus privilegiis ditarunt.

Nunc autem, cum peropportunum visum sit gravibus de causis quaedam immutare de nonnullis Equestribus Pontificiis Ordinibus, Nos collatis consiliis cum dilecto filio Nostro Aloisio S. R. Ecclesiae Diacono Cardinali Macchi, a Brevibus Apostolicis Literis Secretario, et Pontificiae Sedis Equestrium Ordinum Magno Cancellario, omnibus rei momentis attente ac sedulo perpensis, ex certa scientia ac matura deliberatione Nostris haec, quae infrascripta sunt, decernenda existimavimus.

Quod attinet ad Ordinem Militiae Auratae, sive ab Aureo Calcari, auctoritate Nostra ab Ordine Sancti Silvestri Papae seiunctum, animo repetentes vetustissimas et gloriosas Ordinis illius memorias, Nos eum non solum ad pristinum gradum restituere sed novo etiam splendore cohonestare, ac funditus sub coelesti Immaculatae Virginis patrocinio per praesentes instaurare statuimus. Et sane cum Pontificia Sedes Ordine Equestri careat, quod sit sub Virginis praesidio constitutus, hoc potissimum anno a solemni definitione Dogmatis Immaculatae Conceptionis quinquagesimo, atque hac tempestate qua tot tantaque mala videt lugetque christianus orbis, placet Nobis huic Equestri Ordini, in quem dumtaxat fortissimi Ecclesiae Dei vindices atque adsertores erunt cooptandi, coelestem Patronam Immaculatam illam Deiparam Virginem adsignare, quae « terribilis sicut castrorum acies ordinata » draconis inferni caput victrix usque conteret. Quocirca praecipimus ut in Ordinem Militiae Auratae, sive ab Aureo Calcari, ii tantum inserantur praestantissimi viri, qui vel armis, vel scriptis, vel praeclaris operibus rem Catholicam auxerint, et Ecclesiam Dei virtute tutarint, aut doctrina illustraverint, ideoque tribui poterit tum iis qui qualibet alia equestri dignitate sint expertes, cum illis qui iam splendidioribus titulis et ipso Supremo Militiae Iesu Christi Ordine potiantur. Ordo Militiae Auratae constet unica Equitum classi; Nostro et Romani Pontificis pro tempore existentis motu proprio conferatur: liber esto a iuribus Cancellariae;

Equites pro universo Catholico orbe centum numerum non excedant, ne dignitas ex frequentia minuatur. Quoad huius Ordinis propriam Crucem, iuxta tenorem similium Benedicti PP. XIV rec. mem. Nostri Decessoris in forma Brevis Literarum sub die VII Septembris mensis anni MDCCXXXXVII quibus cautum est ne Equites Militiae Auratae Crucem Hierosolymitani Ordinis usurparent, volumus ut Crux‧Ordinis eiusdem Auratae Militiae, sit octogona, aurea, enchausto flavo obducta, cum aureo inferius dependente calcari; referatque in medio parvum numisma album, aureo adversa parte inclusum circulo, et Augustissimo Virginis Mariae Nomine inscriptum, aversa vero numerum referat praesentis anni MDCCCCV et in circulo « Pius X restituit »; Cruci armorum trophaeum ex auro superemineat. Eadem Crux, argenteae stellae radiis super imposita, Ordinis Numisma sit. Careant Equites torqui, sitque eorum vestis rubri coloris tunica, duplici ordine globulorum ex auro, circa collum atque ad extremas manicas serico villoso nigro distincta cum fimbriis aureis. Humeralia sint, tum aureis laciniis, tum Ordinis Emblemate superne ornata. Femoralia praelonga, sint e panno nigro, cum aurea fascia. Calcaria aurea. Oblongus, duplici cuspide, fimbriatus auro galerus, Pontificios referat aureo nodo inclusos colores. Crucem gladii capulus imitetur: vagina sit nigra, balteus aureus cum fimbriis rubris. Sicuti priscis temporibus Ordinis taenia sit rubri coloris, sed circumdata albo. Gestent Equites Crucem taenia serica rubra extremis oris alba, collo circumducta dependentem; inserant ad pectus sinistro lateri Numisma. Quibus animi ingeniique dotibus lectissimos viros, hoc ordine decorandos, praeditos esse oporteat clare superius significavimus, ideoque ut hi semper meritis dumtaxat propriis commendentur, omnes concessiones etiam a Decessoribus Nostris Militiae auratae Equitibus factas, circa privilegium nobilitatis, et Palatini Comitis titulum, quae fortasse nondum sublatae fuerint vi similium Apostolicarum Literarum Gregorii PP. XVI sub die XXXI Octobris anni MDCCCXXXXI, quas ante recensuimus, per praesentes auctoritate Nostra interposita omnino abrogamus, easque in posterum nullius roboris esse decernimus ac statuimus.

Verum tamen expresse mandamus, ne inter Equites eiusdem Militiae discrimen contingat, sed unusquisque Ordo stemmata, insignia, arma atque ornamenta, a Sancta Sede praescripta, servet integerrime, ut praefata insignia Cruces, Numismata, vestes, enses, opera phrygia, atque ornamenta, tum propria Ordinis Militiae Auratae, cum ceterorum quos Apostolica Sedes conferre solet, sint adamussim confecta ad normam exemplarium et declarationum quas a Cancelleria Equestrium Ordinum edi et penes Nostram a Brevibus Apostolicis Literis Secretariam iussimus asservari; utque prae oculis habeantur apposita schemata, quae singulis vicibus cuilibet equestri dignitate aucto de more traduntur.

Haec statuimus, mandamus, praecipimus, decernentes praesentes Literas firmas, validas, atque efficaces semper fore et existere, suosque plenarios atque integros effectus sortiri atque obtinere, illisque ad quos spectat et pro tempore spectabit, in omnibus et per omnia plenissime suffragari: sicque in praemissis per quoscumque iudices ordinarios et delegatos et alios quoslibet quacumque praeeminentia et potestate fungentes, sublata eis et eorum cuilibet quavis aliter iudicandi et interpretandi facultate et auctoritate, iudicari et definiri debere: irritumque et inane si secus quidquam super his a quocumque quavis auctoritàte scienter vel ignoranter contigerit attentari. Non obstantibus Nostra et Cancellariae Apostolicae regula de iure quaesito non tollendo, aliisque Constitutionibus et Ordinationibus Apostolicis, nec non supradictorum et aliorum quorumcumque Equestrium Ordinum etiam iuramento, confirmatione Apostolica, vel quavis firmitate alia roboratis Statutis et consuetudinibus, ceterisque contrariis, licet speciali mentione dignis, quibuscumque: privilegiis quoque, indultis, et Literis Apostolicis, in contrarium praemissorum quomodolibet concessis, confirmatis et innovatis; quibus omnibus et singulis, illorum tenores praesentibus pro plene et sufficienter expressis ac de verbo ad verbum insertis habentes, illis alias in suo robore permansuris, ad praemissorum effectum hac vice dumtaxat specialiter et expresse derogamus. Datum Romae apud Sanctum Petrum sub Annulo Piscatoris die 7 Februarii anno MDCCCCV, Pontificatus Nostri anno secundo.

ALOISIUS Card. MACCHI.

Ex Cancellaria Ordinum Equestrium

Die 7 Februarii 1905.

SSmus Dominus Noster Pius Papa X, animo repetens omnia, quae ab Apostolica Sede sive ad homines virtute formandos sive ad praemia iisdem pro rectefactis rependenda iugiter emanant, iis legibus servanda esse quibus et decori eiusdem Sedis et congrue rationi consultum sit, opportune mentem suam ad Equestres Ordines admovit.

Hinc est quod, re prius acta cum infrascripto Cardinali a Brevibus, Magno Equestrium Ordinum Cancellario, vetustissimum et praeclarum illum, unicum apud Pontifices Maximos per saecula, Ordinem Auratae nempe Militiae sub auspiciis praepotentis illius Virginis, quae primum Dei profligavit inimicum, ad pristinum duxit revocandum esse decus: in quo lectissimi ex omni gradu cives pro suis tantum in religionem meritis adscribi valeant.

Honorarias eiusdem Ordinis praerogativas sartas tectasque voluit per Breve, hoc ipso die datum, et specialia insignia adamussim statuta per leges quae hic sequuntur:

Pro Equitibus Militiae Auratae.

Tunica e panno rubri coloris siet ante pectus duplex.

Circa collum atque ad extremas manicas nigrum gestet sericum villosum, taeniola dentata ex auro fimbriatum.

Duplex pectori globulorum ordo, pro unoquoque latere novem: tres minoris moduli sint manicis, quatuor ad extremas post tergum tunicae oras, duo maioris tamen moduli ad renes globuli sunto.

Humeralia, aureo panno contecta, superne globulo firmentur, Crucemque Ordinis acu pictam referant: aureis sint distincta circumdependentibus ut in schemate fimbriis exercituum Ducum propriis.

Femoralia praelonga e panno nigro sunto: fascia ornentur auro et rubri coloris lineolis contexta.

Galero nigro ex sericis coactilibus aurea fascia fimbriato Pontificium Insigne quatuor ex auro funiculis globulo coniunctis innexum siet.

Globuli, omnes ex auro, Crucem Ordinis propriam caelato opere referant.

Balteus aureus tribus coloris rubri lineis distinctus super tunicam fibula aurea Ordinis Crucem referente nectatur.

Gladii capulus aureus esto et, prouti a schemate apparet, crucis formam imitetur; vagina e corio nigro aureis pariter fulcro, Cruce Ordinis distincto, et cuspide terminetur.

Calcaria aurea sunto.

Crux, Numisma, globuli quoad modulos et formas, taenia quoad colores et altitudinem a schemate non differant.

ALOISIUS Card. MACCHI
MAGNUS CANCELLARIUS ORDINUM EQUESTRIUM.

NOTANDUM. - *Cum aliquem huius Ordinis Equitem ex hac vita migrare contingat, haeredibus curae sit huic Cancellariae decessum significare ut de superstitum Equitum numero ratio semper habeatur.*

Breve Pii Pp. IX pro Equestris Piani Ordinis institutione

PIUS PP. IX

Ad perpetuam rei memoriam. – Romanis Pontificibus Praedecessoribus Nostris, quorum sapientiam non latuit quot uberes lectosque fructus incitamenta honoris producere soleant, non dedecere Apostolicum ministerium visum est certa laudis insignia rebus praeclare gestis tribuere, quo magis hominum animi ad optimas quasque disciplinas et omnigenas virtutes excolendas inflammarentur. Itaque quoniam Nobis, ad summi Apostolatus apicem divina favente clementia evectis, non solum aeternam animarum salutem verum etiam temporalem populi regimini Nostro commissi felicitatem exquirere incumbit; ita ad tantum tamque sublimem finem consequendum eorumdem Praedecessorum Nostrorum vestigia sectantes, praesertim vero fel. rec. Pii IV, qui Equitum Ordinem instituens eos a suo nomine Pianos voluit appellare ac pluribus nobilitatis titulis augere, nova et Nos honoris insignia decernenda statuimus per quae adeo in civili Societate praefulgeant ii, quibus fuerint conlata, ut aliis non modo exemplo, sed stimulo quoque ad egregia facinora obeunda et ad bene de Apostolica Sede merendum esse possint. Maximae porro amoris significationes ab ipso Nostri Pontificatus exordio Nobis oblatae, et eximii indicia obsequii supremae B. Petri Cathedrae in persona Nostrae humilitatis exhibita Nos certam in spem adducunt fore ut benedicente Domino consilium Nostrum ea, quae nunc edere decrevimus, iis ad quos praecipue spectant grato animo respondentibus, felicem sortiantur effectum. Quapropter hisce Nostris Apostolicis Litteris Equestrem Ordinem creamus et constituimus, qui, renovando praedictam illam denominationem a memorato Praedecessore Nostro Pio IV olim inductam, Ordo Pianus a nostro item Nomine nuncupabitur; qua quidem denominatione cum plurium ea de re votis annuere voluimus, tum id potissime propositum habuimus, ut Nostram peculiarius quoque benevolentiam viris praestantibus in Ordinem ipsum adlegendis testaremur. Ordo in duos dividetur gradus, quorum alter Equitibus primae classis, alter Equitibus secundae classis constabit. Qui in primam classem fuerint cooptati privilegio nobilitatis in filios quoque transmittendae potientur: Secundae classis Insigne nobilitatis titulo personam tantummodo afficiet. Proprium Ordinis Insigne ex auro stellae instar superficiem habebit, in octo radios caeruleos divisam, referentem in medio parvum numisma album in quo scriptum sit aureis litteris « PIVS IX »: circulus aureus numisma claudet, in eoque caeruleis literis inscripta sit epigraphe « VIRTVTI ET MERITO »: in parte numismatis aversa scriptum erit « ANNO MDCCCXLVII ». Primae classis Equites Insigne ipsum gestabunt ita ut e taenia collo inserta dependeat; taenia autem erit serica caerulea, duplici linea rubra extremis oris distincta. Equites secundae classis idem Insigne, minoris tamen moduli, eadem ex taenia pendens sinistro pectoris latere iuxta communem equitum morem deferent. Praeterea Equites propriam habebunt vestem caeruleo colore, rubris oris, aureis ornamentis decoratam : quae quidem ornamenta pro vario Equitum ipsorum gradu different; maiora scilicet pro prima classe, minora vero pro secunda erunt iuxta schema cuiusque classis proprium. Poterunt etiam primae classis Equites privilegium adipisci gestandi latere pectoris sinistro magnum Numisma argenteum Insigni simile; declaramus tamen nulli ex Equitibus licere eodem privilegio uti nisi peculiaris et expressa facultas facta sit. Reservamus autem Nobis Romanisque Pontificibus Successoribus Nostris ius eligendi Equites, itemque concedendi Equitibus primae classis memorati argentei Numismatis usum. Ceterum cum huiusmodi Ordo non ad vanitatem ambitionemque fovendam sed ad praemia virtutibus meritisque praestantibus retribuenda unice spectet, plene confidimus illos, qui hisce insignibus fuerint decorati, Pontificiae erga eos voluntati communique bonorum suffragio cumulatius in dies responsuros, splendoremque Ordinis, in quem relati fuerint, amplificaturos. Haec statuimus ac declaramus non obstantibus in contrarium facientibus, etiam speciali mentione dignis quibuscumque.

Datum Romae apud S. Mariam Majorem, sub Annulo Piscatoris, die XVII Junii MDCCCXLVII, Pontificatus Nostri anno primo.

A. Card. LAMBRUSCHINI

Breve Pii Pp. IX de ratione gestandi Insignia Piani Ordinis propria

PIUS PP. IX

Ad perpetuam rei memoriam. — Cum hominum mentes animique ita sint comparati, ut ad virtutis et justitiae semitam terendam atque ad optimas excolendas artes et pulcherrima quaeque peragenda facinora honorum et laudum gloria vehementer excitentur, tum Romani Pontifices Decessores Nostri provido sane consilio Equestres Ordines instituerunt, quo viris de christiana et civili republica ob egregia facta optime meritis debitos tribuerent honores, et alios ejusmodi stimulo ad illustria virtutum exempla imitanda inflammarent. Hac quidem mente per similes Nostras Apostolicas Litteras, die XVII Iunii Anno MDCCCXLVII editas, Equestrem Ordinem a Nostro Nomine Ordinem Pianum appellatum constituimus, illumque in duos gradus divisimus, quorum alterum Equitibus primae classis, alterum vero Equitibus secundae classis attribuimus: atque concessimus, ut primae tantum classis Equites pollerent privilegio transmittendi in filios nobilitatis titulum. Iisdem in Litteris proprium ejusdem Ordinis Insigne statuimus, quod ex auro confectum stellae instar superficiem habet in octo caeruleos radios divisam, parvum album numisma in medio referentem, in quo aureis litteris scriptum « PIVS IX », quod numisma aureo circulo clauditur, et in eo inscriptio caeruleis litteris posita « VIRTVTI ET MERITO », atque in parte aversa numismatis scriptum « ANNO MDCCCXLVII ». Statuimus quoque ut primae classis Equites illud Insigne e taenia serica caerulea, duplici linea rubra extremis oris distincta, collo inserta dependens gestarent, utque secundae classis Equites Insigne ipsum minoris moduli, atque eadem ex taenia pendens in sinistra vestis parte juxta communem equitum morem deferrent. Propriam quoque Equitum vestem sancivimus, quae caeruleo colore, rubris oris, ac variis aureis ornamentis est ornata pro vario ipsorum Equitum gradu. Insuper manifestavimus, primae classis Equites consequi posse privilegium gerendi magnum argenteum Numisma Insigni simile in sinistro pectoris latere innexum, declarantes nulli ex Equitibus licere ejusmodi uti privilegio nisi peculiaris et expressa facultas facta fuisset, ac Nobis et Romanis Pontificibus Successoribus Nostris jus reservavimus tum eligendi Equites, tum concedendi primae classis Equitibus commemorati argentei Numismatis usum. Iam vero hisce Nostris Apostolicis Litteris statuimus, atque decernimus, ut ii omnes qui in posterum Equites Piani Ordinis primae classis fuerint renunciati pollere debeant privilegio gestandi commemoratum magnum argenteum Numisma in sinistro pectoris latere, utque alterum proprium Ordinis Insigne, jam primae classis Equitibus attributum, non amplius e fascia collo inserta dependens veluti antea, sed ita deferant, ut idem Insigne fascia serica praelonga caerulei pariter coloris duplici linea rubri coloris extremis oris distincta dextero humero sustineatur. Et quoniam plures clarissimi Viri a Nobis in primam Piani Ordinis classem fuerunt cooptati cum privilegio gerendi memoratum magnum argenteum Numisma, iccirco per praesentes Litteras declaramus, ut ii tantum primae ipsius Ordinis classis Equites, quibus eiusdem Numismatis usus a Nobis fuit concessus, alterum Ordinis Insigne deferre possint et debeant quemadmodum Nostris hisce Litteris nunc praescribitur. Insuper primae Piani Ordinis classis Equites memoratum magnum argenteum Numisma coruscantibus quoque gemmis exornatum in posterum deferre poterunt, quando tamen id a Nobis et Romanis Pontificibus Successoribus Nostris peculiari et expressa facultate fuerit concessum, sine qua nemini umquam licebit magnum Numisma gemmis ornare. Haec statuimus, concedimus, et declaramus non obstantibus quibuscumque in contrarium facientibus, praesertim vero commemoratis Nostris Apostolicis Litteris die XVII Junii Anno MDCCCXLVII editis, quas in iis omnibus, quae praesentibus hisce Litteris minime adversantur, firmas atque in suo robore permansuras volumus atque mandamus.

Datum Cajetae, sub Annulo Piscatoris, die XVII Junii MDCCCXLIX, Pontificatus Nostri anno tertio.

IACOBUS Card. ANTONELLI

De speciali mandato SSmi

Decretum Pii Pp. IX pro triplici Equitum classe in Piano Ordine constituenda

In ipso Nostri Pontificatus exordio animum mentemque intendentes ad inflammandos hominum animos, ut egregia facinora obire et de Apostolica Sede benemereri contendant, Apostolicis Litteris sub Annulo Piscatoris expeditis die XVII Junii MDCCCXLVII Equestrem Ordinem creavimus et instituimus Pianum appellatum, eumque in duos gradus divisimus, quorum alterum Equitibus primae classis, alterum vero Equitibus secundae classis attribuimus; quorum primis Insigne Ordinis proprium collo appensum, reliquis in sinistra vestis parte gerere fas esset: itemque declaravimus ut Equites primae classis consequi etiam possent privilegium ferendi magnum argenteum Numisma in sinistro pectoris latere innexum.

Aliis praeterea Apostolicis Litteris Cajetae die XVII Junii anni MDCCCXLIX datis statuimus atque decrevimus ut omnes Equites Piani Ordinis primae Classis renunciati pollere deberent privilegio gestandi commemoratum Numisma, itemque praescripsimus ut alterum proprium Ordinis Insigne non quidem taenia e collo inserta penderet sed taenia praelonga e dextero ad sinistrum humerum sustineretur.

Nunc vero, quum opportunum existimavimus eundem Ordinem novo augere decore ejusque gradus amplificare, ut major inde Nobis Nostrisque Successoribus pateat aditus ad virtutem rectaque facta pro merito rependenda, iccirco Motu Proprio plenaque auctoritate Nostra per praesentes decernimus et statuimus ut deinceps Ordo Pianus tribus constet gradibus: nempe Equitum primae classis, Equitum secundae classis, seu Commendatorum, et Equitum tertiae classis; primi Insigne et Numisma prout in commemoratis Litteris XVII Junii MDCCCXLIX praescriptum est: alteri seu Commendatores Insigne tantum e collo appensum: Equites demum tertiae classis Insigne ipsum minoris moduli sinistra vestis parte innexum gerent; firmis tamen remanentibus circa reliqua iis omnibus, queis per hoc Nostrum Decreto minime derogatur. Et quoniam Equites Piani propria utuntur veste caeruleo colore, rubris oris, aureis ornamentis decorata, ita et vestem conformem quae media sit inter primum et tertium Equitum gradum Commendatoribus attributam volumus iuxta schema cum diplomate tradendum. Id statuimus atque decernimus in contrarium facientibus non obstantibus quibuscumque.

Datum Romae ex Nostris aedibus in Quirinali die XI Novembris MDCCCLVI, Pontificatus Nostri anno undecimo.

PIUS PP. IX

Ex Cancellaria Ordinum Equestrium

Die 7 Februarii 1905.

SSmus Dominus Noster Pius Papa X, animo repetens omnia, quae sive ad homines virtute formandos sive ad praemia iisdem pro rectefactis rependenda ab Apostolica Sede proveniunt, iis legibus jugiter moderanda esse quibus et decori eiusdem S. Sedis et congrue rationi consultum sit, opportune mentem suam ad Equestres Ordines admovit.

Hinc est quod re acta cum infrascripto Cardinali a Brevibus, Magno Equestrium Ordinum Cancellario, praeter ordinationes de caeteris Equestribus Ordinibus hoc ipso die latas, voluit ut, quae etiam de Piani Ordinis vestibus et Insignibus propriis illorumque usu adhuc non satis certa et definita viderentur, eadem forent adamussim statuta per leges, quae hic sequuntur:

Equites Primae Classis, seu a Magna Cruce, Ordinis Piani potientur privilegio nobilitatis in filios transmittendae.

Eorum vestis e panno coeruleo nigrante siet in longos post tergum producta limbos.

Circa collum et extremas manicas, itemque super peras, gestet pannum rubri coloris.

Opera phrygia, omnia acu picta ex auro, circa collum, extremas manicas, et supra peras laciniae sint laureas referentes: duplex ante pectus lacinia quae laureas pariter imitetur: dentata insuper taeniola quae extremas totius vestis oras circumeat.

Novem pectori globuli: tres vero sint, minoris moduli, manicis.

Posteriores vestis limbi, inter utramque peram, duobus maioribus globulis nec non laureo serto decorentur; ipsisque peris tres subsint globuli minores.

Sit humeris impositus tortus ex auro funiculus, globulo iuxta collum innexus.

Femoralia praelonga sunto e panno coeruleo nigrante; fascia ornentur ex aureo laureis intexta, cuius altitudo quatuor centesimarum metricae mensurae partium siet.

Galero nigro ex sericis coactilibus, aurea fascia praedivite circumornato, et aureo parvo flocco in utraque cuspide distincto, alba superemineat pluma: eique Insigne Pontificium quatuor ex auro funiculis, globulo coniunctis, innexum sit.

Globuli, omnes ex auro, Insigne Ordinis caelato opere referant.

Item et ensis aurato cingulo suffultus, Insigne Ordinis, prout a schemate apparet, in capulo caelatum referat; capulus ipse sit e concha albida ornatus auro, cum aureo dependente fimbriato funiculo; vagina e corio nigro aureis fulcro et cuspide terminetur.

Numisma Ordinis sit Insigne ipsum argenteae stellae radiis impositum.

Insigne, Numisma, globuli quoad formas et modulos, sic et fascia quoad colores et altitudinem a schemate non differant.

Equites Secundae Classis, seu Commendatores, cum Numismate Ordinis Piani potientur privilegio nobilitatis absque iure transmissionis.

Eorum vestis e panno coeruleo nigrante siet in longos post tergum producta limbos.

Circa collum et extremas manicas, itemque super peras, gestet pannum rubri coloris.

Opera phrygia; omnia acu picta ex auro, circa collum, extremas manicas et supra peras laciniae sint laureas referentes, et dentata taeniola quae extremas totius vestis oras circumeat.

Novem pectori globuli: tres vero sint, minoris moduli, manicis.

Posteriores vestis limbi inter utramque peram duobus maioribus globulis, nec non laureo serto decorentur; ipsisque peris tres subsint globuli minores.

Femoralia praelonga sunto e panno coeruleo nigrante; fascia ornentur ex auro laureis intexta, cuius altitudo quatuor centesimarum metricae mensurae partium siet.

Galero nigro ex sericis coactilibus, duplici transversa utrinque et circum ducta limbos, ut in schemate, nigra undati operis fascia ac parvo aureo flocco in utraque cuspide distincto, nigra superemineat pluma; eique Insigne Pontificium quatuor ex auro funiculis globulo coniunctis innexum sit.

Globuli, omnes ex auro, Insigne Ordinis caelato opere referant.

Item et ensis aurato cingulo suffultus Insigne Ordinis, prout a schemate apparet, in capulo caelatum referat; capulus ipse sit e concha albida ornatus auro, cum aureo dependente fimbriato funiculo; vagina e corio nigro aureis fulcro et cuspide terminetur.

Numisma Ordinis sit Insigne ipsum argenteae stellae radiis impositum.

Insigne, Numisma, globuli quoad formas et modulos, sic et taenia quoad colores et altitudinem a schemate non differant.

Equites Secundae Classis, seu Commendatores, Ordinis Piani potientur privilegio nobilitatis absque iure transmissionis.

Eorum vestis e panno coeruleo nigrante siet in longos post tergum producta limbos.

Circa collum et extremas manicas, itemque super peras, gestet pannum rubri coloris.

Opera phrygia, omnia acu picta ex auro, circa collum, extremas manicas et supra peras laciniae sint laureas referentes, et dentata taeniola quae extremas totius vestis oras circumeat.

Novem pectori globuli: tres vero sint, minoris moduli, manicis.

Posteriores vestis limbi inter utramque peram duobus maioribus globulis, nec non laureo serto decorentur; ipsisque peris tres subsint globuli minores.

Femoralia praelonga sunto e panno coeruleo nigrante; fascia ornentur ex auro laureis intexta cuius altitudo quatuor centesimarum metricae mensurae partium siet.

Galero nigro ex sericis coactilibus, duplici transversa utrinque et circum ducta limbos ut in schemate nigra undati operis fascia ac parvo aureo flocco in utraque cuspide distincto, nigra superemineat pluma; eique Insigne Pontificium quatuor ex auro funiculis globulo coniunctis innexum sit.

Globuli, omnes ex auro, Insigne Ordinis caelato opere referant.

Item et ensis aurato cingulo suffultus Insigne Ordinis, prout a schemate apparet, in capulo caelatum referat; capulus ipse sit e concha albida ornatus auro, cum aureo dependente fimbriato funiculo; vagina e corio nigro aureis fulcro et cuspide terminetur.

Insigne Ordinis et globuli quoad formas et modulos, sic et taenia quoad colores et altitudinem a schemate non differant.

Equitibus Tertiae Classis Ordinis Piani vestis e panno coeruleo nigrante siet in longos post tergum producta limbos.

Circa collum et extremas manicas, itemque super peras, gestet pannum rubri coloris.

Opus phrygium sit circa totius vestis oras, extremas manicas et peras dentata taeniola ex auro.

Novem pectori globuli: tres vero sint, minoris moduli, manicis.

Posteriores vestis limbi, inter utramque peram, duobus maioris moduli globulis necnon parvo laureo serto decorentur: ipsisque peris tres subsint globuli minores.

Femoralia praelonga sunto e panno coeruleo nigrante: fascia ornentur ex auro laureis intexta, cuius altitudo trium centesimarum metricae mensurae partium siet.

Galero nigro ex sericis coactilibus, duplici transversa utrinque et circum ducta limbos, ut in schemate, nigra undati operi fascia ac parvo aureo flocco in utraque cuspide distincto, nigra superemineat pluma; eique Insigne Pontificium quatuor ex auro funiculis globulo coniunctis innexum sit.

Globuli, omnes ex auro, Insigne Ordinis caelato opere referant.

Item et ensis aurato cingulo suffultus Insigne Ordinis, prout a schemate apparet, in capulo caelatum referat; capulus ipse sit e concha albida ornatus auro, cum aureo dependente fimbriato funiculo; vagina e corio nigro aureis fulcro et cuspide terminetur.

Insigne Ordinis et globuli quoad formas et modulos sic et taenia quoad colores et altitudinem a schemate non differant.

ALOISIUS Card. MACCHI
<small>MAGNUS CANCELLARIUS ORDINUM EQUESTRIUM.</small>

Breve Pii Pp. XII de nobilitatis privilegio iam Ordinis Piani proprio abolendo

PIUS PP. XII

Ad perpetuam rei memoriam. — Litteris suis Apostolicis sub anulo Piscatoris obsignatis die decima septima m. Iunii, an. MDCCCXLVII ac die pariter decima septima mensis Iunii, an. MDCCCXLIX, necnon decreto ex Aedibus in Quirinali dato die XI m. Novembris an. MDCCCLVI, Praedecessor Noster Pius Pp. IX Equestrem Ordinem creavit atque instituit, Pianum nuncupatum, qui tribus Equitum classibus constaret. Apostolicis autem Litteris praelaudatis statutum etiam fuit Equites in primam eiusdem Ordinis Classem cooptatos privilegio nobilitatis in filios quoque transmittendae, illos vero, qui secundae Classis insigni essent honestati, nobilitatis titulo ad personam tantummodo gavisuros esse. Quod, habita praesertim temporum nostrorum ratione, minus opportunum videtur, cum ceteri, etiam potiores, Equestres Ordines, quorum insignia a Romanis Pontificibus conferuntur, nullo modo nobilitatis privilegio aliquo fruantur. Itaque, omnibus rei momentis attente perpensis, Nos, ut huiusmodi iure Ordo quoque Pianus ceteris Equestribus Ordinibus adaequetur Pontificiis, motu proprio statuendum censemus ut, iis abolitis quae iam Litteris Apostolicis supradictis decreta fuerant, ex nunc et in posterum omnes et singuli, in quamlibet ex tribus classibus praefati Ordinis Piani classem adsciti, insignibus tantum ac titulo proprio Classis, absque ullo nobilitatis iure privilegioque licite uti, frui possint et queant. Contrariis non obstantibus quibuslibet; decernentes praesentes Litteras firmas, validas atque efficaces iugiter extare ac permanere, suosque plenos atque integros effectus sortiri et obtinere; sicque iudicandum esse ac definiendum, irritumque ex nunc et inane fieri si quidquam secus super his a quoquam, auctoritate qualibet, scienter sive ignoranter attentari contigerit.

Datum Romae, apud Sanctum Petrum, sub anulo Piscatoris, die XI m. Novembris, an. MCMXXXIX, Pontificatus Nostri primo.

A. Card. MAGLIONE
a Secretis Status

Breve Pii Pp. XII de institutione novi gradus, seu torquis aurei, in Ordine Piano

PIUS PP. XII

Ad perpetuam rei memoriam. — Egregio ducti consilio Romani Pontifices Ordines Equestres instituerunt vel institutos amplioribus locupletarunt muneribus vel novis inductis rationibus disposuerunt, ut, qui viri, de re christiana aut publica recte meriti, in eos essent asciti, bene factorum quasi praemia ferrent et ad praeclariora patranda facinora stimulos haberent. Quorum exempla secutis expedire Nobis in praesenti videtur huiusmodi rem, ad maximos honores quod attinet, ita componere, ut cum horum temporum adiunctis satius congruat; scilicet constituere, ut Supremus Ordo D. N. Iesu Christi et Ordo Militiae Auratae seu ab aureo calcari, utpote ad sanctam religionem potissimum pertinentes, tum solummodo in posterum deferantur, cum peculiaris omnino et singularis causa id suaserit. Nolumus tamen Nobis Nostrisque in apostolico munere Successoribus facultatem deesse populorum Moderatoribus aliisque, qui amplissima pollent auctoritate, propensae Summi Pontificis voluntatis signum idque eximium impertiendi. Quam ob rem Ordinem Pianum opportunum visum est ita augeri, ut novus· ei addatur gradus, quo huiusmodi viri honore, gravissimis muneribus suis consentaneo, affici possint. Hic Ordo, e nomine Pii Pp. IV, Decessoris Nostri, nuncupatus, a Pio Pp. IX, paulo postquam ad Summi Pontificatus fastigium est evectus, per Apostolicas Litteras die XVII mensis Iunii anno MDCCCXXXXVII apud Liberianam Basilicam sub anulo Piscatoris editas, institutus fuit seu restitutus, quo viri insignes in civili etiam consortione quasi praecipuo decore praefulgerent. Idem vero Antistes Sacrorum Maximus in eodem Ordine, qui initio duabus tantum continebatur Equitum classibus, quaedam postea immutavit, expeditis ad hoc diplomatis Caietae die XVII mensis Iunii anno MDCCCXXXXVIIII et Romae ex Aedibus in Quirinali die XI mensis Novembris anno MDCCCLVI, quo die eum tribus etiam gradibus constare iussit. Atque Nos ipsi die XI mensis Novembris anno MDCCCCXXXVIIII formam Ordinis, quem diximus, aptiore quadam ratione definivimus. Quibus omnibus perpensis, Nos hisce Litteris Nostraque auctoritate novum in Ordine Piano gradum instituimus, cuius insigne, idem atque huic Ordini usque adhuc proprium, torqui aureo, ex collo dependenti, sit affixum; qui torques alternis clipeolis, Nostri Pontificatus insigne ac decussatas Claves Pontificias referentibus, efficiatur; in medio vero torque, ante pectus, Tiara Romanorum Pontificum habeatur, cui columba utrimque haereat, iuxta schema adnexum; in anteriore denique parte eiusdem Ordinis insignis, ex torque pendentis, haec inscripta sint verba: « ORDO PIANVS A PIO XII AVCTVS », in adversa: « ANNO MDCCCCLVII ». Haec edicentes, statuentes, fore confidimus, ut illustres viri, qui peculiaribus hisce honoris insignibus per Apostolicas sub anulo Piscatoris datas Litteras decoráti fuerint, Petrianam Cathedram praecipua observantia prosequantur. Contrariis quibusvis nihil obstantibus.

Datum Romae, apud Sanctum Petrum, sub anulo Piscatoris, die XXV mensis Decembris, in festo Nativitatis D. N. Iesu Christi, anno MDCCCCLVII, Pontificatus Nostri undevicesimo.

PIUS PP. XII

EX CANCELLARIA ORDINUM EQUESTRIUM
die 25 Decembris 1957

EQUITUM TORQUATORUM ORDINIS PIANI vestis e panno caeruleo nigrante sit in longos post tergum producta limbos.

Circa collum et extremas manicas, itemque super peras, gestent pannum rubri coloris.

Opera phrygia, omnia acu picta ex auro, circa collum, extremas manicas, et supra peras laciniae sint laureas referentes: duplex ante pectus et medium corpus praecingens lacinia quae laureas pariter imitetur: dentata insuper taeniola quae extremas totius vestis oras circumeat.

Novem pectori globuli: tres vero sint, minoris moduli, manicis.

Posteriores vestis limbi, inter utramque peram, duobus maioribus globulis nec non laureo serto quod tribus efficiatur ramulis decorentur; ipsisque peris tres subsint globuli minores.

Sit humeris impositus tortus ex auro funiculus, globulo iuxta collum innexus.

Femoralia praelonga sunto e panno caeruleo nigrante; fascia ornentur ex auro laureis intexta, cuius altitudo quatuor centesimarum metricae mensurae partium siet.

Galero nigro ex sericis coactilibus, aurea fascia praedivite circumornato, et aureo parvo flocco in utraque cuspide distincto, alba superemineat pluma: eique Insigne Pontificium quatuor ex auro funiculis, globulo coniunctis, innexum sit.

Globuli, omnes ex auro, Insigne Ordinis caelato opere referant.

Item et ensis aurato cingulo suffultus, Insigne Ordinis, prout a schemate apparet, in capulo caelatum referat; capulus ipse sit e concha albida ornatus auro, cum aureo dependente fimbriato funiculo; vagina e corio nigro aureis fulcro et cuspide terminetur.

Numisma Ordinis sit Insigne ipsum argenteae stellae radiis impositum.

Insigne, Numisma, globuli quoad formas et modulos, sic et fascia quoad colores et altitudinem a schemate non differant.

BREVE GREGORII PP. XVI PRO INSTITUTIONE
EQUESTRIS ORDINIS S. GREGORII MAGNI

GREGORIVS PP. XVI

Ad perpetuam rei memoriam. – Quod summis quibusque Imperatoribus maximae curae est praemia virtutis et insignia honoris et monumenta laudis iis decernere, quos optime de re publica meritos noverint, id et Romani Pontifices Praedecessores Nostri praestare pro personarum, temporum, actuumque ratione consueverunt erga eos, qui Sanctae Romanae Ecclesiae imperium ope, armis, consiliis, aliisque recte factis iuvarent. Haec reputantibus Nobis, ac de honore iis habendo deliberantibus, qui fidelem assiduamque asperioribus etiam temporibus operam Principatui navarunt, placuit ex more institutoque maiorum Ordinem Equestrem constituere, in quem homines spectatae in Sedem Apostolicam fidei ex Summorum Pontificum auctoritate cooptentur, quos vel praestantia generis, vel gloria rerum gestarum, vel insignium munerum procuratione, vel demum gravibus aliis ex causis dignos ipsi censuerint qui publico Pontificiae dilectionis testimonio honestentur. Inde enim nedum praemium virtuti conferri, sed et stimulos addi ceteris palam est quibus ad bonum rectumque impensius in dies excitentur. Quare hisce Nostris Apostolicis Litteris Equestrem Ordinem constituimus, quem, et ex praecipuo Nostrae in Sanctissimum Praedecessorem Gregorium Magnum venerationis affectu, et ob assumptum ipsius Nomen quando Humilitati Nostrae impositum Pontificatum suscepimus, a Sancto Gregorio Magno volumus nuncupari; reservantes Nobis ac Romano Pontifici pro tempore existenti ius eligendi Equites, quos constet virtutum laude, condicionis honestate, splendore munerum, atque eximia in rebus gerendis sedulitate, communi demum bonorum suffragio commendari. Erit porro peculiare Ordinis Insigne Crux octangula ex auro artificiose elaborata, rubram superficiem habens, in cuius medio, veluti parvo in numismate, exstet affabre caelata imago S. Gregorii Magni. Taenia ad eam sustinendam erit serica rubra, cuius extrema ora flavo colore distinguatur. Cum vero stati quidam in Equestribus Ordinibus gradus dignitatem illorum, qui iisdem accensentur, designent, quattuor in Gregoriano Ordine gradus Equitum praefinimus; quorum primi Equites Magnae Crucis primae classis, secundi Equites Magnae Crucis secundae classis, tertii Equites Commendatores, quarti Equites simpliciter nuncupabuntur. Serica fascia praelonga binis Ordinis coloribus picta, dextero humero imposita, transversaque ad latus sinistrum propendens, et magnam Crucem sustinens, Insigne erit Equitum primi generis; qui insuper medio sinistro latere pectoris innexam vestitui gestabunt alteram maiorem Crucem radiis undique ac gemmis circumornatam, opereque magnifico caelatam. Equites secundae classis Crucem magnam, instar Numismatis, latere pectoris sinistro habebunt, praeter Crucem alteram grandem collo ex fascia serica appensam. Equites Commendatores Crucem magnam gerent, quae e fascia collo inserta dependeat; privilegio tamen carebunt ferendi praedictum numisma seu Crucem alteram in latere pectoris sinistro. Equites quarti ordinis Crucem parvam, iuxta communem Equitum morem, ad pectus apponent in parte vestis sinistra. Ceterum eos omnes, qui publico hoc Pontificiae voluntatis testimonio sint honestati, monitos volumus ut animadvertant sedulo praemia virtutibus addici, nihilque diligentius curandum ipsis esse quam ut rebus praeclare gestis expectationem ac fiduciam quam excitarunt cumulate sustineant, delatoque sibi honore dignos sese in dies magis exhibeant. Haec quidem suscepti huiusce consilii ratio est, haec praecipua muneris ipsius condicio, cui apprime satisfiet constanti erga Deum et Principem fide, prout in aversa Crucis parte scriptum est; atque ita boni omnes et ii praesertim, quorum maxime interest ob Ordinis coniunctionem, de fausto felicique Nostri Instituti progressu gratulabuntur. Haec statuimus ac declaramus non obstantibus in contrarium facientibus, etiam speciali mentione dignis, quibuscumque. Datum Romae apud Sanctam Mariam Maiorem sub Annulo Piscatoris die 1 Septembris MDCCCXXXI, Pontificatus Nostri anno primo.

TH. Card. BERNETTI

BREVE GREGORII PP. XVI PRO TRIBUS TANTUM GRADIBUS IN EQUESTRI GREGORIANO ORDINE SERVANDIS ET PRO INSIGNIBUS SINGULORUM GRADUUM PROPRIIS STATUENDIS

GREGORIVS PP. XVI

A<small>D</small> perpetuam rei memoriam. – Cum amplissima honorum munera iure meritoque parta hominum mentes atque animos ad virtutem amplectendam, gloriamque assequendam vel maxime excitent atque inflamment, tum Romani Pontifices provide sapienterque praecipuos honorum titulos iis tribuere ac decernere semper existimarunt, qui egregiis animi ingeniique dotibus praestantes nihil non aggrediuntur, nihilque intentatum relinquunt, ut de Christiana et Civili Republica quam optime mereri conentur. Hac sane mente in ipso Pontificatus Nostri exordio, ob tantam temporum asperitatem iniucundo ac permolesto, singulare praemium rectefactis impertiri, itemque ad suas cuique partes demandatas impensius obeundas quoddam veluti incitamentum addere in animo habentes illis praesertim viris, qui singulari studio, consilio, fide, integritate Nobis et Romanae Petri Cathedrae omni ope atque opera adhaererent, novum Equestrem Ordinem instituere decrevimus, quem ob praecipuum Nostrae in Sanctissimum Praedecessorem Gregorium Magnum venerationis affectum, et ob assumptum ipsius Nomen quando ad Universae Ecclesiae regimen evecti fuimus, a Sancto Gregorio Magno voluimus nuncupari. Quapropter Apostolicas dedimus Litteras die primo Septembris Anno MDCCCXXXI Annulo Piscatoris obsignatas, quarum vi omnibus notam perspectamque fecimus novi Gregoriani Ordinis institutionem, simulque praescripsimus eius Insigne Crucem esse octogonam ex auro affabre elaboratam, rubra superficie imaginem S. Gregorii Magni in medio referentem, taenia serica rubra, extremis oris flava, sustinendam. Clare insuper significavimus quibus dotibus viros hoc honore decorandos praeditos esse oporteat, Nobisque et Romanis Pontificibus Successoribus Nostris ius reservavimus eiusmodi Equites renuntiandi, quos virtutis et religionis laude, condicionis honestate, muneris splendore, eximia in rebus gerendis sedulitate, communi denique bonorum suffragio pateat esse commendatos. Ad designandam autem eorum dignitatem, qui huic Ordini sunt adscribendi, Nobis opportunum visum est eumdem ipsum in quattuor classes dividere; quarum altera Equitibus Magnae Crucis primi ordinis, altera Equitibus Magnae Crucis secundi ordinis, tertia Equitibus Commendatoribus, quarta Equitibus tantummodo constat. Praescripsimus idcirco, ut Equites a Magna Cruce primi ordinis magnam Crucem e serica fascia praelonga binis Ordinis coloribus picta, dextero humero imposita, transversaque ad latus sinistrum descendente sustineant, ac praeterea medio sinistro pectoris latere innexam vesti gestent alteram maiorem Crucem radiis undique ac gemmis circumornatam: ut Equites a Magna Cruce secundae classis praeter magnam Crucem, ut supra appensam, medio sinistro pectoris latere alteram Crucem nullis coruscantibus gemmis refulgentem deferant: ut Equitibus Commendatoribus liceat Crucem magnam gerere, quae e fascia collo inserta dependeat, haud tamen Crucem alteram in latere pectoris sinistro: ut Equites demum quarti ordinis Crucem parvam ex communi Equitum more in parte vestis sinistra ad pectus apponant. Quin etiam ad removendum quodcumque discrimen, quod in hoc gestando Insigni posset contingere, cuiusque Crucis schema typis excudi mandavimus, novis quibusque Equitibus una cum Diplomate tradendum. Iam vero, cum honoris ac dignitatis splendor eo magis refulgeat quo minor est eorum numerus quibus confertur, Nostris profecto fuisset in votis in Gregoriano Ordine constituendo eorum numerum praefinire, qui in singulas illius classes essent cooptandi. Sed quoniam eo tunc praecipue spectavimus, ut praemium iis potissimum rependeremus, qui incorrupta fide et egregio in Nos atque hanc Sanctam Sedem studio et obsequio effervescentes id temporis seditionis impetus propulsarent, et Religionis causam et Civilem Apostolicae Sedis Principatum pro viribus tuerentur, haud potuimus extemplo consilia Nostra certis quibusdam limitibus circumscribere. Nunc vero rebus divini Numinis ope conversis, atque exoptato in Pontificiis Nostris Provinciis ordine restituto, cum fidis fortibusque viris mercedem proposuerimus, in eam venimus sententiam, aliquid in commemoratis Nostris Litteris immutare, pluraque etiam ab integro decernere, quae ad eiusdem Ordinis splendorem augendum maiestatemque amplificandam pertinere posse videntur. Hisce igitur Litteris statuimus atque mandamus, ut posthac ex utraque classe Magnae Crucis una tantum constet, cui nomen erit primae classis. Nobis vero et Romanis Pontificibus Successoribus Nostris reservamus Magna Cruce gemmis ornata in peculiaribus quibusdam casibus eos decorare, qui Nostro eorumdemque Successorum Nostrorum iudicio singulari ratione honestandi videantur. Quapropter eos omnes qui Magnam Crucem secundae classis iam fuerint adepti, ad primam classem pertinere omnino volumus et declaramus. Itaque deinceps Gregorianus Ordo tribus tantummodo constabit classibus, nempe Equitibus a Magna Cruce, Commendatoribus et Equitibus. Numerum autem cuiuslibet ex tribus iis classibus praefinire volentes, quemadmodum in pluribus Militiis vel Equestribus Ordinibus provide sapienterque factum est et Nos ipsi vehementer optabamus, plena Auctoritate Nostra edicimus atque praecipimus ut Equites a Magna Cruce numerum triginta non praetergrediantur: Commendatores septuaginta, Equites demum tercenti esse possint. Quem quidem singularum classium Equitum numerum pro iis tantum viris, qui Civili Apostolicae Sedis Principatui subsunt praescriptum volumus; proptereaquod ad Nostrum et Successorum Nostrorum arbitrium semper pertinebit homines etiam exterarum gentium in cuiusque classis coetum praeter hunc numerum adlegere. Praeterea, ut huius Ordinis ratio perpetuo servetur neque temporis lapsu diuturna vetustate ullatenus immutetur, mandamus ut Summus ab Actis Gregoriani Ordinis seu, ut dicitur, Magnus Cancellarius sit S. R. E. Cardinalis a Brevibus Apostolicis Litteris; penes quem Equitum nomina, gradus, admissionis dies, ac numerus diligenter servetur. Haec decernimus atque statuimus, non obstantibus editis Nostris Litteris, de quibus habitus est sermo, nec non etiam speciali mentione dignis in contrarium facientibus quibuscumque. Nobis quidem sperare fas est novam hanc consilii Nostri instaurationem optatum exitum assequuturam, eosque simili honore auctos vel in posterum augendos votis Nostris ac fini, ad quem referuntur, quam cumulatissime responsuros, ac Pontificia benevolentia magis magisque dignos futuros, praesertim quod ipso in Insigni inscriptum legant hoc munus eorum potissimum esse, qui Pro Deo et Principe vel maxime praestant. Datum Romae apud S. Petrum sub Anulo Piscatoris die xxx Maii MDCCCXXXIV, Pontificatus Nostri anno quarto.

Pro Domino Card. ALBANO
A. PICCHIONI, substitutus

Ex Cancellaria Ordinum Equestrium
Die 7 Februarii 1905.

SSmus Dominus Noster Pius PP. X, animo repetens omnia, quae sive ad homines virtute formandos sive ad praemia eisdem pro rectefactis rependenda ab Apostolica Sede proveniunt, iis legibus iugiter moderanda esse, quibus et decori eiusdem S. Sedis et congrue rationi consultum sit, opportune mentem suam ad Equestres Ordines admovit.

Hinc est quod re acta cum infrascripto Cardinali a Brevibus, magno Equestrium Ordinum Cancellario, praeter ordinationes de ceteris Equestribus Ordinibus hoc ipso die latas, voluit ut quae etiam de Gregoriani Ordinis vestibus et Insignibus propriis illorumque usu adhuc non satis certa et definita viderentur, servata eiusdem Ordinis, quae hactenus usu venit, in Civilem unam et Militarem alteram Classem partitione, omnia forent adamussim statuta per leges quae hic sequuntur:

Pro Equitibus a Magna Cruce Classis Civilis.

Vestis e panno viridi nigrante siet in longos post tergum producta limbos.

Opera phrygia omnia acu picta ex argento, circa collum, extremas manicas, et supra peras laciniae sint quernea folia referentes: duplex ante pectus lacinia quae folia quernea pariter imitetur: dentata insuper taeniola quae extremas totius vestis oras circumeat.

Novem pectori globuli: tres vero sint, minoris moduli, manicis.

Posteriores vestis limbi, inter utramque peram, duobus maioribus globulis nec non corona querna decorentur; ipsisque peris tres subsint globuli minores.

Sit humeris impositus tortus ex argento funiculus, globulo iuxta collum innexus.

Femoralia praelonga sunto e panno viridi nigrante; fascia ornentur ex argento querneis foliis intexta, cuius altitudo quatuor centesimarum metricae mensurae partium siet.

Galero nigro ex sericis coactilibus, argentea fascia praedivite circumornato, et argenteo parvo flocco in utraque cuspide distincto, alba supereminaet pluma: eique Insigne Pontificium quatuor ex argento funiculis, globulo coniunctis, innexum sit.

Globuli, omnes ex argento, Crucem Ordinis caelato opere referant.

Item et ensis argenteo cingulo suffultus, Crucem Ordinis, prout a schemate apparet, in capulo caelatam referat; capulus ipse sit e concha albida ornatus auro, cum aureo dependente fimbriato funiculo; vagina e corio nigro aureis fulcro et cuspide terminetur.

Crux Ordinis Magna e transversa, ut in schemate, fascia binis Ordinis coloribus distincta dependens, nec non argenteum magnum Numisma, nullis tamen gemmis ornatum, sinistro pectoris lateri ingestum Insignia sunto.

Crucem corona laurea ex enchausto viridi ut in schemate, parva taenia ex auro inferius vincta, supereminaet.

Crux, Numisma, globuli quoad formas et modulos, sic et fascia quoad colores et altitudinem a schemate non differant.

Pro Equitibus Commendatoribus cum Numismate Classis Civilis.

Vestis e panno viridi nigrante siet in longos post tergum producta limbos.

Opera phrygia, omnia acu picta ex argento, circa collum, extremas manicas et supra peras laciniae sint quernea folia referentes, et dentata taeniola quae extremas totius vestis oras circumeat.

Novem pectori globuli: tres vero sint, minoris moduli, manicis.

Posteriores vestis limbi inter utramque peram duobus maioribus globulis, nec non corona querna decorentur; ipsisque peris tres subsint globuli minores.

Femoralia praelonga sunto e panno viridi nigrante; fascia ornentur ex argento querneis foliis intexta, cuius altitudo quatuor centesimarum metricae mensurae partium siet.

Galero nigro ex sericis coactilibus, duplici transversa utrinque et circum ducta limbos, ut in schemate, nigra undati operis fascia ac parvo argenteo flocco in utraque cuspide distincto, nigra superemineat pluma; eique Insigne Pontificium quatuor ex argento funiculis globulo coniunctis innexum sit.

Globuli, omnes ex argento, Crucem Ordinis caelato opere referant.

Item et ensis argenteo cingulo suffultus Crucem Ordinis, prout a schemate apparet, in capulo caelatam referat; capulus ipse sit e concha albida ornatus auro, cum aureo dependente fimbriato funiculo; vagina e corio nigro aureis fulcro et cuspide terminetur.

Praeter Crucem, non aliter ac serica taenia e collo dependentem, Numisma Ordinis argenteum sinistro pectoris lateri ingestum deferre fas esto.

Crucem corona laurea ex enchausto viridi ut in schemate, parva taenia ex auro inferius vincta, superemineat.

Crux, Numisma, globuli quoad formas et modulos, sic et taenia quoad colores et altitudinem a schemate non differant.

PRO EQUITIBUS COMMENDATORIBUS CLASSIS CIVILIS

Vestis e panno viridi nigrante siet in longum post tergum producta limbos.

Opera phrygia, omnia acu picta ex argento, circa collum, extremas manicas et supra peras laciniae sint quernea folia referentes, et dentata taeniola quae extremas totius vestis oras circumeat.

Novem pectori globuli: tres vero sint, minoris, moduli, manicis.

Posteriores vestis limbi inter utramque peram duobus maioribus globulis, nec non corona querna decorentur; ipsisque peris tres subsint globuli minores.

Femoralia praelonga sunto e panno viridi nigrante; fascia ornentur ex argento querneis foliis intexta cuius altitudo quatuor centesimarum metricae mensurae partium siet.

Galero nigro ex sericis coactilibus, duplici transversa utrimque et circumducta limbos, ut in schemate, nigra undati operis fascia ac parvo argento flocco in utraque cuspide distincto, nigra superemineat pluma; eique Insigne Pontificium quattuor ex argento funiculis globulo coniunctis innexum sit.

Globuli, omnes ex argento, Crucem Ordinis caelato opere referant.

Item et ensis argenteo cingulo suffultus Crucem Ordinis, prout a schemate apparet, in capulo caelatam referat; capulus ipse sit e concha albida ornatus auro, cum aureo dependente fimbriato funicolo; vagina e corio nigro aureis fulcro et cuspide terminetur.

Crux tantum non aliter ac per sericam taeniam e collo dependens, Insigne Commendatoribus siet.

Cruci corona laurea ex enchausto viridi ut in schemate, parva taenia ex auro inferius vincta, superemineat.

Crux et globuli quoad formas et modulos sic et taenia quoad colores et altitudinem a schemate non differant.

PRO EQUITIBUS CLASSIS CIVILIS

Vestis e panno viridi nigrante sit in longum post tergum producta limbos.

Opus phrygium sit circa totius vestis oras, extremas manicas et peras taeniola dentata ex argento.

Novem pectori globuli: tres vero sint, minoris, moduli, manicis.

Posteriores vestis limbi, inter utramque peram, duobus maioris moduli globulis necnon parva corona querna ex argento decorentur: ipsique peris tres subsint globuli minores.

Femoralia praelonga sunto e panno viridi nigrante: fascia ornentur ex argento querneis foliis intexta, cuius altitudo trium centesimarum metricae mensurae partium sit.

Galero nigro ex sericis coactilibus, duplici transversa utrimque et circumducta limbos, ut in schemate, nigra undati operis fascia ac parvo argento flocco in utraque cuspide distincto, nigra superemineat pluma; eique Insigne Pontificium quattuor ex argento funiculis globulo coniunctis innexum sit.

Globuli, omnes ex argento, Crucem Ordinis caelato opere referant.

Item et ensis argenteo cingulo suffultus Crucem Ordinis, prout a schemate apparet, in capulo caelatam referat; capulus ipse sit e concha albida ornatus auro, cum aureo dependente fimbriato funicolo; vagina e corio nigro aureis fulcro et cuspide terminetur.

Crucem minoris moduli in sinistro pectoris latere, ut in ceteris Equestribus Ordinibus serica taenia Ordinis coloribus picta pendentem Equitibus gestare ius sit.

Cruci corona laurea ex enchausto viridi ut in schemate, parva taenia ex auro inferius vincta, superemineat.

Crux et globuli quoad formas et modulos sic et taenia quoad colores et altitudinem a schemate non differant.

ALOISIUS Card. MACCHI
MAGNUS CANCELLARIUS ORDINUM EQUESTRIUM

Ex Cancellaria Ordinum Equestrium

Die 7 Februarii 1905.

SS͞mus Dominus Noster Pius PP. X, animo repetens omnia, quae sive ad homines virtute formandos sive ad praemia eisdem pro rectefactis rependenda ab Apostolica Sede proveniunt, iis legibus iugiter moderanda esse quibus et decori eiusdem S. Sedis et congrue rationi consultum sit, opportune mentem suam ad Equestres Ordines admovit.

Hinc est quod, re acta cum infrascripto Cardinali a Brevibus, magno Equestrium Ordinum Cancellario, praeter ordinationes de ceteris Equestribus Ordinibus hoc ipso die latas, voluit ut quae etiam de Gregoriano Ordine adhuc non satis certa et definita viderentur, servata eiusdem Ordinis, quae hactenus usu venit, in Civilem unam et Militarem alteram Classem partitione, omnia forent adamussim statuta per leges quae hic sequuntur:

Equitum Classis, quae Militaris appellatur, ex iis constituitur viris, qui sive in Pontificiis sive in quarumcumque gentium copiis stipendia facientes, suis PRO DEO ET PRINCIPE meritis hoc Ordine cohonestantur.

In hanc Classem adlectis nulla specialis statuitur vestis, cum propriam sui exercitus eorum quisque induatur.

Cruces quidem et Numismata ab unoquoque iuxta suum in Ordine gradum gestentur.

Equitibus a Magna Cruce praeter grande Numisma lateri pectoris sinistro innexum, Magnam Crucem transversa praedivite serica fascia Ordinis coloribus distincta deferre ius esto.

Cruci non laurea corona sed aureum armorum trophaeum, ut in schemate, superemineat.

Numisma argentea stella siet, cuius radiis Crux Ordinis sit superposita.

Crux, Numisma quoad formas et modulos, fascia quoad colores et altitudinem a schemate non differant.

Equitibus Commendatoribus cum Numismate, praeter Crucem serica taenia coloribus Ordinis picta e collo pendentem, etiam Numisma lateri pectoris sinistro innectere fas esto.

Cruci non laurea corona sed aureum armorum trophaeum, ut in schemate, superemineat.

Numisma argentea stella siet, cuius radiis Crux Ordinis sit superposita.

Crux, Numisma quoad formas et modulos, taenia quoad colores et altitudinem a schemate non differant.

Equitibus Commendatoribus Crucem serica taenia Ordinis coloribus picta e collo pendentem gestare ius esto.

Cruci non laurea corona sed aureum armorum trophaeum, ut in schemate, superemineat.

Crux quoad formam et modulos, taenia quoad colores et altitudinem a schemate non differant.

Equitibus Crucem minoris moduli e serica taenia Ordinis coloribus picta pendentem in sinistro pectoris latere deferre ius esto.

Cruci non laurea corona sed aureum armorum trophaeum, ut in schemate, superemineat.

Crux quoad formam et modulos, taenia quoad colores et altitudinem a schemate non differant.

ALOISIUS Card. MACCHI
MAGNUS CANCELLARIUS ORDINUM EQUESTRIUM.

EXCERPTA BREVI SS. D. N. PII PP. X «DE ORDINIBUS
EQUESTRIBUS» PRO ORDINE SANCTI SILVESTRI PAPAE

PIUS PP. X

A D perpetuam rei memoriam. – Multum ad excitandos ad egregia facinora hominum animos praemia virtuti reddita valent, quae, dum ornant egregios bene de re sacra vel publica meritos viros, ceteros exemplo rapiunt ad idem laudis honorisque spatium decurrendum. Hoc quidem sapienti consilio Romani Pontifices Decessores Nostri Equestres Ordines, quasi gloriae stimulos, singulari studio prosequuti sunt, horumque alios instituere, alios iam institutos, vel pristino decori restituerunt, vel novis ac potioribus privilegiis ditarunt.

Nunc autem, cum peropportunum visum sit gravibus de causis quaedam immutare de nonnullis Equestribus Pontificiis Ordinibus, Nos collatis consiliis cum dilecto filio Nostro Aloisio S. R. Ecclesiae Diacono Cardinali Macchi, a Brevibus Apostolicis Literis Secretario, et Pontificiae Sedis Equestrium Ordinum Magno Cancellario, omnibus rei momentis attente ac sedulo perpensis, ex certa scientia ac matura deliberatione Nostris haec, quae infrascripta sunt, decernenda existimavimus.

Neminem latet Ordinem Militiae Auratae, sive ab Aureo Calcari, inter vetustissimos iure esse enumerandum. Sed rerum humanarum ac temporum vicissitudine de veteri splendore ac dignitate excidit. Illum per Apostolicas Literas, die XXXI mensis Octobris anno MDCCCXXXXI eadem hac forma datas, Gregorius PP. XVI rec. mem. Decessor Noster ad pristinum decus curavit revocandum: ipsi vero titulum a Sancto Silvestro Papa tribui iussit, atque exinde novum quasi constituit Equestrem Ordinem Sancti Silvestri Papae, sive Auratae Militiae appellatum. Eundem Ordinem duabus tantum constare classibus praescripsit, Commendatorum et Equitum; sed in praesens iuxtae et rationabiles causae suadent ut etiam Equester Ordo Sancti Silvestri, non minus atque ordines Pianus et Gregorianus, tribus in posterum classibus constet, Equitum scilicet, Commendatorum, et Equitum a Magna Cruce. Nos itaque superiorem classem Ordini Sancti Silvestri tribuentes, eundem a prisco Militiae Auratae Ordine penitus seiungendum esse arbitramur.

Quae cum ita sint, hisce Literis, auctoritate Nostra perpetuum in modum decernimus ac mandamus ut Equester Ordo Sancti Silvestri Papae ab illo Militiae Auratae omnino separetur, atque alterum ab altero per praesentes ita seiungimus, ut duo diversi ac distincti in posterum Ordines exinde efformentur: alter a Sancto Silvestro Papa appellandus, et alter a Militia Aurata sive Aureo ex Calcari. Ordo Sancti Silvestri, non aliter ac Pontificii Ordines supradicti Pianus et Gregorianus, tribus constet classibus: nempe Equitum sive tertia, Commendatorum sive secunda, et Equitum a Magna Cruce sive prima classi. Crux Ordinis propria eadem esto atque hodierna, dempto aureo dependente calcari: sit videlicet aurea, octangula, alba superficie, imaginem cum circum scripto nomine Sancti Silvestri Papae in medio adversa parte referens, aversa vero emblema Pontificium caeruleo inclusum circulo, quo tum Gregorianae instaurationis cum hodiernae renovationis anni aureis literis imprimantur, MDCCCXLI-MDCCCCV. Ipsa Crux argenteae stellae radiis imposita Ordinis numisma sit. Similiter ruber ac niger sint fasciae Ordinis propriae colores. Sit vestis nigri coloris, unico globulorum ordine, et ad extremas manicas et circa collum villoso serico nigro ornata, ac phrygiis ex auro operibus distincta. Femoralia nigra sunto praelonga, cum fascia ex auro. Niger ex sericis coactilibus galerus oblongus, duplici cuspide, emblemate Pontificio ac parvo aurato flocco insignis. Ensi, aurato cingulo innexo, capulus sit e concha albida ornata auro. Tum Crucis moduli ac numismatis, tum vestis opera phrygia, tum galeri ornamenta pro vario Equitum gradu different, minora scilicet pro Equitibus simplicibus, pro superioribus classibus maiora. Gerant Equites Crucem sinistro pectoris latere dependentem e taenia serica, rubro et nigro distincta colore extremis oris rubris. Gerant Commendatores Crucem eandem maioris moduli, simili taenia collo circumducta pendentem, galerum nigra ornent pluma. Equites denique a Magna Cruce gerant Crucem maximi moduli, quae fascia serica praelonga, binis Ordinis coloribus picta, a dextero humero ad extremum sinistrum transversa latus, sustineatur; sinistro item vestis pectori innexum proprium primae classis numisma maius deferant; albam galero plumam imponant. Cum vero contingat ut viri ad gradum Commendatorum evehendi seu iam evecti egregiis iis meritis eniteant, quae quasi potiora Pontificiae voluntatis testimonia exposcant, volumus ut, sicuti fieri interdum solet in ordinibus Piano et Gregoriano, nonnulli etiam Commendatores Ordinis Sancti Silvestri Papae ex singulari prorsus gratia numismate uti queant minori, secundae classis proprio sive Commendatorum, illudque ad pectus sinistro lateri innexum gestent.

Verum tamen expresse mandamus, ne inter Equites eiusdem Militiae discrimen contingat, sed unusquisque Ordo stemmata, insignia, arma, atque ornamenta, a Sancta Sede praescripta, servet integerrime, ut praefata insignia Cruces, Numismata, vestes, enses, opera phrygia, atque ornamenta, tum propria Ordinis Sancti Silvestri Papae, cum ceterorum quos Apostolica Sedes conferre solet, sint adamussim confecta ad normam exemplarium et declarationum quas a Cancelleria Equestrium Ordinum edi et penes Nostram a Brevibus Apostolicis Literis Secretariam iussimus asservari; utque prae oculis habeantur apposita schemata, quae singulis vicibus cuilibet equestri dignitate aucto de more traduntur.

Haec statuimus, mandamus, praecipimus, decernentes praesentes Literas firmas, validas, atque efficaces semper fore et existere, suosque plenarios atque integros effectus sortiri atque obtinere, illisque, ad quos spectat et pro tempore spectabit, in omnibus et per omnia plenissime suffragari: sicque in praemissis per quoscumque iudices ordinarios et delegatos et alios quoslibet quacumque praeeminentia et potestate fungentes, sublata eis et eorum cuilibet quavis aliter iudicandi et interpretandi facultate et auctoritate, iudicari et definiri debere: irritumque et inane si secus quidquam super his a quocumque quavis auctoritate scienter vel ignoranter contigerit attentari. Non obstantibus Nostra et Cancellariae Apostolicae regula de iure quaesito non tollendo, aliisque Constitutionibus et Ordinationibus Apostolicis, nec non supradictorum et aliorum quorumcumque Equestrium Ordinum etiam iuramento, confirmatione Apostolica, vel quavis firmitate alia roboratis Statutis et consuetudinibus, ceterisque contrariis, licet speciali mentione dignis, quibuscumque: privilegiis quoque, indultis, et Literis Apostolicis, in contrarium praemissorum quomodolibet concessis, confirmatis et innovatis; quibus omnibus et singulis, illorum tenores praesentibus pro plene et sufficienter expressis ac de verbo ad verbum insertis habentes, illis alias in suo robore permansuris, ad praemissorum effectum hac vice dumtaxat specialiter et expresse derogamus. Datum Romae apud Sanctum Petrum sub annulo Piscatoris die 7 Februarii anno MDCCCCV, Pontificatus Nostri anno secundo.

ALOISIUS Card. MACCHI

EX CANCELLARIA ORDINUM EQUESTRIUM
DIE 7 FEBRUARII 1905

SS.mus Dominus Noster Pius Papa X, animo repetens omnia, quae ab Apostolica Sede sive ad homines virtute formandos sive ad praemia iisdem pro rectefactis rependenda iugiter emanant, iis legibus servanda esse quibus et decori eiusdem Sedis et congrue rationi consultum sit, opportune mentem suam ad Equestres Ordines admovit.

Hinc est quod, re prius acta cum infrascripto Cardinali a Brevibus, Magno Equestrium Ordinum Cancellario, ad memoriam S. Silvestri I Papae honorificentius excolendam edixit, ut Pontificius Ordo, qui hactenus iuxta literas in forma Brevis a f. r. Gregorio XVI die xxxi Octobris MDCCCXLI datas ab Aurata Militia et a S. Silvestro appellabatur, posthac non quasi adscititium sed proprium unice ab eodem Divo Decessore suo, primo Christianorum Equitum Patrono, nomen mutuetur; utque, item ac alii Equestres Ordines, non Equitibus et Commendatoribus tantum sed et iis et Equitibus a Magna Cruce constet.

Honorarias eiusdem Ordinis praerogativas sartas tectasque voluit per Breve, hoc ipso die datum, et specialia insignia adamussim statuta per leges quae hic sequuntur:

PRO EQUITIBUS A MAGNA CRUCE ORDINIS S. SILVESTRI PAPAE

Vestis e panno nigro siet in longos post tergum producta limbos.

Circa collum et extremas manicas gestet sericum villosum nigri coloris.

Opera phrygia, omnia acu picta ex auro, circa collum, extremas manicas et supra peras taeniola dentata sint et laciniae laureas referentes: duplex ante pectus lacinia, quae laureas pariter imitetur.

Novem pectori globuli; tres vero sint, minoris moduli, manicis.

Posteriores vestis limbi, inter utramque peram, duobus maioribus globulis nec non laureo serto decorentur.

Sit humeris impositus tortus ex auro funiculus, globulo iuxta collum innexus.

Femoralia praelonga e panno nigro sunto: fascia ornentur ex auro laureis intexta et altitudinis quatuor centesimarum metricae mensurae partium.

Galero nigro ex sericis coactilibus, duplici transversa utrinque, ut in schemate, undati operis nigra fascia ac parvo aureo flocco in utraque cuspide distincto, alba superemineat pluma: eique Insigne Pontificium quatuor ex auro funiculis, globulo coniunctis, innexum sit.

Globuli, omnes ex auro, Crucem Ordinis caelato opere referant.

Item et ensis aurato cingulo suffultus Crucem Ordinis, prout a schemate apparet, in capulo caelatam referat: capulus ipse sit e concha albida ornatus auro, cum aureo dependente fimbriato funiculo: vagina e corio nigro aureis fulcro et cuspide terminetur.

Crux, Numisma, globuli quoad modulos et formas, sic et fascia quoad colorem et altitudinem a schemate non differant.

PRO EQUITIBUS COMMENDATORIBUS CUM NUMISMATE ORDINIS S. SILVESTRI PAPAE.

Vestis e panno nigro siet in longos post tergum producta limbos.

Circa collum et extremas manicas gestet sericum villosum nigri coloris.

Opera phrygia, omnia acu picta ex auro, circa collum, extremas manicas, et supra peras taeniola dentata sint et laciniae laureas referentes.

Novem pectori globuli; tres vero sint, minoris moduli, manicis.

Posteriores vestis limbi, inter utramque peram duobus maioribus globulis nec non laureo serto decorentur.

Femoralia praelonga e panno nigro sunto: fiscia ornentur ex auro laureis intexta et altitudinis quatuor centesimarum metricae mensurae partium.

Galero nigro ex sericis coactilibus, duplici transversa utrinque, ut in schemate, undati operis nigra fascia ac parvo aureo flocco in utraque cuspide distincto, nigra superemineat pluma: eique Insigne Pontificium quatuor ex auro funiculis, globulo coniunctis, innexum sit.

Globuli, omnes ex auro, Crucem Ordinis caelato opere referant.

Item et ensis aurato cingulo suffultus Crucem Ordinis, prout a schemate apparet, in capulo caelatam referat: capulus ipse sit e concha albida ornatus auro, cum aureo dependente fimbriato funiculo: vagina e corio nigro aureis fulcro et cuspide terminetur.

Crux, Numisma, globuli quoad modulos et formas, sic et taenia quoad colores et altitudinem a schemate non differant.

PRO EQUITIBUS COMMENDATORIBUS ORDINIS S. SILVESTRI PAPAE

Vestis e panno nigro sit in longos post tergum producta limbos.

Circa collum et extremas manicas gestet sericum villosum nigri coloris.

Opera phrygia, omnia acu picta ex auro, circa collum, extremas manicas, et supra peras taeniola dentata sint et laciniae laureas referentes.

Novem pectori globuli; tres vero sint, minoris moduli, manicis.

Posteriores vestis limbi, inter utramque peram duobus maioribus globulis nec non laureo serto decorentur.

Femoralia praelonga e panno nigro sunto: fascia ornentur ex auro laureis intexta et altitudinis quatuor centesimarum metricae mensurae partium.

Galero nigro ex sericis coactilibus, duplici transversa utrinque, ut in schemate, undati operis nigra fascia ac parvo aureo flocco in utraque cuspide distincto, nigra superemineat pluma: eique Insigne Pontificium quatuor ex auro funiculis, globulo coniunctis, innexum sit.

Globuli, omnes ex auro, Crucem Ordinis caelato opere referant.

Item et ensis aurato cingulo suffultus Crucem Ordinis, prout a schemate apparet, in capulo caelatam referat: capulus ipse sit e concha albida ornatus auro, cum aureo dependente fimbriato funiculo: vagina e corio nigro aureis fulcro et cuspide terminetur.

Crux et globuli quoad modulos et formam, sic et taenia quoad colores et altitudinem a schemate non differant.

PRO EQUITIBUS ORDINIS S. SILVESTRI PAPAE

Vestis e panno nigro sit in longos post tergum producta limbos.
Circa collum et extremas manicas gestet sericum villosum nigri coloris.
Opus phrygium sit circa collum, extremas manicas et peras taeniola dentata ex auro.
Novem pectori globuli; tres vero sint, minoris moduli, manicis.
Posteriores vestis limbi, inter utramque peram, duobus maioribus globulis nec non laureo serto acu picto ex auro decorentur.
Femoralia praelonga e panno nigro sunto: fascia ornentur ex auro laureis intexa et altitudinis trium centesimarum metricae mensurae partium.
Sit galerus niger ex sericis coactilibus, fimbriatus serico undati operis nigro, parvo aureo flocco in utraque cuspide distinctus; eique Pontificium Insigne quatuor ex auro funiculis, globulo coniunctis, innexum sit.
Globuli, omnes ex auro, Crucem Ordinis caelato opere referant.
Item et ensis aurato cingulo suffultus Crucem Ordinis, prout a schemate apparet, in capulo caelatam referat: capulus ipse sit e concha albida ornatus auro, cum aureo dependente fimbriato funiculo: vagina e corio nigro aureis fulcro et cuspide terminetur.

Crux et globuli quoad modulos et formam, sic et taenia quoad colores et altitudinem a schemate non differant.

ALOISIUS Card. MACCHI
MAGNUS CANCELLARIUS ORDINUM EQUESTRIUM

LITTERAE APOSTOLICAE

MOTU PROPRIO

DATAE

DE ORDINUM EQUESTRIUM DIGNITATE
IIS DEFERENDA QUI CIVITATIBUS PRAESUNT

PAULUS PP. VI

EQUESTRES ORDINES a Romanis Pontificibus, varia quidem ratione, instituti sunt vel immutati, amplificati, quibus bonam existimationem, propensam voluntatem, gratum animum ii significarent egregiis Viris, in publica re versantibus aut alio modo spectabilibus et honoris provectione dignis. Hoc inductus consilio, Pius Pp. XII, Decessor Noster rec. mem., Litteris Apostolicis sub anulo Piscatoris die XXV mensis Decembris anno MCMLVII datis, Ordinem Pianum magnopere auxit, aureum torquem inducendo; quem gradum ad populorum Moderatores voluit pertinere vel ad alios, qui amplissima pollerent auctoritate. Iisdem vero Litteris statuit, ut in Supremum Ordinem Militiae D. N. Iesu Christi et in Ordinem Militiae Auratae seu ab aureo calcari, ob peculiarem prorsus et singularem causam, referrentur merentes. Cum vero hac nostra accidat aetate, ut Apostolica Sedes saepius in dies, ac quidem ea ipsa, non aliorum opera, nationum Moderatores attingat atque adeo crebrius humanitatis officia cum his exerceat et ab iisdem accipiat, expedire visum est rem ad praedictos Ordines Equestres spectantem, congruenti ratione componi et accuratius definiri. Itaque, omnibus attente perpensis, haec, quae sequuntur, constituimus atque decernimus:

I. - Torques aureus Ordinis Piani iis tantum, qui Civitatibus praesunt, tribuatur, idemque solus deferatur ob sollemnes eventus, veluti cum ii pro muneris sui officio Summum Pontificem invisunt.

II. – Supremus Ordo Militiae D. N. Iesu Christi et Ordo Militiae Auratae, cum honores sint ob extraordinariam causam conferendi, iis, qui Civitatibus praesunt, solummodo ob maximas celebritates, quibus ipse Summus Pontifex intersit, impertiantur aut propter singulares eventus, qui tanti momenti sint, ut per totum orbem terrarum pervagentur et hominum ubivis incolentium animos moveant. Cum praeterea ambo hi Ordines Equestres indolem potius religiosam praeferant, alter enim nomine D. N. Iesu Christi, alter nomine Beatae Mariae Virginis decoratur, convenire videtur, ut ii tantum Civitatum Moderatores in illos asciscantur, qui fidem profitentur christianam.

Quaecumque autem a Nobis hisce Litteris motu proprio datis sunt decreta, ea omnia firma ac rata esse iubemus, contrariis quibusvis nihil obstantibus.

Datum Romae, apud Sanctum Petrum, die XV mensis Aprilis, anno MCMLXVI, Pontificatus Nostri tertio.

PAULUS PP. VI

LITTERAE APOSTOLICAE

DE HONORIS SIGNO IIS TRIBUENDO
QUI FAUSTUM EVENTUM
SACERDOTALIS IUBILAEI SUMMI PONTIFICIS
SINGULARI STUDIO SUNT PROSEQUUTI.

LEO PP. XIII.

AD FUTURAM REI MEMORIAM.

Quod singulari Dei concessu et munere adeo provecti sunt Nostrae aetatis anni, ut potuerit a Nobis quinquagesimus sacerdotii natalis feliciter agi, id profecto Nos non tam Nostra, quam Ecclesiae atque huius Apostolicae Sedis caussa delectat. Faustitas enim eius eventus plene, cumulateque confirmat, quam miro pietatis ardore quantaque voluntatum consensione soleant catholici homines Iesu Christi Vicarium colere et observare, utque difficultates rerum et temporum dirumpere, aut perturbare nequeant officiorum et studiorum vicissitudinem, quae populis christianis cum Romano Pontifice intercedit. Siquidem ex omnibus orbis terrarum partibus, quacumque invectum est catholicum nomen, tot ac tam praeclarae amoris et obsequii significationes sunt nobis exhibitae, ut institui quodammodo visa sit inter populos voluntatis erga Nos et liberalitatis honesta certatio. De rebus sermo est, quas quidem norunt omnes et quas auctori bonorum omnium Deo Nos referimus acceptas. Ceterum nullum est pietatis testimonium, nullum officii genus, quod christiani homines, ea sibi oblata occasione, Nobis non detulerunt. Revera neminem latet, ut multis in locis festus ille habitus atque auctus sit dies, quo quinquagenariam Sacerdotii Nostri memoriam celebravimus, ut de vita et incolumitate Nostra, tamquam de publico bono, decretae sint gratiarum actiones et gratulationes; ut ad commemorationem auspicati diei non pauca sint christianae plena caritatis opera instituta: videlicet comparata calamitosis adiumenta, aperta perfugia puellis, pueri recepti in scholas, redempta a servitute mancipia. Testis vero est alma Urbs Nostra, quam ingens vis peregrinorum continenter menses huc confluxerit, qui haberent ad Nos aditum et eximia erga Nos animi sensa coram profiteretur. Vidimus sane plurimos genere, sermone, moribus inter se dissimiles non solum ab Europae regionibus, sed vel a dissitis Africae, Asiae, Americae et Oceaniae oris Romam conferre eiusdem omnes fidei et paris observantiae testimonium Pontifici Maximo daturos. Res quidem cum valde per se mirabilis, tum Nobis, qui gentes universas una eademque caritate complectimur, summopere iucunda. Verum sunt alia etiam officia, quorum non excidet Nobis memoria et gratia: ea enim animo tam lubenti, gratoque accepimus, quam obsequenti ac prono sunt delata. De donis nimirum loquimur, muneribusque omnis generis, quae ex orbe terrarum fere universo catholici homines quasi pietatis tributum, Nobis conferenda curaverunt. Sunt ea quidem et plurima numero et genere varia, propter dissimilitudinem locorum, dissimilem rationem habentia: quorum alia divitias et artificia referunt naturae, alia opificum industriam prudentiamque artis testantur: multa vel materia, vel opere valde sunt conspicua, multa contuentium animos vel ipsa peregrinitate delectant. Huiusmodi vero dona cum collecta sint et comportata ab omnibus orbis partibus, omnemque civium ordinem ita attingant, ut pretiosis Regum procerumque donariis proxima videantur munuscula pauperum, Nos non parvi referre ducimus ad Apostolicae Sedis laudem, ea omnia simul congerere et in Nostris Vaticanis aedibus ad spectandum proponere. Quod quidem bene ac prospere cessisse, institutisque rebus exitum contigisse quem optabamus, et laetamur maxime et gratias Deo, uti par est, plurimas agimus et habemus. Sed libet Nobis animum Nostrum et memorem et gratum profiteri etiam viris iis, qui honorum Nobis habendorum fautores extitere. Etsi enim probe novimus ob faustitatem proximi eventus studium populorum alacrius fuisse, quam ut incitari oporteret, non sumus tamen nescii in instituendis sodalitatibus pia peregrinatione ad Nos adeuntibus, in muneribus perferendis, ordinandis, custodiendis, in omnibus denique amoris pietatisque officiis praestandis eorum virorum solertiam industriamque mirifice excelluisse. Iis vero se socias et administras addidisse scimus pias feminas, quae in eiusmodi voluntatis erga Nos significationibus impertiendis suas sibi partes deposcere voluerunt. Quibus e rebus placet Nobis, ut apud eos omnes cum eventus memoria, tum benevolentiae Nostrae maneat testimonium. Idcirco volumus iubemus ex argyrometallo nec non ex auro argentoque conflari insigne formam Crucis habens, quod tamen quatuor interiectis liliis efficiatur octogonon. Media in coniunctione numisma parvum extet, cuius in adversa parte nomen et imago Nostra effingatur; in aversa autem exprimatur Pontificale insigne, inscribaturque « Pro Ecclesia et Pontifice ». Extremae vero partes Crucis, quae obversae sunt, ornentur cometa, qui una cum liliis insigne efficit gentis Nostrae: quae autem aversae, signentur « Pridie Kal. Ianuar. 1888 ». Huiusmodi honoris signo, quod e toenia serica purpurei coloris linea alba flavaque ad utramque oram virgata dependeat, merentium pectus sinistro latere decorari concedimus. Omnibus vero et singulis qui tali honore digni habiti fuerint, auspicem caelestium munerum, Apostolicam benedictionem peramanter in Domino impertimus.

Datum Romae apud S. Petrum sub anulo Piscatoris die XVII Iulii MDCCCLXXXVIII, Pontificatus Nostri anno undecimo.

M. Card. LEDOCHOWSKI

APPENDIX II

1

ADDITIONAL GUIDANCE ON THE WEARING OF THE DRESS UNIFORM OF PAPAL KNIGHTS

Customs and practices of dress have changed considerably since the 1900s. When the rules and regulations for the dress uniform of Papal Knights were published in 1905, it was, for example, taken for granted that an officer or a knight would wear white gloves. Similarly, an appropriate shirt collar was worn, as would black mess boots, yet there is no mention of any of these: such accessories were the norm.

In 1905, gentlemen wore shirts with separate collars and often separate cuffs, and wearing the correct collar with the dress uniform is not a fashion but a very pragmatic necessity. Those who have had their dress uniform cleaned, especially those with gold or silver embroidery, know how prohibitively expensive this can be. The specially stiffened collar and the sleeves which are usually profusely embroidered with gold or silver bullion thread, are normally the first pats to show that the uniform needs cleaning.

In warm conditions, in crowded rooms, or if a knight is caught in the rain while processing in the open, the collar of the uniform and ribbon of the neck-badge (if worn) will soon feel rather uncomfortable and the neck may get red and sore because of the constant irritation. The uniform collar will also absorb moisture and become limp, and the embroidery begins to tarnish. The embroidered sleeves do not suffer as badly as the collar, but eventually a similar effect may be noticed.

The collar problem can easily be alleviated by wearing a shirt made to have a separate collar and use a 'Roman' collar with two studs, such as that worn by priests, or, indeed, by officers wearing dress uniform. These can be had from ecclesiastical and military outfitters, and should be five centimetres high, which allows about five millimetres to show above the uniform collar and thus enhance the general appearance. (See the photograph in the colour section of this book showing H.M. King Juan Carlos of Spain who wears such a collar with a military dress uniform). 'Roman' collars made of a plastic material are now available and they can be wiped clean with a damp cloth. Knights wearing a neck badge place the ribbon between the white collar and the uniform collar with the cross or badge protruding above the top button according to regulations.

There is no regulation salute for Papal Knights. On photographs taken in different countries, one can see different forms of salute when greeting

ADDITIONAL GUIDELINES FOR PAPAL KNIGHTS

each other or when returning the salute of a guard on duty; some knights give a military salute, others touch or doff their hat. As a matter of principal and common courtesy, Papal Knights should always bare their heads when greeting the Pope, a cardinal or bishop, when attending private audiences or entering a church or Cathedral. However, if knights process into a church or Cathedral, it may be arranged that they wear their bi-cornered hats (which are always worn with the cockade facing to the right) and take them off after they have taken their places.

While no particular form of salute is preferred, it adds much to the dignity of an occasion when several uniformed Papal Knights walk together, if the form of salute and other matters of etiquette are arranged beforehand and not left to chance.

The court sword is part of the uniform. It is always worn, except when knights sit down to a meal. The drawing of swords by Papal Knights during the Eucharist to salute the raised Host and the chalice is discouraged in some countries, though it is an inviolable tradition in others, such as the Republic of Poland.

When travelling by air or abroad, transporting the sword can present problems, as security officers consider a court sword a dangerous weapon. The cloth sheath delivered with the sword is unsuitable for any

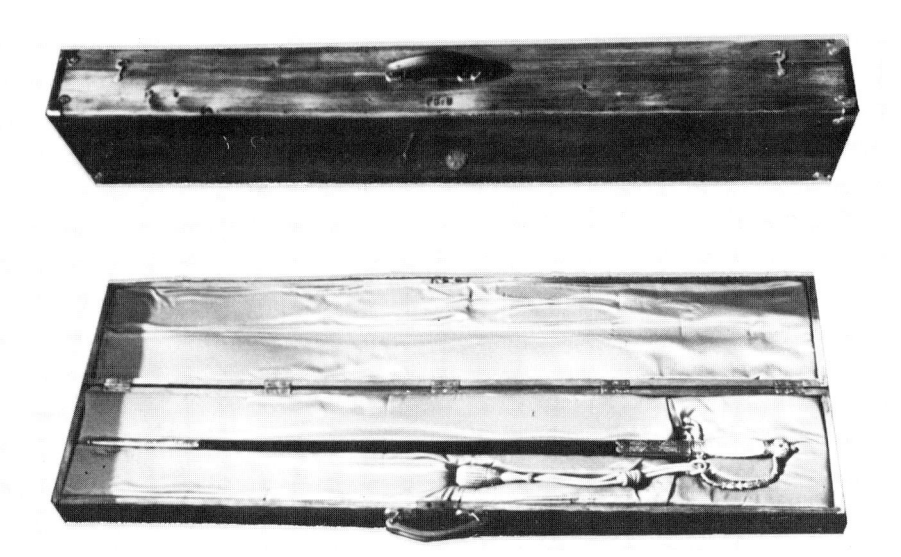

This sword case for travelling was made by a local carpenter using 1 cm thick wood. The eight corners of the case are strengthened with steel corners and a handle fitted above a lock; left and right a catch to secure the closed case. It is lined with foam rubber; the bottom layer has the shape of the hilt and the sword cut out before the foam rubber is lined with cloth. Over-all dimension of closed case 103 cm x 18 cm x 10 cm deep; weight with sword: 4 kg.

transportation, as the scabbard and the sword blade break ..y. To avoid difficulties it is possible to have made a wooden .l with foam rubber cut to shape and covered with a soft cloth. .e needs a lock and two additional clasps to secure it, and if it is to ....ried as hand baggage on an aircraft, knights should ask the airport security officer examining goods for a personal inspection because it always causes difficulties when put through an x-ray machine. Airport authorities normally refuse to permit its transport as hand baggage as it is potentially a lethal weapon. A good advance precaution is to try to arrange with the airline for the captain of the aircraft to secure the sword during the flight, as they are usually most obliging. Problems can arise at customs and security checks abroad, especially on the return journey. A certificate, preferably in the language of the country visited, with a passport-type photograph stamped and signed by the Apostolic Nunciature, will generally put the mind of security officers at rest. Uniformed Papal Knights visiting Rome for a special function, could possibly lease a sword from the suppliers of uniforms for the short period it is needed.

The wearing of decorations on the uniform of Papal Knights is governed by two sets of rules: the national rules appertaining to those decorations which may be worn at state or public functions at which the Head of State is present, and the guidelines laid down by the Apostolic See as far as social and religious functions are concerned. The Apostolic See prohibits the wearing of decorations of self-styled and extinct Orders.

The insignia or decoration of a Papal Knight is part of the uniform; for example, a Knight Commander of a Pontifical Order will always wear the neck badge or cross of the Pontifical Order suspended from its ribbon and protruding above the top button of the uniform as the principle decoration. If that Knight Commander wishes to wear additional neck badges, he will wear the decoration that takes precedence from the second button, and the third neck badge or cross from the third button. The maximum number of stars that can be worn varies from country to country, though four stars on the left side seems to be generally acceptable. Stars designed to be worn on the right side, Crosses of Profession and in some cases Stars of Grand Officers, are worn there. Depending on how four stars are arranged on the left side, the order of precedence is as follows:

```
              2                        1   2
        1         3         or
              4                        3   4
```

Three and two stars are arranged thus:

```
        1                          1
    2       3                  2
```

A single star is positioned centrally on the left breast. Only one sash of a Grand Cross can be worn.

There is no restriction on the number of full-size breast crosses or medals suspended from their ribbons. When wearing dress uniform, a Knight of a Pontifical Order should always wear the Badge or the Cross of his Order as the principal decoration.

The same arrangement of Stars applies when wearing evening dress with white tie,[1] though miniatures are often preferred to full-size medals, and only one neck badge is worn. On morning dress the same number of stars can be worn, the breast medals should be full-size but no sash should be worn.

With evening dress (black tie), one neck badge can be worn and one star. The number of miniature decorations suspended from the medal bar is unrestricted.

With regard to the Pontifical Order of St. Gregory the Great, somebody invented a story that only Knights Commander and Knights Grand Cross may wear a green cloak over their uniform: this is not true. The cloaks are entirely unofficial and do not form part of the prescribed uniform. They came into use at a later date to protect the wearer from the elements and are in my opinion the most useless apparel imaginable, as they are too short to give protection.

Members of the Pontifical Equestrian Orders would do better to acquire an officer's greatcoat, which are available from military outfitters in garrison towns, and who often have excellent and inexpensive second-hand ones in stock. All they need is a change of buttons, which can be purchased from Gammarelli in Rome. Greatcoats are weatherproof, long enough to protect the trouser legs against rain and they keep one warm. They even have inside pockets large enough to hold the bi-cornered hat, the plumes of which would suffer in the rain, and the pockets are made to allow the wearer to hold the hilt of the sword whilst walking. It is the ideal garment to protect the uniformed knight.

---

[1] At functions in the Vatican a black waistcoat is usual, when the sash should be worn under it, rather than above, as with the white waistcoat.

2

PREPARATIONS FOR AN INVESTITURE OF A PAPAL KNIGHT

Investitures of Papal Knights should take place during the celebration of Holy Mass, after the reading of the Gospel and before the Credo. Investitures can take place in the diocesan cathedral, particularly if the Bishop wishes to invest several candidates in his diocese, or in the parish church of a candidate during a visit by the Bishop.

The preparations for an investiture in a cathedral are the same as for those in a parish church, though the organisation will be on a larger scale. The priest responsible for such a function in a cathedral is the Administrator, who is the parish priest of the cathedral, and works closely with the diocesan Master of Ceremonies.

It is exceptional for a newly appointed Papal Knight to have acquired a uniform before his investiture. It is therefore important that one or more uniformed Papal Knights are in attendance. This not only demonstrates the privilege of Papal Knights to be in attendance on ecclesiastical dignitaries, but also the *esprit de corps* of the Papal Knights who welcome a new confrère into the midst of their chivalric fraternity.

One uniformed Papal Knight should act as the candidate's sponsor and present him to the Bishop for the investiture and assist during the ceremony. If other uniformed Papal Knights are present, they can be assigned different ceremonial or liturgical tasks by the Master of Ceremonies. If it proves impossible for a uniformed Papal Knight to be present, the Master of Ceremonies assists the Bishop during the investiture.

Investitures of Papal Knights are relatively rare occasions because of the limited number of knighthoods conferred, and proper preparation for the investiture ensures the dignity of the occasion. Unlike the ceremonial of the conferment of state orders and awards, not even a large diocese has a protocol department to organise such functions. The tasks of a Master of Ceremonies are primarily liturgical, and the guidelines for investitures of Papal Knights were published in *The Cross on the Sword* (1987) to assist in establishing a ceremonial that could be adopted universally while being adapted to national and regional customs and requirements.

Attention to detail in the preparation for an investiture is important because it is the minor omissions that are usually the cause of major mishaps during the event. At secular investitures such matters are routinely handled by protocol departments, and because they are carefully prepared, the ceremonies normally pass without mishap. For example, the fastening mechanism of the Cross or Badge has to be checked to ensure there will be no difficulties when the bishop decorates the candidate: a faulty pin or clasp cannot be repaired during the

The sponsor presenting a newly created knight to the Bishop for the investiture.

Courtesy: F & J Hare Ltd.

ceremony. If a candidate is to receive a decoration that is fastened on the left breast of the uniform or jacket, easy provision can be made in advance to prevent damage to the suit by vertically fastening two safety pins from the inside of the jacket, two centimetres apart, leaving two loops next to each other, through which the usually thick pin at the top of the decoration can be slipped. Those being put round the neck can be difficult to fasten quickly, especially if they have to be tied with a bow.

The plan of the service has to be explained to all participants in advance, and seating plans have to be arranged.

Unless the Bishop is in close contact with the uniformed Papal Knights in his Diocese, his secretary could obtain the names and addresses of Papal Knights with uniforms who live in or near his diocese from the Secretary of the national Association of Papal Knights. The Knights, especially the Knight acting as the sponsor to the candidates, must be informed and invited as early as possible. If robed or uniformed Knights of other Orders attend the ceremony, the Master of Ceremonies has to plan their places in the procession and allocate seats to them.

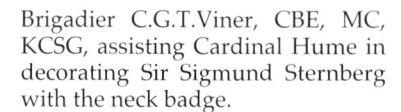

Brigadier C.G.T.Viner, CBE, MC, KCSG, assisting Cardinal Hume in decorating Sir Sigmund Sternberg with the neck badge.

At the liturgy of the Blessing of the new Abbot of Pluscarden, Scotland, Dom Hugh Gilbert, OSB, the Pontifical and the two Religious Orders of Knighthood were represented by members who hold high public office. The Knight Commander in the uniform of the Pontifical Order of St. Gregory the Great is Colonel G.S. Johnston, OBE, TD, DL, the Deputy Lord-Lieutenant of Moray, representing the Crown.

Courtesy: The Moray & Nairn Newspaper Co Ltd.

ADDITIONAL GUIDELINES FOR PAPAL KNIGHTS

The question of precedence among Orders of Knighthood dealt with here in the context of an investiture of Papal Knig[hts;] the same principles apply to religious ceremonies unle[ss] organised by another chivalric Order, in which case Papal K[nights take] the places allocated to them by their hosts.

At religious services Papal Knights are not subject to the same chivalric rules of precedence as other Orders[1]. In as much as Pope St. Pius X decreed in a memorandum to his Master of Ceremonies that the Knights of the Order of St. Gregory the Great should have a place in the papal cortege, Cardinals Casaroli and Martin and the prelates who advised me in preparing an investiture ceremony agreed that in a spirit of confraternal collaboration, all uniformed Papal Knights, irrespective of the Order to which they belong, should have a place in the corteges of cardinals, archbishops and bishops and be in attendance, and not in processions of Knights in front, between or behind other Orders of Knighthood.

Concerning the Pontifical Orders of Knighthood, Pope St. Pius X stated:

THERE IS A FUNDAMENTAL DIFFERENCE BETWEEN THE PONTIFICAL ORDERS OF KNIGHTHOOD AND THE RELIGIOUS-MILITARY, BUT NOT PONTIFICAL, ORDERS OF KNIGHTHOOD, SUCH AS THE SOVEREIGN MILITARY ORDER OF MALTA AND THE EQUESTRIAN ORDER OF THE HOLY SEPULCHRE OF JERUSALEM. THEIR FOUNDATION WAS THE RESULT OF PRIVATE INITIATIVE, ENCOURAGED AND APPROVED BY THE PAPACY; FROM THEIR VERY BEGINNING, LIKE THE EARLY MONASTIC-MILITARY ORDERS OF KNIGHTHOOD, THEY WERE STRONGLY ORIENTED TOWARDS THE CHURCH BY REASON OF THE CONSTITUTION AND MOTIVATION. THE AFORESAID ORDERS ARE FULLY RECOGNISED BY THE HOLY SEE AS RELIGIOUS ORDERS OF KNIGHTHOOD IN THEIR RESPECTIVE DIFFERENT STATUS.

As far as the Religious but not Pontifical Orders of Knighthood are concerned, Masters of Ceremony therefore apply the international rules of precedence when arranging processions. Precedence in order of the date of foundation goes to the Sovereign Military Order of Malta, followed by the Equestrian Order of the Holy Sepulchre of Jerusalem.

It is an extremely difficult task to organise the attendance of Papal Knights on an international basis. Yet on great occasions, for example, when the Pope has appointed a Papal Legate to represent him at an Eucharistic Congress, or there is a special pilgrimage or a festival at a Holy Shrine, Papal Knights have an important rôle to play. It has usually been due to the private initiative of individuals that the Papal Legates received the honours due to them. There has been no firm ruling as to the

---

[1] Prior to Papal Knights being allocated specific tasks, Knights of of Malta always took precedence and walked behind all others; Knights and Dames of the Holy Sepulchre walked first, Papal Knights in between.

After the Pontifical High Mass, His Excellency Archbishop Muszynski of Gniezno, Counsellor of the General Secretariat of the World Synod of Bishops, had two Prelates and two Papal Knights in attendance during the civic reception.

number of Papal Knights that should be in attendance, but the numbers published in 1987 seem to have been generally accepted. A Papal Legate, Cardinals, Apostolic Nuncios, Archbishops and Bishops should each have two Papal Knights in attendance if they are available.

At an investiture, the Papal Knight who acts as the candidates' sponsor either attends on the investing bishop or follows him in the procession if the bishop is attended by the deacon and sub-deacon as well as the Master of Ceremonies.

It is important that the uniformed Papal Knights have their seats allocated in advance, and they should be offered the opportunity of studying the seating arrangements prior to the ceremony. If any of the Knights whose Order is processing is unable to walk at the normal processional pace, arrangements should be made so these Knights can take their places before the procession begins.

The decorations to be conferred and the diplomas should be placed in the order in which they are needed on the altar before the service. Whilst the Knight who presents the candidates to the Bishop will remain standing next to the candidate being presented, the appropriate decoration will be handed to the Bishop by a person appointed to do this; immediately following the investiture, the candidates will be handed the diploma and the case for their decoration.

3
THE INVESTITURE OF A PAPAL KNIGHT

As said above, the guidelines for an investiture of Papal Knights suggested in *The Cross on the Sword* have been widely adopted, and the Knights of St. Columbanus in the Irish Republic, from the ranks of whom many Papal Knights in Ireland have been chosen, have regularly published a liturgy for each investiture. They have used the liturgy of St. Gregory or St. Sylvester, and introduced a set Homily which follows the reading of the Gospel. This is taken from the words of Cardinal Jacques Martin and is designed to place the investiture which follows in perspective:

> 'It is always necessary to underline the essential differences between temporal decorations and those that are conferred by the Sovereign Pontiff. A Papal Knighthood is not to be viewed solely as an honour, as a reward: it also incorporates a duty and a mission, that of serving and protecting the person of the Vicar of Christ.
>
> 'Papal Knights form an army, on the devotion of which the Pope must be able to rely. To the Knights it is not the honour that matters but their obligations and services.'
>
> The Bishop addresses the Knight sponsoring the candidate(s): 'Let the candidate(s) for investiture into the Order of St. Gregory the Great (or/and the Order of Pope St. Sylvester) be brought forward.'

The Sponsor walks toward the candidate(s) and leads him (them) to a position in front of the altar, so that the investiture takes place in full view of the congregation.

The Sponsor will now introduce the candidate(s). To avoid unnecessary repetition, he will name the candidates in the order in which they are to be invested and the rank and Order of which the individual candidates are to become members:

> 'My Lord Bishop, I have the honour of presenting
> ....
> to be invested with the insignia of a...
> of the Pontifical Equestrian Order of St. Gregory the Great" (or the Pontifical Equestrian Order of Pope St. Sylvester).'

The Bishop now addresses the candidates and the congregation. If gentlemen of both the Orders of St. Gregory the Great and of Pope St. Sylvester are being invested, he will read both sections, if only members of one Order are invested, he will read the relevant part:

'The Pontifical Order of St. Gregory the Great was founded in 1831 by Pope Gregory XVI. It is conferred as a reward for services to the Supreme Pontiff, the Holy See and the Church on gentlemen of proved loyalty who must maintain unswerving fidelity to God, the Supreme Pontiff and the Church.'

or/and

'The Pontifical Order of Pope St. Sylvester was founded in 1841 by Pope Gregory the Great and reconstituted as in independent Order in 1905 by Pope St. Pius X. The Order is conferred on gentlemen who are active in the apostolate, particularly in the exercise of their pro fessional duties, and on those who are masters of different arts.'

'The role of a Papal Knight has been defined by Cardinal Agostino Casaroli, for many years the Grand Chancellor of all Pontifical Equestrian Orders, as follows: 'Becoming a Knight does not merely mean receiving a title of honour – even though it is well deserved – but fighting evil, promoting good, and defending the weak and oppressed against injustice.'

If there are more than a single candidate, it is at the discretion of the Bishop if he wishes to read out one translation of the Papal Brief of appointment, but inserting the appropriate names, ranks and Orders of the various candidates, or to read out the translation of the individual Papal Briefs.

'The Papal Brief of appointment reads as follows:

IOANNES PAULUS SECUNDUS PONTIFEX MAXIMUS
JOHN PAUL II SUPREME PONTIFF

Gladly acceding to a request made to Us from which We have learned that you are most deserving as a result of your work for the Holy Catholic Church and its affairs, and in order that We might give a clear sign of Our pleasure and appreciation, We choose, make and declare you

NN ....
of the Diocese of NN ....
a ....[rank]................of the Order of St. Gregory the Great (or: of the Order of Pope St. Sylvester) and We bestow on you the right to use and enjoy all the privileges that go with this high dignity.

Given at St. Peter's in Rome on.............................[Date].............................

IOANNES PAVLVS II PONT. MAX.

PRECIBVS NOBIS ADHIBITIS LIBENTI ANIMO CONCEDENTES, E QVIBVS TE ACCEPIMVS DE ECCLESIAE REIQVE CATHOLICAE BONO ATQVE INCREMENTO BENE MERITVM ESSE, VT PATENS GRATAE NOSTRAE VOLVNTATIS TESTIMONIVM PROMAMVS, TE

Nicolaum Vecchione
ex Archidioecesi Vestmonasteriensi

EQVITEM ORDINIS SANCTI GREGORII MAGNI E CLASSE CIVILI ELIGIMVS, FACIMVS AC RENVNTIAMVS, TIBIQVE FACVLTATEM TRIBVIMVS PRIVILEGIIS OMNIBVS VTENDI, QVAE CVM HAC DIGNITATE SVNT CONIVNCTA.

DATVM ROMAE, APVD S. PETRVM, DIE XI Novembris MCMLXXXVI.

+ A. Card. Casaroli

IOANNES PAVLVS II PONT. MAX.

PRECIBVS NOBIS ADHIBITIS LIBENTI ANIMO CONCEDENTES, E QVIBVS TE ACCEPIMVS DE ECCLESIAE REIQVE CATHOLICAE BONO ATQVE INCREMENTO BENE MERITVM ESSE, VT PATENS GRATAE NOSTRAE VOLVNTATIS TESTIMONIVM PROMAMVS, TE

Gordon Viner
ex Archidioecesi Vestmonasteriensi

EQVITEM COMMENDATOREM ORDINIS SANCTI GREGORII MAGNI E CLASSE CIVILI ELIGIMVS, FACIMVS AC RENVNTIAMVS, TIBIQVE FACVLTATEM TRIBVIMVS PRIVILEGIIS OMNIBVS VTENDI, QVAE CVM HAC DIGNITATE SVNT CONIVNCTA.

DATVM ROMAE, APVD S. PETRVM, DIE XVII Julii MCMLXXXVII.

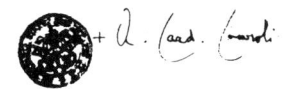

+ A. Card. Casaroli

IOANNES PAVLVS II PONT. MAX.

PRECIBVS NOBIS ADHIBITIS LIBENTI ANIMO CONCEDENTES, E QVIBVS TE ACCEPIMVS DE ECCLESIAE REIQVE CATHOLICAE BONO ATQVE INCREMENTO BENE MERITVM ESSE, VT PATENS GRATAE NOSTRAE VOLVNTATIS TESTIMONIVM PROMAMVS, TE

Petrum Blanchard
ex Urbe

EQVITEM COMMENDATOREM ORDINIS SANCTI GREGORII MAGNI

E CLASSE CIVILI ELIGIMVS, FACIMVS AC RENVNTIAMVS, TIBIQVE FACVLTATEM TRIBVIMVS PRIVILEGIIS OMNIBVS VTENDI, QVAE CVM HAC DIGNITATE SVNT CONIVNCTA.

DATVM ROMAE, APVD S. PETRVM, DIE *XXIX mensis Septembris*, anno *MCMLXXXVI*.

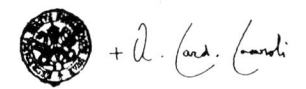

Apostolic Briefs appointing or promoting Pontifical Knights are now signed by the Secretary of State *non de mandato*, without having to ask for a specific mandate to do so. In the Apostolic Constitution *Regimini Ecclesiae Universae* Pope Paul VI transferred the Chancellery of the Pontifical Equestrian Orders to the Papal Secretariat of State; the Cardinal Secretary of State is *ex officio* the Grand Chancellor of all the Pontifical Orders of Knighthood. Opposite, top: The appointment of Nicola Vecchione as Knight of the Order of St. Gregory; below: the promotion of Brigadier C.G.T.Viner, CBE, MC, TD, to Knight Commander of the Order of St. Gregory; above: the appointment of Dott.Pierre Blanchard, Vice Segretario della Amministrazione del Patrimonio della Sede Apostolica (Sezione Straordinaria), Vatican City, as Knight Commander of the Order of St. Gregory the Great. Those living and working in the Vatican City State have as their Diocese *ex Urbe*.

Signed and sealed by the Secretary of State

'I have been delegated by His Holiness Pope John Paul II to invest you with the insignia of the rank and Order to which he has appointed you. Before performing this solemn task, I ask you: Do you promise faithfully to maintain unswerving fidelity to God, the Supreme Pontiff and to the Church, and are you prepared to exercise the office of a Pontifical Knight in accordance with the high ideals and standards expected of you?'

Each candidate should answer individually:

'I promise so to do.'

The Bishop now asks the candidates individually to step forward. The

Sponsor also ascends the steps and assists the Bishop with the task of conferring the insignia. The Bishop addresses each candidate in turn:

'In the name of His Holiness Pope John Paul II I herewith invest you with the insignia of a .... in the Pontifical Order of St. Gregory the Great [or: in the Pontifical Order of Pope St. Sylvester] and I also present to you the Papal Brief of appointment.'

The newly invested Knight bows to the Bishop and takes his place at the foot of the altar steps, where he awaits the other Knights being invested. Finally, the Sponsor bows to the Bishop and leads them back to their seats. The Bishop now continues with the Eucharist. In some regional jurisdictions it has been the practice that a newly invested Knight wishes to speak and express his gratitude to the Holy Father, the Bishop and others. Only if this has been agreed with the Bishop prior to the service, the Knight may do so after the post-communion prayers have been said and before the concluding prayers of the Mass.

4

CONFERMENT OF INSIGNIA UPON NEWLY CREATED MEMBERS OF PONTIFICAL EQUESTRIAN ORDERS

Conferments during an audience with the Holy Father are restricted to honours that have been granted *motu proprio* by the Pope to persons who have given personal service to His Holiness, and sometimes to diplomats who have been accredited to the Holy See for longer than two years and who are paying a visit to take leave of the Supreme Pontiff on being recalled by their government. In most cases, the insignia have been taken by a high dignitary to the recipient prior to his audience with the Pope, and he wears the decoration for the occasion.

The official protocol for the conferment of a papal knighthood on a Head of State in the Apostolic Palace follows traditional guidelines. The Head of State is formally received on arrival in the Vatican by the Prefect of the Pontifical Court who leads him first to a Papal Legate who has been specially appointed to conduct the ceremony of conferment. After the Head of State has been decorated by the Legate with the insignia, the Prefect of the Pontifical Court leads him to the private apartments of the Supreme Pontiff where he receives the Papal Brief.

Knighthoods conferred on lay officials in the Roman Curia and members of the Corps of Swiss Guards in the Vatican (*ex urbe*) are usually bestowed upon the candidate at a brief ceremony by the Cardinal Secretary of State or by one of the Cardinals of the Roman Curia.

Cardinal Agostino Casaroli, Secretary of State, conferring the *Commenda* of the Order of St. Gregory the Great on Dott. Pierre Blanchard – *ex Urbe* – in the offices of the Secretariat of State.

Courtesy: Vincenzo Modica – Roma

In cases of a conferment instead of an investiture, newly created members of a Pontifical Equestrian Order who live abroad receive the insignia either at the Apostolic Nunciature from the Nuncio, or at the Archbishop's or Bishop's House from the Diocesan Bishop. These occasions are usually followed by a reception.

APPENDIX III

CRITERIA FOR, AND THE PROCEDURE OF CONFERMENT OF, THE PONTIFICAL AWARDS OF MERIT 'PRO ECCLESIA ET PONTIFICE' AND 'BENEMERENTI'

Both Pontifical Awards of Merit have their rightful place among the Awards of Merit in the international family of decorations and are classified as Religious Awards. However, the lavishness with which both decorations have been bestowed since the Second Vatican Council in Great Britain justifies a closer examination of the criteria which are applied when an application for one is made to the Holy See. Although no central register is kept for either award, all applications have to go through the Apostolic Nuncio who, once they have been approved by the Secretariat of State, also receives the diplomas and decorations. It appears that the number of 'Pro Ecclesia et Pontifice' Crosses and 'Benemerenti' Medals applied for by the diocesan bishops in Great Britain outnumbers those applied for by the bishops for the rest of Europe, but as there is no central register, it is impossible to obtain any figures.

The criteria for the conferment of one of these two awards probably differ in Great Britain from those applied in other countries of Europe where the awards are not conferred on such a lavish scale.

Parish Priests usually apply to the Local Bishop for the two awards to be made; the applications are forwarded by the Bishop to the Apostolic Nuncio who, if he has no objection, sends them to Rome. The fee, which is payable by the original applicant, includes (unlike the insignia for a knighthood) the Cross or the Medal and a document of conferment which is signed by the *Sostituto* or the *Assessore* of the Section for General Affairs of the Church in the Secretariat of State. Conferments of the 'Pro Ecclesia et Pontifice Cross' and the 'Benemerenti' Medal are not gazetted in the *Acta Apostolicae Sedis*.

In a parish itself, the conferment of a Papal Award is an important event. The recipients are usually well-known members of the parish, and a special ceremony during the celebration of the Eucharist may add to the dignity and importance of the occasion. At the special request of the late Bishop Gerald Mahon, and greatly helped by Canon Adrian Arrowsmith, I also drew up guidelines for such a ceremony, and they were first published in *The Cross on the Sword*. Such a service is not an investiture, as only Knights are invested.

The Local Bishop may confer the Cross or the Medal himself, but more often he delegates the task to the Parish Priest who proposed the recipient for it.

It is not unusual for more than one person to receive a Pontifical Award of Merit on the same occasion. The ceremony should take place after the reading of the Gospel, and the Bishop or Parish Priest will instruct the Master of Ceremonies:

'Please bring to me those upon whom the Holy Father has conferred a Pontifical Award of Merit.'

The Master of Ceremonies leads the recipients to the altar where the Bishop or Parish Priest will address them and the congregation:

'The "Pro Ecclesia et Pontifice" Cross was instituted by Pope Leo XIII in 1888 to mark the occasion of his priestly golden jubilee. It is awarded to men and women as a sign of the Holy Father's recognition of their distinguished service to the Church and Society.'

and/or

'The "Benemerenti" Medal was first awarded by Pope Pius IV in 1775. Similar medals have continued to be bestowed upon men and women who had distinguished themselves by giving special service to the Church or for their accomplishments. In 1891, Pope Leo XIII instituted the Medal "Benemerenti" as a permanent Award of Merit. In 1971, Pope Paul VI changed the medal and adopted a cross for the Award.'

He now reads the Diploma(s) conferring the Award:

'IOANNES PAULUS SECUNDUS PONTIFEX MAXIMUS

JOHN PAUL II, SUPREME PONTIFF

Gladly acceding to a request made to Us from which we have learned that you are most deserving for all that you have done for the Church and the Holy Father, and as a clear sign of Our pleasure, we award you the decoration
    The Cross 'Pro Ecclesia et Pontifice'

or

    The Medal 'Benemerenti'

Given at the Vatican ....

Sostituto '

The recipients are now given their Award and Apostolic Diploma, and the Master of Ceremonies leads the recipient(s) back to their seats in the choir of the church.

CONFERMENT OF PONTIFICAL RELIGIOUS AWARDS

Above: the Sponsor leads three candidates, leaders of the Catholic Scout Movement, to the Bishop who confers on them the Papal Award *Pro Ecclesia et Pontifice* (right).

APPENDIX IV
THE PONTIFICAL MEDAL

The Pontifical Medal has never been a pontifical award or decoration, though until 1982, it was frequently given during a private audience by the Pope as a sign of grateful recognition or of special esteem for the recipient. Since the advent of the Vatican City State in 1929, its government had its own numismatic office where also serious numismatists could acquire copies of the official medals in gold, silver or bronze. They always have been minted for the Vatican State by the Mint of the State of Italy. The complete set in gold, silver and bronze of the annual issue which corresponds to the year of the Pope's pontificate, is usually given by the Pontiff to visiting sovereigns, and prominent public figures. He also gives individual medals in silver, also those minted on special occasions, to important visitors.

There are two types of pontifical medals, *annuale* and *straordinaria*, the annual medal which is always minted in the Italian State Mint, commemorates the accession of a pope to the See of St. Peter and subsequently the anniversary of the event. Extraordinary medals which are struck in the Italian State Mint if they have been officially commissioned, otherwise in private mints, commemorate special events. After the Vatican City State was founded, the first pontifical medal in gold, silver and bronze, was an extraordinary Medal celebrating the signing of the Lateran Treaty. On the obverse it shows the heads of Pope Pius XI, wearing his tiara, facing the crowned head of King Victor Emmanuel III. The photograph used for the reverse of the medal is reproduced in Chapter Two and shows the two principal negotiators of the Treaty, Cardinal Gasparri and Prime Minister Benito Mussolini. Two more extraordinary medals were minted before the first *annuale*, which commemorated the eighth year of the accession of Pope Pius XI to the See of St. Peter.

The form of the pontifical medal has been practically the same for several centuries, starting with Pope Nicholas V (1447-55), until Pope Paul VI decided that the *annuale* commemorating his twelfth anniversary as pope should be oval. As the year 1975 was a Holy Year, a second, but much larger oval medal, not unlike that of the *annuale*, was struck in a limited number to commemorate the Holy Year, apart from a special 'Benemerenti' Medal on that occasion. The *annuale* medal has been circular, with the above-mentioned exception, normally about forty millimetres in diameter, but sometimes reaching seventy-five millimetres in diameter.

The *straordinaria* medals which commemorate special events always

Pope Paul VI had the medal Anno XII (left) struck in an oval shape. This and a special medal *straordinaria* (almost four times the size of the annual medal) commemorated the Holy Year 1975.

carry an image of the reigning pope, his name and its date of issue on the obverse and a representation of the event being commemorated on the reverse. Pope Paul VI, a great admirer of modern art, introduced several new forms and tried to combine contemporary with ancient styles.

When Pope John Paul II declared 1983 an extraordinary Holy Year, he used the pontifical *annuale* medal as a 'Benemerenti' medal, suspended from a yellow and white ribbon, which was chiefly awarded to members of the Pontifical Swiss Guards.

Other medals are struck on the occasion of *Sede Vacante*, following the death of a pope and the election of his successor. These medals mark the *interregnum* and the government of the Church by the cardinals under the Cardinal Camerlengo of the Holy Roman Apostolic Church. On the obverse of the medal is the *Ombrelino* (open umbrella) above the crossed keys of St. Peter, the wording *Sede Apostolica Vacante* and the year[1], on the reverse are the armorial bearings of the Cardinal Camerlengo, his name and title.

Pontifical medals are of great value from artistic, iconographic and historic points of view, and they reflect highlights in the history of the Church and the Papacy.

A third official pontifical medal came into being with Pope Paul's

---

[1] In 1978, Pope Paul VI and Pope John Paul I died within a month of each other.

Six of the Pontifical Medals struck during the Pontificate of Pope Paul VI, who introduced many new form which represent both ancient and modern styles. For example, the medal reproduced bottom left (Anno V) shows on the reverse the images of SS. Peter and Paul as they have always appeared on the seals of Papal Bulls. The reverse of the medal reproduced bottom right (Anno VII) recalls the Pope's seminal encyclical letter of that year, *Humanae Vitae*. The artist's interpretation caused as much controversy as the encyclical letter.

The medal *Sede Vacante*, reproduced above left was struck after the death of Pope Paul VI in 1978; in the centre left is the medal *Sede Iterum Vacante*, struck about a month later after Pope John Paul I had died. The medals reproduced centre right and bottom left and right commemorate the first three years of the pontificate of Pope John Paul II. The medals *Sede Vacante* and *Sede Iterum Vacante* were struck by order of the Camerlengo of the Holy

Roman Church whose task it is to convene the conclave for the election of the new pope. Cardinal Jean Villot was Camerlengo on both occasions and the medals bear his coat of arms on the reverse. The medal Anno I always bears the new Pontiff's coat of arms. The medal reproduced top right was struck retrospectively by order of John Paul II to commemorate the short pontificate of his predecessor.

The obverse of the medals Anno IV, Anno V and Anno VI, commemorating those years of the Pope's pontificate.

travels abroad, a practice enthusiastically adopted by Pope John Paul II. Whenever the Pope visits a country, a special medal is minted to commemorate the event, and these are given by the Pontiff personally to meritorious persons.

Beginning with fourth year of the pontificate of John Paul II, the Secretariat of State in collaboration with the Governatorato of the Vatican City State made use of the increasing interest shown in pontifical medals by collectors and numismatists. In the same way that Vatican Postal Stamps had proved a great attraction for philatelists and secured a substantial income to the Vatican Post Office, the Ufficio Numismaticato in the Vatican now issues certificates of authenticity with the medals, which give information regarding the number of medals struck in gold, silver and bronze, their metal content, diameter and exact details of obverse, reverse and edge inscriptions and sculptures. Each medal is engraved on the edge with the words E CIVITATE VATICANA, and the incised number corresponds to that on the certificate.

His Holiness still presents sets of these commemorative pontifical medals to some visitors, but it is fair to say that they have become mainly numismatic attractions, now also available from shops in Rome.

Those wishing to place orders for pontifical medals can do so by writing to:

>Governatorato della Città del Vaticano
>Ufficio Numismatico
>00120 Città del Vaticano.

APPENDIX V

THE PONTIFICAL CORPS OF GUARDS

On 14 September 1970, Pope Paul VI abolished three of the four Corps of Pontifical Guards, 'il Corpo della Guardia d'Honore di Sua Santità' (the Corps of the Guards of Honour of His Holiness), better known as 'il Corpo delle Guardie Nobili Pontificie' (the Corps of the Pontifical Noble Guard); 'il Corpo della Guardia Palatina d'Honore' (the Corps of the Palatine Guard of Honour); and 'il Corpo della Gendarmeria Pontificia' (the Corps of the Pontifical Gendarmerie). The only Corps of Guards Paul VI retained was 'il Corpo della Guardia Svizzera Pontificia' (the Corps of the Pontifical Swiss Guards). All four corps provided a personal life guard for the Pope, but their main task was ceremonial.

In his Apostolic Constitution *Regimini Ecclesiae Universae* of 15 August 1967, he had already reorganised most departments of the Holy See, transferred ('suppressed') secretariats, tribunals and chancelleries to other, larger departments, such as to the Secretariat of State or to the Prefettura della Casa Pontificia.

There is no doubt that between 1967 and 1970, the ceremonies In St. Peter's Basilica and in the Apostolic Palace, especially on the occasion of official visits by sovereigns, heads of states and governments, or processions on St. Peter's Square, became less colourful and more modest events, without the splendour millions of pilgrims had come to see and participate in. It was not only the disappearance of the Corps of Guards, but the abolition of many traditional features that changed the ceremonial highlights in the Vatican. Perhaps the most striking feature was the absence of the *Sedia Gestatoria*, the portable throne on which the Supreme Pontiff was carried by twelve *Palafrenieri* on solemn occasions, that was changed for a jeep in which Pope Paul VI first made his entrance into St. Peter's Square. The offices of many of the attendants and chamberlains no longer existed, and consequently the pontifical cortège was curtailed.

The Corpus Christi procession, which in every Holy Year takes place on St. Peter's Square, has also taken on a different character. In 1950 Pope Pius XII was accompanied by the highest dignitaries of Church and the Italian State, all the Corps of Guards, and the Prelates of the Roman Curia as well as visiting honorary chamberlains from all over the world and representative groups from all the religious Orders and seminaries were part of the pontifical entourage. Twenty-five years later Pope Paul VI carried the monstrance while being driven round St. Peter's Square on a converted jeep with floral decorations; a few seminarians carried a baldachin, and the Holy Father was followed by four prelates, some priests, monks and nuns.

Surrounded by members of all the corps of guards and gendarmes, private chamberlains and followed by the staff of the Papal Court, Pope Pius XII on the *Sedia Gestatoria*, follows the procession of cardinals and high prelates when entering St. Peter's Basilica for the Holy Year 1950.

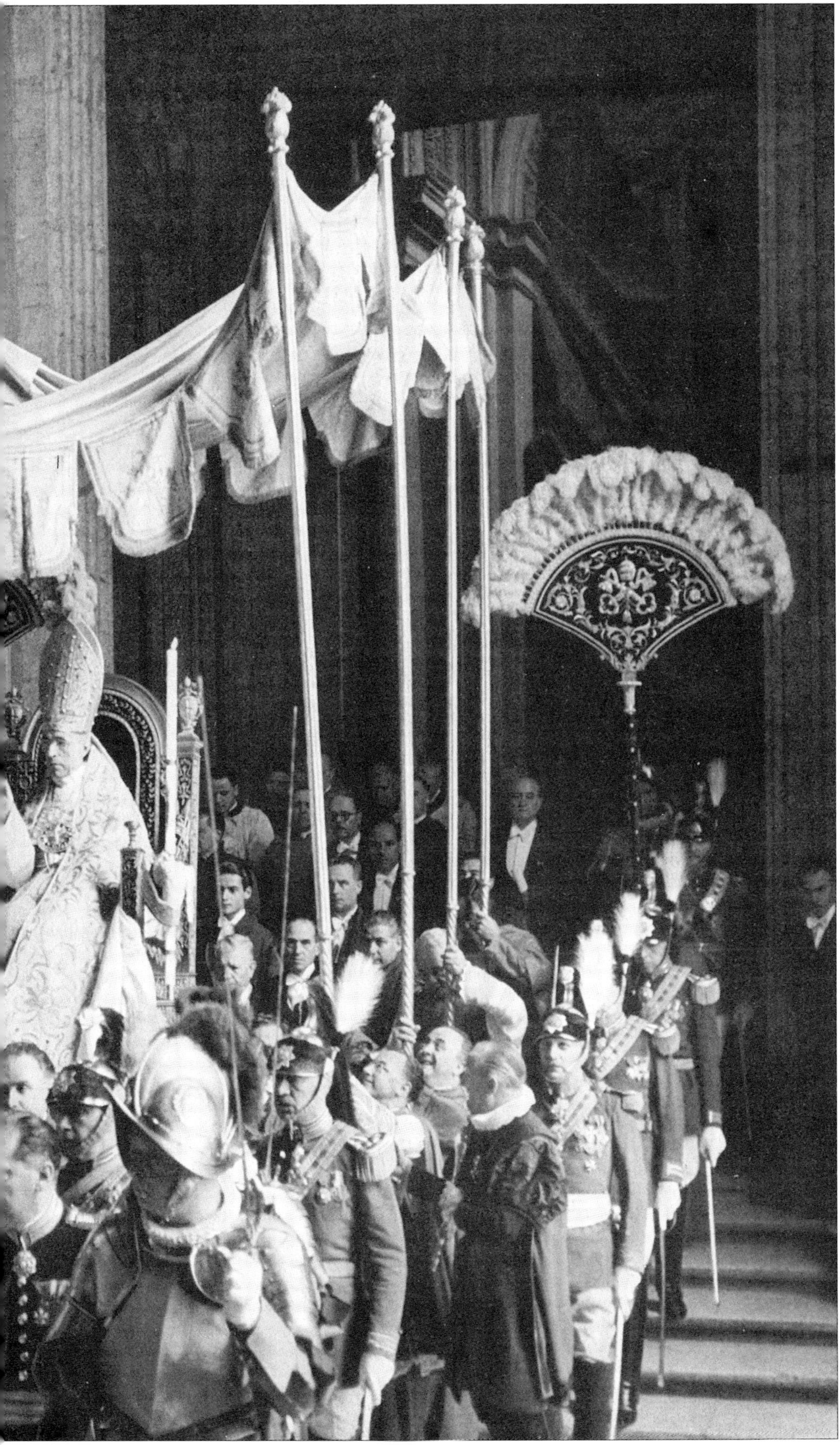

The illustrations I have reproduced show how the ceremonial in the Vatican itself has changed in these twenty-five years. Thirty years after Paul VI ceased using the *Sedia Gestatoria*, a spokesman of the Apostolic See informed the world press that its re-introduction in a slightly modified form is under consideration. Because Pope John Paul II finds walking the very long aisles of St. Peter's and standing for long periods of time in the 'Popemobile' difficult, the portable throne, carried by twelve *Palafrenieri*, appears an obvious solution. The two *Flabella*, the large fans, made of ostrich feathers surmounting heavy gold embroidery, that were always carried on either side of the Pope, are unlikely to be used. The *Daily Telegraph* (London, 22 April 1995) commented: 'the *Sedia* would be a dignified way of moving among his people.'

The disbandment of the Corps of Guards which Paul VI ordered was just one aspect of how he wished to emphasize even in outward appearance, the religious nature of the mission of St. Peter's successor.[1]

Almost all members of the different Corps of Guards were Papal Knights, many of whom continued to participate in some ceremonies. Nowadays it is not infrequent for Knights of the Pontifical Equestrian Orders to carry out duties previously reserved to the Corps of Guards whose duties in the Apostolic Palace were allocated to them by the Prefect of the Apostolic Palaces. The long service the Corps of Guards have given to the Apostolic See has earned them a place in this book, especially as four hundred years ago the Pontifical Noble Guards used to be the Guards of the Pontifical Knights.

1

THE CORPS OF THE PONTIFICAL NOBLE GUARD

The principal corps was 'il Corpo delle Guardia Nobili Pontificie', the Corps of the Pontifical Noble Guard or Corps of the Guard of Honour of His Holiness.[2] It was founded by Pope Innocent VIII in 1485 as 'il Guardia de Cavalleggeri', the 'Guard of Knights', and the Senate and the People of Rome reconstituted them in 1555 as 'il Cavalieri di Guardia di Nostro Signore'. (Knights of the Guard of Our Lord) in honour of Pope Paul IV.

This élite corps was disbanded in 1798 when the French occupied Rome, and reconstituted as 'il Guardia Nobile del Corpo di Nostro Signore' in 1801 by Pope Pius VII, and it was a mark of great distinction to be appointed to it. The Captain Commandant held the rank of a Lieutenant-General, the two Colonels, each commanding a Brigade, held the rank of Brigadier-General, while its members held the ranks of Captain, First and

---
[1] *The Vatican and Christian Rome*, Libreria Editrice Vaticana, 1974.
[2] *Annuario Pontificio* [Note Storiche], an offical annual publication of the Holy See, first published in 1716.

Members of the Corps of the Pontifical Noble Guard, who were called in 1555 'the Knights of the Guard of Our Lord'.

Courtesy: Pontifical Photographic Archives

Second Lieutenant. The Corps of the Pontifical Noble Guard was organised and administered by the Cardinal Secretary of State and their service rota was the responsibility of the Prefect of the Apostolic Palace.

2

THE CORPS OF THE PONTIFICAL SWISS GUARD

'Il Corpo della Guardia Svizzera Pontificia',[1] the Corps of the Pontifical Swiss Guards, was officially founded in 1506 by Pope Julius II and consisted of Swiss mercenaries, who since the previous century had been in the service of Italian princes and cities, as well as Pontiffs, such as Sixtus IV (1471-84), in the Papal States. Their most glorious and bravest deed was the defence of Rome in May 1527 when imperial troops sacked Rome, and the Swiss Guard defended St. Peter's Basilica fighting up to the papal altar. Of its members, 147 died in that battle, whilst the forty-two survivors rescued the Pope, Clement VII, and protected him in the fortified Castel Sant'Angelo. Pope Paul VI retained the Swiss Guard as the only Corps of Guards after he had disbanded the Corps of the Noble

[1]Ibid. and *Begegnung mit der Päpstlichen Schweizergarde im Vatikan*, Frauenfeld, Switzerland, 1984.

The Corps of the Pontifical Swiss Guards on parade.

Courtesy: *L'Osservatore Romano*

Guard, the Palatine Guard and the Gendarmerie in his Decree of 14 September 1970. Although directly under the Supreme Pontiff, they are administered by the Government of the Vatican City State and are responsible for the personal security of the Pope and the Vatican City State as well as police services.

Today, the Corps of the Pontifical Swiss Guard is a highly trained and well disciplined military unit that, in spite of the traditional appearance of their uniforms designed – so folklore has it – by Michelangelo, faces the same dangers as any guard protecting a head of state. All members of the corps are multilingual, and their duties embrace not only the protection of the Supreme Pontiff, but each member has to be able to cope with the thousands of visitors who turn to them for help and advice. They are expected to aid and assist a visiting dignitary or diplomat as much as taking care of a child lost among the tens of thousands that visit the Vatican. They have to learn to be patient with hundreds of amateur photographers, protect the better-known prominent dignitaries from being exposed to the curious and sometimes excited crowds, and at the same time smile and make the pilgrims feel welcome.

The conditions for joining the Swiss Guards and the qualifications required of them are rigorous and demanding. The present Commandant of the Corps, Colonel Buchs, has raised the standards required of recruits, and serving guardsmen have passed their tests in many disciplines and skills, so that they are on a par with the best units in any army. The Corps of the Pontifical Swiss Guard is a professional unit, loyal and devoted to

A member of the Swiss Guards on duty in the Prefettura della Casa Pontificia. The Prefect of the Papal Court arranges with the Colonel Commandant of the Swiss Guards the duties of the guards in the Apostolic Palaces and at pontifical functions.

Courtesy: *L'Osservatore Romano*

the Supreme Pontiff and an asset of the highest value to the Pope, the Church and most certainly the Vatican City State.

The Swiss Guards on duty for the reception of a dignitary who pays an official visit to the Supreme Pontiff.

Courtesy: *L'Losservatore Romano*

3

THE CORPS OF THE PALATINE GUARD OF HONOUR

'Il Corpo della Guardia Palatina d'Honore', the Corps of the Palatine Guard of Honour[1] was established by Pope Pius IX in 1850 by amalgamating two existing civic corps, 'il Corpo della Milizia Urbana', the Urban Militia, and 'il Corpo dalla Civica Scelta', an élite unit of a specially trained Civic Guard, both of which had been founded in the eighteenth century. The corps, of two battalions under a Colonel Commandant, was made up of approximately 500 volunteers, all living either in the Vatican City or in Rome so they could be called upon to serve at short notice. They had various duties assigned to them, and they were under the direct control of the Cardinal Secretary of State, and as far as their services to His Holiness were concerned, they were at the disposal of the Prefect of the Apostolic Palace. During the period of *Sede Vacante* they were at the disposal of the Cardinal Camerlengo and the Marshal of the Conclave.

[1] *Annuario Pontificio*.

An Officer and a Corporal of the Corps of the Palatine Guard of Honour.

Courtesy: Pontifical Photographic Archives

4

THE CORPS OF THE PONTIFICAL GENDARMERIE

In 1816 Pope Pius VII founded by special decree 'il Corpo dei Carabinieri Pontifici' for specific police duties and in the service of the Judiciary. In 1850, Pope Pius IX renamed the corps 'il Corpo della Gendarmeria Pontificia',[1] and placed their administration with the Cardinal Secretary of State. After the foundation of the Vatican City State in 1929, Pope Pius XI placed the Gendarmerie under the Governor of the Vatican City State and in 1946, Pope Pius XII transferred their administration to the Cardinal President of the Commission for State. Among their various duties was the personal protection of the Supreme Pontiff, the defence of the territory of the Vatican City State, general police duties, internal security and law enforcement.

[1]*Ibid.*

A member of the Corps of the Pontifical Gendarmerie (right) and a Private Chamberlain to His Holiness (left).

Courtesy: Pontifical Photographic Archives

APPENDIX VI

PERROT'S LIST OF EXTINCT ORDERS OF KNIGHTHOOD

In 1820, A.M. Perrot published his *Tableau Chronologique des Ordres Eteints*. This has been the only list of expressly extinct Orders of Knighthood compiled by a historian. As previously mentioned, it is not complete and inevitably out of date, as many Orders that are featured in Perrot's *Collection Historique des Ordres de Chevalerie* were extant in 1820 but have since ceased to exist.

Unfortunately, Perrot does not distinguish between short-lived and long-lived Orders, but he is the only historian who has given dates of foundation (with a few exceptions) and a detailed description of the Orders' insignia, which are featured on two plates.

The ninety-nine Orders I have retained in the list of Perrot can also be found among the 252 Orders listed in *Haydn's Dictionary of Dates*. Those I have taken out cannot be found in cross references or were very short-lived nineteenth century non-Catholic-founded Orders of Merit, founded in connection with the Napoleonic conquests.

The names of many of Perrot's extinct Orders of Knighthood appear in the Chapter on self-styled Orders.

Order / Illustration	*Place of Foundation*	*Date*
THE ORDER OF ST. ANTHONY	Ethiopia	370 Plate I – 1
THE ORDER OF THE HOLY VIAL	France	496 Plate I – 2
THE ORDER OF THE SWAN	Flanders	500 Plate I – 3
THE ORDER OF THE DOG AND COCK	France	500 Plate I – 4
THE ORDER OF THE OAK	Navarre	722 Plate I – 5
THE ORDER OF THE DOGE	Venice	Plate I – 6
THE ORDER OF THE GENET	France	732 Plate I – 7
THE ORDER OF ST. MARK	Venice	? Plate I – 8
THE ORDER OF ST. CATHERINE	Holy Land	? Plate I – 9
THE ORDER OF THE ROYAL CROWN	France	802 Plate I – 10
THE ORDER OF THE CROWN	Germany	793 Plate I – 11
THE ORDER OF OUR LADY OF THE LILY	Spain	1023 Plate I – 12
THE ORDER OF THE MARTYRS	Holy Land	1030 Plate I – 13
THE ORDER OF THE LION	France 1180	Plate I – 14
THE ORDER OF THE HOLY SAVIOUR	Spain	1104 Plate I – 15
THE ORDER OF THE TEMPLARS	Jerusalem	1119 Plate I – 16
THE ORDER OF ST. BLAISE AND OF THE VIRGIN MARY	Holy Land	12th cent. Plate I – 17
THE ORDER OF AUBRAC	Flanders	1120 Plate I – 18

THE ORDER OF THE HATCHET	Spain	1149 Plate I – 19
THE ORDER OF DOBRIN	Poland	1153 Plate I – 20
THE ORDER OF ST. MICHAEL'S WING	Portugal	1171 Plate I – 21
THE ORDER OF MONTJOIE	Spain	1180 Plate I – 22
THE ORDER OF ST. GEREON	Holy Land	1190 Plate I – 23
THE ORDER OF SILENCE or OF THE SWORD	Cyprus	1195 Plate I – 24
THE ORDER OF THE SWORD BEARERS	Livonia	1202 Plate I – 25
THE ORDER OF THE HOLY GHOST OF MONTPELLIER	France	1195 Plate I – 26
THE ORDER OF ST. GEORGE OF ALFAMA	Spain	1201
THE ORDER OF THE HOLY GHOST OF SAXIA	Italy	1207 Plate II – 33
THE ORDER OF OUR LADY OF THE ROSARY	Spain	1209 Plate I – 27
THE ORDER OF THE BROTHERS HOSPITALLER OF BURGOS	Spain	1212 Plate I – 28
THE ORDER OF THE BEAR OF THE ABBEY OF ST. GALLEN	Germany	1215 Plate I – 29
THE ORDER OF THE MILITIA OF JESUS CHRIST or ST. DOMINIC	Italy/France	1216 Plate I – 30
THE ORDER OF THE FAITH OF JESUS CHRIST	Italy/France	1225 Plate II – 38
THE ORDER OF OUR LADY OF RANSOM	Spain	1218 Plate I – 31
THE ORDER OF OUR LADY OF MERCY	Spain	1228 (same Order?)
THE ORDER OF ST. MARY or OF THE BROTHERS OF JUBILATION	Italy	1233 Plate I – 32
THE ORDER OF SS. JOHN AND THOMAS	Holy Land	1261 Plate I – 34
THE ORDER OF THE SPURS OF NAPLES	Two Sicilies	1266
THE ORDER OF THE CRESCENT	Two Sicilies	1268 Plate I – 35
THE ORDER OF THE SHIP AND THE SHELL	France 1269	Plate I – 36
THE ORDER OF ST. JAMES OF THE SHELL	Holland	1290 Plate I – 37
THE ORDER OF ST. GEORGE IN CARINTHIA	Empire	1273 Plate I – 38
THE ORDER OF THE SCALE	Spain	1318 Plate I – 39
THE ORDER OF THE STAR	Two Sicilies	1351 Plate I – 40
THE ORDER OF THE STAR OF THE NOBLE HOUSE	France	1351 Plate I – 41
THE ORDER OF THE KNOT	Sicily	1360 Plate I – 42
THE ORDER OF ST. BRIDGET OF SWEDEN	Sweden	1366 Plate I – 43
THE ORDER OF THE GOLD ESCUTCHEON	France	1369 Plate I – 44
THE ORDER OF THE PASSION OF CHRIST (founded by Richard II of England in 1380 and adopted by Charles VI of France in 1400)	Holy Land	1400 Plate I – 45
THE ORDER OF THE FOOLS	France	1380 Plate I – 46
THE ORDER OF THE ERMINE AND THE EAR OF CORN	Bretagne	1381 Plate I – 47
THE ORDER OF ST. ANTHONY	Bavaria	1381 Plate I – 48
THE ORDER OF THE ARGONAUTS	Two Sicilies	1382 Plate I – 49

PERROT'S LIST OF EXTINCT ORDERS

THE ORDER OF THE REEL AND THE LIONESS	Two Sicilies	1386 Plate II – 1
THE ORDER OF ST. GEORGE OF BURGUNDY or OF MIOLANS	France	1390 Plate II – 2
THE ORDER OF THE PORCUPINE	France	1394 Plate II – 3
THE ORDER OF THE DEFEATED DRAGON	Empire	1418 Plate II – 5
THE ORDER OF ST.JAMES-DU-HAUT-PAS	France	1400 Plate II – 6
THE ORDER OF OUR LADY OF BETHLEHEM	Papal	1459
THE ORDER OF THE ERMINE	Two Sicilies	1461 Plate II – 7
THE ORDER OF ST. GEORGE	Genoa	1472 Plate II – 8
THE ORDER OF ST. GEORGE	Papal	1492
THE DAMES OF CORDELLIER	France	1498 Plate II – 9
THE ORDER OF SS.PETER AND PAUL		Plate II – 10
(Leo X founded the Order of St.Peter in 1520 which Paul III merged with the Order of Paul in 1534)		
THE ORDER OF ST. GEORGE	Papal	1534 Plate II – 11
THE ORDER OF TUNIS	Germany	1535 Plate II – 13
THE ORER OF THE LILY	Papal	1546 Plate II – 12
THE ORDER OF TUSIN		1564 Plate II – 14
THE ORDER OF THE LAMB OF GOD	Sweden	1561 Plate II – 15
THE ORDER OF OUR LADY OF VICTORY	Lepanto	1571
THE ORDER OF OUR LADY OF LORETO	Papal	1582 Plate II – 16
THE ORDER OF CHRISTIAN CHARITY	France	1589 Plate II – 17
THE ORDER OF THE PRECIOUS BLOOD	Mantua	1608 Plate II – 35
THE ORDER OF MADELAINE	France	1614 Plate II – 18
THE ORDER OF JESUS AND MARY	Papal	1615 Plate II – 19
THE ORDER OF THE VIRGIN	Italy	1618 Plate II – 36
THE ORDER OF THE CONCEPTION	Germany/Italy	1618 Plate II – 21
THE ORDER OF THE CELESTIAL COLLAR OF THE ROSARY	France	1645 Plate II – 20
THE ORDER OF THE HEAD OF DEATH (Female)	Germany	1652 Plate II – 22
THE ORDER OF THE AMARANTH	Sweden	1653 Plate II – 23
THE ORDER OF THE NAME OF JESUS	Sweden	1656 Plate II – 24
THE ORDER OF LOUISE ULRIQUE	Sweden	1744 Plate II – 31
THE ORDER OF LOYALTY	France	1770 Plate II – 32

PLATE I

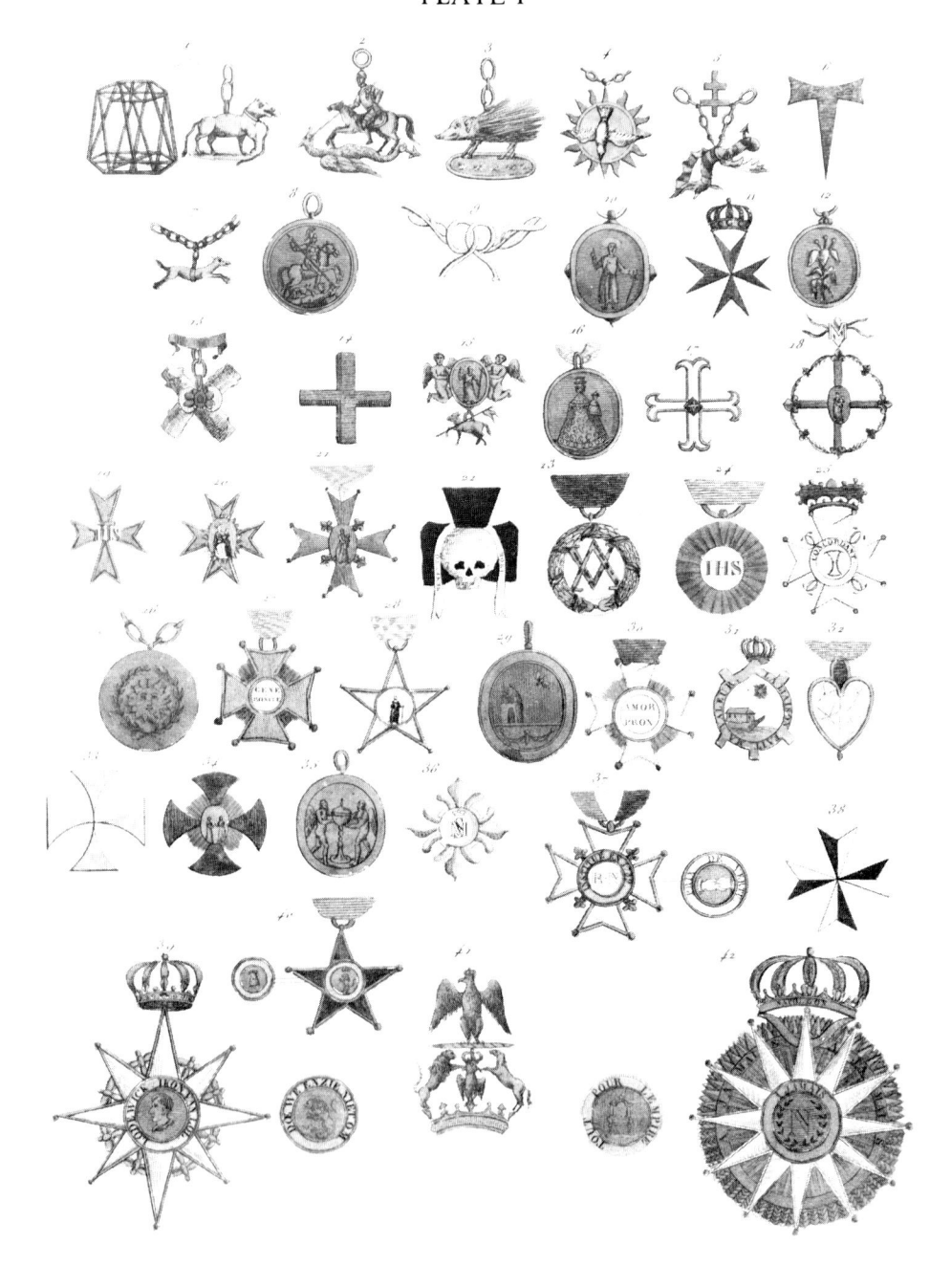

PERROT'S LIST OF EXTINCT ORDERS 645
PLATE II

APPENDIX VII

ON CHRONOLOGICAL LISTS OF ORDERS
OF KNIGHTHOOD (extant and extinct)

As I endeavoured to explain in chapter nine, it is rare, if not impossible, to find lists of Orders of Knighthood that give the same dates for the Order's year of foundation, and even rarer, lists that mention when an Order became extinct. Perhaps the most referred to reference book is the Austrian publication *Handbuch der Ritter und Verdienstorden* by Maximilian Gritzner, published in 1893, the translation of its full title being *Handbook of Orders of Knighthood and of Merit of all civilised States in the World*.

It is interesting to note that Gritzner features the Apostolic See among the civilised states, although the Papal States had been annexed by the House of Savoy in 1870, and he mentions several of the extant Orders prior to the reformation of the Pontifical and Religious Orders by Pope St. Pius X in 1905; he also gives the Order of the Holy Sepulchre of Jerusalem as a Knighthood of the Papal States.

The Sovereign Military Order of Malta is declared extinct as a Religious Order of Knighthood from 1814 onwards when the remnants of the 'Malteser Orden' (the Maltese Order) had been divided up between different countries after the Czar of Russia had been elected Grand Master. Then Gritzner continues to list 'Malteser Johanniter' Orders in various countries but no longer in Russia. In the light of the decree published by 1803 by Czar Alexander I, and the final legal act of 1817, with which the Czar abolished not only the Order of Malta in Russia but the right under which heirs to family commanderies could bear that title or in future inherit it, Gritzner must have been aware of the decree and the legal act promulgated by Czar Alexander I. The Teutonic Order is attributed by Gritzner to Austria, and he does not mention any extinct Orders, but he continues to list the Kingdom of the Two Sicilies, the Grand Duchy of Tuscany, and the Duchy of Parma, creating the impression that their Orders now belonged to Italy. Otherwise, Gritzner remains valid – with the exception of Portugal which became a Republic in 1910 – until the First World War.

Perrot (Paris, 1820) gives a chronological list of the foundation of all Orders of Knighthood, marking the extinct Orders with an asterisk. In his list of extinct Orders (Appendix VI) he only gives the date of extinction for two Napoleonic Orders, neither of which I placed on the list, (the Royal Order of Westphalia, [Plate II/41], founded by Jérôme Bonaparte in 1809, abolished by the new government of Westphalia in 1815; and the

Order of the Reunion, [Plate II/42], founded by Napoleon in 1811, and abolished by King Louis XVIII in 1815).[1]

In 1841, the London firm of Ward, Lock & Co. published the first of many editions of *Haydn's Dictionary of Dates and Universal Information Relating to all Ages and Nations*. It claimed to contain the complete history of the world up to the date of the appropriately revised edition. *Haydn's Dictionary* was one of the best researched and reliable records available. If there are errors in the dates of the foundation of some Orders of Knighthood, at least one knows that few reference books agree on dates.

Under the heading 'Principal Military, Religious and Honorary Orders of Knighthood', Mr. Joseph Haydn and his successors present an alphabetical list of approximately 250 Orders of Knighthood, giving dates of foundation, or merger with another Order or reconstitution, but no distinction is made between extant and extinct Orders, and judging by the dates, they are not copied from Perrot.

In 1860 the prestigious Parisian publishing house Larousse published the first edition of an illustrated Encyclopaedia of the World. After a colour plate on crowns, coronets, heraldic helmets and achievements, it features a monochrome plate 'Colliers et Insignes de Chevalerie' with sixty-three insignia of Orders of Knighthood. Apart from the fact that many of them look distinctly different from those illustrated by Perrot, the engravers, Rougeron, Vignerot and Demoulin, were not too particular about their accuracy, even when it came to the French motto of the Order of the Garter, nor does the table give any dates of foundation or information as to whether the Order is extant or extinct.

There have been later lists and many other illustrated books on Orders of Knighthood. In most cases I have found that the best informed and reliable ones are those published either by the Royal House or the State that conferred the Orders, though scholars of phaleristics are always advised to exercise caution and crosscheck information if there has been a division in the dynasty, more than one claimant to the position of Grand Master, or, in a republic, if the published history of the Orders is used to denigrate a former regime, i.e. a monarchy.

Another problem with new editions of statutes and rules of dynastic Orders of Knighthood or Merit is the possible inclusion of Orders that either should not be on a list of extant Orders or, worse, Orders that have been founded by non-regnant successors to monarchs who, under international law are not entitled to institute new Orders, which is a prerogative reserved to reigning monarchs.

A non-regnant successor to a monarch can, if circumstances make it

---

[1]Perrot also mentions 'The Military Imperial Order of the Three Golden Fleeces', founded by Napoleon by decree of 15 August 1809, but never instituted or conferred. A prototype (in ormulu) exists in the Musée National de la Légion d'Honneur et des Ordres de Chevalerie in Paris. It shows the crowned French Eagle, holding three fleeces, and weighs nine ounces.

648 ORDERS OF KNIGHTHOOD AND OF MERIT

COURONNES (COLLIERS ET INSIGNES DE CHEVALERIE).

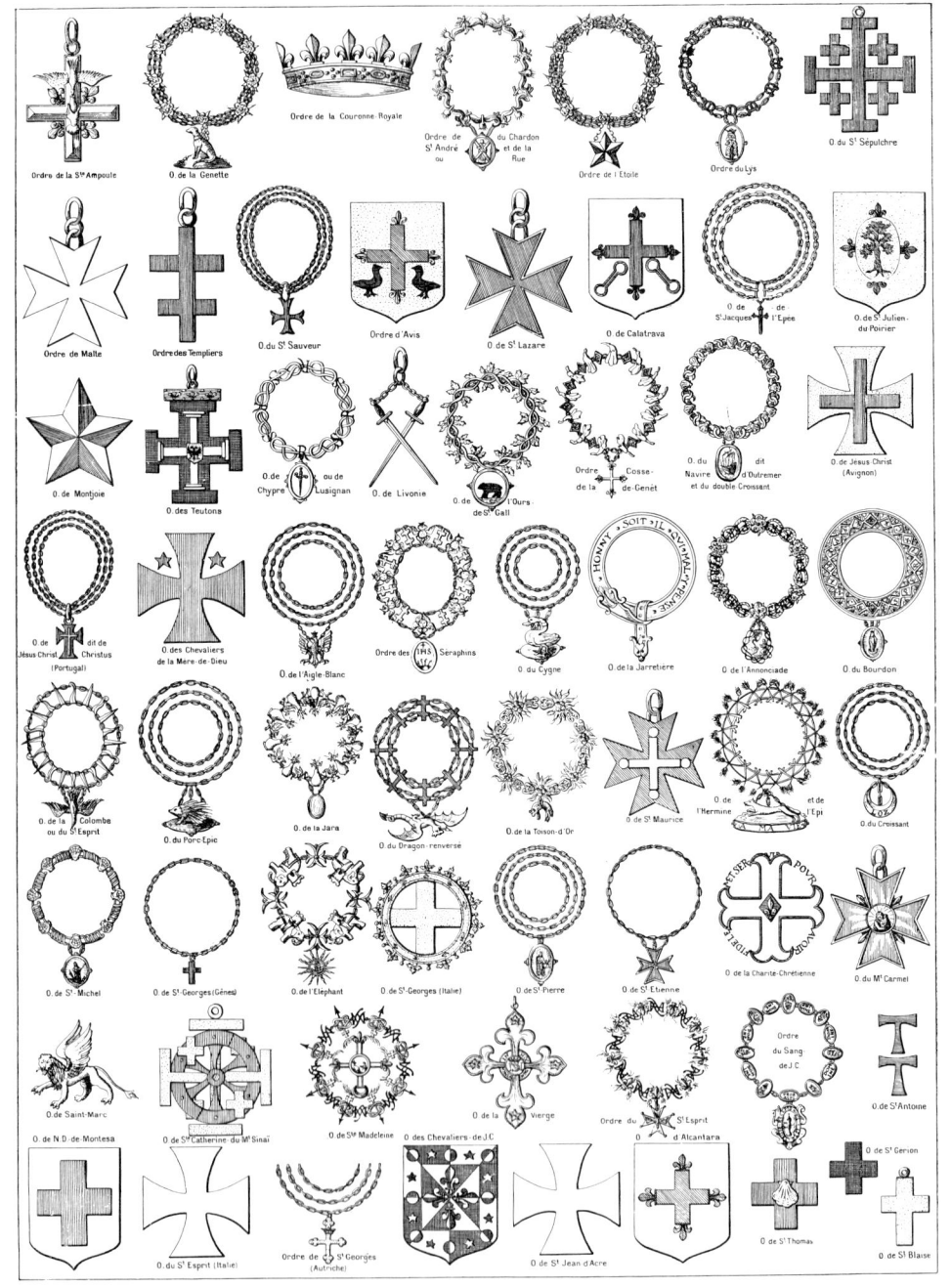

- Ordre de la Ste Ampoule
- O. de la Genette
- Ordre de la Couronne Royale
- Ordre de St André ou du Chardon et de la Rue
- Ordre de l'Etoile
- Ordre du Lys
- O. du St Sépulchre
- Ordre de Malte
- Ordre des Templiers
- O. du St Sauveur
- Ordre d'Avis
- O. de St Lazare
- O. de Calatrava
- O. de St Jacques de l'Epée
- O. de St Julien du Poirier
- O. de Montjoie
- O. des Teutons
- O. de Chypre ou de Lusignan
- O. de Livonie
- O. de St Ours de St Gall
- O. de la Cosse de Genêt
- O. du dit Navire d'Outremer et du double Croissant
- O. de Jésus Christ (Avignon)
- O. dit de Jésus Christ Christus (Portugal)
- O. des Chevaliers de la Mère de Dieu
- O. de l'Aigle Blanc
- Ordre des Séraphins
- O. du Cygne
- O. de la Jarretière
- O. de l'Annonciade
- O. du Bourdon
- O. de la Colombe ou du St Esprit
- O. du Porc-Epic
- O. de la Jarre
- O. du Dragon renversé
- O. de la Toison d'Or
- O. de St Maurice
- O. de l'Hermine et de l'Epi
- O. du Croissant
- O. de St Michel
- O. de St Georges (Gênes)
- O. de l'Elephant
- O. de St Georges (Italie)
- O. de St Pierre
- O. de St Etienne
- O. de la Charité-Chrétienne
- O. du Mt Carmel
- O. de Saint-Marc
- O. de N.D. de Montesa
- O. de St Catherine du Mt Sinaï
- O. de Ste Madeleine
- O. des Chevaliers de J.C
- O. de la Vierge
- Ordre du St Esprit
- Ordre du Sang de J.C
- O. d'Alcantara
- O. de St Antoine
- O. de St Gerion
- O. du St Esprit (Italie)
- Ordre de St Georges (Autriche)
- O. de St Jean d'Acre
- O. de St Thomas
- O. de St Blaise

Les insignes des ordres de chevalerie sont figurés dans le tableau ci-dessus tels qu'ils ont été déterminés par les actes de fondation; on remarquera que les uns ont disparu avec l'ordre dont ils étaient le symbole, et que la composition ou la disposition des autres a subi des modifications. — V. CROIX, DECORATIONS, MEDAILLES, ORDRES, etc.

necessary, change certain parts of the statutes concerning conferment, change part of the name of the Order if it is necessary to distinguish the old from the new version of the same Order, and change grades of rank in the Order, or add medals of merit to it. However, one must avoid setting oneself up as judge, jury and executioner if one finds something in print that gives rise to a misunderstanding. As I explained in Chapter Seven in the section of the Royal House of Savoy, it was after I made enquiries of H.R.H. Prince Victor Emmanuel, Duke of Savoy, the son of the late King Umberto, that I learned that the secular dynastic Order 'Ordine Civile di Savoia', founded in 1831 by Carlo Alberto, King of Sardinia, Duke of Savoy, had been brought up to date and appropriately modified in 1988 by Prince Victor Emmanuel who renamed it 'Ordine Al Merito Civile di Savoia'. This was a legitimate and necessary act if the Order was to be relevant to today's needs and the changed conditions relating to the Order and its recipients. At first glance, and without checking with the Chancellery of the Royal Savoyan Orders, I might have concluded that a new Order had been founded by a non-regnant successor to a monarch.

APPENDIX VIII

THE PREROGATIVES OF THE DUKES OF BRAGANÇA TO CONFER THE ANCIENT TITLES OF NOBILITY, THE *FOROS*

Among the Heads of the non-regnant Catholic dynasties, the Dukes of Bragança, the legitimate heirs and successors to the Crown of Portugal, are unique in as much as the inherent rights and prerogatives they have always possessed as sovereign Dukes of Bragança, were never surrendered to the Crown of Portugal and continued to exist in parallel with the rights and prerogatives they exercised as monarchs of the Kingdom of Portugal.

To exercise these rights the Dukes of Bragança never needed apostolic or ministerial approval or advice. The act of giving to the Portuguese Council of Nobility the right of approving and keeping a register of the Duke's appointments, was an act of courtesy by Dom Duarte Nuno, Duke of Bragança, who had instituted the Council of Nobility after his return from exile in 1950. Juridically only the Duke of Bragança is the legitimate *fons honorum* who can confer *Foros*, which are six ancient hereditary titles of nobility, solely conferred by the Heads of the House of Bragança, even when not rulers of Portugal.

These *Foros* were often conferred as complementary to the royal titles bestowed by the monarchs as Sovereigns of Portugal on those singled out for special distinction, and they were conferred separately. Thus, those honoured with the highest *Foro*, FIDALGO CAVALEIRO, prior to 1640, were appointed FIDALGO CAVALEIRO DO DUQUE – Ducal Peer -, and those whom the Monarch appointed after 1640 were created FIDALGO CAVALEIRO DA CASA REAL – Peer of the Royal House.

Since 1910, when Portugal became a Republic, the Dukes of Bragança can only confer dukedoms and other royal titles of nobility upon actual members of the Royal Family, who must be approved and named by the Assembleia da República, the Portuguese Parliament. However he has the unrestricted right of conferring *Foros* because the Ducal House of Bragança never surrendered that prerogative to the Crown of Portugal. As mentioned above, royal titles which need renewing under the clauses of the relevant Royal Letters Patent are now ratified and confirmed by the Council of Nobility of Portugal.

Royal Portuguese titles of nobility were conferred for one, two or at most three generations, after which they had to be renewed. It is the prerogative of the Duke of Bragança to approve the renewal of a title. His approval is indicated to the President of the Council of Nobility, who will then discuss the matter in Council. Requirement for renewal of title does not apply to the *Foros* which have always been conferred in perpetuity. Dom Duarte Nuno, Duke of Bragança, delegated the responsibility for examining and deciding on claims of legitimate successors to royal titles to the Council of Nobility of Portugal. The titles, which have to be renewed periodically, and to which lawful and legitimate succession has to be proven by the petitioner before the Duke of Bragança recommends ratification of a renewal, are those of Duque, Marquàs, Conde, Visconde and Barâo, these being titles conferred by a Monarch before 1910.

The Duke of Bragança can also grant permission and give his personal *Nihil Obstat* for foreign titles of nobility that have been conferred upon Portuguese citizens by foreign Monarchs to be born as a foreign titles in Portugal, and the *Tratamento*, the appellation 'Dom' which is used by distinguished nobles, is in his personal gift.

In exceptional cases the Dukes of Bragança have conferred a *Foro* upon a foreign citizen. The Duke of Bragança informs the Council of Nobility and the proposed recipient of the *Foro* he intends to confer. The Council will then ratify and register the title of the newly created holder and an *Alvará* or Letters Patent will be issued.

A separate document is issued by the Associacâo da Nobreza Histórica de Portugal, a public body in the Republic, which gives the date of ratification of the title, the date of publication of the document, its enrolment number as well as issuing a badge of nobility.

The *Foros da Casa Real*, fall into two categories: the higher and lesser nobility:

Higher Nobility:
    FIDALGO CAVALEIRO DA CASA REAL
    FIDALGO ESCUDEIRO DA CASA REAL
    MOÇO FIDALGO DA CASA REAL

Lesser Nobility:
    CAVALEIRO FIDALGO DA CASA REAL
    ESCUDEIRO FIDALGO DA CASA REAL
    MOÇO DA CAMERA DA CASA REAL.

As can be seen, the distinction between the first and the fourth, and the second and the fifth *Foro* has been the position of the word FIDALGO. If it was placed first, it presupposed that the bearer of the title was considered a Peer of the House of Bragança of Portugal. From the second half of the sixteenth century to the first half of the seventeenth century, only twenty gentlemen were created FIDALGO. Initially they were appointed FIDALGO DO DUQUE[1], which was changed after 1640 to FIDALGO DA CASA REAL.

On 2 December 1991 Dom Duarte Pio, Duke of Bragança decreed that

---

[1] See *Mercàs de D. Theodósio II Duque de Bragança*, Lisboa 1967.

from that date the two principal *Foros* of Higher Nobility should both be registered by the Council of Nobility in the *Alvará* as FIDALGO DA CASA REAL – Peer of the Royal House – as the original distinctions relating to positions at Court no longer apply, although the Duke of Bragança will continue to confer the titles of FIDALGO CAVALEIRO and FIDALGO ESCUDEIRO at his discretion. No decision with regard to the *Foros* of Lesser Nobility has been taken, as none has been conferred since 1896.

Those holding a *Foro* are listed in the *Anuário da Nobreza de Portugal*, updated editions of which are published periodically. The Duke of Bragança has also issued a decree to make it clear that holders of the first and second class ranks of the Order of Our Lady of the Conception of Vila Viçosa, do not receive a Foro by right, as has been stated in some publications, his prerogatives as successor to the Crown of Portugal and to the Dukedom of Bragança being quite separate.

I am endebted to Mr. John Bury, a foremost scholar and authority in Iberian history, for providing me with a comprehensive history and definition of a *Foro*. Mr. Bury[1] has made a particular study of the era from the fifth to the eighth Duke of Bragança. *Foro* DO DUQUE and *Foro* DA CASA REAL are ancient Portuguese phrases, best translated as largess, charter or grant bestowed by the Head of the Sovereign Ducal House of Bragança. A *Foro* or a largess of a FIDALGO consisted of the actual title, annuities and privileges.[2] The word *Foro* is primarily used in modern parlance for a charter conferring privileges on cities and towns.

As far as titles connected with Royal or Ducal Houses are concerned, they tend to use archaic terms that can create problems when an up-to-date interpretation or a translation into another language is sought. Mr. Bury cited several reference works that analyse the appellation FIDALGO and show that it is a contraction of the words *filho,* son, and *d'algo,* meaning of wealth, of riches, of honour; (in the 16th and 17th and 18th centuries it always implied that the person was a member of the nobility and armigerous). In his researches, Mr. Bury also discovered that, particularly in the sixteenth century, the *Foro* granting the title FIDALGO was quite distinct from those granting lesser ranks of nobility, as each group constituted a different possibility of promotion and position that could be held at Court. He cautioned against drawing any comparison between persons holding a *Foro* in Portugal, which confers actual nobility, with those using the appellation *Nobile*, sometimes granted with a Pontifical Order of Knighthood. The appellation *Nobile*, does not confer or denote actual nobility and the recipient is therefore listed as 'untitled

[1] Mr. John Bury drew my attention to the *Mappa de Portugal* by Joâo Bautista de Castro (Lisboa, 1762) which he considers the best source of information on the two parallel ladders of promotion from MOÇO through ESCUDEIRO to CAVALEIRO DA CASA DO DUQUE and CASA REAL DE PORTUGAL. This practice prevailed in Portugal from at least the early sixteenth century.
[2] See the official publication *Privilegios da Nobreza, e Fidalguia de de Portugal*, Anno dé 1806, com Licença da Meza do Sesembargo do Paço.

nobility' or it can be used as a courtesy title for a person of high social standing.

By courtesy of Mr. Bury the following extracts have been reproduced: from *Mappa de Portugal Antigo, E Moderno pel Padred Joâo Bautista de Castro* (Lisbon, 1762), the relevant pages referring to FIDALGUIA PORTUGUESA, and from his own work *Juan de Herrera y el Escurial* (Madrid: Patrimonio Nacional, 1995), a comparison between FIDALGOS and Knights in Spain.

MAPPA DE PORTUGAL
ANTIGO, E MODERNO

PELO PADRE

JOAÕ BAUTISTA
DE CASTRO,

Beneficiado na Santa Basilica Patriarcal de Lisboa.

TOMO PRIMEIRO.
PARTE I. E II.

Nesta segunda ediçaõ revisto, e augmentado pelo seu mesmo Author: e contém huma exacta descripçaõ Geografica do Reino de Portugal com o que toca à sua Historia Secular, e Politica.

LISBOA,
Na Officina Patriarcal de Francisco Luiz Ameno.

M. DCC. LXII.
Com as licenças necessarias, e Privilegio Real.

Governo da Casa Real.

CAPITULO IX.
Do Governo antigo, e moderno da Casa Real.

1 Ainda que alguns Escritores nossos se inclinassem (1) a que os officios, com que se servio a Casa Real até ElRey D. Fernando, fossem sómente Mordomo da Corte, Alferes, e Trinchante, (2) todavia varios outros Officiaes tiveraõ muitos dos Reys, que lhe precederaõ, dos quaes daremos breve informação por aquella ordem, que nos for lembrando, sem darmos exacta preferencia aos taes officios, que requer a grandeza da sua dignidade.

2 *Mordomo Mór.* He entre todos os officios titulares da Casa Real o que tem o primeiro lugar. No Regimento, que fez Gomes Annes de Azurara, (se acaso naõ foy Martim Affonso de Mello) dos officios Móres do Reino por mandado delRey D. Affonso V. que foy o Principe, que reduzio a singular ordem a Fidalguia Portugueza nos empregos de Palacio, se lê, que em outras Cortes chamavaõ à preeminencia deste officio *Senescal*, que vale o mesmo que *Senex calculi*, ou Presidente das contas, (3) porque

---

[1] Naõ fazem menção de outros Officiaes até o dito tempo Fr. Antonio Brandaõ, Ruy de Pina, e Duarte Nunes, sendo estes dos mais principaes Chronistas entre os nossos. [2] Os que contaõ em hum dos tres officios ao Trinchante, he porque entendem que isto significava *Dapifer*; mas enganaõ-se, porque este officio corresponde ao de Veador, entre o qual, e o de Mordomo Mór naõ havia antigamente differença. Danet. in Diction. antiq. Roman. verb. *Comes*. Castr. Palat. Ducange verb. *Dapifer*. [3] Veja-se a Bluteau no vocab. *Mordomo Mór*, e *Senescal*, e a Gil Gonçalves Davila no Theatro de las grandezas de Madrid p. 513. Nunes de Castro no livro *Solo Madrid es Corte* liv. 1. cap. 10. Villasboas na Nobiliarq. Port. cap 12. Lima Geograf. Histor. tom. 1. p. 481, Solan. Succo de Pegas tom. 2. p. 376. verb. *Æconomus*.

422   *Mappa de Portugal.*

que a seu cargo toca tomallas de todas as despezas dos Reys; porém Scipiaõ Amirato affirma, que Senescalco era o Architriclino antigo, e que o officio de Mordomo Mór tivera origem no Reino de França, donde se derivou a outras Cortes da Europa.

3 Neste Reino devia começar com o Conde D. Henrique; porque em tempo delRey D. Affonso seu filho assina, e confirma muitas vezes as doações o Mordomo Mór Gonçalo Rodrigues. O que temos por infallivel he, que esta dignidade andou sempre nos principaes Senhores de Portugal. ElRey D. Diniz honrou com ella a seu filho illegitimo D. Affonso Sanches, de quem foy summamente affeiçoado. O Conde D. Nuno Alvares Pereira foy Mordomo Mór delRey D. Joaõ I. e assim a tiveraõ outros muitos Cavalheros da primeira Nobreza.

4 Além da superintendencia, que o Mordomo Mór tem na Casa Real, entende particularmente em receber todos os criados, e moradores della; e porque antigamente em lugar do verbo *Tomar* se dizia *Filhar*, conserva ainda hoje esta palavra, chamando-se a estas recepções *Filhamentos.* Os Fóros, que ha na Casa Real, em que entraõ os novamente filhados, saõ estes: *Moços da Camera, Moços da Guardaroupa, Escudeiros Fidalgos, Cavalleiros Fidalgos, Moços Fidalgos, Fidalgos Escudeiros, Fidalgos Cavalleiros, Fidalgos do Conselho.*

5 No foro de *Moços Fidalgos* filha o Mordomo Mór aos filhos, e netos dos já filhados, ou a outros, a quem ElRey faz mercê de novo, ainda que seus antepassados naõ fossem filhados. O filhamento dos primeiros he ordinario, porque naõ se póde negar ao filho do criado delRey o foro, e moradia de seu pay. Chegando os Moços Fidalgos a vinte annos, os accrescentaõ a *Fidalgos Escudeiros*; e depois sendo armados Cavalleiros em algum acto de guerra, lhe daõ foro de *Fidalgos Cavalleiros*; porém nisto póde haver dispensa com facilidade. O ultimo
                                                                accres-

Governo da Caſa Real. 423

accreſcentamento he de *Fidalgos do Conſelho*, porém naõ he accreſcentamento ordinario, nem os filhos o podem requerer, mas ElRey dá eſte titulo a quem lhe parece, e anda annexo a todos os Arcebiſpos, e Biſpos, Priores Móres de Aviz, e Santiago, a todos os Inquiſidores do Conſelho Geral do Santo Officio, a todos os Condes, Deſembargadores do Paço, Chancelleres da Caſa da Supplicaçaõ de Liſboa, e Relaçaõ do Porto, e Chanceller Mór, Reitor da Univerſidade de Coimbra, Governador do Algarve, aos Governadores das Praças de Africa, Braſil, e Angola, e preſentemente o concedeo Sua Mageſtade aos ſetenta e dous Mon-Senhores Prelados da Santa Igreja Patriarcal.

6 Os moradores da Caſa delRey, que naõ entraõ por Moços Fidalgos, ſaõ tomados por *Moços da Camera*, e depois ſe accreſcentaõ a *Eſcudeiros Fidalgos*, e ultimamente a *Cavalleiros* com a terceira, ou quarta parte mais de moradia, conforme ſuas qualidades. Os Moços da Capella, Porteiros, Repoſteiros, e toda a mais gente daqui para baixo tem accreſcentamento ordinario a Eſcudeiro ſómente, e eſſe menor, e de quantia certa.

7 O foro dos *Fidalgos Cavalleiros*, que ſómente ſe dava em algum famoſo acto militar, mais era dignidade que foro, e começou neſte Reino a ſer accreſcentamento ordinario depois da tomada de Alcacere, como diz Gomes Annes de Azurara; porque até entaõ como o Reino eſtava ſem Conquiſtas, naõ havia ocaſiaõ, ſenaõ rara, de alcançar ſemelhante honra; e os que hiaõ buſcalla fóra do Reino, eraõ poucos, e por iſſo eſta dignidade era taõ eſtimada, que todos os Principes daquelle tempo a procuravaõ alcançar com grande cuidado: aſſim lemos que para eſte effeito vieraõ a Heſpanha, e Portugal grandes Senhores em varios tempos; e os que neſta parte alcançaraõ mayor gloria, foraõ os noſſos Infantes, filhos delRey D. Joaõ I. porque

Apéndice III
Juan de Herrera, ¿Hidalgo y Caballero?

PARA COMPRENDER la condición social de Herrera es necesario hacer algunas consideraciones acerca de la hidalguía. Esta clase se consideraba en España perteneciente a la nobleza (al revés que el equivalente inglés de *gentry*), pero como los hidalgos carecían de los títulos de los rangos nobiliarios más altos, se esforzaban por marcar las diferencias que los distinguían del resto de la población. Estos signos distintivos eran primordialmente el que todos los auténticos hidalgos tenían escudo de armas; su posesión era una señal *sine qua non* de nobleza; en segundo lugar, ningún hidalgo verdadero se dedicaba a oficios manuales ni al comercio, aunque se permitía excepcionalmente que fuera criado de una casa noble. Las mejores familias hidalgas (hidalgos de solar conocido) poseían una casa solariega (en inglés *family seat*). Las familias hidalgas se dividían también por su origen en las creadas por el Rey (hidalgos de privilegio) y las que habían probado su titularidad ante la ley (hidalgos de ejecutoria).

Los hidalgos, por ser nobles, estaban extensos de tributos. Este privilegio, aparte del estado social del rango, hacía muy deseable acceder a la hidalguía; y como la Corona, siempre escasa de caudales, estuvo dispuesta, a partir de 1520, a vender ejecutorias de hidalguía, las compraba todo el que podía pagarlas, poniéndose gran ingenio en la con-

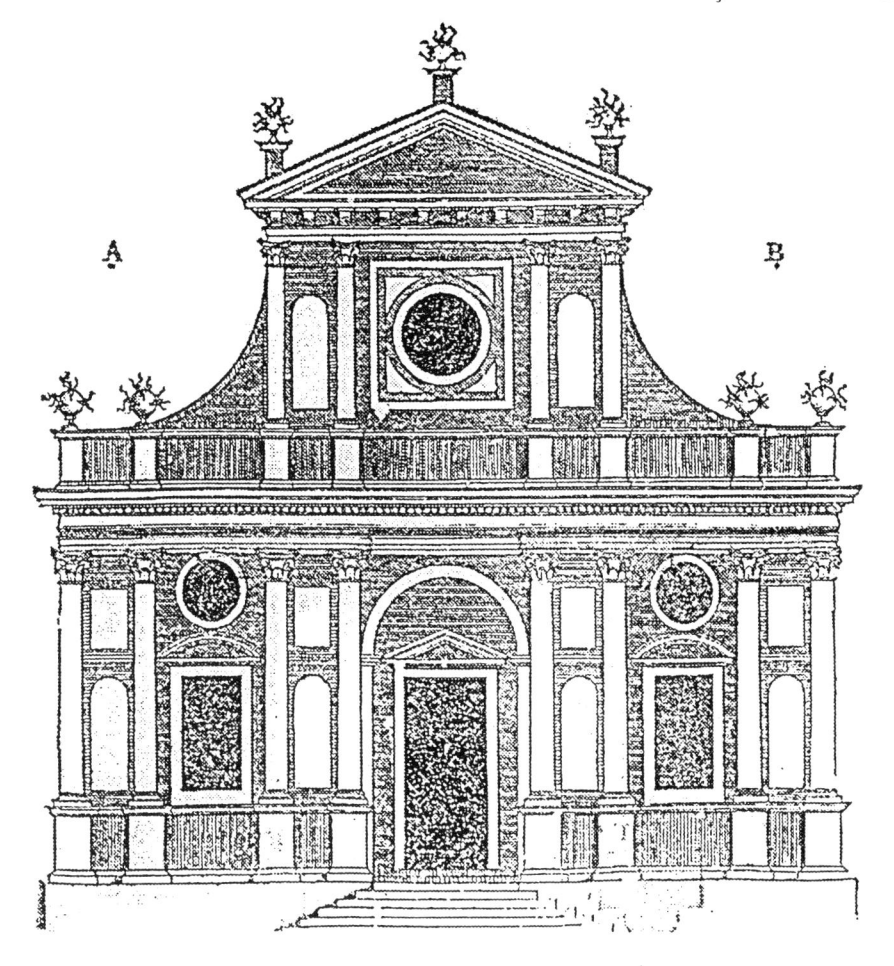

fección de genealogías para los muchos indeterminables nuevos ricos que las pedían (J. H. Elliott, *Imperial Spain 1469-1716*, London, 1963, p. 104). Se sabe que los funcionarios de la corte de origen humilde estaban entre las clases más probablemente ansiosas de alcanzar, mediante compra, el rango de hidalgo (John Lynch, *Spain under the Habsburgs*, Oxford, 1964, Vol I, p. 105).
La clase hidalga era una élite relativamente pequeña extendida por toda España, excepto en el *NO* del país donde, paradójicamente, el concepto acostumbrado del hidalgo estaba a todos los efectos vuelto del revés. Todos los vascos, por ejemplo, gozaban de exención de impuestos y del servicio militar (a cambio de defender la frontera) por los fueros concedidos por los primeros reyes y confirmados por sus

sucesores; y como estas exenciones eran privilegio de la hidalguía, toda la nación vasca se consideraba con derecho a la condición de hidalgo, lo que daba lugar a descripciones de oficios contradictorias en sí mismas, como hidalgo çapatero. Pero, por supuesto, esos obreros manuales y comerciantes vascos que se autotitulaban hidalgos no tenían escudo, de modo que era difícil que sus aspiraciones de hidalguía se aceptaran fuera de las Vascongadas.

En la provincia de la Montaña, de donde procedía Herrera, aproximadamente un cuarto de los habitantes aseguraban ser hidalgos. No se ha comprobado si el linaje de Herrera estaba o no entre los que afirmaban tal cosa. Pero en cualquier caso no parece que tuviera blasón, porque cuando probó su nobleza con éxito ante los "señores alcaldes de hijosdalgo" de la Cancillería de Valladolid, probablemente en la década de 1580, le dieron con la ejecutoria un escudo de armas "industrial" referido a su apellido (derivado de herrería) "integrado por dos calderas sobrepuestas". Esta ejecutoria aparece en el inventario de sus bienes hecho a su fallecimiento (Ruiz de Arcaute, *op. cit.*, nota 10 anterior. p. 170).

El motivo que figura en el escudo de armas de Juan de Herrera es según Ruiz de Arcaute *(op. cit,* 127) al parecer un conjunto de "dos calderas sobrepuestas", pero no revela Arcaute la fuente de esta afirmación. Si fuera verdad, entonces es que probablemente los heraldos en Valladolid estaban bajo el influjo de la igualdad de nombres entre nuestro Herrera, el aposentador, y Melchor Gómez de Herrera, (recientemente nombrado por Felipe II marqués de Auñón), a pesar de no existir relación entre ambas familias. El escudo de armas del viejo linaje madrileño de Gómez de Herrera estaba compuesto por "dos calderas sobrepuestas en campo de sangre y doze calderas por orla"; la orla era necesaria para distinguir el escudo de los Gómez de Herrera del de los Pacheco, Manrique, Nuñez de Lara y Guzmán, que tambien mostraban el mismo motivo de dos calderas sobrepuestas. Véase Gonzalo Argote Molina, *Nobleza de Andalucía* (Sevilla 1588) Jaén 1867, reimpreso en Jaén en 1957 p. 645; y véase igualmente López de Haro, *Nobiliario,* Madrid, 1622, Vol. II p. 487.

José Camón Aznar *(La arquitectura y la orfebrería españolas del XVI,* Madrid, 1970, p. 436) dice, sin citar la fuente, que Herrera fue hecho caballero de Santiago. Ruiz de Arcaute *(op. cit.,* p. 140), que tampoco cita la fuente, añade que Herrera fue enterrado en la iglesia madrileña de Santiago por ser caballero de la Orden. Esto contradice a Llaguno y Ceán *(op. cit.,* II, p. 150).

Si hemos de creer a Ruiz de Arcaute, Herrera debe haber sido caballero poco antes de su muerte (enero de 1597) porque no aparece la insignia de la Orden en el detallado inventario de sus ropas y otros efectos personales que se hizo en Marzo de 1595 a la muerte de su mujer Inés. Más aún, esta calidad de caballero debe haberse olvidado después de fallecido, porque no se menciona en el acta de defunción, ni en las memorias de la familia de 1802. Y cuando en 1765 se hizo una búsqueda oficial de sus huesos, la comisión no los buscó en la iglesia de Santiago, sino en la de San Nicolás, donde Herrera en su testamento indicó que le enterraran y donde Llaguno afirma muy positivamente que fue en efecto inhumado (Llaguno y Ceán, *op. cit.* pp. 150, 368-9).

APPENDIX IX

BULLA FUNDATIONIS MILITIAE D.N. IESU CHRISTI
IOANNES XXII P.M. A.D. MCCCIXX
et
ACCEPTATIO, ET RATIFICATIO DOMINI REGIS DIONYSII

In 1319 Pope John XXII (1316-34) promulgated the Papal Bull *Ad ea ex quibus* which concerned the foundation of the Equestrian Order known as the Militia of Our Lord Jesus Christ or the Order of Christ. The Bull made this Order the lawful successor to the Order of the Knights Templars which had been ruthlessly annihilated between 1307 and 1314 by Philip of France (1285-1314) with the support of his nominee the French Pope Clement V (1305-14), who had finally suppressed the Order in 1312 and allocated their possessions to the Crown and different Orders, in France mainly to the Order of St. John.

King Dinis I of Portugal (1279-1325) had requested the foundation of the Order in 1317, and Pope John XXII agreed and issued the above-mentioned Bull. Portugal, both as a Kingdom and as a Republic has always rejected the widely-spread statement that the Papacy had the right also to appoint knights to the Portuguese Order, and the Secretary-General of the Portuguese Orders, Dr. José Vicente de Bragança explained to me, that in the eighteenth century the Apostolic See believed this too, and actually tried to appoint knights to the Order. Many books on Orders of Knighthood have perpetuated this grave error, referring to the Bull *Ad ea ex quibus*, but Pope John XXII does not refer to a papal prerogative to create knights in the Portuguese Order. Other historians state that this prerogative was established in 1522 when the Apostolic See freed the knights from their solemn vows, and before the grand-mastership became the property of the Crown of Portugal. This assumption is as erroneous as the first. The Bull of Foundation of 1319 is the sole basis upon which the Order of Christ was built and evolved.

Although I was unable to find the Bull *Ad ea ex quibus* and any acceptance or ratification of the Bull by King Dinis I of Portugal during my search in the Vatican, the Presidency of the Portuguese Republic made both documents available to me.

In his Papal Brief *De Ordinibus Equestribus* Pope St. Pius X makes a fleeting reference to his predecessor John XXII who in 1318[1], after the Order of the Knights Templars had been destroyed, followed the wish of Dinis I, King of Portugal, and founded the Order of the Militia of Our

---

[1] The date MCCCVIII in the 1905 edition of the Papal Brief in the Order's statutes, signed by Cardinal Macchi, may be a misprint.

Lord Jesus Christ, but continues: '*Ioanne XXII rec. mem. Praedecessore Nostro instituit, hunc Equestrium Pontificiae Sedis Ordinum Supremum esse auctoritate Nostra per praesentes edicimus ac mandamus, quo non alter sit dignitate potior, sed ceteris amplitudine ac splendore superemineat*'.

It is most probable that Pope St. Pius X signed the seminal Papal Brief concerning the Pontifical Equestrian Orders, which undoubtedly was prepared for him by Cardinal Macchi, the Secretary of Papal Briefs and newly appointed Grand Chancellor of all Pontifical Equestrian Orders, without direct reference to the Papal Bull of Foundation.

It is my belief that the errors concerning the history of the Order of Christ have been perpetuated for so long because the Bull of Foundation was either unavailable to researchers, or they thought it unnecessary to check it, relying on earlier historians whose statements were simply copied. It is a pit into which many scholars who rely too much on secondary sources often fall.

Scholars who wish to consult the Papal Bull that founded the Order of Christ can now do so because *Ad ea ex quibus* and the reply of King Dinis I are reproduced on the following pages.

JOannes Episcopus, servus servorum Dei. Ad perpetuam rei memoriam. Ad ea, ex quibus cultus augeatur divinus, fidelium quies in quiete proficiat, & defensionis murus, & vallum fidei inexterminabile adversus incursus infidelium hostium opponatur, adhibemus plenis affectibus solicitudinis nostræ curas. Sanè dudum felicis recordationis Clemens Papa V. Prædecessor noster quondam Ordinem Militiæ Templi Hierosolymitani ex certis rationalibus causis, ejusque statum, habitum, ac nomen in Concilio Viennensi, eodem approbante Concilio, irrefragabili, & perpetuo valitura sustulit sanctione, illum perpetuæ prohibitioni supponens, ac districtiùs inhibens, ne quis dictum Ordinem, vel habitum ejus suscipere, seu deferre, vel pro Templario se gerere quomodolibet attentaret, bonis omnibus dicti Ordinis Apostolicæ Sedis ordinationi specialiter reservatis, dictusque Prædecessor attendens, quòd dilecti filii, & Magister, & Fratres Hospitalis Sancti Joannis Hierosolymitani fidei Orthodoxæ cultores industrii, & Christianæ Religionis in transmarinis præcipuè partibus strenui defensores, pro defensione illarum partium, & recuperatione Terræ Sanctæ ducebant, sicut & ducunt, pericula quælibet in contemptum, post deliberationem super hoc cum suis Sanctæ Romanæ Ecclesiæ Cardinalibus, necnon Patriarchis, Archiepiscopis, Episcopis, aliis, & nonnullis Principibus, & illustribus viris, necnon Prælatorum absentium, Capitulorumque, atque Conventuum Ecclesiarum, seu Monasteriorum Procuratoribus, tunc in dicto Concilio constitutis, præhabitam diligentem, omnia bona dicti quondam Ordinis Templi, quæ idem Ordo tempore, quo Magister, & nonnulli ex Fratribus dicti quondam Ordinis in Regno Franciæ communiter capti fuerunt, videlicet, anno Domini millesimo trecentesimo octavo, mense Octobris, per se, vel quoscumque alios habebat, tenebat, & possidebat ubilibet, vel ad dictum Ordinem, ipsosque Magistrum, & Fratres ipsius pertinebant, seu pertinere poterant, & debebant, Ordini dicti Hospitalis, ipsique Hospitali donavit concessit, univit, incorporavit, applicavit, & annexuit in perpetuum de Apostolicæ plenitudine potestatis, (bonis illis, quæ idem Ordo Templariorum in Regnis, & terris charissimorum in Christo filiorum nostrorum Castellæ, Aragonum, Portugaliæ, & Maioricarum Regum illustrium

ex-

extra Regnum Franciæ habebat, feu poffidebat, & ad eum poterant debitè quomodolibet pertinere, dumtaxat exceptis) quæ dictus Prædeceffor certis ex caufis pro parte Regum ipforum prætenfis à donatione, conceffione, unione, incorporatione, & annexatione prædictis excepit fpecialiter, & excuffit, ea nihilominùs difpofitioni, & ordinationi Apoftolicæ refervando; fed ne propter prætentionem caufarum hujufmodi dictorum bonorum in dictis Regnis, & terris confiftentium, ordinatio diutiùs differretur, idem Prædeceffor certum terminum dictis Regibus per fuas literas peremptorium affignavit, in quo per Procuratores, feu Nuntios idoneos plenum ad hoc fpeciale mandatum habentes cum omnibus rationibus, & monumentis ad caufas pertinentibus memoratas Apoftolico fe confpectui præfentarent, informaturi eum de veritate caufarum, & effentia prædictarum, ejusque fuper illos ordinationis beneplacitum audituri; poft hac autem chariffimus in Chrifto filius nofter Dionyfius Portugaliæ, & Algarbii Rex illuftris propter hoc ad prædecefforis ejufdem, & fubfequènter ad noftram (poftquam fuimus, Domino permittente, ad apicem Apoftolicæ dignitatis affumpti) præfentiam Nuntios fuos diverfis vicibus deftinavit, proponi faciens diverfas rationes, & caufas, propter quas bona ipfa in Regnis fuis exiftentia uniri, & incorporari non poffe memorato Ordini Hofpitalis, abfque fuo, & Regnorum fuorum evidenti præjudicio, & difpendiofo periculo afferebat. Cujus in hac parte caufis, & rationibus coram Nobis, & Fratribus noftris expofitis diligenter auditis, poft longam caufam, & diuturnam examinationem, quam cum dilectis filiis Petro Petri Canonico Colimbricenfi, & nobili viro Joanne Laurentii de Monte Seratio, Milite, Nuntiis, & Procuratoribus dicti Regis ad hoc legitimum mandatum habentibus, & etiam fpeciale, cujus mandati copiam præfentibus inferi juffimus ad cautelam, habuimus diligentem. Inter alia per Procuratores eofdem expofitæ Nobis fuerunt graves injuriæ, innumera damna, & alia multiplicia, & enormia mala non facile commemoranda præfentibus, quæ hoftes Fidei Sarraceni perfidi jam retrò antiquitus & continuatis fucceffivè temporibus, partibus illis, quas fideles inhabitant, hoftibus ejufdem continuis intulerunt, & inferre non ceffant; qui inter cætera adhibenda remedia ad eorumdem hoftium molimina refrænanda, utpotè de conditionibus illarum partium plenam notitiam obtinentes, ac de ipfius Regis confcientia ad plenum inftructi aperuerunt Nobis plures caufas neceffarias, ac evidentes, & probabiles rationes, quòd in Caftro Marino, Sylvenfis Diœcefis in dicto Regno Algarbii conftituto caftro, (utpote valido) quod inexpugnabile quodammodo reddit loci difpofitio naturalis, in fronteria dictorum

rum hostium Fidei consistente, eisque contiguo, nova Militia pugilum Christi, qui dimissis vanitatibus sæculi Sanctæ Religionis spontanei professores circa zelum veræ Fidei sint accensi, poterat collocari, quorum ope, & prompto præsidio, prædictis injuriis, damnis, & malis, quorum illationi fera manus hostilis jam dudum vocavit, liberiùs obviari salubriter poterit in futurum, & via præstari facilior, non solùm ad resistendum hostium congressibus, sed etiam ad impetus, & conatus conterendos ipsorum, ac propulsandum eosdem, & recuperandum partes alias intermedias per ipsorum hostium jam olim fraudulentis insidiis occupatas. Exposuerunt quoque nobis Procuratores prædicti, quo occurrit acceptius votis nostris, quòd idem Rex præmissa commoda Fidei in examen attentæ considerationis inducens, tanquam Princeps Christianissimus Deo devotus, dictum Castrum, ex quo sibi non parva proveniebat utilitas temporalis, ob tantum bonum eidem Fidei proventurum, cum mero, & mixto imperio, omnibusque juribus, & jurisdictionibus paratus erat prædictæ novæ Militiæ novi Ordinis inibi ordinandæ ex sua propria munificentia, donatione perpetua elargiri. Propter quod Procuratores prædicti Nobis ex parte ipsius Regis humiliter supplicarunt, ut ejus in hac parte pio desiderio annuentes, novam Militiam pugilum Christi religiosè viventium in dicto Castro constituere dignaremur. Nos itaque prædictis causis, & rationibus diligentiùs intellectis, easque in attentæ meditationis indaginem deducentes, propter securitatem Fidelium, & tutelam, plurimaque bona exinde, annuente Domino, proventura, cum Fratribus nostris super his diligenti deliberatione præhabita, ejusdem Regis laudabile in hac parte propositum disposuimus favorabiliter prosequendum. Propter quod de ipsorum Fratrum consilio, & Apostolicæ plenitudine potestatis ad infrascriptam ordinationem, divinum super hoc invocantes auxilium, duximus procedendum. Cùm enim illa fœda dictorum Sarracenorum natio, & impia Christiani nominis inimica in fronteria dicti Regni Algarbii contiguis terminis, ut prætangitur, constituta Regnum ipsum, ejusque Fideles in summi Regis offensam per successus (proh dolor!) retrò temporum diversorum tribulationibus multis afflixerit, periculis subjecerit variis, & feritatem frequenter armaverit, sicut & armare conatur in exterminium eorumdem,

1 Nos eidem Regi, & Regno, ac Fidelibus adversus eorumdem hostium conatus nefarios deprimendos, assistente nobis divino præsidio, prospicere cupientes, in prædicto Castro-Marino Domum novi Ordinis pugilum Christi providimus ordinandam, quam quidem Domum ipsius Ordinis caput esse decernimus.

2 Et

2 Et eidem Parochialem Ecclesiam Sanctæ Mariæ ejusdem Castri dictæ Silvensis Diœcesis, cum omnibus juribus, & pertinentiis suis donamus, concedimus, annectimus, & unimus, ac ad honorem Dei, & exaltationem Catholicæ Fidei, tutelam Fidelium, & depressionem infidelium prædictorum in dicta Domo prædictum Ordinem instituimus auctoritate Apostolica, & etiam ordinamus.

3 In quo præfata Militia Fidei athletarum, qui Ordinem proprium profiteantur, sub observatione regulæ de Calatrava ejusdem regulares observantias servaturi, idonei, & in Fidei soliditate præstantes, debeat collocari, ut sic idem Regnum, & Fideles eò ferventiùs dictis hostibus resistere valeant, quò plurium viribus conflatis in unum maiori potentia fulciantur, auctoritate Apostolica de ipsorum Fratrum consilio statuentes, quòd Ordo prædictorum Militum ejusdem novæ Militiæ, Ordinis Militiæ Jesu Christi perpetuis futuris temporibus nuncupetur, ac dilectum Ægidium Martini, olim Magistrum Domûs Ordinis Militiæ Calatravensis de Avisio, Elborensis Diœcesis, ejusdem Calatravensis Ordinis professorem, de cujus vitæ munditia, Religionis zelo, morum maturitate, strenuitate personæ, integritate Fidei, & aliis innatæ sibi probitatis meritis laudabilia Nobis testimonia sunt relata, eidem Ordini Militiæ Jesu Christi de ipsorum Fratrum consilio, auctoritate prædicta præficimus in Magistrum, ipsum à Magisterio prisci Ordinis Calatravensis de Avisio, auctoritate præsentium absolventes, sibique curam, gubernationem, & administrationem dicti Ordinis Militiæ Jesu Christi plenariè committentes, alienatione bonorum immobilium dicti novi Ordinis sibi, & suis successoribus, & membris ejus omnibus penitùs interdicta, nisi in casibus à jure permissis, & forma juris debitè observata, dilectis filiis, Fratribus dictæ Domûs de Avisio, vel iis, vel ei, ad quos, vel quem Magistri præfatæ Domûs electio, vel provisio pertinet eligendi sibi personam idoneam, vel providendi de persona idonea in Magistrum, dantes, tenore præsentium, liberam facultatem.

4 Dictumque Ordinem, Magistrum, qui nunc, & qui pro tempore fuerit, ac Fratres ejusdem Ordinis, ejusdem privilegiis, libertatibus, & indulgentiis gaudere volumus, quibus Magister, & Fratres Calatravenses gaudent.

5 Cui quidem Ordini plena super hoc cum eisdem Fratribus deliberatione præhabita, & de ipsorum consilio ex causa præmissa Castrum-Album, Langroviam, Thomarium, & Almourol, necnon omnia alia castra, fortalitia, & bona mobilia, & immobilia, universa, & singula quæcumque, & in quibuscumque consistentia, tàm Ecclesiastica, quàm mundana, necnon nomina, actiones, jura, jurisdictiones,

nes, imperium merum, & mixtum, honores, homines, & vassallos quoslibet, cum Ecclesiis, Capellis, & Oratoriis quibuscumque, ac suis juribus, terminis, & pertinentiis universis, quæcumque Ordo quondam Templi in præfatis Portugaliæ, & Algarbii Regnis tenebat, habebat & habere debebat, quæcumque sint, & in quibuscumque consistant, & quocumque nomine censeantur, & ad eum quacumque ratione, vel causa debeant, vel poterant pertinere, auctoritate prædicta concedimus, donamus, unimus, incorporamus, annectimus, & in perpetuum applicamus. Decernentes irritum, & inane, si secùs super prædictis Castris, à quoquam quavis auctoritate, scienter, vel ignoranter attentatum forsan est hactenùs, vel contigerit in posterum attentari.

6 Dictique Procuratores, procuratorio nomine dicti Regis, prout de speciali mandato eis super hoc facto à Rege prædicto poterant, donaverunt dictum Castrum-Marinum pura, & irrevocabili donatione Deo, & dicto Ordini, ac Nobis recipientibus pro Ordine novæ Militiæ Jesu Christi, & Magistro prædictis cum omni jurisdictione, mero, & mixto imperio, hominibus, vassallis, homagiis fidelitatis, seu alterius juramenti præstationibus, juribus, & pertinentiis universis, quæcumque sint, & in quibuscumque consistant, & quocumque nomine censeantur, & cum pleno, ac libero, & integro exercitio eorumdem, & quidquid juris in proprietate, dominio, seu possessione, vel quasi jure patronatûs, jurisdictione, mero, & mixto imperio, hominibus, vassallis, homagiis fidelitatis, seu alterius juramenti præstationibus, honoribus, hominibus, actionibus, seu aliàs quovis modo eidem Regi in prædictis Castris nominatis, & aliis Castris, terris & locis non expressis, fortalitiis, & bonis, cum terminis, & pertinentiis suis, quæ prædictus Ordo quondam Templi tempore dictæ captionis Magistri, & Fratrum prædictorum tenebat, habebat vel habere debebat, quæcumque sint, & in quibuscumque consistant, & quocumque nomine censeantur, & ad eum quacumque ratione, vel causa debebant seu poterant pertinere, in Regnis, & terris Regis ejusdem, dictus Rex habebat, vel ad eum in eisdem possint quomodolibet pertinere, eidem novo Ordini Militiæ Jesu Christi in nostra, & dictorum Fratrum præsentia concesserunt dederunt, & donaverunt liberè, munificè, purè, simpliciter, & irrevocabiliter inter vivos, promittentes procuratorio nomine dicti Regis, prout similiter in mandatis habebant, quòd idem Rex, postquam ad eum præmissa pervenerint, quamprimum commodè poterit, dictum Castrum-Marinum, necnon universa Castra, fortalitia, terras, loca, bona, & jura prædicta præfatis Magistro, & Fratribus ejusdem novi

Or-

Ordinis faciet tradi, & affignari integraliter cum effectu, ipfosque dictorum Caftrorum, terrarum, locorum, bonorum, jurifdictionis, meri, & mixti imperii, & aliorum jurium prædictorum, plena, & pacifica poffeffione, & quafi gaudere, amotis quibuslibet detentoribus ab eifdem, eisque de ipforum fructibus, redditibus, proventibus, juribus, & obventionibus, & aliis univerfis integrè refpondere.

7 In prædicto autem Ordine per Nos, ut præmittitur, noviter inftituto dilectus filius Abbas Monafterii de Alcobaça Cifterciensis Ordinis Ulisbonenfis Diœcefis, qui eft, & erit pro tempore, vifitationis, & correctionis officium tàm in capite, quàm in membris, quoties expedierit, debeat exhibere corrigens, reformans in eo futuris temporibus, quæ correctionis, & reformationis auxilio indigere profpexerit, quæcumque licet Ordini Cifterciensi in Calatravenfi Ordine, contradictores per cenfuram Ecclefiafticam, appellatione poftpofita, compefcendo.

8 Volumus infuper, quòd præfatus Abbas, qui eft, & pro tempore fuerit, vel ejus locum tenens, vel, loco vacante, Adminiftrator Monafterii à dicto Magiftro novi Ordinis Militiæ Jesu Chrifti, qui eft, & fuccefforibus ejus, qui pro tempore fuerint, juramentum fidelitatis nomine noftro, & Romanæ Ecclefiæ recipere debeat fub forma infrà fcripta, quoties in eodem novo Ordine Magifter aliquis affumetur; dictusque Abbas formam juramenti prædicti, quod dictus Magifter præftabit, quàm citiùs commodè poterit, Sedi Apoftolicæ deftinare procuret.

9 Dictoque juramento præftito, ac nihilominùs poftea pro plena fecuritate ipforum, Regis, & Regnorum Portugaliæ, & Algarbii, & ad propellenda imminentia fibi quæque pericula, quo præfatus Magifter Ordinis Militiæ Jesu Chrifti, & fucceffores fui Magiftri novi Ordinis memorati, qui erunt pro tempore, vel, dictis Magiftris abfentibus, eorum loca tenentes, antequàm adminiftrationi hujufmodi bonorum fe ingerant, coram dicto Rege, qui nunc eft, vel qui pro tempore fuerit, fi Regem ipfum tunc in aliquo dictorum Regnorum Portugaliæ, feu Algarbii fore contigerit, perfonaliter fe præfentent, eique præftent juramentum perfonale, & homagium faciant fub hac forma, videlicet, quòd ipfe Magifter fidelis erit dicto Regi, & per fe, vel alium nunquam aliquid faciet, vel fieri, feu procurari confentiet publicè, vel occultè, propter quod eidem Regi, & fuis, vel Regnis, aut terris ejus aliquod damnum valeat evenire; quòd fi fortè fciret aliquid procurari, vel fieri, quod in damnum dicti Regis, aut Regnorum, & terrarum ipfius effet, vel cedere poffet, id eidem Regi, quàm citò poterit, intimabit, vel faciet intimari, & nihilominùs im-

pe-

pediet juxta poſſe, quòdque de Caſtris, villis, locis, & bonis, & juribus, ac hominibus, quæ dictus novus Ordo Militiæ JESU Chriſti habet ad præſens, vel habebit in poſterum in Regnis, & terris prædictis, nunquam dicto Regi, vel Regnis, ac terris, vel ſubditis ſuis, eodem Magiſtro ſciente, volente, mandante, aut ratum habente, aliquod damnum eveniat in futurum; quòd ſi forte id ſciverit, vel ſenſerit, totis impediat viribus, & quantum in eo fuerit, amovebit. Juramentum verò, & homagium ſupradicta per dictum Magiſtrum non ratione dictorum bonorum, ſed ratione perſonæ præſtantis Regi, præſtari, & fieri volumus ſupradicto, nullumque ipſi Regi ex juramento, vel homagio ſupradictis in bonis eiſdem quomodolibet jus acquiri.

10 Quod quidem juramentum, & homagium idem Rex intra decem dierum ſpatium, poſtquàm à Magiſtro, qui eſt, & erit pro tempore, fuerit requiſitus, ab eodem Magiſtro offerente recipere teneatur. Quòd ſi Rex ipſe juramentum, & homagium hujuſmodi intra terminum ipſum forte recipere non curaret, liceat dicto Magiſtro, qui eſt, & erit pro tempore, abſque prædictorum præſtatione, & Regis ipſius licentia recedere, & officium Magiſterii bonorum hujuſmodi exercere liberè, & ſicut pro utilitate novi Ordinis ſibi videbitur expedire, adminiſtrare plenariè in eiſdem; ſi verò in primo ejuſdem Magiſtri dicti novi Ordinis Militiæ JESU Chriſti adventu, quem nunc præficimus, & qui præficietur pro tempore ad Regna prædicta, dictum Regem, qui nunc eſt, vel qui pro tempore fuerit, ab ipſis Regnis abeſſe forte contigerit, idem Magiſter locum tenenti dicti Regis teneatur juramentum præſtare, & homagium facere, ſicut ſuperiùs eſt expreſſum; & ſi contigerit fortaſſis interdum, quòd Ordini, & bonis prædictis Magiſter aliquis non præeſſet, locum tenens ipſius, aut ille, qui bonorum ipſorum adminiſtrationem habuerit, præfato Regi, vel ejus locum tenenti, ipſo Rege à prædictis Regnis abſente, juramentum præſtet, & homagium faciat ſupradicta.

11 Inferiores quoque Præceptores dicti Ordinis Militiæ JESU Chriſti, eorumque locum tenentes, cùm Præceptores ipſos à dictis Regnis ejuſdem Regis abeſſe contigerit, antequàm incipiant in bonis adminiſtrare prædictis, afferre juramentum, & homagium hujuſmodi dicto Regi, ſi ipſe in aliquo loco dictorum Regnorum, in quo Præceptoria hujuſmodi fuerit, præſens extiterit, alioquin locum tenenti ejus intra prædictum tempus hujuſmodi juramentum præſtare, & homagium facere teneantur; quo elapſo, ſive dictum juramentum, & homagia ſint recepta, vel etiam non recepta, liceat prædictis inferioribus Præceptoribus, vel ipſorum loca tenentibus ad eorum loca redire,

dire, & absque praedictorum praestatione, & Regis ejusdem, seu locum tenentis ipsius licentia in bonis administrare liberè supradictis.

12   Volumus tamen, quòd Magister ipse, aut Praeceptor maior praedicti Ordinis Militiae Jesu Christi, seu ipsius locum tenens, eo absente, & Praeceptores alii, seu eorum loca tenentes, qui fuerint sub eodem in Regnis, & terris ejusdem Regis, ad Curias ipsius Regis accedant, & ei, & suis haeredibus, ac successoribus omnia faciant, quae Ordo Hospitalis Sancti Joannis Hierosolymitani in Regnis praedictis consistens sibi, & praedecessoribus suis facere consuevit, reservatis etiam omnibus juribus, & servitiis praefato Regi, & successoribus suis à praefato Ordine Militiae Jesu Christi praestandis, quae dictus Rex, & praedecessores sui à dicto Ordine Hospitalis in Regnis praefatis existente retroactis temporibus habere consueverunt, & adhuc etiam habere noscuntur.

13   Statuimus praetereà, & etiam ordinamus, quòd, quoties per cessionem, seu decessum ipsius Magistri dicti novi Ordinis, vel quocumque alio modo eumdem novum Ordinem proprio carere Magistro contigerit, aliqua Militaris, & Religiosa persona eumdem novum Ordinem expressè professa, à Fratribus ejusdem novi Ordinis juxta morem hactenùs in Calatravensi Ordine observatum seligi debeat in Magistrum, qui, absque alia confirmatione, pro confirmato eo ipso auctoritate Apostolica habeatur, quòdque à tempore vacationis per ejusdem Magistri obitum, vel alio quocumque modo novi Ordinis memorati illi Milites, & Fratres ejusdem novi Ordinis bona ipsius in eodem novo Ordine liberè administrent, quousque eidem novo Ordini fuerit, ut praemittitur, de Magistro provisum, qui juxta observantias dicti Calatravensis Ordinis (quas circa hoc in praedicto novo Ordine volumus observari) ad administrationem hujusmodi fuerint deputati, & nihilominùs dicti Procuratores promiserunt se bona fide facturos, & curaturos, quòd praedictus Rex ea omnia, & singula, prout ad eum pertinebit, seu pertinere poterit, & debebit, approbabit, rata habebit, & grata, eaque servare, & adimplere curabit, ullo unquam tempore in contrarium non venturus. Tenor autem procuratorii, seu mandati dictorum Petri, & Joannis per omnia talis est. Noverint universi praesentis procurationis litteras inspecturi, quòd nos Dionysius Dei gratiâ Rex Portugaliae, & Algarbii, constituimus, facimus, ac etiam ordinamus Procuratores nostros veros, legitimos, & sufficientes, ac Nuntios speciales, nobilem virum Joannem Laurentii Militem, & discretum virum Petrum Petri Colimbricensem Canonicum, familiares nostros, latorem, seu latores praesentium, utrumque

b ii   ipso-

ipsorum in solidum, itaque non sit melior conditio occupantis, sed quod unus incœperit, alter mediare valeat, & finire, super quibuscumque gratiis pro Nobis, & dictis Regnis nostris à Sanctissimo Patre, ac Domino Domino Joanne, Divinâ providentiâ Sacrosanctæ Romanæ, ac universalis Ecclesiæ Summo Pontifice, impetrandis; necnon ad tractandum, ordinandum, & compositionem faciendum, seu componendum cum dicto Summo Pontifice, & cum aliis quibuscumque, qui sua crediderint interesse, super omnibus, & singulis bonis, quæ à Fratribus Ordinis quondam Templariorum in Regnis nostris tenebantur, & super omnibus aliis bonis, quæ in eisdem Regnis nostris à quolibet alio Ordine Militari tenentur, seu teneri consueverunt, & super ponendis, seu ordinandis Magistro, seu Magistris in omnibus præfatis bonis, prout dictis Procuratoribus nostris, & cuilibet eorum videbitur expedire, concedentes sibi, & utrique ipsorum plenam, generalem, & liberam administrationem super negotiis prædictis, & quolibet eorumdem, & generaliter ad omnia alia, & singula faciendum, & exercendum, quæ circa præmissa, seu præmissorum quodlibet fuerint necessaria, seu etiam opportuna, & quæ Nos facere possemus, si personaliter præsentes essemus, etiamsi mandatum exigant speciale, promittentes Nos firmum, & ratum perpetuò habituros quidquid per dictos Procuratores nostros, seu per alterum ipsorum actum, seu procuratum fuerit in præmissis, & in quolibet præmissorum, sub hypotheca, & obligatione omnium bonorum nostrorum. In cujus rei testimonium has nostræ procurationis litteras sigillo nostro dependenti fecimus communiri. Datum Ulyssipone quarta decima die mensis Augusti. Rege mandante Dominicus Joannes notavit, œra millesima trecentesima quinquagesima sexta. Forma verò juramenti, quod idem Ægidius Martini Magister dictæ Domûs Ordinis Militiæ Jesu Christi, & quilibet successorum suorum præstabit, talis est. Ego N. Magister Domûs Militiæ Jesu Christi ab hac hora in antea fidelis, & obediens ero Beato Petro, Sanctæ Apostolicæ Ecclesiæ Romanæ, & Domino meo PP. suisque successoribus canonicè intrantibus; non ero in consilio, aut consensu, vel facto, ut vitam perdant, aut membrum, vel capiantur mala captione; consilium verò, quod mihi credituri sunt per se, aut per Nuntios suos, sive per litteras, ad eorum damnum, me sciente, nemini pandam. Papatum Romanum, & Regalia Sancti Petri adjutor eis ero ad retinendum, & defendendum, salvo meo Ordine, contra omnem hominem. Legatum Apostolicæ Sedis in eundo, & redeundo honorificè tractabo, & in suis necessitatibus adjuvabo. Vocatus ad Synodum veniam, nisi præpeditus fuero canonica præpeditione.

14 Apostolorum limina singulis trienniis visitabo, aut per me, aut per meum Nuntium, nisi Apostolica absolvar licentia. Possessiones verò ad Domum meam, & Ordinem prædictum spectantes non vendam, nec donabo, nec impignorabo, nec denuò infeudabo, vel aliquo modo alienabo, inconsulto Romano Pontifice ; sic me Deus adjuvet, & hæc Sancta Euangelia Dei. Nulli ergo omninò hominum liceat hanc paginam nostrarum constitutionum, donationum, concessionum, annexationum, unionum, institutionis, ordinationum præfectionis, absolutionis, commissionis, dationis, voluntatum, incorporationis, applicationis, & statuti infringere, vel ei ausu temerario contraire. Siquis autem hoc attentare præsumpserit, indignationem Omnipotentis Dei, & Beatorum Petri, & Pauli Apostolorum ejus se noverit incursurum. Datum Avenione, Idib. Martii, Pontificatûs nostri anno tertio.

ACCEPTATIO, ET RATIFICATIO DOMINI
Regis Dionyſii.

NOs verò præfatus Rex, qui pervigili cura foliciti continuò circa indemnitates ſtudiosè flectimur ſubjectorum, voluntariosque labores aſſumimus, ut eiſdem præparantes quietem, ubi maximè Fides invaleſcit Catholica, non conſideratis opibus, ſed mente jucunda, ac Chriſtianæ Religionis zelo ferventi eos cum omni providentia ſervemus illæſos, omnibus, & ſingulis in nota prædicti Nobis per dictum noſtrum Militem præſentata contentis, & per eumdem relatis oraculo vivæ vocis, inſpectis, intellectis, & efficaciter examinatis, ac diligenti deliberatione habita ſuper eis, conſiderantes præfatam ordinationem de prælibato Ordine Militiæ Jesu Chriſti, utpotè ſanctè, & providè inſtitutam, ad Dei ſervitium tendere, & honorem, Divinique cultûs augmentum, & exaltationem Fidei Orthodoxæ, & Regni noſtri Algarbii, ſubditorumque noſtrorum ſtatum pacificum, & tranquillum, ut per Chriſti pugiles, tanquam inexpugnabili muro, infidelium bellatorum inſultus, & amaritudo vitetur, incurſus opprimatur hoſtilis, & enervetur immanitas barbaricæ feritatis, eamdem ordinationem per eumdem Dominum noſtrum Summum Pontificem, ſicut præmittitur, inſtitutam, gratam habemus, ac laudabilem reputamus; & aſſentientes eidem, donationes, & conceſſiones prædictas per dictos Procuratores noſtros nomine noſtro factas, & præmiſſa omnia, & ſingula per eoſdem facta pro Nobis, & nomine noſtro, & geſta, prout ad Nos pertinet, & pertinere poteſt, & debet, approbamus, ratificamus, ac firma, rata, ſeu valida, grataque habemus, eaque ſervare, & adimplere curabimus, ullo unquam tempore in contrarium non venturi. In cujus rei teſtimonium has noſtras patentes litteras per Dominicum Joannis Notarium noſtrum, ac Regnorum noſtrorum Tabellionem publicum, & generalem ſcribi mandavimus, eaſque ſigillo noſtro plumbeo ad maiorem firmitudinem fecimus communiri, ejuſdemque Tabellionis ſigno ſignari. Et ego Dominicus Joannis Notarius prædictus, ac auctoritate Regali publicus, & generalis Tabellio in prædictis Regnis Portugaliæ, & Algarbii, qui ad inſtantiam, & mandatum prædicti Domini Regis præmiſſis litterarum Apoſtolicarum, & notæ, ſeu formæ ordinationis prælibati Ordinis Militiæ Jesu Chriſti per Dominum Summum Pontificem inſtituti, & de novo creati, dictoque Domino Regi per dictum Joannem Laurentii Militem præſentationibus factis, & etiam gratificationi, aſſenſioni, approbationi, ac ratificationi de contentis in ordinatione prædicta per eumdem Dominum Regem, ut præmittitur, præſtitis, &

omni-

omnibus aliis, & fingulis ibidem actis, five geftis unà cum teftibus infrafcriptis præfens fui de mandato ipfius Domini Regis, de prædictis omnibus, & fingulis fuprafcriptis has præfentes litteras manu propria fideliter fcripfi, & in eifdem fignum meum confuetum appofui, quod tale eft in teftimonium præmifforum. Acta fuerunt hæc omnia, & fingula fupradicta Sanctarenæ, Ulisbonenfis Diœcefis, in Aula prædicti Domini Regis quinta die menfis Maii, æra millefima trecentefima quinquagefima feptima, fub anno etiam Nativitatis Domini millefimo trecentefimo decimo nono, præfentibus etiam Reverendiffimo in Chrifto Patre Domino N. Divina miferatione Elborenfi Epifcopo, & nobilibus viris Domino Alfonfo Sancii Domino de Albuquerque, & Maiordomo præfati Domini Regis, Domino Joanne filio fereniffimi Domini Alfonfi Hifpani, ac difcretis viris Domino Francifco Dominici, Priore Ecclefiæ Sanctæ Mariæ de Alcaçova Santarenfi Ulisbonenfis Diœcefis, Valafco Martini de Riparia Colimbrienfi Canonico, Stephano Aric. Clericis, & Stephano de Guardia prædicti Domini Regis Secretario teftibus ad præmiffa vocatis fpecialiter, & rogatis.

APPENDIX X

INSIGNIA AS *OBJETS D'ART*

Several books have been written on Orders as *objets d'art*. The authors use, as has become common practice, the word 'order' for insignia and decorations. Prince Michael of Greece[1] wrote that it became fashionable in the seventeenth and eighteenth centuries, notably in Germany, for sovereigns and princes to have their own insignia made in precious stones. This practice goes back much further, and far more insignia have been made into jewellery for men and women than can be found in the crown jewels of the European royal houses.

It was not only the insignia of Europe's principal Orders, the Garter, the Golden Fleece, St. Andrew of Russia or the Elephant of Denmark of which copies, richly encrusted with the most precious stones and pearls were made because the original insignia conferred, especially collars, had to be returned to the Orders's Chancelleries after the recipients had died, but the badges, crosses and stars of almost all Orders were turned into – sometimes very beautiful – *objets d'art*, worn by their owners and became family heirlooms. In Russia almost every noble had his Cross of the Order of St.Anne made of gold and profusely decorated with large diamonds, rubies, sapphires and emeralds.

Sometimes, presumably at the insistence of whoever ordered it, goldsmiths used so many precious stones – often regardless of their colour – that the jewel bore little or no likeness to the original insignia. A typical example is the Polish Order of the White Eagle which King Augustus of Saxony had awarded himself when he also became King of Poland.[2] The cross of the Order is a gold, ball-tipped Maltese cross, red-enamelled with a white border and the crowned Eagle of Poland superimposed on it, between the arms of the cross is a burst of gold rays. The jewel fashioned for King Frederick Augustus II stands out because of the sixteen large emeralds, each surrounded by a ring of cut diamonds, although emerald-green is a colour not in the original insignia; there are four rather small rubies, and the rest of the very large badge is completely covered in large diamonds. It is quite impossible to see any resemblance between the Order of the White Eagle and the jewel which supposedly represents it. Fortunately, few such travesties have survived.

King Christian IV of Denmark (1588-1648) had a special jewel made

---

[1] *Crown Jewels of Britain and Europe*, London, 1983.
[2] *Ibid.*

in which he had the Order of the Elephant combined with the Order of the Mailed Arm, which he founded and fell into disuse soon afterwards.[1]

The Golden Fleece has often been made into personal jewels, perhaps most splendid example being that made in Brazil for King João VI of Portugal when he and the Royal Family were in exile there. The original, which of course had to be returned on his death, was given him by King Carlos III of Spain in 1785 when João was an Infante of Portugal. After Queen Maria I of Portugal had added the emblem of the Sacred Heart to the combined insignia of the Orders of Christ, of Avis and of Santiago in 1789, several jewels of the Badge and the Star were made for members of the royal family.[2]

The Star of the Portuguese Order of the Conception of Our Lady of Vila Viçosa, also made in Brazil for King João VI,[3] is a gold plaque covered with hundreds of cut diamonds, and were it not for the blue enamelled circle surrounding the centre medallion, it would be difficult to recognise the decoration. It is interesting to compare King João's diamond encrusted star of the Order with the 'mini insignia' of the same star[4] (24mm. high/20mm. wide) made by the papal engraver Prof. Rudolf Niedballa.[5] This also was a private commission and was made of eighteen carat enamelled yellow and white gold. The mini-insignia are not miniatures worn from a bar on a ribbon, but exquisite replicas, showing

Professor Rudolf Niedballa, the Papal Engraver, whom Pope John Paul II created a Knight Commander of the Order of St. Gregory the Great, uses glasses and microscopic instruments with up to forty-fold magnification when making the mini-orders in precious metals and enamel.

---

[1] Apart from a reference to the Order of the Mailed Arm in the book about crown jewels by Prince Michael, I have been unable to find a reference to that Order elsewhere.
[2] See: colour plate on insignia as *objets d'art* in this work.
[3] See: colour plates on the Royal House of Bragança.
[4] See: colour plates on insignia as *objets d'art*.
[5] Prof.Rudolf Niedballa, D-51515 Kürten, Deutschland.

the smallest details of the originals, and are worn as a single decoration on the lapel, perhaps instead of a rosette. I am reproducing in colour three of Prof. Niedballa's mini-insignia: the Star of the above-mentioned Order, the Cross of the Pontifical Equestrian Order of St. Gregory the Great and the royal insignia of the Savoyan Order of St. Maurice and St. Lazarus, all made of 18 carat gold and enamelled. When working on these mini-insignia Prof. Niedballa uses glasses with up to fortyfold magnification. Just how exact these *objets d'art* are can only be appreciated under a powerful magnifying glass; in fact, they are in many details far more accurately made than the original insignia which are many times larger. They are the twentieth century descendants of the decorations that were commissioned from outstanding craftsmen in the seventeenth and eighteenth centuries in gold and precious stones.

The Collars of the Pontifical Orders of Christ, of the Golden Spur and of the Pian Order, with their silver-gilt and enamelled badges and stars, are *objets d'art* of the highest standard and no recipient has thought to improve on them by commissioning his own version. The craftsman who makes them for the Holy See is Sig. Giorgio Guccione,[1] who also makes the collars and decorations for the Order of the Holy Sepulchre and other Orders of Knighthood.

Although not a Catholic-founded Order, the Grand Master's Collar of the Brazilian Imperial Order of the Rose, founded in 1829 by Emperor Dom Pedro II of the House of Orléans e Bragança, and still worn by the Head of the Dynasty, has often been described as the most beautiful decoration ever made. Particularly striking are the roses, all of which are carved rose quartz.

Sig. Giorgio Guccione makes the Collars reserved for Heads of State and other Pontifical decorations for the Papal Secretariat of State as well as the insignia for the Order of the Holy Sepulchre of Jerusalem and the Constantinian Order.

[1]Studio Giorgio Guccione, Via dell'Orso, 17-18, 00186 Roma, Italia.

APPENDIX XI

ORDERS AND DECORATIONS OF THE REPUBLIC OF POLAND AFTER 22 DECEMBER 1990.

DZIENNIK USTAW – Rzeczypospolitej Polskiej – Warszawa – dnia grudnia 1992 r. Nr 90, the issue of the *Law Gazette* of the Polish Republic, published in Warsaw on 8 December 1992, dealt with all matters relating to Orders and Awards in the Republic. Because this is the first official publication giving the exact details about Orders and Decorations in the Republic of Poland, it is reproduced here with some relevant extracts from the *Gazette*.[1]

1) GENERAL: Orders and Decorations are awarded by the President of Poland. The Commander in Chief of the Armed Forces is empowered to award Orders and Decorations in the Armed Forces during an armed conflict and for five years after cessation of hostilities.

Within six months of publication of this Law Gazette a Provisional Chapter of the Order of the White Eagle will be established and present its first recommendations.

The President of the Republic will appoint a Chancellor and a Chapter for the Order of 'Virtuti Militari'.

The President of the Republic will appoint members to the Chapter of the Order of 'Polonia Restituta'.

2) ORDERS:

The Order of the White Eagle

    The Order of 'Virtuti Militari'
    I   Grand Cross
    II Commander's Cross
    III Knights Cross
    IV Gold Cross
    V Silver Cross

The Order of 'Polonia Restituta'
    I   Grand Cross
    II Commander with Star (Grand Officer)
    III Commander
    IV Officer
    V Knight

[1] Mr. Krzysztof Barbarski, the Curator of the Sikorski Museum in London, obtained the official *Law Gazette* specifically for this book and also translated the relevant sections on Orders and Decorations.

The Order of Merit of the Polish Republic
(Grades as for the Order of 'Polonia Restituta')

[In order to distinguish the Riband of this Order from the Order of the White Eagle, the colour of light blue-celeste has been changed to a darker blue, similar to that of the National Order of Merit of France]

3) DECORATIONS AND MEDALS RECOGNISED BY THE POLISH REPUBLIC:
    (*) instituted by the Polish Government in Exile.
    (**) no longer awarded.
    (***) no longer awarded after 8 May 1995.

Cross of Valour
Gold Cross of Merit with Swords (*) (**)
Gold Cross of Merit
Silver Cross of Merit with Swords (*) (**)
Silver Cross of Merit
Bronze Cross of Merit with Swords (*) (**)
Bronze Cross of Merit
Medal for Sacrifice and Bravery
Medal for long-lasting marriage (50 years)
Army Medal (*) (**)
Navy Medal (*) (**)
Air Force Medal (*) (**)
Polish Merchant Navy Medal (*) (**)
1939 September Campaign Cross (*) (**)
Monte Casino Cross (*) (**)
Home Army Cross (*) (***)
Peasant Battalions Cross (***)
National Armed Forces Cross (***)

4) The following Decorations are approved but are no longer awarded after 8 May 1995:
The Silesian Uprising Cross; Greater Poland Uprising Cross; Partisans Cross; Warsaw 1939-45 Medal; Oder, Nyse and Baltic Medal; 1939 Campaign Medal; Warsaw Uprising Cross; Auschwitz Cross; Battle of Lenino Cross; 1918-21 War Cross.

There remained one very important issue unresolved: while the legitimate succession of Presidents of the Republic had been laid down, no authoritative statement had been published that expressly named those who had been entitled to award Orders of Knighthood and Awards of Merit, particularly after the second World War when Poland was under Soviet domination. In addition, a more embarrassing than legal irregularity had brought to the fore questions about the activities of a Mr. Juliusz Nowina-Sokolnicki, who claimed for some decades to be the President of Poland in exile and who had provided, with the help of the popular press, ample copy for the newspapers. He lavishly sold and bestowed Polish decorations, titles of Consul General, Consul and all manner of honours to unsuspecting recipients who believed that he represented the legitimate Polish Government in exile and was its President. On 27 September 1994, *Dziennik Polski* published in London the following official statement in Polish, which is followed by an English translation.

Problem stopni wojskowych i odznaczeń

Ponieważ kwestia uznawania przez prezydenta RP stopni wojskowych, przyznawanych wcześniej przez polskie władze na uchodźstwie, budzi kontrowersje wśród i samych zainteresowanych, i niektórych prawników — chciałbym przedstawić wykładnię prawną decyzji, które podejmuje prezydent Lech Wałęsa w tych przypadkach.

Art. 11 ust. 1 ustawy z 25 października 1991 roku o zmianie ustawy o powszechnym obowiązku obrony oraz niektórych innych ustaw (Dz. U. nr 113 poz. 491) zobowiązał organa właściwe do mianowania na stopnie wojskowe — prezydenta i ministra obrony narodowej — do uznawania stopni wojskowych nadanych przez władze Rzeczypospolitej Polskiej w okresie do 22 grudnia 1990 r.

Pod pojęciem „władze Rzeczypospolitej Polskiej" należy rozumieć organa państwowe na uchodźstwie działające z mocy przepisów ustawy konstytucyjnej z 23 kwietnia 1935 roku. Za takie zaś można uznać jedynie prezydentów Rzeczypospolitej: gen. Bolesława Wieniawę-Długoszowskiego, Władysława Raczkiewicza, Augusta Zaleskiego, Stanisława Ostrowskiego, Edwarda Raczyńskiego, Kazimierza Sabbata, Ryszarda Kaczorowskiego oraz powoływane przez nich organa państwowe. Oni to bowiem są — w świetle przepisów ustawy konstytucyjnej z 23 kwietnia 1935 r. jak i faktów historycznych — następcami prezydenta Ignacego Mościckiego, a ostatni z nich prezydent Ryszard Kaczorowski, w przeprowadzeniu w kraju wolnych i powszechnych wyborów prezydenckich w 1990 r. uznał za zakończone funkcje i zadania prezydenta Rzeczypospolitej na uchodźstwie, składając jednocześnie insygnia II Rzeczypospolitej w ręce prezydenta Lecha Wałęsy.

Mając to na uwadze należy przyjąć, że panu Juliuszowi Nowinie-Sokolnickiemu nie przysługiwały przymioty „władz Rzeczypospolitej Polskiej" i w związku z tym nie mogą być honorowane jego czynności natury państwowej, w tym także nie mogą zostać uznane, na podstawie art. 11 ust. 1 cytowanej na wstępie ustawy, nadane przez niego stopnie wojskowe.

Art. 11 ust. 2 cytowanej wcześniej ustawy upoważnił prezydenta RP do określenia zasad i trybu postępowania oraz organów właściwych w sprawach o uznawanie stopni wojskowych.

Andrzej Drzycimski
sekretarz stanu
rzecznik prasowy prezydenta RP

Wyciąg z oświadczenia opublikowanego w *Prawie i Życiu* nr 20, czerwiec 1994

Translation[1]

Article 11 of Bill 1 of 25 October 1991 (113.491), while giving the President and the Minister of Defence of the Polish Republic the power and obligation to promote to military [knightly] rank, also recognises this power as being bestowed by Authority of the Polish Republic up to 22 December 1990.

The phrase 'the Authority of the Polish Republic' should be understood to mean the organs of the state institutions abroad based on the Polish Constitution of 23 April 1935. It therefore recognises as Presidents of the Polish Republic General Boleslaw Winiawe-Dlugoszowski, Wladyslaw Raszkiewicz, August Zaleski, Stanislaw Ostrowski, Edward Raczynski, Kazimierz Sabbat, and Ryszard Kaczorowski, as well as the state organs appointed by them. According to the Constitution of 23 April 1935 and historical fact they are the successors of President Ignacy Moscicki.

The last mentioned, President Ryszcard Kaczorowski, acknowledges that, following free elections in Poland and the election of the President in

[1] Courtesy: Prof. Dr. M. Sas-Skowronski, VM.

1990, the activities of the President-in-Exile terminated when he handed the insignia of the Second Polish Republic to President Lech Walesa.

With this in mind, it should be stated that Mr. Juliusz Nowina-Sokolnicki did not possess the authority of the Polish Republic and therefore his activities purporting to be actions of the state [as a result of calling himself President-in-Exile of the Polish Republic] cannot be honoured, and according to Article 11 of Bill 1, the ranks granted by him are not recognised.

(signed)
Andrzej Drzycimski
State Secretary
Press Spokesman of the President of the Polish Republic.

APPENDIX XII

On 16 December 1994, His Majesty King Juan Carlos I of Spain, with the approval of the Cortes, appointed his cousin H.R.H. Don Carlos de Borbón-Dos Sicilias y Borbón Parma an Infante of the Kingdom of Spain, granting him all the privileges, style and honours due to an Infante in line of succession to the Crown of Spain.

As can be seen in Chapter Seven in the section on the Royal House of Bourbon of the Two Sicilies, the appointment of H.R.H. Don Carlos as a Spanish Infante has changed the *status quo* that has existed since the death of his Father, H.R.H. Don Alfonso, Infante of Spain.

His Royal Highness belongs to the regnant dynasty of Bourbon of Spain and genealogically to the non-regnant dynasties of Bourbon of the Two Sicilies (both through his father and grandfather), and Bourbon Parma (through the lineage of his mother). The dynasty of Bourbon of Spain is regarded as the senior Bourbon branch; the other extant Bourbon dynasties, including those of Orléans and Orléans-Bragança of Brazil, are autonomous and formerly sovereign Royal Houses. Though interrelated many times through marriage, each Bourbon branch has retained its independent and sovereign status even when non-regnant.

The arguments whether an Infante of Spain can be the Head of the Royal House of Bourbon Two Sicilies has been dealt with at length in Chapter Seven.

As to the title 'Duke of Calabria', this has traditionally always been the title of the son of the Duke of Castro, who would succeed as the Head of the House of the Two Sicilies. On several occasions, the Dukes of Castro have given the Duke of Calabria the grand-mastership of the Sacred Military Constantinian Order of St. George prior to his succession to the title 'Duke of Castro' and to the headship of the Royal House.

I have no intention of entering into further discussion on the question of the headship of the House of the Two Sicilies and the grand-mastership of the dynastic Orders of Knighthood in the light of H.R.H. Don Carlos de Borbón-Dos Sicilias y Borbón Parma having been created an Infante of Spain by H.M. The King of Spain.

When King Juan Carlos bestowed the high honour upon his cousin, I was immediately informed of this fact. I am much obliged to His Excellency the Marquis de la Conquista Real, Madrid, and Mr. Guy Stair Sainty of New York for sending me the original document of appointment for publication and for supplying me at my request with an independent translation of the Royal Decree. I have also received several comments as to the meaning of the decree.

After reproducing the Royal Decree in full, I also reproduce the independent translation which has been accepted by all parties.

I was also informed of the legal interpretation, given by a member of the Council of the Grandees of Spain who is a constitutional jurist. The excellent and independent translation I was furnished with might be misleading because it did not take into account the intricate juridical points contained in the Royal Decree. According to this information, 'the exceptional circumstances that coincide in His Royal Highness don Carlos de Borbón-Dos Sicilias e Borbón-Parma,' lie in the fact that he is a representative of a dynastic line that is historically linked to the Crown of Spain, and that His Royal Highness was created an Infante of Spain as representative of a second, though junior, Spanish dynastic line.

I am not sufficiently acquainted with Spanish dynastic law to make any personal comment on this matter. It is a strictly Spanish matter which has no bearing on the tenor of this book.

JEFATURA DEL ESTADO

27905 *REAL DECRETO 2412/1994, de 16 de diciembre, por el que se concede la Dignidad de Infante de España a don Carlos de Borbón-Dos Sicilias y Borbón-Parma.*

Las circunstancias excepcionales que concurren en Su Alteza Real don Carlos de Borbón-Dos Sicilias y Borbón-Parma, como representante de una línea dinástica vinculada históricamente a la Corona española, constituyen razones por las que le juzgo digno de la merced y Dignidad de Infante de España, por lo que, de conformidad con lo establecido en el artículo 3.º, 2, del Real Decreto 1368/1987, de 6 de noviembre,

DISPONGO:

Artículo único.

Se concede la Dignidad de Infante de España a Su Alteza Real don Carlos de Borbón-Dos Sicilias y Borbón-Parma con los honores y tratamientos anejos a la citada Dignidad.

Dado en Madrid a 16 de diciembre de 1994.

JUAN CARLOS R.

El Presidente del Gobierno,
FELIPE GONZALEZ MARQUEZ

Translation of the Royal Decree, published in the *Boletín Oficial del Estado* on Saturday, 17 December 1994:

LEADERSHIP OF THE STATE

27905 Royal Decree 2412/1994 of 16 December, by which is conferred the Dignity of Infante of Spain on don Carlos of Bourbon-Two Sicilies and Bourbon Parma.

The exceptional circumstances which coincide in His Royal Highness don Carlos of Bourbon-Two Sicilies and Bourbon Parma, as representative of a dynastic line historically linked to the Spanish Crown, constitute reasons for which he is judged worthy of the favour and Dignity of Infante of Spain, for which, conforming with what is established under article 3.o,2, of the Royal Decree 1368/1687, of 6 November.

IT IS DECIDED

Article One.

The Dignity of Infante of Spain is granted to His Royal Highness don Carlos of Bourbon-Two Sicilies and Bourbon Parma with the honours and titles annexed to the cited Dignity.

Given at Madrid on 16 December 1994

JUAN CARLOS R.

The President of the Government,
FELIPE GONZALEZ MARQUEZ

SELECT BIBLIOGRAPHY

ACTA APOSTOLICAE SEDIS – Bollettino Ufficiale della Santa Sedis, Città del Vaticano.
ALEXIS de ANJOU, *La Verdadera Historia De Los Caballeros De San Juan*, Madrid, 1990.
ANNUARIO PONTIFICIO – Annuario Ufficiale della Santa Sedis, Città del Vaticano.
L'ATTIVITA' DELLA SANTA SEDE – Annuario non ufficiale della Santa Sede, Città del Vaticano.
ASHMOLE, Elias, *The Institution, Laws and Ceremonies of the Most Noble Order of the Garter*, London, 1672.
Associaçâo da Nobreza Histórica de Portugal, Estatutos, Lisboa, 1984.
BANDER van DUREN, P., *The Cross on the Sword*, Gerrards Cross, 1987.
——, see also under CARDINALE, H.E.
BASCAPÉ, Giacomo, *Gli Ordini Cavallereschi in Italia*, Milano, 1972.
—— and Monterisi, M., *Storia politica dell'Ordine di Malta*, 2 vols., Milan, 1940.
BEGENT, Peter J., *The Most Noble Order of the Garter: Its History and Ceremonial*, Colnbrook/Slough, 1991.
BELARD DA FONSECA. Francisco, *A Ordem Militar de Nossa Senhora da Conceiçâo de Vila Viçosa*, Lisboa, 1955.
BERTOUCH, E. von, A. Mittelstaed, & J. Preto, *Mönchsund Ritterorden*, München, 1984.
BIGOSZEWSKA, W., *Polskie Ordery I Odznaczenia*, Warszawa, 1989.
BOND, Maurice, *St. George's Chapel, Windsor*, Gerrards Cross, 1975.
BURKE, Sir Bernard, *The Book of Orders and Knighthood and Decorations of Honour*, London, 1858.
BURNETT, Charles J. and BENNETT, Helen, *The Green Mantle*, National Museums of Scotland, 1987.
BURY, John, *Juan de Herrera y el Escurial*, Patrimonio Nacional, Madrid, 1995.
CALO, Renato, *Le Medaglie del Vaticano 1929-1972*, Roma, 1973.
CARDINALE, H.E., *The Holy See and the International Order*, Gerrards Cross, 1976.
——, *Orders of Knighthood, Awards and the Holy See*, Gerrards Cross, 1983; edited and revised by Peter Bander van Duren, 1984, 1985.
CASTRÉN, Klaus, *Les Ordres Nationaux de la Finlande*, Helsinki, 1975.
CHAFFANJON, A. & FLAVIGNY, B.G., *Ordres & contre-ordres de chevalerie*, Paris, 1982.

CHANCELLARIA DAS ORDENS MILITARES DE REAL CASA DE PORTUGAL, *Estatutos da Ordem de Nossa Senhora da Conceiçâo de Vila Viçosa*, Reino Unido de Portugal, do Brazil e Algarves, 1819.
CONSTANTINIAN CHRONICLER (edited by Colin Smythe), Nos. 1-4, Gerrards Cross, 1990-92.
CORNET, René, *Les Ordres Nationaux Belges*, Bruxelles, 1982.
CRAILSHEIM, Freiherr Hanns-Jürgen von, *Der Königlich-Bayrische Hausritterorden vom Heiligen Georg*, München, 1979.
CHRONACHE COSTANTINIANE, Gran Cancellaria dell'Ordine Costantiniano di S.Giorgio, Napoli, Roma, 1992-.
Code of Canon Law, The, London, 1983.
CODEX IURIS CANONICI, Sede Apostolica, Vaticano, 1917.
CODEX IURIS CANONICI, Santa Sede, Vaticano, 1983.
CUOMO, R., *Ordini Cavallereschi Antichi e Moderni*, Napoli, 1894.
DA SILVA PEREIRA OLIVEIRA, Luiz, *Privilegios da Nobreza, e Fidalguia de Portugal*, Lisboa, 1806.
DANIEL, P.E., *A Bibliography for the History of the Order of the Holy Sepulchre of Jerusalem in the British Isles (1100-1954)*, Redhill (Surrey), 1992.
de BRAGANÇA, Dr. José Vicente, *The Portuguese Orders of Merit, A Brief Account*, Chancelaria das Ordens Honorificas Portugueses, O Secretário-Geral da Presidància da República, Lisboa, .
de CASTRO, Joâo Bautista, *Mappa de Portugal*, Lisboa, 1762.
DE FESTI, Cesare, *Sull'Origine Istituzione e Prerogative dei Conti Palatini e dei Cavalieri Aurati*, Pisa, 1888. *Denmark, Official Handbook*, Ministry of Foreign Affairs, Kobenhavn.
De SIBERT, GAUTIER and de SAISSEVAL, Guy Coutant, *History of the Military and Hospitaller Order of Saint Lazarus of Jerusalem*, Paris, 1772 (trans. & completed, 1988).
de la BERE, Ivan, *The Queen's Orders of Chivalry*, London, 1961.
dell'AJA, P.Gaudenzio, *Per la Translazione in Santa Chiara di Napoli dei Resti Mortali degli ultimi Sovrani delle Due Sicilie*, Napoli, 1984.
Der Bayrische Hausritterorden vom Heiligen Georg 1729-1979, München, 1979.
de VILLARREAL de ALAVA, Marques, *La Maison Royal des Deux Siciles, l'Ordre Constantinien de Saint-Georges et l'Ordre de Saint-Janvier*, Madrid, 1964.
di LORENZO, Achille, *Il Sacro Militare Ordine Costantiniano di San Giorgio, A Cura del Gran Magistero dell'Ordine*: Volume I (1698-1966), Napoli, 1966; Volume II (1860-1966), Napoli, 1966; Volume III, Napoli, 1971; Volume IV, Napoli, 1978; Volume V, *Ricerche Storiche sull'Ordine Costantiniano di San Giorgio*, Napoli, 1978.
——, *The World Crisis In Our Time*, Naples, 1975.
——, *La Crisi Mondiale Dei Nostri Tempi*, Napoli, 1975.

——, *Sovrintendenza Generale E Magistrale per la Promozione e Realizzazione Culturale e Delegazione Magistrale di Studi Storici ed Umanistici*, Roma, 1985.
——, *S.M.O. Costantiniano di San Giorgio: Réplicas A Hidalguia – Documentos*, Napoli, 1982.
——, *S.M.O. Costantiniano di S.Giorgio – Napoli.* Cassette tape, side A: 'Inno del Re' (Band), 'Tocchi di Guerra', 'Assemblea'; Side B: 'Inno del Re' (Organ), 'Marcia del 1822', 'Marcia del 1830', Napoli, 1984.
——, 'Who is the legitimate Grand Master of the Sacred Military Order of St. George of Naples?', in *Constantinian Chronicler*, No. 2, 1990, pp. 3-22.
——, 'Matters concerning the true history of the Dynastic Order of Chivalry of the Royal House of Bourbon Two Sicilies', in *Constantinian Chronicler*, No. 4, 1992, pp. 3-32.
——, *Sacro Ordine Costantiniano di San Giorgio*: Cassette tape, side A: 'Messagio'; Side B: 'Preghiera a Sua Santità Giovanni Paolo II P.M.', Napoli, 1993.
——, *Il Tramonto del Sacro Ordine Costantiniano di San Giorgio*, Napoli, 1993.
DOS SANTOS, Armando Alexandre, *A Legitimiadade Monárquica No Brazil*, Sâo Paulo, 1988.
——, *Ser ou nâo ser Monarquista – Eis a questâo!*, Sâo Paulo, 1990.
DOYLE, W.J., *The Origins, Structure and Present Work of the Equestrian Order of the Holy Sepulchre of Jerusalem*, La Jolla, CA, 1974.
DUPUY de CHINCHAMPS, Ph., *La Cavallerie*, Paris, 1961.
DURNIN, P. *Liturgies for Ceremonies of Investiture for the Pontifical Equestrian Orders of St. Gregory the Great and of Pope St. Sylvester*, c/o The Knights of St. Columbanus, Rosaire, Moneymore, Drogheda, Co. Louth, Ireland.
DUROV, V.A., *The Orders of Russia*, Moscow, 1993.
ELVIN, C.N., *A Dictionary of Heraldry*, London, 1969.
FARMER, D.H., *The Oxford Dictionary of Saints*, Oxford, 1978.
FERNANDEZ de la PUENTE y GOMEZ, F., *Condecoraciones Españolas*, Madrid, 1953.
FILIPOW, K. *Order Virtuti Militari 1792-1945*, Waszawa, 1990.
FUNDAÇAO DA CASA DE BRAGANÇA, *Mercàs de D. Theodósio II, Duque de Bragança*, Lisboa, 1967.
GILLIAT-SMITH, E., *Some Notes Historical and Otherwise Concerning the Sacred Constantinian Order*, London, 1922.
GILLINGHAM, A.E., *Italian Orders of Chivalry and Medals of Honours*, Rochester, NY, 1967.
GRAN MAGISTERO dell'Ordine, *Statuto dell'Ordine Costantiniano di San Giorgio*, Napoli, 1973.
GRAN MAGISTERO dell'Ordine, *Statuto dell'Ordine Equestre del Santo Sepolcro di Gerusalemme*, Vaticano, 1977.
GRAN MAGISTERO dell'Ordine, *Statuto dell'Ordine Supremo della SS. Annunziata*, Torino, 1990.

GRAN MAGISTERO dell'Ordine, *Statuto dell'Ordine dei Santi Maurizio e Lazzaro*, Torino, 1990.
GRITZNER,Maximilian, *Handbuch der Ritter und Verdienstorden aller Kulturstaten der Welt innerhalb des XIX Jahrhunderts*, Leipzig, 1893, (Reprinted Graz, 1968).
GUIRAUD-DARMAIS, Jacques, *Ordres et Decorations Monegasques*, Palais de Monaco, 1985.
HARTWELL, R., *Guide to Orders of Chivalry*, Torrence, CA, 1974.
—— (General Editor), *The Augustan Society Omnibus*, Torrence, CA, Vols. 1-14, 1967-.
HAYDN, Joseph, *Haydn's Dictionary of Dates*, first published London, 1841; twenty-five editions (edited by Benjamin Vincent, 1898-1910), twenty-fifth edition, London, 1911.
——, *The Book of Dignities*, first published London, 1851; twelfth edited and revised edition (Edited by Horace Ockerby), London 1894; facsimile edition with prefaces of previous editions (edited by Norris and Ross McWhirter), London, 1969.
HEIM, B.B., *Heraldry in the Catholic Church, its origin, customs and laws*, Gerrards Cross, 1981.
'Historia', in *Les Chevaliers Teutoniques, Les Chevaliers de Malte, les Ordres Militaires et Hospitaliers*, n.403 bis (special issue), Paris, 1980.
HIERONYMUSSEN, P., *Handbuch Europäischer Orden in Farben*, Berlin, 1966.
——, *Orders, Medals and Decorations of Britain and Europe*, London, 1967, 1975.
Il Cavaliere – La Revista degli Ordini Cavallereschi, Il Cavaliere, Presidente R. Trabucco, Roma, 1993.
Imperial Society of Knights Bachelor, The, 26th Edition, London, 1981.
JACOB, J.R., *Court Jewellers of the World*, London, 1978.
JENKINS, D., *Equestrian Order of the Holy Sepulchre of Jerusalem – Historical Notes*, London, 1979.
JOSLIN, E.C., *The Standard Catalogue of British Orders Decorations and Medals*, (annual publication of Spink & Son Ltd.), London.
——, *The Observer's Book of British Awards and Medals*, London, 1974.
KELLY, J.N.D., *The Oxford Dictionary of Popes*, Oxford, 1986.
KIRCHNER, H., & TRUSZCZYNSKI, G.von, *Ordensinsignien und Auszeichnungen des Souveränèn Malteser-Ritterordens*, Köln, 1974.
KLIETMANN et alii, Ordenskunde – *Beiträge zur Geschichte der Auszeichnungen*, Nos. 1-29, Berlin, 1957-67.
KLIMEK, S., *Im Zeichen des Kreuzes – die anerkannten geistlichen Ritterorden*, Stuttgart, 1986.
KRANTZ, H.V., *Handbuch Europäischer Orden in Farben*, Berlin, 1966.
KRIEG, Mons. P., *The Papacy and the Vatican: The Holy Year*, Zurich, 1950.
L'Ordre du Saint-Sepulcre de Jerusalem et la Terre Sainte, Musée de Fourière, Lyon, 1990.

MALECOT, *Décorations Françaises*, Paris, 1956.
MARTIN, Cardinal Jacques, *Heraldry in the Vatican [L'Araldica in Vaticano] [Heraldik im Vatikan]*, Gerrards Cross, 1987.
MENENIUS, F., *Deliciae Equestrium seu Militarium Ordinum*, Coloniae, 1608.
MENESTRIER, F., *De la Chevalerie Ancienne et Moderne*, Paris, 1683.
MERICKA, V. *Orden und Auszeichnungen*, Praha, 1966.
——, *Orders and Decorations*, London, 1969.
——, *Orden und Ehrenzeichen der ôsterreichischen-Ungarischen Monarchie*, Wien, 1974.
MICHAEL of GREECE, Prince, *Crown Jewels of Britain and Europe*, London, 1983.
MIGNE, W., *Dictionnaire Encyclopédique des Ordres de Chevalerie Civile et Militaire Crée chez les Differents Peuples depuis les Temps les plus Reculés*, Paris, 1861.
NEUBECKER, O., *Ordens-Lexikon*, Berlin, 1955. *Order of the Orthodox Hospitallers, The*, Colnbrook/Slough, 1987.
PEDROSA DOS SANTOS GRAÇA, Luís Maria, *Convento de Cristo*, Lisboa, 1991.
PERROT, A.-M., *Collection Historique des Ordres de Chevalerie Civilis et Militaires, Existant Chez les différens Peuples su Monde, Suivie d'un Tableau Chronologique des Ordres Éteints*, Paris, 1820.
POLSKI UNIWERSYTET NA OBCZYZNIE, *Polonia Restituta*, (Sabbat/Sas-Skowronski/Barbarski, edited by Peter Bander van Duren) Gerrards Cross, 1989.
Portuguese and International Orders, Banco Portuguàs do Atlântico, Lisboa, 1995.
PRESIDENCIA DA REPUBLICA PORTUGUESA, *Ordens Honoríficas Portuguesas*, Lisboa, 1968.
PROKOPOWSKI, Rudolf, *Ordre Souverain et Militaire Jérosolymitain de Malte*, (French, Italian, English, Spanish, German), Rome, 1950.
PROSSER, R.E., *The Order of the Golden Fleece*, Iowa, 1981.
——, *The Royal Prerogative*, Iowa, 1981.
RAUFFER, Franz Karl, *Statutenbuch – Der Königlich-Bayrische Hausritterorden vom Heiligen Georg*, München, 1768.
RAWLINSON OF EWEL, Lord, and Draper G.I.A.D., *Opinion, The Royal Dynasty and Family of Bourbon-Two Sicilies and The Sacred Military Constantinian Order of St.George*, London, 1990.
RENWICK, E.D., and WILLIAMS, I.M., *The Order of St. John*, London, 1958.
REPUBLICA PORTUGUESA, *Palácio da Ajuda*, Lisboa, 1986.
REPUBLICA DI SAN MARINO, *Gli Ordini Equestri*, San Marino, 1982.
Revista Internazionale, SMOM, Rome.
RISK, James C., *British Orders and Decorations*, New York, 1945.

——, *History of the Order of the Bath*, London, 1972. *Royalty, Peerage and Nobility of the World, The*, London, 1976.
RUBBI, Ugo, *Ordini Cavallereschi Esisti ed Esistenti nel Mondo*, Roma, 1948.
SAINTY, Guy Stair, *The Sacred Military Order of Constantine of Saint George: History and Statutes*, Burgess Hill, 1974.
——, *Sacred Military Order of Constantine of Saint George. Origins of the Dispute, Recent Events*, Madrid, 1976.
——, *La Sucesión a la Jefatura de la Casa Real de los Dos Sicilias y el Gran Magisterio de la Orden Constantinina*, Madrid, 1977.
——, *The Orders of Chivalry of the Bourbon Two Sicilies Dynasty*, Madrid, 1989.
——, *The Orders of Saint John*, New York, 1991.
——, *The Orders of Saint John and the Great Confraternal Orders of Chivalry still extant*, New York, 1996.
SCHAUFELBERGER, Prof.Dr. Walter, *Begegnung mit der Päpstlichen Schweizergarde im Vatikan*, Frauenfeld, 1984.
SCICLUNA, Sir Hannibal P., *The Order of St. John of Jerusalem*, Malta, 1969.
SECRETARIA STATUS SEU PAPALIS, *De Supremo Equestri Ordine Militiae D. N. Iesu Christi*, Palazzo del Vaticano, 1905.
——, *De Equestri Ordine Militiae Auratae*, Palazzo del Vaticano, 1905.
——, *De Equestri Ordine Piano*, Palazzo del Vaticano, 1905, Città del Vaticano 1958.
——, *De Equestri Ordine S. Gregorii Magni*, Palazzo del Vaticano, 1905, Città del Vaticano, 1947, 1979.
——, *De Equestri Ordine S. Silvestri Papae*, Palazzo del Vaticano, 1905, Città del Vaticano, 1968, 1969, 1976.
SEWARD, D., *Italy's Knights of St. George: The Constantinian Order*, Gerrards Cross, 1986.
Silva's Leilâo Portugal-Brazil, Lisboa, 1989.
SOLANO, Emma, *La Orden de Calatrava en Siglo XV*, Sevilla, 1978.
SOVEREIGN MILITARY ORDER OF MALTA, *Constitutional Charter of the Sovereign Military Hospitaller Order of St. John of Jerusalem of Rhodes and of Malta*, Rome, 1961/1979.
Code of the Sovereign Military Order of St. John of Jerusalem of Rhodes and of Malta, Rome, 1966/1979.
SPADA, Dott. Antonio, *Onori e Glorie*, Vol. I & II, Brescia, 1981/82.
——, *Sovrano Militare Ordine di Malta*, Brescia, 1981.
——, *Ordini Dinastici della Real Casa di Borbone delle Due Sicilie: Insigne Reale Ordine di San Gennaro e Sacro Militare Ordine Costantiniano di San Giorgio*, Brescia, 1983.
——, *Ordini Dinasti della Real Casa di Savoia: Ordine Supremo della Santissima Annunziata, Ordine dei Santi Maurizio e Lazzaro, e Ordine Civile di Savoia*, Brescia, 1985.
TEIXEIRA, José, *O Paço Ducal de Vila Viçosa*, Lisboa, 1983.

TOUMANOFF, Frà Cyril, Prince, *L'Ordre de Malte et l'Empire de Russie*, Rome, 1979.
——, *The Order of Malta, Yesterday and Today*, Palazzo di Malta, Rome.
——, *Catalogue de la Noblesse Titrée de l'Empire de Russie*, Rome, 1982.
——, *Les Dynasties de la Caucasie Chrétienne de l'Antiquité jusqu'au XIXe siécle. Tables généalogiques et chronologiques*, Rome, 1990.
TUMLER, M., *Der Deutsche Orden*, Bonn, 1974.
YOUNGER, Stuart G. Morris of Balgonie, *The Insignia and Decorations of the Military and Hospitaller Order of Saint Lazarus of Jerusalem*, Coupar Angus, 1986.

INDEX

INDEX

This index starts with the Introduction. Colour plates are paginated in roman numerals, and are fully indexed at the end of relevant entries. For individual members of Royal Houses, see under their names or titles. Extinct Orders of Knighthood are indicated by an asterisk preceding the entry. Saints appear under their names, but Orders that use the term Saint in their title, will be found under that honorific, for example 'St. Gregory, Order of'.

Unless otherwise indicated the terms 'Emperor' and 'Empire' refer to the Holy Roman Empire. Once the title had effectively become hereditary to the House of Habsburg-Lorraine, holders were often known as Emperors of Germany. In 1806 Emperor Francis II changed the title to become Emperor Francis I of Austria.

Aboukir Bay, Battle of, 175
absolutism, 49
Accademia dei Nobili Ecclesiastici, *see* Pontificia Academia Ecclesiastica
Accademia di San Luca, 24
Acre, Siege of, 356
Acta Apostolicae Sedis, 32, 33, 35, 59, 61, 132, 143, 144, 176
Acta Sanctae Sedis, 35, 144
Adelaide Sophie zu Löwenstein-Wertheim-Rosenberg, Princess, 254
Adenauer, Dr. Konrad, 70, 74
Admission to Papal Orders of Knighthood, 12-13, 126-27, 142-44, 606-20
Adrian VI, Pope, 65, 77, 399-400, 405, 406, 434, 437
*Advocates of St. Peter, Cross of the, 459, 460, X
Agustin de Iturbide, Emperor of Mexico, 473
Albano, Cardinal, 588
Albert of Apeldera, Bishop of Livonia, 466
Albert I, Sovereign Prince of Monaco, 378
Albert, Hereditary Prince of Monaco, 378, XXXVI
Albert, King of the Belgians, 243
Albert, Prince Consort to Queen Victoria, 430
Albert von Brandenberg, 213
Albert von Mecklenburg, King of Sweden, 449
Albigenses, 487
Albrecht, Prince, Duke of Bavaria, 319, 324
Alcantara, Military Order of (Spain), 22, 217, 224, 426, 434, XXXV

Alcobaça, Abbot of the Monastery of, 521
Alexander I, Czar of Russia, 557, 646
Alexander III, Pope, 414, 434, 436, 437, 465
Alexander IV, Pope, 47
Alexander VI, Pope, 65, 195, 405, 437, 487
Alexander, Prince of Yugoslavia, 556, 557
Alexandra, Queen, wife of Edward VII, 357
Alfonso, 1st Duke of Bragança, 249
Alfonso, King of Naples and Aragon, 152
Alfonso I Henriques, 1st King of Portugal, 408, 519
Alfonso II, King of Portugal, 409
Alfonso V, King of Portugal, 347, 399, 414
Alfonso XII, King of Spain, 429
Alfonso XIII, King of Spain, 241, 425, 426, 430
Alfonso, Count of Caserta, Duke of Castro, 271, 273, 275, 277, 278, 291, 292, 469
Alfonso, Infante Don (Bourbon of Spain), 275, 277, 279, 290, 291, 292, 294, 299
'Al Merito della Repubblica Italiana', Order of, 306
'Al Merito Civile di Savoia', Order of, *see* Ordine Al Merito Civile di Savoia
Amadeo of Savoy, King of Spain, 429
Amadeus V, Count of Savoy, 312
Amadeus VI, Count of Savoy, 312
Amadeus VIII, 1st Duke of Savoy, Antipope, 309, 312, 314
Amalia Walburga, Princess of Saxony, 303
Amelia, Queen of Portugal, 153
Amiens, Treaty of (1802), 175
*Ancient Nobility of the Four Emperors, Order of the, 478-79
Anders, General Wladislaw, 307, 319

Angelo Maria Angelo, Prince, 296
Anglo-Saxon Chronicle, 374
Anna, Princess of Lithuania, 386
Anna Maria von Dernbach, 478
Anna Maria Sophia of Bavaria, 477
Anne, Queen of Great Britain, 368
'Anno Iubilaei MCML, Benemerenti' Medal, 162
'Anno Iubilaei Romae MCMLXXV' Medal, 162
'Anno Santo MCMXXV' Medal, 161
Annuario Pontificio, 32
Annunciation, Supreme Order of the Most Holy, *see* SS. Annunziata, Supreme Order of
Antonelli, Cardinal Iacobus, 576
Antonio Farnese, Duke of Parma, 464
Antonio, Prior of Crato, King of Portugal, 406
Antonio Statella, Prince of Cassero, 469
Anuário das Ordens Honoríficas Portuguesas, 393
Apostolic Briefs and Constitutions, *see under* Encyclical Letters, Pontifical,
Apostolic See, as opposed to Holy See, 7-9, 19, 37, 39
Arena, Dr. Manuel de Noronha e Andrade, Marquês de, XIX
Arnold of Egmont, 324
Arrowsmith, Canon Adrian, 14, 136
Arthur, Prince, Duke of Connaught & Strathearn, 187, 256
Arundel, John, Dean of St. George's Chapel, Windsor, 356
Augustine, Rule of St., 344, 413, 437, 466
Aureate Knights *see* 'Torquati Aurati'
Avellino, Marino Caracciolo, Prince of, 295, 296
Avignon, Popes' stay at, 480
Avis, The Military Order of St. Benedict of (Portugal), 22, 65, 345, 393, 396, 397, 398, 400, 401, 406, 408-13, 414, 677, XXXIX
*Avis, Military Order of (Brazil), 411
Avis, Royal House of, 248

Baggio, Cardinal Sebastiano, 178, 179, 186
Baldwin II, King of Jerusalem, 483
Balley Brandenburg des Ritterlichen Ordens St. Johannis vom Spital zu Jerusalem, 187, 189
Bander van Duren, Peter, *The Cross on the Sword*, 6, 10, 14, 15, 29, 126-27, 129, 135, 138, 144, 147, 223, 231, 495, 517, 519, 550, 551, 610, 615, 621
*Bar, Order of the, 489
Barbarito, Archbishop Luigi, Apostolic Nuncio, 12, 59, 61, 62
Barbarski, Krzysztof, 384, 679
Barcelona, Count of, Don Juan de Bórbon y Battenburg, 224, 241, 287, 425, 426, 433
Barlassina, Mons., Patriarch of Jerusalem, 203
Barwig, Prior Regis, 538
Basel, Council of (1439), 309, 411
Basil, Rule of St. 75, 344, 465
Bath, The Most Honourable Order of the, 22, 345, 368-73
Bath King of Arms (England), 371
Baudouin I, King of the Belgians, 10, 70, 72, 186, 241
Bavaria-Wittelsbach, Royal House of, 319-21, 324
Baw, Catherine, 47
Beatrix, Queen of the Netherlands, 222, 357, 361, 430
Begent, Peter, 356
Belgians, Royal House of the (Saxe-Coburg-Gotha), 235
Belgium, Order of, 488
Belgium, Royal House of, 4,
Benedict IX, Pope, 480
Benedict XIII, Antipope (Pietro de Luna), 322, 436, 487
Benedict XIV, Pope, 75, 197, 303, 337
Benedict XV, Pope, 199, 203, 320, 518
Benedict, Rule of St. 344, 408, 434, 484, 519; *see also*Avis, Military Order of St. Benedict of
Benelli, Cardinal Giovanni, 3
'Benemerenti' Medal, Pontifical Award of Merit, 14, 142, 145, 149, 150, 157-58, 160-65, 621-23, IX, X
Bennett, Helen, 366
Bernadin, Cardinal Joseph, 104
Bernard of Clairvaux, St., 484
Bernadotte, Royal House of (Sweden), 449
Bernetti, Cardinal Th., 585
Bertie, Frà Andrew, Prince and Grand Master of SMOM, 172, 177, 178, 179, 182, 183, 186, 299, 538, XI
Birdwood, Field Marshal Lord,
Bismarck, Prince Otto von, 9, 56-57, 70, 319

Blanchard, Dr. Pierre, 618
Blasco, Alfred, J., 206
Boniface VIII, Pope, 410, 414, 480
Borges Grainha, Prof. Manuel, <it. Historia de Franco – Maconaria em Portugal, 521
Boselli, Minster, 278
Bourbon of France, Royal House of, 328-29, 425
Bourbon-Orléans, Royal House of, 224
Bourbon of Spain, Royal House of, 224, 234, 425, 426, 427, 433, 439
Bourbon-Two Sicilies, Royal House of, 271-94, 425, XXIV, XXV, XXVI
Bowen, Michael, Archbishop of Southwark, 208
Bragança, Royal House of, and Dukes of, 6, 227, 248, 345, 516, 524, 650-61, XVI, XVII, XVIII
Brandenburg, Bailiwick of St. John, 187, 192
British Empire, Most Excellent Order of the, 376
*Brotherly Love, Order of, 463
Bruno, St., 19
Bulgarian Orders of Knighthood (Communist), 49
Bull, Papal, *see under* Encyclical Letters, Pontifical,
Bull, Sir William, 375
Burgundy, Duke of, Founder of the Order of the Golden Fleece, *see* Philip the Good, Duke of Burgundy
Burgundy, Royal House of, 235
Burnett, Charles, Ross Herald of Arms, 347, 364, 365-66
Bury, John, 652-53; *Juan de Herrera y el Escurial*, 653-61

Calatrava, Military Order of (Spain), 22, 217, 224, 408, 412, 426, 434-35, 465, 485, 486, XXXV
Calatrava, Order for Ladies (Spain), 435
Callaghan, James, Baron Callaghan of Cardiff, 361
Callistus II, Pope, 195
Calò, Renato, *Le Medaglie del Vaticano 1929-1972*, 157-58
Cambrai, Congress of, 235, 239
Camerlengo, 40, 625, 628-29
Campoformio, Treaty of (1797), 241
Canali, Cardinal Nicola, 3, 137, 168, 170, 198-99, 203, 205
Cannes, Act of (1909), 277

Caprio, Cardinal Giuseppe, 171, 202, 205, XV
Cardinale, Archbishop Hyginus Eugene, 1-5, 16, 37, 38, 40, 43, 44, 48, 56, 59, 60, 116, 167, 170, 217, 275, 280, 287, 288, 290, 306, 335, 337-38, 393, 442, 447, 452, 455, 480, 553; *The Holy See & the International Order*, 7, 11, 39, 40, 454, 509; *Orders of Knighthood, Awards & the Holy See*, 1, 5-6, 7, 9, 11, 13, 15, 16, 17, 46, 52, 129, 136, 145, 167, 219, 227, 230, 231, 287, 346-47, 381, 427, 451, 452, 454, 495, 522, 526, 546, 548, 551, 554; *Le Saint-Siége et la Diplomatie*, 454
Cardinals, Tribunal of, 168, 175
Caritas (aid organisation), 531
Carl Gustav XVI, King of Sweden, 446
Carlo di Borbone delle Due Sicilie, Prince, Duke of Calabria, 289, 297, 298
Carlo Alberto, King of Sardinia & Duke of Savoy, 225, 309, 649
Carlo Emmanuel I, King of Sardinia & Duke of Savoy, 309
Carlo Felix, King of Sardinia & Duke of Savoy, 309
Carlos I, King of Portugal, 254, 255
Carlos II, King of Spain, 239
Carlos III, King of Spain (formerly King Carlo VII of the Two Sicilies), 297, 303, 438, 677
Carlos III, Most Distinguished Order of (Spain), 23, 220, 303, 425, 430, 438-40, XXXIV
Carlos, Don, son of Count of Caserta, Infante of Spain, 275, 277, 278, 279, 280, 281, 287, 291, 299, 469
Carlos, Don, de Bórbon y Bórbon, also Bórbon Dos Sicilias y Bórbon Parma, Infante of Spain, 224, 279, 280, 281, 286, 291, 292, 426-27, 433, 684-85, XXXV
Carlota Joaquina, Princess of Spain, Queen of Portugal, 48, 270
Carlowitz, Treaty of (1699), 478
Caroline Islands, 56
Casaroli, Cardinal Agostino, 1, 5, 6, 16, 27, 29, 31, 37, 53, 133, 136, 138, 167, 170, 228-29, 290, 515, 516, 517, 518, 519, 525-26, 613, 620
Caserta, Don Alfonso, Count of, *see* Alfonso, Count of Caserta
Casimir III, King of Poland, 386
Casimira, Queen of Poland, 153
Cassation, Court of (Italy), 168, 175

Catholic Encyclopedia, 406
Catholic Knights, International Alliance of, 519
Cavaliere, Il, 465
*Celestial Collar of the Holy Rosary, Order of, 463
Celestine II, Pope 409
Celestine III, Pope,
Celestine V, Pope, 410
Chaffanjon, A., & B. Galimard Flavigny, *Ordres & Contre-Ordres de Chevalerie* 552, 553
Chambord, Count of, 326, 331,333
Charles I, Emperor of Austria, 243
Charles I, King of England and Scotland, 375
Charles II, King of England and Scotland, 335, 370
Charles II, Duke of Mantua, 246
Charles II, Duke of Lucca and Parma, 469
Charles III, Duke of Bar, 489
Charles III, Duke of Lucca and Parma, 312, 469
Charles III, Prince of Monaco, 378
Charles III, King of Spain, and Most Distinguished Order of (Spain), *see* Carlos III
Charles IV, Emperor, 479
Charles IV, Duke of Bar, 489
Charles V, Emperor, King Carlos I of Spain, 77, 174, 237, 239, 294, 435, 466
Charles VI, Emperor, 239, 241,243
Charles VIII, King of Sweden, 449
Charles IX, King of France, 239
Charles X, King of France, 333, 510
Charles the Bold, Duke of Burgundy, 237, 238, 243
Charles Borromeo, St., 220, 378, 475
Charles Louis, Duke of Lucca, 469
Charles, Prince of Wales, 263, 368, XXVIII
Charles Edward Stuart, The Young Pretender, 368
Charles Theodor, Elector of Bavaria, 478
Charlotte, Grand Duchess of Luxembourg, 153, 156
Charlotte, Princess of Monaco, 378
Chaucer, Geoffrey, *The Canterbury Tales*, 375
chevalière, use of as title, 47
Chibesakunda, Ambassador, of Zambia, 59, 90, 145
Chigi Albani della Rovere, Prince and Grand Master Frà Ludovico, 68, 70, 167, 168
Chivalry, spirit of Christian, 525-43
Christ, Supreme Order of (Pontifical), 9, 23, 25, 30, 55, 56-57, 58, 64-74, 142, 217, 221, 235, 346, 442, 563-68, 600-01, 678, II
Christ, The Military Order of (Portugal), 22, 64-65, 235, 345, 393, 396, 397, 398, 400, 404-08, 435, 480, 486, 546, 662-75, 677, XXXIX
Christian I, King of Denmark, 348
Christian II, King of Denmark, 350
Christian III, King of Denmark, 350
Christian IV, King of Denmark, 350, 676
Christian V, King of Denmark, 346, 350, 351, 353
Christian VII, King of Denmark, 352
*Christian Militia, Order of the, 463
Christina, Queen of Sweden, 335
Chronicle of the Cistercians, 519
Churchill, Sir Winston Spencer, 350, 361
Ciechanowiecki, Count Andrzej, 288
Cisneros, Order of (Spain), 426. 442, 444
Cistercians, Rule of the, 344
Claves Sancti Petri, 42
Clement IV, Pope,
Clement V, Pope, 22, 65, 404, 414, 480, 481, 485, 552, 662
Clement VI, Pope, 356
Clement VII, Pope, 77, 174, 195, 240, 635
Clement VIII, Pope, 8, 152
Clement IX, Pope, 246
Clement XI, Pope, 149, 271, 293, 294, 296, 487
Clement XII, Pope, 337
Clement XIII, Pope, 75, 298, 478
Clement XIV, Pope, 438
Clovis, King of the Franks, 464
Codex Iuris Canonici (1917), 37
Codex Iuris Canonici (1983), 7, 8, 37, 39, 40, 148, 218, 219, 220, 221, 508, 548
Coggan, Rt. Rev. Donald, Baron of Canterbury, 130, 194
Cole, Sir Colin, former Garter King of Arms, 373-74; *The Roll of Knights Bachelor*, 374
Collegia Militum, 23
Collegium Militum Sancti Pauli, 24
Collegium Sancti Petri, 23-24
Columba, Knights of St. (Great Britain), 519
Columbus, Association of the Knights of (North & South America), 515, 516, 517-19, XLVIII

Comes Palatinus Maior, 35-36, 75, 76; *see also* Palatine, Papal Counts
Comes Palatinus Minor, 36, 75
Commonwealth, British, 531
*Conception of Our Lady, Order of the, 463
'Concilium Oecumenicum Vaticanum II' Medal, 161, 164
Conrad, Duke of Massovia, 213
Conry, Mons. Kieran, 131
Constance, Council of (1414-18),
Constantine, Emperor (Roman Empire), 75, 294
Constantine II, King of the Hellenes (in exile), 224-25
Constantinian Chronicler, The, 293
Constantinian Order of St. George, Sacred and Military Order of (Two Sicilies), 2, 9, 22, 37, 43, 44, 52, 75, 100, 117, 130, 182, 217, 219, 222, 226, 227, 271-94, 294-303, 316, 338, 346, 453, 464, 548, XXIV, XXV, XXVI, XXXII
'Cope of Reconciliation', 192, 194, XIV
Coppa, Archbishop Giovanni, 70
Corripio Ahumada, Cardinal Ernesto, 504, XLVII
Cortes (Spanish), 224, 426, 443
Cortes (Portuguese), 257
Cosimo d'Medici, Duke of Florence, Grand Duke of Tuscany, 337, 339
Cossiga, Francesco, President of Italy, 286, 298
Council of Europe, 175
Counts Palatine, *see* Palatine, Papal Counts
Counts of the Holy Roman Empire, 36, 77
Courland, Duchy of, 466
Court of St James, (Royal Court of Great Britain), 59
Coutant de Saisseval, Guy, 500
Couve de Murville, Maurice, Archbishop of Birmingham, 103
Cravanzolla, Ditta, 143
Crosses of Merit (Poland), 386
Crusaders, Crusader Knights, 195
Crusades, 19-24, 49, 50, 75, 152, 195, 212
Curia, Roman, 7, 8, 10, 12, 31, 37, 39, 58, 60, 142, 286, 293, 310, 454, 455, 495, 499, 504, 507, 511, 512, 515, 517, 631
Cyprus, 556

da Gama, Vasco, 20
Da Gama, Knights of, 519

d'Alboquerque, Affonso, 20
d'Andalò, Count Loderigo, 47
D'Angiò, Count Fulco, 152
'Dank für Polenhilfe' Medal, 500, XLV
Dannebrog, Cross of Honour of Men of (Denmark), 352
Dannebrog, Order of the (Denmark), 22, 345, 346, 351-54, 451, XLII, XLIII
de Balben, Frà Auger, 173
de Beauharnais, Prince August, 254
de Besalú, Armengal, 19,
de Boack, Felix, 116
de Bouillon, Godefroy, 195
de Bragança, Dr. José Vicente, 662; 'The Portuguese Orders of Merit; A Brief Account', 396, 398, 404, 406, 409,
de Brissac, Pierre de Cossé, 12th Duc, 500
de Brissac, François de Cossé, 13th Duc, 504, 505, 512, XLVI
de Brissac, Duchesse de, 505
de Castro, João Bautista, *Mappa de Portugal Antigo*, 652, 653
de Cisneros, Cardinal Francisco Jiménez, 444
de Fürstenberg, Cardinal Maximilien, 170-71, 199, 202, 205
de Gaulle, General Charles, President of France, 73, 350
de la Conquista Real, Marquis, 684
de La Sierragorda, Joaquån Martinez-Correcher, Count, 290, 429, 430
de La Valette, Grand Master Frà Jean, 174
de Lisboa, Frei António, 405
de Lopez y Santa Anna, Antonio, President of Mexico, 473, 475
de' Medici, Allesandro, ruler of Tuscany, 337
de' Medici, Cosimo, Duke of Florence, 337
de Mojana di Cologna, Frà Angelo, Prince & Grand Master of SMOM, 10, 167, 182, 185-86, 268
de Molay, Jacques, Grand Master, Order of the Templars, 481, 482
de Moraes, Prof. Arq. Marcello, 103, 264, XIX
de Payens, Hugues, Founder of Knights Templars, 483, 484
de Polignac, Count Pierre, later Grimaldi, 378
de Polignac, Prince, 426
de Saint-Lazare, Marquis Française, 510
de Valera, Éamon, President of Ireland, 74
de Villaret, Frà Foulques, 174

de Villiers, Frà Jean, 173
Dechant, Virgil C., Supreme Knight, Assoc. of the Knights of Columbus, 515, 518, XLVIII
Dell' Acqua, Cardinal Angelo, 3
DeSantis, Comm. Anthony, 104, I
de Sousa Lara, Dom Antonio, 259
Diário da República (Portugal), 393
Dias de Sousa, Grand Master Dom Lopo, 405
Dick, Mons. Klaus, Auxiliary Bishop of Cologne, 498
di Lorenzo, Bali don Achille, Marchese, 182, 277, 278, 281, 284, 285, 286, 288, 291, 292, 298, 299
di Mojana di Cologna, Prince and Grand Master Frà Angelo, 70
Dinis I, King of Portugal, 64, 404, 409, 410-11, 414, 435, 486, 662, 674-75
Diocletian, Roman Emperor, 419
Docwra, Grand Prior Thomas (Venerable Order), 189, 191
Donizetti, Gaetano, 49
*Dove, Order of the, 462
Duarte I, King of Portugal, 411
Duarte Nuno, Dom, Duke of Bragança, 223, 228, 256, 257, 258, 259, 263, 521, 650, 651
Duarte Pio, Dom, Duke of Bragança, 48, 223, 228, 249, 252, 258, 259, 260-61, 262, 263, 264, 265, 268, 270, 516, 517, 521, 522, 524, 651, XVII, XVIII
Double Tressure, The, 366
du Puy, Frà Raymond, 173
Durnin, Peter, 138, 139, 519
Dutch East India Company, 335
Duvalier, Jean Claude, President of Haiti, 10, 145

Eastman, Canon D.I.T., 356
Eden, Sir Anthony, 1st Earl of Avon, 361
Edward II, King of England, 481, 482, 486
Edward III, King of England, 356, 481
Edward IV, King of England, 237, 238, 356
Edward VI, King of England, 364
Edward VII, King of Great Britain, 62, 187, 189, 234
Edward VIII, King of Great Britain (subsequently Duke of Windsor), 256, 312, 361-62, 430
Eisenhower, General, Dwight D., President of the USA, 350

Eleanor Gonzaga, Empress (Habsburg-Lorraine), 246, 470
Elena di Savoia, Queen of Italy, 153
Elephant, Order of the (Denmark), 22, 23, 345, 348-51, 366, 676, XXXII, XLII
Elizabeth, St., of Thuringia, Queen of Hungary, 471
Elizabeth, Empress of Brazil, 153
Elizabeth, Queen of the Belgians, 153
Elizabeth I, Queen, 189, 191
Elizabeth II, Queen, 188, 194, 354, 357, 361, 371, 376, 398, 403, XXVIII, XL, XLIV
Elizabeth the Queen Mother, Queen, 357, 359, 362, 368, XXVIII
Elizabeth Augusta, Countess of Sultzbach, 478
Emanuele Filiberto, Prince of Savoy, 183, 307, XXII
Encyclical Letters, Pontifical
  Ad Anglos (Leo XIII, 1895), 151
  Ad ea ex quibus (John XXII, 1319), 65, 404, 435, 546, 553, 662
  Ad Providam (Clement V, 1312) 482
  Aeterni Patris (Leo XIII, 1880),
  Apostolicae Curae (Leo XIII, 1896),
  Constante fide (Leo X, 1516), 65
  Cum amplissima honorum (Gregory XVI, 1834), 101
  Cum hominum mentes (Gregory XVI, 1834), 79, 115
  Cum ob nonnullas, 8
  De Ordinibus Equestribus, see *Multum ad excitandos*
  Equestres Ordines (Paul VI, 1966), 9, 55, 67, 79, 85, 133
  Ex Cancellaria Ordinum Equestrium, 67
  Eximiae devotionis (Adrian VI, 1522), 65
  Humanae Vitae (Paul VI, 1968), 626
  Inter caetera (Boniface VIII), 410, 411
  Litteris suis (Pius XII, 1939), 87
  Militantis Ecclesiae (Clement XI, 1718), 271
  Multum ad excitandos (St. Pius X, 1905), 25, 55, 67, 76, 79, 99, 101, 104, 147, 152, 406, 528, 662
  Nostrae Ætate (Paul VI, 1965), 127
  Pastoralis officii (Nicholas IV, 1288), 410, 414
  Praeclara Clarissimi (Julius III, 1551), 396
  Quod singulari Deo concessu (Leo XIII, 1888), 157
  Quod summis quibusque (Gregory XVI, 1831), 99

Quotiens postulatur (Clement III, 1191), 211
Quoties a nobis (Gregory VIII, 1187), 409
Redemptoris et Domini Nostri (Clement IX, 1668), 246
Regimini Ecclesiae Universae (Paul VI, 1967), 9, 31, 32, 33, 136, 142, 145, 147, 546, 618, 631
Religiosis vitam eligentibus (Innocent III, 1201), 409
Rerum Novarum (Leo XIII, 1891), 151
Romanis Pontificibus (Pius IX, 1847), 87
Satis Cognitum (Leo XIII, 1896),
Vox in excelso (Clement V, 1312), 482
equitessa, use of as title, 47
Ermenhild (Hermynhild), St., 443
Eugene IV, Pope, 30, 309, 405, 411, 414
Eugene, Archduke of Austria, 213, 214
Eugene, Prince of Savoy, 21, 237, 309, 478
Eugénie, Express of France, 153
European Economic Community, European Community, 3, 499, 501, 507
Eusebius, 295
Évora Militia of Calatrava, *see* Avis, Military Order of
Extinct Orders, 641-45; *see also under their names*. Note that those appearing only in Perrot's list do not appear elsewhere in this index.

Fabiola, Queen of the Belgians, 72
Farouk, King of Egypt, 310
Fatimid Caliphs, 173
Faustinus, St., 476
Federsel, Prof. Franz Josef, 500, 502, XLVI
Felici (papal photographers), 2
Felix V, Antipope, *see* Amadeus VIII, 1st Duke of Savoy
Ferdinand I, Emperor of Austria, 243
Ferdinand I, King of Naples, 237, 238, 467
Ferdinand II (Ferdinand the Catholic), King of Aragon and Castile, 437, 440, 444
Ferdinand II, King of León and Galicia, 413, 434, 436
Ferdinand II, King of the Two Sicilies, 87, 153, 161, 297, 462
Ferdinand II, King of Portugal, 254
Ferdinand II, Grand Duke of Tuscany and Würzburg), 478
Ferdinand III, Archduke of Austria, Grand Duke of Tuscany, 340, 341
Ferdinand III, Emperor, 246

Ferdinand IV, King of the Two Sicilies, 297, 303, 466, 467
Ferdinand VI, King of Spain, 297
Ferdinand VII, King of Spain, 425, 427, 438, 440, 443
Ferdinando Maria di Borbone delle Due Sicilie, Prince, Duke of Castro, 182, 281, 284, 286, 287, 291, 292, 293, 294, 295, 305, XXIV
Ferdinando Pio di Borbone delle Due Sicilie, Prince, Duke of Castro, 273, 273, 275, 277, 278, 280, 281, 284, 291, 292, 293, 294, 299, 469
Fernandez Barrientos, Don Suero & Don Gómez, 434
Fernando, Dom, of Portugal, son of Joâo I, 397
Ferrara, Marquis de, 77
Ferri IV, Duke of Lorraine, 485
Festing, Frà Matthew, 177, 191
'Fidei et Virtuti' Medal (papal), 161
Filastre, Bishop Guillaume, 244
*Fleet, Order of the (France), 463
fons honorum, fontes honorum, 33, 35, 42, 47, 126, 133, 145-48, 224, 231, 233, 234, 307, 309, 338, 368, 431, 451, 455, 512, 650
Foros (Royal House of Bragança), 48, 262, 650-53
*Four Emperors, Order of the (Limburg-Luxemburg), 478-79
Francis I Farnese, Duke of Parma, 296
Francis I, Emperor of Austria, formerly Emperor Francis II of Germany (Holy Roman Empire), 243, 472
Francis I, King of France, 239
Francis I, King of the Two Sicilies, 305
Francis II, King of France, 239
Francis II, last King of the Two Sicilies, 227, 271, 285, 303, 461, 462. 467, 469
Francis, Duke of Habsburg-Lorraine, Grand Duke of Tuscany, 337
Franco Bahamonde, Generalissimo Don Francisco, Head of State, Spain, 224, 402, 425, 426, 438, 441, 442, 444
Frankish Kings, Merovingian dynasty, 76
Franz I, Emperor, 243
Franz, Crown Prince of Bavaria, 319
Franz-Josef I, Emperor of Austria, 243, 471
Frederick I, Emperor, 319
Frederick I, King of Denmark, 350
Frederick II, King of Denmark, 350
Frederick III, Emperor, 387
Frederick II, Elector of Brandenburg, 488

Frederick VI, King of Denmark, 352, 353
Frederick IX, King of Denmark, 83
Frederick Augustus I, Elector of Saxony, King of Poland, 386
Frederick Augustus II, Elector of Saxony, King of Poland, 303, 490, 676
Frederick, Crown Prince of Denmark, XLI
Frederik I, King of Sweden, 447, 449, 450
French Revolution, 244, 335, 340
Friedrich, Duke of Swabia, 212
Friedrich I Barbarossa, Emperor, 212, 378
Friedrich Wilhelm III, King of Prussia, 187
Friedrich Wilhelm IV, King of Brandenburg, 489
Friedrich Wilhelm IV, King of Prussia, 187
Frotz, Bishop, 497
Fundação da Casa de Bragança, 269

Gabrielczyk, Comm. R. J., 115, 116
Gammarelli, Ditta Annibale, 143
Gantin, Cardinal Bernardin, 102
Garrison, David, Jr., 302, XXVI
Garter, Most Noble Order of the (England), 22, 23, 234, 255-56, 305, 345, 355-64, 430, 431, 451, 676, XXVII, XXVIII, XXIX, XXX, XLIII
Gasparri, Cardinal Pietro 57, 58, 273, 279, 280, 510, 624
George the Martyr, St., 525
George I, King, 368, 370
George II, King, 368
George III, King, 368
George IV, King, 368, 371, 427
George V, King, 187, 375, 398, 430
George VI, King, 234, 398, 431
Gerard, the Blessed, 173
Gerhard V, Duke of Jülich-Berg, 324
Gian Andrea Angelo, Prince, 296, 464
Gilbert, Dom Hugh, Abbot of Pluscarden, 612
Giovanni Angelo, Prince, 295
Giustiani, Abbot Bernardo, *Historie Cronologiche dell'Origine degl'Ordini Militari e di tutte le Religione Cavalleresche*, 521
Glemp, Cardinal Josef, 102, 117
*Glorious Saint Mary, Order of the, 47
Gluck, Christoph Willibald, 79
*Golden Collar, Knights of, 464
Golden Fleece, Order of (Habsburg, Habsburg-Lorraine, Austria), 9, 37, 197, 217, 219, 222, 235, 242-45, 305, 346, 426, 429, 431, 432, 472, 676, XX, XLIII

Golden Fleece, Order of (Burgundy), 4, 22, 23, 235-42, XLIII
Golden Fleece, Order of (Spain), 34, 197, 217, 231, 222, 223, 234, 235, 258, 305, 345, 424, 426, 427-32, 676, 677, XXXIV
Golden Militia, Knights of the (Papal), *see* Golden Spur, Order of
Golden Rose, The (Papal), 149, 152-56, 366, X
Golden Spur, Order of, or Golden Militia (Papal), 23, 25, 30, 35, 36, 55, 57, 70, 72, 73, 74, 75-83, 115, 135, 142, 146, 147, 217, 221, 280, 346, 377, 569-72, 600-01, 678, III
Gottfried, Archduke of Habsburg-Lorraine, 337-38
Grace, Princess of Monaco, 378
Greco, Bishop, 518
Greek Orthodox Church, 197
Green, Mons. Peter, 138, 139
Gregory VII, Pope, 20, 414
Green Crescent (aid organisation), 531
Gregory IX, Pope, 466
Gregory XIII, Pope, 22, 239, 306, 312, 465, 505
Gregory XVI, Pope, 30, 35, 36, 76, 79, 87, 99, 115, 161, 175, 254, 584, 586, 616
Gregory, Sir William, 376
Gregory, Lady, née [Isabella] Augusta Persse, 376, 429
Grey, Sir Edward, 1st Viscount, 361
Grimaldi, The Sovereign Princely House of, 376
Gritzner, Maximilian, *Handbuch der Ritter- und Verdiensorden*, 326, 474, 489, 646
Guccione, Giorgio, 58, 143, 677
Guedes, Prof. Dr. Antonio de Sousa Lara, Conte di, 103, 385, XIX
Gustav Adolf VI, King of Sweden, 85
Gustavus I Wasa, King of Sweden, 447, 449
Gustavus III, King of Sweden, 448

Haakon VII, King of Norway, 447
Habsburg and Habsburg-Lorraine, Imperial and Royal House of, 20, 37, 239, 441, XX
Habsburg-Tuscany, Ducal House of, 337-38, 342
Hailsham, Baron of St. Marylebone, 130, 131
Hans Adam, Prince of Liechtenstein, 324, 325
*Hatchet, Order of the, or Hacha, 47, 463-64
Haydn's Dictionary of Dates, 406, 461, 641, 647

INDEX 705

Heath, Sir Edward, 361
Heim, Archbishop Bruno Bernard, 102
Helena, St., Empress (mother of Emperor Constantine), 155
Henri III, King of France and Poland, 329, 331
Henri IV, King of France, 331, 489, 506
Henri, Prince, Count of Paris 328-29, 342
Henrik, Prince of Denmark, XLI
Henrique, Cardinal, King of Portugal, 406
Henrique, Infante, Dom, of Portugal ('the Navigator'), 20, 397, 405
Henrique, Infante, Dom, Duke of Coimbra, 258, 259, 262, XVIII
Henry I, King of England, 374
Henry II, Saxon emperor, 490
Henry III, King of England, 375
Henry IV, King of England, 369
Henry VII, Emperor, 479
Henry VII, King of England, 237
Henry VIII, King of England, 184, 189, 190, 237, 240, 357
Henry, Prince, Duke of Gloucester, 187, XIV
Heuss, Dr Theodor, President of the Federal Republic of Germany, 82
Hickey, Cardinal James Aloysius, XI
Hieronimo Angelo, Count of Drivasto, 295
Hirohito, Emperor of Japan, 357, 430
Hitler, Adolf, 493
Holbein, Hans, 239
Holstein, Duke of, 212
Holy Ghost, Order of the (France), 23, 329-31, 334
*Holy Ghost of Montpelier, Order of the (France), 487
*Holy Land Pilgrim's Cross, 457, 459
Holy Roman Emperors and Empire, 77
Holy See, as opposed to Apostolic See, 7-9, 19, 37, 39
Holy Sepulchre, Equestrian Order of the, 6, 22, 24, 29, 34, 43, 44, 52, 130, 170-71, 195-209, 217, 219, 220, 221, 453, 512, 515, 613, 646, XV, XVI
Holy Sepulchre, Guardian (or Custodian) of, 195, 197
*Holy Vial, Order of the (France), 464
Honorius III, Pope, 351
Hood, Sir Harold, 100
Hornes, House of, 47
Horthy de Nagybanjya, Admiral Nicholas Vitéz, 'Reichsverweser of the Kingdom of Hungary, 491

Hulton, Sir Geoffrey, Bart., 102
Hume, Cardinal Basil, Archbishop of Westminster, 13-14, 129, 130, 131
Hungarian Orders of Knighthood (Communist), 49
Hussein I, King of Jordan, 346
Huydecoper, Jonkheer Johann, 334, 335

*Immaculate Conception, Order of the, 463
Imperial Society of Knights Bachelor, 375
Innes of Learney, Thomas, Lord Lyon King of Arms, 366
Innocent II, Pope, 484
Innocent III, Pope, 155, 409, 414, 436, 487
Innocent VIII, Pope, 465, 634
Isaac II Comnenus, Byzantine Emperor, 295
Isabel la Catolica, Order of (Spain), 220, 440-41, XXXIV
Isabella the Catholic, Queen of Castile, 437, 440, 444
Isabella II, Queen of Spain, 153, 425, 429
Isabella, Infanta of Portugal, 235
Islam, 15, 19-22, 50, 51, 195, 344, 413, 434, 435, 436, 487, 530

Jagellon, Grand Duke, 213
Jaime, Don, Duke of Segovia, 425, 425
Jakobovits, Chief Rabbi Sir Immanuel, 130
James I, King of Aragon, 466
James I, King of England (James VI of Scotland), 482
James II, King of Aragon, 435
James III, King of Scotland, 364, 366
James IV, King of Scotland, 364
James V, King of Scotland, 365
James VII, King of Scotland (James II of England), 347, 364, 365, 368
James Francis Edward Stuart, The Old Pretender, 368
Jean, Grand Duke of Luxembourg, 72, 429, 430
Jean I, Prince of Monaco, 378
Jenkins, Douglas, 208
Jérôme Bonaparte, King of Westphalia, 646
Jerusalem, Kingdom of, 173
Jerusalem, Latin Patriarch of, 195, 197, 203
*Jesus and Mary, Order of, 463
Joachim, Prince of Denmark, XLI
João I, King of Portugal, 249, 397, 405, 411, 414

João III, King of Portugal, 65, 405, 406, 415
João IV, King of Portugal, 248, 262, 406
João VI, King of Portugal & Emperor of Brazil, 48, 252, 253, 266, 270, 347, 398, 400, 411
João, Dom, of Portugal, son of João I, 397, 414
João, Bishop of Lamego, 405
Johann Wilhelm, Duke, of Neuburg, Elector Palatine, 324
Johannes Ernst von Thun, Prince Archbishop of Salzburg, 478
Johanniter Orden, 187, 189, 192, 452
John, King of Austria, 152
John II. King of Sicily, 237, 238
John XII, Pope, 77
John XXII, Pope, 65, 404, 405, 410, 411, 414, 435, 436, 466, 486, 546, 547, 553, 662
John XXIII, Pope, 11, 42, 70, 72, 73, 82, 90, 157, 164, 165, 167, 176, 205, 275, 277, 280-81, 287, 288, 290, 299, 354
John Paul I, Pope, 40-41, 46
John Paul II, Pope, 1, 9, 11, 13, 16, 17, 38, 42, 45-46, 51, 53, 55, 58, 59, 70, 86, 127, 145, 151, 159, 160, 163, 165, 171, 186, 192, 196, 211, 228, 268, 269, 295, 296, 354, 459, 496, 497, 500, 501, 511, 516, 616, 618, 622, 625, 629, XXIII, XLVI
John Sobieski, King of Poland, 21,
Johnston, Col. G. S., 612
Jorge de Lancastre, Duke of Coimbra, 406
Joseph II, Emperor, 243, 487
Joseph Arpád, Archduke of Austria, 268
Joseph Charles, Count Palatine of Sultzbach, 478
Josef Clemens, Duke of Bavaria-Wittelsbach, Archbishop & Elector of Cologne, etc., 326
Joseph Bonaparte, King of Naples, 467
Joslin, E.C., 375
Journal of the Orders and Medals Research Society, 293
Juan Carlos I, King of Spain, 10, 34, 72, 86, 219, 224, 231, 234, 241, 280, 290, 291, 303, 359, 424, 425, 426, 429, 430, 433, 440, 606, 684-85, XXXIII
Juliana, Queen of the Netherlands, 357
Julius II, Pope, 34, 65, 405, 635
Julius III, Pope, 65, 77, 396, 406, 411, 415

Kaczorowski, Ryszard, President of Poland-in-Exile, 383, 384, XLIV
Karl I, Emperor of Austria, 243

Karl VI, Emperor, 239, 241, 243
Karl von Habsburg, Archduke, 241
Karl of Hohenzollern, Prince, 187
Karl Albrecht, Duke of Wittelsbach, Elector of Bavaria, 318, 322
Karl Theodor, Duke of Neuburg, and Bavaria-Wittelsbach, 324
Kendall, Dr Russell, 171, 206
Kent, Duke of, 362, XXVIII
Kettler, Gothard, 466
Kingston, Richard, Dean of St. George's Chapel, 356
Knighthood, imitation and unrecognised orders of, 229-31, 482-83, 504, 545-558
Knights Bachelor (Great Britain), 373-76
*Knights of the Lily, Order of (Papal), 24
Knox, Cardinal James Robert, 102
Knut IV, King of Denmark, 348
Kulturkampf, 56, 57, 320
Kyprianou, Spyros, President of Cyprus, 556

Lambruschini, Cardinal A., 574
Lancellotti, Prince Paulo Enrico Massiomo, 512
Lateran Council, Fourth (1215), 414, 436
Lateran Cross (religous, in abeyance), 457, 458
Lateran Treaty (1929), 8, 19, 35, 37, 40, 43, 44, 57, 279, 280, 624
L'Attività della Santa Sede, 32
Lauretan Cross (religious, in abeyance), 24, 457, 458
*Lauretan Knights, Order of (Papal), 24
Lavinia, Duchess of Norfolk (widow of 16th Duke), 360
Lazarus Hilfswerk, 496, 497, 498, 500, 501, 531, 539-43
Lech I, Prince of Poland, 386
Ledochowski, Cardinal Mieczyslaw Halka, 56, 57, 605
Legion d'Honneur, 49, 50
Leo II, Pope, 8
Leo IX, Pope, 20, 152
Leo X, Pope, 23, 34, 65, 77, 197, 405, 406
Leo XIII, Pope, 24, 56, 57, 149, 150, 151, 157, 158, 456-57, 458, 459, 602, 622
Leonor, Queen of Portugal, 399
Leopold I, Emperor, 239, 246, 470, 478
Leopold II, Emperor, 243
Leopold I, King of the Belgians, 149, 203
Leopold, Duke of Lorraine and Bar, 489
Lepanto, Battle of, 152, 174

INDEX 707

Liberman, Dr. Henryk, 383
Liechtenstein, Royal House of, 235
Lomas, Countess Mary Frances, 203
Loredan, Francesco, Doge of Venice, 152
Loreto, Holy House of, 24
Los Angeles, Archbishop of, 13,
Louis I, King of Portugal, 254, 415
Louis I, Sovereign Duke of Bar, 489
Louis II, Sovereign Prince of Monaco, 378
Louis IX, St., King of France, 463
Louis XI, King of France, 333
Louis XII, King of France, 378
Louis XIV, King of France, 21, 239, 331, 334, 335, 489
Louis XV, King of France, 342, 489
Louis XIV, King of France, 489
Louis XVIII, King of France, 331, 333, 335, 461, 488, 489, 647
Louis Philip, Crown Prince of Portugal, 254
Louis Philippe I, King of France, 333
Ludwig I, King of Bavaria, 326
Ludwig II, King of Bavaria, 319-20, 321
Ludwig III, King of Bavaria, 319
Luitpold, Regent of Bavaria, 319
Luther, Martin, 20
Luxembourg (Nassau), Royal House of, 235

McAuliffe, Bishop Michael F., 205
McCahey, F. Miller, XLVII
McGivney, Fr. Michael J., 518
McInnes, Rt Rev. Fr V.A., 500
McKiernan, Thomas E., 205
Macchi, Cardinal Luigi, 30, 564, 565, 571, 584, 591, 593, 596, 599, 662, 663
Macharski, Cardinal, 495, 497, 498, 500, 540
*Magdalen, Order of, or of Mary Magdalen, 463
Maglione, Cardinal A., 581
Magnus I Ladulæs, King of Sweden, 449
Mahon, Bishop Gerald, 14, 130, 136, 137, 621
*Mailed Arm, Order of the (Denmark), 350, 676-77
Makarios III, Archbishop, President of Cyprus, 556
Malachy, St., 44
Malloch, Russell J., 'Register of Knighthood, Part III', 365
Malta, imitation orders of, 229-30, 231, 504, 554-57

Malta, Sovereign Military Order of (SMOM), 2, 3, 5, 10, 14, 22, 24, 29, 34, 37, 43, 52, 136, 137, 167, 168, 169, 170, 171-86, 190, 191, 195, 203, 212, 217, 219, 220, 221, 229-30, 231, 235, 258, 293, 396, 426, 452, 453, 465, 481, 482, 485, 486, 487, 490, 504, 505-06, 509, 515, 529, 538, 547, 553, 554, 613, 662, XI, XII, XIII
Malteser Hilfdienst, 531, 536-37
Mantua, Duke of, 463
Manuel I, King of Portugal, 65, 152
Manuel II, King of Portugal, 223, 254, 255, 256, 257, 258, 263, 266, 361, 452, 521
Marcellus II, Pope, 77
Margrethe, Queen of Denmark, 449
Margrethe II, Queen of Denmark, 233, 349, 357, 430, XLI
Mari, Arturo, 2
Maria I, Queen of Portugal, 65, 393, 397, 400, 401, 406, 411, 415, 417, 677
Maria II, Queen of Portugal, 252, 254
Maria Christina, Queen of Spain, 153
Maria Christina, Princess of the Two Sicilies, 285
Maria Grazia Pia, Princess of Naples/Two Sicilies, 153
Marie Henriette, Queen of the Belgians, 153
Maria Pia di Savoya, Princess, 153, 254
Maria Sophia, last Queen of the Two Sicilies, 285
Maria Teresa, Queen of Sardinia, 153
Maria Theresia, Queen of Hungary, 491
*Maria Theresia, Order of, 491
Marie de Bourgogne, 237
Marie Françoise de Orléans Bragança, Princess, 258
Marie Louise, Empress of France, then Duchess of Parma, 298
Marinus, founder of San Marino, 419
Martin V, Pope, 7, 405, 414
Martin, Cardinal Jacques, 2, 6, 14, 16, 29, 30, 31, 32, 40-41, 67, 100, 104, 132, 133-35, 136, 144, 148, 151, 497, 498, 517, 613, XXVIII
Martinez Somalo, Archbishop Eduardo, 495
Mary I, Queen of England, 189, 190
Mary, Queen (with William III), 234
Mary, Queen (consort of George V), 357
Mary, Queen of Scots, 365
Mater et Magistra, Apostolic See's rôle as, 22, 37, 42, 52, 225, 343, 348, 447, 545

Mateusz, Bishop, 116
Mathias, Emperor, 239
Maxentius, Roman Emperor, 295
Maximilian I, Emperor, 237, 487
Maximilian, Emperor of Mexico, 473, 475
Maximilian Josef, 1st King of Bavaria, 324, 326
Maximilian II Josef, King of Bavaria, 326
Maximilian IV, Elector of Bavaria, 477
Maximos III Mazlñm, Greek Melchite Catholic Patriarch of Antioch, 510
Maximos V Hakim, Greek Melchite Catholic Patriarch of Antioch, 504, 505, 512, XLVI
Médici, Emílio Garastazu, President of Brazil, 403
Mercedes, Princess of the Asturias, 277
*Mercy, The Order of, 461
Merit, Order of (British), 234
Merit, Decorations and Medals of (Poland), 680
Merit, Order of (Holy Sepulchre), 209
Merit, Order of the Polish Republic, 385, 680
Merit, Order of (SMOM), 184
*Merit for Catholic Priests in Military Service, Order of (Empire), 472-73
Michael, Prince of Greece, 676
Miguel I, King of Portugal, 223, 252, 254, 257, 521
Miguel II, Duke of Bragança, 254, 256, 258, 262
Miguel de Bragança, Infante, Dom, Duke of Viseu, 103, 258, 259, 522, XVIII
*Military Cincture, Order of the (Sicily), 464-65
Military Orders of Portugal, 396-418
*Militia of Jesus Christ, Order of the, *or* of St. Dominic, 462
Milvian Bridge, Battle of the (312), 295
Miolans, Order of, 488
Model, Richard, 385
Mohamed Reza Pahlavi, Shahinshah of Iran, 82
Montesa, Order of (Spain), 22, 224, 404, 426, 435-36, 485, 486, 487, XXXV
*Montfrac, Order of (Spain), 465
Montgomery of Alemein, Fieldmarshal the Viscount, 350
*Montjoie, Order of (Spain), 464
*Moretto, Equestrian Order of the (Papal), 24
morganatic marriages, 218

Moscicki, President of Poland, 381, 384
Mowbray, Segrave & Stourton, Baron, 495
Mozart, Wolfgang Amadeus, 79
Muslims, *see* Islam
Mussolini, Benito, 43, 57, 279, 280, 310, 624
Muszynski, Archbishop Henryk Josef, 140, 614

Napoléon Bonaparte, Emperor of France, 174-75, 213, 252, 319, 337, 426, 647
Narutowics, Gabriel, President of Poland, 383
National Orders of Merit of Portugal, 396
Nelson, Admiral Viscount Horatio, 175, 467
Nicholas IV, Pope, 410, 414
Nicholas V, Pope, 309, 399, 624
Niedballa, Prof. Rudolf, 677, 678, XXVII
Norfolk, 17th Duke of, Hereditary Earl Marshal of England, 90, 363
November Insurrection (Polish), 388

Oddi, Cardinal Silvio, 104
Olav V, King of Norway, 86, 368
*Old Nobility, The Knightly Order of the (Limburg-Luxembourg), 478-79
Ordine Al Merito Civile di Savoia (*formerly* Ordine Civile di Savoia), 225
Oscar I, King of Norway, 447
Osservatore Romano, L', 2, 35, 59, 62, 76, 457, 465, 483, 508, 518, 519, 526, 545, 547, 550, 552, 553-54
Ostrowski, Stanislaw, President of Poland-in-Exile, 384
Otto I, Emperor, 77
Otto I, King of Bavaria, 319
Otto von Wittelsbach, Duke of Bavaria 319
*Our Lady of Bethlehem, Order of (Papal States), 465, 486
*Our Lady of Guadalupe, Order of (Mexico), 461, 473-75
*Our Lady of Loreto, Order of, 463
*Our Lady of Mercy, Sacred & Military Order of Spain), 466
*Our Lady of Mount Carmel, Order of, 506, 510, 516
*Our Lady of Mount Carmel & St. Lazarus of Jerusalem (amalgamated), Order of, 22, 461, 487, 489-90, 506, 510, 512
*Our Lady of Ransom, Order of (Spain), 466
Owen, John, 21,

INDEX 709

Palatine Guard of Honour, Corps of the, 631, 636, 638
Palatine, Papal Counts, 25, 35, 75-76, 77, 79, 115
Palatine, Secular Counts, 76-77
Pallavicini, Bali Frà Giancarlo, 178
Pallavicini, Frà Oberto, Marchese, 168, 183
Palm of Jerusalem (Holy Sepulchre), 209
Papal Briefs, *see under* Encyclical Letters, Pontifical,
Papal Guards, corps of, 161
Papal knights, 129-48
Papal States, 24, 40, 58, 99, 161, 279, 310
Papal titles, hereditary, 35
Paris, Pact of (1922), 223, 257, 521
Parma, Royal House of, 271
Pascal II, Pope 173
Passigato, Mons. Rino, 102, 131
Paul I, Czar, 175, 556, 557
Paul II, Pope, 465, 487
Paul III, Pope, 23, 75, 77, 465
Paul IV, Pope, 77, 415, 634
Paul V, Pope, 22, 463
Paul VI, Pope, 2, 6, 11, 31, 32, 37, 45, 55, 60, 67, 74, 79, 83, 85, 86, 90, 105, 135, 146, 155, 157, 158, 162, 163, 164, 165, 221, 286, 292, 346, 457, 459, 553, 600-01, 618, 624, 625-28, 631, 635
Paul, King of the Hellenes, 241
Pedro I, Emperor of Brazil, *see* Pedro IV, King of Portugal
Pedro II, Emperor of Brazil, 252
Pedro II, King of Aragon, 487
Pedro I, King of Portugal, 405
Pedro IV, King of Portugal, also Pedro I, Emperor of Brazil, 252, 254, 401
Pedro V, King of Portugal, 254
Pedro, Dom, Duke of Coimbra, 414
Perrot, A. M., *Collection Historique des Ordres de Chevalerie*, 335, 347, 400, 489, 641; *Tableau Chronologique des Ordres Eteints*, 641
Peter, St., Prince of the Apostles, 8
Peter, St., See of, 8, 11
Peter I, Czar of Russia, 'the Great', 386
Peter II, King of Yugoslavia, 426, 556, 557
Peyrefitte, Roger, *Chevaliers de Malte*, 137; *Les Clefs de St.Pierre*, 137
Philibert of Miolans, 488
Philip IV 'the Fair', King of France, 22, 480-81, 485, 486, 662
Philip the Good, Duke of Burgundy, 235, 236, 426, 430

Philip the Handsome, King, 237, 244
Philip II, King of Spain (and I of Portugal), 190, 239, 357, 406, 411
Philip III, King of Spain (and II of Portugal), 406
Philip IV, King of Spain (and III of Portugal), 237, 248, 406
Philip V, Philip d'Anjou, King of Spain, 239, 240
Philip, Prince, Duke of Edinburgh, 54, 354, XL
Philip Ferdinand, Duke of Limburg, 478
Philippa of Lancaster, 405
Pian Order, Golden Collar of, 10, 55, 72, 85-87, 115, 142, 145, 583-86, 600-01, 678, IV
*Pian Knights, Order of (Papal), 24
Picchioni, Mons. A., 588
Pilgrim's Shell (Holy Sepulchre), 209
Pilsudski, Marshal Jósef, Chief of State of Poland, 384, 389
Pius II, Pope, 486
Pius IV, Pope, 75, 77, 79, 160
Pius V, St., Pope, 337
Pius VI, Pope, 298, 397, 406, 411, 438, 487
Pius VII, Pope, 24, 25, 26, 75, 79, 220, 440, 634, 639
Pius VIII, Pope, 22
Pius IX, Pope, 24, 87, 88, 153, 161, 162, 197, 203, 227, 271, 278, 310, 311, 316, 338, 462, 464, 460, 573, 575, 577, 638
Pius IX, Order of (*see also* Pian Order, Golden Collar of), 3, 25, 30, 45, 55, 59, 60, 61, 87-98, 104, 105, 142, 145, 217, 221, 258, 343, 346, 515, 526, 573-82, V
Pius X, St., Pope, 2, 25, 29, 33, 35, 40, 55, 58, 67, 76, 79, 99, 101, 104, 105, 134, 135, 137, 144, 147, 151, 163, 203, 206, 528, 563, 569, 594, 613, 616, 646, 662, 663
Pius XI, Pope, 22, 35, 43, 44, 68, 203, 212, 213, 273, 279, 280, 510, 624, 639
Pius XII, Pope, 24, 25, 28, 43, 68, 82, 84, 85, 87, 137, 153, 155, 156, 162, 167, 168, 175, 200, 203, 209, 217, 221, 227, 228, 258, 259, 306, 320, 338, 377, 442, 464, 581, 583-84, 632, 639
Pokolm, Klaus-Peter, 497, 498, 500, 505, 540, XLVI
Poland, Kings of, 213
Poland, Orders and Decorations of Republic of, 679-83
Poletti, Cardinal Ugo, XXIII
Polish Catholic Mission, 115-16,

Polish Government-in-Exile, 46, 682-83
Polish Law Gazette, 14, 679
'Polonia Restituta', Order of, 100, 383, 385, 389-92, 452, 679, XLV
Polska Zbrojna, 384
Pontifical Gendarmerie, Corps of the, 631, 636
Pontifical Medals, 624-30
Pontifical Noble Guard, Corps of the, 631, 634-36
Pontifical Orders of Knighthood, Grand Chancellors of, 25, 30, 133; *see also under individual names*
Pontifical Religious Awards of Merit, 149-65
Pontifical Swiss Guards, Corps of the, 90, 105, 161, 163, 625, 631, 635-38
Pontificia Academia Ecclesiastica (*formerly* Accademia dei Nobili Ecclesiastici), 149
Pope St. Sylvester, Order of, *see* St. Sylvester, Pontifical Equestrian Order of Pope
Porte, The Sublime, 197
Portugal, Crown/Kings of, 65
Portugal, President of, as Grand Master of State Orders, 393, 394, 396
Portuguese Civil Orders of Merit, 396
'Prammatica' (1759), separating Spain and the Two Sicilies, 297
'Pro Ecclesia et Pontifice' Cross, 14, 58, 142, 145, 149, 150, 157-60, 164, 621-23, VIII
Projet de D écret de Reconnaissance, 509
*'Pro Petri Sede' Medal (Papal), 161
Prosser, R. E., *The Royal Prerogative*, 337

Raczkiewicz, Wladislaw, President of Poland-in-Exile, 381, 384
Raczynski, Count Edward, President of Poland-in-Exile, 382, 384
Rainier I, Prince of Monaco, 378,
Rainier II, Prince of Monaco, 378
Rainier III, Sovereign Prince of Monaco, 377, 378, XXXVI
Ramón de Barcelona, Count Berenguer, 19
Ranieri Maria, Prince, Duke of Castro, 43, 182, 275, 277, 278, 281, 284, 286, 287, 291, 292, 294, 299
Ratisbon, Diet of, 20-21
Ratzinger, Cardinal Joseph, 303
Rawlinson of Ewell, Lord, 293
Raymond Berengarius, Count of Barcelona, 463

Red Cross, International, 501, 531
Reformation, 20
Regina, Archduchess, 247
Res Publica Christiana, 9, 343, 344, 346, 347, 526, 545
Richard I, King of England, 356
Richard II, King of England, 369
Richard, Duke of Gloucester, 187, 192, 535
Risorgimento, 273, 278, 309
Rodolph, Emperor, 239
Rodrigues, Grand Master Don Nuno, 405
Roger I, Duke of Lucca and Parma, 469
Roger I, Grand Count of Sicily, 464
Rose, Kenneth, 151, 234, 367, 431
Rose, Order of the (Brazil), 678
Royal Victorian Chain, 234
Royal Victorian Order (UK), 151, 234
Rubin, Cardinal Wladyslaw, 116
Rudolph I, Emperor, 487
Ruprecht, Prince, Duke of Bavaria, 319
Russian and Soviet Military Awards, 49
Russian Orders (Communist), 49
Russian Revolution (1917), 220

Sabbat, Kazimierz, President of Poland-in-Exile, 384, 385, XLIV
Sacred Congregation *De Propaganda Fide*, 57
*St. Andrew, Order of (Russia), 676
St. Andrew, Order of, *see* Thistle, Order of
St. Agatha, Order of (San Marino), 418, 423
*St. Anne, Order of (München-Bavaria), 477
*St. Anne, Order of (Russia), 676
*St. Anne, Order of (Würzburg-Bavaria), 478
SS. Annunziata (the Most Holy Annunciation), Order of (Savoy), 22, 23, 183, 219, 222, 227, 237, 258, 306, 307, 312-14, 338, 456, XXII
*St. Anthony of Hainault, Order of, 462-63
*St. Anthony of Vienna, Order of, 462
St. Benedict of Avis, Military Order of, *see* Avis, The Military Order of
*St. Bridget of Sweden, Order of, 456, 463
*St. Cecilia, Equestrian Order of (Papal), 24
St. Cecilia, Musical Academy of, 24
*St. Charles, Order of (Mexico), 461, 475-76
St. Charles, Order of (Monaco), 220, 378-80, XXXV

INDEX

St. Columbanus, Knights of (Ireland), 138-39, 519, 615
*St. Dominic, Order of, *see* Militia of Jesus Christ, Order of the
*St. Elizabeth, Imperial Order of (Austro-Hungarian Empire), 471-72
*St. Faustin, Order of (Haiti), 461, 476-77
St. Ferdinand, Military Order of (Spain), 443
*St. Ferdinand & of Merit, Order of (Two Sicilies), 461, 466-67, 468
*St. George of Austria, Order of, 487
St. George, Order of (Bavaria-Wittelsbach), 318, 320, 321, 322-23, 342, 548, XXVII
*St. George, Order of (France), 461
*St. George in Carinthia, Order of (Empire), 487-88
*St. George of Alfama, Order of (Aragon/Spain), 436, 487
*St. George of Burgundy, Order of (Belgium), 488
*St. George of Ravenna, Order of (Papal States), 465
*St. George of the Reunion, Order of (Two Sicilies), 462, 467-49
St. Gothard, Battle of, 21,
St. Gregory the Great, Order of (Pontifical), 10-11, 13, 25, 29, 30, 33, 45, 55, 59, 60, 61, 99-114, 115, 126-27, 129, 130, 133, 137, 142, 146-47, 217, 221, 343, 346, 515, 526, 586-93, 609, 613, 615-20, 678, VI, XXVII
*St. Henry, Military Order of (Saxony), 490-91
St. Hermenegildus, Royal & Military Order of (Spain), 443
St. Hubert, Order of (Bavaria), 22, 217, 320, 324-25, 550, XX
*St. Hubert of Lorraine, or the Bar, Order of, 489
St. Isabel, Royal Order of (Portugal), 6, 48, 249, 270-71, 402, 516
*St. James of Altopascio, Order of, 486
St. James of Holland, Order of, 452-53
St. James of the Sword, Military Order of (Portugal), 22, 65, 345, 393, 396, 397, 398, 400, 406, 409, 411, 413-18
St. James of the Sword, Order of (Spain), 22; *see* Santiago, Military Order of (Spain)
St. Januarius, Order of (Two Sicilies), 23, 217, 275, 284, 299, 303-306, 438, XXIV, XLIII

St. John Ambulance, 190, 194, 531, 532-33, 535
St. John Opthalmic Hospital, Jerusalem & Gaza, 190, 531, 534
*St. John, Royal Prussian Order of, 187
St. John, Sovereign Military Order of, *see* Malta, Sovereign Military Order of
St. John Lateran, Order of, 463
St. John of Jerusalem, Most Venerable Order of (British), 169-70, 187-94, 453, 504, 531, 547, 553, XIV
*SS. John and Thomas, Order of, 462
St. Joseph, Order of (Tuscany), 337-38, 340, 341
St. Julian Pereiro, Knights of, *see* Alcantara, Military Order of
St. Lazarus of Jerusalem, Military & Hospitaller Order of, 22, 37, 52, 53, 314, 453, 489-90, 495-513, 516, 517, 526, CLVI, XLVII
St. Lazarus, imitation orders of, 504
*St. Louis, Order of (Lucca/Parma), 461, 469-70
St. Louis, Royal & Military Order of (France), 329, 331-33
*St. Mark, Order of, 462
*St. Mary, Order of the Glorious, 462
St. Maurice, Order of (Savoy), 22, 314, 506, 510, 516
SS. Maurice and Lazarus, Order of (Savoy), 183, 217, 222, 226, 227, 278, 279, 306, 307, 314-17, 319, 338, 456, 510, 548, 678, XXII, XXIII, XXVII
St. Michael, Order of (Bavaria), 320, 326-28
St. Michael, Order of (France), 22, 329, 331, 333-36, 366
St. Michael of the Wing, Order of, Secret Society of, now Knightly Order/Association (Portugal), 222, 249, 252, 254, 516, 517, 519-24
St. Olaf, Order of (Norway), 447
St. Raymond of Peñafort, Order of the Cross of (Spain), 426, 442, 444-45
*St. Remi, Order of, *see* Holy Vial, Order of
*St. Rose, Order of (Honduras), 461
*St. Rupert of Salzburg, Order of, 478
*St. Stephen the Apostolic King, Royal Hungarian Order of, 472, 491-93
St. Stephen, Order of (Tuscany), 337-38, 339-40, 486
St. Sylvester, Pontifical Equestrian Order

of Pope, 25, 30, 45, 55, 59, 60, 61, 76, 79, 90, 104, 105, 115-25, 130, 137, 142, 146, 147, 217, 221, 343, 346, 526, 615-20, VII
Sainty, Guy Stair, 224, 433, 684; *The Orders of Chivalry and Merit of the Bourbon Two Sicilies Dynasty*, 293; *The Orders of St. John*, 417
Saladin, Sultan of Egypt, 212
Joan, Countess of Salisbury, 356
Salisbury, Marquess of, 151
Sancho I, King of Portugal, 409
Sancho III, King of Castile, 434
San Marino, 419-23
San Marino, Equestrian Order of, 419-22
Santa Iria, Marquês of, XIX
Santiago, Military Order of (Spain), 48, 217, 224, 413, 426, 435, 436-37, 677, XXXV, XXXIX
Sapieha, Eustachy, 381
Saragat, Giuseppe, President of Italy, 9
Sas-Skowronski, Prof. M., 301, 303
Savoy, Royal House of (Italy), 22, 217, 225, 306-10, 345, 646, 649, XXI, XXII, XXIII
Szcepanik, Prof. Edward, Polish Prime Minister-in-exile, 383
Schleswig-Holstein-Sinderburg-Glücksburg, Royal House of (Greece), 225
Sczaniecki, Comm. A. M. A., 115, 116, 130
Sebastiâo, King of Portugal, 406
Secretariat and Secretary of State, Papal, 25, 26, 30, 31, 32, 43, 53, 59, 62, 68, 91, 101, 104, 133, 142, 143, 145, 146, 147, 221, 381, 498, 511, 551, 618, 630, 634
Sede Vacante, 39, 625, 628
Sede Iterum Vacante, 625, 628
Sedia Gestatoria, 632-33, 634
Segni, Antonio, President of Italy, 73
Sejm (Polish parliament), 383, 384, 386, 388
Seraphim, Most Noble Order of the (Sweden), 22, 447, 449-50
Seville, Don Francisco de Bórbon y de la Torre, 3rd Duke of, 510
Seward, Desmond, *Italy's Knights of St. George*, 293, 305
Sforza-Cesarini, Ducal House of S. Fiora, 77
*Ship and the Crescent, Order of the (France), 463
Sigismund, Emperor, King of Hungary, 309, 479
Sikorski, General Wladislaw, 381
Sikorski Museum, London, 679

Silvia, Queen of Sweden, 446
Siri, Cardinal Giuseppe, 303
Simon, Judge Caroline K., 555
Sistine Chapel, 153
Sixtus IV, Pope, 153, 366, 400, 487, 506, 635
Sixtus V, Pope, 24, 48, 436, 443
*Slaves of Virtue, Order of the (Empire), 246, 470
Smythe, Colin, 5, 16-17
Soares, Dr. Mário, President of Portugal, 394, 395, 403, XXXVII, XL
Soares, Mme., XL
Sophia, Queen of Spain, 86, 159
Sotheby's, London, 334-35
Soulouque, General St. Faustin, Emperor of Haiti, 476
Southern Cross, Knights of the (Australia), 519
Southern Cross, Knights of the (New Zealand), 519
Sovereign Military Order of Malta, *see* Malta, Sovereign Military Order of
Spada, Dr Antonio, 305, XXVI
Spain, Royal House of Bourbon of, XXXIII, XXXIV, XXXV
Spink & Son Ltd., 489, 549, 550; *Catalogue of British Orders, Decorations and Medals*, 375
Stanislaus Augustus Poniatowski, King of Poland, 388
Starry Cross, Order of the Dames of the, 246-47, XX
Stephen, St., Apostolic King of Hungary, 40, 491
Sternberg, Sir Sigmund, 127, 129, 130, 146, 612
*Swan, Order of the (Brandenburg), 488-89
Swierczynski, Mons. Stanislaw, 117, 140
Swiss Guards, Corps of the Pontifical, *see* Pontifical Swiss Guards, Corps of the
*Sword, Order of the, *see under* Tower and the Sword, Military Order of the
Sword, Royal Order of the (Sweden), 22, 447-49
*Sword Bearers, Military Order of (Lithuania), 212-13, 466
Sylvester I, St., Pope, 75
Szkopiak, Prof. Zygmunt, Polish Foreign Minister-in-exile, 385

Tablet, The, 59
*Templars, Order of the (Order of the Poor Knights of Christ and the Temple of

Solomon), 22, 64-65, 173, 212, 404, 405, 435, 436, 480-82, 483-86, 506-07, 546, 547, 662; *see also* Christ, Order of (Portugal)
Temple, Inner and Middle, Inns of Court, 482
Teodosio II, Duke of Bragança, 249
Terracina, Laura Bacio, 364
Teutonic Order, 22, 24, 211-16, 237, 273, 485, 646
Teutonic Order, Nazi invention, 213, 215
Texas Catholic Herald, The, 58-59
Thatcher, Margaret, Baroness, 361
Thistle, Most Noble Order of the, (Scotland), 234, 345, 347, 364-68, 431, 451, XXIX, XXXI
Three Golden Fleeces, Military Order of the, 647
Three Orders, Riband of the (Portugal), 393, 396-99, XXXII, XXXVII, XXXVIII
Tisserant, Cardinal Eugene, 199, 204-05
Tokarzewski-Karaszewics, General Michael, 383
Tomaszewski, Tadeusz, 383
*Torquati Aurati, 464
Toumanoff, Frà Cyril, Prince, 168, 179, 229-30, 512, 555; *Les Dynasties de la Caucasie Chrétienne*, 230
Tower and the Sword, of Valour, Loyalty & Merit, Military Order of the (Portugal), 347, 399-404, XLIX, XL
Tribunal de Grand Instance de Paris, 552
Troyes, Council of (1128), 484
*Truxillo, Order of (Spain), 465
*Two Moons, Order of the (France), 463
*Two Orders, Riband of the (Portugal), 398, XXXVIII
Two Sicilies, Royal House of Bourbon of the, 9, 14, 17, 37, 43, 271-94, 294-303 *passim*

Umberto I, Count of Savoy, 309
Umberto I, King of Italy, 310, 311
Umberto II, King of Italy, 183, 217, 225, 227, 306, 307, 309, 310, 316, 649
UNESCO, 175
United Nations Organization (UNO), 10, 175, 509, 529-30
Urban II, Pope, 19, 152
Urban VIII, Pope, 174, 295, 463
Utrecht, Treaty of (1713), 239, 426

Vatican, the, 58, 68
Vatican Archives, 29, 34

Vatican City State (international juridical entity), 62, 87, 146, 157, 624, 639
Vatican Council, Second, ('Vatican II'), 60, 127, 455, 513, 547
Vecchione, Nicola, 100, 618
Venerable Order of St. John, *see* St. John of Jerusalem, Venerable Order of
Ventura, Mons. Luigi, 6, 31
Versailles, Treaty of (1919), 243
Vestey, 3rd Baron, 192
Victor Amadeus II, King of Sicily & of Sardinia, 309
Victor Emmanuel II, King of Sardinia and 1st King of Italy, 254, 309, 310, 311, 429
Victor Emmanuel III, King of Italy, 58, 310, 624
Victor Emmanuel, Prince, Duke of Savoy, 183, 217, 306, 307, 309, 649, XXI, XXII
Victoria, Queen Empress, 149, 151, 191
Vienna, Treaty of (1815), 298
Vila Viçosa, Order of the Conception of Our Lady of (Portugal), 6, 23, 219, 222, 226, 227, 249, 253, 258, 265, 266-69, 402, 452, 455, 516, 524, 548, 652, 677, XVII, XVIII, XXVII
Villot, Cardinal Jean, 629
Viner, Brigadier Gordon, 100, 130, 612, 618
'Virtuti Militari', Order of (Poland), 385, 679
von Habsburg, Archduke Dr. Otto, 241, 242, 429, 501
von Hindenburg, Field Marshal Paul, President of Germany, 241
von Leden, Dr. Hans, 500, 501, 512, 513, XLVI, XLVII
von Metternich-Winneburg, Paul Alfons, 6th Prince, 499
von Metternich-Winneburg, Princess Tatiana, 499, 540
von Slatin, Baron Dr Heinz Peter, 500
Voskresenie & the Government of the Russian Federation, 557

Waldemar II, King of Denmark, 346, 351, 353
Waldheim, Dr Kurt, President of Austria, 10,
Walesa, Lech, President of Poland, 46, 383, 384, 500, 540, 681-83 XLIV
Weatherill, Baron, 131
Wellington, 1st Duke of, Duke of Ciudad Rodrigo, 312, 427, 428, 430

Wenzel I, Emperor, 479
Westphalia, Royal Order of, 646
White Eagle, Order of the (Poland), 6, 15, 22, 46, 381, 383, 384, 385, 386-89, 451, 455, 456, 490, 676, 679, XLV
Wilhelm II, Kaiser, 57, 356
Wilhelm, Duke of Jülich-Berg, 324
William II, King of England, 374
William III, King, and Queen Mary, 234
William IV, King (Great Britain), 357
Wilson, Harold, 1st Baron Wilson of Rievaulx, 361
Wladimir, Grand Duke, 556, 557
Wojciechowski, Stanislaw, President of Poland, 384

World War I, 225, 243, 320, 646
World War II, 44, 50, 115, 187, 203, 215, 225, 228, 350, 361, 383, 384, 493, 551
Württemberg, Duke of 1993, 324, 325
Wyszowadski, Mons. Wladislaw, 140

Yonnes, Doña Gazelas Maria, 435

Zacchi, Archbishop Cesare, 14, 50, 132, 149, 356, 495, 498
Zaleski, August, President of Poland-in-Exile, 384
Zita, Empress of Austria, 247
zu Loewenstein, Prince Rupert, 293